ENGLISH DICTIONARY

ENGLISH DICTIONARY

PUBLISHED BY PETER HADDOCK Ltd.
BRIDLINGTON, ENGLAND
By arrangement with Purnell & Sons Ltd.

© Purnell
Printed in HUNGARY

INTRODUCTION

This dictionary is intended for general use, and therefore has three main functions. First, and most important of all, is the clear definition of words. Second is the spelling of words, and third is their pronunciation.

In compiling a dictionary the editor is confronted with various problems such as the constant changes in a living language; old words going out of fashion, while new ones are being coined. This is especially true of the technological age in which we live today.

Furthermore there is virtually no limit to the details that a dictionary can contain, and the dividing line between dictionary and encyclopaedia is accordingly very thin. There must, however, be a limit to each individual entry, and so decisions must be made in relation to the inclusion or omission of words, particularly in the semi-scientific and technical fields. Thus, the English Dictionary has concentrated on a vocabulary that will be invaluable to the average family, and prove to be a standard reference book in every household.

On the question of pronunciation it should be remembered that the English language is spoken by such a large proportion of the world's population that it is subject to considerable variation; not only between different countries; but even between different districts and divisions of the same country. Fashion and taste through the ages also dictate changes of pronunciation. In the English Dictionary Therefore, simplicity has been the guiding principle.

The most important factor in pronunciation is the accent. The accent is placed *immediately after* the syllable which is to be accented or stressed. Where the accent follows a vowel this vowel will invariably be long, but where the accent follows a consonant the preceding vowel usually becomes short. For example in "la'dle" the "a" is pronounced as in "bay", but in "lam'inate" the "a" becomes short as in "lamb". When exceptions are made to this rule, an explanation has been given in the text. One general exception occurs, however, when "a" and "r" are combined, and the accent usually becomes long when they are followed by another vowel; thus in "ripar'ian" the "ar" sound is pronounced like "air". In the case of the double "r", even when the accent has to be placed between the two (r'r) the "ar" sound becomes short as in "car".

The system of accenting has also been used occasionally in the case of monosyllables when the long vowel sound is required; thus "po'st" instead of the short sounding word "lost".

To avoid the use of phonetic signs long sounds which do not conform to the rule above have been indicated by syllables derived from other commonly known words in which there is no ambiguity of pronunciation.

The ending "-tious" is invariably pronounced "-shus", even when the accent comes after the "t" or in some cases "c". It has sometimes been necessary to place the accent after these letters to emphasise the preceding short "i".

Where the vowel is followed by the consonant and another vowel, its sound, generally speaking, is long, although there are exceptions to this. For example while "a" obeys the rule when followed by "l" and a vowel ("pale"), it does not become short when it is followed by a double "l" at the end of a word, but becomes "aw" as in "pall" or "fall". (Other vowels, however, follow the rule in similar circumstances, e.g. "fell" or "sell"). But when the double "l" is followed by another syllable the "a" remains short, as in 'fallacious".

Explanations of pronunciation have been inserted on the basis of obviously known sounds. In the case of "g" the sound is soft or hard according to the vowel. When it is followed by

"a", "o", or "u" it is invariably hard; when followed by "e"
or "i" it is sometimes hard as in "get" or "give", but more
usually soft. Where there is any doubt a "j" sound has been
indicated.

The parts of speech have been indicated by the customary
abbreviations placed immediately after the main entry. Where
the meaning of a derivative part of speech (e.g. the noun
"baldness" from the adjective "bald") is obvious from the
first definition, it has been thought sufficient to include the
word itself and indicate the appropriate part of speech without
including a further definition. Nor has it been felt essential
to include the adverb as well as the adjective, for in most
cases this is simply a matter of adding the ending "-ly" or
"-ily". And it has not been thought necessary to define the
meaning of verbs or substantives when this is clear from the
main entry.

Finally it is hoped that those who use this dictionary will
find it both enjoyable and profitable. Exploring the riches of
the English language can be a greatly rewarding and pleasur-
able occupation.

ABBREVIATIONS

a. adjective.
abbrev. abbreviation.
adv. adverb.
Amer. American.
anat. anatomy, anatomical.
arch. archaic.
archit. architecture,
   architectural.
auxil. auxiliary.
biol. biology, biological.
bot. botany, botanical.
chem. chemistry, chemical.
coll. collective, collectively.
colloq. colloquial.
comp. comparative.
conj. conjunction.
dial. dialect.
E. east.
elec. electricity, electrical.
esp. especially.
fem. feminine.
fig. figurative.
Fr. French.
geol. geology, geological.
gram. grammar.
incl. including.
interj. interjection.
iron. ironical.
Jap. Japanese.
leg. legend, legendary.

lit. literary, literal.
masc. masculine.
maths. mathematics.
med. medicine, medical.
mil. military.
mus. music, musical.
myth. mythology,
   mythological.
N. north.
nav. naval.
naut. nautical.
occ. occasionally.
orig. original, originally.
pl. plural.
pref. prefix.
prep. preposition.
pron. pronoun.
rel. religion.
S. *south.*
sing. singular.
sl. slang.
sup. superlative.·
suff. suffix.
U.S. United States.
us. usually.
v. verb.
v.i. verb intransitive.
v.t. verb transitive.
W. west.
zool. zoology.

A

A, An, *indefinite article.* One in quantity or number.

A-, *prefix* denoting without, e.g. **a-moral.**

An, *arch.* if.

A1 (one), first-rate, fit, esp. ship in Lloyd's Register of Shipping.

Aback', *adv.* backwards, taken aback, person surprised or ship forced back by wind.

Ab'acus, *n.* apparatus for counting with beads on parallel wires.

Abaft', *adv. & prep.* stern of ship, towards the stern.

Aban'don, *v.t.* to give up or relinquish completely, leave sinking vessel or give up project or idea. **Aban'doned,** *a.* of person given up to evil. **Aban'donment,** *n.* self-surrender, impulsiveness.

Abase', *v.t.* to humiliate, make lower. **Abase'ment,** *n.*

Abash', *v.t.* to cause feeling of awkwardness, confuse.

Abate', *v.t.* to slacken, lessen. **Abate'ment,** *n.*

Abattoir', *n.* slaughterhouse.

Abb'ot, *n.* head of monastery or abbey. **Abb'ess,** *n.* head of convent.

Abb'ey, *n.* monastery, church that was formerly this.

Abbre'viate, *v.t.* to shorten, chiefly in lit. sense. **Abbrevia'-tion,** *n.* shortened version of name, sentence etc.

Ab'dicate, *v.t.* to relinquish, esp. throne. **Abdica'tion,** *n.*

Abdo'men, *n.* belly. **Abdom'inal,** *a.* to do with this.

Abduct', *v.t.* to kidnap, carry off. **Abduc'tion,** *n.*

Abeam', *adv.* (*naut.*) abreast: 'in line abeam', vessels sailing in formation parallel to each other.

Aberra'tion, *n.* deviation from path or type, mental failing.

Abet', *v.t.* to encourage or help someone in wrongful intent. **Abett'or,** *n.*

Abey'ance, *n.* condition of suspended activity, temporary disuse.

Abhor', *v.t.* to detest, loathe. **Abhor'rence,** *n.* **Abhor'rent,** *a.* hateful, loathsome.

Abide', *v.t.* to dwell stay; also put up with in sense of terms or conditions. **Abode',** *n. arch.* place of residence.

Ab'ject, *a.* degraded, miserable.

Abjure', *v.t.* to relinquish or renounce on oath. **Abjura'tion,** *n.*

Ablaze', *a.* on fire, *fig.* e.g. burning with enthusiasm.

A'ble, *a.* competent, skilled. **Abil'ity,** *n.* **Able-bod'ied,** *adj.* esp. in a.-b. seaman.

Ablu'tion, *n.* cleansing the person.

Ab'negate, *v.t.* to renounce belief or right. Abnega'tion, *n.* self-sacrifice, denial.

Abnor'mal, *a.* not normal, irregular. Abnormal'ity, *n.*

Abol'ish, *v.t.* to do away with, e.g. customs, laws etc. Aboli'-tion, *n.* Aboli'tionist, *n.* person campaigning to abolish an evil, esp. slavery, liquor.

Abom'inate, *v.t.* to loathe, detest. Abom'inable, *a.* Abomina'tion, *n.* object or act deserving to be detested.

Aborig'ines (-eez), *n.pl.* original inhabitants. Aborig'inal, *a.*

Abort', *v.i.* to miscarry, have premature natal delivery. Abor'-tion, *n.* Abort'ive, *a.* of project failing to materialize.

Abound', *v.i.* to be plentiful.

About', *adv.* all round; nearly. *prep.* dealing with, near. *Naut.* 'go about', *v.t.* to turn round.

Above', *adv.* overhead, more than, higher than.

Abrade', *v.t.* to injure by rubbing, skin etc., scrape. Abra'-sion, *n.* place so injured.

Abreast, *adv.* abeam, side by side.

Abridge', *v.t.* to abbreviate, esp. of book. Abridge'ment, *n.*

Abroad', *adv.* away in foreign country; at large.

Ab'rogate, *v.t.* to cancel, as of laws. Abroga'tion, *n.*

Abrupt', *a.* brusque in manner, sudden, steep.

Ab'scess (-sess), *n.* collection of pus.

Abscind', *v.t.* to cut off, esp. *surg.* Abscis'sion, *n.*

Abscond' (-sk), *v.i.* to make off illegally.

Ab'sent, *a.* not present. Absent', *v.t.* to stay away; absentee'ism, *n.* irresponsible staying away from work. Absent-minded, *a.* inattentive.

Absolve', *v.t.* to free from blame. Absolu'tion, *n.* Ab'solute, *a.* complete, unconditional.

Absorb', *v.t.* to soak up liquid. Absorp'tion, *n.* Absorb'ent, *n.*

Abstain', *v.i.* to refrain from, e.g. alcohol or voting. Absten'-tion, *n.* Ab'stinence, *n.*

Abste'mious, *a.* frugal in eating or drinking.

Ab'stract, *a.* separate, not material, of the mind. Abstract', *v.t.* to take away from. Abstract', *n.* a precis or summary.

Abstruse' *a.* not clear, difficult to understand.

Absurd', *a.* ridiculous, unreasonable. Absurd'ity, *n.*

Abun'dance, *n.* large quantity, plentiful. Abun'dant, *a.*

Abuse' (-buze), *v.t.* to use badly, misuse, address someone in coarse terms. Abuse' (-buce), *n.* Abu'sive, *a.*

Abut', *v.i.* to have a common border or wall with; abut'ment, *n.* architectural support.

Abyss', *n.* deep chasm or pit. Abys'mal (-z), *a.* very deep.

Acad'emy, *n.* higher form of school, society for honouring or cultivating the arts or sciences. Academ'ic, *a.* learned, theoretical.

Accede' (Aks-), *v.i.* to agree to request, to enter position or office, e.g. throne. Acces'sion, *n.*

Accel'erate (Aks-), *v.i. & t.* to increase speed. Accelera'tion, *n.* Accel'erator, *n.* attachment in machine for increasing speed, pes. in vehicle.

Ac'cent (Aks-), *n.* stress in speech, a mark to denote this.

Accent', *v.t.* **Accent'uate**, *v.t.* **Accentua'tion**, *n.*

Accept' (Aks-), *v.t.* to receive, admit. **Accept'able**, *a.* **Accept'ance**, *n.*

Ac'cess (Aks-), *n.* entrance, approach. **Access'ible**, *a.* easy to approach. **Access'ary**, *n.* assistant, esp. in crime. **Access'ory**, *a.* & *n.* additional, contributing, something that does this.

Ac'cident (Aks-), *n.* chance happening, mishap. **Accident'al**, *a.*

Acclaim', *v.t.* to applaud loudly. **Acclama'tion**, *n.* **Acclam'atory**, *a.*

Accli'matize, *v.t.* to get used to a new climate, new conditions. **Acclimatiza'tion**, *n.*

Acclivi'ty, *n.* upward slope of hill.

Accolade', *n.* ceremonial stroke on shoulder with sword during ceremony of bestowing knighthood.

Accomm odate, *v.t.* to provide lodging, *fig.* agree with. **Accommoda'tion**, *n.* lodging.

Accom'pany, *v.t.* to escort, go with; *mus.* play for. **Accom'paniment**, *n.*

Accom'plice, *n.* companion in crime or dubious action.

Accom'plish, *v.t.* to achieve, complete. **Accom'plished**, *a.* skilled, talented. **Accom'plishment**, *n.* achievement.

Accord', *v.t.* to settle amicably, *v.i.* to agree. **Accord'ance**, *n.* **Accord'ingly**, *adv.* as the circumstances indicate.

Accord'ion, *n.* hand wind-instrument worked by bellows, with keyboard.

Accost', *v.t.* to speak to, approach, usually aggressively.

Accouche'ment, (-oosh) *n.* confinement, delivery in childbirth.

Account', *v.t.* to reckon up money, give explanation or description. **Accoun'tant**, *n.* person who professionally draws up financial balance or statement. **Account'able**, *a.* responsible.

Accou'tre (-ooter), *v.t.* to equip or harness in arch. sense. **Accou'trements**, *n.pl.* military equipment.

Accred'it, *v.t.* to appoint officially, e.g. ambassador.

Accre'tion, *n.* addition, growth.

Accrue' (-oo), *v.i.* to be added, esp. financially.

Accu'mulate, *v.t.* to gather, increase. **Accumula'tion**, *n.* **Accu'mulator**, *n.* apparatus for storing electricity.

Acc'urate, *a.* correct, precise. **Acc'uracy**, *n.* state of exactness.

Accurs'ed, *a.* hateful, living under a curse.

Accuse', *v.t.* to charge with evil or criminal act, to blame. **Accu'ser**, *n.* **Accusa'tion**, *n.* **Accu'satory**, *a.* **Accu'sative**, *n.* *gram.* objective case.

Accus'tom, *v.t.* to make used to. **Accus'tomed**, *a.* usual, habitual.

Ace, *n.* the one in dice or cards etc. *fig.* person highly skilled in certain sport or activity.

Acerb'ity, *n.* bitterness.

Ace'tic, *a.* like vinegar, sour.

Acet'ylene, *n.* an illuminating gas of calcium carbide and water.

Ache (Ake), *n.* a constant pain. *v.i.* to suffer pain.

Achieve', *v.t.* to accomplish, complete. **Achieve'ment**, *n.*

Ac'id (-s), *a.* bitter, sharp in taste or manner. *n.* a sour chemical or substance. **Acid'ify**, *v.t.* to make acid or sour. **Acid'ity**, *n.* **Acido'sis**, *n.* condition of acidity in blood. **Acid'ulate**, *v.t.* to render slightly acid.

Acknowl'edge (Ak-nol'ij), *v.t.* to admit truth of, recognize. **Acknowl'edgement**, *n.* recognition of service done.

Ac'me, *n.* perfect state of success, highest point, *fig.*

Ac'ne, *n.* pimply skin disease.

Ac'olyte, *n.* attendant on priest.

Acous'tic (-koo or -kow), *a.* having to do with sense of hearing. **Acous'tics**, *n.pl.* the science of this.

Acquaint', *v.t.* to inform, get to know. **Acquaint'ance**, *n.* person one knows, less than a friend.

Acquiesce', *v.i.* to agree tacitly, consent, esp. reluctantly. **Acquiescence**, *n.* **Acquiescent**, *a.*

Acquire', *v.t.* to obtain, get hold of. **Acquisi'tion**, *n.* act of doing this.

Acquit', *v.t.* to declare innocent, discharge. **Acquitt'al**, *n.* act of declaring not guilty in court.

A'cre (-ker), *n.* measure of land, 4840 square yards.

Ac'rid, *a.* bitter.

Ac'rimony, *n.* bitter feeling among persons. **Acrimo'nious**, *a.*

Ac'robat, *n.* physically skilled and agile person in circus. **Acrobat'ic**, *a.*

Across, *adv.* & *prep.* crosswise, on the other side.

Acros'tic, *n.* poem or other composition in which first and or last letters of lines compose a word or sentence.

Act, *n.* a thing done or accomplished; section of play; law passed by parliament. *v.i.* to do, behave. **Act'ing**, *n.* performance of theatrical or artificial part. **Ac'tion**, *n.* deed, lawsuit, motion. **Ac'tionable**, *a.* liable to lawsuit. **Act'ive**, *a.* strong, lively. **Activ'ity**, *n.* exertion of energy. **Act'or** (*fem.* **act'ress**), *n.* one who performs on stage.

Ac'tinism, *n.* property of sun's rays whereby chemical changes are induced, e.g. in photography.

Ac'tivate, *v.t.* to make active, stimulate.

Ac'tual, *a.* existing in fact, real. **Actual'ity**, *n.* **Ac'tually**, *adv.*

Ac'tuary, *n.* professional authority on rates of mortality and accident insurance.

Ac'tuate, *v.t.* to cause to do or move.

Acu'men, *n.* keenness of wit, common-sense.

Acute', *a.* sharp, severe as in pain, critical. **Acute'ness**, *n.*

Adage (-ij), *n.* proverb, old saying.

Ad'agio (-jo), *a.* & *adv.* (*mus.*) slowly; *n.* slow movement.

Adamant, *a.* very hard, unrelenting.

Adapt, *v.t.* to fit, alter. **Adapta'tion**, *n.* different version of original work. **Adapt'able**, *a.* **Adaptabil'ity**, *n.*

Add, *v.i.* & *t.* to join something on, increase. **Addi'tion**, *n.* sum. **Additional**, *a.*

Add'er, *n.* poisonous snake, viper.

Add'ict, *n.* person obsessed with habit, esp. vicious one. **Addic'tion**, *n.*

Ad'dle, *v.i. & t.* to confuse (*fig*);
to become or make rotten.

Address', *v.t.* to speak to or
write to; send, direct. *n.* a
speech; skill; direction on letter; place where one lives. Ad-
dressee', *n.* person addressed or
written to. Address'es, *n.pl.*
arch. form for courtship.

Adduce', *v.t.* to produce as proof
or example. Adduc'tion, *n.*

Ad'enoids, *n.pl.* spongy tissue
between throat and back of
nose. Adenoidal, *a.* unclear way
of speaking because of this.

Adept', *a.* skilled. *n.* an expert.

Ad'equate, *a.* enough, suitable.
Ad'equacy, *n.*

Adhere', *v.i.* to stick to. Adhe'-
rent, *n.* follower. Adhe'sion, *n.*
adhering. Adhe'sive, *a.*

Ad'ipose, *a.* fatty. Adipos'ity, *n.*

Adja'cent, *a.* close by, near.

Ad'jective, *n.* word preceding
noun to indicate quality. Ad-
jecti'val, *a.*

Adjoin, *v.i. & t.* to lie next do.
Adjoin'ing, *a.* alongside.

Adjourn (-jurn), *v.i. & t.* to
postpone esp. meeting. Adjourn'ment, *n.*

Adjudge', *v.t.* to pronounce
verdict, act as referee in
competition.

Adju'dicate, *v.i. & t.* to sit in
judgement, to try. Adjudica'-
tion, *n.* Adju'dicator, *n.* one
who judges.

Ad'junct, *a.* of something added
or incidental to. *n.*

Adjure', *v.t.* solemnly to request. Adjura'tion, *n.*

Adjust', *v.t.* to put right or make
suitable. Adjust'ment, *n.* Ad'-
justable, *a.*

Ad'jutant, *n.* chief assistant to
military officer of higher rank.

Admin'ister, *v.t.* to look after,
manage. Administra'tion, *n.*
Admin'istrative, *a.* Admin'-
istrator, *a.*

Ad'miral, *n.* highest ranking
naval officer. Ad'miralty, *n.*
formerly title of board controlling Royal Navy.

Admire', *v.t.* to regard with much
approval, look up to with respect. Ad'mirable, *a.* person or
object worthy of this. Admira'-
tion, *n.* Admir'er, *n.*

Admit', *v.i. & t.* to allow en-
trance to; accept as correct.
Admiss'ible, *a.* Admis'sion, *n.*
Admitt'ance, *n.*

Admix'ture, *n.* blend of different
substances.

Admon'ish, *v.t.* to reprove, warn.
Admoni'tion, *n.* Admon'itory, *a.*

Ado', *n.* fuss, esp. unnecessary.

Adoles'cent, *a.* immature, growing up. *n.* person in this state.
Adoles'cence, *n.*

Adopt', *v.t.* to take person esp.
child into family or relationship; accept an idea or resolution. Adop'tion, *n.* Adopt'ive, *a.*

Adore', *v.t. & i.* to reverence,
love deeply. Ador'able, *a.*
Adora'tion, *n.*

Adorn', *v.t.* to deck with ornaments, beautify. Adorn'ment,
n. Ornament, embellishment.

Adre'nalin, *n.* hormone secreted
by adrenal glands.

Adrift', *a. & adv.* off course, out
of control.

Adroit', *a.* adept, skilled. Adroit'-
ness, *n.*

Adula'tion, *n.* excessive praise.
Ad'ulatory, *a.*

Adult', *n.* grown-up person. *a.*
mature.

Adul'terate, *v.t.* spoil or corrupt
by addition of inferior matter.

Adul'terated, a. Adul'teration, n.

Adul'tery, n. illicit sexual intercourse by a husband or wife with another person. Adul'terer, n.

Ad'umbrate, v.t. to indicate in outline. Adumbra'tion, n.

Advance', v.t. & i. to move or bring forward; encourage, promote; make a loan. Advance'ment, n. promotion or improvement in position.

Advan'tage, n. gain; superior position. Advanta'geous, a.

Ad'vent, n. arrival, coming. rel. the coming of Christ. Advent'ual, a.

Adventitious, a. by chance, accidental.

Adven'ture, n. risky enterprise, bold deed. v.t. & i. to take a chance or to risk.

Ad'verb, n. word preceding verb, adjective or other adverb to qualify meaning. Adverb'ial, a.

Ad'verse, a. hostile, contrary to. Ad'versely, adv. Ad'versary, n. opponent. Advers'ity, n. misfortune.

Advert', v.i. refer to. Advert'ence, n. Advert'ent, a.

Ad'vertise, v.t. to make known, give notice of, esp. in print. Ad'vertiser, n. Advert'isement, n. Ad'vertising, a. & n.

Ad'vice, n. counsel; opinion given; statement. Advise', v.t. to give counsel, inform. Advi'sable, a. expedient, prudent. Advi'ser, n. one who counsels.

Ad'vocate, n. legal defender. v.t. to recommend. Ad'vocacy, n. Advoca'tion, n.

Advow'son, n. rel. right of presentation to a church benefice.

Adze, n. tool for cutting away surface of wood, with arched blade at right angles to haft.

Ae'gis (e-jis), n. fig. protection, sponsorship.

A'erate, v.t. expose to air; charge with gas. A'erator, n. Aera'tion, n.

Aer'ial, n. apparatus used in transmitting or receiving radio messages etc. a. pertaining to the air.

A'ero — pref. pertaining to aircraft. Aerobat'ics, n.pl. flying of a sensational nature. A'erodrome, n. airfield. Aerodynam'ics, n. science dealing with motion of air and other gases. A'erofoil, n. aeroplane wing or lifting surface of aircraft. A'erolite or -lith, n. meteorite. A'eronaut, n. aircraft pilot. Aeronau'tics, n.pl. science of flying and navigating aircraft. A'eroplane, n. flying machine heavier than air.

Aesthet'ic (Ees-), a. pertaining to beauty and good taste. Aesthetics, n.pl. Aes'thete, n. iron. person professing excessive love of culture.

Ae'stivate, v.i. zool. spend summer in state of torpor.

Aetiol'ogy, n. philosophy or study of causes.

Afar', adv. far off, at a distance.

Aff'able, a. friendly, benign. Affabil'ity, n.

Affair', n. private or business matter. pl. operations or matters in general.

Affect', v.t. to practise, use; assume (form or character etc.) show a liking or preference for. Affecta'tion, n. insincere manner. Affect'ed, a. making a pretence. Affec'tion, n. fondness, almost love. Affec'tionate, a. Affect'ing, a. stirring the feelings, pathetic.

A'fferent, a. conducting inwards, esp. of nerves connected with brain.

Affi'ance, v.t. to betroth.

Affida'vit, n. statement made on oath and signed in presence of witness.

Affil'iate, v.t. to join e.g. a society or federation; attribute to. Affilia'tion, n.

Affin'ity, n. mutual attraction, relationship. Affin'itive, a.

Affirm', v.t. & i. to state positively, declare formally. Affirma'tion, n. Affirm'ative, a. & n.

Affix', v.t. to attach, fasten to. Aff'ix, n. an addition.

Affla'tion, n. act of breathing or blowing on. Affla'tus, n. iron. inspiration, us. as divine afflatus.

Afflict', v.t. to give or cause pain or grief. Afflic'tion, n.

Aff'luent, a. prosperous. n. a tributary. Aff'luence, n. wealth.

Afford', v.t. to be able to purchase; yield supply of.

Affray', n. riot or breach of the peace.

Affright', v.t. to terrify.

Affront', v.t. to insult grossly. n. an insult. Affront'ed, adj.

Afield', adv. about, in or on the field, abroad.

Afire', adv. on fire.

Aflame', adv. ardent, passionate.

Afloat', adv. floating, at sea.

Afoot', adv. astir; in preparation.

Afore', adv. & prep. before, us. in compounds, e.g. aforesaid.

Afraid', a. timid, in fear.

Afresh', adv. once again, anew.

Afrikan'der, n. S. African of European descent. Afrikaans', n. S. African language originating from 17th-century Dutch.

Aft, adv. near or towards stern of vessel.

Af'ter, adv. behind, later. prep. in imitation of, e.g. after Velasquez; as prefix as in e.g. afterbirth, n. membrane extruded after birth; aftermath. second crop, esp. of hay. Af'terwards, adv. later on.

Again', adv. once more, besides.

Against', prep. opposed to; leaning on.

Agape', a. or adv. open-mouthed in astonishment etc.

Ag'ate, n. precious stone of various kinds.

Age, n. length of time person or object exists; a period of time or history. v.t. to make old. v.i. to grow old. A'ged, a. old. Age'less, a. undying, immortal. Age'long, a.

Agen'da, n.pl. list of items to be dealt with at meeting.

A'gent, n. person acting for someone else; representative. chem. substance causing certain action. A'gency, n. active operation, office of agent.

Agglom'erate, v.t. & i. to collect into a mass. Agglom'erate, n. geol. mass of volcanic matter united by great heat. Agglomera'tion, n.

Agglu'tinate, v.t. to unite as with glue. Agglutina'tion, n.

Agg'randize, v.t. to make greater in importance or size. Aggrand'dizement, n.

Agg'ravate, v.t. to increase degree of offence or pain. Aggrava'tion, n. Agg'ravating, a.

Agg'regate, v.t. & i. to collect together. n. total, mass, score.

Aggre'ssion, n. pugnacity, unprovoked attack. Aggress'ive, a. pugnacious. Aggress'or, n.

Aggrieve', *v.t.* to distress, cause pain.

Aghast', *a.* horrorstruck.

Ag'ile, *a.* nimble, quick. Agil'ity, *n.*

Ag'itate, *v.t.* to disturb, shake up, make nervous. Agita'tion, *n.* Agi'tator, *n. us.* person who seeks to disturb politically or industrially.

Aglow', *adv.* & *a.* glowing, bright, excited.

Agnos'tic, *n.* person who believes that humanity can know nothing of things or life outside material world. Agnos'ticism, *n.*

Ago', *a.* & *adv.* in the past, since.

Agog', *a.* & *adv.* excited, eager.

Ag'ony, *n.* great pain or suffering. Ag'onize, *v.i.* Ag'onizing, *a.*

Agra'rian, *a.* relating to farming and management of land.

Agree', *v.i.* to consent, be of same opinion. Agree'able, *a.* consenting, pleasant. Agree'ment, *n.* contract, pact.

Ag'riculture, *n.* the practice of cultivating the soil, farming. Agricul'tural, *a.* Agricul'turist, *n.* farmer.

Agron'omy, *n.* rural economy, farming.

Aground', *adv.* stranded, esp. of vessel.

A'gue, *n.* shivering fever.

Ahead', *adv.* in advance, in front of, forward.

Ahoy', *interj. naut.* call to attract attention of another ship.

Aid, *v.t.* to help. *n.* help, assistance.

Aide-de-Camp, *n. us.* as A.D.C. chief staff officer assisting superior, viceroy's assistant.

Ail, *v.t.* & *i.* to sicken, trouble. Ail'ing, *a.* Ail'ment, *n.* illness.

Ai'leron, *n.* movable flap on aircraft wing.

Aim, *v.t.* & *i.* to direct at, e.g. effort, projectile; throw or strike. *n.* direction, object, purpose. Aim'less, *a.* purposeless.

Air, *n.* mixture of gases enveloping the earth; *mus.* a tune. *pl.* artificial manner. *v.t.* to expose to the air. Air'ily, *adv.* lightly. Air'ing, *n.* to have an outing, put clothes in open.

Air, as prefix, e.g. aircraft. **airfield, airgun, airtight** etc.

Aisle, *n.* division of church, passage between pews.

Ait, *n.* small island in river.

Ajar', *adv.* partly open, esp. door.

Akim'bo, *adv.* hands on hips and elbows turned outwards.

Akin', *a.* related by blood or type; similar to.

Al'abaster, *n.* stone resembling marble.

Alack', *interj. arch.* ejaculation of distress.

Alac'rity, *n.* quickness, cheerful readiness.

Alarm', *n.* warning cry or sound. *v.t.* to arouse to danger, call to action or arms. Alarm'ing, *a.* & *adv.* Alar'um, *n. arch.* form of alarm.

Alas', *interj.* cry of grief or distress.

Albe'it, *conj. arch.* even though, notwithstanding.

Albi'no, *n.* animal (inc. human) with white hair and pink eyes due to faulty pigmentation. Al'binism, *n.*

Al'bum, *n.* book with blank leaves for mounting stamps, photographs, etc.

17   **Allitera'tion**

Albu'men, *n.* white of egg. **Albu'-minous,** *a.*

Al'chemy, *n.* mediaeval form of chemistry. **Al'chemist,** *n.*

Al'cohol, *n.* pure spirit of wine; any intoxicating liquor. **Alcohol'ic,** *a.* & *n.* **Al'coholism,** *n.* poisoning caused by excess of alcohol.

Al'cove, *n.* a recess.

Al'dehyde, *n.* volatile fluid obtained by oxidization of alcohol.

Al'derman, *n.* co-opted member of city or borough council. **Alderman'ic,** *a.*

Ale, *n.* liquor made with fermented malt, flavoured with hops. **Ale'-house,** *n. arch.* form of inn.

Alert', *a.* watchful. *n.* warning of possible attack, state of readiness.

Alfres'co, *n.* & *a.* in the open-air, informal.

Al'gebra, *n.* manner of calculation by means of symbols. **Algebra'ic,** *a.*

Alge'sia, *n.* extreme sensitivity to pain.

A'lias, *adv.* otherwise. *n.* an assumed name.

Al'ibi (-by), *n.* proof that a person was elsewhere when a crime was committed.

A'lien, *a.* foreign; different in nature. *n.* a foreigner. **A'lienate,** *v.t.* to estrange. **Aliena'tion,** *n.* **A'lienist,** *n.* specialist in mental disorders.

Alif'erous, *a.* possessing wings. **Al'iform,** *a.* wing-shaped. **Alig'-erous** (-j), *a.* winged.

Alight', *v.i.* to descend, settle.

Alight', *a.* on fire, radiant.

Align', *v.t.* to bring into line. **Align'ment,** *n.*

Alike', *a.* similar, same.

Al'iment, *n.* food. **Aliment'ary,** *a.* nourishing. **Alimenta'tion,** *n.*

Al'imony, *n.* maintenance paid to ex-wife by divorced husband.

Al'iquot, *n.* part contained by a whole a certain number of times without remainder.

Alive', *a.* living, active.

Al'kali, *n. chem.* substance combining with acid to form a salt. **Al'kaline,** *a.* **Al'kaloid,** *n.* & *a.*

All (Awl), *a.* & *n.* total, entire, everyone. **All-in,** *a.* & *adv.* including everything. **All round,** *a.* versatile. **All clear,** *n.* signal denoting end of alarm.

Al'lah, *n.* Arabic name for God.

Allay', *v.t.* to lessen, relieve.

Allege', *v.t.* & *i.* to make accusation, affirm. **Allega'tion,** *n.*

Alle'giance, *n.* duty of a subject to his sovereign or to a cause, loyalty.

All'egory, *n.* story with a meaning other than literal one. **Allego'rical,** *a.* figurative manner of speaking or writing.

Alle'gro, *adv. mus.* briskly. **Allegret'to,** *a.* less briskly.

Al'lergy, *n.* extreme sensitivity to certain substances. **Aller'gic,** *a.*

Alle'viate, *v.t.* to make easier, lighter. **Allevia'tion,** *n.*

All'ey, *n.* narrow passage or lane; enclosure for skittles.

Alli'ance, *n.* condition of being allied or joined; union of states by pact or families by marriage.

All'igator, *n.* member of crocodile family found in the Americas.

Allitera'tion, *n.* commencement of consecutive words with same letters, e.g. 'Around the rugged

rocks the ragged rascals ran'.
Allit'erative, *a.*

All'ocate, *v.t.* to assign, portion
out. Alloca'tion, *n.*

All'ocution, *n.* formal address,
esp. by pope.

Allot', *v.t.* to distribute share.
Allot'ment, *n.* distribution, payment; small vegetable plot.

Allo'tropy, *n.* substance's property of appearing or existing
in different forms, e.g. carbon
in form of diamond and coal.

Allow', *v.t.* to permit, grant.
Allow'able, *a.* Allow'ance, *n.*
fixed payment other than salary or wage.

Alloy', *n.* mixture of different
metals.

Allude', *v.i.* to refer to inciden-
tally. Allu'sion, *n.* Allu'sive, *a.*

Allure', *v.t.* to tempt, win over,
attract strongly. Allu'ring, *a.*
Allure'ment, *n.*

Allu'vium, *n.* deposit of silt washed down by river. Allu'vial, *a.*

Ally', *v.t.* to make an alliance.
Al'ly *n.* partner.

Al'manac (Awl-), *n.* calendar of
months and tides etc.

Almi'ghty (Awl-), *a.* all-powerful.
n. God.

Al'most (Awl-), *adv.* nearly, all
but.

Alms (Ahms), *n.* gifts to the needy. Alm'oner, *n. lit.* distributor
of alms; now official of hospital. Alms'house, *n.* charitable
house for poor people.

Aloft', *adv.* overhead; *naut.* in
the rigging.

Alone', *a.* solitary, by oneself.
adv. separately.

Along', *adv.* lengthwise, together
with.

Aloof', *adv.* cold in manner,
keeping apart.

Aloud', *adv.* in a clear voice.

Alp, *n.* high mountain, us. as
alps. Al'pine, *a.* very high, characteristic of high places. Al'-
pinist, *n.* mountaineer.

Alpac'a, *n.* cloth made from
wool of Peruvian sheep.

Al'penstock, *n.* walking staff
iron-shod for use in climbing.

Al'pha, *n.* first letter of Greek
alphabet; also used to denote
high mark in examinations etc.

Al'phabet, *n.* letters used in a
language. Alphabet'ical, *a.* following order of letters in alphabet.

Already (Awl-), *adv.* by this time,
previously.

Al'so (Awl-), *adv.* in addition, as
well as.

Al'tar (Awl-), *n.* form of table or
raised place deriving from
sacrificial stone; in Christian
church place where priest con-
secrates eucharist.

Al'ter (Awl-), *v.t. & i.* to make or
become different. Al'terable, *a.*
us. when as negative unalter-
able. Altera'tion, *n.*

Alterca'tion, (Awl-) *n.* wordy
dispute. Al'tercate, *v.i.*

Al'ternate (Awl-), *v.t. & i.* to happen or cause to happen by turn.
Alter'nate, *a.* Alter'native, *a.*
& n. offering choice of two
different things or courses.

Although' (Awl-), *conj.* though,
admitting that.

Altim'eter, *n.* instrument for
measuring height esp. in aircraft.

Al'titude, *n.* height above sea
level.

Al'to, *n. mus.* male voice of
highest pitch.

Altogeth'er (Awl-), *adv.* entirely,
in conjunction.

Al'truism, *n.* principle of living and acting for benefit of others. Altruis'tic, *a.*

Al'um, *n.* a mineral salt, double sulphate of aluminium and potassium.

Alumin'ium, *n.* very light untarnishable metal.

Alum'nus, *n.* pupil, graduate of college (Amer.)

Al'ways (Awl-), *adv.* forever, at all times.

Amal'gam, *n.* compound of different substances, alloy of mercury and other metal. Amal'gamate, *v.t.* to combine, mix, join. Amalgama'tion, *n.*

Amanuen'sis, *n.* *arch.* person who writes at another's dictation, secretary in special way.

Amass', *v.t.* to gather in quantity, esp. of money.

Am'ateur (-ter), *n.* person who engages in sporting or other activity for pleasure and not for payment. Amateur'ish, *a.* of poor quality.

Am'atory, *a.* pertaining to or causing love.

Amaze'.*v.t.*to astonish, astound. Ama'zing, *a.* Amaze'ment, *n.* great surprise or astonishment.

Am'azon, *n.* a female warrior; masculine type of woman.

Ambass'ador, *n.* diplomatic representative. Ambassado'rial, *a.*

Am'ber, *n.* fossil resin of yellow colour. *a.* made of or coloured like amber.

Am'bergris, *n.* wax-like, fragrant substance produced in sperm whale and used for making perfume.

Ambidex'trous, *a.* able to use both hands equally well. Ambidexter'ity, *n.* ability with both hands.

Ambig'uous, *a.* unclear, open to double meaning. Ambigu'ity, *n.*

Am'bit, *n.* extent, precincts, bounds.

Ambi'tion, *n.* desire to better oneself, to gain power or honour. Ambi'tious, *a.*

Ambiv'alence, -ency, *n.* simultaneous attraction to and repulsion from something.

Am'ble, *v.i.* to proceed at leisurely pace.

Ambro'sia, *n.* *orig.* food of the gods, anything delicious. Ambro'sial, *a.*

Am'bulance, *n.* vehicle for transporting sick or wounded.

Ambuscade', *n.* more usually ambush, *n.* military force concealed to make surprise attack. *v.t.*

Ame'liorate, *v.t. & i.* to make better, improve. Ameliora'tion, *n.*

Ame'nable, *a.* easy to be persuaded or led. Amenabil'ity, *n.*

Amend', *v.t. & i.* to make or grow better, change in detail. Amend'ment, *n.* Amends, *n. pl.* reparation. To make amends, to compensate for.

Ame'nity, *n.* pleasantness; us. as *n. pl.* pleasant ways or facilities.

A'miable, *a.* kindly, friendly. Amiabil'ity, *n.*

Am'icable, *a.* friendly.

Amice, *n.* religious vestment.

Amid', Amidst', *prep.* among.

Amid'ships, *adv.* in middle of ship.

Amiss', *a.* wrong. *adv.* faulty.

Ammo'nia, *n.* pungent alkaline gas.

Ammuni'tion, *n.* military projectiles and weapons.

Amne'sia, *n.* loss of memory.

Am'nesty, n. a general pardon of prisoners.

Amoe'ba, n. Microscopic animalcule. Amoe'bic, a.

Among, Amongst', prep. making part of, mixed with.

Amor'al (A-), a. without morals.

Am'orous, a. quickly moved to love, in love.

Amorph'ous, a. shapeless.

Amount', v.i. to come to in total. n. the whole.

Am'pere, n. unit of current in electricity.

Amphib'ious, a. living or capable of moving both on land and in water. Amphib'ian, n.

Amphithe'atre, n. open-air building with curved tiers of seats.

Am'ple, a. enough, full, plenty. Am'plify, v.t. to make louder or bigger. Am'plifier, n. apparatus for increasing sound. Amplifica'tion, n. Am'plitude, n. plenitude.

Am'putate, v.t. surg. to cut off limb Amputa'tion, n.

Amuck', Amok', adv. us. only in 'to run amok', berserk or murderous frenzy.

Am'ulet, n. object worn as a charm.

Amuse', v.t. to occupy pleasantly, divert, arouse sense of fun. Amu'sing, a. Amu'sement, n.

Anabap'tist, n. person believing that baptism should be adult only.

Anac'hronism, n. error in computing time, wrongful attribution of phenomena to certain period.

Anae'mia, n. lack of blood. Anae'mic, a.

Anaesthet'ic, n. surg. drug to cause insensibility during operation. a. Anaes'thetist, n. med.

professional who administers anaesthetics.

An'agram, n. sentence or word composed by rearranging letters of another sentence or word.

Anal'ogy, n. similarity, parallel. Anal'ogize, v.t. Anal'ogous, a.

Anal'ysis, n. detailed explanation or description. pl. anal'yses. An'alyse, v.t. An'alyst, n. Analyt'ical, a.

An'archy, n. without government, polit. doctrine holding that government should be abolished. An'archist, n. Anarc'hical, a.

Anath'ema, n. accursed thing, rel. official curse, anything detested. Anath'ematize, v.t.

Anat'omy, n. science of the study of the body; surg. dissection of the body. Anatom'ical, a. Anat'omist, n.

An'cestor, n. relations from whom one's family is descended. Ancestral', a. An'cestry, n. lineage.

An'chor, n. naut. instrument for keeping vessel in position when not moving. v.t. & i. An'chorage, n.

Anc'horite, n. rel. a hermit.

An'cient, a. old, out of date. n. an old person.

An'cillary, a. subordinate, subservient.

Andan'te, adv. mus. moderately slowly. n.

An'ecdote, n. very short story us. recounted verbally.

Anemom'eter, n. instrument for measuring strength of wind. Anemomet'tric, a. Anemom'etry, n.

An'eroid, a. barometer working without use of mercury.

Anew', *adv*. afresh, again.

An'gel, (-jel) *n*. divine messenger; *fig*. extremely kindly person. Angel'ic, *a*.

An'ger, *n*. ire, wrath. *v.t*. to offend. An'gry, *a*.

Angi'na, (-jy-) *n*. inflammation of the throat.

An'gle, *v.i*. to fish. An'gler, *n*. fisherman (rod).

An'gle, *n*. a corner, meeting of two lines, point of view. An'gular, *a*. sharp, awkward.

An'glican, *a*. of the Church of England.

An'glicise, *v.t*. to express something foreign in English. An'glicism, *n*. idiomatic English.

An'glo- *pref*. English, e.g. Anglo-Catholic, Anglo-American.

An'guish, *n*. extreme pain or distress.

Anhy'drous, *a*. free from water.

Animadvert', *v.i*. to criticise or censure. Animadver'sion, *n*.

An'imal, *n*. organism endowed with life and power of movement; a beast. An'imalism, *n*.

An'imate, *v.t*. to put life into, to enliven. An'imated, *a*. gay, lively. Anima'tion, *n*.

An'imism, *n*. primitive religion, belief in spirits.

Animos'ity, *n*. enmity, mutual dislike.

An'kle, *n*. joint between foot and leg.

Ann'als, *n.pl*. records of events kept year by year. Ann'alist, *n*.

Anneal', *v.t*. to toughen metal or glass by heating and slow cooling.

Annex', *v.t*. to seize, esp. of territory, to add. Ann'exe, *n*. an additional building, something added. Annexa'tion. *n*. forcible seizure.

Anni'hilate, *v.t*. to destroy utterly. Annihila'tion, *n*.

Anniver'sary, *a*. yearly return of a date and its celebration.

Ann'otate, *v.t*. to make notes upon. Annota'tion, *n*.

Announce', *v.t*. to make known, proclaim. Announce'ment, *n*. Announ'cer, *n*. us. broadcasting official who reads news or gives out announcements.

Annoy', *v.t*. to vex, irritate. Annoy'ance, *n*.

Ann'ual, *a*. yearly. *n*. magazine or book published once a year, plant that lives only one year.

Annu'ity, *n*. sum paid yearly.

Annul', *v.t*. to abolish. Annul'ment, *n*.

Ann'ular, *a*. ring-shaped.

Annuncia'tion, *n*. announcement; esp. *rel*. Gabriel's to the Virgin Mary. Annun'ciate, *v.t*. proclaim.

An'odyne, *a*. relieving pain. *n*. a drug for this.

Anoint', *v.t*. to smear with ointment or oil; *rel*. to consecrate with oil. Anoint'ment, *n*.

Anom'alous, *a*. abnormal, irregular. Anom'aly, *n*.

Anon', *adv*. *arch*. in a short time, soon.

Anon'ymous, *a*. without name. Anonym'ity, *n*.

Anoth'er, *pron*. someone else, a different one. *a*. different.

An'swer, *v.t*. & *i*. to reply to, satisfy, meet needs of. An'swerable, *a*.

Antag'onist, *n*. an opponent. Antag'onism, *n*. hostility. Antag'onise, *v.t*. to offend, make enemy of. Antagonis'tic, *adv*.

Antarc'tic, *a*. of the south polar regions. *n*.

An'te, *n.* stake in poker. *v.t.* to put up a stake in this.

Ante- *pref.* meaning going before, e.g. ante-chamber, ante-date, etc. **Antedilu'vian,** *a.* before the flood, i.e. *fig.* out of fashion.

Antenn'a, *n.* an insect's feelers; an aerial.

Ante'rior, *a.* before or previous.

An'them, *n.* a piece of sacred or official music.

Anthol'ogy, *n.* a selection of writings, esp. poems. **Anthol'ogist,** *n.* person who makes such a selection.

An'thracite, *n.* a kind of hard coal.

An'thrax, *n.* a contagious disease esp. among cattle and certain wild animals, e.g. elephant; also communicable to man.

An'thropoid, *n.* an ape resembling man. *a.*

Anthropol'ogy, *n.* the study of mankind. **Anthropol'ogist,** *n.* scientist specialising in this.

Anthropormorph'ism, *n.* the attribution of human form or characteristics to deities and animals.

Anti- *pref.* meaning against, e.g. anti-cy'clone, anti-cli'max, etc.

An'tic, *n.* us. *n. pl.* grotesque or amusing movement.

Antic'ipate, *v.t.* to foresee, forestall, enjoy in advance, **Anticipa'tion,** *n.* **Antic'ipatory,** *a.*

An'timony, *n.* a brittle metal.

Antip'athy, *n.* firm aversion or dislike. **Antipathet'ic.** *a.*

Anti'phonal, *a. & n.* sung alternately; *mus.* or *lit.* composition.

Antip'odes, *n.pl.* region or regions diametrically opposite to each other.

Antique', *a.* ancient, old-fashioned. *n.* relic of ancient art or craft.

Antiq'uity, *n.* former times. **Antiqua'rian,** *a.* connected with the study of antiquities.

Antith'esis, *n.* exact opposite, contrast. **Antithet'ical,** *a.*

Ant'ler, *n.* branched horns on deer's head.

An'tonym, *n.* a word of opposite meaning to another.

A'nus, *n.* posterior opening of alimentary canal in animals.

An'vil, *n.* iron block on which blacksmith works metal.

Anx'ious, *a.* disquieted, uneasy. **Anxi'ety,** *n.*

An'y, *a. & pron.* somebody or something, some.

Apace', *adv.* briskly, at a quick pace.

Apache (-ash), *n.* desperado, esp. in Paris formerly.

Apartheid (Afrikaans), *n.* racial segregation.

Apart'ment, *n.* a room or rooms, esp. as flat.

Ap'athy, *n.* lack of interest or feelings. **Apathet'ic,** *a.*

Ape, *n.* a monkey; *fig.* imitator. *v.t.* to imitate.

Ape'rient, *n.* mild laxative. *a.*

Aper'itif, *n.* alcoholic drink taken before meal.

Ap'erture, *n.* an opening, gap.

A'pex, *n.* peak, highest point.

Apha'sia, *n.* sudden loss of speech as result of stroke, etc.

Aph'orism, *n.* a maxim, succinct saying. **Aphoris'tic,** *a.*

Aphrodis'iac, *n.* anything that excites sexually. *a.*

A'piary, *n.* place where bees are kept. **A'piarist,** *n.* beekeeper.

Apiece', *adv.* severally, each.

Aplomb, *n.* self-possession, poise.

Apoc'alypse, *n.* a revelation, esp. that of St John. Apocalyp'tic, *a.*

Apoc'rypha, *n.* any writing. esp. rel. of dubious authenticity. apoc'ryphal, *a.*

Ap'ogee, *n.* point of sun's or moon's orbit farthest from the earth.

Apol'ogy, *n.* something uttered in defence; acknowledgement of an offence and expression of regret for this; a poor substitute for something. Apol'ogize, *v.i.* Apol'ogist, *n.* Apologet'ic, *a.*

Ap'oplexy, *n.* sudden stroke; *fig.* great anger. Apoplec'tic, *a.*

Apos'tasy, *n.* betrayal of one's religion. Apos'tate, *n.* one who abandons or betrays his faith.

Apos'tle, *n. rel.* follower or champion of new belief, esp. in Christianity. Apostol'ic, *a.*

Apos'trophe, *n.* sign of omission of letter or possessive case; exclamatory address. Apos'trophise, *v.t.*

Apoth'ecary, *n. arch.* name for chemist.

Apotheo'sis, *n.* deification, deified ideal.

Appal'(-awl), *v.t.* to horrify, to dismay greatly. Appall'ing, *a.*

Appara'tus, *n.* machine or equipment for carrying out operation or experiment, etc.

Appar'el, *n.* clothing in a formal sense.

Appa'rent, *a.* obvious, clear. seeming. Appa'rentness, *n.*

Appari'tion, *n.* ghostly appearance.

Appeal, *v.i.* to call upon earnestly, e.g. for help or advice. *Leg.* refer to higher court. *n.* Appeal'ing, *a.* pitiable. Ap-

pell'ant, *n.* one who appeals to court.

Appear', *v.i.* to become visible, to come, to seem. Appear'ance, *n.*

Appease', *v.t.* to pacify, satisfy, us. in sense of weakness. Appease'ment, *n.*

Appela'tion, *n.* form of name.

Append', *v.t.* to add, join on. Append'age, *n.* addition.

Append'ix, *n.* addition to book etc; part of intestines. Appendici'tis, *n. surg.* inflammation of appendix.

Appertain', *v.i.* to relate to, belong to.

App'etence, *n.* strong desire, longing after.

App'etite, *n.* desire, inclination, e.g. for food.

Applaud', *v.t.* to praise loudly, by word or clapping hands. Applause', *n.*

Apply', *v.t.* to put close to, use, administer, address oneself to. Appli'ance, *n.* equipment or apparatus. App'licant, *n.* one who asks for something. Application, *n.* App'licable, *a.*

Appoint', *v.t.* to nominate to an office, fix, settle, equip. Appoint'ment, *n.* job, position, agreement to meet at certain time.

Appor'tion, *v.t.* to divide out in shares. Appor'tionment, *n.*

App'osite, *a.* apt, suitable. Apposi'tion, *n.* placing side by side.

Appraise', *v.t.* to determine value. Apprais'al, *n.*

Appre'ciate, *v.t.* to value properly. *v.i.* to increase in value. Apprecia'tion, *n.* Appre'ciative, *a.*

Apprehend', *v.t.* to arrest; understand. **Apprehen'sion**, *n.* **Apprehen'sive**, *a.* fearful.

Appren'tice, *n.* person bound legally to master in order to learn certain trade. *v.t.* **Appren'ticeship**, *n.*

Apprise', *v.t.* to inform.

Approach', *v.i.* to come near.

Approba'tion, *n.* approval, sanction.

Appro'priate, *a.* fitting, suitable. *v.t.* to take hold of, devote. **Appro'priateness**, *n.* **Appropria'tion**, *n.*

Approve', *v.t.* to think well of, sanction. **Approv'al**, *n.*

Approx'imate, *a.* nearly correct or resembling. *v.t.* & *i.* to bring or come near. **Approxima'tion**, *n.* **Approx'imative**, *a.*

Appurt'enance, *n.* an accessory, thing which appertains to.

A'pron, *n.* piece of cloth or leather worn to protect person working.

Apse, *n.* arched recess in church.

Apt, *a.* suitable, quick-witted. **Apt'itude**, *n.*

Aqua'rium, *n.* tank for keeping fish and other water creatures in.

Aquat'ic, *a.* living or growing in water, pertaining to water.

Aq'ueduct, *n.* artificial channel for carrying water.

A'queous, *a.* watery.

Aq'uiline, *a.* relating to the eagle ; hooked like eagle's beak.

Ar'ab, *n.* native of Arabia or similar countries; pedigree horse. **Ar'abic**, *n.* language of Arabian countries.

Arabesque', *n.* fanciful decoration.

Ar'able, *a.* land used for tilling crops. *n.*

Arb'iter, *n.* umpire, judge. **Arbitra'tion**, *n.* **Arb'itrator**, *n.* one who settles dispute between others. **Arbit'rary**, *a.* despotic, unrestrained.

Arbo'real, *a.* pertaining to trees.

Arb'our, *n.* part of garden sheltered by trees.

Arc, *n.* part of circle or curve.

Arcade, *n.* covered walk, lined with buildings.

Arca'num, *n.* mystery, secret.

Arch, *n.* curved structure in architecture. *v.t.* to make into an arch.

Arch, *a.* roguish. **Arch'ness**, *n.*

Arch, *a.* chief, e.g. **arch-villain.** But in arch-angel = ark.

Archaeology, (-ke-ol-) *n.* the study of antiquities. **Archaeo'gical**, *a.* **Archaeol'ogist**, *n.*

Archa'ic (-k-), *a.* outmoded, primitive. **Archa'ism**, *n.* an obsolete custom or expression.

Arch'er, *n.* bowman. **Arch'ery**, *n.*

Arch'ctype (-k-), *n.* an original pattern or type. **Arc'hetypal**, *a.*

Archipel'ago (-k-), *n.* group of many islands.

Arch'itect (-k-), *n.* designer of buildings. **Architect'ure**, *n.* the art of building. **Architec'tural**, *a.*

Arch'ives (-k), *n. pl.* public records, place where these are kept. **Arc'hival**, *a.* **Arc'hivist**, *n.* person who keeps such records and documents.

Arc'tic, *a.* of the northern polar regions. *n.*

Ard'ent, *a.* passionate, enthusiastic. **Ard'our**, *n.*

Ard'uous, *a.* laborious, difficult to accomplish.

Ar'ea, *n.* extent, scope, .yard round house.

Are'na, *n.* open space in amphitheatre for performances of various kinds.

Ar'gent, a. silvery-white, esp. in heraldry.

Arg'osy, n. large, richly laden merchant-ship (arch.)

Arg'ue, v.t. & i. to discuss, offer reasons, dispute. Arg'uable, a. Arg'ument, n. Argument'a-tive, a.

A'ria, n. song in opera.

Ar'id, a. dry, parched. Arid'ity, n.

Aright', adv. correctly, rightly.

Arise', v.i. to get up, rise, result.

Aristoc'racy, n. government by best citizens; the noble classes; an elite. Arist'ocrat, n. Arist'o-cratic, a.

Arith'metic, n. the science of numbers, computation. Arith-met'ical, a. Arithmeti'cian, n.

Ark, n. chest, box; vessel used by Noah during flood.

Arm, n. limb extending from shoulder; any projecting limb as in branch of sea etc.

Arm, n. military weapon, us. n. pl. v,t. & i. to supply with weapons, take up weapons. Arm'ament, n. esp. n. pl. mil. weapons and supplies.

Arma'da (-ahdah), n. fleet of warships.

Arm'ature, n. defensive covering of animal etc, essential part of dynamo.

Arm'istice, n. mil. a truce between opposing armies.

Arm'our, n. defensive covering. Arm'ourer, n. a maker of weapons. Arm'oury, n. mil. store-place for weapons etc.

Arm'y, n. mil. large organized body of soldiers, a great number.

Aro'ma, n. pleasant odour. Aro-mat'ic, a.

Around', adv. on every side.

Arouse', v.t. to awaken.

Arraign' (-rain), t.v. to accuse, indict. Arraign'ment, n.

Arrange', v.t. to set in order, settle, adjust. Arrange'ment, n.

Ar'rant, a. notorious, down-right.

Array', v.t. to set in order, to dress up. n.

Arrear', n. something undone or unpaid; us. n. pl.

Arrest', v.t. to stop, person or object, apprehend by legal war-rant. n. seizure of criminal or suspect by police.

Arrive', v.i. to reach a destina-tion; Arri'val, n.

Ar'rogate, v.t. claim unduly. Ar'rogance, n. overbearing pride. Ar'rogant, a.

Ar'row, n. pointed missile fired from bow.

Ars'enal, n. establishment for construction or storage of armaments.

Ars'enic, n. a violent mineral poison.

Ars'on, n. the crime of setting fire to property.

Art, n. human skill as opposed to nature; skill applied to paint-ing, literature, music, etc. A craft or profession, a system. Art'ist, n. Artis'tic, a.

Art'ery, n. a vessel or tube car-rying blood from the heart. Arte'rial, a. to do with the arteries; now us. as main, im-portant, as in a. road.

Arte'sian, a. of a well sunk for water which rises by internal pressure.

Art'icle, n. a thing or object; a clause or section in a law or agreement. v.t. to apprentice to a profession, e.g. solicitor. n. a journalistic or literary composition.

Artic'ulate, *v.t.* to utter clearly, to joint. *a.* **Articula'tion**, *n.*

Art'ifice, *n.* device, contrivance. **Artif'icer**, *n.* craftsman or mechanic. **Artifi'cial**, *a.* not genuine.

Artill'ery, *n.* large guns or cannons; branch of army using these.

Artisan', *n.* workman, craftsman.

Ar'yan, *a.* pertaining to the Indo-European people and languages.

As, *adv.*, *conj.* so far, since, because, while, in similar manner.

Asbes'tos, *n.* fibrous non-flammable mineral.

Ascend', *v.i.* to rise, mount. **Ascension'**, *n.* **Ascent'**, *n.* act of ascending. **Ascend'ancy**, *n.* domination, supremacy over.

Ascertain', *v.t. & i.* to find out, make sure.

Ascet'ic, *n.* person who lives austerely. *a.* abstinent, austere. **Ascet'ism**, *n.* **Ascet'ical**, *adv.*

Ascribe', *v.t.* to attribute, assign. **Ascri'bable**, *a.* **Ascrip'tion**, *n.*

Asep'tic (A-), *a.* clean, free from germs. **Asep'sis**, *n.*

Asex'ual (A-), *a.* without sex.

Ash, *n.* residue of burnt material.

Ashamed', *a.* filled with shame.

Ashore', *adv.* on shore, run aground.

Aside', *adv.* on one side, privately, in an undertone. *n.*

As'inine, *a.* like an ass. **Asinin'ity**, *n.*

Ask, *v.t.* to request, invite, inquire of.

Askance', *adv.* sideways esp. to look at askance, to regard suspiciously.

Askew', *adv.* awry, crookedly.

Aslant', *adv.* obliquely, not straight.

Asleep', *a. & adv.* sleeping, at rest.

As'pect, *n.* view, appearance, look, direction in which house or other object faces.

Asper'ity, *n.* brusqueness, harshness.

Asperse', *v.t.* to bespatter, calumniate. **Asper'sion**, *n.* unjustifiable remark about someone.

As'phalt, *n.* bituminous substance used, e.g. in road-making.

Asphyx'ia, *n.* suffocation. **Asphyx'iate**, *v.t.* **Asphyxia'tion**, *n.*

As'pic, *n.* savoury meat jelly.

As'pirate, *a. & n.* the sound of "h".

Aspire', *v.i.* to aim high in ambition, desire eagerly. **As'pirant**, *n.* one who aspires. **Aspira'tion**, *n.*

Assail', *v.t.* to attack. **Assail'ant**, *n.*

Assass'in, *n.* murderer us. in polit. sense, paid murderer. **Assass'inate**, *v.t.* **Assassina'tion**, *n.*

Assault', *n.* a sudden attack. *v.t.* to make violent attack on.

Assay', *v.t.* to test genuineness of metal. *n.*

Assem'ble, *v.t. & i.* to collect, gather together. **Assem'blage**, *n.* **Assem'bly**, *n.*

Assent', *n.* agreement. *v.i.* to agree, concur.

Assert', *v.t.* to insist upon one's rights, declare strongly. **Asser'tion**, *n.* strong declaration. **Assert'ive**, *a.*

Assess', *v.t.* establish the value of something, fix an amount, of fine or taxation etc. **Assess'-**

able, *a.* **Assess'ment,** *n.* **Assess'-or,** *n.*

Ass'ets, *n.pl.* property of value, esp. in sense of available to cover debts.

Asse'verate, *v.t.* to declare solemnly. **Assevera'tion,** *n.*

Assid'uous, *a.* persevering. **Assidu'ity,** *n.* devotion to work.

Assign', *v.t.* allot as a share, make over, fix. **Assigna'tion,** *n.* apportionment, appointment. **Assign'ment,** *n.* legal transference.

Assim'ilate, *v.t.* to make like, to absorb. **Assimila'tion,** *n.*

Assist', *v.t.* to help. **Assis'tance,** *n.* **Assis'tant,** *a.*

Assize', *n.* us. as *n. pl.* periodical county court.

Asso'ciate, *v.t. & i.* to join with, combine, go with. *n.* a companion, partner. **Associa'tion,** *n.*

Ass'onance, *n.* resemblance of sound, e.g. in rhyming syllables. **Ass'onant,** *a.*

Assort', *v.t. & i.* to classify, group with others. **Assort'ed,** *a.* **Assort'ment,** *n.* things of different kinds.

Assuage' (-sw-), *v.t.* to soften **Assuage'ment,** *n.*

Assume', *v.t.* to take upon oneself, to take for granted; to simulate. *v.t.* to enter upon duty or office. **Assum'ing,** *a.* tending to be arrogant. **Assump'tive,** *a.* **Assump'tion,** *n.*

Assure', *v.t.* to impart confidence, tell definitely, make safe. **Assur'ed,** *a.* **Assur'ance,** *n.*

As'terisk, *n.* star (*) used in printing to mark words for reference or distinction.

Astern', *adv.* behind, to go astern, reverse engines, backwards (*naut.*).

Asth'ma (-sm-), *n.* a disease of respiration. **Asthmat'ic,** *a. & n.*

Astig'matism, *n.* defect of sight. **Astigmat'ic,** *a.*

Astir', *adv.* on the move, out of bed.

Aston'ish, Astound', *v.t.* to surprise greatly, amaze. **Astonish'ment,** *n.*

As'tral, *a.* of the stars.

Astray', *adv.* lost, out of the correct way.

Astride', *adv.* with legs apart.

Astrin'gent, *a.* binding, severe, austere. *n.* a binding medicine. **Astrin'gency,** *n.*

Astrol'ogy, *n.* pretence or art of forecasting events by study of stars. **Astrol'oger,** *n.*

Astron'omy, *n.* scientific study of heavenly bodies. **Astron'omer,** *n.* **Astronom'ical,** *a.*

Astute', *a.* shrewd, quick-witted.

Asun'der, *adv.* in pieces, apart.

Asy'lum, *n.* a sanctuary; esp. as lunatic asylum, place for treatment of people suffering from mental illness.

At'avism, *n.* resemblance to remote ancestors. **Atavis'tic,** *a.*

A'taxia, *n. med.* irregularity of nerves and muscles.

A'theism, *n.* disbelief in existence of God. **A'theist,** *n.*

Ath'lete, *n.* competitor in physical contests, robust, healthy person. **Athlet'ic,** *a.* **Athlet'ics,** *n. pl.* organized running etc.

Athwart', *prep.* lying across.

At'las, *n.* a collection of maps in book form.

At'mosphere, *n.* the air and its constituents, the mass of gas surrounding an astral body. Mental or moral environment. **Atmospher'ic,** *a.* **Atmospher'-ics,** *n.pl.* distortions in radio reception due to electrical disturbances.

Atoll', *n.* a small coral island.

At'om, *n.* the smallest particle of matter in chemical combination; anything very small. Atom'ic, *a.*

Atone', *v.i.* to make reparation for. Atone'ment, *n.*

Atro'cious, *a.* extremely wicked or cruel. Atro'city, *n.*

At'rophy, *n.* gradually wasting away through non-usage. *v.i.*

Attach', *v.t.* to fasten, connect, join on to. Attach'ment, *n.* affectionate connection.

Attache' (-tashay), *n.* member of diplomatic staff. Attaché-case, *n.* small flat case for carrying documents etc.

Attack', *v.t.* to assault, assail, criticize sharply; affect by disease, etc. *n.* an assault, seizure.

Attain', *v.t.* to reach, arrive at, accomplish. Attain'able, *a.* Attain'ment, *n.* Achievement, accomplishment.

Attain'der, *n.* consequences of sentence for treason. Attaint', *v.t.* to subject to attainder, convict.

Att'ar, *n.* scented oil made from roses.

Attempt', *v.t.* to endeavour, try. *n.* effort.

Attend', *v.t.* & *i.* to wait upon, wait for, give mind to. Attend'-ance, *n.* Attend'ant, *n.* Attention, *n.* Atten'tive, *a.*

Atten'uate, *v.t.* to draw out, make thin, reduce. *v.i.* to become weak. Attenua'tion, *n.*

Attest', *v.t.* to certify, put on solemn oath. Attesta'tion, *n.* evidence, testimony.

Att'ic, *n.* small room in roof.

Attire', *v.t.* to array, dress. *n.*

Att'itude, *n.* point of view, posture, behaviour. Attitu'dinise, *v.i.* to strike a pose,

Attor'ney (-ter-), *n.* a solicitor; legal agent.

Attract, *v.t.* to draw towards, to engage the fancy, entice. Attraction', *n.* Attractive, *a.*

Attrib'ute, *v.t.* to ascribe, assign. Att'ribute, *n.* a characterictic or quality. Attrib'utable, *a.*

Attri'tion, *n.* a wearing out, exhaustion, friction.

Attune', *v.t.* to put in tune.

Au'burn, *a.* reddish brown.

Auc'tion, *n.* sale of property to highest bidder at public sale. *v.i.* Auctioneer', *n.*

Auda'cious, *a.* bold, daring. Auda'city, *n.*

Au'dible, *a.* capable of being heard,

Au'dience, *n.* spectators, assembly of hearers, formal interview.

Au'dit, *n.* formal inspection of accounts. *v.t.* Auditor, *n.*

Audi'tion, *n.* trial hearing of singer or musician; power of hearing. Audito'rium, *n.* concert hall.

Au'ger, *n.* carpenter's tool for boring.

Augment', *v.t.* & *i.* to increase, enlarge. Augmenta'tion, *n.*

Au'gur, *n.* Roman religious official who foretold future. *v.t.* to foretell. Au'gury, *n.* sign, omen.

August', *a.* dignified, majestic.

Aunt, *n.* sister of person's father or mother; wife of person's uncle.

Au'ra (Aw-), *n.* subtle emanation, atmosphere created by person or event.

Au'ral, *a.* of the ear.

Aur'eole, *n.* gold disc surrounding heads in primitive paintings.

Au'reomycin, *n.* an antibiotic drug.

Au'ricle, *n.* the outer ear. *n.pl.* upper cavities of heart. Auric'ular, *a.* of the ear.

Aurif'erous, *a,* bearing or yielding gold.

Au'rist, *n.* ear-doctor.

Auro'ra, *n.* luminous atmospheric phenomena emanating from earth's northern and southern poles.

Aus'pice, *n. orig.* observation of birds in connection with omens ; *n.pl.* patronage. Auspi'cious, *a.* favourable.

Austere', *a.* severe, harsh, frugal. Auster'ity, *n.*

Aus'tral, *a.* southern.

Authen'tic, *a.* genuine, trustworthy. Authen'ticate, *v.t.* Authenti'city, *n.* genuineness.

Au'thor, *n.* writer of a book, originator.

Author'ity, *n.* legal power or right, influence, person or book entitled to be believed, a government or body in control. Author'itative, *a.* Au'thorize, *v.t.* Authoriza'tion, *n.*

Au'to, *pref.* meaning self, e.g. autobiography, autograph.

Au'tocrat, *n.* absolute ruler, despot. Autoc'racy, *n.* Autocrat'ic, *a.*

Automa'tion, *n.* mechanical control of machines by means of electronic devices etc.

Autom'obile, *n.* motor-car.

Auton'omy, *n.* political self-government. Auton'omous, *a.*

Autop'sy, *n.* post-mortem examination.

Au'tumn, *n.* third season of year, preceding winter. Autum'nal, *a.*

Auxil'iary, *a.* subsidiary, helping. *n.*

Avail', *v.t. & i.* afford help, be of value *n.* benefit. Availabil'ity, *n.*

Av'alanche, *n.* mass of snow etc. descending rapidly down mountainside.

Av'arice, *n.* greed for wealth. Avari'cious, *a.*

Avaunt', *interj.* begone!

Avenge', *v.t.* to inflict retribution, satisfy oneself for wrong done. Aven'ger, *n.*

Av'enue, *n.* road or walk bordered by trees; an approach.

Aver', *v.t.* to declare true, affirm. Aver'ment, *n.*

Av'erage, *n.* the ordinary standard, the mean value or quantity. *a.* medium, ordinary, *v.t.* to calculate a mean.

Avert', *v.t.* to ward off, turn away. Averse', *a.* disinclined.

Aver'sion, *n.* dislike; person or object disliked strongly.

A'viary, *n.* a large cage or place for keeping birds.

Av'id, *a.* eager, greedy. Avid'ity, *n.*

Avoca'tion, *n.* minor occupation, calling.

Avoid', *v.t.* to keep clear of, escape, elude. Avoid'able, *a.* Avoid'ance, *n.*

Avoirdupois', *n.* British system of weights except for precious stones.

Avow', *v.t.* to admit, confess. Avow'al, *n.*

Await', *v.t.* to wait for, stay for.

Awake', Awa'ken, *v.t. & i.* to rouse from sleep, cease from sleep.

Award', *v.t.* to grant, assign. *n.* prize, judgement.

Aware', *a.* informed, knowing. Aware'ness, *n.*

Awash', *adv.* level with surface of water, washed by waves.

Away', *adv.* absent, at a distance, apart.

Awe, *n.* reverential fear or wonder. Awe'some, *a.* Aw'ful, *a.*

Awhile', *adv.* for a short time.

Awk'ward, *a.* ungainly, clumsy; difficult to cope with; embarrassed. Awk'wardness, *n.*

Awl, *n.* shoemaker's tool for pricking leather.

Awn'ing, *n.* canvas covering to protect against weather.

Awry' (A-rye), *adv.* crookedly, wrongly.

Axe, *n.* bladed tool for chopping wood.

Ax'iom, *n.* maxim, established principle. Axiomat'ic, *a.* self-evidently true.

Ax'is, *n.* imaginary line about which a body, e.g. earth, rotates. *polit.* an alliance between states of similar views.

Ax'le (Ak'sl), *n.* spindle or bar on which wheels revolve.

Ay (Eye), *interj. & n.* yes. *pl.* Ayes.

Aye (A), *adv.* ever, always (*poet.*)

A'zimuth, *n.* arc of heavens reaching from zenith to horizon which it cuts at right angles.

Az'ure, *a.* sky coloured, clear blue. *n.*

B

Bab'ble, *v.i.* to talk like a baby, talk foolishly. *v.t.* to utter thoughtlessly. *n.* Bab'bling, *n.* Bab'bler, *n.*

Babe, *n.* baby, infant. Ba'by, *n.* Ba'byish, *a.* Ba'byhood, *n.*

Ba'bel, *n.* many voices talking at once; a confused scene, tumult.

Bacc'arat (-rah), *n.* game of cards for stakes.

Bacc'hanal (-ka-), *n.* drunken rite or orgy in praise of Bacchus, god of wine. Bacchana'lian, *a.*

Bach'elor, *n.* unmarried man; university graduate on taking first degree. Bach'elorhood, *n.*

Bacill'us (-sil), *n.* a microbe, microscopic organism often causing disease. Bacill'i, *n. pl.* Bacill'iform, *a.* rod-shaped.

Back, *n.* the rear part. *a.* situated behind. *v.t.* to support, to cause to recede or retreat. *v.i.* to retreat or move backwards. *v.t.* to line or strengthen something. *adv.* in return, into the past, into a previous condition or position. Back'bencher, *n.* rank-and-file member of Parliament. Back'bite, *v.t.* to criticize or slander person in his absence. Back'blocks, *n. pl.* interior of Australia. Back'bone, *n.* spinal column, sturdiness of character. Back'chat, *n.* impertinence. Back'cloth, *n.* principal part of stage scenery. Backfire', *v.i.* to ignite faultily, to go wrong. Back'slide, *v.i.* to transgress, fall back into past bad ways. Back'ward, *adv.* to the rear, from a better to a worse state. **Back'water,** *n.* arm of river or creek away from main stream.

Back'sheesh, *n.* tip, gratuity. As Army slang: **Buck-shee,** *a. & adv.* of something obtained free.

Ba'con, *n.* cured back and sides of pig-meat.

Bacte'rium, *n.* microbe, us. as *n. pl.* **Bacteria. Bacte'rial,** *a.* **Bacteriol'ogy,** *n.* study of microbes. **Bacteriol'ogist,** *n.* **Bac'tericide,** *n.* agent or means which destroys bacteria.

Bad, *a.* not good, wicked, faulty, rotten.

Badge, *n.* an emblem or sign.

Badg'er, *v.t.* to harry, worry, chivvy. *n.* grey-coated nocturnal mammal. **Badger-digging,** *n.* brutal pastime in which terriers are set against handicapped badger.

Bad'minton, *n.* game played with rackets and shuttlecocks.

Baf'fle, *v.t.* to puzzle deeply, frustrate.

Bag, *n.* apparatus for carrying articles, pouch, sack, satchel. *v.t.* to catch, seize, kill as game, etc.

Bagatelle, *n.* game resembling billiards; a trifle.

Bagg'age, *n.* luggage; worthless female.

Bag'pipe, *n.* us. as *n. pl.* Scottish wind instrument.

Bail, *n. leg.* surety for accused person's reappearance in court after remand. *v.t.* to release on this basis.

Bail, *n.* part of wicket in game of cricket. **Bail out,** *v.i.* to drop from aircraft by parachute when in danger. **Bale out,** *v.t.*

empty out water from leaky or swamped boat.

Bail'ie, *n.* Scottish justice of peace.

Bail'iff, *n.* sheriff's officer. **Baili'wick,** *n.* district administered by bailiff. **Water-bailiff,** *n.* fishing equivalent of gamekeeper.

Bairn', *n.* child (*Sc*).

Bait, *n.* food to lure animals, etc.; any enticement. *arch.* food eaten at work or on journey. *v.t.* to set a trap, to entice; to tease, persecute.

Baize, *n.* coarse woollen cloth.

Bake, *v.t. & i.* to cook or harden by heat, make bread; *fig.* to become scorched by sun. **Ba'ker,** *n.* **Ba'kery, bake'house,** *n.*

Balalai'ka (-ly-), *n.* Russian stringed instrument.

Bal'ance, *n.* equilibrium, surplus; pair of scales. *v.t.* to adjust, make equal. **Balance-sheet,** *n.* detailed statement of financial position.

Bal'cony, *n.* a platform or gallery attached to outer wall.

Bald (bawld), *a.* hairless of head; plain, outspoken. **Bald'ness,** *n.*

Bal'derdash (Bawl-), *n.* utter nonsense.

Bal'dric (Bawl-), *n.* shoulder-belt for sword or bugle.

Bale, *n.* package. *v.t.* to make into bundles, i.e. of hay.

Bale, *n.* evil, woe, destruction. **Bale'ful,** *a.*

Ball (Bawl), *n.* round object, us for certain sports; a globe bullet (*arch.*) *v.i.* to clog.

Ball (Bawl), *n.* social gathering for dancing.

Ball'ad, *n.* narrative in song-form.

Ball'ast, *n. naut.* material loaded in ship to provide steadiness; material laid between railway lines. *v.t.* to load thus.

Ball'et (-ay), *n.* theatrical dance composed of formalized steps and movements. Balfetomane', *n.* devotee of ballet. Balleri'na, *n.* principal female dancer in ballet.

Ballis'ties, *n. pl.* science dealing with motion of projectiles.

Balloon', *n.* round or pear-shaped airtight container expanding when filled with gas to make it rise in air. *v.i.* to puff out, make expand.

Ball'ot, *n.* method of voting secretly. *v.i.* Ball'ot-box, *n.* sealed container in which votes are kept until counted.

Ballyhoo, *n. sl.* nonsense, inflated publicity.

Balm (Bahm), *n.* healing ointment or influence, aromatic substance. Balm'y, *a.* mild.

Bal'uster, *n.* short pillar supporting staircase rail. Balustrade', *n.* banister.

Bam'boozle, *v.t.* to hoax, mystify.

Ban, *n.*a prohibition, a denunciation. *v.t.* to forbid, outlaw.

Ba'nal, *a.* trite, commonplace. Banal'ity, *n.*

Band, strip of cloth or other material. Ban'dage, *n.* the same for binding wounds. *v.t. & i.*

Band, *n.* a company, esp. of musicians, dance-orchestra. *v.t & i.* join together for some project.

Bandann'a, *n.* richly coloured, patterned handkerchief.

Ban'dit, *n.* robber, highwayman.

Ban'dolier', *n.* shoulder-belt with pouches for cartridges.

Ban'dy, *n.* game resembling hockey. *v.t.* to hurl from one to another, esp. *fig.* verbally. Ban'dy, bandy-legged, *a.* having outwardly curved legs.

Bane, *n.* poison. Bane'ful, *a.*

Bang, *n.* heavy blow or sound; explosion. *v.t.* to beat violently, buffet.

Ban'gle, *n.* bracelet or anklet.

Ban'ish, *v.t.* to exile. Ban'ishment, *n.*

Ban'ister, *n.* guard-rail along stairway.

Ban'jo, *n. mus.* stringed instrument.

Bank, *n.* margin of lake or river, boundary of field, ridge of earth thrown up for this, shoal in sea. *v.t. & i.* to pile up as of earth; aircraft: to tilt on turning.

Bank, *n.* place for keeping money; commercial firm specializing in this. *v.t. & i.* to place in bank for keeping, to deal with bank. Bank'er, *n.* professional financier.

Bank'rupt, *n.* person defaulting on debts. Bank'ruptcy, *n.* financial insolvency.

Bann'er, *n.* flag bearing emblem.

Banns, *n. pl.* official announcement in church of forthcoming wedding.

Ban'quet, *n.* official dinner or feast. *v.t. & i.*

Ban'shee, *n. Gael.* spirit portending death.

Ban'tam, *n.* miniature fowl closely resembling orig. jungle-fowl; small person; category in boxing.

Ban'ter, *n., v.t. & i.* humourous teasing, good-natured fun or ridicule.

Ban'tling, *n.* brat, young child, urchin.

Baptize', *v.t. relig.* to immerse in or sprinkle with water ceremonially; to christen. **Bap'tism**, *n.* **Bap'tist**, *n.* member of relig. sect believing in baptism by immersion only. **Baptis'mal**, *a.*

Bar, *n.* barrier of any kind, rail, sandbank at entrance to harbour. *Leg.* collection of lawyers, rail in courtroom; counter in public house; band of colour; additional award to medal already given. *v.t.* to fasten door, keep out, prevent. *prep.* us. in betting, except.

Barb, *n.* part of arrow or fish-hook recurved from point; *arch.* beard. **Barb'ed wire**, *n.*

Barb'arous, *a.* uncivilized, savage. **Barba'rian**, *n.* primitive savage, uncultivated person. **Barbar'ic**, *a.* **Barb'arism**, *n.*

Bar'becue, *n.* outdoor meal at which meat cooked on spits. Apparatus for this.

Barb'er, *n.* hairdresser, esp. for men.

Barbitu'rate, *n. med.* compound used in nervous tension.

Bard, *n.* poet, minstrel. **Bard'ic**, *a.* us. in connection with Welsh cultural festivals.

Bare, *a.* naked, scanty, empty, uncovered. *v.t.* to make thus. **Bare'ly**, *adv.* scarcely. **Barefaced**, *a.* blatant, impudent.

Barg'ain, *n.* an advantageous purchase; a contract or agreement. *v.i.* to make an agreement, to haggle over terms.

Barge, *n.* flat-bottomed vessel for carrying freight. *v.t. & i.* knock into or over violently.

Bar'itone, *n.* male voice between bass and tenor; singer with this.

Ba'rium, *n.* metallic element.

Bark, *n.* rind or outer skin of tree. *v.t.* to take this off tree; to scrape or rub off.

Bark, *v.i.* to utter warning cry, esp. of dog. *n.* **Bark'er**, *n.* tout trying to attract customers.

Bar'ley, *n.* cereal used for food and in brewing certain liquor.

Barm, *n.* yeast.

Barm'y, *a. sl.* daft, foolish.

Barn, *n. agric.* building for storing produce or implements. **Barn-dance**, *n. orig.* part of harvest celebrations.

Barn'acle, *n.* shellfish able to cling tightly to rocks or ships' bottom; *fig.* person difficult to shake off.

Bar'ney, *n. sl.* humbug, false talk; dispute.

Barom'eter, *n.* instrument for forecasting weather by atmospheric pressure. **Baromet'ric**, *a.* **Bar'ograph**, *n.* barometer that records variations.

Bar'on, *n.* peer of lowest rank. **Bar'oness**, *n.* **Bar'onage**, *n.* **Baro'nial**, *a.* **Bar'ony**, *n.*

Ba'ronet, *n.* hereditary knighthood. **Ba'ronetcy**, *n.*

Baroque', *a.* whimsical or decorated style in art or architecture.

Barque, *n.* three-masted sailing-ship.

Barr'ack, *n.* us. as *n. pl.* large building for soldiers etc.; *fig.* any large ugly building.

Barr'ack, *v.t. & i.* to jeer at players during game.

Barr'age (-ahzh), *n.* dam built across stretch of water; concerted artillery fire.

Barr'el, *n.* cask, round wooden container for wine etc.

Barr'en, *a.* bare, sterile.

Barricade', *n.* temporary forti-

fication across road or pass.
v.t. to fortify in hasty fashion.

Barr'ier, *n.* obstruction, fence,
bar.

Barr'ister, *n.* leg. lawyer who
pleads in higher court.

Barr'ow, *n.* small wheeled handcart; *archeol.* ancient burial-
mound.

Bart'er, *v.t. & i.* to give or exchange goods or services for
others in return; to part with
for worthless consideration. *n.*

Bas'alt (-awlt), *n.* dark-coloured igneous rock.

Base, *n.* foundation, bottom,
starting-place for project. *v.t.*
to establish, found. **Base'less**,
a. **Base'ment**, *n.* lowest storey
of building, us. below surface.

Base, *a.* contemptible, low,
mean. **Base'born**, *a.*

Base'ball, *n.* Amer. ball game
resembling rounders.

Bash, *v.t.* to strike violently,
smash.

Bash'ful, *a.* shy, modest.

Ba'sic, *a.* fundamental.

Basil'ica, *n.* orig. royal palace;
now us. church with double
colonnade and apse.

Bas'ilisk, *n.* legendary reptile
with fiery breath and eye;
person resembling this, *fig.*

Ba'sin, *n.* deep circular receptacle for cooking; dock for
ships; territory drained by
river-system.

Ba'sis, *n.* foundation. *pl.* **Ba'ses.**

Bask (-ahsk), *v.i.* to lie or revel
in warmth; *fig.* in praise.

Bask'et (-ahsk), *n.* receptacle for
carrying articles. **Bas'ket-ball**,
n. team ball-game.

Bas-relief', *n.* shallow sculpture
carved on background.

Bass (Base), *n.* lowest part in

harmonized music, lowest male
voice; singer with such a voice.
a. deep-sounding.

Bassinet', *n.* hooded cradle or
perambulator (not us.).

Bassoon', *n.* wood-wind instrument.

Bast, *n.* inner bark of tree yielding fibrous material.

Bast'ard, *n.* child of unmarried
parents. *a.* spurious, not
genuine.

Baste, *v.t.* to apply fat to roast-
ing meat.

Baste, *v.t.* to stitch together
roughly.

Baste, *v.t.* to thrash.

Bastina'do, *n.* to beat on soles of
feet with stick.

Bas'tion, *n.* projecting part of
fortress.

Bat, *n.* flat club used esp. in
cricket. *v.i.* to use this. **Bats'-
man**, *n.* **Batt'ing**, *n.*

Bat, *n.* winged mammal.

Batch, *n.* number or quantity of
articles, esp. loaves.

Bath (-ahth), *n.* vessel for bathing in; act of washing in this.
v.t.

Bathe, *v.t. & i.* to immerse in
water for washing or swimming. **Ba'ther**, *n.* one who
enters sea for pleasure.

Ba'thos (-thos), *n.* descent from
sublime to ridiculous.

Bat'man, *n.* officer's servant.

Bat'on, *n.* weapon carried by
policeman; staff for conducting
orchestra; marshal's staff of
office.

Battal'ion, *n.* mil. division of
infantry regiment, us. about
one thousand strong.

Ba'tten, *n.* long narrow piece of
wood. *v.t.* to strengthen or
fasten with battens.

Batt'er, *v.t.* to strike repeatedly, assault. *n.* cooking mixture.

Batt'ery, *n. mil.* division or section of artillery; the infliction of blows; set of electric cells.

Bat'tle, *n.* violent encounter between armed forces.

Bat'tlement, *n. us.* as *n. pl.* fortified parapet.

Bau'ble (Baw-), *n.* a trifle, worthless thing.

Baulk (Baw-), *n.* balk, *v.t.* to hinder, frustrate; *v.i.* to swerve, refuse jump, as with horse. *n.* term in billiards.

Bau'xite, *n.* clay yielding aluminium.

Bawd, *n.* procuress. Bawd'y, *a.* & *adv.* obscene, vulgar.

Bawl, *v.i.* to shout stridently. *n.*

Bay, *a.* reddish-brown, esp. of horse.

Bay, *n.* wide-mouthed opening of sea-coast.

Bay, *n.* recess, division of wall between columns. Bay'-window, *n.,* protruding window.

Bay, *n.* laurel-tree.

Bay, *n.* deep bark, cry of hounds in full cry. *v.t.* & *i.* At bay, cornered, confronting pursuers.

Bay'onet, *n.* stabbing blade attachable to rifle-barrel. *v.t.*

Bazaar (-zahr), *n. esp.* oriental market, any market or general shop.

Bazoo'ka, *n.* portable mortar.

Be, *v.i.* to exist, live.

Beach, *n.* sea-shore. *v.t.* to run a boat ashore. Beach'head, *n.* base established on enemy coast at commencement of attack. Beach'comber, *n.* lazy person living by what he picks up.

Bea'con, *n.* warning mark or fire.

Bead, *n.* tiny ball or globule. Bead'ing, *n.* pattern or decoration on woodwork.

Bea'dle, *n.* parish official, mace-bearer

Bea'gle, *n.* small hound used for hunting hare.

Beak, *n.* bill of bird, mandibles, anything pointed.

Beak'er, *n. arch.* large drinking-cup; glass vessel used in chem.

Beam, *n.* long squared piece of timber; bar of balance; ray of light. *v.t.* & *i.* to emit in beams, to shine; direct radio message etc.

Bean, *n.* leguminous plant, seed of.

Bear (Bare),*v.t.*to support, carry; produce young or crops; press upon. Bear'ing, *n.* carriage, way a person moves or acts.

Bear (Bare), *n.* large carnivore; *fig.* financier who speculates on a fall in the stock market. Bear'-skin, *n.* fur head-dress worn by guardsmen.

Beard (Beerd), *n.* growth of hair on chin and cheeks. *v.t.* to defy.

Beast, *n.* an animal, a brutal person. Beast'ly, *a.*

Beat, *v.t.* to strike, thrash, gain victory over, throb, surpass; sail against wind. *n.* stroke, rhythm, pulsation; regular journey or patrol.

Beat'ify (Be-at'-), *v.t.* to make happy; *rel.* to pronounce eternally in bliss. Beatifica'tion, *n. rel.* first step towards canonization. Beatif'ic, *a.* Beat'itude, *n.*

Beau (Bo), *n.* a fop, dandy, suitor. *n.pl.* Beaux.

Beauty (Bu-),*n.* loveliness. Beau'-tiful, *a.* Beauti'cian, *n.* artificial word for person specialising in beauty treatment.

Bea'ver, *n*. amphibious rodent quadruped; its fur; hat made of this.

Becalm', *v.t.* to make calm, deprive of wind.

Because', *adv. & conj.* by reason, on account of.

Beck, *n*. significant gesture, nod.

Beck'on, *v.t. & i.* to call by sign, signal without words.

Become', *v.t.* to come to be. *v.t.* to suit, befit. **Becom'ing**, *a*. pleasing (in appearance, dress).

Bed, *n*. place to sleep on; bottom of river or lake; part of garden set aside for plants. *v.t.* to lay in a bed, plant out. **Bedd'ing**, *n*. sheets and blankets etc. **Bed'ridden**, *a*. confined to bed. **Bed'rock**, *n. us. fig.* basis, foundation. **Bed'room**, *n*. **Bed'-spread**, *n*. coverlet. **Bed'stead**, *n*. frame of bed.

Bedeck', *v.t.* to decorate, adorn.

Bedi'zen (-y-zn), *v.t.* to dress out gaudily. **Bedi'zened**, *a*.

Bed'lam, *n*. uproar; lunatic asylum.

Bed'ouin (-oo-in), *n*. nomadic Arab.

Bee, *n*. winged social insect producing honey. **Bee'hive**, *n*. **Bee'line**, *n*. shortest, most direct way. **Bees'wax**, *n*. wax used for polishing.

Beef, *n*. flesh of bullock; bullock for slaughter. *pl.* **Beeves**. **Beef'y**, *a*. thickset, stolid **Beef'steak** (-stake), *n*.

Beef'eater, *n*. yeoman of guard, Tower of London warder.

Beer, *n*. fermented alcoholic liquor made with malt and flavoured with hops. **Beer'-**house, *n*. **Beer'y**, *a*. smelling of or affected by beer.

Beet, *n*. root-plant of various kinds.

Bee'tle, *n*. tool for ramming, etc., large mallet.

Bee'tle, *v.i.* overhang, of cliffs, etc. *a*. projecting, shaggy, scowling.

Bee'tle, *n*. a coleopterous insect. **Bee'tle-crushers**, *n.pl.* large boots.

Befall' (-awl), *v.i.* to happen; *v.t.* to happen to.

Befit', *v.t.* to be suitable to. **Befitt'ing**, *a*.

Before', *prep.* in front of, in presence of, earlier than, in preference to. *adv.* earlier, in front of. *conj.* sooner than. **Before'hand**, *adv.* before (in time).

Befoul' (-owl), *v.t.* to soil, make dirty.

Befriend', *v.t.* come to the aid of, help.

Beg, *v.t.* to entreat, beseech. *v.i.* to ask for alms or charity. **Begg'ar**, *n*. **Begg'ary**, *n*. to beg the question, take for granted truth of matter in dispute.

Beget', *v.t.* to produce, generate. **Begott'en**, *p.p.* **Begett'er**, *n*.

Begin', *v.i.* to start, commence. *v.t.* to originate, initiate.

Begrudge', *v.t.* to envy someone else a certain advantage or possession.

Beguile' (-gyle), *v.t.* to lure, cheat.

Behalf', *n*. favour, benefit (us. as, e.g., on behalf of).

Behave', *v.i.* to conduct. bear oneself. **Beha'viour**, *n*. way in which person acts, conduct.

Behead', *v.t.* to execute by chopping off the head.

Behest', *n*. order, command.

Behind', *prep*. in rear of. *adv*. in the rear. Behind'hand, *adv*. late, in arrears.

Behold', *v.t*. to watch or see, esp. in rhet. sense.

Behold'en, *a*. obliged to (someone), bound in gratitude.

Behove', *v.i*. to be necessary, fitting.

Beige (Bayzh), *n*. woollen cloth; colour of this.

Be'ing, *n*. life, existence; a person or animal.

Bela'bour, *v.t*. to beat or thrash.

Bela'ted, *a*. late, esp. in deplorable sense; half-hearted.

Belay', *v.t. naut*. to make fast a rope or hawser by coiling it round a cleat or bollard.

Belch, *v.i*. to emit wind noisily from mouth; to emit smoke or fumes from chimney etc.

Bel'dam, *n.arch*. hag, old woman.

Beleag'uer (-lee-ger), *v.t*. to lay siege to.

Bel'fry, *n*. church-tower with bells.

Belie' (-ly), *v.t*. give false notion of, fail to justify promise etc.

Believe', *v.t*. to accept as true; *v.i*. to have faith. Belief, *n*. Believ'er, *n*. us. meant in rel. sense. Believ'able, *a*.

Belitt'le, *v.t*. to dispraise, make light of. Belitt'lement, *n*.

Bell, *n*. hollow metal vessel widening at mouth to emit ringing sound when struck by clapper. *naut*. way of marking half-hours. Bell'-boy, *n*. hotel page-boy.

Bell'icose, *a*. war-like, pugnacious. Bellicos'ity, *n*.

Belli'gerent (-ij-), *a*. pugnacious, waging war. *n*. nation engaged in war.

Bell'ow, *v.i*. to shout loudly, roar like bull. *n*.

Bell'ows (-oes), *n*. hand-instrument for pumping air into fire etc.

Bell'y, *n*. part of human body containing stomach and bowels. *v.t. & i*. to swell out.

Belong', *v.i*. to be the property of, be connected with. Belong'-ings, *n. pl*. possessions.

Belov'ed, *a*. greatly loved. *n*. sweetheart.

Below' (-o), *adv*. beneath. *prep*. inferior to, lower than.

Belt, *n*. a girdle round waist. *v.t*.

Bemoan', *v.t*. to regret deeply, bewail.

Bemuse', *v.t*. to confuse, stupefy.

Bench, *n*. a long seat; body of judges or magistrates, etc. Bench'er, *n*. senior lawyer belonging to one of the inns of court.

Bend, *v.t*. to curve, stoop down. *v.i*. to take a curved shape. *n*. a curve, esp. in road.

Beneath', *prep*. lower than. *adv*. in a lower position.

Benedic'tion, *n*. official blessing.

Ben'efit, *n*. profit, advantage, good. *v.t*. to do good to. *v.i*. to receive advantage from. Benefac'tion, *n*. Ben'efactor, *n*. Benef'icent, *a*. Benef'icence, *n*. Benefic'ial, *a*. Benefi'ciary, *n*. Ben'efice, *n*. an ecclesiastical living.

Benev'olent, *a*. kindly, tolerant. Benev'olence, *n*.

Benight'ed, (-ny-ted), *a*. overtaken by night when travelling, stranded; *fig*. in intellectual darkness.

Benign' (-nine), *a*. gentle kindly. Benig'nant (be-nig-nant), *a*. Benig'nancy, *n*.

Ben'ison, *n.* blessing.

Bent, *n.* inclination turn of mind.

Benumb', *v.t.* to deaden by pain or shock.

Bequeath', *v.t.* to leave by will. **Bequest',** *n.* a legacy.

Bereave', *v.t.* to rob of, esp. by death. **Bereave'ment,** *n.*

Berr'y, *n.* small stoneless fruit.

Berth, *n. naut.* anchorage, place in dock for ship, place to sleep, situation. *v.t.* to dock, moor a ship.

Beseech', *v.t.* to entreat earnestly, implore.

Beset', *v.t.* to attack, surround.

Beshrew', *v.t.* now *iron.* only as mild imprecation.

Beside', *prep.* alongside, near, distinct from. **Besides',** *adv. & prep.* in addition.

Besiege', *v.t.* to cut off fortress with armed forces.

Be'som (Biz-), *n.* broom of twigs.

Bespeak', *v.t.* to arrange or engage beforehand.

Bes'tial, *a.* like a beast, horribly brutal. **Bestial'ity,** *n.*

Bestir', *v.t.* to rouse up, take action.

Bestow (-o), *v.t.* to give, confer. **Bestow'al,** *n.*

Bestride', *v.t.* to stand over with legs apart.

Bet, *n.* a wager. *v.t. & i.* to gamble.

Betide', *v.i.* to happen.

Betimes', *adv.* in good time, early.

Betok'en, *v.t.* to presage, foreshadow, signify by certain sign.

Betray', *v.t.* to be disloyal to, mislead seriously, give person up to enemy. **Betray'al,** *n.* **Betray'er,** *n.*

Betroth (-othe) *v t* to pledge in marriage, engage. **Betroth'al,** *n.* **Betrothed',** *n.* fiancé.

Between', *prep.* in the middle of two other objects. *adv.* midway. **Betwixt,** *arch.* or *poet.* form of this.

Bev'el, *n.* carpenter's tool for setting off angles; sloping surface at edge of woodwork. *v.t.*

Bev'erage, *n.* nourishing liquid.

Bev'y. *n.* group, flock, company.

Bewail', *v.t.* to bemoan, lament.

Beware', *v.i.* to be on one's guard, alert.

Bewil'der, *v.t.* to mystify, puzzle. **Bewil'derment,** *n.*

Bewitch', *v.t.* to influence by witchcraft, enchant.

Beyond', *adv.* farther away. *prep.* on farther side of, out of reach.

Bezique', *n.* game of cards.

Bi-(By), *pref.* meaning twice or double, e. g. bilateral, binocular, etc.

Bi'-annual, *a.* appearing twice in a year.

Bi'as (By-), *n.* prejudice, one-sided inclination. *v.t.* to influence in partial way.

Bib, *n.* cloth tied under child's chin when feeding.

Bi'ble (By-), *n.* collection of sacred Christian and Hebrew writings. **Bib'lical,** *a.*

Bibliog'raphy, *n.* history of books, collection of details of books and their authors. **Bibliograph'ical,** *a.* **Bibliog'rapher,** *n.* **Bib'liophile,** *n.* book-lover, in expert sense.

Bib'ulous, *a.* given to alcoholic drinking, tipsy.

Bi'ceps (By-), *n.* muscle with double head, esp. in upper arm.

Bick'er, *v.i.* to dispute in pointless fashion.

Bicus'pid (By-), *n.* tooth with double fang.

Bi'cycle (By-ci-), *n.* two-wheeled vehicle powered by foot-pedals. *v.i.* **Bi'cyclist,** *n.*

Bid, *v.t.* to make offer for, command, *n.* an offer, esp. at sale. **Bidd'er,** *n.* **Bidd'ing,** *n.* order.

Bide, *v.i.* to remain.

Bienn'ial (By-), *a.* occurring every two years. *n.* plant which lives for two years.

Bier (beer), *n.* wooden frame on which coffin is carried.

Bifo'cal (By-), *a.* us. of spectacles with two different segments for near and distant sight.

Big, *a.* large, great.

Big'amy, *n.* the crime of marrying again when legal spouse is still alive and undivorced. **Big'amist,** *n.* **Big'amous,** *a.*

Bight (Byte), *n.* a bay; loop of cord.

Big'ot, *n.* obstinately prejudiced person. **Big'otry,** *n.* excessive prejudice.

Bi'jou (-joo), *n.* trinket, jewel.

Bile, (Byle) *n.* fluid secreted by liver; *fig.* bad feeling, anger. **Bil'ious,** *a.* sickly.

Bilge, *n.* bottom of ship's hull, foul water collecting there. *sl.* nonsense.

Biling'ual (By-), *a.* able to speak two languages equally well. **Biling'ualism,** *n.*

Bill, *n.* a bird's beak. *v.i.* to caress with bills, us. as *iron.* **bill and coo.**

Bill, *n.* an account of charges or expenses ; advertising placard ; draft of parliamentary Act.

Bill'et, *n.* civilian quarters for military personnel; resting-place, comfortable niche; a piece of firewood. *v.t.* to quarter troops etc.

Bill'iards (-yrds), *n.* game played on large table with balls and cues.

Bill'ion, *n.* a million millions; *Amer.* a thousand millions. **Bill'ionaire,** *n.*

Bill'ow, *n.* small swelling wave. *v.i.*

Bin, *n.* receptacle for storing corn or wine, etc.

Bind (Bynd), *v.t.* to tie up or round, tie fast; unite; of book, protect with outer covering. **Binding',** *a.* obligatory, *n.* cover of book.

Binn'acle, *n.* box containing ship's compass.

Binoc'ular, *n. us.* in *pl.* field-glasses for both eyes.

Bino'mial (By-), *n.* consisting of two terms, as in algebra, etc.

Bio-(By-o), *pref.* meaning life or of life; e.g. **biom'etry,** *n.* **biochemistry,** *n.* chemistry of living things, **biog'raphy,** *n.* story of person's life, told by someone else; **biol'ogy,** *n.* the science of life.

Bi'ped, (By-), *a* two footed animal.

Bi'plane, (By-) *n.* aircraft with two sets of wings, one above the other.

Birch, *n.* cane-rod for beating as punishment. *v.t.*

Bird, *n.* a feathered animal.

Birett'a, *n.* Roman Catholic priest's cap.

Birth, *n.* a coming to life, beginning, parentage. **Birth'day,** *n.* anniversary of day person was born.

Bis (Beess), *adv. mus.* over again; cry of applause requesting second performance of same item.

Bis'cuit (-kit), *n*. hard baked flat unleavened cake.

Bisect (By-), *v.t.* to cut in halves. **Bisect'ion**, *n*.

Bish'op, *n*. priest in charge of a diocese. **Bishop'ric**, *n*. bishop's position or extent of jurisdiction.

Bis'muth, *n*. a reddish-white metal.

Bi'son (By-), *n*. wild ox, often mistakenly called buffalo.

Bissex'tile, *n*. leap-year.

Bit,*n*.a fragment; part of boring tool; mouthpiece of bridle.

Bitch, *n*. female dog.

Bite, *v.t.* to cut into with teeth. *n*. act of biting, wound made by animal's teeth; a mouthful.

Bitt'er, *a*. sharp, harsh, piercing, opposite of sweet. **Bitt'erness**, *n*. resentful or regretful feeling.

Bit'umen, *n*. a mineral pitch such as asphalt. **Bitu'minous**, *a*.

Bi'valve (By-), *n*. mollusc having double shell.

Biv'ouac, *n*. temporary open-air camp, *v.i.*

Bizarre', *a*. fantastic, quaint.

Blab', *v.i.* give away secret.

Black, *a*. dark, without colour, gloomy. *n*. darkest colour.

Black'ball, *v.t.* to vote against, esp. in respect of someone's entry to club, to reject.

Black'board, *n*. large dark board on easel or wall for writing on with chalk in schools etc.

Black'guard (Blaggard), *n*. a scoundrel, knave.

Black'mail, *n*. money extorted by threatening person with exposure of past misdemeanour. *v.t.*

Black'out, *n*. failure of electrical supply; temporary uncon sciousness. *v.t.* & *i.*

Black'smith, *n*. artisan working in iron, esp. shoeing horses' hooves.

Bladd'er, *n*. part of body containing and processing liquids.

Blade, *n*. leaf of plant; main part of stabbing or thrusting weapon, etc. *fig.* a dashing fellow.

Blame, *v.t.* to find fault with, put responsibility for wrong happening on. *n*. censure. **Blame'worthy**, *a*.

Blanch, *v.t.* & *i.* to whiten, make white, bleach, turn pale.

Bland, *a*. smooth in manner.

Bland'ish, *v.t.* coax, flatter. **Bland'ishment**, *n*.

Blank, *a*. empty, unmarked; witless confused; rhymeless.

Blank'et, *n*. woollen covering for bed. *v.t.* to cover with this, to smother.

Blare, *v.i.* to roar loudly. *n*.

Blar'ney, *n*. facile persuasive talk. *v.t.* & *i.*

Blaspheme', *v.t.* to speak profanely of; *v.i.* to talk profanely. **Blas'phemy**, *n*. **Blasphe'mer**, *n*. **Blas'phemous**, *a*.

Blast, *n*. violent current of air, explosion, *v.t.* to blow up, destroy.

Blast-fur'nace, *n*. smelting-place in steel-works, etc.

Bla'tant, *a*. barefaced, noisy, vulgar.

Blaze, *n*. fierce fire, outburst, display. *v.i.*

Blaze, *v.t.* to mark a trail for others.

Bla'zer, *n*. coloured flannel sports jacket.

Bla'zon, *n*. heraldic shield or emblem. *v.t.* to proclaim.

Bleach, *v.t.* to whiten. *v.t.* to turn white. *n.* chemical for whitening clothes etc.

Bleak, *a.* cheerless, cold, exposed.

Blear, *a.* inflamed, esp. of eyes. **Blear'y,** *a.*

Bleat, *n.* cry of sheep or goat. *v.t. & i.*

Bleed, *v.t.* to take blood from; *fig.* to extort money from; *v.i.* to lose blood.

Blem'ish, *n.* a fault. *v.t.* to spoil.

Blench, *v.i.* to flinch, quail.

Blend, *v.t.* to mix, esp. liquids. *n.*

Bless, *v.t.* to invoke favour on, to consecrate, make happy. **Bless'ing,** *n.* **Bless'edness,** *n.*

Bleth'er, *n.* useless chatter. *v.i.* to babble.

Blight (Blyt), *n.* mildew, blackfly. *v.t.* to affect with this, spoil, wither.

Blind (Blynd), *a.* without sight, bigoted, heedless; shut at one end. *v.t.* to dazzle with light, make blind. *n.* a curtain or screen to shut out cold or darkness.

Blink, *v.i.* to shut and open eyes rapidly; to shine intermittently; *n.* a gleam. **Blink'ers,** *n. pl.* leather pads to prevent horse from seeing sideways and being alarmed.

Bliss, *n.* perfect happiness. **Bliss'ful,** *a.*

Blis'ter, *n.* vesicle on skin caused by chafing. *v.t.* to cause a blister.

Blithe, *a.* gay, happy, carefree. **Blithe'some,** *a.*

Blizz'ard, *n.* violent storm of snow and wind.

Bloa'ted, *a.* puffy, swollen.

Bloat'er, *n.* salted and smoked herring.

Bloc, *n.* group of nations with similar views.

Block, *n.* massive piece of wood; any coherent mass; a group of buildings; *hist.* large piece of wood on which victim laid head before execution. *v.t.* to obstruct, stop up. **Block'head,** *n.* numbskull, stupid person.

Blockade', *n.* the cutting off of supplies to an enemy. *v.t.*

Blonde, *a.* light, fair-haired. *n.* girl with fair hair.

Blood (Blud), *n.* red fluid in veins of animals; kin, parentage; passion, character. *v.t.* to draw blood from, to accustom to blood or violence.

Blood'sport, *n.* sport in which animals are pursued and killed for human pleasure.

Blood'test, *n. med.* examination of blood to ascertain category.

Blood'thirsty, *a.* cruel, liking violence.

Bloom, *n.* flower of plant, prime, perfection; powdery deposit on skin of fruit etc. *v.i.*

Bloom'er, *n.* stupid blunder.

Bloss'om, *n.* a flower. *v.i.* to flower, develop.

Blot, *n.* a blemish, mark of disgrace; *v.t.* to spot; dry with blotting-paper. **Blott'ing-pad,** *n.*

Blotch, *n.* dark patch on skin etc. *v.t.* to make spotted.

Blouse (-ow-), *n.* woman's loose upper garment.

Blow (Bloe), *v.t.* to send air upon, to drive by blowing air upon; to spout (of whales); *v.i.* to pant, make current of air, sound a blast on whistle etc. *v.i.* to melt because of excess heat, as in elec. fuse.

Blow (Bloe), *n.* a punch, violent stroke, set-back.

Blow'zy, *a.* coarse in bloated way, dishevelled.

Blubb'er, *n.* whale-fat.

Blubb'er, *v.i.* to weep.

Bludg'eon (Bluj'n), *n.* thick club or truncheon. *v.t.* to assault with this.

Blue (Bloo), *a.* coloured like sky or deep sea and various shades resembling these; *fig.* depressed. *n.* the colour. *v.t.* to make blue. Blue baby, *n.* infant sufferer from certain heart affliction. Blue'jacket, *n.* sailor. Blue, *n.* student chosen to play in university team, esp. Oxford and Cambridge. Blue'stocking, *n. iron.* woman affecting literary tastes.

Bluff, *a.* steep, abrupt; of person, forthright, hearty. *n.* a cliff, steep bank.

Bluff, *v.t.* to deceive by pretence.

Blun'der, *v.i.* to make a clumsy mistake, move clumsily. *n.* a serious mistake. Blun'derer, *n.*

Blun'derbuss, *n. arch.* form of hand-gun.

Blunt, *a.* not sharp, with coarse edge; abrupt in manner. *v.t.* to dull, spoil cutting edge.

Blur, *n.* a smudge, stain. *v.t.* to dim, obscure.

Blurt, *v.t.* to speak impetuously.

Blush, *v.i.* to become red in face, to be ashamed. *n.* a suffusion of colour.

Blus'ter, *v.i.* to blow roughly, of wind or manner. *n.* a blast. Blus'terer, *n.* loud-mouthed swaggerer. Blust'ery, *a.*

Bo'a, *n.* large pythonlike snake; long fur carried round neck.

Boar, *n.* male of the swine family.

Board, *n.* broad flat strip of wood, plank. table, meals; authorized body of people; thick, stiff paper. *v.t.* to cover with wooden planks; to accommodate; to attack a ship by sending men onto it. *v.i.* to take meals and lodging. Board'er, *n.* Board'ing-house, *n.* Board'ing-school, *n.*

Boast, *v.t. & i.* to brag, talk loudly of one's possessions etc. *n.*

Boat, *n.* small open vessel powered by oars or sails. Boat'ing, *n.* Boat'-hook, *n.* hooked tool for holding on to quayside or other boat. Boat'swain (Bose'n), *n.* ship's officer in charge of boats, sails, work etc. Boat'er, *n.* flat straw hat.

Bob, *v.i.* to duck, move up and down jerkily.

Bobb'in, *n.* spool or reel of thread.

Bobb'y, *n. col.* a policeman (after Sir Robert Peel, founder of modern police).

Bode, *v.t.* to portend, foretell, esp. evil.

Bod'ice (-is), upper part of woman's dress.

Bod'kin, *n.* tool for piercing holes.

Bod'y, *n.* entire physical frame of animal: main part of this; main part of any object or work; substance, a mass, a person; matter as distinct from spirit. Bod'iless, *a.* Bod'ily, *a. & adv.* Bod'yguard, *n.* man or men employed to protect important person. Bod'y-line, *a.* as applied to form of aggressive bowling in cricket intended to intimidate batsman.

Boer (Boor), *n.* South African of Dutch descent.

Boff'in, *n.* World War 2 sl. for expert or scientist.

Bog, *n.* soft wet ground. *v.t.* to submerge in bog. **Bogg'y,** *a.*

Bo'gey, *n.* goblin, bugbear.

Bog'gle, (**Bog'l**) *v.i.* to hesitate, demur, equivocate.

Bo'gie, *n.* low truck on four wheels, revolving undercarriage.

Bo'gus, *a.* fake, spurious, sham.

Bohem'ian, *n.* person who lives in unorthodox way, gypsy.

Boil, *n.* an inflamed swelling.

Boil, *v.t.* to cook by boiling; *v.i.* to bubble up from action of heat, to be angry. **Boil'er,** *n.*

Boi'sterous, *a.* spirited, wild, turbulent.

Bold, *a.* adventurous, daring, distinctly marked, presumptuous.

Bole, *n.* trunk of a tree.

Bole'ro, *n.* Spanish dance; also bodice worn when performing this.

Bol'ster, *n.* long pillow or pad. *v.t.* to hold up, support.

Bolt, *n.* a metal bar or pin; *arch.* an arrow; a flash of lightning; a sudden departure. *v.t. & i.* to run away, swallow greedily, fasten with bolt.

Bo'lus, *n. med.* large pill.

Bomb, *n.* explosive charge dropped from aircraft or shot from mortar, a grenade. *v.t.* to attack with this. **Bombard',** *v.t.* to shell by artillery. **Bombard'ment,** *n.* **Bombardier',** *n.* artillery non-commissioned officer. **Bomb'er,** *n.* aircraft used for dropping bombs.

Bom'bast, *n.* pompous language. **Bombas'tic,** *a.*

Bo'na fi'de, *adv.* or *a.* in good faith, genuine.

Bond, *n.* a link, close connection, written promise in finan-

cial matters; *v.t.* to store goods such as liquor and tobacco until excise is paid on them.

Bond'age, *n.* slavery. **Bond'man,** *n. hist.* man bound to serve a mediaeval lord.

Bone, *n.* part of animal skeleton. *v.t.* to take bones out of meat. **Bo'ny,** *a.*

Bon'fire, *n.* open-air fire of garden-rubbish etc.

Bon'homie (-om-), *n.* geniality, general friendliness.

Bonn'et, *n.* old-fashioned hat with strings.

Bonn'y, *a.* handsome, in good health.

Bo'nus, *n.* extra payment.

Boob'y, *n.* a blockhead, dunce. **Boob'y-prize,** *n.* consolation prize for last in contest. **Boob'y-trap,** *n.* disguised or hidden trap.

Book, *n.* a literary work; a division of such; a bound collection of sheets of paper. *v.t.* to enter in a book, reserve a ticket or place. **Book'ish,** *a.* sedulously learned. **Book'-maker,** *n.* person who traffics in betting professionally. **Book'-worm,** *n.* a voracious reader.

Boom, *n.* a long spar; a barrier defending estuary, etc.

Boom, *n.* loud resonant noise. *v.i.*

Boom, *n.* sudden commercial prosperity. *v.t. & i.* to prosper, become active, expand.

Boo'merang, *n.* curved wooden missile used by Aus. aborigines, which, when thrown, returns.

Boon, *n.* a favour, blessing. *a.* convivial.

Boor, *n.* uncouth fellow. **Boor'-ish,** *a.*

Boost, *v.t.* to help on, lift up. *n.* praise, publicity.

Boot, *n.* leather covering for foot and ankle. **Boot'jack**, *n.* implement for taking off riding-boots, etc. **Boots**, *n.* hotel-servant who cleans boots and runs errands.

Boot, *n. arch.* gain, profit. (To) **boot**, as well, in addition.

Booth, *n.* a stall at market or fair; polling-place.

Boot'y, *n.* plunder.

Booze, *n. vulg.* alcohol, a drinking-bout. *v.i.* to drink too much alcohol.

Borac'ic, *a.* of borax.

Bo'rax, *n.* crystalline salt used as antiseptic.

Bord'er, *n.* edge, frontier, boundary, garden-bed. *v.t.* to edge, adjoin. *v.i.* to approach, be adjacent to.

Bore, *v.t.* to pierce through lengthways; to weary by dull talk or inactivity. *n.* the calibre of a gun; a tedious person; a hole, esp. as of a well.

Bore, *n.* tidal wave in some rivers.

Bo'rough (Bu-ru), *n.* a municipality, town with corporation. *Sc.* **Burgh.**

Bor'row (-ro), *v.t.* to obtain on loan; to copy fashion.

Bos'cage (Bosk-ij), *n.* woodland, thick foliage.

Bo'som, (-zm), *n.* human breast; *fig.* a refuge.

Boss, *n.* chief, manager, head of gang etc.; a knob. *v.i.* to bully, give orders.

Bot'any, *n.* the study of plants. **Bot'anist**, *n.* **Botan'ical**. *a.* **Bot'anize**, *v.i.* to study plants.

Botch, *v.t.* to do something clumsily.

Both, *a. & pron.* the pair of, the two. *adv.* equally.

Both'er, *v.t. & i.* to annoy, worry, give trouble. *n.* nuisance, trouble. **Both'ersome**, *a.*

Both'y, *n. Sc.* shepherd's hut.

Bot'tle, *n.* glass vessel for containing liquids. **Bottle'neck**, *n.* a delay in production because of lack of materials or strike; abrupt narrowing of road.

Bott'om, *n.* lowest part, bed of sea or river; *naut.* a ship.

Bott'omry, *n.* using ship for financial security.

Bot'ulism, *n.* violent kind of food poisoning.

Boud'oir (Bood-wahr), *n.* lady's private room.

Bough (Bow), *n.* branch of a tree.

Boul'der (Bole-), *n.* large rock.

Bounce (Bownce), *v.i.* to bound, throw oneself about. *n.* **Bounc'ing**, *a.* pert, swaggering.

Bound, *v.i.* to leap, jump. **Bound'er**, *n.* a cad.

Bound, *n.* limit, boundary. **Bound'less**, *a.* unlimited. **Bound'ary**, *n.* limit of cricket field etc, a score at cricket.

Bound, *a.* ready to go, obliged.

Boun'ty, *n.* generous giving, liberality, a premium. **Boun'teous**, **Boun'tiful**, *a.*

Bouquet (Book-kay), *n.* a formal bunch of flowers; aroma of wine; *fig.* a compliment.

Bour'geois (Boor-zhwah), *a.* middle-class, dull.

Bout (Bowt), *n.* spell, round, turn. attack.

Bo'vine, *a.* oxlike, stupid.

Bow (Bo), *n.* weapon for shooting arrows; knot of ribbon or cord; a bend; implement for playing violin, etc. **Bow-legged,** *a.* bandy.

Bow (Bow), *v.i.* to bend the body, to submit. *v.t.* to bend downwards. *n.* act of bowing in respect.

Bow (Bow), *n.* fore end of ship or boat, us. as *n. pl.* **bows.**

Bowd'lerize (Bowd-), *v.t.* to cut out passages from a book to tamper with literary work for different edition from original.

Bow'el (Bow-), *n.* an intestine; *pl.* entrails; pity, as in bowels of compassion.

Bow'er (Bow-), *n.* an arbour, garden shelter.

Bowl (Bo-), *n.* a basin, round vessel, hollow part of something.

Bowl (Bo-), *n.* a wooden ball used in game of bowls. *v.t. & i.* to roll or project a ball.

Bow'sprit (Bow-), *n.* spar projecting from bows of vessel.

Box, *n.* a wooden or metal container with lid; a set of private seats at theatre. *v.t.* to pack in box.

Box, *n.* tree with very hard timber.

Box, *v.t. & i.* to fight with gloved fists. **Box'er,** *n.* **Box'ing,** *n.* **Box,** *n.* a light blow.

Box, *n. arch.* as present in box, hence **Boxing-Day.**

Boy, *n.* male child. **Boy'hood,** *n.* **Boy'ish,** *a.*

Boy'cott, *n.* an organized refusal to have relations with. *v.t.*

Brace, *n.* a carpenter's tool, a clamp: a pair (of game, etc.). *naut.* a rope used in rigging. *n.pl.* trouser-suspenders. *v.t.* to stretch, support, make firm. **Bra'cing,** *a.* invigorating.

Brace'let, *n.* ornamental ring round wrist or arm.

Bra'chial, *a.* pertaining to the arm, resembling an arm.

Brack'en, *n.* a kind of fern.

Brack'et, *n.* a support to hold a shelf etc; *pl.* in writing and printing a sign to enclose words parenthetically. *v.t.* to enclose thus, couple together.

Brack'ish, *a.* saltish (of water).

Brad, *n.* a small thin nail.

Brad'-awl, *n.* small boring tool.

Brag, *v.i.* to boast. **Bragg'art,** *n.* boastful person.

Braid, *n.* woven band, plait of hair. *v.t.* to trim with braid, plait.

Braille (Brale), *n.* system of raised printing for blind people to read by means of fingers.

Brain, *n.* nervous organ in skull; the intellect. *v.t.* to strike on the head so as to kill or injure. **Brain'storm,** *n.* fit of madness. **Brains trust,** *n.* panel of experts answering questions.

Braise, *v.t.* to stew in covered pan.

Brake, *n.* bracken, brushwood.

Brake, *n.* device for checking speed of vehicle or machine. *v.t.*

Bram'ble, *n.* prickly skrub, blackberry-bush.

Bran, *n.* husks separated from flour.

Branch (Brahnch), *n.* limb or tree, tributary of river, etc.; off-shoot, subsidiary office or shop. *v.i.* to diverge, to bear branches.

Brand, *n.* a mark, a trade-name, a burning piece of wood, a category of goods. *v.t.* to mark, esp. with hot iron. **Brand-new,** *a.* completely new.

Bran'dish, *v.t.* to wave, flourish, e.g. a weapon.

Bran'dy, *n.* cognac, spirit made from wine.

Brash, *a.* impudent, presumptuous.

Brass,*n.*alloy of zinc and copper; *sl.* impudence.

Brass'erie, *n.* eating-place where alcohol also served.

Bras'siere, *n.* woman's underbodice.

Brat, *n.* child, in contemptuous sense.

Brava'do (-vah-), *n.* boastful show of courage.

Brave, *a.* courageous. *n.* a Red Indian warrior. *v.t.* to meet boldly, defy. Bra'very, *n.*

Bravu'ra, *n. mus.* brilliant execution, florid manner.

Brawl, *v.i.* to quarrel rowdily. *n.*

Brawn, *n.* muscular strength; pickled,choppedpork.Brawn'y, *a.* tough, strong.

Bray, *n.* cry of donkey. *v.i.*

Braze, *v.t.* to solder with alloy of zinc and brass, to cover with brass.

Bra'zen, *a.* shameless, impudently bold; made of brass.

Bra'zier, *n.* worker in brass; container for burning charcoal or coke.

Breach, *n.* infringement, gap, opening, breaking of rules, etc. *v.t.* to make a gap in.

Bread (Bred), *n.* flour baked in loaves.

Breadth (Bredth), *n.* extent across, width; broadness of mind, view, etc. Breadthways, Breadthwise, *adv.*

Break (Brake), *v.t. & i.* to separate forcibly, to burst asunder, to become shattered, to ruin, to part company. *n.* a fracture, fault; in billiards, etc. a series of consecutive scoring strokes. *col.* a respite, piece of luck.

Break'down, *n.* a failure, *v.i.*

Break'fast (Brek-), *n.* first meal of day. *v.i.*

Break'water (Brake-), *n.* protective harbour-wall.

Breast (Brest), *n.* milk-secreting organ in mammals; the human chest; *fig.* the heart, affections. *v.t.* to mount, face, make clean breast of, to confess.

Breast'work, *n.* outer fortification.

Breath (Breth), *n.* respiration, air used by lungs; life; a faint breeze. Breathe, *v.i.* to inhale and exhale air, to live; whisper, pause. Brea'ther, *n.* a short pause.

Breech, *n.* hinder part of gun etc.; lower part of body at back. *n. pl.* trousers. *v.t.* to put in trousers.

Breed, *v.t.* to produce young, generate. *n.* race, kind, strain, offspring.

Breed'ing, *n.* ancestry, good manners.

Breeze, *n.* a soft wind. *coll.* a disturbance, quarrel. Breez'y, *a.* Breez'ily, *adv.* careless in manner.

Breve, *n. mus.* longest note in use, equal to two semi-breves.

Brev'et, *n.* nominal rank.

Bre'viary, *n.* book of daily services in R.C. Church.

Brev'ity, *n.* briefness, in speech or writing.

Brew (Broo), *v.t. & i.* to make liquor by fermentation, to infuse concoct, to be in process. Brew'er, *n.* Brew'ery, *n.* place for brewing beer.

Bri'ar (Bry-), *n.* tobacco-pipe made from heather-root.

Bribe, *n.* a payment to corrupt or influence illegally. *v.t.* Bri'bery, *n.*

Bric'-à-Brac, *n.* worthless curios, fancy objects.

Brick, *n.* building-block of baked clay. *v.t.* to make with bricks. Brick'-layer, *n.* skilled workman in housebuilding, etc. *coll.* a social blunder, esp. as drop a brick.

Bride, *n.* woman about to be or just married. Bri'dal, *a.* pertaining to a wedding. Bride'groom, *n.* man about to be married.

Brides'maid, *n.* girl who is member of bride's retinue at wedding.

Bridge, *n.* structure for crossing river, railway, etc.; part of nose; *naut.* raised platform on ship for navigation, etc.; game of cards. *v.t.* to span, make bridge over.

Bri'dle, *n.* harness for horse's head; any restraint. *v.t. & i.* to restrain, put bridle on; *fig.* to show offence.

Brief, *a.* short. *n.* *leg.* summary of a case for guidance of barrister, instructions.

Bri'er, *n.* wild rose.

Brig, *n.* square-rigged, two-masted sailing-ship.

Brigade', *n.* a mil. division, organized band. Brigadier', *n.* mil. rank, commander of brigade.

Brig'and, *n.* robber. Brig'andage, *n.*

Brig'antine, *n.* two-masted sailing-ship square-rigged on foremast only.

Bright (Brite), *a.* shining, cheerful, clever (*col.*). Bright'en, *v.t. & i.*

Brill'iant (-yant), *a.* shining, sparkling, very clear, extremely clever. Brilliance, *n.*

Brim, *n.* edge of vessel etc. *v.t. & i.* to be full or fill to the top. Brim'stone, *n.* sulphur.

Brin'dled, *a.* streaked, tawny with streaks.

Brine, *n.* salt water. Bri'ny, *a.* very salt.

Bring, *v.t.* to fetch, carry with one, cause to come.

Brink *n.* edge of steep place, margin.

Briquette', *n.* block of ice-cream or compressed coal-dust.

Brisk, *a.* active, lively.

Bris'ket, *n.* breast of animal in butchery.

Bris'tle, *n.* short stiff hair. *v.t. & i.* to stand erect like this.

Brit'tle, *a.* fragile, easily broken.

Broach, *n.* roasting-spit, boring-tool. *v.t.* to open cask, raise for discussion.

Broad (Brawd), *a.* wide, open, extensive; outspoken, pronounced (of accent); indelicate. *pl.* expanse of water.

Broad'cast, *n.* radio transmission. *v.t.* to sow, scatter freely.

Broad'side, *n.* naval discharge of guns simultaneously on one side of ship.

Brocade, *n.* cloth woven with raised pattern.

Brochure' (-shoor), *n.* a pamphlet, booklet.

Brogue, *n.* a stout leather shoe for; a way of speaking, esp. Irish.

Broil, *v.t. & i.* to grill, cook on gridiron. *n.* noisy dispute.

Bro'ker, *n.* agent, middleman,

dealer who acts for others. **Bro'-
kerage**, *n.* his commission.

Bro'mide, *n.* a sedative, photograph printed on paper treated
with silver bromide.

Bro'mine, *n.* element resembling
chlorine.

Bronchi'al, *a.* to do with bronchi
or windpipe and its branches.
Bronchi'tis (-ky-tis), *n.* inflammation of these.

Bronc'o, *n.* Amer. unbroken
horse.

Bronze, *n.* alloy of tin and copper. *a.* **Bronzed**, *a. coll.* sunburnt.

Brooch (Broche), *n.* ornamental
clasp or safety-pin.

Brood (-oo-), *n.* family of young
birds, a strain, race. *v.t.* to sit
as bird on eggs; *fig.* to meditate gloomily. **Brood'y**, *a.* of
hen sitting on eggs or *fig.* of
person in sullenly meditative
mood.

Brook, *n.* a small stream.

Brook, *v.t.* to tolerate, put up
with.

Broom, *n.* brush for sweeping;
wild yellow-flowered shrub.

Broth, *n.* thick meat soup.

Broth'el, *n.* house of prostitu-
tion.

Broth'er (Bruth-), *n.* a son of the
same parents, associate, equal.
Brethren, *arch. pl.* form. **Broth'-
erhood**, *n.* friendly company,
relationship. **Broth'er-in-law**, *n.*
the brother of a husband or
wife. **Broth'erliness**, *n.*

Brow, *n.* the protective ridge
above eyes, the forehead, edge
of hill. **Brow'beat**, *v.t.* to intimidate, bully.

Brown, *a.* between orange and
black in colour. *v.t. & i.* to
make or become brown.

Browned-off, *a. sl.* bored, disap-
pointed.

Brown'ie, *n.* a fairy, goblin;
junior girl-guide.

Browse, *v.i.* to feed on leaves
and shoots of trees; to glance
cursorily through a book.

Bruise (-ooze), *v.t.* to strike,
damage. *n.* discoloration caused
by blow.

Bruit (Broo-), *n. arch.* rumour,
report. *v.t.* to report.

Brunette', *n.* woman with dark
hair and complexion.

Brunt', *n.* chief shock or stress.

Brush, *n.* implement with bristles
for smoothing hair, sweeping,
etc.; fox's tail; a skirmish;
undergrowth. *v.t. & i.* to clean,
smooth, sweep, touch lightly.
Brush-off, *n. & v.t. sl.* rebuff,
to rebuff.

Brusque (Broosk), *a.* abrupt in
manner. **Brus'querie**, *n.* a curt
expression.

Brute (Broot), *n.* beast, unkind
person. *a.* **Bru'tal**, *a.* cruel,
unkind, grossly sensual. **Bru'-
tish**, *a.* **Brutal'ity**, *n.* **Bru'talise**,
v.t. to render insensitive to
violence, etc.

Bub'ble, *n.* hollow globe of liquid
filled with air; anything empty
or fraudulent. *v.i.* to form bubbles.

Buccaneer', *n.* sea-rover, pirate.

Buck, *n.* male of deer, rabbit,
etc.; a dandy. *v.t. & i.* of a
horse, to leap with arched back
and stiff legs in an attempt to
throw rider.

Buck'et, *n.* pail, vessel for water.

Buc'kle, *n.* metal clasp for strap.
v.t. to fasten with buckle. **Buck'-
ler**, *n. arch.* shield.

Buck'ram, *n.* coarse, stiffened
cloth.

Buckshee', *a. & adv. sl.* free, windfall.

Buco 'ic (Bew-), *a.* rustic. *n.* pastoral poem.

Bud, *n.* first shoot of flower, stem, leaf etc. *v.i.* to start to grow, open out.

Buddh'ism (Bood-), *n.* religion founded on the teachings of Gautama, Hindu sage of 6th century B.C. Buddha, his sacred name.

Budge, *v.i.* to give way, move.

Bud'gerigar, *n.* Australian love-bird kind of parakeet.

Budg'et, *n.* an annual financial statement or forecast. *v.i.* to prepare this. *n.* a bag with its contents, stores, etc.

Buff, *n.* light yellow colour; the bare skin.

Buff'alo, *n.* various kinds of wild ox.

Buff'er, *n.* shield to reduce shock of collision; *sl.* an old man.

Buff'et, *n.* a slight blow; misfortune. *v.t.* to strike or slap.

Buff'et (Boo-fay), *n.* refreshment bar.

Buffoon', *n.* a clown. Buffoon'ery, *n.*

Bug, *n.* flat red blood-sucking insect.

Bug'bear, *n.* object of dislike or terror, great annoyance.

Bug'gy, *n.* light horse-drawn vehicle.

Bu'gle, *n.* brass instrument resembling trumpet. Bu'gler, *n.*

Build (Bild), *v.t. & i.* to erect, construct, shape, depend (on). Build'er, *n.* Build'ing, *n.*

Bulb, *n.* rooted plant-bud like narcissus or onion, etc. Bulb'-ous, *n.* shaped like this.

Bulge, *n.* a swelling or protuberance. *v.i.*

Bulk, *n.* volume, size; the larger part of anything; a cargo. *v.i.* to be of importance, to weigh heavily. Bulk'y, *a.* Bulk'iness, *n.*

Bulk'head, *n.* wall or partition in ship.

Bull, *n.* male of cattle; financier speculating for a rise in stocks. Bull'ock, *n.* a castrated bull. Bull's-eye', *n.* the centre of a target, a lantern.

Bull, *n.* a Papal edict; a ridiculous contradiction in speech.

Bull'dozer, *n.* machine for excavating soil. Bull'doze, *v.t.* to use this; *fig.* to act ruthlessly.

Bull'et, *n.* projectile fired from rifle., etc.

Bull'etin, *n.* official statement on progress of conference, famous person's illness, etc.

Bull'ion, *n.* gold or silver in mass, not as coin.

Bully, *n.* domineering person. *v.t.* to intimidate, treat badly.

Bul'rush, *n.* tall water-rush.

Bul'wark, *n.* raised side of ship; a defence.

Bum'ble-Bee, *n.* large social bee.

Bumm'aree, *n.* middleman in fish-trade, esp. at Billingsgate.

Bump, *n.* a slight collision, a blow, a lump caused by a blow. *v.t.* to collide with or strike against.

Bump'er, *n.* a full glass; motor-car fender. *a.* abundant, as of harvest.

Bump'kin, *n.* peasant, rustic.

Bump'tious, *a.* self-assertive.

Bun, *n.* small round soft cake; hair gathered in ball at nape of neck.

Bunch, *n.* a number of things tied together or similar. *v.t. & i.*

Bun'dle, *n.* a bulky package; a number of things tied together.

v.t. to tie in a bundle; bundle (off), *v.t.* dismiss abruptly.

Bung, *n.* a stopper for a cask; large cork. *v.t.* to stop up.

Bun'galow (Bung-ga-loe), *n.* single-storied dwelling. **Bung'-aloid,** *a.* of ugly spread of such outside towns.

Bun'gle, *v.t.* to perform awkwardly; to spoil by clumsy action. **Bun'gler,** *n.*

Bun'ion, *n.* inflamed swelling on toe.

Bunk, *n.* a sleeping place, a berth in ship.

Bunk, *v.i. sl.* as do a bunk, run away.

Bunk'er, *n.* bin for coal; hazard on golf-course.

Bunk'um, *n.* bombastic nonsense.

Bunt'ing, *n.* flags, material for flags.

Buoy (Boi), *n. naut.* floating mark anchored in sea, for ships' guidance or mooring. *v.t.* to mark with buoy, to keep afloat. **Buoy'ant,** *a.* floating, cheerful. **Buoy'ancy,** *n.*

Bur, *n.* prickly headed plant; *fig.* person difficult to shake off.

Burd'en, *n.* a load, cargo, something heavy or difficult to bear. *v.t.* to load heavily, encumber.

Burd'en, *n.* chorus of a song.

Bu'reau (-roe), *n.* a writing-desk, an office. **Bureau'cracy** (-ok'-), *n.* government by officials, centralized government.

Bu'reaucrat, *n.* self-important official. **Bu'reaucratic,** *a.*

Bur'gess, *n.* citizen, inhabitant of municipality.

Burg'lar, *n.* thief who breaks into private premises. **Burg'le,** *v.t. & i.* **Burg'lary,** *n.*

Bur'gundy, *n.* name given to various wines from that part of France.

Bur'ial (Ber'-), the act of interment, funeral.

Burke, *v.t.* to smother, avoid issue.

Burles'que (-esk), *n.* travesty, humorous imitation. *v.t.*

Bur'ly, *a.* sturdy, thickset.

Burn, *v.t. & i.* to destroy by fire, be on fire; to glow. *n.* mark or injury caused by burning.

Burn'ish, *v.t.* to polish highly.

Burr'ow (-roe), *n.* rabbit's hole. *v.t.* to make hole in ground.

Burs'ar, *n.* a keeper of official purse, treasurer, esp. of college or school; scholar winning grant or award.

Burst, *v.t. & i.* to break violently, shatter, fly apart, break into fragments. *n.* an explosion, a sudden acceleration.

Bur'y (Ber'-i), *v.t.* to enter, put in a grave or underground, conceal.

Bus'by (Buz-), *n.* hussar's fur hat.

Bush (Boo-), *n.* small shrub, wild scrub-jungle in Africa.

Bush'el (Boo-), *n.* measure of capacity, eight gallons.

Business (Biz-ness), *n.* livelihood, employment; trade, company; affairs in general; duty; stage action without real dialogue. **Bus'iness-like,** *a.* efficient, well-organized.

Bust, *n.* upper part of human body, chest; statue of person's head and shoulders.

Bus'tle (-sl), *v.i.* to move about briskly, fussily. *n.* lively activity, fuss; formerly pad to make skirt stand out.

Bus'y (Biz-), *a.* actively occupied, industrious. *v.t.* **Bus'y-body,** *n.* meddler, fussy person.

But, *prep. & conj.* that not, yet, unless, still, besides.

Bu'tane, *n.* gas from paraffin hydrocarbon.

Butch'er (Boo-), *n.* tradesman selling meat, person who kills animals for meat; *fig.* a savage person. *v.t.* to slaughter, kill.

But'ler, *a.* head manservant.

Butt, *n.* large tub or cask; a blow with the head; a target for ridicule; wooden end of rifle etc. *v.t. & i.* to strike with the head.

Butt'er, *n.* edible oily solid obtained by churning cream. *v.t.* to spread with butter; *fig.* to flatter excessively.

Butt'erfly, *n.* diurnal insect with large coloured wings.

Butt'ermilk, *n.* milk remaining after churning.

Butt'erscotch, *n.* kind of toffee.

Butt'ery, *n.* store-room, pantry esp. in large establishment.

Butt'ocks, *n. pl.* the rump.

Butt'on, *n.* disk for fastening dress or suit etc. *v.t.*

Butt'ress, *n.* a prop, a structure to reinforce a wall. *v.t.* to support.

Bux'om, *a.* plump and lively, in glowing health, esp. of woman.

Buy (Bye), *v.t.* to obtain by payment, to purchase.

Buzz, *n.* humming sound as of bees etc. *v.i.*

Buzz'ard, *n.* kind of hawk.

By, *prep.* near, beside, along, through agency of, as soon as. **By and by,** soon. **By and large,** in general, more or less. **By'-stander,** *n.* casual spectator, onlooker.

By-elec'tion, *n.* election held separately from General Election.

By, Bye, in general prefix meaning sub-ordinate, e.g. **By'-pass, By'-law,** etc.

Byre, *n.* cow-shed, shippen.

By'word, *n.* familiar saying; object of ridicule.

C

Cab, *n.* a vehicle for public hire. **Cab'man,** *n.*

Cabal', *n.* political plot, body organizing this.

Cab'aret (-ay), *n.* song and dance entertainment in night club.

Cabb'age, *n.* green vegetable with tight-leaved green head. **Cabb'age-rose,** *n.* fragrant old-fashioned rose.

Cab'in, *n.* small room on ship, a hut. *v.t.* to confine.

Cab'inet, *n.* highest executive part of government; a chest of drawers.

Ca'ble, *n.* a hawser or strong rope; submarine telegraph system, message sent by this. *v.t. & i.* to signal by cable. **Ca'ble-gram,** *n.* a cabled message.

Cache (Cash), *n.* secret store or hiding-place.

Cach'et (-ay), *n.* mark of authenticity, distinctive character or refinement. *Med.* capsule containing medicine.

Cachou', *n.* perfumed lozenge for sweetening the breath.

Cac'kle, *n.* fussy cry, cry of hen, etc., strident empty talk. *v.i.*

Cacoph'ony, *n.* discordant sound. Cacoph'onous, *a.*

Cac'tus, *n.* prickly plant growing in desert. *pl.* cac'ti, cac'tuses. Cactac'eous, *a.*

Cad, *n.* mean, ill-behaved person. Cadd'ish, *a.*

Cadav'erous, *a.* corpse-like. Cadav'er, *n.* a corpse.

Cadd'ie, *n.* youth or man employed to carry golfer's bag.

Ca'dence, *n.* intonation, rhythm, modulation of voice.

Caden'za, *n. mus.* ornamental flourish.

Cadet', *n.* younger son; student-officer in military college or corps.

Cadge (Kaj), *v.t. & i.* to obtain by begging, beg. Cadg'er, *n.* loaf, lazy fellow; formerly hawker.

Caesar'ean, *n.* operation for delivering child by incision in abdomen.

Ca'fé (-fay), *n.* small restaurant or coffee-bar.

Cafete'ria, *n.* restaurant at which customers serve themselves.

Caff'eine, *n.* alkaloid found in coffee and tea plants.

Caf'tan, *n.* long, wide-sleeved eastern garment.

Cage, *n.* box, enclosure, equipped with bars for keeping birds and animals. *v.t.*

Cairn, *n.* a pile of stones for landmark or monument.

Cais'son, *n.* large water-tight chamber for building dams, etc.

Cai'tiff, *n. arch.* villain, contemptible person.

Cajole', *v.t.* wheedle, coax by flattery or deceit. Cajo'lery, *n.*

Cake, *n.* various kinds of sweet baked confections; hard mass of soap, etc. *v.t. & i.*

Calam'ity, *n.* profound misfortune. Calam'itous, *a.*

Calca'reous, *a.* containing lime.

Calc'ify, *v.t. & i.* convert or be converted into lime.

Cal'cine, *v.t. & i.* reduce to quick-lime.

Cal'cium, *n.* Basis of lime.

Cal'culate, *v.t.* to reckon, compute. *v.i.* Calcula'tion, *n.* Cal'culable, *a.* Cal'culator. Cal'culating, *a.* scheming, cunning.

Cal'endar, *n.* table of months and days, system for reckoning date, register, etc.

Cal'ender, *n.* steam mangle, machine for smoothing cloth, etc.

Calf (Kahf), *n.* young of cow, whale, elephant, etc. *pl.* Calves. Calve (Kahve), *v.i.* to give birth to calf.

Calf (Kahf), *n.* fleshy hinder part of leg between knee & ankle.

Cal'ibre, *n.* internal bore of gun or rifle; character, quality. Cal'ibrate, *v.t.*

Cal'ico, *n. & a.* cotton cloth.

Ca'liph, *n. arch.* title of Moslem rulers.

Call (Kawl), *v.t. & i.* to cry out, summon, shout, pay a short formal visit, make a bid as in bridge, etc., name, designate, speak to on telephone. *n.* a cry, a visit, a bid, etc.

Callig'raphy, *n.* handwriting, esp. decorative writing.

Call'ipers, *n.* instrument with two movable arms for measuring diameters.

Callisthen'ics, *n.* gymnastics for helping strength and beauty.

Call'ous, *a.* insensitive, unfeeling, hard.

Call'ow, *a.* naive, inexperienced.

Calm (Kahm), *a.* peaceful, quiet, undisturbed. *v.t.* & *i.* to make or become quiet, soothe. *n.* absence of wind, stillness. **Calma'tive,** *n. med.* sedative.

Cal'omel, *n. med.* purgative made from preparation of mercury.

Cal'ory, *n.* unit of heat, unit of energy produced by food. **Calorif'ic,** *a.* heat-producing.

Cal'umny, *n.* a slander, false charge. **Calum'niate,** *v.t.* **Calumnia'tion,** *n.* **Calum'niator,** *n.* slanderer.

Calv'ary, *n.* place of the Crucifixion, representation of this.

Ca'lyx, *n. bot.* leaf-covering of flower-bid.

Cam, *n.* projecting part of wheel for changing rotary into reciprocating motion.

Camarad'erie, *n.* comradeship.

Cam'ber, *n.* convexity in surface of road or aircraft wing.

Cam'bric, *n.* fine white linen.

Cam'el, *n.* long-necked, humped quadruped used for desert transport.

Cam'eo, *n.* gem carved in relief.

Cam'era, *n.* apparatus for making photographs. **In camera** *leg.* not in open court.

Cam'isole, *n.* under-bodice.

Cam'ouflage, *n.mil.* disguise to hide ship, guns etc. from enemy observation. *v.t.*

Camp, *n.* an open-air resting-place with fire or tent; collection of military tents, bivouac, etc. *v.i.* **Camp-follower,** *n.* hanger-on.

Campaign' (-pane), *n.* series of military operations, political programme. *v.i.* to serve in military operation, to agitate for some objective. **Campaign'er,** *n.* experienced soldier.

Campanol'ogy, *n.* bell-lore. **Campan'ile,** *n.* high tower with bells.

Cam'phor, *n.* white, transparent substance volatile in character. **Cam'phorated,** *a.*

Cam'shaft, *n.* rotating shaft in automobile engine.

Can, *v.i.* to be able, to have right to, be allowed to.

Can, *n.* a metal container for carrying liquid. *v.t.* to preserve in tin or can.

Canal', *n.* an artificial waterway; *med.* a duct in the body. **Can'alise,** *v.t.*

Can'ard (-ar), *n.* false rumour.

Cana'ry (-airy), *n.* yellow songbird; light sweet wine.

Can'cel, *v.t.* to obliterate, countermand, cross out. **Cancella'tion,** *n.*

Can'cer, *n.* the Crab, fourth sign of Zodiac; constellation of stars; a malignant disease.

Candela'brum, *n.* ornamental candlestick with branches.

Can'did, *a.* frank, outspoken. **Can'dour,** *n.*

Can'didate, *n.* person seeking election or appointment. **Can'didature,** *n.*

Can'dle, *n.* long round stick of wax with wick for burning as light. **Can'dlestick,** *n.*

Can'dy, *n.* crystallized sugar. **Can'died**, *a.*

Cane, *n.* stem of dwarf palm or large tropical grasses; a walking-stick. *v.t.* to thrash. **Cane-sugar**, *n.* made from sugar-cane as opposed to sugar made from beet.

Ca'nine, *a.* pertaining to the dog.

Can'ister, *n.* small box or case for holding tea etc. *arch.* type of shrapnel.

Cank'er, *n.* ulcerous sore or growth, anything that destroys by eating away. *v.t. & i.* to corrupt, decay. **Cank'erous**, *a.*

Cann'ibal, *n.* one who eats flesh of other human-beings, any animal feeding on its own species. **Cann'ibalism**, *n.* **Cann'-ibalize**, *v.t.*

Cann'on, *n.* large mounted gun. **Cannonade'**, *n.* **Cann'on-bone**, *n.* horse's bone between fetlock and hock.

Cann'on, *n.* scoring combination in billiards.

Cann'y, *a. Sc.* shrewd, cautious.

Canoe' (-noo), *n.* light boat with curved ends and powered by hand-paddle.

Can'on, *n.* a church dignitary, an eccl. law or rule, list of books accepted as authentic. **Can'-onise**, *v.t.* to proclaim a saint. **Canonisa'tion**, *n.* **Canon'ical**, *a.*

Can'opy, *n.* awning over bed, throne, etc. *v.t.*

Cant, *n.* hypocritical talk, humbug; thieve's jargon. *v.i.*

Cant, *n.* slanting surface, inclination. *v.t. & i.* to slope, tilt.

Cant'aloup, *n.* kind of melon.

Cantan'kerous, *a.* irritable, ill-natured.

Canta'ta (-tah-tah), *n.* choral work resembling oratorio.

Canteen', *n.* tea-bar or café in factory or barracks; a case of cutlery.

Can'ter, *n.* unextended gallop. *v.t. & i.*

Can'ticle, *n.* short hymn.

Cant'le, *n.* rear part of saddle.

Can'to (-toe), *n.* division of long poem.

Can'ton, *n.* division of country, esp. in Switzerland; group of villages in France.

Can'vas, *n.* strong coarse cloth made of hemp or flax; a painting, sails of vessel.

Can'vass, *v.t. & i.* to ask for votes or support, examine opinion.

Can'yon, *n.* deep gorge.

Cap, *n.* a covering for the head, a lid etc. *v.t.* to cover with such; outdo.

Ca'pable, *a.* efficient, able, competent. **Capabil'ity**, *n.*

Capac'ity, *n.* power of holding or grasping; volume; ability, character. **Capa'cious** (-pay-), *a.* roomy, extensive.

Capar'ison, *n.* rich harness for horse. *v.t.*

Cape, *n.* loose, sleeveless robe.

Cape, *n.* a tongue of land jutting into the sea.

Ca'per, *v.i.* to frisk, skip about. *n.* a frolic or escapade.

Capill'ary, *a.* hair-like, of hair. *n.* tube with tiny bore, thin blood-vessel.

Cap'ital, *n.* chief city of country; top of pillar; large-sized letter; accumulated wealth as opposed to income, stocks, funds. **Cap'italism**, *n.* system based on individual ownership. **Cap'-italise**, *v.t.* to convert property

into money, take advantage.
Cap'ital punishment, *n.* death penalty for murder, etc.

Capita'tion, *n.* a tax or grant per head of population.

Capit'ulate, *v.i.* to yield, surrender. **Capitula'tion,** *n.*

Ca'pon, *n.* castrated cock.

Caprice' (-preess), *n.* a whim, passing fancy. **Capri'cious,** *a.* inconstant.

Cap'ricorn, *n.* the Goat, tenth sign of Zodiac; southern tropic.

Capsize', *v.t.* & *i.* to upset, be upset, esp. when in boat.

Cap'stan, *n. naut.* apparatus for winding up anchor, etc.

Cap'sule, *n.* soluble case containing dose of medicine, metal envelope or container.

Cap'tain (-tin), *n.* a leader, commander, commanding officer of ship, naval rank below Rear-Admiral, mil. rank below major. **Cap'taincy,** *n.*

Cap'tion, *n.* explanatory wording beneath photograph or illustration.

Cap'tious, *a.* quick to criticize.

Cap'tive, *n.* prisoner. *a.* imprisoned. **Captiv'ity,** *n.* state of being a prisoner. **Cap'ture,** *n.* act of being seized or taken prisoner. **Cap'tor,** *n.*

Cap'tivate, *v.t.* to fascinate.

Car, *n.* a wheeled vehicle.

Carafe', *n.* glass water or wine bottle for table.

Car'amel, *n.* kind of sweet, burnt sugar for culinary purposes.

Cara'pace, *n.* hard upper shell of crab, tortoise, etc.

Car'at, *n.* measure of weight for gems, gold, etc.

Car'avan, *n.* convoy of merchants, covered dwelling-wagon.

Car'avel, *n. arch.* fast small ship.

Carb'ide, *n.* compound of carbon with second element.

Carb'ine, *n.* a short rifle. **Carabin'eer,** *n.* mounted soldier armed with this.

Carbol'ic, *n.* esp. as **c. acid,** disinfectant made from coaltar.

Carb'on, *n.* non-metallic element, the substance of pure charcoal; thread of c. used as glowing end of electric lamp. **Car'bon copy,** *n.* copy made from using paper treated with carbon; something identical with another. **Carbonif'erous,** *a.* coal-bearing.

Carb'oy, *n.* large glass vessel protected by wicker-work.

Carb'uncle, *n.* precious stone; an inflamed boil.

Carb'urettor, *n.* device for inducing explosion of oil-vapour and air in motor engine.

Carc'ass, Carc'ase, *n.* corpse, dead body of animal.

Card, *n.* toothed instrument for combing wool; piece of pasteboard used as postcard, playing-card etc; dial of compass. *sl.* an amusing character. *v.t.* to comb out wool with card. **Card-sharper,** *n.* person who cheats at cards, esp. for money.

Card'iac, *a.* pertaining to the heart.

Card'igan, *n.* knitted woollen jacket.

Card'inal, *n.* highest rank in R.C. church below Pope. *a.* principal, chief.

Car'diogram, *n.* record showing heart-beats obtained by cardiometer.

Care, *n.* concern, anxiety, cause

of this. *v.i.* to be concerned or anxious, heed, look after, like. Care'ful, *a.* Care'worn, *a.* exhausted by worry. Caretak'er, *n.*

Careen', *v.t. & i.* to tilt vessel on side in order to clean or repair bottom.

Career', *n.* a chosen job or course of action. *v.i.* to move along at full speed.

Caress', *v.t.* to treat with affection, fondle, stroke. *n.* act or expression of affection.

Car'et, *n.* a mark in printing or writing denoting where something is to be inserted.

Car'go, *n.* a ship's freight, a load.

Ca'ribou (-boo), *n.* N. Amer. reindeer.

Car'icature, *n.* likeness made ridiculous or exaggerated. *v.t.*

Car'illon, *n.* a concerted peal of bells, set of bells.

Car'ious, *a.* decayed, as of teeth.

Car'mine, *n. & a.* brilliant crimson colour.

Carn'age, *n.* slaughter.

Carn'al, *a.* of the flesh, sensual, worldly, lustful.

Carna'tion, *n.* rosy pink colour; flower like pink.

Carn'ival, *n.* festivity, esp. week preceding Lent.

Carniv'orous, *a.* flesh-eating. Carn'ivore, *n.*

Car'ol, *n.* joyful Christmas song; *v.t. & i.* Car'oller, *n.*

Carouse', *n.* loud, drunken revelry. *v.i.* Carous'al, *n.*

Carp, *n.* large freshwater fish.

Carp, *v.i.* to find fault in niggling fashion.

Car'pal, *a. anat.* pertaining to the wrist.

Carp'enter, *n.* a worker in timber. Carp'entry, *n.*

Carp'et, *n.* floor-covering of woven cloth. *v.t.* Carp'etbagg'er, *n.* political opportunist.

Car'riage (-ij), *n.* horse-drawn vehicle; bearing, conduct; cost or act of carting goods.

Car'rion, *n.* dead putrefying flesh.

Car'ronade, *n. arch.* small naval gun.

Car'rot, *n.* long, edible root-vegetable of reddish colour.

Car'ry, *v.t. & i.* to transport, bear, behave, reach, take.

Cart, *n.* light two wheeled vehicle for pulling or pushing; *v.t.* to carry in such. Cart'age, *n.* Cart'er, *n.* Cart'age, *n.*

Cart-wheel, *n.* sideways somersault on arms and legs in turn.

Car'tel, *n.* combination of manufacturers to fix prices.

Cart'ilage, *n.* gristle, elastic tissue in body.

Cartog'raphy, *n.* the craft of map-making. Cartog'rapher, *n.*

Cart'on, *n.* cardboard container.

Cartoon', *n.* preparatory drawing for larger work ; humorous drawing ; film made up from number of drawings.

Cart'ridge, *n.* metal or cardboard case containing charge for gun.

Carve, *v.t.* to cut up meat; to make sculpture out of wood or stone.

Cascade', *n.* small waterfall. *v.t.*

Case, *n.* a box, trunk, container, sheath. *v.t.*

Case, *n.* an example, instance, lawsuit.

Case'mate, *n.* armoured protection for warship's gun.

Case'ment (-sm-), *n.* hinged window.

Cash, *n.* money, coin. *v.t.* to turn into money.

Cashier', *n.* clerk in charge of money.

Cashier', *v.t.* to dismiss officer with ignominy.

Cash'mere, *n.* very soft wool from Cashmere goat; shawl of this.

Cas'ino (-seeno), *n.* public building for gambling or dancing.

Cask, *n.* a barrel.

Cask'et, *n.* small case for jewels etc.

Casque', *n. arch.* a helmet.

Cass'erole, *n.* fireproof dish for cooking.

Cass'ock, *n.* long black garment worn by clergyman.

Cast (Kahst), *v.t. & i.* to shed, leave off, throw away; to allot parts in play, to shape, mould. *n.* a mould, set of actors. Cast'ing-vote, *n.* decisive vote of chairman.

Cas'tanets, *n.pl.* small ivory or wooden instruments held in hand and clicked as accompaniment to Spanish dance.

Cast'away, *n.* shipwrecked person.

Caste, *n.* a social group, esp. in India ; rank.

Cas'tigate, *v.t.* to punish, chastise, admonish. Cas'tigator, *n.* Castiga'tion, *n.*

Cas'tle, *n.* stronghold, fortified house; piece in chess.

Cast'or, *n.* small wheel on foot of chair etc.

Cast'or oil, *n.* vegetable oil for purging or lubricating.

Cas'trate, *v.t.* to geld, remove testicles, emasculate. Castra'tion, *n.*

Cas'ual (-z-), *a.* chance, accidental, unprepared, occasional.

Cas'ualty, *n.* instance of bodily injury through war or accident.

Cas'uist, *n.* quibbler; person who studies cases of conscience. Cas'uistry, *n.*

Cat, *n.* member of feline order, tame or domesticated. *fig.* a spiteful woman. Cat's-paw, *n.* dupe; light breeze. Cat-walk, *n.* narrow temporary footway used during bridge-building.

Cata-, Cath, prefix meaning down or downwards, as in catadromous, cataract, etc.

Cat'aclysm, *n.* deluge, violent upheaval.

Cat'acomb, *n.* subterranean gallery with recesses for tombs.

Cat'alepsy, *n. med.* disease causing suspension of senses and physical powers; a trance. Catalep'tic, *a.*

Cat'alogue (-og), *n.* an alphabetical descriptive list, a sales list. *v.t.* to make a list or inventory.

Cat'apult, *n. arch.* military apparatus for hurling stones; forked stick with elastic thongs for hurling pebbles, etc. *v.t. & i.* to hurl forward violently.

Cat'aract, *n.* a large steep waterfall; an eye-disease.

Catarrh', *n.* inflammation of mucous membrane, a cold. Catar'rhal, *a.*

Catas'trophe (-fi), *n.* great calamity, disaster. Catas'trophic, *a.*

Catch, *v.t. & i.* to take, grasp, lay hold of, comprehend, to get ensnared. *n.* a thing caught or taken, a prize; a decisive action in cricket. Catch'ment, *n.* area in which water is collected for use. Catch'penny, *a.* cheap and showy. **Catch′word,** *n.* popular idea or phrase.

Cat′echize (-kize), *v.t.* to teach by question & answer, to question closely, as in rel. matters. **Cat′echism,** *n.* **Cat′echist,** *n.*

Cat′egory, *n.* class, order. **Cat′egorize,** *v.t. & i.* to name in detail, put into categories. **Categor′ical,** *a.* precise, exact.

Ca′ter, *v.i.* to provide food, amusement, allow for. **Ca′terer,** *n.*

Ca′terpillar, *n.* grub or larva of insect, esp. moth or butterfly. *n.* moving, endless track for enabling vehicle to proceed over difficult ground.

Cat′erwaul, *n.* cry of tom-cat, esp. when quarrelling. *v.i.*

Cathar′tic, *n. & a.* purgative. **Cathar′sis,** *n.* emotional relief produced by art.

Cathe′dral, *n.* head church of a diocese, housing bishop's throne.

Cath′ode, *n.* negative pole of electric current.

Cath′olic, *a.* universal, all-embracing; of the Anglican church, of the Roman Catholic Church, of all Christian religions. *n.* **Cathol′icism,** *n.*

Cat′tle, *n.* livestock, esp. of bovine orders.

Cau′cus (Kaw-), *n.* small powerful political group or committee.

Caul′dron, *n.* large iron vessel for boiling.

Cauli′flower (Kol-), *n.* kind of cabbage with large white fleshy flower-head.

Caulk (Kawk), *v.t.* to make seams of ship, etc. watertight with pitch and oakum.

Cause (-z), *n.* anything that produces an effect, reason, motive; principle for which people work. *v.t.* to bring into being, to put into effect. **Caus′al,** *a.* relating to cause. **Causal′ity,** *n.* condition of being a cause. **Causa′tion,** *n.* causing an effect

Cause′way, *n.* a raised thoroughfare across wet or marshy place.

Can′stic, *a.* burning, biting, sarcastic.

Cau′terise, *v.t.* to disinfect by burning with hot iron. **Cauterisa′tion,** *n.*

Cau′tion, *n.* a warning, heedulness. *v.t.* to warn. **Cau′tious,** *a.* prudent, careful. **Cau′tionary,** *a.*

Cavalcade′, *n.* procession of horsemen.

Cavalier′, *n.* a horseman, esp. a supporter of King Charles I. *a.* haughty, disdainful.

Cav′alry, *n.* body of mounted troops.

Cave, *n.* a hollow recess or tunnel in the earth. **Cav′ern,** *n.* a very deep cave. **Cav′ernous,** *a.* **Cav′ity,** *n.* a small hole or hollow.

Caviare′, *n.* salted sturgeon roe.

Cav′il, *v.i.* to criticize without reason.

Caw, *n.* corvine cry. *v.t.*

Cayenne′, *n.* hot red pepper.

Cease, *v.t. & i.* to discontinue, stop.

Ce′dar, *n.* large handsome evergreen tree with fragrant timber.

Cede, *v.t.* to surrender rights or territory.

Cei′ling (See-), *n.* inner roof of room, lining of this; lower level of cloud formation: maximum height to which aircraft can reach.

Cel′ebrate, *v.t.* to make famous,

to mark with ceremony, keep anniversary, etc. **Celebra'tion,** *n.* **Celeb'rity,** *n.* well-known person.

Celer'ity, *n.* speed, swiftness.

Cel'ery, *n.* vegetable with long white succulent stalks.

Celes'tial, *a.* heavenly, divine.

Cel'ibacy, *n.* unmarried state. **Cel'ibate,** *n.* & *a.*

Cell, *n.* place for prisoner, small room in monastery; unit of living matter; division of electric battery; subversive political group. **Cell'ular,** *a.*

Cel'lo (Chel-), *n. mus.* abbr. for violoncello.

Cell'uloid, *n.* plastic material made from camphor & guncotton.

Cell'ulose, *n.* starchlike substance in vegetable cells.

Cement', *n.* mortar, mixture of lime & water for fixing together bricks, etc. *v.t.*

Cem'etery, *n.* burial-ground.

Cen'otaph, *n.* monument to people buried elsewhere.

Cen'ser, *n.* church vessel for burning incense in.

Cen'sor, *n.* official who examines plays and films for offensive material. *v.t.* **Censo'rial,** *a.* **Censo'rious,** unnecessarily fault-finding. **Cen'sorship,** *n.* official overseeing of news, etc. esp. in time of war.

Cen'sure, *n.* severe reproof. *v.t.*

Cen'sus, *n.* official calculation of number of inhabitants.

Cen'taur, *n.* a legendary creature, half man, half horse.

Cente'nary, *n.* celebration of a hundredth anniversary. **Centena'rian,** *n.* person one hundred years old. **Centenn'ial,** *a.* having lasted or existed a hundred

years. **Cen'tury,** *n.* a hundred years; in cricket, one hundred runs.

Cent'igrade, *n.* system of measuring heat with freezing-point as nought degrees and boiling-point one hundred degrees. *a.*

Cent'ipede, *n.* small segmented animal with hundred or many legs.

Cen'tre, *n.* the middle point, the interior, source, headquarters, pivot, axis. **Cen'tral,** *a.* **Cen'tralise,** *v.t.* to concentrate, esp. power, organization, etc. **Centralisa'tion,** *n.* **Centrif'ugal,** *a.* tending to move away from centre. **Centrip'etal,** *a.* tending to move towards centre.

Centu'rion, *n.* Roman officer commanding one hundred men.

Ceram'ic, *a.* pertaining to the art of pottery; us. as *n.pl.* the art of pottery.

Ce'real, *a.* pertaining to edible grain. *n.* esp. as *n.pl.*

Cer'ebral, *a.* pertaining to the brain. **Cerebra'tion,** *n.* action of brain, process of thought.

Cer'emony, *n.* a sacred or official rite, traditional courtesy. **Ceremo'nial,** *a.* & *n.* **Ceremo'nious,** *a.* with formal observance.

Cert'ain, *a.* positive, reliable, sure, inevitable; some, one. **Cert'ainty, Cert'itude,** *n.*

Cert'ify, *v.t.* to acknowledge as correct or certain. **Certif'icate,** *n.* official declaration of person's ability, position, etc.

Cervic'al, *a.* of the neck.

Cerv'ine, *a.* pertaining to deer.

Cessa'tion, *n.* a discontinuance, a stopping.

Cess'ion, *n.* a surrendering, giving up.

Cess'pool, n. large pit for household drainage.

Cetac'ean, a. & n. of whale family, a member of this.

Chafe, v.t. & i. to make sore or warm by rubbing, to irritate. Chafing-dish, n. vessel for keeping food hot on table.

Chaff, n. husks of grain, worthless material; banter. v.t. to tease.

Chaff'er, v.i. to bargain, haggle.

Chagrin (Sha-), n. vexation, deep disappointment. v.t.

Chain, n. a series of links joined one to the other, a fetter, a consecutive series of happenings, a surveyor's measure. v.t. to bind, secure, restrict. Arch. Chain-armour, chain-mail, n. Chain'-shot, n. cannon-shot linked by chain to cut down rigging.

Chair, n. a movable seat for one person; the office of professor, a position of authority. v.t. to carry in triumph. Chair'man, n. head man of committee. Chair'manship, n.

Chaise (Shaze), n. light horse-carriage. Chaise-longue, n. lit. a long chair on which person can rest legs.

Cha'let (Shal-lay), n. mountain cottage.

Chal'ice (-iss), n. cup, esp. for communion.

Chalk (Chawk), n. carbonate of lime, crayon for writing on board etc. v.t. & i. to mark with this.

Chall'enge (Chal-), v.t. to summon to contest or battle, to dispute truth of something, to hail and question, as of sentry. n. Chall'enger, n.

Chalyb'eate (Kal-ib-), a, containing iron, esp. of water. Chalyb'-ean, a.

Cha'mber, n. room, assembly room, an official body.

Cha'mberlain, n. official in royal household. Cha'mbermaid, n. maid-servant responsible for care of bedrooms. Cha'mber-music, n. music to be played in a room as opposed to concert-hall.

Chame'leon (Kam-eel-), n. small lizard capable of adapting its colour to merge with any background.

Cham'fer (Sham-), v.t. to bevel symmetrically, channel, groove. n.

Cham'ois (Sham-wah), n. mountain antelope; soft leather made from its skin.

Champ', v.t. & i. to bite and chew noisily and continuously, esp. of horse.

Champagne (Sham-pane), n. sparkling white French wine.

Cham'pion, n. most successful competitor; person who fights for honour of somebody else; a hero, a superb sportsman. v.t. to defend, fight for. Cham'-pionship, n.

Chance, n. fortune, opportunity, that which happens. v.t. & i. to risk, happen. a. unexpected, fortuitous.

Chan'cel, n. eastern part of church where altar is situated.

Chan'cellor, n. high state or legal official, principal of university. Chan'cellorship, n. Chan'-cellery, n. office of chancellor, department of embassy.

Chan'cery, n. a division of High Court of Justice.

Chandelier', (Shan-), n. branched hanging support for, orig., candles, now electric bulbs.

Change, *v.t. & i.* to alter, make or become different, to dress in different clothes, to convert money into smaller units. *n.* alteration, substitution, variation; small coins, balance of money remaining after purchase. **Change'able,** *a.*

Chann'el, *n.* navigable part of waterway, deep strait, bed of stream, gutter, a means of conveying or communicating. *v.t.*

Chant (Chahnt), *v.t. & i.* to recite in musical manner. *n.* a church melody, a formal song. **Chant'-ry,** *n. rel.* chapel devoted to singing of masses.

Cha'os (Kay-), *n.* utter confusion, complete lack of form or order. **Cha'otic,** *a.*

Chap, *v.t. & i.* of skin, to split or chafe because of cold. *n.*

Chap, *n. col.* a man, lad.

Chap'el, *n.* small place of worship attached to private house or institution or subsidiary to main church; Nonconformist place of worship.

Chap'eron (Sh-), *n.* older woman who accompanies young unmarried woman for sake of propriety. *v.t.*

Chap'lain, *n.* priest attached to warship, regiment, family, institution etc. **Chap'laincy,** *n.*

Chap'ter, *n.* section of a book, official assembly of priests.

Char, *v.t. & i.* to scorch, discolour by burning, turn to charcoal. **Char'coal,** *n.* form of carbon obtained by special method of burning wood.

Char, *n.* fish of trout family.

Char, *v.t. & i.* to scrub floors, clean house in general. **Charwoman,** *n.*

Charabanc, *n.* (Sharra-bang) long open coach with transverse seats.

Char'acter (Ka-), *n.* moral qualities, temperament, reputation ; a prominent feature, a letter, distinguishing mark; person in novel or drama, an eccentric person. **Characteris'tic** *a,* **Char'acterise,** *v.t.* **Characterisation,** *n.*

Charade' (Shar-rahd), *n.* game in which object is to guess particular word which has been acted] or represented by syllables.

Charge, *v.t. & i.* advance on at a run, attack, load, enjoin, accuse, fill with electricity, demand as a price. *n.* price, task, commission, accusation. **Charge'able,** *a.* **Char'ger,** *n.* warhorse.

Char'iot, *n. arch.* two-wheeled horse-drawn military or sporting vehicle. **Charioteer',** *n.* driver of such.

Char'ity, *n.* generosity to the needy, love towards others, instinctive kindness. **Char'itable,** *a.*

Charl'atan (Sharl-), *n.* an imposter, quack, pretender. **Charl'atanism,** *n.*

Charm, *n.* attractive quality, magic spell, amulet worn to avert evil. *v.t.* to attract greatly, fascinate, cast spell over.

Charn'el-house, *n.* vault containing bones of the dead.

Chart, *n.* a map of the sea showing depth of water etc. *v.t. & i.* **Chart'-house,** *n.* room or cabin behind ship's bridge in which navigator plots course.

Chart'er, *n.* a document in evidence of rights or privileges. *v.t.* to grant privilege, to hire, esp. of aircraft.

Char'y (Chare-), *a.* cautious, sparing. **Char'ily**, *a.*

Chase, *v.t.* to pursue, run after, drive from. *n.* a pursuit, a hunt.

Chase, *v.t.* to emboss, engrave.

Chasm (Kazm), *n.* deep fissure, abyss.

Chas'sis (Shass-ee), *n.* basic framework of vehicle.

Chaste (Chased), *a.* pure, virgin, modest. **Chas'tity**, *n.*

Cha'sten, *v.t.* to correct by discipline or punishment.

Chastise', *v.t.* to punish, beat. **Chas'tisement**, *n.*

Chat, *v.i.* to talk casually. *n.* **Chatt'er**, *v.i.* to talk idly, rattle teeth as with fear or cold. *n.* idle talk.

Chatt'el, *n. us. pl.* movable possessions.

Chauffeur' (Sho-fer), *n.* motorcar driver.

Chau'vinism (Sho-vin-izm), *n.* aggressive, exaggerated patriotism of dangerous kind. **Chau'vinist**, *n.* **Chauvinist'ic**, *a.*

Cheap, *a.* low-priced, easily got, worthless. **Cheap'en**, *v.t. & i.* to make or become cheap, lose value.

Cheat, *v.t. & i.* to deceive, swindle, play falsely. *n.* person who does this.

Check, *v.t. & i.* to bring, come to a halt, restrain, control, examine. *n.* move threatening king in chess, a sudden set-back, repulse, ticket. **Checkmate'**, *n.* in chess, winning move. *v.t.* to defeat.

Cheek, *n.* side of face between eye and jaw-bone; *sl.* impudence. *v.t.* to address impudently.

Cheer, *n.* mood, food, cry of applause. *v.t. & i.* to encourage, comfort, shout applause. **Cheer'ful**, *a.* **Cheer'ily**, *adv.*

Cheese, *n.* curds of milk formed into more or less hard mass. **Cheese'paring**, *a.* mean, stingy.

Chef (Shef), *n.* a male cook, esp. in hotel, restaurant etc.

Chem'ical (Kem-), *n.* substance produced or used in chemistry. *a.* pertaining to chemistry. **Chem'istry**, *n.* science treating of properties, combinations & reactions of substances. **Chem'ist**, *n.*

Chemise' (Shemeez), *n.* woman's under-garment.

Chenille' (Shen-), *n.* silk or worsted cord used for trimming.

Cheque (Check), *n.* private money order on bank holding person's money. **Cheque'-book**, *n.*

Che'quer (Checker), *n.* pattern of squares in alternate colours. *v.t.*

Cher'ish, *v.t.* to treat with affection, to value highly, protect, encourage, foster.

Cheroot' (Sh-), *n.* cigar with both ends already cut.

Cher'ry, *n.* tree with sweet stone fruit; its fruit.

Cher'ub, *n.* angel in child-form, nice child. **Cheru'bic**, *a.*

Chess, *n.* ancient game played with thirty-two pieces of different strength able to be moved in different directions on chequered board of sixty-four squares.

Chest, *n.* large strong box; upper part of human body protected by ribs.

Chest′nut, *n.* large handsome tree of different kinds, one of which bears edible fruit, the other inedible; reddish-brown colour. *a.*

Chev′ron (Sh-), *n.* V-shaped mil. badge denoting non-commissioned rank in army or long service in Royal Navy.

Chew (Choo), *v.t. & i.* to masticate, grind with teeth.

Chic (Sheek), *n.* stylish, very smart.

Chica′nery, *n.* verbal trickery, false dealing.

Chick, *n.* newly hatched bird, young child (*fig.*) **Chick′en,** *n.* young of domestic hen. **Chick′-en-hearted′,** *a.* cowardly. **Chick′-en-pox,** *n.* mild eruptive infantile disease.

Chide, *v.t. & i.* to scold, admonish, find fault with.

Chief, *n.* a leader, head man *a.* principal, main, foremost. **Chief′tain,** *n.* leader of tribe or clan.

Chil′blain, *n.* inflamed swelling on toes, etc. caused by cold.

Child (Chyld), *n.* an infant, small boy or girl, offspring. **Child′ren** (Chil-), *n.pl.* **Child′ish** (Chyl-), *a.*

Chill, *n.* feeling of cold, sickness caused by exposure. *a.* frigid, formal. *v.t. & i.* to make or become cold, discourage.

Chime, *n.* harmonious ringing of bell or bells, set of bells. *v.t. & i.* to ring harmoniously, strike bell.

Chime′ra (Kim-), *n.* fabulous creature composed of parts of different animals, bogey, outlandish idea. **Chime′rical,** *a.*

Chim′ney, *n.* narrow vertical passage us. of bricks for smoke to escape from building.

Chimpanzee, *n.* African ape with resemblance to man.

Chin, *n.* part of face below mouth.

Chi′na (Chy-), *n.* porcelain, fine earthenware, household utensils made of this. *a.*

Chink, *n.* sound of coins or other metal pieces striking together, a small hole or cleft. *v.t. & i.*

Chintz, *n.* cotton cloth printed with coloured patterns.

Chip, *n.* small fragment or slice. *v.t. & i.* to shape by knocking small pieces from, to chop into pieces.

Chirop′ody, *n.* care of hands and feet. **Chirop′odist** (Kir-op-), *n.* professional expert in this.

Chis′el (-zl), *n.* carpenter's tool with square cutting edge. *v.t. & i. sl.* to cheat in mild way.

Chit, *n.* signed voucher in lieu of immediate payment, note; child, girl.

Chiv′alry (Sh-), *n.* mediaeval system of knighthood, gallantry, courtesy. **Chiv′alrous,** *a.* courteous.

Chlo′rine (Kl-), *n.* an element, a gas with suffocating qualities. **Chlo′ride,** *n.* compound of chlorine. **Chlo′rate,** *n.* salt of chloric acid. **Chlo′rinate,** *v.t.* to disinfect or bleach with chlorine.

Chlo′roform (Kl-), *n.* liquid used as anaesthetic. *v.t.*

Chlo′rophyll (Kl-), *n.* green colouring matter in plants.

Chock, *n.* wooden wedge or block to stop cask or wheel from moving. *v.t.* **Chock-full,** *n.* crammed tight.

Choc′olate, *n.* drink or sweetmeat made from cacao beans.

Choice, *n.* selection, object

chosen, alternative. *a.* of high quality, chosen with care.

Choir (Kwyre), *n.* organized group of singers, esp. in church; part of church in which they sing.

Choke, *v.t. & i.* to stifle, throttle, stop breath of. Choke′bore, *n.* shot-gun with muzzle narrower than breech of barrel.

Chol′er (K-), *n.* intense anger. Chol′eric, *a.* irascible, easily given to anger.

Chol′era (K-), *n.* infectious and deadly disease affecting bowels.

Choose, *v.t. & i.* to make choice, decide course of action, select.

Chop, *v.t. & i.* to hack, cut by striking, hew in pieces. *n.* a sharp blow, a slice of meat from ribs of animal. Chop′per, *n.* bladed tool for hewing wood.

Chop, *v.t.* esp as chop and change, to shift, be inconstant.

Chop′sticks, *n.pl.* ivory or bamboo sticks used by Chinese instead of spoon or fork.

Chop, Chap, *n.* the jaw, us. in *pl.* Chap′fallen, *a.* dejected, put out.

Cho′ral (K-), *a.* of, for, sung by choir.

Chord (K-), *n. mus.* combination of harmonic notes, string of mus. instrument; straight line uniting ends of arc.

Chore, *n.* insignificant task, domestic job.

Choreog′raphy (K-), *n.* the formal notation or composition of dancing steps esp. for ballet. Choreog′rapher, *n.* Choreog′-raphic, *a.*

Cho′rus (K-), *n.* organized band of singers, refrain of song. *v.t.* to speak or sing in unison.

Chris′tian, *n.* believer in the doctrines of Christ. *a.* relating to the Christian religion. Christ′-en (Kris′n), *v.t.* baptize and give name to, admit into Christian religion. Christian′-ity, *n.* Chris′tendom, *n.* that part of the world believing in Christianity.

Chromat′ic, (K-), *a.* pertaining to colour; *mus.* of or having notes not included in particular passage or sca e.

Chron′ic (K-), *a.* esp. of disease, constantly recurring, of long duration.

Chron′icle, *n.* record of events in sequence of happening. Chron′icler, *n.* official keeper of records or history.

Chronol′ogy, *n.* system of reckoning dates, keeping record of events. Chronolo′gical, *a.* in proper order according to time.

Chronom′eter, *n.* specially accurate watch used in navigation.

Chrys′alis, *n.* pupal form or stage of insect before emerging in final state.

Chuck, *v.t.* to throw idly, playfully tap, esp. as chuck under chin. *n.* pet, darling.

Chuc′kle, *v.i.* to laugh quietly. *n.*

Chukk′er, *n.* period of play in game of polo.

Chunk, *n.* thick lump or piece of wood, etc.

Church, *n.* building devoted to Christian worship, a sect or body of Christians, the clergy as a whole. *v.t.* to offer thanks in church esp. for woman after child-birth.

Churl, *n. arch.* boor, rustic. Churl′ish, *a.* ungrateful, surly.

Churn, *n.* vessel for containing

large quantity of milk or for making butter. *v.t.* to agitate in churn, to disturb violently.

Chute (Shoot), *n.* partly enclosed channel or large groove for transporting things down, smooth waterfall.

Chut'ney, *n.* spiced Indian pickle or relish, esp. with curry.

Chyle (Kyle), *n.* milky fluid produced by eaten food and passed into blood.

Ci'der (Sy-), *n.* alcoholic drink made from apple-juice.

Cigar', *n.* elongated roll of tobacco-leaf for smoking.

Cigarette', *n.* shredded, chemically treated tobacco wrapped in paper for smoking.

Cinch, *n.* girth of saddle; *sl.* easy job.

Cin'der, *n.* ember, fragment of burnt coal.

Cin'ema, *n.* motion pictures, places where films are shown. **Cinematog'rapher,** *n.* professional taker of moving pictures or films, now us. camera-man. **Cine-projector,** *n.* apparatus for showing moving pictures on screen.

Cinerar'ium, *n.* repository for ashes of dead people who have been cremated.

Ci'pher, Cy'pher, *n.* zero, nought, a single figure, a person of no account; a secret way of writing; a monogram. *v.t. & i.* to put into secret writing, to work with figures.

Cir'cle, (Ser-kl), *n.* perfectly round figure, a ring, a gathering of people, a group with similar views or interests. *v.t. & i.* to move round, revolve. **Circ'ular,** *a.* round. *n.* duplicated or printed letter. **Circ'-**

ulate, *v.i.* to move round, keep moving. **Circula'tion,** *n.* movement of blood; number of copies newspaper sells.

Circ'uit (-kit), *n.* a circular course, a round of official visits, esp. of judge, an area, the path of an electric current, a detour. **Circu'itous,** *a.* indirect, involved.

Circ'umcise, *v.t.* to cut off foreskin of, esp. as rel. rite. **Circumcis'ion,** *n.*

Circum'ference, *n.* the line enclosing a circle, the distance round a circular object.

Circumlocu'tion, *n.* involved speech.

Circumnav'igate, *v.t.* to sail round. **Circumnaviga'tion,** *n.*

Circumscribe', *v.t.* to limit, restrict.

Circ'umspect, *a.* prudent, discreet, cautious. **Circumspec'-tion,** *n.*

Circ'umstance, *n.* an occurrence, incident, matter of fact. *n. pl.* state of life or affairs, condition. **Circumstan'tial,** *a.* detailed, indirect. **Circumstan'-tiate,** *v.t.* to verify in detail.

Circumvent, *v.t.* to outwit, avoid or frustrate by ruse. **Circumven'-tion,** *n.*

Circ'us, *n.* entertainment of acrobats, clowns, performing animals, etc; place where this is held; row of houses built in form of arc.

Cir'rhosis, *n.* hardened condition esp. of liver.

Cir'rus, *n.* highest form of cloud.

Cis'tern, *n.* tank for holding water.

Cit'adel, *n.* fortress commanding or protecting city.

Cite, *v.t.* to quote as authority, summon to appear in law-court, mention as example. **Cita'tion,** *n.* Amer. description of deed for which decoration is awarded.

Cit'izen, *n.* townsman, inhabitant of city, member of a state. **Cit'izenship,** *n.*

Cit'ron, *n.* lemon-like fruit. **Cit'ric,** *a.* **Ci'trate** (Sy-), *n.* salt of citric acid.

Cit'y, *n.* large town.

Civ'et, *n.* catlike animal from whose musk perfume is made.

Civ'ic, *a.* pertaining to city or citizenship. **Civ'ics,** *n. pl.* principles or study of good citizenship.

Civ'il, *a.* of citizens or the state, not ecclesiastical or military; polite, obliging; *leg.* not criminal. **Civil'ity,** *n.* politeness. **Civil'ian,** *n.* private non-military person. **Civ'ilise,** *v.t.* to instruct in human refinements. **Civilisa'tion,** *n.* the social condition evolved during mankind's history.

Claim, *v.t.* to demand as a right, call for, seize as one's own. *n.* a right, demand, title. **Clai'-mant,** *n.*

Clairvoy'ance, *n.* power of second sight, of seeing non-material things. **Clairvoy'ant,** *n.*

Clam', *n.* edible shell-fish.

Clam'ant, *a.* insistent, noisy, demanding attention.

Clam'ber, *v.i.* to climb laboriously.

Clamm'y, *a.* moist and sticky.

Clam'our, *n.* loud discordant outcry. *v.i.* **Clam'orous,** *a.*

Clamp, *n.* tool for holding securely, brace. *v.t.* fasten with this, very firmly.

Clan, *n.* tribal unit under leadership of chief, esp. *Sc.* **Clan'nish,** *a.* **Clans'man,** *n.*

Clandes'tine, *a.* secret, surreptitious.

Clang, *n.* loud ringing sound esp. of metal. *v.t. & i.*

Clang'our, *n.* discordant ringing sound.

Clank, *n.* sharp metallic sound. *v.t. & i.*

Clap, *n.* sharp, explosive sound, noise of thunder. *v.t. & i.* to applaud with hands, strike together, to put, place, thrust abruptly. **Clapp'er,** *n.* tongue or striker of bell.

Claque (Klack), *n.* group of paid applauders, sedulous supporters.

Clar'et, *n.* fine red Bordeaux wine.

Clar'ify, *v.t.* to make clear or comprehensible, explain. **Clarifica'tion,** *n.*

Clar'ion, *n.* stirring call to action, a trumpet.

Clar'inet, *n.* wood-wind instrument.

Clash, *n.* a collision, violent dispute, loud noise. *v.t. & i.*

Clasp, *n.* fastening for a dress or box, etc., an embrace, a hold; bar on medal ribbon. *v.t. & i.* to seize or grasp firmly.

Class, *n.* a division or section of school, a social division, set of recruits of same year. *v.t.* to categorize, put into proper division. **Class'ify,** *v.t.* to arrange in classes or detailed order. **Classifica'tion,** *n.*

Class'ic, *a.* of acknowledged standard or excellence, esp. lit. **Class'ical,** *a.* pertaining to ancient Greek and Roman literature. **Class'ics,** *n. pl.* study of Greek and Latin. **Class′-icist,** *n.*

Clatt′er, *n.* rattling noise, strident conversation. *v.t. & i.*

Clause (-z), *n.* article in a formal document, part of a sentence.

Claus′trophobia, *n.* morbid terror of enclosed places. **Claus′-trophobic,** *a.*

Clav′ichord (-k), *n. mus.* instrument, forerunner of piano.

Clav′icle, *n.* collar-bone.

Claw, *n.* hooked nail or talon of bird or beast, any claw-like object. *v.t. & i.* to seize as with claw, to rend.

Clay, *n.* stiff tenacious soil; *fig.* human body.

Claymore′, *n. arch.* Sc. Highlander's broadsword.

Clean, *a.* unsoiled, pure, free from dirt or blemish, absolute. *v.t.* to remove dirt from. **Clean′liness** (Klen-), *n.* **Cleanse** (Klenz), *v.t.*

Clear, *a.* comprehensible, plain, unsullied, limpid, free from clouds, open, transparent. *v.t. & i.* to make or become clear; to acquit, to make as profit. **Clear′ance,** *n.* **Clear′ing-house,** *n.* central bank where cheques are cleared. **Clear′ing-station,** *n. mil.* first-aid post where wounded are first treated. **Clear′ing,** *n.* open space in woodland.

Cleat, *n.* iron or wooden projection on vessel for making fast rope.

Cleave, *n.* west-country valley or coombe.

Cleave, *v.t. & i.* to split asunder, cut in two. **Clea′vage,** *n.*

Cleave, *v.i.* to be faithful to.

Clef, *n.* sign to show pitch of stave in mus.

Clem′ent, *a.* gentle, soft, benignant. **Clem′ency,** *n.* mercy.

Clench, *v.t. & i.* to close tightly, secure.

Clere′story, *n.* upper part of inner church walls with unglazed windows.

Cler′gy, *n.* priests of the Christian church. **Cler′gyman,** *n.*

Cler′ic, *a.* a priest.

Clerk (-ark), *n.* a clergyman, an assistant in office, secretary of a board.

Clev′er, *a.* able, skilled, intelligent. **Clev′erness,** *n.*

Cli′ché (-shay), *n.* trite phrase, hackneyed saying.

Click, *n.* small sharp sound.

Cli′ent (Kly-), *n.* a customer, person employing professional expert. **Cli′entele** (-tell), *n.* body of clients.

Cliff, *n.* sheer rock face.

Climacter′ic, *n.* turning-point in human life or career.

Cli′mate, *n.* weather conditions of country or region. **Cli′matic,** *a. arch.* Clime, *n.*

Cli′max, *n.* the culmination of an event, highest point of interest or excitement in a story.

Climb (Klime), *v.t. & i.* to ascend, rise, mount with effort.

Clinch, *v.t. & i.* to confirm a deal, settle an argument.

Cling, *v.t. & i.* to hold on to, attach.

Clin′ic, *a.* place where medical treatment or advice can be obtained. **Clin′ical,** *a.* medical, of the sick-bed.

Clink, *n.* sharp metallic sound. *v.t. & i.*

Clink′er, *n.* hard slag or cinder.

Clink′er-built, *a. naut.* of vessel built with boards or plates overlapping.

Clip, *n.* metal fastener. *v.t.* to fasten together.

Clip, *v.t.* to snip with scissors, cut short. *n.* yield of sheep-wool at shearing.

Clipp'er, *n.* fast sailing vessel.

Clique (Kleek), *n.* small exclusive group of people.

Cloak, *n.* loose sleeveless overcoat; a disguise. *v.t.* to cover with cloak, hide. **Cloak'room,** *n.* place for leaving outer clothes.

Cloche (Klosh), *n.* bell-shaped or sloping glass protection for plants; a close-fitting hat.

Clock, *n.* an instrument for marking the time. *v.t. & i.* to register the time of arrival, esp. as to clock in, out.

Clock'work, *n.* machinery powered by wound-up spring. **Clock'-wise,** *a.* in direction of clock's hands.

Clod, *n.* blockhead; lump of earth.

Clog, *v.t. & i.* to block up, impede, choke. *n.* an obstruction; a wooden shoe.

Cloi'ster, *n.* arcade, open on one side, in monastery or college.

Close (-s), *a.* sultry, tight, reticent, mean, near, dense. *adv.* closely, nearly. *n.* a private enclosed place among buildings, esp. precincts of cathedral or college. **Close-fisted,** *a.* mean. **Close-season,** *n.* time when certain kinds of fish and game are protected.

Close (-z), *v.t. & i.* to shut, stop up, finish, draw together, grapple. *n.* end.

Clos'et (-z-), *n.* small private room, cupboard, water-closet. **Closeted with,** having private interview with.

Clo'sure (-z), *n.* ending of debate by vote or ruling.

Clot, *n.* mass, coagulation. *v.t. & i.* to coagulate.

Cloth, *n.* woven material, woollen stuff. **Clothes,** *n. pl.* garments, dress. **Clo'thing,** *n.* **Clothe,** *v.t. & i.* to dress, put clothes on.

Cloud (Clowd), *n.* mass of water-vapour in sky; a threatening prospect; mass of smoke. *v.t. & i.* to overshadow, obscure.

Clout (Clowt), *n.* cloth, garment; a blow. *v.t.* to patch, strike.

Clove, *n.* dried aromatic bud used for flavouring.

Clo'ver, *n.* plant of trefoil family used as cattle-fodder.

Clown, *n.* entertainer in circus, buffoon

Cloy, *v.t.* to fill to satiety, to sicken by sweetness.

Club, *n.* thick stick as weapon, an instrument used in golf etc.; a suit at cards; a private association for social purposes. *v.t. & i.* to beat as with a club, to band together for common object.

Clue, *n.* sign or guide to solution of crime or mystery.

Clump, *n.* cluster of trees, plants.

Clump, *v.t.* to tread heavily.

Clum'sy (-z-), *a.* awkward, ill-made, unwieldy. **Clum'sily,** *a.*

Clus'ter, *n.* a group, bunch. *v.t. & i.* to grow or gather together.

Clutch, *v.t. & i.* to grip, embrace, seize hold of. *n.* a firm grip, a device in engine, a set of eggs, the birds hatched from these.

Coach, *n.* a motor-bus, a railway carriage, a horse-drawn vehicle. **Coach,** *v.t. & i.* to teach privately, to train. *n.* a tutor or instructor.

Coag'ulate, *v.t. & i.* to form into clots, curdle. **Coagula'tion,** *n.*

Coal, *n.* mineral used for fuel, formed from fossilized trees; a piece of this, especially when burning. *v.t. & i.* to supply with or take in coal, esp. of ship.

Coalesce (Co-al-ess), *v.i.* to unite, merge, form coalition. **Coali'tion,** *n.* alliance of several polit. parties.

Coarse, *n.* harsh, rough; inferior, ill-mannered, obscene.

Coast, *n.* sea-shore. *v.t. & i.* to sail near shore, to free-wheel, drive easily. **Coast'er,** *n.* vessel trading round coasts. **Coast'-guard,** *n.* officer keeping watch for smugglers, wrecks etc.

Coat, *n.* outer jacket or garment with sleeves; animal's hide or fur; a layer of paint etc. *v.t.* to cover with layer.

Coax, *v.t. & i.* to persuade by flattery, wheedle.

Cob, *n.* stocky riding pony; composition of clay and straw for building; male swan.

Cobalt', *n.* brittle metallic element, deep blue pigment.

Cob'ble, *n.* round paving-stone. *v.t.* to pave with this.

Cob'ble, *v.t.* to mend roughly, to mend footwear. **Cob'bler,** *n.* shoe-mender.

Co'bra, *n.* venomous Afric. & As. snake.

Cob'web, *n.* snare made by spider, collection of dust.

Cocaine', *n.* drug used as local anaesthetic.

Coch'ineal, *n.* scarlet edible dye made from certain beetles.

Cock, *n.* a male bird; hammer of gun; tap. *v.t. & i.* to become or make erect, to make gun ready to fire, tilt hat, etc. **Cock-a-hoop,** *a.* triumphant, exultant.

Cock, *n.* a heap, esp. of hay.

Cockade', *n.* rosette, badge, knot of ribbons.

Cockatoo', *n.* crested parrot.

Cock'erel, *n.* young cock, esp. fowl.

Coc'kle, *n.* edible shell-fish.

Cock'ney (-ni), *n.* Londoner born within sound of Bow Bells; his dialect.

Cock'pit, *n.* enclosure for cock-fighting; pilot's seat in small aircraft.

Cock'roach, *n.* kind of beetle-like insects.

Cocks'comb, *n.* over-confident youth.

Cock'sure, *a.* over-confident.

Cock'tail, *n.* drink made from mixture of various alcohols.

Co'coa, *n.* powder of ground beans from tropical tree.

Co'conut, *n.* tropical palm bearing large heavy fruit containing milky fluid.

Cocoon', *n.* silky sheath woven by grub when entering pupal stage.

Cod, *n.* large white-fleshed sea-fish. *v.t. sl.* to deceive.

Cod'dle, *v.t.* to pamper, nurse excessively.

Code, *n.* systematic set of rules or laws; secret form of signalling.

Cod'icil, *n.* an addition to a will.

Co-educa'tion, *n.* the teaching of boys and girls in same classes.

Coeffi'cient, *n.* thing that acts in conjunction with another.

Coerce (Co-erse), *v. t.* to force, compel. **Coer'cive,** *a.* **Coer'-cion,** *n.* force, restraint.

Coe'val, *a.* of same age, contemporary.

Coexist', *v.t.* to exist together, to compromise. Coexis'tence, *n.*

Coff'ee, *n.* beverage made from roasted seeds of coffee-shrub.

Coff'er, *n.* chest or box for valuables.

Coff'in, *n.* box for dead body.

Cog, *n.* toothed projection on rim of wheel for engaging with other. *fig.* unimportant person.

Co'gent, *a.* convincing, reasoned. Co'gency, *n.*

Cog'itate (Koj-), *v.t.* & *i.* to ponder, think deeply, plan. Cogita'tion, *n.*

Cogn'ac (Konyak), *n.* French brandy.

Cog'nate, *a.* coming from same stock, closely related.

Cog'nisance, *n.* awareness, legal notice. Cogni'tion, *n.* knowledge, act of perception.

Cogno'men, *n.* surname.

Cohab'it, *v.i.* to live together as husband and wife. Cohabita'tion, *n.*

Cohere', *v.i.* to remain or stick together, be consistent. Cohe'rent, *a.* Cohe'rence, *n.* clearness of speech or thought.

Co'hort, *n.* tenth part of Roman legion; *pl.* troops, followers.

Coiff'ure (Kwof-), *n.* style of hairdressing. Coiff'eur, *n.* haidresser.

Coil, *v.t.* & *i.* twist into rings or spirals, to adopt a winding shape. *n.* length of rope, series of rings; *elec.* spiral wire for transforming current.

Coin, *n.* a piece of money; money in general. *v.t.* to turn into money; to invent phrase.

Coincide (Ko-in-), *v.i.* to occur at same time, occupy same position, to agree exactly. Coin'cident, *a.* Coin'cidence, *n.*

Coke, *n.* coal from which gas has been extracted.

Col'ander, *n.* a sieve.

Cold, *a.* without heat, unfeeling, unemotional. *n.* minor illness; lack of heat, low temperature.

Col'ic, *n.* griping pains in abdomen.

Coli'tis, *n.* inflammation of colon.

Collab'orate, *v.i.* to co-operate, work together. Collab'orator, *n.* Collabora'tion, *n.*

Collapse', *v.i.* to fall down, fail, give way. Collaps'ible, *a.* esp. of things made to fold up for convenience.

Coll'ar, *n.* band worn round neck as part of dress or harness. *v.t.* to seize by collar, to catch hold of, get control of.

Collate', *v.t.* to examine and compare in detail, esp. *lit*; *rel.* to appoint to a living.

Colla'tion, *n.* a light meal.

Collat'eral, *a.* descended from same ancestor, accompanying, subordinate. *n.* kinsman, security.

Coll'eague (-eeg), *n.* associate in same profession or office.

Collect', *v.t.* & *i.* to gather or come together, assemble. Collect'ed, *a.* cool, self-possessed. Collect'ive, *a.* jointly. *n.* Soviet farm worked by all peasants of district. Collect'ivism, *n.* polit. theory that State should own and run means of production. Collec'tion, *n.* money collected for certain cause; group of objects gathered because of interest or rarity. Collect'or, *n.*

Coll'ect, *n.* brief prayer for special occasion.

Coll'ege, *n.* unit of university, society of cardinals or scholars, institution for higher education. **Colle'giate,** *a.*

Collide', *v.i.* to clash together violently, strike against. **Colli'sion,** *n.*

Col'lie, *n.* long-haired sheepdog.

Coll'ier, *n.* coal-miner; ship for transporting coal. **Coll'iery** (-yeri), *n.* coal-mine.

Collo'dion, *n.* solution of gun-cotton & ether for photographic purposes.

Coll'oid, *a.* gluelike, gummy.

Coll'oquy, *n.* dialogue. **Coll'-oquial,** *a.* of words or speech in common usage. **Collo'quialism,** *n.*

Collu'sion, *n.* secret understanding us. for dubious purposes. **Collu'sive,** *a.*

Co'lon, *n.* punctuation mark denoting break in sentence.

Co'lon, *n. med.* large intestine.

Colonel (Kurnel), *n. mil.* rank. commander of army regiment. **Colonel'cy,** *n.* status or position of such.

Colonnade', *n.* a series of columns flanking pathway.

Col'ony, *n.* overseas country settled by people still owing allegiance to parent state. **Colo'nial,** *a.* **Col'onist,** *n.* a settler. **Col'onise,** *v.t.* **Colonisa'tion,** *n.*

Coloss'us, *n.* a giant, very big man, huge statue. **Coloss'al,** *a.* huge, immense.

Col'our (Kull-er), *n.* hue, tint, pigment, complexion, paint. *pl.* flags, regimental banners. *v.t. & i.* to give colour to, become coloured, to blush, paint.

Colt, *n.* young male horse.

Col'umn, *n.* large pillar, body of troops, division of printed page. **Colum'nar,** *a.*

Co'ma, *n.* state of insensibility, stupor. **Co'matose,** *a.* unconscious, drowsy.

Comb (Coam), *n.* instrument with long teeth for arranging hair; ornament for hair; a bird's crest; group of honeycells. *v.t.* to arrange hair with comb.

Com'bat, *v.t.* to fight. **Combat',** *n.* a fight, struggle. **Com'-batant,** *n.* one taking part in fight. **Com'bative,** *a.* aggressive, prepared to fight.

Combine', *v.t. & i.* to unite closely, join together. **Combina'tion,** *n.* **Com'bine,** *n.* esp. as c. **harvester,** *ag.* machine carrying out all processes of harvesting and threshing etc.; trading companies grouped for mutual benefit.

Combus'tion, *n.* process of burning. **Combus'tible,** *a.* easily made to burn.

Come (Kum), *v.i.* to arrive, approach, happen, reach, originate from.

Com'edy, *n.* amusing play, anything humorous or amusing. **Come'dian,** *n.* person who acts to amuse. **Com'ic,** *a.* amusing, ridiculous, laughable.

Come'ly (Kum-), *a.* handsome, esp. of woman. **Come'liness,** *n.*

Comes'tible, *n.* food, esp. in *pl.* *a.* edible.

Com'et, *n.* heavenly body with train of light.

Com'fort (Kum-), *n.* consolation in distress, relief from trouble, physical ease. *v.t.* to console, look after. **Comfortable,** *a.* making for pleasant ease.

Com'ity, *n.* friendliness, esp. as c. of nations.

Comm'a, *n.* punctuation mark dividing words or clauses in a sentence.

Command', *v.t. & i.* to order, control, compel, dominate, exercise authority over. *n.* an order; a district or body of troops under commanding officer. **Command'er**, *n.* **Commandant'**, *n.* **Command'ment**, *n.* rule, esp. biblical. **Commandeer'**, *v.t.* to seize esp. for mil. purposes.

Comman'do (-doe), *n.* orig. group of Boer guerillas; compact, mobile and highly efficient body of troops for special operations; member of such.

Commem'orate, *v.t.* to celebrate memory by ceremony or writing. **Commem'orative**, *a.* **Commemora'tion**, *n.*

Commence', *v.t. & i.* to start, begin. **Commence'ment**, *n.*

Commend', *v.t.* to recommend, praise, entrust. **Commend'able**, *a.* **Commenda'tion**, *n.* praise for meritorious action.

Commen'surate, *a.* proportionate to, adequate, equal in size or length of time.

Comm'ent, *n.* remark, a note of criticism or appraisal. *v.i.* to make a comment or remark. **Comm'entator**, *n.* person who describes event for benefit of others, esp. on radio or TV. **Commen'tary**, *n.*

Comm'erce, *n.* trade, merchant intercourse, buying & selling. **Commer'cial**, *a.*

Commina'tion, *n.* threat of divine denunciation, vengeance. **Commina'tory**, *a.*

Commis'erate (-z-), *v.t. & i.* to sympathise with, to pity. **Commisera'tion**, *n.*

Com'missar, *n.* head of a Communist ministry or governmental department. **Com'missary**, *n.* deputy. **Com'missariat**, *n.* mil. supply department.

Commis'sion, *n.* business or duty allocated to someone, authority to act, document appointing officer, official body investigating something, errand. *v.t.* to appoint, employ to do specific job, such as writing book etc. **Commis'sioner**, *n.* official empowered to act, member of commission.

Commit', *v.t. & i.* to do, perpetrate, consign. **Commit'ment**, *n.* obligation. **Committ'al**, *n.* act of committing.

Committ'ee, *n.* body elected or appointed from larger body to deal with business.

Commode', *n.* chest of drawers in bedroom, chamber-pot enclosed in stool.

Commo'dious, *a.* spacious, roomy.

Commod'ity, *n.* article for sale.

Comm'odore, *n.* naval rank between captain and rear-admiral; senior captain of merchant line, president of yacht-club.

Comm'on, *a.* public, usual, ordinary, belonging equally to more than one person, inferior, vulgar. *n.* open land on which local inhabitants have certain rights. *n. pl.* lower and dominant House of Parliament. **Comm'onalty**, *n.* the common people, people in general. **Comm'oner**, *n.* private person without title. **Comm'-**

'onplace, *a.* dull, ordinary.
Comm'onwealth,*n.hist.* republic
set up in Britain after execution
of Charles I; the countries once
comprising the Brit. Empire
but now a voluntary organisation of independent states.

Commo'tion, *n.* loud confusion,
physical disturbance.

Commune', *v.t. & i.* to have
intimate conversation with.

Communica'tion, *n.* information,
connection, means of getting in
touch. *v.t. & i.* to be in contact,
exchange news etc.

Commu'nion, *n.* rel. rite. Commu'nicant, *n.* one who takes
part in this.

Commu'nicative, *a.* prepared to
give information. Comm'unique
(-kay), *n.* official announcement, official message, esp.
regarding foreign affairs.

Comm'unism, *n. polit.* doctrine
that each should work according to his ability and receive
according to his needs. Com-
m'unist, *n.* supporter of this.

Comm'unity, *n.* organized body
of people living on similar
basis and in same locality.

Commute', *v.t. & i.* exchange,
change, reduce, as in punishment; to travel daily from
home to work in different
locality. Commut'er, *n.* Com-
muta'tion, *n.*

Com'pact, *n.* an agreement.
Compact', *a.* tightly packed,
neat, concentrated. *n.* a case
containing face-powder and
mirror.

Compan'ion, *n.* comrade, friend.
Compan'ionable, *a.* Compan'-
ionship, *n.*

Compan'ion, *n. naut.* esp. as
c.-way, a staircase in ship.

Com'pany (Kum-), *n.* gathering
of people, trading firm, guests,
mil. division of battalion.

Compare', *v.t. & i.* to note
similarities between, liken, contrast, be like. Com'parable, *a.*
Compar'ative, *a.* relative, not
absolute. Compar'ison, *n.*

Compart'ment, *n.* division of
ship, railway carriage.

Com'pass (Kum-), *n.* naviga-
tional instrument whose magnetic needle always indicates
north ; range of voice ; scope,
space. *v.t.* to contrive, cause to
happen. As *n.pl.* dividing instrument for drawing circle.

Compas'sion, *n.* feeling for
others' distress, pity. Compas'-
sionate, *a.*

Compat'ible, *a.* agreeable with,
fitting in with, consistent. Compat'ibility, *n.*

Compat'riot, *n.* fellow-country-
man.

Compeer', *n.* companion, equal.

Compel', *v.t.* to constrain, force.
Compul'sion, *n.* Compul'sory,
a. obligatory.

Compend'ium, *n.* summary or
abridgement. Compend'ious, *a.*

Com'pensate, *v.t.* to make up
for, recompense. Compensa'-
tion, *n.* Compensa'tory, *a.*

Compete', *v.i.* to contend, strive
against others. Competi'tion,
n. Compet'itive, *a.* Compet'itor,
n. one who competes.

Com'petent, *a.* efficient, able,
qualified, proper. Com'petence,
n. sufficiency, adequate income.
Com'petency, *n.*

Compile', *v.t.* to gather together
from various sources, esp. in
lit., amass. Compila'tion, *n.*

Compla'cent, *a.* self-satisfied.
Compla'cence, *n.*

Complain', *v.i.* to express a grievance, find fault. **Complaint'**, *n.* statement of grievance or wrong. **Complai'nant**, *n.* one who goes to law about grievance.

Com'plaisant (-plaze-), *a.* anxious to please, obliging. **Com'plaisance**, *n.*

Com'plement, *n.* a complete allowance or equipment, a ship's company. *v.t.* to form complement to. **Complemen'tary**, *a.*

Complete', *a.* entire, finished, perfect. *v.t.* to finish, accomplish. **Comple'tion**, *n.*

Com'plex, *a.* involved, intricate. *n.* various kinds of mental abnormality or inhibition. **Complex'ity**, *a.*

Complex'ion (-ekshn), *n.* texture and colour of skin, appearance.

Com'plicate, *v.t.* to make difficult or involved. **Complica'tion**, *n.*

Compli'city, *n.* partnership in crime.

Com'pliment, *n.* expression of praise or flattery. *v.t.* **Complimen'tary**, *a.*

Compline', *n.* evening service in R.C. Church.

Comply', *v.i.* to act as requested, consent. **Compli'ant**, *a.* **Compli'ance**, *n.*

Compo'nent, *n.* an essential part.

Comport', *v.t.* & *i.* to conduct oneself, behave, agree, accord. **Comport'ment**, *n.*

Compose', *v.t.* & *i.* to form, make up, write, settle, adjust. **Composed'**, *a.* self-possessed. **Compo'ser**, *n.* writer of mus. compositions. **Com'posite**, *a.* made up of different parts or elements **Composi'tion**, *n.* **Compo'sure**, *n.* calmness, self-possession.

Compos'itor, *n.* skilled typesetter.

Com'post, *n.* fertilizing mixture for garden or farm.

Compound', *v.t.* & *i.* to make up, mix, arrange settlement of debt by partial down-payment; to condone, esp. offence. **Com'pound**, *a.* not simple, composed of several parts.

Com'pound, *n.* esp. in Orient, open space enclosed by bungalows or other buildings.

Comprehend', *v.t.* to understand, to comprise, include. **Comprehen'sion**, *n.* power of understanding. **Comprehen'sive**, *a.* all-inclusive. **Comprehen'sible**, *a.* intelligible.

Compress', *v.t.* to squeeze or press into smaller size or space. **Com'press**, *n. med.* wet bandage applied to swelling or wound. **Compres'sion**, *n.* condensation, concentration.

Comprise', *v.t.* to contain, include, consist of.

Com'promise (-ize), *n.* peaceful solution of dispute by mutual concessions. *v.t.* & *i.* to make such an arrangement; to endanger one's reputation.

Compunc'tion, *n.* scruple, regret at misbehaviour.

Compute', *v.t.* & *i.* to calculate, estimate, count. **Comput'able**, *a.* **Comput'er**, *n.* electronic machine for calculating. **Computa'tion**, *n.*

Com'rade, *n.* friend, companion. **Com'radeship**, *n.*

Con, *v.t.* to check course of ship; to study. **Conn'ing-tower**, *n.* bridge of submarine.

Concat'enate, *v.t.* to link together. **Concatena'tion**, *n.* a linking together.

Con'cave, *a.* hollow, curving inwards. Concav'ity, *n.*

Conceal', *v.t.* to hide, keep secret. Conceal'ment, *n.*

Concede', *v.t.* to grant, admit, give up. Conces'sion, *n.*

Conceit', *n.* vanity, excessive self-opinion; lit. an extravagant notion.

Conceive', *v.t.* & *i.* to become pregnant, imagine, form mentally, understand. Conceiv'able, *a.* imaginable. Concep'tion, *n.* act of conceiving.

Concen'sus, *n.* general agreement.

Con'centrate, *v.t.* & *i.* to direct one's thoughts, bring together in one place, compress into smaller space, gather at one place. Concentra'tion, *n.* Concentra'tion camp, *n.* brutal institution for mass-murder perpetrated by Nazis.

Con'cept, *n.* an abstract idea. Concep'tual, *a.* pertaining to abstract ideas. Concep'tion, *n.*

Concern', *v.t.* to make anxious, to relate to, matter to. *n.* business, matter that concerns one. Concern'ing, *prep.* about.

Concert', *v.t.* to act or plan together. Con'cert, *n. mus.* performance; union, harmony. Concert'ed, *a.* unified, planned. Concert'o (-cher-), *n. mus.* composition for solo instrument and orchestra. Concerti'na (-tee-), *n. mus.* instrument worked by bellows and keys.

Conch, *n.* large spiral marine shell ; a trumpet made from this.

Conchol'ogy, (Kon-kol-) *n.* study of shells and shell-fish.

Concierge. (-si-) *n.* caretaker in a block of flats.

Concil'iate, *v.t.* to pacify, make friendly. Concilia'tion, *n.* Concil'iatory, *a.*

Concise', *a.* succinct, brief. Concise'ness, *n.*

Con'clave, *n.* private meeting, assembly of cardinals.

Conclude (-ood), *v.t.* & *i.* to bring or come to an end; to infer, resolve. Conclu'sion, *n.* Conclu'sive, *a.* definite, final.

Concoct', *v.t.* to make by mixing, to fabricate. Concoc'tion, *n.* mixture.

Concom'itant, *a.* & *n.* accompanying.

Conc'ord, *n.* agreement, harmony. Concord'ance, *n.* pact, agreement. Concord'ant, *a.*

Conc'ourse, *n.* a great throng, a gathering together.

Con'crete, *a.* existing as matter, real, not abstract. *n.* mixture of sand and cement, etc. for building purposes.

Conc'ubine, *n.* woman cohabiting with man but not married to him. Concu'binage, *n.*

Concup'iscence, *n.* lust, sexual desire. Concup'iscent, *a.*

Concur', *v.i.* to agree, coincide, occur together. Concur'rence, *n.* Concur'rent, *a.*

Concus'sion (-shn), *n.* violent injury to brain by blow or fall. Con'cuss, *v.t.* to cause this.

Condemn', *v.t.* to pronounce guilty, to blame, rate as unfit for use. Condemna'tion, *n.* Condem'natory, *a.*

Condense', *v.t.* & *i.* reduce to smaller size or volume, compress, shorten, change from vapour into liquid. Condensa'tion, *n.* Condens'er, *n.* apparatus for storing elec. energy or converting steam into water.

Condescend, *v.i.* to patronise, assume superior attitude, deign. **Condenscen'sion,** *n.*

Condign' (-ine), *a.* merited, adequate.

Con'diment, *n.* relish, seasoning.

Condi'tion, *n.* mode of living, rank, situation, fitness; a factor on which a statement or occurrence, etc. depends. **Condi'tional,** *a.* not absolute, relative to conditions.

Condole', *v.i.* to share other's sorrow, sympathise with in grief. **Condo'lence,** *n.*

Condone', *v.t.* to overlook, esp. fault, forgive. **Condona'tion,** *n.*

Conduce', *v.i.* to tend to cause, to contribute to causing of. **Conduc'ive,** *a.*

Conduct', *v.t.* & *i.* to direct, lead, manage, transmit. **Con'duct,** *n.* behaviour. **Conduct'or,** *n.* person in charge of orchestra or bus etc. **Conduc'tion,** *n.* **Conduct'ive,** *a.* **Conductiv'ity,** *n.*

Con'duit (-dit), *n.* water-channel, aqueduct.

Cone, *n.* solid figure with circular base and other end tapering to a point ; fruit of conifer. **Con'ical,** *a.* **Co'nifer,** *n.* pine, fir, other trees bearing fruit-cones. **Conif'erous,** *a.*

Confec'tion, *n.* sweetstuff, sweet cakes. **Confec'tioner,** *n.* shopkeeper selling sweets etc. **Confec'tionery,** *n.*

Confed'erate, *n.* an ally, accomplice. **Confederate',** *v.t.* & *i.* to unite, us. in polit. sense. **Confed'eracy,** *n.* **Confedera'tion,** *n.* an alliance, of states or industrial interests.

Confer', *v.t.* & *i.* to consult; bestow. **Confer'ment,** *n.* bestowal, of honours etc. **Con'-ference,** *n.* meeting for consultation or discussion.

Confess', *v.t.* & *i.* to admit, acknowledge, to hear confession of sins, to declare one's sins. **Confes'sion,** *n.* **Confes'-sional,** *n.* box in R.C. church for hearing confession. **Confess'or,** *n.* priest who hears confession; person who retains faith in spite of persecution.

Confett'i, *n.pl.* small coloured shapes of paper scattered at weddings as symbol of corn.

Confide', *v.t.* & *i.* to trust in, have confidence in. **Confidant',** *n.* person entrusted with intimate news or secrets. **Con'-fidence,** *n.* trust, self-assurance. **Con'fidential,** *a.* private, almost secret.

Confine', *v.t.* to shut up, restrict, imprison, keep in bed. **Con'-fines,** *n.pl.* limits, boundaries. **Confine'ment,** *n.* childbirth.

Confirm', *v.t.* to verify, make authoritative, make strong, corroborate, admit into Ang. church. **Confirma'tion,** *n.* **Confirm'ative, Confir'matory,** *a.* **Confirmed',** *a.* permanent, habitual.

Con'fiscate, *v.t.* to seize by authority. **Confisca'tion,** *n.* **Con'-fiscatory,** *a.*

Conflagra'tion, *n.* a catastrophic fire.

Con'flict, *n.* quarrel, fight, violent dispute. **Conflict',** *v.t.* to clash, be inconsistent with.

Con'fluence, *n.* a meeting-place of rivers. **Con'fluent,** *a.* uniting, flowing together.

Conform', *v.t.* & *i.* to follow same custom or rule, to comply. **Conform'able,** *a.* corresponding, consistent with. **Conforma'-**

77 Con'science

tion, *n.* adaptation, structure. Conform'ity, *n.*

Confound', *v.t.* to overthrow, frustrate, mix up.

Confront (-unt), *v.t.* to face, oppose. Confronta'tion, *n.* encounter of opposing persons or ideas.

Confuse', *v.t.* to perplex, obscure, mistake one person or thing for another, mix up. Confu'sion, *n.* disorder, embarrassment.

Confute', *v.t.* to defeat in argument, prove wrong. Confuta'tion, *n.*

Congeal' (-j-), *v.t. & i.* to coagulate, to solidify. Congela'tion, *n.*

Conge'nial (-jee-), *a.* compatible, agreeable, of similar outlook. Congenial'ity, *n.*

Congen'ital (-je-), *a.* existing at or dating from birth.

Con'ger (Kong-ger), *n.* large sea-eel.

Conge'ries (-je-), *n. or n.pl.* a collection, mass.

Conges'tion (-jes-), *n.* overcrowding; *med.* accumulation of blood. Conges'ted, *a.* overcrowded.

Conglom'erate, *a.* grouped together in mass. *v.t. & i.* to gather into ball or mass. Conglomera'tion, *n.*

Congrat'ulate, *v.t.* to express praise or pleasure at success or good fortune of other person. Congratula'tion,, *n.* Congrat'ulatory, *a.*

Con'gregate, *v.t. & i.* to assemble, gather together. Congrega'tion, *n.* an assembly for rel. purposes. Congrega'tional, *a.* rel. sect in which each church & its congregation are self-governing.

Con'gress, *n.* formal assembly of deputies, a legislative body, as in U.S.A. Congres'sional, *a.* Con'gressman, *n.*

Con'gruent, *a.* suitable, fitting, in agreement. Con'gruence, *n.* Con'gruous, *a.* Congru'ity, *n.*

Conjec'ture, *n.* a guess. *v.t. & i.* to guess, surmise. Conjec'tural, *a.*

Con'jugal, *a.* pertaining to marriage. Conjugal'ity, *n.*

Con'jugate, *v.t. & i.* to join sexually; to name different parts of verb. Conjuga'tion, *n.*

Conjunc'tion, *n.* a simultaneous happening, a union; *gram.* a word linking other words or clauses.

Conjure', *v.t. & i.* to entreat, implore solemnly.

Con'jure (Kun-), *v.t. & i.* to produce trick effects by sleight-of-hand, juggle; to invoke. Con'jurer, *n.*

Connect', *v.t. & i.* to unite, link, associate mentally. Connec'tion, *n.* relation, link, association.

Connive', *v.i.* to help in offence by failure to prevent or condemn. Conni'vance, *n.*

Connoisseur' (Kon-as-ser), *n.* discriminating expert, esp. in art etc.

Connote', *v.t.* to indicate, imply. Connota'tion, *n.*

Connu'bial, *a.* pertaining to marriage.

Con'quer (-ker), *v.t. & i.* to defeat, to be victorious, to master. Con'queror (-ke-), *n.* Con'quest, *n.*

Consanguin'ity, *n.* blood-relationship. Consanguin'eous, *a.*

Con'science (-shens), *n.* sense of right and wrong. Conscien'-

tious, *a.* scrupulous, persevering.

Con'scious, *a.* aware of, awake to one's physical surroundings. Con'sciousness, *n.* state of being conscious, perception.

Con'script, *n.* person forcibly enlisted in armed forces. Conscrip'tion, *n.* national service.

Con'secrate, *v.t.* to set aside as sacred, dedicate to holy use, devote. Consecra'tion, *n.*

Consec'utive, *a.* successive, happening or following in regular order.

Consen'sus, *n.* unanimity, general agreement.

Consent', *v.i.* to agree to. *n.* permission.

Con'sequence, *n.* outcome, result. Con'sequent, *a.* Consequen'tial, *a.* resultant, self-important.

Conservatoire' (-twar), *n.* academy of music.

Conserve', *v.t.* to keep from decay or destruction, to preserve, safeguard. Conserva'tion, *n.* rational protection of natural resources from destruction. Conserv'ative, *a.* opposed to change or innovation.

Conserv'atory, *n.* greenhouse.

Consid'er, *v.t. & i.* to examine merits of, think over, take into account, to hold opinion. Considera'tion, *n.* Consid'erable, *a.* of importance, sizeable. Consid'erate, *a.* heedful of others' interests.

Consign, *v.t.* to commit, despatch goods to, hand over. Consig'nor, *n.* person who sends; Consig'nee, *n.* person to whom goods are sent. Consign'ment, *n.* batch of goods sent.

Consist', *v.i.* to be comprised of,

made up of. Consist'ent, *a.* uniform, regular. Consist'ence, *n.* degree of density.

Console', *v.t.* to support in grief or disappointment. Consola'tion, *n.* Consol'atory, *a.*

Con'sole, *n.* as c. table, c. mirror, supported by bracket against wall.

Consol'idate, *v.t. & i.* to strengthen, unify into single whole. Consolida'tion, *n.*

Consomm'é (-ay), *n.* meat soup.

Con'sonant, *n.* alphabetical letter other than vowel, sound combining with vowel to make syllable. *a.* agreeing with, consistent with. Con'sonance, *n.* accord, agreement.

Con'sort, *n.* husband or wife, esp. of queen or king; ship accompanying a larger one. Consort', *v.i.* to associate with, accompany. Consort'ium, *n.* association of states or commercial interests.

Conspic'uous, *a.* standing out, prominent.

Conspire, *v.i.* to plot for criminal purposes. Conspir'ator, *n.* Conspir'acy, *n.* a plot. Conspirator'ial, *a.*

Con'stable (Kun-), *n.* a policeman; *arch.* a high officer of state, warden of castle. Constab'ulary, *n.* body of policemen.

Con'stant, *a.* unceasing, unvarying, regular, faithful. Con'stancy, *n.*

Constella'tion, *n.* group of stars.

Consterna'tion, *n.* great dismay.

Constipa'tion, *a.* costiveness, sluggishness of bowels. Con'stipate, *v.t.* to cause this.

Con'stitute, *v.t.* to appoint, establish, form. Constitu'tion, *n.* composition, health, method by which state is organized. **Constitu'tional**, *a.* legal.

Constit'uency, *n.* body of electors, area in which they reside. **Constit'uent**, *n.* an elector.

Constrain', *v.t.* to prevent forcibly, to force. **Constraint'**, *n.* restrain, compulsion.

Constric'tion, *n.* tightness, compression. **Constrict'**, *v.t.* **Constrict'ive**, *a.* **Constric'tor**, *n.* snake that kills by crushing prey.

Construct', *v.t.* to build, erect, make. **Construc'tion**, *n.* **Construct'ive**, *a.* creative, helpful.

Construe', *v.t. & i.* to translate. word for word, analyse structure of sentence.

Con'sul, *n.* diplomatic official safeguarding nationals in foreign countries; Roman magistrate, *arch.* **Con'sular**, *a.* **Con'sulate**, *n.* office or dwelling of consul.

Consult', *v.t. & i.* to confer with, seek advice or information. **Consulta'tion**, *n.*

Consume', *v.t. & i.* to devour, use up, destroy. **Consump'tion**, *n.* using up; tuberculosis. **Consump'tive**, *a.* tending to be affected by tuberculosis.

Con'sumer, *n.* person who buys and uses for consumption, as opposed to producer.

Con'summate, *v.t.* to complete, bring to perfection. **Consumm'ate**, *a.* perfect, complete. **Consumma'tion**, *n.*

Con'tact, *n.* a state of being in communication with, connection, touch. **Conta'gion**, *n.* disease transmitted by contact or touch. **Conta'gious**, *a.*

Contain', *v.t.* to enclose, hold, keep under control. **Contain'er**, *n.*

Contam'inate, *v.t.* to spoil, make impure. **Contamina'tion**, *n.*

Con'template, *v.t. & i.* to regard steadily, meditate, intend. **Contempla'tion**, *n.* **Contem'plative**, *n.* thoughtful, grave.

Con'temporary, *a.* of present times, existing at same period. *n.* person living at same time as oneself. **Contempora'neous**, *a.* another form of contemporary.

Contempt', *n.* scorn, disgrace. **Contempt'ible**, *a.* despicable, mean. **Contempt'uous**, *a.* scornful.

Contend', *v.t. & i.* to strive, dispute, hold opinion. **Conten'tion**, *n.* **Conten'tious**, *a.* argumentative.

Contest', *v.t. & i.* to dispute, fight for or against. **Con'test**, *n.* struggle, conflict, competition. **Contest'ant**, *n.* one who takes part in such. **Contest'able**, *a.*

Con'text, *n.* parts preceding or following passage in text.

Contig'uous, *a.* touching. **Contigu'ity**, *n.* proximity, contact.

Con'tinent, *a.* chaste, temperate. **Con'tinence**, *n.* abstinence, self-restraint esp. in sexual matters.

Con'tinent, *n.* large mainland mass. **Continent'al**, *a.*

Contin'gent (-j-), *a.* dependent on, incidental to. **Contin'gency**, *n.* chance happening, possibility. **Contin'gent**, *n.* body of troops.

Contin'ue, *v.t. & i.* to proceed, go on, last, resume. **Contin'ual**, *a.* unceasing. **Continua'tion**, *n.* **Continu'ity**, *n.* sequence, unbroken progression. **Contin'uous**, *a.* uninterrupted.

Contort', *v.t.* to twist or pull out

of normal shape. **Contor'tion,** *n.* **Contor'tionist,** *n.* acrobatic entertainer.

Con'tour (-toor), *n.* outline, marks on map denoting heights etc.

Con'tra, *pref.* meaning against, e.g. **contradict, contravene,** etc.

Con'traband, *n.* illegal traffic in goods, smuggled goods. *a.* forbidden to be imported. **Con'trabandist,** *n.* smuggler.

Con'traception, *n.* birth-control. **Contracep'tive,** *a.* & *n.* of appliance to prevent conception.

Con'tract, *n.* a formal agreement. **Contract',** *v.i.* to make such an agreement; to diminish in size. **Contrac'tor,** *n.* person making a contract, esp. builder, road-engineer, etc.

Contradict', *v.t.* to assert contrary of, deny, be at variance with. **Contradict'ory,** *a.* **Contradic'tion,** *n.*

Contral'to, *n.* lowest female voice, singer with this.

Con'trary, *a.* opposed, opposite, unfavourable. *n.* the opposite. **Contrari'ety,** *n.*

Contrast', *v.t.* & *i.* to compare, show differences, be strikingly different from. **Con'trast,** *n.* marked difference.

Contravene', *v.t.* to infringe law, to conflict with. **Contraven'tion,** *n.*

Contrib'ute, *v.t.* & *i.* to help in bringing about, to make payment into fund, to write for. **Contribution,** *n.* **Contrib'utor,** *n.* person who contributes to fund, author or journalist writing articles etc. for publications. **Contrib'utory,** *a.* contributing.

Con'trite, *a.* deeply penitent or sorrowful for crime committed. **Contri'tion,** *n.*

Contrive', *v.t.* to bring about, devise, succeed in implementing. **Contri'vance,** *n.* mechanical device, scheme.

Control (-ole), *n.* command, power of regulating or directing; check, restraint; mechanical device in engine; checkpoint in motor-rally etc. *v.t.* to command, direct, check. **Controll'able,** *a.* **Controll'er** (-oler), *n.* **Controlroom,** *n.* place for direction of operations.

Con'troversy, *n.* argument, dispute. **Controvert',** *v.t.* to refute, argue against. **Controver'sial,** *a.* disputable, causing argument. **Controver'sialist,** *n.* person given to argument.

Con'tumacy, *n.* obstinate disobedience. **Contuma'cious,** *a.*

Con'tumely, *n.* scornful language, abuse, disgrace. **Contume'lious,** *a.*

Contuse' (-tuze), *v.t.* to bruise. **Contu'sion,** *n.* a bruise, a wound that does not break skin.

Conun'drum, *n.* a riddle.

Convales'cent, *a.* in state of recovering from illness. *n.* person in this state. **Convales'cence,** *n.* period of recovery.

Convene', *v.t.* & *i.* to call together, arrange a meeting, assemble. *n.* **Conven'tion,** *n.* a treaty, formal meeting for agreement. **Conven'or,** *n.* one who calls a meeting. **Conven'ticle,** *n.* meeting-house, esp. for secret purposes.

Conve'nient, *a.* suitable, comfortable, handy. **Conve'nience,** *n.*

Con'vent, *n.* community of nuns.

Conven'tion, *n.* social custom, traditional usage.

Conven'tional, *a.* ordinary, following social custom. **Conventional'ity,** *a.*

Converge', *v.t. & i.* to approach towards one point, incline together. **Conver'gent,** *a.* **Conver'gence,** *n.*

Converse', *v.i.* to speak with. **Con'verse,** *n.,* **conversa'tion,** *n.* talk, discussion. **Conversa'tional,** *a.* **Con'versant,** *n.* acquainted or familiar with.

Con'verse, *n.* the opposite in sense or order. *a.*

Convert', *v.t.* to change into different form, persuade to take up different religion or opinion. **Con'vert,** *n.* person so converted. **Conver'sion,** *n.* **Convert'ible,** *a.* **Convertibil'ity,** *n.*

Con'vex, *a.* curving outwards. **Convex'ity,** *n.*

Convey (-vay), *v.t.* to transmit, transport, carry, impart, transfer. **Convey'ance,** *n. leg.* transaction transferring property etc. **Convey'ancer,** *n.*

Convict', *v.t.* to pronounce or find guilty. **Con'vict,** *n.* criminal in prison. **Convic'tion,** *n.* being found guilty; firmly held belief, opinion.

Convince', *v.t.* to persuade absolutely, satisfy by firm proof. **Convin'cing,** *a.*

Conviv'ial, *a.* festive, jovial, **Convivial'ity,** *n.*

Convoke', *v.t.* to summon to assemble, call together. **Convoca'tion,** *n.* an assembly, esp. rel. or univ.

Convolu'tion, *n.* fold, twist, coil, spiral. **Convo'lute,** *a.*

Convoy', *v.t.* to escort, accompany for protection. **Con'voy,** *n.* escorting force, esp. of ships.

Convulse', *v.t.* to shake violently, throw into great agitation or convulsions. **Convuls'ive,** *a.* **Convul'sion,** *n.*

Co'ny, Co'ney, *n. arch.* or *leg.* form for rabbit; hyrax or rock-badger.

Coo, *n.* note or cry of pigeon. *v.i.*

Cook, *n.* person who prepares meals. *v.t. & i.* to prepare food for table. **Cook'ery,** *n.*

Cool, *a.* fresh, somewhat cold; self-composed; unfriendly. *v.t. & i.* to make or become cool. **Cool'ness,** *n.*

Cool'ie, *n.* Asiatic labourer.

Coomb, Combe, *n.* small valley, esp. in west-country.

Coop, *n.* hutch or run for fowls. *v.t.* to shut up in such; to confine strictly.

Coop'er, *n.* craftsman who makes casks. **Coop'erage,** *n.*

Co-op'erate, *v.i.* to work together. **Co-opera'tion,** *n.* **Co-opera'tive,** *a. & n.* for mutual benefit or profit. **Co-op'erator,** *n.*

Co-opt', *v.t.* to invite onto body or committee without previous election. **Co-op'tion,** *n.*

Co-ord'inate, *a.* equal in rank, degree, etc. *v.t.* to bring into proper order or relation. **Co-ordina'tion,** *n.*

Cope, *n.* long ceremonial cloak worn by priest.

Cope, *v.t. & i.* to deal successfully, manage.

Co'per, *n.* us. as horse-coper, a dealer.

Co'ping, co'ping-stone, *n.* top masonry or protection of wall.

Co'pious, *a.* abundant, plentiful. **Co'piousness,** *n.*

Copp'er, *n.* reddish ductile malleable metal; small coin; cauldron for washing clothes. *v.t.* to cover with copper. **Copperbottom,** *v.t.* to protect ship's hull with copper against shipworm etc. **Copper-plate,** *n.* fine, formal writing.

Cop'ra, *n.* dried coconut kernels for commercial use.

Copse, Copp'ice, *n.* small wood, esp. of small trees for brushwood.

Cop'ulate, *v.i.* to join in sexual intercourse. **Copula'tion,** *n.* **Cop'ulative,** *a.*

Cop'y, *v.t. & i.* to imitate, reproduce, use as model. **Copy,** *n.* an imitation, exact reproduction. **Cop'yhold,** *n.* form of land-tenure. **Cop'yright,** *n. leg.* right of ownership over literary work etc. **Copy-writer,** *n.* writer of material for advertisements.

Coquette' (-ket), *n.* a woman who trifles with men's feelings, skittish woman. **Coquett'ish,** *a.* **Coquet',** *v.i.* to flirt. **Co'-quetry,** *n.*

Cor'acle, *n.* circular wickerwork fishing-boat covered with hide.

Cor'al, *n.* Hard calcareous substance formed by sea-polyps and found in pink, red, or white reefs and other formations. **Cor'alline,** *a.*

Cord, *n.* fine rope or thick string, ribbed fabric, measure of firewood. *v.t.* to tie with cord. **Cord'age,** *n.* ropes in ship's rigging etc.

Cord'ial, *a.* friendly, openhearted, warm. *n.* a warm drink. **Cordial'ity,** *n.* warm friendliness.

Cor'dite, *n.* smokeless explosive.

Cord'on, *n.* body of troops or police encircling certain area;

ornamental braid or ribbon. **Cordon bleu,** *n.* first-class cook.

Cor'duroy, *n.* coarse thick ribbed material with soft surface; temporary road made of treetrunks across wet land.

Core, *n.* inner part of fruit containing seeds, central or essential part of anything. *v.t.* to remove core.

Co-respon'dent, *n.* person proceeded against for adultery in divorce case.

Cor'gi, *n.* small Welsh breed of dog.

Coriac'eous, *a.* leathery, of leather.

Corin'thian, *a.* of Corinth; of architectural style based on this. *n. arch.* man of fashion or sport.

Cork, *n.* bark of the cork-tree; round bottle-stopper made of this. *v.t.* to stop up with cork. **Cork-screw,** *n.* implement for drawing cork from bottles. **Cork'y,** *a.* light, like cork; *fig.* lively, frivolous.

Cor'morant, *n.* fish-eating seabird; *fig.* greedy person.

Corn, *n.* grain, cereal. **Corn'-flour,** *n.* finely ground maize or rice. **Corn-chandler,** *n.* grain and seed merchant.

Corn, *n.* horny painful place esp. on foot.

Corn, *v.t.* to preserve meat with salt.

Corn'ea, *n.* transparent membrane in eye.

Corn'er, *n.* angle, point where lines, walls, streets, etc. meet. *v.t.* to monopolise, force into position impossible to get out of.

Corn'et, *n. mus.* trumpet-like instrument with valves; *arch.*

junior cavalry officer; ice-cream cone.

Corn'ice (-iss), *n.* horizontal moulding on pillar or wall.

Cornuco'pia, *n.* ornamental horn filled with fruit & flowers symbolising plenty.

Coroll'ary, *n.* natural deduction, result, additional proposition self-evident from one already demonstrated.

Coro'na, *n.* crown, top, fiery halo round sun.

Corona'tion, *n.* ceremonial crowning of monarch.

Cor'oner, *n.* crown officer who inquires into causes of death.

Cor'onet, *n.* small crown; lowest part of horse's pastern.

Corp'oral, *n.* non-commissioned officer below sergeant in army.

Corp'oral, *a.* pertaining to the body, material. Corpor'eal, *a.* of the body.

Cor'porate, *a.* united in a body or corporation. Corpora'tion, *n.* legally constituted organization, town council, etc. *sl.* a round belly. Cor'porative, *a.*

Corps (Kor), *n.* Corps (Korz), *n. pl.* large mil. force; two army divisions.

Corpse, *n.* dead human body.

Corp'ulent, *a.* very fat, stout. Corp'ulence, *n.*

Corp'uscle (-ussl), *n.* blood-cell, minute particle.

Corral' (-ahl), *n.* stockade for enclosing horses, cattle. *v.t.* to drive into or keep in this.

Correct', *a.* exact, right, precise, conforming to facts. *v.t.* to set right, admonish. Correc'tion, *n.* Correct'ive, *n.* & *a.* Correct'-ness, *n.* Correc'titude, *n.* rightness of conduct.

Cor'relate, *v.t.* & *i.* to have a mutual relation, to bring into this. *n.* Either of two related things or words. Correla'tion, *n.* Correl'ative, *a.*

Correspond', *v.i.* to exchange letters, to agree, answer, have similarity to. Correspond'ence, *n.* Correspond'ent, *n.* person contributing news or articles to newspaper; letter-writer.

Cor'ridor, *n.* a narrow passage in building or railway-train, etc.

Corrigen'da (-jen-), *n. pl.* things to be corrected. *sing.* Corrigen'-dum.

Corrob'orate, *v.t.* to confirm formally or by evidence. Corrobora'tion, *n.* Corrob'-orative, *a.*

Corrode', *v.t.* & *i.* to destroy, wear away slowly. Corro'sive, *a.* Corro'sion, *n.* decay, gradual destruction.

Cor'rugated, *a.* with ridged or furrowed surface. Corruga'tion, *n.* Cor'rugate, *v.t.* & *i.* to form or bend in undulating ridges.

Corrupt', *v.t.* & *i.* to make or become rotten or evil, to bribe, to influence in evil manner. Corrupt'ible, *a.* Corrup'tion, *n.* rottenness, bribery.

Cors'air, *n.* a pirate, pirate-ship.

Cors'et, *n.* stays, stiffened bodice.

Cors'let, *n. arch.* protective body armour.

Cortege' (-tezh), *n.* funeral procession, attendants.

Cor'uscate, *v.i.* to flash, glint, sparkle. Corusca'tion, *n.*

Corvette', *n.* warship, escort vessel.

Cosmet'ic, *n.* beauty preparation.

Cos'mic (Koz-), *a.* of the universe.

Cos'mo, *pref.* meaning universe or of the universe, as in e.g. **Cosmogony,** *n.* theory of origin of universe; **Cosmography,** *n.* charting or mapping of universe; **Cosmology,** *n.* science of universe as orderly system.

Cos'mos, *n.* the universe.

Cosmopol'itan, *a.* of all parts of the world, without national connections or prejudices. *n.* **Cosmop'olite,** *n.*

Cos'sack, *n.* member of various Soviet clans renowned as horsemen.

Coss'et, *v.t.* to pamper, fuss over.

Cost, *v.t.* involve payment, sacrifice, loss; to fix price of. *n.* price, expense. *n. pl.* expenses of lawsuit. **Cost'ly,** *a.* of great value, entailing much expense.

Cos'ter, Cos'termonger, *n.* trader who sells from street-barrow.

Cos'tume, *n.* style of dress, theatrical clothes, woman's coat & skirt. **Costu'mier,** *n.* dealer in costumes, woman's tailor.

Cot, *n.* child's enclosed bed, swinging bed in ship.

Cote, *n.* house or shelter for birds or animals, as in **dovecote.**

Co'terie, *n.* clique, circle of people with same interests.

Cotill'ion, Cotill'on, *n.* lively dance.

Cott'age, *n.* small house.

Cott'on, *n.* a plant; soft white fibrous hairs covering its seeds from which material or thread is made. **Cotton-wool,** *n.* raw cotton. **Cotton-cake,** *n.* cattle-fodder made from compressed c.-seed. **Cotton-gin,** *n.* machine for processing cotton-seed fibres.

Couch (Kowch), *n.* piece of furniture for lying on in daytime; sofa. *v.t. & i.* to lie down; to hold spear or lance ready for action.

Couch, *v.t.* to express, term, put into words.

Cough (Kof), *v.i. & t.* to expel air from lungs with violent noise or effort. *n.* the act of coughing, a disease of respiratory organs.

Coun'cil, *n.* administrative or deliberative body or assembly. **Coun'cillor,** *n.* member of such.

Coun'sel, *n.* legal adviser, barrister, serious advice. *v.t.* to advise, warn, recommend. **Coun'sellor,** *n.*

Count, *v.t. & i.* to number, reckon, calculate, consider to be, to be of importance, depend on. *n.* a reckoning, *leg.* one of various charges or indictments.

Count, *n.* foreign title equivalent to earl.

Count'enance, *n.* the face, its expression; approval, support. *v.t.* to give approval or support.

Count'er, *n.* token used for scoring in certain games; bar in bank or shop; part of ship's stern.

Count'er, *adv. & a.* in opposite direction, contrary.

Coun'ter, *pref.* meaning against, rival, opposite, retaliatory; e.g. **Counteract,** *v.t.* to act in opposition to, neutralize; **Counter-attack,** *v.t.* to attack immediately after enemy attack; **Counter-balance,** *v.t.* to act against in equal strength or weight; **Counter-claim,** *n. leg.* action in reply to one made by other person. **Counter-irritant,** *n. med.* application to relieve inflammation. **Counter-march,** *v.i.* to march in opposite direction to.

Count′erfeit, *a.* forged, spurious. *n.* a forgery. *v.t.* to forge. **Count′erfeiter,** *n.*

Count′erfoil, *n.* part of bank cheque, receipt, sweep-ticket, etc. retained for checking purposes.

Countermand, *v.t.* to cancel order.

Count′erpane, *n.* bed-quilt, covering.

Count′erpart, *n.* a duplicate, person or thing exactly similar to another; complementary object or part.

Count′erpoint, *n. mus.* method of combining melodies; melody added to another as accompaniment.

Count′ersign, *n.* password given in response to sentry's challenge. *v.t.* to sign in authorisation in addition to another's signature.

Coun′tersink, *v.t.* to sink screwhead by means of bevelling hole in wood.

Coun′try (Kun-), *n.* a nation's territory, a region, district, rural area. **Coun′tryside,** *n.* rural land as opposed to town. **Coun′trified,** *a.* rustic in manner, old-fashioned.

Coun′ty, *n.* shire, division of country.

Coup (Koo), *n.* a sudden successful action.

Coup′le (Kup-), *n.* two of similar kind, an engaged man & woman, husband and wife. *v.t. & i.* to join or link together, to associate in the mind. **Coup′ling,** *n.* chain-connection

between railway carriages etc. **Coup′let,** *n.* two lines of rhyming verse.

Cou′pon (Koo-), *n.* a voucher, detachable ticket exchangeable for food, money, etc.

Cour′age (Kur-), *n.* bravery. **Coura′geous,** *a.*

Cou′rier (Koo-), *n.* official messenger, guide for tourists.

Course (Kors), *n.* progress or movement in space or time; direction of this, line of action or conduct; a layer of bricks; a series of lessons or lectures or treatment; one of series of dishes at meal. *v.t. & i.* to run freely, swiftly; to hunt hare with greyhounds. **Cours′er,** *n. arch.* a swift horse.

Court (Kort), *n.* space surrounded by buildings, area enclosed for various games, a residence, retinue or establishment of a monarch, body with judicial powers, place where it assembles. *v.t.* to woo, to seek friendship of. **Court′ier,** *n.* person who attends royal court. **Court′ly,** *a.* elegant, ceremoniously polite. **Court-martial,** *n.* judicial court of mil. or naval officers. **Courtyard,** *n.* paved space among or in front of buildings. **Court-card,** *n.* in cards the king, queen, jack.

Courtesan′, *n.* a high-class whore.

Cour′tesy (Kur-), *n.* courteous behaviour or manner. **Court′-eous,** *a.* C. title, title used by custom but without legal right.

Cous′in (Kuz-), *n.* son or daughter of aunt or uncle.

Cove, *n.* a small sheltered bay.

Cov′enant (Kuv-), *n.* a solemn agreement, a contract. *v.t. & i.*

Cov'enanter, *n.* 17th cent. supporter of Sc. National Covenant in defence of rel. liberty.

Cov'er (Kuv-), *v.t.* to protect, hide, spread over, insure, *journ.* to report upon, aim at with gun. *n.* a protection, shelter, wrapping, book-binding. **Cov'erlet,** *n.* quilt, bed-covering.

Cov'ert, *a.* secret, furtive. *n.* a small dense wood, copse.

Cov'et (Kuv-), *v.t.* to desire jealously or eagerly, esp. someone else's property. **Cov'etous,** *a.*

Cov'ey (Kuv-), *n.* brood of partridges.

Cow, *n.* female ox, elephant, whale etc. *v.t.* to intimidate.

Cow'ard, *n.* person without courage. **Cow'ardice,** *n.* lack of courage, faint-heartedness.

Cow-boy, *n.* Amer. cattle-hand; *fig.* wild person who acts irresponsibly.

Cow'er, *v.i.* to cringe in fear.

Cowl, *n.* hooded vent for chimney, monk's hood.

Cox'comb, *n.* self-opinionated young man.

Cox'swain (Kok'sn), **Cox,** *n. naut.* petty officer in charge of steering and management of boat, steersman in racing boat.

Coy, *a.* bashful, shy in exaggerated fashion.

Coyo'te (Ky-yoti), *n.* Amer. prairie-wolf.

Coz'en (Kuz-), *v.t. & i.* to beguile, cheat, deceive.

Crab, *n.* ten-legged edible crustacean.

Crab, *v.t. & i.* to carp at, criticise meanly. **Crabb'ed,** *a.* ill-natured; of writing, hard to read.

Crack, *v.t. & i.* to split, break sharply, make a sharp sound, make a joke, open bottle; of voice, to become uneven. *a.* smart, excellent, e.g. **crackship, crack-shot. Crack'er,** *n.* firework, paper toy used for table decoration at Christmas, a kind of biscuit. **Crack'le,** *n.* series of small crackling sounds. **Crack'ling,** *n.* sliced skin of roast pork.

Cra'dle (Kray-), *n.* a baby's cot on rockers, supporting frame under vessel being constructed, place of origin. *v.t.* to rock or hold or place as in cradle.

Craft, *n.* skill, cunning, a skilled trade or art; boat, vessel (*pl.* craft). **Crafts'man,** *n.* **Crafts'manship,** *n.,* **Craft'y,** *a.* cunning.

Crag, *n.* a steep rugged rock. **Cragg'y,** *a.* **Crags'man,** *n.* rock-climber, esp. in Lake District.

Cram, *v.t. & i.* to stuff, pack full, feed to excess, prepare privately and rapidly for examination. **Crammer,** *n.* private tutor.

Cramp, *n.* painful contraction of muscles; masonry clamp. *v.t.* to affect with cramp, to hamper, restrict, write too small. **Cram'pon,** *n.* spiked iron device worn as climbing aid on boot.

Cran, *n.* a Sc. measure of herrings.

Cran'berry, *n.* wild red sour berry used for sauce.

Crane, *n.* machine for lifting heavy loads; tall wading bird with long legs and bill. *v.i.* to stretch out neck.

Cra'nium, *n.* the skull. **Cra'niology,** *n.* study of skull for purpose of determining characteristics.

Crank, *n.* an odd, unconventional person; lever attached to shaft of engine for turning. *v.t.* & *i.* to turn, wind by crank.

Crann'y, *n.* a crevice, small cleft.

Crash, *n.* a violent collision or collapse, faulty landing by aircraft, large outburst of sound. *v.t.* & *i.*

Crass, *n.* exceedingly stupid.

Crate, *n.* slatted box or packing-case. *v.t.* to pack in such.

Cra'ter, *n.* mouth of volcano, shell-hole.

Cravat', *n.* necktie, neckcloth, small silk scarf.

Crave, *v.t.* & *i.* to have great desire for, to ask humbly. **Cra'ving,** *n.*

Cra'ven, *a.* cowardly. *n.* a coward.

Crawl, *v.i.* to creep, move on hands and knees, move very slowly; to swim by crawl-stroke.

Craw'fish, Cray'fish, *n.* fresh-water crustacean resembling small lobster.

Cray'on, *n.* pencil or stick of coloured chalk, a drawing made with such.

Craze, *n.* extreme enthusiasm, mania for something. *v.t.* to make insane. **Cra'zy,** *a.* daft, foolish, mad, shaky.

Creak, *n.* shrill squeaky sound. *v.i.*

Cream, *n.* rich oily part of milk, best part, choice. *v.t.* & *i.* to remove cream or best part from. **Cream'y,** *a.* **Cream'ery,** *n.* dairy, butter and cheese factory.

Crease (-eess), *n.* a wrinkle, line caused by folding; in cricket line limiting batsman's and bowler's positions. *v.t.* & *i.* to make creases in, spoil by this.

Create (Kree-ate), *v.t.* & *i.* to bring into being, to make, produce, give rise to. **Crea'tion,** *n.* **Crea'tor,** *n.* God, maker. **Crea'ture** (Kreetyur), *n.* living being; insignificant person. **Crea'tive,** *a.* having power to create, positive, progressive.

Creche (Kraysh), *n.* public nursery.

Cre'dence, *n.* belief. **Creden'tials,** *n. pl.* letters of introduction, documents proving person's status. **Cred'ible,** *a.* believable.

Cred'it, *n.* belief, trust, good name or reputation, trust in another's ability to pay, deferred payment, amount of money remaining at person's disposal in bank, side or page of cash-book on which sums received are entered. *v.t.* to believe, to place on credit side of account, to attribute to. **Cred'itable,** *a.* praiseworthy. **Cred'itor,** *n.* person to whom another owes money.

Cred'ulous, *a.* over-quick to believe, easily deceived.

Creed, *n.* system of rel. belief, exposition or summary of Christian religion.

Creek, *n.* narrow inlet.

Creel, *n.* rod-fisherman's basket.

Creep, *v.i.* to crawl, move silently, stealthily, cringe, have sensation of skin moving through horror. **Creep'er,** *n.* creeping or climbing plant. **Creep'y,** *a.* uncanny. **Creepy-crawly,** *n.* insect, any small creature.

Cremate', *v.t.* to consume body

by fire. **Crema'tion,** *n.* practice of burning corpses instead of burying. **Cremato'rium,** *n.* place where this is carried out.

Cre'ole, *n.* a native of Sp. Amer. or W. Indies having European ancestry.

Cre'osote, *n.* oily protective liquid made from wood-tar.

Crepe (Krape), *n.* gauzy wrinkled fabric of silk or artificial silk.

Crepus'cular, *a.* of or appearing at twilight.

Crep'itate, *v.i.* to make crackling sound. **Crepita'tion,** *n.*

Crescen'do (-shen-), *a.* gradually increasing in loudness or intensity esp. in mus. *n.*

Cres'cent, *n.* figure of moon in first or last quarter, this as Muslim emblem, any similar shape, row of houses in c.-shape. *a.* increasing.

Cress, *n.* kinds of plants with edible leaves.

Crest, *n.* tuft of hair or feathers on animal's head, plume on helmet, top of hill or ridge, top of wave, armorial device on top of shield. *v.t. & i.* to equip with crest, reach to the top of. **Crest'fallen,** *a.* dejected by failure or disappointment.

Creta'ceous (-shus), *a.* chalky.

Cret'in, *n.* deformed idiot. **Cret'-inism,** *n.* **Cret'inous,** *a.*

Cretonne', *n.* unglazed cotton cloth with printed coloured patterns.

Crevasse', *n.* deep fissure in glacier.

Crev'ice (-iss), *n.* deep cleft or fissure.

Crew (Kroo) *n.* a ship's company, a set, a mob.

Crib, *n.* manger, child's cot, a piece of plagiarism. *v.t. & i.*

to copy illegally, to cramp, confine.

Cribb'age, *n.* a card game.

Crick, *n.* sudden cramp in back or neck. *v.t.*

Crick'et, *n.* jumping chirping insect.

Crick'et, *n.* open-air game played with ball and bat and between teams of eleven players each. **Crick'eter,** *n.*

Crime, *n.* evil act, serious violation of the law. *v.t.* army *sl.* to charge with offence. **Crim'inal,** *n. & a.* **Criminal'ity,** *n.* **Criminol'ogy,** *n.* science of crime. **Crim'inous,** *a.* guilty of crime. **Crim'inate,** *v.t.* charge with crime, censure.

Crimp, *v.t.* to compress into folds or frills, corrugate.

Crimp, *n.* agent paid to lure seamen to serve in another ship. *v.t.*

Crim'son, (-zn), *n.* deep-red colour. *a.*

Cringe, *v.i.* to cower, creep in fear, fawn.

Crin'kle, *v.t. & i.* to wrinkle, crumple, *n.*

Crin'oline (-leen), *n. arch.* a woman's hooped petticoat.

Crip'ple, *n.* a lame or disabled person. *v.t.* to disable.

Cri'sis, *n.* decisive or dangerous moment, turning-point. *pl.* **Cri'ses. Crit'ical,** *a.*

Crisp, *a.* hard and brittle, bracing, brisk, curly. *v.t. & i.* to make or become crisp, to harden by baking.

Crite'rion (Kry-), *n.* principle, standard.

Crit'icise, *v.t.* to discuss in detail, to censure, to analyse in lit. sense. **Crit'ic,** *n.* person who does this. **Crit'icism,** *n.*

expert appraisal or judgement,
fault-finding. **Crit'ical,** *a.*

Croak, *n.* a low harsh cry or
sound. *v.t. & i.* **Croak'er,** *n.*
dismal, pessimistic person.

Cro'chet (-shay), *n.* kind of fine
knitting done with hooked
needle. *v.t. & i.*

Crock, *n.* an earthenware pot or
jar; broken-down horse or car.
v.t. & t. to make or become
unfit. **Crocked,** *a.* temporarily
unfit.

Crock'ery, *n.* household earthenware utensils.

Croc'odile, *n.* large amphibious
reptile. **C. tears,** humbug.
hypocrisy.

Croft, *n.* Sc. small-holding.
Croft'er, *n.* one who farms
this.

Crom'lech (-lek), *n.* prehistoric
structure with flat stone supported by upright stones.

Crone, *n.* a witch, shrivelled old
woman.

Cro'ny, *n.* pal, bosom-friend.

Crook, *n.* a thief, criminal,
swindler; a shepherd's hooked
staff. *v.t.* to bend into the shape
of a hook. **Crook'ed,** *a.*
dishonest, bent.

Croon, *v.t. & i.* to sing softly.
Croon'er, *n.* entertainer who
sings in informal or unskilled
fashion.

Crop, *n.* a season's produce from
certain plants, harvest; a bird's
pouch; stock of a whip; a
close-cut style of hairdressing,
e.g. crew-cut. *v.t. & i.* to clip,
bite down grass, to raise
cultivable plants.

Cro'quet (-kay), *n.* lawn game
played by driving wooden balls
through hoops. *v.t.* to hit away
opponent's ball.

Croquette (-ket), *n.* a kind of
rissole.

Cro'sier (-z-), *n.* bishop's staff.

Cross, *n.* structure with upright
and crossbar near top; mark
made by intersection of right-
angled lines; an intermingling
of breeds. **The C.,** cross on
which Christ was crucified, thus
symbol of Christian church.

Cross, *n.* something difficult
to bear, an affliction. *v.t. & i.*
to thwart, to go from one side to
another, to intersect, to hybrid-
ize. *a.* transverse, contrary, ill-
tempered. **Cross'bow,** *n. arch.*
mechanical bow. **Cross-benches,**
n.pl. in parl. seats where independent members sit. **Cross-
examine,** *v.t.* in law to question
severely, esp. witness of other
party. **Cross-grained,** *n.* irritable. **Cross-section,** *n.* surface
revealed by cutting solid at
right-angles; a representative
sample.

Crotch'et, *n. mus.* symbol equal
to half a minim; a fad. **Crotch'-
ety,** *a.* faddy, irritable.

Crouch (Krowch), *v.i.* to stoop
down, huddle, prepare to
spring.

Croup (Kroop), *n.* rump, hind-
quarters of horse.

Croup (Kroop), *n.* inflammatory
disease of throat in children.

Crow (Kroe), *n.* black or grey
and black carrion-eating bird.
Crow's nest, *n.* masthead shelter
for look-out. **Crow-bar,** *n.* iron
bar used as lever.

Crow, *n.* cry of cock. *v.i.* to utter this, to exult.

Crowd, *n.* large gathering of
people. *v.t. & i.* to throng
together, fill with people.

Crown, *n.* a monarch's formal

headdress; the royal power; top of head, hill, road, etc.; ceremonial wreath for head; a five shilling piece; the completion, consummation of a project. *v.t.*

Cru'cial (-shal), *a.* critical, decisive.

Cru'cible, *n.* melting-pot.

Cru'cify, *v.t.* to put to death by hanging on a cross. Crucifix'ion, *n.* Cru'cifix, *n.* image of Christ on the cross.

Crude (krood), *a.* rough, uncouth, unfinished, raw. Cru'dity, *n.*

Cru'el (Kroo-), *a.* brutal, enjoying others' pain or distress, callous. Cru'elty, *n.*

Cru'et, *n.* set of small bottles for sauces or condiments.

Cruise (Krooz), *v.i.* to sail or move in leisurely fashion. *n.* a pleasure voyage. Cruis'er, *n.* warship faster but smaller than battleship.

Crumb (-m), *n.* small fragment of bread, the soft part of a loaf.

Crum'ble, *v.t. & i.* to disintegrate, to break or fall into pieces, to collapse.

Crum'pet, *n.* flat soft round cake for toasting.

Crum'ple, *v.t. & i.* to make or become spoilt by wrinkling or crushing, to crush in hand. Crum'pled, *a.* ruffled, bent, creased.

Crunch, *n.* gritty sound caused by treading or biting. *v.t. & i.*

Crupp'er, *n.* strap securing saddle by passing under horse's tail; hindquarters of horse.

Crusade', *n.* mediaeval Christian campaign to drive Muslims out of Holy Land; any intense or earnest campaign

or movement against public evil. *v.i.* Crusa'der, *n.*

Cruse (Krooz), *n. arch.* a small earthenware jar or pot.

Crush, *v.t. & i.* to compress in violent manner, to overwhelm, squash, disconcert. *n.* a mass of people.

Crust, *n.* hard outer part of loaf, a scrap of bread, the outside or hard surface of object. Crus'ty, *a.* hard, short-tempered.

Crust'acean, *n.* hard-shelled animal such as crab, lobster, etc. Crusta'ceous (-shus), *a.*

Crutch, *n.* staff or prop with cross-piece to fit under armpit of injured or crippled person for support.

Crux, *n.* a difficult problem, essential point.

Cry, *v.t. & i.* to call out, to proclaim, to weep. *n.* the call of a bird, a bout of weeping, a catchword.

Crypt, *n.* vault beneath church. Cryp'tic, *a.* mystical, secret. Cryp'togram, *n.* a message in cipher.

Cry'stal (Kris-), *n.* transparent quartz, very fine glass, *chem.* body in geometrical form. Crys'talline, *a.* Crys'tallise, *v.t. & i.* to take shape, to become or form into crystals. Crystal-set, *n.* simple form of radio receiver.

Cub, *n.* the young of various animals, e.g. bear, fox, wolf. *v.t. & i.* to produce young.

Cube, *n.* regular solid with six equal square sides; cube-shaped block; product of a number being multiplied by itself twice. Cu'bic, *a.* of three dimensions. Cu'bical, *a.* Cu'bicle, *n.* small sleeping-compartment separated from others by partition.

Cu'bit, *n. arch.* measure of length of about eighteen inches.

Cuck'oo, *n.* a migratory bird so named from its call (Kook-oo).

Cuck'old, *n.* husband of unfaithful wife. *v.t.* to make cuckold of.

Cu'cumber (Ku-), *n.* long fleshy green juicy fruit or vegetable produced by plant of same name.

Cud, *n.* food brought up from first stomach by ruminant in order to chew and digest at leisure.

Cud'dle, *v.t. & i.* to hug affectionately, to nestle against.

Cud'gel, *n.* bludgeon, club. *v.t.* to beat with such. **To cudgel one's brains,** to think hard; **take up the cudgels,** defend or argue vigorously.

Cue, *n.* signal for actor to take the stage; hint or signal in general.

Cue, *n.* long tapering rod or stick in billiards; pigtail.

Cuff, *n.* end of sleeve, starched linen band worn round wrist.

Cuff, *v.t.* to strike lightly.

Cuirass (Kwir-), *n.* defensive armour for torso.

Cui'sine (Kwiz-), *n.* cookery, style of cooking, kitchen.

Cul-de-sac, *n.* blind alley.

Cul'inary, *a.* pertaining to cooking.

Cull, *v.t.* to gather, pick, select.

Cul'minate, *v.i.* to reach a climax, reach highest point. Culmina'tion, *n.*

Cul'pable, *a.* blameworthy. Culpabil'ity, *n.* Cul'prit, *n.* an offender, guilty person.

Cult, *n.* a system of religious belief, a sedulous devotion to person or object.

Cul'tivate, *v.t.* to till the soil, raise crops; improve, refine, civilize, acquire acquaintance of. Cultiva'tion, *n.* Cul'tivator, *n.*

Cul'ture, *n.* intellectual development, refinement of enlightenment & taste; artificially reared set of bacteria. Cul'tural, *a.* pertaining to intellectual pursuits.

Cul'vert, *n.* channel or drainpipe carrying water under road, canal, etc.

Cum'ber, *v.t.* to burden, hamper. Cum'bersome, Cum'brous, *a.*

Cumm'erbund, *n.* waist sash.

Cu'mulative, *a.* tending to accumulate or increase. Cu'mulate, *v.t. & i.*

Cu'mulus, *n.* (*pl.* Cumuli) heaped up mass of clouds on top of each other.

Cunn'ing, *n.* artfulness, furtive skill. *a.*

Cup, *n.* drinking vessel with handle; ornamental vessel as prize or trophy. Cup'board (Kubb-), *n.* shelved cabinet for cups, etc. *v.t.* Cup, to hold in hands like cup ; *arch. med.* to bleed a person.

Cupid'ity, *n.* greed of gain.

Cu'pola (Ku-), *n. arch.* a dome of bulbous or pointed shape.

Cur, *n.* a mongrel, worthless dog, despicable person.

Cur'ate (Kure-), *n.* assistant to parish priest. Cur'acy, *n.*

Cur'ative (Kure-), *a.* tending to cure, esp. disease.

Cura'tor, *n.* keeper of museum, art gallery, etc. Cura'torship, *n.*

Curb, *n.* part of bridle used to check horse, a check, restraint. *v.t.* to restrain.

Curd, *n.* coagulated milk used in cheese-making. **Cur'dle,** *v.t. & i.* to congeal, turn into curd.

Cure, *n.* a remedy, course of med. treatment. *v.t. & i.* to restore or be restored to health; to preserve fish, etc. by salting.

Cur'few, *n.* signal or time after which inhabitants of town or region under martial law must remain indoors.

Cu'rious (Kure-), *a.* inquisitive, anxious to know; strange, mystifying; carefully done or wrought in detailed way. **Curios'ity,** *n.* inquisitiveness, anxiety to know ; rare or unusual object. **Cu'rio,** *n.* rare or unusual object of art.

Curl, *v.t. & i.* to form or be formed in coiled, twisted shape, to bend, curve. *n.* a ringlet of hair, a curving motion or shape. **Cur'ling,** *n.* game resembling bowls played on ice.

Curmudg'eon, *n.* miserly fellow, skinflint.

Curr'ant, *n.* fruit of various bushes, dried fruit of small grape.

Curr'ent, *a.* in general use or circulation. *n.* a body of air or water in motion, the general flow of a river, transmission of electricity. **Curr'ency,** *n.* time during which something is in use ; money in actual use.

Curric'ulum, *n.* (*pl.* curricula) organized course of study.

Curr'y, *v.t. & i.* to groom, rub down, esp. of horse; to win favour by flattery; to dress leather. **Curr'ier,** *n.* leather-dresser.

Curr'y, *n.* Eastern dish of rice with highly spiced meat, etc. *v.t.*

Curse, *n.* malediction, invocation of evil. *v.t. & i.* to swear, blaspheme, afflict.

Curs'ive, *a.* writing with letters joined.

Curs'ory, *a.* superficial, hasty, perfunctory. **Curs'orily,** *a.*

Curt, *a.* abrupt, brusque.

Curtail', *v.t.* to cut short. **Curtail'ment,** *n.*

Curt'ain, *n.* suspended cloth as protective screen, moveable screen between stage and auditorium. *v.t.* to hide or protect with curtain.

Curt'sy, *n.* woman's salutation made by bending knees and ducking body. *v.i.*

Curve, *n.* bend, a line without any straight part. *v.t. & i.* **Curv'ature,** *n.* a bent form, e.g. of spine. **Curvet',** *n.* bounding action of horse by arching its back. *v.i.* **Curvilin'ear,** *a.* consisting of or contained by curved lines.

Cush'ion (Koosh-), *n.* mass of soft material contained in silk or cloth envelope; the inside edges of a billiard table. *v.t.* to protect or provide with cushion.

Cusp, *n.* sharp point, crown of tooth, apex.

Cus'tard, *n.* mixture of milk & eggs, sweetened & flavoured.

Cus'tody, *n.* guardianship, safe-keeping, temporary imprisonment pending trial. **Custo'dial,** *a.* **Custo'dian,** *n.* keeper, gaoler.

Cus'tom, *n.* usual or accepted practice, business patronage, as *n. pl.* duties payable on imported goods. **Cus'tomary,** *a.* usual. **Cus'tomer,** *n.* person who patronizes shop or business. **Cus'toms officer,** *n.* government official collecting duties payable on imported goods.

Cut, *v.t.* & *i.* to divide, sever, wound, strike, hit; to ignore somebody; to curtail, interrupt, as in film-making. *n.* a choice slice of meat, a wound made by knife, etc.

Cuta'neous (Ku-), *a.* of the skin. **Cu'ticle,** *n.* outer or superficial skin.

Cute, *a.* clever, shrewd, compact, neat.

Cut'lass, *n.* seaman's short heavy sword.

Cut'ler, *n.* craftsman who makes knives, dealer in these. **Cut'lery,** *n.* cutler's trade, knives esp. for domestic use.

Cut'let, *n.* small chop of meat, slice of veal.

Cut'purse, *n.* pickpocket.

Cut'tle, *n.* us. as **c.-fish,** tentacled mollusc capable of ejecting black fluid as defence.

Cutt'er, *n.* warship's small boat for visiting, taking messages, etc.

Cy'anide, *n.* prussic acid. **Cyan'ogen,** *n.* colourless poisonous gas of nitrogen & carbon.

Cy'cle, *n.* recurrent series of phenomena or events; body of poems with main theme, complete series of anything, regular period of time, *v.i.* to progress in cycles ; to pedal a bicycle. **Cy'clic, Cy'clical,** *a.* **Cy'clist,** *n.* a bicycle-rider. **Cyclom'eter,** *n.* instrument for recording distances on bicycle. **Cy'clone,** *n.* violent circular tempest, system of winds circling round centre of extremely low barometric pressure. **Cyclon'ic,** *a.*

Cyg'net (Sig-), *n.* a young swan.

Cyl'inder (Sil-), *n.* round, straight sided body with flat circular ends; piston-chamber of engine. **Cylin'drical,** *a.*

Cym'bal (Sim-), *n.* us. as *n.pl.* round brass plates used as percussion instruments in mus.

Cy'mometer, *n.* instrument for calculating frequency of elec. waves.

Cyn'ic (Sin-), *n.* person sceptical of goodness of things. **Cyn'ical,** *a.* sneering, shameless, sceptical of goodness.

Cyn'osure, *n.* centre of admiration or attraction; guiding star.

Cyst (Sist), *n.* bladder or organ secreting liquid, sac filled with pus.

Czar, Tsar (Zahr), *n.* title of Russian monarch until 1917. **Czar'ina,** *n.* his wife.

D

Dab, *v.t.* to touch lightly, strike feebly, wipe gently with sponge, damp cloth. *n.* a gentle blow, a lump of butter etc., a small flat fish. *a. coll.* expert. **Dabhand,** *n.* an expert.

Dab'ble, *v.t.* & *i.* to splash about in, engage desultorily in some project.

Dacoit', *n.* Indian or Burmese bandit.

Da'daism, *n.* a school of art &

lit. aiming at the suppression of any relation between thought and expression.

Da'do, *n.* lower part of room-wall when painted or panelled separately from rest.

Dae'mon (De-), *n.* genius, supernatural being, impelling influence, spirit of good or evil. **Daemon'ic**, *a.* supernatural.

Daft, *a.* silly, crazy.

Dagg'er, *n.* short stabbing weapon with pointed and sharp blade.

Da'go, *n.* abusive term for Spaniard or Italian etc.

Daguerre'otype (Da-gerrio-), *n.* 19th cent. photographic process.

Dail'y, *a.* performed, done, published, etc. every day. *adv.* every day. *n.* a daily newspaper, domestic help.

Dain'ty, *a.* delicate, fastidious, prettily elegant. *n.* a tidbit of food. **Dain'tiness**, *n.*

Dair'y, *n.* a place for handling or processing milk and its products.

Dais, (Day-iss) *n.* a low raised platform in hall.

Dale, *n.* valley, esp. in north country. **Dales'man**, *n.*

Dall'y, *v.i.* to delay, waste time idly, trifle, make love in light-hearted way. **Dall'iance**, *n.*

Dalmat'ic, *n.* ceremonial wide-sleeved garment worn by kings & bishops.

Dam, *n.* mother, esp. of animals.

Dam, *n.* embankment or other construction to impede flow of water ; water confined by this. *v.t.* to restrain with or build a dam.

Dam'age, *n.* injury, harm. *pl. leg.* payment claimed or award-ed as compensation. *v.t.* to injure, cause harm to.

Dam'ask, *n.* table-linen with pattern revealed by reflection of light, **d.-rose**, *n.* old-fashioned rose brought orig. from Damascus. *a.* made of damask.

Dame, *n. arch.* or *poet.*, a lady; title of woman member of Order of the British Empire and equiv. of knight.

Damn (Dam), *v.t. & i.* to condemn, censure, doom to hell, curse. Interj. *a.* curse, expression of anger. **Dam'nable**, *a.* worthy of being damned, detestable. **Damna'tion**, *n.*

Damp, *a.* slightly wet, moist. *n.* moisture, dangerous gas in coal-mines. *v.t.* to make damp, moisten, depress, smother. **Damp'en**, *v.t. & i.* **Damp'er**, *n.* sliding plate for controlling chimney flue.

Dam'sel (-zel), *n. arch.* or *poet.*, a girl.

Dam'son (-zn), *n.* small purple plum, the tree bearing this.

Dance, *v.t. & i.* to leap or move in rhythmic patterns, esp. to mus., to caper, act or gesture joyfully, skip, bob up and down, to perform a dance. *n.* a dancing motion, an organized series of intricate steps performed to mus., a tune for this, a party for dancing. **Danc'er**, *n.*

Dan'druff, *n.* scurf, scaly formation on skin of scalp.

Dan'dy, *n.* a fop, person obsessed by clothes.

Dan'ger (-jer), *n.* menace, liability or exposure to harm or injury. **Dan'gerous**, *a.*

Dan'gle, *v.t. & i.* to hang and swing loosely.

Dank, *a.* unhealthily damp, oozy.

Dapp'er, *a.* neat and smart, esp. in small way.

Dap'ple, *v.t. & i.* to mark or become marked with patches and spots of varying colour.

Dare, *v.t.* to be bold enough to, to venture, to defy. **Dar'ing,** *a. & n.* **Dare-devil,** *n.* reckless person.

Dark, *a.* without light, gloomy, sombre, deeply tinted, almost black in colour, brown or black haired with brown complexion, furtive, wicked. *n.* night, absence of light or knowledge. **Dark'en,** *v.t. & i.* to make or become dark or obscure. **Dark'-ness,** *n.* **Dark'ling,** *adv. poet.* in the dark. **Darkroom,** *n.* light-proof room for photographic process.

Dar'ling, *n.* term of endearment, person greatly loved. *a.* very precious.

Darn, *v.t.* to mend hole in sock or clothes by knitting over with wool. *n.* a hole thus mended. **Darn'ing,** *n.*

Dart, *n.* light throwing weapon with point, sudden movement. *v.t. & i.* to move swiftly and suddenly. *n.pl.* indoor game in which feathered darts are thrown at board divided into numbered sections. **Dart--board,** *n.*

Dash, *v.t. & i.* to run swiftly and suddenly, to throw down, to shatter, to flavour. *n.* a sudden rush, vigorous smartness, a small quantity esp. to flavour something, a short line as punctuation mark. **Dash'ing,** *a.* with spirit. **Dash'board,** *n.* mud-shield in front of horse-drawn vehicle, instrument-board in automobile.

Das'tard, *n.* treacherous coward.

Date, *n.* a sweet single-stoned fruit, the palm bearing this.

Date, *n.* day or time of happening, a period to which art etc. belongs, statement of day, month & year on letter or newspaper etc.; *sl.* an appointment, rendezvous. *v.t. & i.* to mark with date, to originate from a certain time, to reckon time or period. **Dateless,** *a.* undated, without date. **Out of date,** old-fashioned, obsolete. **Up to date,** modern.

Da'tive (-tiv), *a. & n.* gram. case indicating indirect object.

Da'tum, *n.* fact or thing known or granted, logical assumption. *n.pl.* **Da'ta.**

Daub, *v.t. & i.* to smear over with paint, paint badly. *n.* a poorly executed picture. **Daub'er,** *n.* a slap-dash artist.

Daught'er (Daw-), *n.* female child. **Daughter-in-law,** *n.* wife of one's son.

Daunt (Daw-), *v.t.* to discourage, intimidate. **Daunt'less,** *a.* brave.

Dau'phin (Doh-), *n.* eldest son of French king when France was a monarchy.

Dav'enport, *n.* small writing-desk.

Dav'it, *n.* apparatus for lowering or raising ship's boat.

Da'vy Jones's Locker, *n.* bottom of the sea, watery grave.

Da'vy Lamp, *n.* miner's safety lamp.

Daw'dle, *v.i.* to loiter, waste time.

Dawn, *n.* daybreak, first appearance or sign of something.

v.i. to begin to grow light, to start to appear. **Dawn'ing,** *n.*

Day, *n.* daily period when sun is above horizon; twenty-four hours from midnight to midnight. **Dar'ly,** *a.*, *adv.* & *n.* **Day'-light,** *n.* light of sun. **Daylight-saving,** *n.* gain of extra daylight by advancing clock one hour.

Daze, *v.t.* to bewilder, stupefy. *n.* **Dazed,** *a.*

Daz'zle, *v.t.* & *i.* to blind temporarily by brilliant light, to overwhelm by outstanding performance or beauty.

De-, *pref.* meaning down, away, off, from etc., e.g. defend, **deduce, denaturalize, declare,** etc.

Dea'con, *n.* minor priest or church official. **Dea'coness,** *n.* female church official. **Dea'-conry,** *n.* office of deacon, priest's dwelling.

Dead (Ded), *a.* without life, extinct, inanimate, dull, without spirit. *n.* a dead person, dead persons in general. *adv.* exact, complete, e.g. in dead-sure, dead-right. **Dead'en,** *v.t.* to numb, make insensible, muffle. **Dead'ly,** *a.* fatal. **Dead'heat,** *n.* a race in which two or more competitors finish simultaneously. **Deadloss,** *n.* complete loss without compensation or profit. **Deadletter,** *n.* law no longer enforced. **Dead-march,** *n.* funeral music. **Deadeye,** *n.* a kind of pulley. **Dead-fall,** *n.* trap worked by falling weight. **Dead-light,** *n.* in ship, shutter over porthole. **Deadlock,** *n.* a standstill through clash of interests.

Deaf (Def), *a.* unable or unwilling to hear. **Deaf'ness,** *n.* **Deaf'-en,** *v.t.* deprive of hearing by noise.

Deal, *n.* timber of pine or fir.

Deal, *v.t.* & *i.* to do business with, distribute cards, inflict. *n.* a business arrangement, a share. **Deal'er,** *n.* trader, person whose turn it is to distribute cards at bridge etc.

Dean, *n.* chief priest of cathedral, head of college or university. **Dean'ery,** *n.* dwelling-house of dean.

Dear, *a.* costly, much loved. *n.* someone much loved. *adv.* expensive. **Dear'ness,** *n.*

Dearth (Durth), *n.* scarcity, lack.

Death (Deth), *n.* end of life, dying, destruction. **Death'less,** *a.* immortal. **Death'ly,** *a.* like death, still, pale. **Death-mask,** *n.* plaster or wax cast of person's face made immediately after death. **Death-blow,** *n.* blow or happening causing death. **Death-rate,** *n.* proportion of population dying annually.

Deba'cle, (Day-bahkl), *n.* complete collapse, utter disaster.

Debar', *v.t.* to exclude, shut out.

Debase', *v.t.* to lower value of, bring shame to, adulterate. **Debase'ment,** *n.*

Debate', *v.t.* & *i.* to discuss in reasoned fashion, to consider seriously. *n.* organized discussion. **Deba'table,** *a.*

Debauch' (-bawtsh), *v.t.* to corrupt, seduce, lure from virtue. *n.* orgy, sensual indulgence. **Debauch'ery,** *n.*

Deben'ture, *n.* bond of company or corporation guaranteeing payment before other liabilities.

Debil'ity, *n.* feebleness of health.

Debil'itate, *v.t.* to enfeeble. Debilita'tion, *n.*

Deb'it, *n.* entry in account book of sum owed, page of account book used for this. *v.t.* to charge, to enter as debt owing.

Debonair', *a.* gay, carefree, amiable.

Deb'ris (-bree), *n. & n.pl.* wreckage, broken pieces after accident or destruction.

Debt (Det). *n.* a sum owed, an obligation. Debt'or, *n.* person who owes.

De'bunk, *v.t.* to show up, remove false glamour from, reveal sham.

Debut (Day-bu), *n.* first appearance in public. De'butante, *n.* girl making first appearance in high society.

Dec'ade, *n.* a period of ten years.

Dec'adent, *a.* decaying, corrupted. Dec'adence, *n.* morbid or corrupted taste or way of life.

Dec'agon, *n.* a plane figure with ten sides or angles. Decag'onal, *a.* Decahe'dron, *n.* solid with ten faces. Decahe'dral, *a.* Dec'alogue, *n.* the ten commandments.

Decamp', *v.t.* to make off, skedaddle.

Decant', *v.t.* to pour wine or other liquid from one vessel into another. Decant'er, *n.* fine glass wine container.

Decap'itate, *v.t.* to behead. Decapita'tion, *n.*

Decarb'onise (-ize). *v.t.* to remove carbon or carbon deposit from. Decarbonisa'tion, *n.*

Decath'lon, *n.* athletics contest comprising ten different events.

Decay', *v.t. & i.* to deteriorate, decompose, crumble away. *n.*

Decease', *n.* death. Deceased', *a. n.* a dead person.

Deceive', *v.t. & i.* to delude, mislead. Deceit', *n.* Deceit'ful, *a.* Deceiv'er, *n.*

Decel'erate, *v.i.* to slacken speed. Decelera'tion, *n.*

Decem'ber, *n.* last month of year.

Decenn'ial, *a.* happening every ten years. Decennary, *n.* period of ten years.

De'cent, *a.* seemly, respectable, adequate. De'cency, *n.* modesty, goodness of behaviour.

Decep'tion, *n.* fraud, illusion. Decep'tive, *a.* misleading.

Decide', *v.t. & i.* to determine, pass judgement, settle. Deci'ded, *a.* well defined, without hesitation. Decis'ion, *n.* ruling, act of making up one's mind. Deci'sive, *a.* conclusive.

Decid'uous, *a.* cast periodically, esp. leaves, antlers; not evergreen.

Dec'imal (Dess-), *a.* system of reckoning by multiples of ten. *n.* a fraction in this. D. system, *n.* system of currency or weight or other measurements in which each denomination is ten times the preceding one.

Dec'imate, *v.t. lit.* to kill every tenth man, us. to kill large number. Decima'tion, *n.*

Deci'pher, *v.t.* to decode, change from secret into ordinary writing. Deci'pherable, *a.* readable.

Deck, *n.* flooring of ship. *v.t.* to cover with planking etc; to adorn, decorate.

Dec'kle, *n.* gauge on papermaking machine. D.-edge, *n.* uneven edge of hand-made paper.

Declaim', *v.t. & i.* to speak

dramatically or in exaggerated fashion. **Declama'tion,** *n.* **Declam'atory,** *a.*

Declare', *v.t. & i.* to proclaim, announce, affirm, admit having dutiable imports, in cricket to close innings before all team has batted. **Declare for** or **against,** take sides with or against. **Declara'tion,** *n.* formal announcement, e.g. of war, intent, etc.

Declen'sion, *n.* case inflexion of noun.

Decline', *v.t. & i.* to slope downwards, to deteriorate, to refuse. **Declina'tion,** *n.* a downward slope.

Decliv'ity, *n.* a downward slope.

Declutch', *v.i.* to disengage clutch in motor-engine.

Decoc'tion, *n.* an essence obtained by boiling. **Decoct',** *v.i.*

Decode', *v.t.* to change from code or cipher into clear language.

Décoll'eté (Day-kol-tay), *a.* low-necked, wearing low-neck dress.

Decompose', *v.t. & i.* to rot, break up into elements. **Decomposi'tion,** *n.*

Decompress', *v.t.* to slacken air-pressure. **Decompress'ion,** *n.* **Decompression chamber,** *n.* device for safe and gradual relief of pressure on deep-sea diver.

Decontamina'tion, *n.* the neutralisation or removal of contaminating agents, e.g. poison gas. **Decontam'inate,** *v.t.*

Decontrol', *v.t.* to free from restriction.

Decor (Day-), *n.* decoration for theatre stage.

Dec'orate, *v.t.* to beautify,

adorn; invest with medal or order. **Decora'tion,** *n.* ornament, medal. **Dec'orative,** *a.* pleasant to the eye. **Dec'orator,** *n.* house-painter.

Deco'rum, *n.* proper behaviour, dignity. **Dec'orous,** *a.*

Decoy', *v.t.* to lure, entice, *n.* model or dead bird set up to attract others within range of gun.

Decrease', *v.t. & i.* to diminish, grow less. **De'crease,** *n.*

Decree', *n.* an official order. *v.t.*

Dec'rement, *n.* decrease, amount of decrease.

Decrep'it, *a.* old and feeble, useless. **Decrep'itude,** *n.*

Decry', *v.t.* to disparage, belittle.

Dedans', *n.* in Real Tennis gallery at open end of court.

Ded'icate, *v.t.,* to devote solemnly, set apart for some special purpose, inscribe book as compliment to someone. **Dedica'tion,** *n.* **Ded'icatory,** *a.*

Deduce', *v.t.* to draw conclusions from facts. **Deduc'tion,** *n.*

Deduct', *v.t.* to subtract, take away from. **Deduc'tion,** *n.* amount subtracted.

Deed, *n.* act, exploit, legal document.

Deem, *v.t.* to consider, believe. judge.

Deep, *a.* extending far down, profound, difficult to comprehend, intense. *n.* a deep place in the sea, the ocean in general. **Deep'en,** *v.t. & i.* to make or become deeper.

Deer, *n.* ruminant with deciduous antlers. *pl.* **deer.**

Deface', *v.t.* to disfigure, mar. **Deface'ment,** *n.*

De'falca.e, *v.i.* to embezzle

funds held in trust. **Defalca'-tion**, *n*. **De'falcator**, *n*.

Defame', *v.t.* to slander, take away good name. **Defama'tion**, *n*. **Defam'atory**, *a*.

Default, *n*. want, absence, neglect of duty, failure to pay. **Default'er**, *n*. person who defaults, serviceman guilty of crime.

Defeas'ance, *n*. *leg*. annulment. **Defeas'ible**, *a*. able to be annulled.

Defeat', *v.t.* to overthrow, vanquish, frustrate. *n*. a lost battle or contest. **Defeat'ist**, *a*. & *n*. inclined to surrender without fighting, person like this. **Defeat'ism**, *n*.

Def'ecate, *v.t.* & *i*. to void excrement, purify. **Defeca'-tion**, *n*.

Defect', *n*. a fault, blemish. **Defec'tion**, *n*. desertion, failure to carry out duty. **Defect'ive**, *a*. imperfect. **De'fect**, *v.i.* to desert.

Defend', *v.t.* to protect, guard, champion. **Defence'**, *n*. **Defend'ant**, *n*. *leg*. person defending lawsuit. **Defend'er**, *n*. **Defens'-ible**, *a*. **Defens'ive**, *a*. serving for defence. *n*. esp. as on the d., ready to defend.

Defer', *v.t.* & *i*. to postpone. **Defer'ment**, *n*.

Defer', *v.i.* to give in to another's opinion, authority or position. **Def'erence**, *n*. respect. **Deferen'-tial**, *a*.

Defi'ance, *n*. open resistance, refusal to submit. **Defi'ant**, *a*.

Defy', *v.t.* to challenge, resist.

Defic'ient, *a*. inadequate, falling short of requirement. **Defic'-iency**, *n*.

Defile', *v.t.* to sully, pollute. **Defile'ment**, *n*.

Defile', *n*. a narrow valley. *v.i.* to march in single file.

Define', *v.t.* to indicate clear, fix limits or powers, describe precisely. **Defi'nable**, *a*. **Defini'-tion**, *n*. **Def'inite**, *a*. distinct, clear, absolute. **Defin'itive**, *a*. conclusive.

Deflate', *v.t.* to release air from, to lower inflation of economy, to prick someone's dignity. **Defla'tion**, *n*.

Deflect', *v.t.* & *i*. to deviate, cause to turn aside. **Deflec'-tion**, *n*.

Deflower', *v.t.* to ravish, strip of flowers.

De'foliate, *v.t.* to strip of leaves. **Defolia'tion**, *n*.

Deform', *v.t.* to mar shape or appearance of, twist unnaturally. **Deform'ity**, *n*. **Deforma'-tion**, *n*.

Defraud', *v.t.* to swindle, cheat.

Defray', *v.t.* to pay cost of. **Defra'yal**, **Defray'ment**, *n*.

De'frock, *v.t.* unfrock, as of priest.

Deft, *a*. nimble, skilled. **Deft'-ness**, *n*.

Defunct', *a*. & *n*. dead, no longer extant.

Degen'erate, *v.i.* to deteriorate, become slack or corrupt. **Degenera'tion**, *n*. **Degen'era-cy**, *n*.

Degrade', *v.t.* & *i*. to reduce in rank, to lower oneself in dignity. **Degrada'tion**, *n*.

Degree', *n*. status, relative rank, condition, university mark of qualification, relative guality or intensity, unit of measurement in temperature and navigation etc.

Degress'ion, *n.* a going down in general, a lowering of taxation.

Degust', *v.t.* to sample food, taste. **Degusta'tion,** *n.*

Dehy'drate, *v.t.* to remove water from. **Dehydra'tion,** *n.*

De-ice, *v.t.* to free or protect aircraft wings from formation of ice.

De'ify, *v.t.* to worship as a god, make god of. **Deifica'tion,** *n.*

De'ity, *n.* a god.

Deign (Dane), *v.t. & i.* to condescend.

Deject', *v.t.* to depress, dishearten. **Dejec'-tion,** *n.*

Delay', *v.t. & i.* to be late, cause to be late, hinder, put off. *n.*

Delect'able, *a.* delightful, delicious. **Delecta'tion,** *n.*

Del'egate, *v.t.* to send as representative to assembly, conference etc., commit duty, business to. *n.* representative. **Delega'tion,** *n.* body of delegates.

Delete', *v.t.* to erase, strike out. **Dele'tion,** *n.*

Deleter'ious, *a.* harmful.

Delft, *n.* make of glazed earthenware.

Delib'erate, *v.t. & i.* to reflect upon, consider carefully, debate. *a.* intentional. **Delibera'-tion,** *n.* careful reflection, purposeful movement.

Del'icate, *a.* fragile, finely made or performed, needing careful or diplomatic handling. **Del'-icacy,** *n.* refinement.

Del'icacy, *n.* fine or dainty foodstuff. **Delicatess'en,** *n.* shop specializing in preserves, cooked meats of special kinds.

Deli'cious, *a.* exceedingly pleasant to the senses.

Delight', *v.t. & i.* to give pleasure, take pleasure in. **Delight'ful,** *a.*

Delimit', *v.t.* to define boundaries, powers etc. **Delimita'-tion,** *n.*

Delin'eate, *v.t.* to depict, draw, indicate in outline. **Delinea'-tion,** *n.*

Delin'quent, *n.* an offender, *a.* neglecting duty. **Delin'quency,** *n.* misdeed, offence. **Delict,** *n.* offence in law.

Deliquesce', *v.i.* to melt, become liquid. **Deliques'cent,** *a.*

Delir'ious, *a.* highly excited, not in possession of senses. **Delir'-ium,** *n.* fevered mental disorder.

Deliv'er, *v.t.* to set free, to make speech, to bring something, to give birth to. **Deliv'ery,** *n.* **Deliv'erance,** *n.* a setting free.

Dell, *n.* small wooded hollow.

Del'ta, *n.* alluvial land at mouths of large river. **Del'toid,** *a* triangular.

Delude', *v.t.* to deceive. **Delu'-sion,** *n.* mistaken belief. **Delus'-ive,** *a.*

Del'uge, *n.* huge flood of rain or other water. *v.t.* to flood, overwhelm.

Delve, *v.t. & i.* to dig, research into.

Demag'netize, *v.t.* to deprive of magnetic properties.

Dem'agogue, *n.* political agitator, mob leader. **Demagog'ic,** *a.* **Dem'agogy,** *n.*

Demand', *v.t.* to ask as an order, to request brusquely. *n.* a peremptory request, requirement.

Demarc'ate, *v.t.* to mark out, delimit. **Demarca'tion,** *n.* limit, boundary.

Demean', *v.t.* to debase oneself.

Demean'our, *n.* behaviour, bearing.

Dement'ed, *a.* crazy, mad. **Demen'tia**, *n.* madness caused by enfeeblement of mind.

Demerar'a, *n.* kind of brown sugar.

Demer'it, *n.* unworthy quality.

Demers'al, *a.* living or found in deep water (zool.)

Demesne' (-mane), *n.* estate, freehold possession of land.

Dem'i-, *pref.* meaning half.

Dem'igod, *n.* creature half divine, half human.

Dem'ijohn, *n.* large glass container protected by wickerwork.

Demise' (-ize), *n.* death. *v.t.* to convey by lease or will.

Demit', *v.t. & i.* to abdicate, resign office. **Demiss'ion**, *n.*

Demo'bilize, *v.t.* to disband armed forces. **Demobiliza'tion**, *n.*

Democ'racy, *n.* government by the people, universal franchise, a state based on this principle. **Dem'ocrat**, *n.* supporter of democracy. **Democ'ratize**, *v.t.* to make freer, introduce d.

Demog'raphy, *n.* statistics of country's births, deaths etc.

Demol'ish, *v.t.* to destroy, pull down. **Demoli'tion**, *n.*

De'mon, *n.* devil, evil spirit, cruel or wicked person. **Demo'niac**, *a.* frenzied, possessed by devils. **Demonol'ogy**, *n.* the study of superstitious beliefs about demons.

Dem'onstrate, *v.t. & i.* to prove, to explain, show by reasoned process, manifest feelings about something. **Demon'strable**, *a.* **Demonstra'tion**, *n.* **Demon'strator**, *n.* **Demon'strative**, *a.* showing feelings, conclusive.

Demor'alize, *v.t.* to harm morally, pervert, cause to lose courage or discipline. **Demoraliza'tion**, *n.*

Demote', *v.i.* reduce to lower rank or grade. **Demo'tion**, *n.*

Demot'ic, *a.* vulgar, popular.

Demur', *v.i.* to take exception, object. *n.*

Demure', *a.* modest, reserved.

Den, *n.* animal's lair, hole, private study.

Dene, Dean, *n.* small coombe.

Den'igrate, *v.t.* to defame, belittle. **Denigra'tion**, *n.*

Den'izen, *n.* inhabitant, animal.

Denom'inate, *v.t.* to designate, name. **Denomina'tion**, *n.* religious sect, name, designation.

Denom'inator, *n.* divisor in vulgar fraction.

Denote', *v.t.* to distinguish, point, out, mark.

Denoue'ment (Day-noo-mong), *n.* climax of plot or story, culminating situation.

Denounce', *v.t.* to inform against, speak critically of in public, condemn, repudiate. **Denuncia'tion**, *n.* **Denun'ciatory**, *a.*

Dense, *a.* closely packed, impenetrable, stupid. **Dens'ity**, *n.*

Dent, *n.* small hollow left on surface by blow or collision. *v.t.*

Dent'al, *a.* pertaining to teeth or dentistry. **Dent'ate**, *a.* toothed. **Dent'ist**, *n.* dental surgeon. **Denti'tion**, *n.* arrangement or formation of teeth.

Denude', *v.t.* to strip, make bare. **Denuda'tion**, *n.* ruining of soil by erosion etc.

Deo'dorize, *v.t.* to take away smell from. **Deod'orant**, *n.*

Depart', *v.t. & i.* to leave, go away, die. **Depart'ure**, *n.*

Depart'ment, *n.* office or division of business or administration. **Department'al**, *a.*

Depend', *v.i.* to rely, be conditional on. **Depend'able**, *a.* trustworthy, reliable. **Depend'ant**, *n.* someone maintained by another. **Depend'ent**, *a.* conditional on. **Depend'ence**, *n.* **Depend'ency**, *n.* subject country.

Depict', *v.t.* describe, draw, delineate.

Dep'ilate, *v.t.* to remove hairs from. **Depil'atory**, *n.* substance for doing this.

Deplen'ish, *v.t.* to empty, exhaust stock from.

Deplete', *v.t.* to empty, exhaust or run down stocks etc. **Deple'tion**, *n.*

Deplore', *v.t.* to regret greatly, lament. **Deplor'able**, *a.*

Deploy', *v.t. & i. mil.* to change formation from column to line. **Deployment**, *n.* now, general use of resources.

Depo'nent, *n.* witness making deposition; *gram.* verb passive in form but active in meaning.

Depop'ulate, *v.t.* to reduce population. **Depopula'tion**, *n.*

Deport', *v.t.* to banish, send out of country. **Deporta'tion**, *n.*

Deport'ment, *n.* bearing, carriage.

Depose', *v.t. & i.* to remove from office, dethrone; to give sworn evidence. **Deposi'tion**, *n.* sworn evidence.

Depos'it, *v.t.* to put down, leave in keeping of bank etc., give part payment as pledge of good faith. *n.* sediment, money in bank. **Depos'itor**, *n.* **Depos'-**

itary, *n.* person to whom money etc. is consigned. **Depos'itory**, *n.* place for safe-keeping, storehouse.

Dep'ot (-o), *n.* railway yard, mil. barracks or stores, storehouse.

Deprave', *v.t.* to lead astray morally, pervert. **Deprav'ity**, *n.* moral rottenness.

Dep'recate, *v.t.* to disapprove of. **Depreca'tion**, *n.* **Dep'recatory**, *a.*

Depre'ciate, *v.t. & i.* to fall in value, to denigrate. **Deprecia'tion**, *n.* **Depre'ciator**, *n.* person who belittles another. **Depre'ciatory**, *a.*

Depreda'tion, *n.* pillage, plundering. **Dep'reda r**, *n.*

Depress', *v.t.* to deject, lower. **Depres'sion**, *n.* dejection, trade recession, hollow, lowering of barometric pressure.

Deprive', *v.t.* to dispossess, take away from. **Depriva'tion**, *n.*

Depth, *n.* deepness, profundity.

Depute', *v.t.* to delegate, authorize as substitute. **Dep'uty**, *n.* assistant, delegate. **Deputa'tion**, *n.* representative body of people speaking for others. **Dep'utize**, *v.i.* to act for.

Derail', *v.t.* to cause train etc. to leave rails. **Derail'ment**, *n.* accident caused by this.

Derange', *v.t.* to confuse, madden. **Derange'ment**, *n.* disorder, mental disorder.

Der'by (Dar-), *n.* famous horse-race; bowler-hat (Amer.)

Der'elict, *a.* in ruins, abandoned. *n.* something abandoned. **Derelic'tion**, *n.* neglect, esp. of duty.

Deride', *v.t.* to mock at, laugh to scorn. **Deris'ion**, *n.* **Deri'-**

sive, *a*. Deri'sory, *a*. laughable, worthy of scorn.

Derive', *v.t*. & *i*. to originate from, obtain. Deriva'tion, *n*. origin, source. Deriv'ative, *a*. esp. of art, lit., not original, imitative.

Dermati'tis, *n*. inflammation of the skin. Derm'atoid, *a*. skin-like. Dermatol'ogy, *n*. science or study of the skin.

Der'ogate, *v.i*. to detract, disparage. Deroga'tion, *n*. Derog'-atory, *a*. discrediting, disparaging.

Derr'ick, *n*. ship's hoisting-apparatus, crane.

Der'vish, *n*. Muslim friar, holy man.

Des'cant, *n*. melody, song, counterpoint to plainsong. *v.i*. to talk at length and enthusiastically.

Descend', *v.i*. to go or come down, to originate from in ancestry, to attack suddenly, to slope downwards. Descend'-ant, *n*. person descended from another. Descent', *n*. a descending, a sudden attack, line of ancestry.

Describe', *v.t*. to show clearly in words, trace out, follow certain course. *n*. Descrip'tive, *a*. Descrip'tion, *n*. detailed account in words.

Descry', *v.t*. to catch sight of suddenly.

Des'ecrate, *v.t*. to profane, violate holy place. Desecra'-tion, *n*.

Des'ert (Dez-), *n*. a waterless, barren wilderness. *a*.

Desert', *v.t*. & *i*. to forsake, abandon. Deser'tion, *n*. defection to the enemy. Desert'-er, *n*.

Desert', *n*. us. as *n. pl*. virtues, merits, what person deserves.

Deserve' (-zerv), *v.t*. & *i*. to be worthy of, have claim to, merit. Deserv'edly, *adv*. justly. Deserv'ing, *a*. meritorious.

Deshabillé' (dayz-a-bi-yay), undressed.

Des'iccate, *v.t*. & *i*. to dry or become dried up. Desicca-tion, *n*.

Desid'erate, *v.t*. to desire greatly, feel need of. Desidera'tum, *n*. a conscious want or need (*pl*. desiderata).

Design', *v.t*. & *i*. to make working plan or drawing of, to sketch pattern, to intend. *n*. a pattern, scheme, project. Design'er, *n*. craftsman who makes patterns or fashions.

Des'ignate, *v.t*. to appoint, distinguish. *a*. appointed but not yet entered in office. Designa'tion, *n*. title, description.

Desire', *v.t*. & *i*. to wish for greatly, long for, request. *n*. longing, request, object or person wished for. Desi'rable, *a*. pleasing, fitting. Desi'rous, *a*. wishful to do or to have. Desirabil'ity, *n*.

Desist', *v.i*. to cease, refrain from.

Desk, *n*. table with flat or sloping top for writing or reading.

Des'olate, *a*. neglected, barren, abandoned, bare, wretched. *v.t*. to despoil, destroy, make unhappy. Desola'tion, *n*.

Despair', *v.i*. to lose hope. *n*. absence or loss of hope, thing or person causing this. Des'-perate, *a*. very serious or dangerous, without hope. Despera'tion, *n.* **Despera'do** (-ah-), *n.* outlaw, bandit.

Despise', *v.t.* to look down on. **Des'picable**, *a.* contemptible, unworthy.

Despite', *n.* outrage, injury, malice. *prep.* in spite of.

Despoil', *v.t.* to plunder. pillage.

Despond', *v.i.* to lose courage or hope. **Despond'ent,** *a.* **Despond'-ency,** *n.*

Des'pot, *n.* autocrat, tyrant. **Despot'ic**, *a.* **Des'potism**, *n.* autocratic state.

Dessert' (-z), *n.* fruit and sweets served as last course at dinner.

Des'tine (-tin), *v.t.* to set apart, ordain beforehand, decide future. **Des'tiny**, *n.* providence, one's pre-determined future. **Destina'tion**, *n.* place to which a person is going.

Des'titute, *a.* poverty-stricken. **Destitu'tion**, *n.*

Destroy', *v.t.* to wipe out, pull down, efface, demolish. **De-stroy'er**, *n.* fast warship with torpedoes & depth-charges.

Destruc'tion, *n.* great damage, destroying, being destroyed. **Destruc'tive**, *a.* damaging, un-helpful. **Destruc'tor**, *n.*

Des'uetude (Dezwi-), *n.* disuse.

Des'ultory, *a.* intermittent, unco-ordinated.

Detach' (-atch), *v.t.* to separate, unfasten, disconnect. **Detach'-ed**, *a.* separate, disinterested. **Detach'ment**, *n.* small body of soldiers; impartiality.

De'tail, *n.* single part of whole, small item, small group of soldiers for guard duty etc. **Detail'**, *v.t.* to describe fully, to allocate men for duty.

Detain', *v.t.* to hold in custody, to delay, to keep waiting.

Deten'tion, *n.* form of imprison-ment or punishment.

Detect', *v.t.* to find out, find clue, discern. **Detect'or**, *n.* **Detec'tion**, *n.* **Detect'ive**, *n.* policeman or private investi-gator tracking criminals.

Deter', *v.t.* to hinder, dissuade. **Deterr'ent**, *n.* something that deters.

Deter'gent, *n.* substance for superficial cleansing. *a.*

Dete'riorate, *v.t.* & *i.* to make or become worse in condition or quality. **Deteriora'tion**, *n.*

Deter'mine, *v.t.* & *i.* to come to a decision, resolve, fix, ascer-tain, end. **Deter'minable**, *a.* **Deter'minant**, *a.* & *n.* **Deter'-minate**, *a.* limited or fixed. **Determina'tion**, *n.* resolution, clearness of purpose. **Deter'-mined**, *a.* strong-minded. **Deter'minism**, *n.* belief that human life and action is determined by outside forces; opposite of free will.

Detest', *v.t.* to dislike extremely, loathe. **Detest'able,** *a.* **Detesta'-tion**, *n.*

Dethrone', *v.t.* to depose, remove from throne. **Dethrone'-ment**, *n.*

Det'onate, *v.t.* & *i.* to explode with loud report. **Detona'tion**, *n.* **Det'onator**, *n.* device for setting off explosive.

Detour' (Day-toor), *n.* round-about way, deviation.

Detract', *v.t.* & *i.* to disparage, take away from. **Detrac'tion**, *n.* **Detract'or**, *n.*

Detrain', *v.t.* & *i.* to alight or cause to alight from train.

Det'riment, *n.* loss, harm, dis-advantage. **Detrimental**, *a.* harmful.

Detri'tus, *n.* silt, river-debris, gravel.

Deuce (Duce), *n.* card or dice with two spots, score of forty-all in tennis; the devil, mischief in general.

Deval'uate, *v.t.* to reduce value, esp. of currency. **Devalua'tion,** *n.* adjustment of currency to logical level.

Dev'astate, *v.t.* to lay waste, ravage, destroy, **Devasta'tion,** *n.*

Devel'op, *v.t. & i.* to bring or come to fulfilment or maturity, to expand, evolve, start part of photographic process. **Devel'oper,** *n.* **Devel'opment,** *n.* expansion, growth.

De'viate, *v.i.* to turn aside from main course or route. **Devia'tion,** *n.* **De'vious,** *a.* involved, tortuous.

Device', *n.* an apparatus, contrivance, scheme, heraldic emblem. **Devise',** *v.t.* to contrive, plan, work out.

Dev'il, *n.* demon, spirit of evil. *v.t. & i.* to do work for which employer takes credit, esp. barrister. Devil's advocate, *n. fig.* person defending evil. **Dev'ilish,** *a.* wicked, fiendish. **Dev'ilry,** *n.* Devil-may-care, *a.* reckless, carefree. **Dev'il,** *v.t. & i.* to grill and season highly, e.g. kidneys.

Devoid', *a.* empty, completely lacking.

Devolve', *v.t. & i.* to hand on duty etc. to another, transfer. **Devolu'tion,** *n.*

Devote', *v.t.* to apply oneself exclusively, to dedicate, set apart. **Devo'ted,** *a.* loyal or very affectionate. **Devotee',** *n.* enthusiast. **Devo'tion,** *n.* great loyalty or love, dedication, rel. worship. *n. pl.* prayers, worship. **Devo'tional,** *a.* **Devout',** *a.* pious.

Devour', *v.t.* to consume utterly, eat up, destroy. **Devour'er,** *n.*

Dew, *n.* moisture from air forming on ground at night. *v.t. & i.* to form or cover with dew. **Dew'y,** *a.* Dew-drop, *n.* head of moisture hanging from nose. **Dewlap,** *n.* fold of skin under throat of cattle. **Dew'pond,** *n.* artificial downland pond. **Dew-claw,** *n.* rudimentary inner toe of certain dogs.

Dexter'ity, *n.* skill, deftness, right-handedness. **Dex'terous,** *a.* **Dex'ter,** *a.* in heraldry right-hand side of shield from bearer's viewpoint.

Diabe'tes (-tez), *n.* urinary disease with allergy to sugar. **Diabet'ic,** *n.* person suffering from this. *a.*

Diabol'ic, Diabol'ical, *a.* devilish, fiendish. **Diab'olism,** *n.* devil-worship, evil behaviour.

Di'adem, *n.* a crown.

Diaer'esis (Dy-er-), *n.* mark consisting of two dots over vowel to indicate that it is pronounced separately from a preceding vowel.

Diag'nose, *v.t.* to determine nature of disease from symptoms. **Diagno'sis,** *n.* skill or act of doing this. **Diagnos'tic,** *a.* **Diagnosti'cian,** *n.* doctor specializing in diagnosis.

Diag'onal, *a.* oblique, going from corner to corner across middle of rectangle. *n.* diagonal line.

Di'agram, *n.* plan in outline, chart, geometrical figure. **Diagrammat'ic,** *a.*

Di'agraph, *n.* instrument or apparatus for enlarging plans, maps etc. mechanically.

Di'al, *n.* face of a clock, various indicators etc. *v.t.* to call number on telephone, indicate on dial.

Di'alect, *n.* regional variation of a language, accent.

Dialect'ic, *n. us.* as *n.pl.* the art of logical debate or discussion. **Dialec'tical materialism,** *n.* the original doctrine of Communism as expounded by Karl Marx. **Dialecti'cian,** *n.* one skilled in logic.

Di'alogue, *n.* conversation, conversational passage in fiction.

Diam'eter, *n.* transverse measurement, straight line passing through centre of circle. **Diamet'rical,** *a.* directly opposite.

Di'amond, *n.* precious stone of pure carbon, lozenge-shaped formation, suit at cards. **Diamond jubilee, d. wedding,** sixtieth anniversary.

Diapa'son, *n.* swelling burst of harmony, organ-stop, range of voice.

Di'aper, *n.* linen fabric worked with diamond pattern ; towel, napkin, decorate with this. *v.t.* to decorate with diaper.

Diaph'anous, *a.* transparent, gauzy.

Diaph'oretic, drug causing perspiration. *a.*

Di'aphragm (-fram), *n.* muscular wall between chest and stomach; vibrating device in certain apparata.

Di'archy, *n.* government by two separate powers.

Diarrhoe'a (-re-a), *n.* unnatural looseness of bowels.

Di'ary, *n.* record of daily events, opinions; journal for this.

Di'arist, *n.* person who keeps diary.

Di'atribe, *n.* bitterly critical speech.

Dib, *n.* us. *n.pl.* children's game. *sl.* money.

Dib'ble, *n.* gardener's tool for making holes for plants. *v.t.*

Dich'otomy (Dyk-), *n.* division into two, repeated divergence.

Dictate', *v.t. & i.* to utter or read for other person to record in writing; to command authoritatively. **Dic'tate,** *n.* a command. **Dicta'tion,** *n.* **Dicta'tor,** *n.* tyrant. **Dictato'rial,** *a.* tyrannical, overbearing. **Dic'taphone,** *n.* instrument for recording letters etc. dictated.

Dic'tion, *n.* verbal style, choice of words.

Dic'tionary, *n.* a book with alphabetical list of words and their meanings in same or other language.

Didac'tic, *a.* intended to instruct, having the manner of a teacher.

Did'dle, *v.t.* to swindle in mild way.

Die (Dye), *v.i.* to perish, cease to live. **Die'hard,** *n.* person resisting progress to the end.

Die, *n,* small cube with faces numbered with spots from one to six, used for gambling. *pl.* **Dice.** *v.i.* to play or gamble with dice. **Die,** *n.* engraved stamp for embossing notepaper, making coin etc. *pl.* **Dies.**

Die'sel (Deezl), *a.* of internal combustion engine powered by crude oil. *n.*

Di'et, *n.* the food one lives on, prescribed way of feeding. *v.t. & i.* to restrict amount & kind of food. **Di'etary,** *n.* al-

lowance of food. *a.* of diet.
Dietet'ic, *a.* as *n.pl.* the science
of diet. **Dieti'cian**, *n.* medical
expert in dietetics.
Di'et, *n.* equivalent of parliament in some countries.
Diff'er, *v.i.* to disagree, be different from. **Diff'erence**, *n.*
unlikeness, what is left after
part has been subtracted. **Diff'-
erent**, *a.* unlike. **Differen'tial**,
n. mechanical device enabling
rear wheels of motor-car to
revolve at different speed for
rounding corners ; difference
in wages between skilled &
unskilled. **Differen'tiate**, *v.t.* &
i. to distinguish between, make
difference clear. **Differentia'-
tion**, *n.*
Diff'icult, *a.* hard to do or understand, involved. **Diff'iculty**, *n.*
obstacle, hindrance, matter
hard to overcome.
Diff'idence, *n.* shyness, disinter-
estedness, lack of self-
confidence. **Diff'ident**, *a.*
Diffuse' (-fuze), *v.t.* & *i.* to give
forth, shed. **Diffuse'** (-s), *a.*
imprecise, verbose. **Diffu'sion**,
n. **Diffu'sive**, *a.*
Dig, *v.t.* & *i.* to open up soil,
excavate, delve into.
Digest', *v.t.* & *i.* to pass food
through natural processes, to
take in, meditate on. **Di'gest**,
n. a summary. **Digest'ible**, *a.*
Digest'ive, *a.* **Diges'tion**, *n.*
Dig'it (Dij-), *n.* finger or toe,
any figures nought to nine.
Dig'nify, *v.t.* to give or do honour
to, exalt, make worthy. **Dig'-
nity**, *n.* stateliness, worthy behaviour, a person with these
qualities or in high office. **Dig'-
nitary**, *n.* person in high church
office etc.

Digress', *v.i.* to deviate from
subject, turn aside verbally.
Digres'sion, *n.*
Dihe'dral, *a.* solid or shape with
two plane faces.
Dike, Dyke, *n.* embankment
against water, ditch.
Dilap'idate, *v.t.* & *i.* to bring or
fall into ruined state. **Dilap'-
idated**, *a.* neglected, tumbling
down. **Dilapida'tion**, *n.*
Dilate' (Dy-), *v.t.* & *i.* to expand,
to make or become larger, to
talk at length on. **Dila'tion**, *n.*
Dil'atory, *a.* slack, inclined to
delay or put off. **Dil'atori-
ness**, *n.*
Dilem'ma, *n.* an embarrassing or
difficult choice, position in
which this happens.
Dilettan'te (Dilli-tanti), *n.* devotee of or expert in the fine
arts, esp. in amateur sense.
pl. -ti.
Dil'igence, *n.* unremitting application, painstaking work.
Dil'igent, *a.* industrious.
Dilute', *v.t.* to decrease strength
by adding water. **Dilu'ted**, *a.*
Dilu'tion, *n.*
Dim, *a.* obscure, indistinct. *v.t.*
& *i.* to make or become obscure.
Dimen'sion, *n.* size, extent,
measurement. **Dimen'sional**, *a.*
Dimin'ish, *v.t.* & *i.* to lessen,
make or become smaller. **Di-
minu'tion**, *n.* **Dimin'utive**, *a.*
tiny.
Dim'ple, *n.* small hollow in chin
or cheek.
Din, *n.* loud discordant sound.
v.t. & *i.* to assail with noise,
to repeat something continually.
Dine, *v.t.* & *i.* to take dinner, to
give dinner to. **Di'ning room**, *n.*
room where meals are eaten.

Di'ning-car, di'ner, *n.* restaurant-car on train. **Di'ner,** *n.* person eating dinner.

Din'ghy (Ding-ee), *n.* small sailing-boat.

Din'gle, *n.* small wooded dell or hollow.

Din'gy (-ji), drab, shabby. **Din'giness,** *n.*

Dinn'er, *n.* main meal of day.

Dint, *n.* form of dent. **By dint of,** by force or reason of.

Di'ocese, *n.* district under jurisdiction of bishop. **Dioc'esan,** *a.* of this. *n.* bishop, priest or member of diocese.

Dio'rama, *n.* scenic painting with effects provided by special lighting.

Diox'ide, *n. chem.* compound containing two parts oxygen and one part of metal.

Dip, *v.t. & i.* to go lower, to immerse briefly in liquid, slope downwards. a slope, a bathe. **Dip'stick,** *n.* gauge for measuring liquid in tank.

Diphther'ia, *n.* dangerous infectious disease of throat.

Diph'thong, *n.* union of two vowels to form a compound sound.

Diplo'ma, *n.* official document proving person's qualification, academic certificate.

Diplo'macy, *n.* the practice of peaceful international relations. **Dip'lomat,** *n.* official representative in this. **Diplo'matist,** *n.* **Diplomat'ic,** *a.* tactful, to do with conduct of foreign relations.

Dipsoma'nia, *n.* uncontrollable addiction to alcohol. **Dipsoman'iac,** *n.*

Dip'tych (-tik), *n.* painting on two hinged wooden boards.

Dire, *a.* terrible, dangerous, acute.

Direct', *v.t. & i.* to order, keep under control, show way to, address letter etc. *a.* straight, undeviating, forthright. **Direc'tion,** *n.* instruction, command, guidance, course. **Direct'or,** *n.* one who directs, member of controlling body of organization, manager. **Direct'orship,** *n.* **Direct'ory,** *n.* book containing names, addresses of residents and businesses in town etc.

Dirge, *n.* a lament, a funeral song.

Dir'igible, *a.* of something that can be steered or directed. *n.* airship.

Dirk, *n.* dagger worn by Highlanders.

Dirt, *n.* filth, dust, foulness in general, earth. **Dirt'y,** *a.*

Dis-, pref. with various meanings us. neg., apart from, not, reverse, deprivation, the cancelling of an action etc., opposite of main word, e.g. **disarray, disarticulate, disassimilation, disavow, disband, disbelieve, disbench, disburden, discolour, discompose, disconnect, discontinue, discourage, discountenance, discredit,** etc.

Disa'ble, *v.t.* to cripple, incapacitate, render unfit. **Disabil'ity,** *n.* an incapacity, an obstacle.

Disabuse', *v.t.* to disillusion, undeceive.

Disas'ter, *n.* terrible and sudden mishap. **Disas'trous,** *a.*

Disburse', *v.t. & i.* to pay out money officially. **Disbursement',** *n.*

Discard', *v.t. & i.* to throw away, get rid of, take off.

Discern, *v.t.* to perceive, distinguish. **Discern'ment,** *n.* perception, insight. **Discern'ible,** *a.*

Discharge', *v.t.* to dismiss, release, unload cargo from ship etc.

Disci'ple, *n.* follower, esp. in rel. sense.

Dis'cipline, *n.* obedience to rule, to the dictates of conscience, strict training of character, a system of rules. *v.t.* to train to obedience, keep under control. **Dis'ciplinary,** *a.*

Discom'fit (-kum), *v.t.* to upset, defeat, throw into confusion. **Discom'fiture,** *n.*

Disconcert', *v.t.* to confuse, disturb self-possession.

Discon'solate, *a.* forlorn, downcast.

Dis'cord, *n.* lack of harmony. **Discord'ant,** *a.* not in agreement, unharmonious.

Dis'count, *n.* reduction on price charged. **Discount',** *v.t.* to lessen, leave out of consideration, ignore.

Dis'course, *n.* a speech, weighty conversation. **Discourse',** *v.t.* to speak, utter at length.

Discov'er, *v.t.* to find out, reveal. **Discov'ery,** *n.* **Discov'erer,** *n.*

Discreet', *a.* tactful, careful in speech and action. **Discre'tion,** *n.*

Discrep'ancy, *n.* a faulty difference, a sum lacking between two sets of accounts or figures, a conflicting statement.

Discrim'inate, *v.t. & i.* to distinguish difference between, to judge between good and evil. **Discrimina'tion,** *n.*

Discurs'ive, *a.* deviating from the main subject.

Dis'cus, *n.* athletics throwing disk.

Discuss, *v.t.* to talk about, exchange views on. **Discus'sion,** *n.*

Disdain', *n.* contempt, feeling of superiority. *v.t.* to scorn, look upon as inferior. **Disdain'ful,** *a.*

Disease', *n.* sickness of malignant, infectious or contagious nature. **Diseased',** *a.* decaying, rotten, infected.

Disfig'ure, *v.t.* to mar or injure. **Disfig'urement,** *n.*

Disgrace', *n.* shame, cause of shame, dishonour. *v.t.* to bring dishonour to. **Disgrace'ful,** *a.*

Disgrun'tled, *a.* vexed, dissatisfied.

Disguise' (-gyze), *v.t.* to conceal real appearance or identity, misrepresent. *n.* false appearance.

Disgust', *n.* strong distaste or dislike, loathing. *v.t.* to offend by unpleasant behaviour, taste etc.

Dish, *n.* shallow utensil for holding or cooking food; food cooked and served in a particular way.

Dishev'elled (Di-shev-), *a.* with ruffled hair.

Disinfect'ant, *n.* chemical germicide for protection against infection. **Disinfect',** *v.t.* **Disinfec'tion,** *n.*

Dis'locate, *v.t.* to put out of joint, disarrange. **Disloca'tion,** *n.*

Dis'mal, *a.* gloomy, depressing.

Disman'tle, *v.t.* to strip of furnishings, take to pieces.

Dismay', *v.t.* to discourage. *n.* consternation.

Dismiss', *v.t.* to send away, discharge from job or duty, put from mind. **Dismiss'al,** *n.*

Disown', *v.t.* to refuse to acknowledge.

Dispar'age, *v.t.* to speak slightingly of, to belittle. **Dispar'agement**, *n.*

Dis'parate, *a.* completely different, opposite.

Dispas'sionate, *n.* phlegmatic, unemotional.

Dispatch', **Despatch'**, *n.* official message. *v.t.* to send off.

Dispel', *v.t.* to drive away, clear away.

Dispense', *v.t. & i.* to deal out, to distribute, make up medicine, do without. **Dispens'er**, *n.* doctor's assistant or chemist who makes up medicines. **Dispens'ary**, *n.* place where this is done.

Dispensa'tion, *n.* religious exemption or pardon.

Disperse', *v.t. & i.* to scatter, drive off, break up (of crowd etc.). **Dispers'al**, *n.*

Dispir'it, *v.t.* to discourage, depress.

Displace', *v.t.* to remove from position or office, to take the place of, put in place of.

Display', *n.* exhibition, show. *v.t.*

Dispose', *v.t. & i.* to get rid of, settle, arrange, to feel inclined. **Disposi'tion**, *n.* arrangement, inclination, temperament. **Dispos'al**, *n.*

Dispute', *v.t. & i.* to argue, oppose, call in question, *n.* **Disputa'tion**, *n.* learned discussion.

Disquisi'tion, *n.* a learned discourse or treatise.

Disrupt', *v.t.* to break violently, shatter, disturb. **Disrup'tive**, *a.* **Disrup'tion**, *n.*

Dissect', *v.t.* to cut up body for anatomical examination, to examine minutely. **Dissec'tion**, *n.*

Dissem'ble, *v.t. & i.* to disguise feelings, deceive.

Dissem'inate, *v.t.* to sow, scatter abroad. **Dissemina'tion**, *n.*

Dissent', *v.t.* to disagree, differ in opinion. **Dissen'sion**, *n.*

Disserta'tion, *n.* learned address.

Diss'ident, *a.* disagreeing, conflicting. **Diss'idence**, *n.*

Dissim'ulate, *v.t. & i.* to dissemble, pretend not to have, deceive. **Dissimula'tion**, *n.*

Diss'ipate, *v.t. & i.* to waste, squander, disperse. **Dissipa'tion**, *n.* corrupt way of life.

Disso'ciate, *v.t.* to separate from, disavow. **Dissocia'tion**, *n.*

Dissolve', *v.t. & i.* to cause to become decomposed, esp. in liquid, put an end to, vanish, melt. **Dissolu'tion**, *n.* disintegration, official termination of e.g. parliament. **Diss'olute**, *a.* depraved. **Dissolu'tion**, *n.* laxity of morals, loose living.

Diss'onance, *n.* discord, disharmony. **Diss'onant**, *a.*

Dissuade' (-swaid), *v.t.* to persuade not to, advise against. **Dissua'sion**, *n.* **Dissua'sive**, *a.*

Dis'tance, *n.* length of space between two points. **Dis'tant**, *a.* far off, aloof.

Distaste', *n.* dislike, aversion. **Distaste'ful**, *a.* unpleasant.

Distend', *v.t. & i.* to swell out. **Disten'sion**, *n.*

Distil', *v.t. & i.* to heat substance till it turns to vapour, cool till it condenses and collect liquid so obtained ; draw out the essence of. **Distilla'tion**, *n.* **Distill'er**, *n.* manufacturer of whisky etc.

Distinct', *a.* clear, quite separate, sharp. **Distinc'tion**, *n.* characteristic difference, making such a difference, distinguished in character, status, etc.

Distin'guish, *v.t. & i.* to tell difference between, to recognize, to draw a distinction. **Distin'guishable**, *a.* **Distin'guished**, *a.* celebrated, eminent.

Distort', *v.t.* to misrepresent, falsify, twist out of shape. **Distor'tion**, *n.*

Distract', *v.t.* to divert, interrupt concentration, bewilder. **Distrac'tion**, *n.* relaxation, interruption of concentration. **Distract'ed**, *a.* frantic, maddened.

Distrait' (-tray), *a.* distracted, vague, absent-minded.

Distraught', *a.* highly anxious, distressed, crazy.

Distress', *n.* great trouble, grief. *v.t.*

Distrib'ute, *v.t.* to give out. **Distribu'tion**, *n.*

Dis'trict, *n.* region, locality, area of administration.

Distrust', *v.t.* to suspect, not to trust.

Disturb', *v.t.* to disarrange, to interrupt, trouble, upset, worry. **Disturb'ance**, *n.* disorder, commotion.

Ditch, *n.* long narrow drainage trench.

Diur'nal, *a.* of or in the daytime, daily.

Divan', *n.* long backless sofa convertible into bed.

Dive, *v.i.* to plunge into esp. water. *n. sl.* an underground bar, to descend suddenly, to dip. **Di'ver**, *n.* esp. as one who descends into sea-depths.

Diverge', *v.t. & i.* to separate, go in different directions. **Diver'gence**, *n.* **Diver'gent**, *a.*

Di'vers, *a.* sundry, several. **Diverse'**, *a.* different, varied. **Divers'ity**, *n.* great variety. **Diversifica'tion**, *n.*

Divert', *v.t.* to amuse, distract, turn aside, ward off. **Diver'sion**, *n.*

Divest', *v.t.* to dispossess, strip, unclothe.

Divide', *v.t.* to separate, cut up or deal out in separate parts. **Divis'ion**, *n.* act of dividing, part of whole, large army organization, a vote in parliament. **Divis'ible**, *a.* **Divis'ional**, *a.* **Divi'sor**, *n.*

Divine', *a.* sacred, heavenly, pertaining to God. *n.* a clergyman or theologian. **Divin'ity**, *n.* a god, the study of theology.

Divine', *v.t. & i.* to guess, perceive. **Divi'ner**, *n.* esp. as wa'ter diviner, *n.* person with ability to discover underground water. **Divining-rod**, *n.* rod of hazelwood which he uses for this.

Divorce', *n.* legal separation of husband & wife. *v.t.* to separate in this way.

Divulge', *v.t.* to make known, reveal a secret.

Dizz'y, *a.* have dazed or unsteady feeling.

Do, *v.t. & i.* perform, accomplish, act, be adequate, progress.

Do'cile, *a.* passive, submissive, easily led. **Docil'ity**, *n.*

Dock, *v.t.* to cut short, esp. of horse's tail.

Dock, *n.* harbour, quay, *v.t. & i.* to bring or go into dock.

Doc'tor, *n.* graduate holding degree or doctorate in medicine, philosophy, music or other faculty; one who practises medicine. **Doc'torate**, *n.*

Doc'trine, *n.* the teaching of or beliefs in religion, what is taught. **Doctri'nal**, *a.*

Docu'ment, *n.* official declaration or certificate.

Dodge, *v.t. & i.* to avoid, swerve away from, *n.* a trick, deceit, idea.

Doe (Doh), *n.* female of deer, rabbit etc.

Dog, *n.* four-legged domesticated animal. *v.t.* to pursue or follow closely. **Dogg'ed**, *a.* persistent, sedulously resolute.

Dogg'erel, *n.* slipshod poetry us. of satirical kind.

Dog'ma, *n.* authoritative belief, body of rel. beliefs. **Dogmat'ic**, *a.* pertaining to dogma, arrogant in assertion of beliefs, intolerant. **Dog'matism**, *n.*

Dol'drums, *n.pl.* region of calms and light winds near equator difficult for sailing-ships to proceed in; *fig.* state of depression.

Dole, *n.* charitable or official dealing out of money for poor or unemployed. *v.t.* to deal out sparingly.

Dole'ful, *a.* dismal, disconsolate.

Doll, *n.* miniature model of human as child's toy. *v.t.* to dress up smartly.

Dol'phin, *n.* highly intelligent sea-mammal.

Dolt, *n.* idiot, stupid fellow.

Domain', *n.* lands or territory ruled over by landlord.

Dome, *n.* rounded roof.

Domes'tic, *a.* of the home, of animals trained by man for work, of home affairs as opposed to foreign. *v.t.* **Domes'-ticate**, *v.t.* to train for home purposes. **Domestica'tion**, *n.* **Domestic'ity**, *n.*

Dom'icile, *n.* person's usual residence, esp. as termed in official documents.

Dom'inate, *v.t. & i.* to overshadow, overlook, control, exert influence over. **Domma'tion**, *n.* **Domin'ion**, *n.* supreme power, sovereignty.

Don, *v.t.* to put on clothes.

Don, *n.* fellow or tutor in university.

Donate', *v.t.* to give to fund, subscribe. **Dona'tion**, *n.* gift of money.

Donk'ey, *n.* an ass; stupid person.

Doom, *n.* destiny, fate, ruin. *v.t.* to condemn.

Door, *n.* hinged entrance to room or building.

Dope, *n.* opiate, drug. *v.t.* to drug, render senseless. **Dope-peddler**, *n.* person who traffics in drugs.

Dorm'ant, *a.* inactive, in state of sleep or suspension. **Dorm'-ancy**, *n.*

Dorm'itory, *n.* bedroom for several persons.

Dor'mouse, *n.* hibernating rodent.

Dor'sal, *a.* pertaining to the back.

Dose, *n.* amount of medicine prescribed. *v.t.* to administer this. **Dos'age**, *n.*

Dote, *v.t.* to be foolishly fond of, to sentimentalize over, to be weak-minded through age. **Do'-tage**, *n.* senility.

Dott'le, *n.* tobacco left in pipe.

Dou'ble, *a.* in two parts, twice as much as. *n.* person exactly like someone else. *v.t.* to fold in two, increase in quantity or size by as much again, perform two parts in same play.

Doubt (Dowt), *v.t. & i.* to mistrust, be uncertain of, suspect. **Doubt'ful,** *a.* **Doubt'less,** *a.* certainly.

Dought'y, *a. arch.* bold, valiant.

Dour, *a.* stubborn, grim.

Douse (Dowse), *v.t.* to drench, put out light.

Dove, *n.* bird of pigeon family. **Dovecote,** *n.* house or loft for doves. **Dove'tail,** *n.* in carpentry a joint made by tenon & mortise. *v.t. & i.* to fit together closely.

Dow'ager, *n.* widow of titled person, e.g. **dowager marchioness, dowager queen** etc. *coll.* stately matron.

Dow'dy, *a.* drab, dull, ill-kempt.

Dow'er, *n.* a widow's portion.

Dow'ry, *n.* a wedding portion, property bride brings on marriage.

Down, *n.* stretch of undulating open grassland.

Down, *n.* soft inner feathers of birds.

Down, *adv.* to a lower position, in same direction as, in a prone position, *prep.* along, to or towards a lower level, at a lower level. **Down'cast,** *a.* dejected, directed down. **Down'-fall,** *n.* defeat, ruin, disgrace heavy rain. **Down'pour,** *n.* heavy rain. **Down'right,** *a. & adv.* thorough, utter. **Down'-trodden,** *n.* oppressed, feeble.

Doze, *v.i.* to sleep lightly, be almost asleep. *n.* a nap.

Dozen, *n. & a.* twelve.

Drab, *a.* dowdy, colourless. *n.* an ill-kempt woman.

Draft, *n.* detachment of troops, new batch of recruits, outline of scheme, moneyorder. *v.t.*

Drag, *v.t. & i.* to draw along with difficulty, proceed slowly, search with net, esp. of pond or river. *n.* a brake, a hindrance.

Drag'on, *n.* kind of pigeon and lizard, mythical monster.

Dragoon', *n.* sort of cavalryman. *v.t.* to coerce.

Drake, *n.* male duck.

Dra'ma, *n.* theatrical piece or composition, exciting event. **Dramat'ic,** *a.* of drama, striking, exciting. **Dram'atist,** *n.* writer of theatrical plays. **Dram'atize,** *v.t.* to turn into drama, to exaggerate.

Drape, *v.t.* to cover loosely with cloth, to arrange cloth in folds. **Dra'per,** *n.* merchant who deals in cloths and fabrics, etc. **Dra'pery,** *n.*

Dras'tic, *a.* severe, rigorous.

Draught (Draft), *n.* current of air, long drink. **Draught'y,** *a.* uncomfortable because of current of air.

Draughts'man, *n.* skilled designer. **Draughts'manship,** *n.*

Draw, *v.t. & i.* to pull along, to attract, to take up water, take out money, depict.

Drawl, *v.t. & i.* to speak lazily or slowly. *n.*

Dray, *n.* low cart with sides.

Dread (Dred), *n.* great fear, terror. *v.t.* to fear greatly, hold in awe. **Dread'ful,** *a.* shocking.

Dream, *n.* a vision during sleep, a hopeful fancy or wish. *v.t. & i.*

Drear'y, *a.* dull, dismal, drab, boring.

Dredge, *v.t.* to scrape or clear bottom, esp. of sea or river, to bring up from bottom. **Dredg'-**

er, *n.* ship with mechanical buckets for clearing channel or harbour.

Dregs, *n. pl.* worthless sediment, base part.

Drench, *v.t.* to soak, give purgative medicine to cattle.

Dress, *v.t. & i.* to put on clothes, prepare, apply dressing, correct alignment of ranks of parading troops.

Drift, *n.* tendency of conversation or sea etc., snow driven by wind. *v.i.* to move while out of control, to act in haphazard way. **Drif'ter,** *n.* kind of fishing-boat which drifts with nets out.

Drill, *n.* tool for boring holes. *v.t.* to use this.

Drill, *n.* exercise for troops. *v.t.* to exercise troops on parade, to smarten, instill sense of discipline.

Drink, *v.t. & i.* to swallow liquid, partake of alcohol frequently. *n.*

Drip, *v.t. & i.* to fall or let fall in drops. *n.* a tiny amount of liquid, drop. *coll.* person who is always complaining.

Drive, *v.t. & i.* to ride in vehicle, to go, to force on, impel. *n.* energy, forcefulness, a ride in a vehicle, an organized shoot when game is driven towards guns.

Driv'el, *n.* nonsense, idiotic talk. *v.t.*

Droll, *a.* oddly amusing.

Drom'edary, *n.* riding-camel.

Drone, *n.* honeybee that does not work but only mates with queen, lazy person, humming sound, dreary tone. *v.t. & i.* to talk or hum in monotonous fashion.

Droop, *v.t. & i.* to wilt, hang limply, tire.

Drop, *n.* small round globule of liquid, small amount. *v.t. & i.* to fall or let fall, to fall in drops.

Dross, *n.* scum of molten metal, worthless part, impurity.

Drought (Drowt), *n.* long period without rain, great thirst.

Drove, *n.* flock of cattle, pathway along which cattle are habitually driven. **Dro'ver,** *n.* shepherd or stockman who drives animals across country to market etc.

Drown, *v.t. & i.* to suffocate or cause to suffocate in water; make inaudible by louder sound.

Drow'sy, *a.* sleepy, dull, not fully awake. **Drowse,** *v.i.* to doze.

Drub, *v.t.* to beat, thrash, defeat. **Drubb'ing,** *n.* a beating.

Drudge, *v.i.* to work hard and monotonously. **Drudg'ery,** *n.* mean, uninteresting work.

Drug, *n.* medical substance for relieving pain or deadening senses. *v.t.* to administer drug.

Drum, *n. mus.* percussion instrument of skin stretched on round frame and beaten with knobbed sticks; any object shaped like a drum, an oil-barrel. *v.t. & i.* **to beat a drum,** to beat or throb continually.

Drunk, *a.* intoxicated. *n.* person under influence of alcohol. *fig. a.* in grip of strong emotion, e.g. **drunk with desire.**

Dry, *a.* not wet, arid, without rain, uninteresting.

Du'al, *a.* twofold, double, in a pair.

Dub, *v.t.* to name, nickname, confer knighthood on.

Du′bious, *a.* doubtful, open to question. **Dubi′ety,** *n.*

Duck, *n.* short-legged water-bird of various kinds; *coll.* a nice person. *v.t. & t.* to plunge into water, to stoop to avoid something.

Duct, *n.* conduit, tube, channel.

Duct′ile, *a.* malleable, capable of being drawn into wire.

Dud, *n.* shell or bomb that fails to explode, anything that fails.

Dude, *n.* dandy, fop.

Dudg′eon, *n.* offence, anger, indignation.

Due, *a.* owing, merited, proper, timed for. *n.* fair share, charge. **Du′ly.** *a.*

Du′el, *n.* fight with weapons between two persons over question of honour; *fig.* a keen contest, dispute. *v.i.* **Du′ellist,** *n.*

Duet′, *n.* piece of mus. for two performers.

Duke, *n.* highest rank in nobility. **Du′cal,** *a.* **Duch′ess,** *n.* wife of duke.

Dul′cet, *a.* sweet sounding.

Dul′cimer, *n.* stringed mus. instrument played with special hammers.

Dull, *a.* unclear, overclouded, sluggish, stupid. **Dull′ard,** *n.* blockhead, stupid person.

Dumb, *a.* bereft of power of speech, silent, *sl.* stupid. **Dumb′-bell,** *n.* a weight for muscular exercise. **Dumbfound′,** *v.t.* to astonish, disconcert.

Dumm′y, *n.* model for fitting clothes, imitation construction or object, baby's rubber teat, useless, lifeless person, imaginary player at bridge. *v.i.* at rugby football to pretend to pass the ball.

Dump, *n.* a rubbish-tip, a dull place, a depot. *v.t.* to put down in heap, to export cheap goods in mass.

Dump′ling, *n.* small round suet pudding with various contents.

Dun, *a.* of dull grey-brown colour.

Dun, *v.t.* to press persistently for payment of debts. *n.* person who does this.

Dunce, *n.* slow-witted person.

Dune, *n.* long mound of sand.

Dun′derhead, *n.* blockhead, stupid person.

Dung, *n.* animal excrement, farmyard manure.

Dun′garee, *n.* us. as *n. pl.* overalls.

Dun′geon, *n.* underground cell in castle or fortress.

Dupe, *n.* person deceived, victim of fraud. *v.t.* to cheat.

Du′rable, *a.* strong, long lasting, resisting wear and tear. **Durabil′ity,** *n.*

Du′rance, *n.* imprisonment. **Du′ress,** *n.* restraint, illegal compulsion.

Du′ring, *prep.* in course of, in time of.

Dusk, *n.* later stage of twilight preceding darkness. **Dusk′y,** *a.* dark-coloured.

Dust, *n.* powder, fine particles of sand, dry soil etc. *v.t.* to sprinkle with dust, to wipe clean of dust. **Dust′er,** *n.* small cloth for wiping furniture.

Du′ty, *n.* obligation, function, customs or excise tax.

Dwarf, *n.* undersized, stunted person or creature, miniature plant. *a. v.t.* to overshadow, cause to seem small by comparison. **Dwarf'ish,** *a.*

Dwell, *v.i.* to reside, fix thoughts on, talk or write at length on. **Dwell'ing,** *n.* house, abode.

Dwin'dle, *v.i.* to diminish, grow less.

Dye, *n. chem.* or vegetable matter for colouring. *v.t.* to colour with this. **Dye'ing,** *n.* **Dy'er,** *n.*

Dynam'ic, *a.* of force, forceful, energetic. *n. pl.* branch of physics relating to force as producing motion or power.

Dy'namite, *n.* high explosive made with nitro-glycerine. *v.t.* to blow up with this.

Dy'namo, *n.* electrical generator, machine for conversion of energy.

Dyn'asty (Din-), *n.* succession of rulers of same ancestry. **Dynas'-tic,** *a.*

Dys'entery (Dis-), *n.* serious bowel disease.

Dyspep'sia, (Dis-). *n.* indigestion. **Dyspep'tic,** *a. & n.*

E

Each, *a. & pron.* every one taken separately.

Ea'ger, *a.* ardent, enthusiastic, keenly desirous. **Eag'erness,** *n.*

Ea'gle, *n.* large predatory bird famous for keen sight. **Ea'glet,** *n.* young eagle.

Ea'gre (-ger), *n.* large tidal wave in estuary, bore.

Ear, *n.* organ of hearing; *mus.* appreciation, attention. **Ear'-mark,** *n.* mark in sheep or other animal's ear to denote ownership. *v.t.* to mark in this way, to assign for special purpose or use. **Ear'shot,** *n.* hearing distance.

Ear, *n.* head of corn.

Earl (Erl), *n.* nobleman ranking above viscount and below marquis. **Earl'dom,** *n.*

Earl'y (Erl-), *adv. & a.* soon, in good time, beginning, not late good time, beginning, not late.

Earn (Ern), *v.t.* to receive as reward for labour or effort.

Earn'ings, *n. pl.* wages, salary.

Earn'est (Ern-), *a.* serious, sincere, *n.* a sum paid to show good faith before completion of transaction, a pledge.

Earth, *n.* the world, this planet, soil, fox's den. *v.t. & i.* to cover with earth, to connect elec. apparatus with ground as safety measure. **Earth'en,** *a.* **Earth'enware,** *n.* baked clay, vessels made of this. **Earth'-quake,** *n.* violent convulsion of earth's surface. **Earth'work,** *n.* prehist. or mediaeval fortification. **Earth'ly,** *a.* material, not spiritual. **Earth'y,** *a.* coarse, unrefined.

Ease, *n.* comfort, freedom from pain or trouble, idleness, informality. *v.t. & i.* to make easier, relieve from pain, slacken, relax. **Ease'ful,** *a.* **Eas'y,** *a.* not difficult. **Eas'ily,** adv. **Eas'y-going,** *a.* not hard to please, tolerant.

Eas'el, *n.* frame for supporting artist's painting or school blackboard.

East, *n.* quarter in which sun rises, countries of the eastern part of world. *a. & adv.* to or from the east. **East'erly,** *a. & adv.* towards the east, from the east. **Eas'tern,** *n.* of or dwelling in eastern country. **East'erner,** *n.* **East'ward (s),** *a. adv. & n.*

East'er, *n.* Christian festival of the Resurrection.

Eat, *v.t. & i.* to consume food, chew and swallow, destroy gradually. **Eat'able,** *a.* **Eat'-ables,** *n. pl.* food in general.

Eaves, *n. pl.* projecting and overhanging edge of roof. **Eaves'dropper,** *n.* person who listens secretly.

Ebb, *n.* the outflowing movement of a tide. *v.i.* to flow back.

Eb'ony, *n.* kinds of very hard black wood. *a.*

Ebull'ient, *a.* exuberant, boiling. **Ebull'ience,** *n.* **Ebull'ition,** *n.* bubbling outburst.

Eccen'tric (Eks-), *a.* odd, irregular, peculiar, whimsical. *n.* an unconventional person with unusual tastes. **Eccentri'city,** *n.*

Ecclesias'tical, *a.* pertaining to the church.

Ech'elon (Esh-), *n.* formation of troops in series of steps.

Ech'o (Ek-), *n.* repetition of sound by reflection, an imitation. *v.t. & i.* to resound, emit echo.

Eclat (A-kla), *n.* striking effect, verve.

Eclec'tic, *a.* selecting the best from various sources, esp. of philosophy, of broad views. *n.*

Eclipse', *n.* a complete or partial darkening of sun or moon etc. by another astral body. *v.t.* to obscure, blot out, surpass. **Eclip'tic,** *a.*

E'cology, *n.* study of living organisms and their habits in relation to their habitat. **E'cologist,** *n.*

Econ'omy, *n.* regulation and management of the resources of a country, the best use of resources in general, lack of waste, thrift. **Econom'ic,** *a.* **Econom'ics,** *n. pl.* science of planning nation's resources. **Econom'ical,** *a.* frugal, thrifty. **Econ'omist,** *n.* expert in economics. **Econ'omize,** *v.t. & i.* to live or plan more sparingly, to lessen expenditure.

Ec'stasy, *n.* rapturous delight, great joy, emotional frenzy. **Ecstat'ic,** *a.*

Ec'toplasm, *n.* emanation from spiritualistic medium.

Ec'zema, *n.* disease of the skin.

Edd'y, *n.* small whirl of smoke or water. *v.t. & i.* to move round and round, whirl.

Edge, *n.* border, limit, cutting side of knife etc. *v.t.* to provide with edge or border, sharpen, proceed gradually. **Edge'ways, Edge'wise,** *adv.*

Ed'ible, *a.* eatable. **Edibil'ity,** *n.*

E'dict, *n.* a decree, authoritative order.

Ed'ifice (-fiss), *n.* large building, esp. church etc.

Ed'ify, *v.t.* to teach, instruct, evoke moral improvement. **Edifica'tion,** *n.*

Ed'it, *v.t.* to prepare, gather for publication, oversee production of magazine or newspaper, arrange final version of film, radio programme etc. **Edi'tion,** *n.* form in which book is published and number of copies published at one time, an issue. Ed'itor, *n.* person who edits or manages magazine etc. Edito'rial, *a. n.* official article stating views of newspaper.

Ed'ucate, *v.t.* to train by teaching, to instruct scholastically, to bring up. Educa'tion, *n.* Educa'tional, *a.* Ed'ucator, *n.* Educa'tionist, *n.* person skilled in or advocating education. Ed'ucative, *a.* instructive, helpful to learning.

Educe', *v.t.* to deduce, infer, bring out.

Eel, *n.* kinds of serpent-like fish.

Ee'rie, *a.* uncanny, unnerving, weird.

Efface', *v.t.* to wipe out, rub out, cause to disappear. Efface'-ment, *n.*

Effect, *n.* the consequence or result of action or thought, impression. *n. pl.* movable property, possession. *v.t.* to bring about, accomplish. Effect'ive, *a.* striking, having effect. *n. pl.* troops ready for action. Effect'ual, *a.* answering purpose. Effect'uate, *v.t.* to fulfil, put into effect.

Effem'inate, *a.* unmanly, womanly as applied to men.

Effervesce' (-vess), *v.i.* to froth up, give off bubbles. Efferves'-cent, *a.* Efferves'cence, *n.*

Effete', *a.* spent, worn out, degenerate.

Effica'cious, *a.* effective, producing result. Eff'icacy, *n.*

Effi'cient, *a.* able, competent, capable. Effi'ciency, *n.*

Eff'igy, *n.* image, likeness.

Eff'luent, *n.* tributary flowing from larger river or lake, sewage tank. *a.* flowing out. Eff'luence, *n.* a flowing out.

Efflu'vium, *n.* poisonous vapour. *pl.* -via.

Eff'ort, *n.* attempt, endeavour, exertion. Effortless, *a.* without difficulty.

Effront'ery (-frun-), *n.* gross impertinence.

Efful'gent, *a.* radiant, shining forth. Efful'gence, *n.*

Effu'sion, *n.* an outpouring; *iron.* a literary composition. Effu'sive, *a.* talkative, demonstrative. Effuse, *v.t.* to shed, pour out.

Egg, *n.* oval body containing germ of young and produced by birds etc.

Egg, *v.t.* esp. as to Egg on, to encourage.

Eg'o, *n.* the self. Eg'oism, *n.* self-opinionation, theory that bases morality on self-interest. Eg'-oist, *n.* Egois'tic, *a.* Eg'otism, *n.* self-praise in obsessive way. Eg'otist, *n.*

Egre'gious, *a.* outstanding in an unfortunate way.

E'gress, *n.* right of going out, way out.

Eight (Ait), *a. & n.* cardinal number one above seven. Eighth, *a.* ordinal number. Eight'fold, *a.* Eighteen, *a. & n.* eight more than ten. Eight'y, *a. & n.* ten times eight.

Eith'er, *a. & pron.* one or the other, one of two, each. *adv.* or *conj.*

Ejac'ulate, *v.t. & i.* to utter suddenly, eject. Ejacula'tion, *n.* Ejac'ulatory, *a.*

Eject', *v.t.* to expel, throw out, get rid of. Ejec'tion, *n.* Eject'-or, *n.* Eject'ment, *n.*

Eke (eek), *v.t.* to supplement,

esp. as to **Eke out,** subsist with difficulty.

Elab'orate, *v.t.* to work out in detail, to make more finished, complete properly. *a.* complicated, done in detail. **Elabora'-tion,** *n.*

Elapse', *v.i.* to pass (of time).

Elas'tic, *a.* returning to normal shape after being distorted, springy, flexible. **Elastic'ity,** *n.*

Ela'tion, *n.* great joy, high spirits. **Elate',** *v.t.* to make happy, raise spirits.

El'bow, *n.* joint or bend of arm, any joint or angle. *v.t. & i.* to thrust, jostle.

El'der, *a.* older, senior. *n.* person of advanced years, official of certain churches and institutions. **El'derly,** *a.* becoming old.

Elect', *v.t.* to choose, esp. by vote. *a.* chosen, selected. **Elec'-tion,** *n.* a selection by voting. **General Election,** *n.* election of an entirely new House of Commons. **By-election,** *n.* election of new single member after death or resignation of previous one. **Electioneer',** *v.t.* to work in election propaganda. **Elect'-or,** *n.* person with right to vote. **Elect'oral,** *a.* **Elect'orate,** *n.* the body of voters in general.

Electric'ity, *n.* natural force or agency developed by friction, magnetism, heat etc. **Elec'tric,** *a.* **Elec'trify,** *v.t.* charge with electricity, enliven, excite. **Electrifica'tion,** *n.* **Electri'cian,** *n.* skilled worker in electricity. **Elec'tron,** *n.* fundamental particle charged with electricity. **Elec'trocute,** *v.t.* to execute by electricity.

Elec'tro, *pref.* meaning of, pertaining to, caused by electricity.

El'egance, *n.* refinement in taste and movement. **El'egant,** *a.* refined, cultured, graceful.

El'egy, *n.* poem or song of lamentation, esp. for the dead. **Ele'giac** (-jy-), *a.* **Ele'gize,** *v.t. & i.* to lament in poetry or song.

El'ement, *n.* ingredient, component part, basic substance that cannot be broken down or analysed further. *n. pl.* the powers of nature, rudiments. **Element'al,** *a.* pertaining to the elements or powers of nature. **Elemen'tary,** *a.* simple, primary.

El'ephant, *n.* very large thick-skinned quadruped with trunk and ivory tusks. **Elephan'tine,** *a.* huge, ponderous.

El'evate, *v.t.* to lift up, raise. **Eleva'tion,** *n.* high place, altitude, angle of gun, architectural drawing, a raising up, promotion, ennoblement. **El'-evator,** *n.* lift.

Elev'en, *a. & n.* one more than ten, a team of players in certain games. **Elev'enth,** *a. & n.* ordinal number, one above ten.

Elf, *n.* a sprite, fairy. *pl.* **Elves.**

Elic'it, *v.t.* to educe, evoke, draw out.

El'igible, *a.* suitable, fit to be chosen or elected, qualified. **Eligibil'ity,** *n.*

Elim'inate, *v.t.* to disqualify, wipe out, remove. **Elimina'tion,** *n.*

Elite' (A-leet), *n.* the best, the finest part, superior class.

El'ixir, *n.* alchemist's concoction claimed to be able to prolong life, stimulate love or produce gold from base metals.

Ellipse', *n.* a regular oval. **Ellip'-tical,** *a.*

Ellip′sis, *n.* omission of words where they are not needed to make sense. *pl.* -ses. **Ellip′-tical,** *a.*

Elocu′tion, *n.* art of oral delivery, esp. in public. **Elocu′tionist,** *n.* person skilled in public recitation. **Elocu′tionary,** *a.*

E′longate, *v.t. & i.* to stretch out, make longer. **Elonga′-tion,** *n.*

Elope′, *v.i.* to run away with lover when lacking parents' approval. **Elope′ment,** *n.*

El′oquence, *n.* fluent, persuasive use of language. **El′oquent,** *a.*

Else, *adv.* otherwise, besides, in addition, if not.

Elu′cidate, *v.t.* to explain, make clear, cast light upon. **Elucida′-tion,** *n.* **Elu′cidatory,** *a.*

Elude′, *v.t.* to avoid, escape from, dodge. **Elu′sion,** *n.* **Elu′sive,** *a.* **Elu′sory,** *a.*

Ema′ciate, *v.t.* to make lean or thin, to waste away. **Emacia′-tion,** *n.* thinness, haggardness of appearance.

Em′anate, *v.t.* to originate from, issue from. **Emana′tion,** *n.*

Eman′cipate, *v.t.* to liberate, set free from bondage. **Emancipa′-tion,** *n.* **Eman′cipator,** *n.*

Emas′culate, *v.t.* to castrate, spoil lit. work by bowdlerization. **Emascula′tion,** *n.*

Embalm′ (-bahm), *v.t.* to preserve dead body by special processes.

Embankment′, *n.* raised earth or stone structure for carrying road or railway or protecting land from flood. **Em′bank,** *v.t.*

Embar′go, *n.* official order stopping movement of ships or goods. *v.t.*

Embark′, *v.t. & i.* to go or put on board ship, to start on project. **Embarka′tion,** *n.*

Embar′rass, *v.t.* to disconcert, make uncomfortable mentally, to hinder. **Embarr′assment,** *n.*

Em′bassy, *n.* ambassador's mission, office or official residence.

Embell′ish, *v.t.* to beautify, decorate, enrich. **Embell′ish-ment,** *n.*

Em′ber, *n.* fragment of live fuel in neglected fire.

Embezz′le, *v.t.* to misappropriate money not one's own. **Embezz′-ler,** *n.* **Embezzle′ment,** *n.*

Embitt′er, *v.t.* to make bitter, resentful.

Embla′zon, *v.t.* to adorn with heraldic devices. **Emblaz′-onry,** *n.*

Em′blem, *n.* heraldic device, symbol, badge. **Emblemat′ic,** *a.*

Embod′y, *v.t.* to give body to, make actual, express clearly. **Embod′iment,** *n.*

Embol′den, *v.t.* to encourage.

Emboss′, *v.t.* mould or carve in relief.

Embrace′, *v.t. & i.* to enclose in arms, include. *n.*

Embra′sure, *n.* opening in fortress wall for cannon.

Embroca′tion, *n.* *med.* lotion for rubbing bruised or strained parts of the body.

Embroi′der, *v.t.* to decorate with special needlework, to exaggerate story. **Embroi′-dery,** *n.*

Embroil′, *v.t.* to involve in argument or conflict. **Embroil′-ment,** *n.*

Em′bryo (-brio), *n.* offspring of animal before birth, anything undeveloped. **Embryon′ic,** *a.* **Embryol′ogy,** *n.* science or study of the embryo.

Emend', v.t. to correct. Emenda'-tion, n.

Em'erald, n. green precious stone. a. the colour of this.

Emerge', v.i. to come out, rise up, come to notice. Emer'-gence, n. Emer'gent, a.

Emer'gency, n. crisis, urgent happening or need.

Emet'ic, n. a medicine to induce vomiting. a.

Em'igrate, v.t. & i. to leave one's own country & settle in another. Emigra'tion, n. Em'ig-rant, a.

Em'inent, a. notable, distin-guished, prominent. Em'inence, n. distinction, title of cardinal, prominent geog. feature.

Em'issary, n. person sent on dubious mission.

Emit', v,t, to give out, put forth. Emiss'ion, n.

Emoll'ient, a. & n. making soft or supple, application with this ability.

Emol'ument, n. salary, profit.

Emo'tion, n. agitation of mind, excited state of feeling. Emo'-tive, a. of or causing emotion.

Empanel', v.t. to enrol, esp. on jury.

Em'peror, n. monarch ruling over empire. Em'press, n. fe-male counterpart or wife of this.

Em'pire, n. territory or state comprised of several countries governed by supreme ruler.

Em'phasize, v.t. to put stress on, underline, state forcibly. Em-phat'ic, a. Em'phasis, n.

Empir'ic, a. based on trial and error, not on theory. Empir'-icism, n.

Emplace'ment, n. gun-site, situa-tion.

Employ', v.t. to make use of, to use services of for pay. Employ'er, n. person using & paying workers. Employee', n. a paid worker. Employ'ment, n.

Empo'rium, n. large store or supermarket.

Empow'er, v.t. to authorize, enable.

Emp'ty, a. containing nothing, vacant, blank, devoid of con-tents, foolish. v.t. & i. to be-come or make empty.

Em'ulate, v.t. to imitate, esp. in good qualities. Emula'tion, n. Em'ulative, a.

Emul'sion, n. milky fluid con-taining oily properties.

En- pref. meaning to put into or on, effect, e.g. encase, en-camp, enrage, enact, enchain, encircle, enclose, encompass, encourage, etc.

Enam'el, n. opaque, glassy coat-ing for coating pottery etc. v.t. to coat with this.

Enam'our, v.t. to charm, inspire with love.

Enchant', v.t. to bewitch, delight greatly. Enchant'ment, n. a spell, extreme attraction. En-chant'er, Enchant'ress, n.

En'clave, n. territory surrounded by that of another state. Enco'-mium, n. eulogy, formal praise.

En'core (On-), interj. shout of applause meaning again. n. repetition or request for re-petition of song or mus. per-formance.

Encoun'ter, v.t. to meet with, come up against in hostility. n.

Encroach', v.i. to intrude, tres-pass. Encroach'ment, n,

Encrust, Incrust, v.t. & i. to cover with crust.

Encum'ber, v.t. to hamper, bur-den, impede. Encum'brance, n.

Encyc'lical, *n.* papal letter. *a.*

Encyclopae'dia, Encyclopedia, *n.* reference book containing information on many or all branches of knowledge. **Encyclopedic,** *a.* all-embracing.

End, *n.* conclusion, extremity, finish, limit, purpose. *v.t.*

Endeav'our (-devver), *v.i.* to attempt earnestly, to try. *n.*

Endem'ic, *a.* regularly occurring in country or among country's population, esp. of disease.

Endorse', *v.t.* to write or sign on back of, to confirm, to enter conviction. **Endorse'ment,** *n.*

Endow', *v.t.* to give income or property to, to furnish, invest with. **Endow'ment,** *n.*

Endure', *v.t. & i.* to last, undergo, put up with. **Endu'rance,** *n.* act or power of enduring, stamina. **Endu'ring,** *a.* lasting.

En'ema, *n. med.* injection for freeing bowels.

En'emy, *n.* foe, opponent, hostile person or state. *a.*

En'ergy, *n.* activity, force, drive, vigour. **Energet'ic,** *a.* active, lively. **En'ergise,** *v.t.* to put life or energy into, stir into action.

En'ervate, *v.t.* to weaken, deprive of energy. **Enerva'tion,** *n.*

Enfilade', *v.t. mil.* to rake enemy troops with fire from end to end. *n.*

Engage', *v.t. & i.* to betroth, pledge, bind by promise or contract, involve, start to fight, employ. **Engage'ment,** *n.* formal betrothal, appointment, obligation.

Engen'der, *v.t.* to beget, give rise to.

En'gine (-jin), *n.* a machine, locomotive, motor, mechanical apparatus. **Engineer',** *n.* skilled person who makes or drives engines. **Engineer,** *v.t.* to construct, bring about. **Engineer'ing,** *n.* the skill or profession of dealing with or designing engines.

Engrave', *v.t. & i.* to carve figures on surface, to cut drawing on metal for printing, to impress unforgettably. **Engra'ving,** *n.* sketch or picture printed from engraved metal plate. **Engra'ver,** *n.* craftsman in this art.

Engross', *v.t.* to absorb, occupy completely, to express in legal form or large writing.

Enhance', *v.t.* to add to value, intensify. **Enhance'ment,** *n.*

Enig'ma, *n.* a puzzle, riddle, mystifying person or thing. **Enigmat'ic,** *a.*

Enjoin', *v.t.* to command, prescribe, earnestly recommend.

Enjoy', *v.t.* to take pleasure from or in, have use of or benefit from. **Enjoy'ment,** *n.* pleasure. **Enjoy'able,** *a.*

Enlight'en, *v.t.* to make clear, instruct. **Enlight'enment,** *n.*

Enlist', *v.t. & i.* to enrol or engage esp. for mil. service. **Enlist'ment,** *n.*

En'mity, *n.* hostility, hatred.

Enor'mous, *a.* immense. **Enor'mity,** *a.* extreme wickedness.

Enough' (-nuf), *a.* sufficient, as many or much as necessary.

Enrol', Enroll', *v.t.* to enlist, accept as member, enter. **Enrol'ment,** *n.*

Ensconce', *v.t.* to establish or settle oneself snugly.

Ensemble' (On-sembl'), *n.* the general effect, kind of theatrical collective performance, esp. singing & dancing.

Enshrine', *v.t.* to enclose in shrine, to hold up to reverence or affection.

Enshroud', *v.t.* to drape over, cover up, conceal.

En'sign (-sn), *n.* a banner, a flag, esp. mil. or naval.

En'silage (-ij), *n.* hay, etc. preserved in pit or silo with molasses. Ensile', *v.t.*

Ensue', *v.t. & i.* to result, happen subsequently.

Entail', *v.t.* to necessitate, impose, involve, settle. *n.* an inherited property that can only be passed on according to conditions made.

Entente' (on-tont), *n.* a cordial atmosphere or understanding, esp. between nations.

En'ter, *v.t. & i.* to go or come into, to be admitted, to take up position on stage, to become member of, to put name down as entrant in competition etc., to start upon talks etc. En'trance, *n.* the act of coming or going in, a doorway or other means of entering, the right of admission, payment made for this. En'trant, *n.* person who takes part in competition or contest.

Enteri'tis, *n.* typhoid fever, inflammation of the bowels Enter'ic, *n. & a.*

En'terprise, *n.* a project of an adventurous or progressive kind. En'terprising, *a.* bold, ready for positive action.

Entertain', *v.t.* to amuse, divert, have as guests, sanction, consider. Entertain'er, *n.* e.g. professional raconteur, dancer, singer etc. Entertain'ment, *n.* us. in sense of public amusement.

Enthral', Enthrall' (-awl), *v.t.* to charm, hold spellbound.

Enthuse', *v.i.* to show great keenness, admiration etc. Enthu'siasm, *n.* keen interest, great zeal. Enthu'siast, *n.* Enthusias'tic, *a.*

Entice', *v.t.* to attract in dubious manner, to allure. Entice'ment, *n.*

Entire', *a.* whole, complete, unqualified. Entire'ty, *n.* the whole, the total.

En'tity, *n.* a reality, a living being.

Entomol'ogy, *n.* the study of insects. Entomolo'gist, *n.* Entomolo'gical, *a.*

Entourage' (-ahzh), *n.* important person's attendants.

En'trails, *n.pl.* intestines.

Entrance', *v.t.* to captivate, charm, send into trance.

Entreat', *v.t. & i.* to implore, beg earnestly. Entreat'y, *n.*

Entree' (-tray), *n.* privilege or right of admission, a dish at table served between fish and meat courses.

Enu'merate, *v.t.* to specify items, count. Enumera'tion, *n.*

Enun'ciate, *v.t.* to express clearly, pronounce. Enuncia'tion, *n.*

Envel'op, *v.t.* to cover, encircle completely, smother. Envel'opment, *n.*

En'velope, *n.* cover for a letter.

Envi'ron, *n.* us. as *n.pl.* outskirts of a town. Envi'ronment, *n.* surroundings in general.

Envis'age, *v.t.* to conceive mentally, imagine.

En'voi, En'voy, *n.* short concluding verse in poem.

En'voy, *n.* ambassadorial messenger.

En'vy, *n.* chagrin at someone

else's greater fortune or position. *v.t.* **En'viable**, *a.* **En'vious**, *a.*

En'zyme (-zeem), *n.* any of various substances made by both vegetable & animal cells and capable of causing chem. action in other substances while remaining unchanged themselves.

E'on, *n.* an immeasurable period, an age of the universe.

Ep'aulette, *n.* shoulder ornament in mil. uniform denoting rank.

Ephem'eral, *a.* in insects, living only for a day, very short-lived.

Ep'ic, *a.* heroic, on a grand or historic scale. *n.* a narrative describing the lives and deeds of heroes.

Ep'icure, *n.* person devoted to pleasure, person with fine tastes in food. **Epicure'an**, *a.* & *n.*

Epidem'ic, *n.* disease attacking many people at same time, *coll.* a widespread occurrence of anything.

Epider'mis (-dur), *n.* the outer layer of animal skin.

Epiglott'is, *n.* leaf-shaped lid of cartilage covering upper part of windpipe during act of swallowing.

Ep'igram, *n.* short poem or saying with witty point. **Epigrammat'ic**, *a.*

Ep'ilepsy, *n.* chronic nervous disease attended by convulsions & unconsciousness. **Epilep'tic**, *n.* person afflicted by this. *a.*

Ep'ilogue, *n.* poem or speech recited at end of play.

Epiph'any, *n.* festival of the visit of the Magi to Jesus Christ.

Epis'copal, *a.* pertaining to a bishop. **Epis'copacy**, *n.* bishops as a group, the government of a bishop. **Episcopa'lian**, *a.* pertaining to the **E. church**. **Epis'copate**, *n.* the office of bishop.

Ep'isode, *n.* an incident within a chain of events but not essential to the rest. **Episod'ic**, *a.*

Epis'tle (-s'l), *n.* a formal letter, esp. as in New Test. **Epis'tolary**, *a.* pertaining to letters & letter writing.

Ep'itaph, *n.* a memorial inscription on a tomb.

Ep'ithet, *n.* an adjective expressing some quality or characteristic.

Epit'ome (-mee), *n.* a synopsis, summary, essence.

E'poch (-pok), *n.* an era, period marked by historic events.

Ep'onym, *n.* person from whom place or discovery takes its name. **Epon'ymous**, *a.*

Eq'uable, *a.* steady, unchanging, tranquil, serene. **Equabil'ity**, *n.*

E'qual, *a.* same in size, value, number, rank etc, evenly balanced. *v.t.* & *n.* **Equal'ity**, *n.* **E'qualize**, *v.t.* & *i.* to make equal, same. **Equalisa'tion**, *n.*

Equanim'ity, *n.* serenity, evenness of temperament.

Equate', *v.t.* to make equal or treat as equal. **Equa'tion**, *n.* a mathematical statement that two things are equal.

Equa'tor, *n.* an imaginary line around the earth equally distant from N. & S. Poles. **Equator'ial**, *a.* pertaining to the Torrid Zone; of or near the equator.

Eq'uerry, *n.* royal officer formally in charge of horses, a royal attendant or aide.

Eques'trian, *a.* pertaining to horses & horsemanship. *n.* a horseman. **Eq'uine,** *a.* pertaining to or like the horse.

Equi', *pref.* meaning equal, e.g. equid stant, equilateral, etc.

Equilib'rium, *n.* state of balance between opposing weights, forces, action, opinions etc.

E'quinox, *n.* either of two occasions during year when sun crosses equator and night and day are equal in duration. **Equinoc'tial,** *a.*

Equip', *v.t.* to fit out for an undertaking, supply adequately. **Equip'ment,** *n.* **Equ'ipage,** *n.* arms & supplies of mil. character, carriage and servants etc. of person of rank.

E'quinoise, *n.* equilibrium.

Eq'uity, *n.* fair dealing, justice. **Eq'uitable,** *a.* fair, impartial.

Equiv'alent, *a.* equal in value, same in meaning. *n.* **Equiv'-alence,** *n.*

Equiv'ocal, *a.* of uncertain or doubtful meaning. **Equiv'ocate,** *v.i.* to speak with double meaning, to conceal truth by verbal subterfuge.

E'ra (Eer-), *n.* period of time with historic characteristics.

Erad'icate, *v.t.* to wipe out, destroy. **Eradica'tion,** *n.*

Erase', *v.t.* to rub out, obliterate. **Era'sure,** *n.*

Ere (Air), *prep. & conj.* before, rather than (poet.).

Erect', *v.t.* to construct, build, raise up. *a.* upright, standing up. **Erec'tion,** *n.* building, construction. **Erect'or,** *n.*

Er'mine (Ur-), *n.* fur made from skin of member of weasel family and esp. as used for ceremonial robes.

Erode', *v.t. & i.* to wear or be worn away. **Ero'sion,** *n.* esp. of soil or rock being worn away by water etc. **Ero'sive,** *a.*

Erot'ic, *a.* pertaining to sexual love. **Erot'icism,** *n.*

Err (Ur), *v.i.* to be at fault, go astray. **Errat'ic,** *n.* inconsistent, irregular, eccentric. **Erra'tum,** *n.* a mistake in writing or printing (*pl.* -ta.). **Erro'neous,** *a.* incorrect, mistaken. **Err'or,** *n.* a mistake, fault. **Err'ant,** *a.* roving in search of romance or adventure, erring.

Err'and, *n.* à commission, a duty or brief journey to carry out an order or request.

Erst'while (Urst-), *a.* formerly, long ago.

Eructa'tion, *n.* a belch.

Er'udite, *a.* scholarly, learned. **Erudi'tion,** *n.*

Erupt', *v.i.* to burst forth violently. **Erup'tion,** *n.* **Erup'-tive,** *a.*

Erysip'elas, *n.* (Er-i-) infectious disease of the skin.

Es'calator, *n.* a moving stairway.

Escapade', *n.* a reckless adventure, a scrape.

Escape', *v.t. & i.* to elude, to get free from capture, to avoid, break loose, flow out, be unaffected by. **Escap'ism,** *n.* a wish to get away from the complications and stupidities of daily life.

Escape'ment, *n.* mechanism ensuring regularity in clocks etc.

Escarp'ment, *n.* steep slope under hill or fortification.

Eschatol'ogy (Es-ka-), the study & doctrine of death and life after death.

Eschew', *v.t.* to shun, avoid.

Es'cort, *n.* a protective body or

convoy of ships, armed men etc. Escort', *v.t.* to accompany for protection or as compliment.

Es'culent, *a.* fit to eat.

Escutch'eon (-un), *n.* armorial shield.

Es'kimo, *n.* one of race of people inhabiting arctic N. Amer.

Esoter'ic, *a.* pertaining to and understood only by a learned elite.

Es'pionage (-ij or -aajh), *n.* spying, employment of secret agents.

Esplanade', *n.* an open walk or carriage way along sea front, a promenade.

Espouse (-spowz), *v.t.* to marry, give in marriage, become a supporter of. Espous'al, *n.*

Esquire', *n. orig.* a knight's attendant or son; now a courtesy form of address in writing.

Essay', *v.t.* to make an attempt, try difficult thing. Ess'ay, *n.* an experimental attempt, a lit. composition on special subject. Ess'ayist, *n.*

Ess'ence, *n.* the characteristic or most important part of anything, the extract of a substance dissolved in alcohol. Essen'tial, *a.* pertaining to the real character of something, an indispensable element, something absolutely necessary. *n.*

Estab'lish, *v.t.* to set up, to confirm, settle, prove. Estab'-lishment, *n.* a business organization; *iron.* the ruling clique.

Estate', *n.* condition of life, property, esp. in land, property left in will.

Esteem', *v.t.* to value highly, to consider. *n.* respect, good opinion.

Es'timable, *a.* deserving esteem, worthy.

Es'timate, *v.t.* to reckon, form an approximate opinion of, calculate probable cost. Estima'tion, *n.* respect, favourable opinion.

Estrange', *v.t.* to disrupt pleasant relations, cause a coolness of feeling. Estrange'ment, *n.*

Es'tuary, *n.* the broad mouth of a tidal river.

Etch (Ech), *v.t.* to engrave upon copper plate etc. by means of wax and acid. Etch'ing, *n.*

Eter'nal, *a.* everlasting, for ever. Eter'nity, *n.* indefinite time, time without beginning or end.

E'ther, *n.* liquid anaesthetic, upper pure air or sky beyond clouds. Ethe'real, *a.* exquisite, heavenly, disembodied.

Eth'ical, *a.* morally right, pertaining to moral things. Eth'-ics, *n. pl.* the science of morals, the practice & principles of good.

Ethnol'ogy, *n.* science treating of races of men and their characteristics. Eth'nic, *a.* of race. Ethnol'ogist, *n.* specialist in ethnology.

E'tiolate, *v.t. & i.* to make or turn pale through lack of light. Etiola'tion, *n.*

Et'iquette (-ket), *n.* conventional rules of conduct in social intercourse.

Etymol'ogy (Etti-), *n.* science dealing with origin & history of words. Etymol'ogist, *n.*

Eu'charist (U-k-), *n.* in many Chr. churches, holy communion. Eucharis'tic, *a.*

Eugen'ics (U-), *n. pl.* science of

improving the human race by selective breeding.

Eu'logy, *n.* great praise. **Eu'logize,** *v.t.*

Eu'nuch (-uk), *n.* castrated man as attendant in harem or singer.

Eu'phemism, *n.* the use of a mild or polite expression instead of more accurate but harsher one. **Euphemis'tic,** *a.*

Eu'phony, *n.* pleasantness of sound. **Eupho'nious,** *a.* **Eupho'nium,** *n. mus.* bass instrument of saxhorn type.

Euthana'sia, *n.* gentle, easy death, esp. as induced deliberately in case of incurable sickness.

Evac'uate, *v.t.* to empty, abandon possession of, withdraw, discharge. **Evacua'tion,** *n.* **Evac'uee,** *n.* person moved from disaster area or occupied territory.

Evade', *v.t.* to elude, avoid, escape from. **Eva'sion,** *n.* artful avoidance. **Eva'sive,** *a.* elusive, difficult to pin down verbally etc.

Eval'uate, *v.t.* to calculate value of. **Evalua'tion,** *n.*

Evanes'cent, *a.* vanishing, fleeting. **Evanes'cence,** *n.*

Evangel'ical, *a.* pertaining to or according to the Gospels, of many Protestant churches. **Evan'gelist,** *n.* one of the four writers of the gospels, person who spreads the word of the gospels. **Evan'gelize,** *v.t.* to convert or preach in Chr. sense. **Evangeliza'tion,** *n.*

Evap'orate, *v.t. & i.* to change from solid or liquid into vapour, to vanish completely. **Evapora'tion,** *n.*

Eve (Eev), *n.* the evening or day before important event or festival.

E'ven, *n. poet.* evening. **Eventide,** *n.*

E'ven, *a.* level, smooth, equal in place, parallel, impartial, uneventful. *v.t.* to make smooth or equal. *adv.* just, simply, imparting emphasis.

E'vening (Eevning), *n.* close of day, beginning of nightfall. *a.* pertaining to this.

Event', *n.* an occurrence, happening, result, item in athletic programme etc. **Event'ful,** *a.* momentous, important.

Event'ual, *a.* depending on a future event or contingency. **Eventual'ity,** *n.* possible contingency. **Event'uate,** *v.i.* to turn out, result.

Ev'er, *a.* at some or any time, everlasting, always, in any degree.

Ev'ermore, *adv.* forever, always.

Ev'ery, *a.* all, taken one at a time, each, all possible.

Evict', *v.t.* to eject by force, esp. by legal process. **Evic'tion,** *n.*

Evi'dence, *n.* proof, facts from which judgement can be made. **Ev'ident,** *a.* obvious. clear to the senses, in view, conspicuous. **Eviden'tial,** *a.*

E'vil, *a.* wicked, sinful. *n.* **Evil-doer,** *n.* **Evil-minded,** *a.*

Evince', *v.t.* to show, make evident.

Evoke', *v.t.* to call forth. **Evoca'tion,** *n.*

Evolu'tion, *n.* gradual development from earlier forms. **Evolu'tionary,** *a.* **Evolve',** *v.t.* to develop, expand, unfold.

Ewe (U), *n.* female sheep.

Ew'er (U-er), *n.* large water pitcher.

Ex- *pref.* meaning out, from, beyond, out of, former.

Exac'erbate, *v.t.* to annoy, aggravate. **Exacerba'tion,** *n.*

Exact', *a.* correct, precise. **Exac'titude,** *n.*

Exact', *v.t.* to require, insist on, compel. **Exac'tion,** *n.* an excessive demand.

Exag'gerate (-jer-), *v.t.* to overstate, enlarge beyond limits of truth or reason. **Exaggera'tion,** *n.* **Exag'gerator,** *n.*

Exalt' (-zawlt), *v.t.* to delight, elate, raise up in rank or glory. **Exalta'tion,** *n.* elation, a raising up in position or dignity.

Examina'tion, *n.* an investigation or inquiry, a test of fitness or knowledge. *v.t.* to inspect or probe into closely. **Exam'iner,** *n.* **Exam'inee,** *n.* person being examined or sitting for examination.

Exam'ple, *n.* a person or object worthy to be imitated, a specimen.

Exas'perate, *v.t.* to enrage, annoy, irritate. **Exaspera'tion,** *n.*

Ex'cavate, *v.t.* to dig, hollow out, reveal by digging. **Excava'tion,** *n.* **Ex'cavator,** *n.*

Exceed', *v.t.* to go beyond the limit, to surpass, excel. **Excess',** *n.* abundance, more than sufficient, intemperance. **Excess'ive,** *a.*

Excel', *v.t. & i.* to possess very high qualities, to surpass, be superior to. **Ex'cellent,** *a.* extremely good. **Ex'cellence,** *n.* **Ex'cellency,** *n.* title of honour.

Except', *v.t. & i.* to omit, leave out of account, raise objection to. *prep.* not including, outside of. **Excep'ting,** *prep.* not including. **Excep'tion,** *n.* an omission, exclusion, thing not included. **Excep'tional,** *a.* unusual. **Excep'tionable,** *a.* open to objection.

Excerpt', *n.* a selection or extraction from book or piece of music.

Exchange', *v.t.* to give in return for something else, trade, barter *n.* the action of this, an institution where business and financial transactions are carried out.

Excheq'uer (-checker), *n.* treasury, government department in charge of finances.

Ex'cise, (-size) *n.* tax on home-produced goods. **Exciseman,** *n.* officer who collects this. **Excise',** *v.t.* to cut out. **Excis'ion,** *n.*

Excite', *v.t.* to stir up, to agitate mentally, incite. **Exci'table,** *a.* **Excitaoil'ity,** *n.* **Excite'ment,** *n.*

Exclaim', *v.i.* to cry out, speak suddenly or sharply. **Exclama'tion,** *n.* **Exclam'atory,** *a.*

Exclude' (-klood), *v.t.* to shut out, debar, prevent from entering. **Exclu'sive,** *a.* shutting out, open only to members or privileged people, select. **Exclu'sion,** *n.*

Excommun'icate, *v.t.* to punish by denying membership or communion of the church. **Excommunica'tion,** *n.*

Ex'crement, *n.* dung, waste matter voided from bowels. **Excrete',** *v.t.* to get rid of waste matter from body. **Excre'tion,** *n.*

Excres'cence, *n.* an unnatural and disfiguring growth.

Excrucia'ting, *a.* acutely painful. Excru'ciate, *v.t.*

Ex'culpate, *v.t.* to free from blame, declare guiltless. Exculpa'tion, *n.* Exculpa'tory, *a.*

Excur'sion, *n.* a journey made for pleasure.

Excuse', *v.t.* to pardon from blame or obligation, to justify, make apology for, remit. *n. & n. pl.* apology, pleas in mitigation, reasons for not doing something. Excu'sable, *a.* forgivable, pardonable.

Ex'ecrable, *a.* outrageous, detestable. Ex'ecrate, *v.t.* to curse, abhor. Execra'tion, *n.*

Ex'ecute, *v.t.* to put into effect, complete, kill officially. Execu'tion, *n.* Execu'tioner, person employed officially to put criminals to death. Exec'utant, *n.* a performer. Exec'utive, *n.* administrative branch of government, business director. Exec'utor, *n.* person appointed by legator to carry out terms of will.

Exemp'lary, *a.* praiseworthy, serving as a model or example. Exem'plar, *n.* model, worthy example. Exem'plify, *v.t.* to illustrate, show by example.

Exempt', *v.t.* to excuse or release from duty etc. *a.* Exemp'tion, *n.* freedom from obligation, duty, payment.

Ex'ercise, *v.t. & i.* to practise, employ e.g. mind or muscles actively, to do organized physical movements, to make anxious, worry, to take exercise. *n.*

Exert', *v.t.* to put forth, bring into action. Exer'tion, *n.* effort.

Exhale', *v.t. & i.* to breathe out, give off as vapour. Exhala'tion, *n.*

Exhaust (-zawst), *v.t.* to tire out, wear out, empty, discuss extensively. *n.* escape of gas or steam from engine, device for drawing this off. Exhaus'tion, *n.* utter fatigue. Exhaus'tive, *a.* thorough, complete.

Exhib'it (-zibbit), *v.t.* to show, display, present publicly. *n.* thing shown in evidence, object displayed, entered in competition etc. Exhib'ition, *n.* a public display; a form of university scholarship. Exhib'itionism, *n.* morbid desire to show off.

Exhil'arate (ex-zil-), *v.t.* to gladden, make joyous. Exhilara'tion, *n.*

Exhort', *v.t. & i.* to advise strongly, urge earnestly. Exhorta'tion, *n.* Exhort'atory, *a.*

Exhume', *v.t.* to disinter, to dig up something already buried. Exhuma'tion, *n.*

Ex'igency (-jen-), *n.* urgency, pressing necessity. Ex'igent, *a.*

Ex'ile, *n.* banishment from one's own country, person so banished. *v.t.*

Exist', *v.i.* to live, have actual being, to be found, to occur. Exist'ence, *n.* the state of being. Exist'ent, *a.*

Ex'it, *n.* a way out, the act of going out, departure of an actor from stage.

Ex'odus, *n.* a departure, going out on a large scale.

Exon'erate, *v.t.* to declare guiltless, Exonera'tion, *n.*

Exorb'itant, *a.* excessive, esp. regarding price. Exorbi'tance, *n.*

Ex'orcise, *v.t.* to expel an evil spirit by invocation, to cast out. Ex'orcism, *n.* Ex'orcist, *n.*

Exot'ic, *a.* foreign, introduced from abroad, e.g. of plants etc.

Expand', v.t. & i. to spread out, enlarge, develop. **Expan'sion**, n. **Expan'sive**, a. large, unrestrained, effusive. **Expan'sile**, a. **Expanse'**, n. a wide uninterrupted space.

Expa'tiate, (-sshe-ate) v.i. to discourse or write at length.

Expa'triate, n. an exile. v.t. to banish. **Expatria'tion**, n.

Expect', v.t. to anticipate, regard as likely or due. **Expect'ant**, a. **Expect'ancy**, n. **Expecta'tion**, n.

Expect'orate, v.t. & i. to spit out. **Expectora'tion**, n.

Expe'diency, n. action conditioned by advantage regardless of rightness. **Expe'dient**, a. practical, fitting.

Ex'pedite, v.t. to hasten, help on. **Expedi'tious**, a. speedy.

Expedi'tion, n. an enterprise for purposes of exploration etc. **Expedi'tionary**, a.

Expel', v.t. to drive away, turn out forcibly. **Expul'sion**, n. **Expul'sive**, a.

Expend', v.t. to pay out, spend, use up. **Expendi'ture**, n. money or effort paid out or used. **Expense'**, n. n. pl. charges entailed. **Expens'ive**, a. high in price.

Expe'rience, n. knowledge of skill acquired by practice, observation or life in general. v.t. to live through, undergo.

Experi'ment, n. a trial or test to prove theory or discover something hitherto unknown. **Experiment'al**, a.

Ex'pert, a. skilled, dexterous. n.

Ex'piate, v.t. to atone or make amends for a crime. **Expia'tion**, n. **Ex'piatory**, a.

Expire', v.t. & i. to breathe out, to die. **Expira'tion**, n. **Expi'-**ratory, a. **Expi'ry**, n. termination.

Explain', v.t. to make clear, give meaning of, account for. **Explana'tion**, n. **Explan'atory**, a. **Ex'plicable**, a.

Ex'pletive, n. an oath, a word added for emphasis. a.

Ex'plicable, a. capable of being explained. more us. as neg. viz.: inexplicable.

Explic'it, a. definite, expressed in detail.

Explode', v.t. & i. to burst or cause to burst violently and with loud noise, to refute or disprove. **Explo'sion**, n. **Explo'sive**, a. & n.

Ex'ploit, n. a heroic act, notable deed. v.t. to make use of, esp. selfishly. **Exploita'tion**, n.

Explore', v.t. to search thoroughly, esp. unknown country. **Explora'tion**, n. **Explor'atory**, a. **Explo'rer**, n.

Expo'nent, n. person who explains or interprets.

Ex'port, v.t. to send goods abroad in trade. n. pl. such goods. **Exporta'tion**, n. **Export'er**, n.

Expose', v.t. to uncover, lay open to view, disclose. **Expo'sure**, n. the act of making known, unprotected state, e.g. to weather, etc., a photographic process.

Expos'tulate, v.i. to remonstrate, protest. **Expostula'tion**, n. **Expos'tulatory**, a.

Expound', v.t. to explain. **Exposi'tion**, n. a formal explanation or demonstration.

Express', v.t. to utter, put in words, make known, send by fast delivery. a. plainly stated, special. n. fast train. **Expres'-**

sion, *n.* a manner of speech, the act of expressing. **Express'ive**, *a.* full of meaning.

Ex'purgate, *v.t.* to tamper with book on grounds of eliminating offensive passages. **Expurga'-tion**, *n.*

Ex'quisite (-iz-it), *a.* delicately beautiful, intense.

Extemp'orary, *a.* without notes or preparation.

Extend', *v.t. & i.* to reach to, to enlarge, stretch out, increase, offer. **Exten'sion**, *n.* something added or offered. **Exten'sive**, *a.* spacious, large. **Extent'**, *n.* size, scope.

Exten'uate, *v.t.* to lessen blame, make excuses for. **Extenua'-tion**, *n.*

Exte'rior, *n.* the outside of anything. *a.* **Extern'al**, *a.*

Exterm'inate, *v.t.* to destroy utterly. **Extermina'tion**, *n.*

Extinct', *a.* no longer living, inactive.

Exting'uish, *v.t.* to destroy, put out. **Exting'uisher**, *n.* fire-fighting apparatus.

Extol', *v.t.* to praise highly.

Extort', *v.t.* to obtain by threats or force. **Extor'tion**, *n.* **Extor'-tionate**, *a.*

Extra, *a.* additional, of greater quality.

Extra- *pref.* meaning beyond, outside of, besides. e.g. **extraor-dinary, extra-mural, extra-sen-sory, extra-territorial, extra-judicial** etc.

Extract', *v.t.* to draw out by force, obtain by pressure or distillation, to take passage from book. **Ex'tract**, *n.* passage from book, concentrated essence. **Extrac'tion**, *n.* extracting, descent. **Extract'or**, *n.*

Extradi'tion, *n.* handing over of criminal by one country to another under treaty. **Ex'-tradite**, *v.t.*

Extra'neous, *a.* not essential, added from outside.

Extrav'agant, *a.* wasteful, over-spending needlessly, excessive. **Extrav'agance**, *n.* **Extrav'-aganza**, *n.* wildly ornate mus. composition, speech, writing.

Extreme', *a.* at the highest degree, furthest away, most severe. *n.* first or last of series or comparison. **Extre'mist**, *n.* person prepared to go to extremes esp. in polit. matters. **Extrem'ity**, *n.* extreme need or distress, end. *n. pl.* hands and feet.

Ex'tricate, *v.t.* to disentangle, set free, get out of. **Extrica'-tion**, *n.*

Extrin'sic, *a.* external, not belonging.

Ex'trovert, *n.* outward looking person without inhibitions. **Ex'troversion**, *n.*

Extrude', *v.t.* to thrust or jut out. **Extru'sion**, *n.*

Exu'berance, *n.* an overflowing or abundance esp. of high spirits. **Exu'berant**, *a.*

Exude', *v.t. & i.* to ooze out, give out moisture. **Exuda'tion**, *n.*

Exult', *v.i.* to rejoice exceedingly. **Exulta'tion**, *n.* **Exult'ant**, *a.*

Eye, *n.* organ of sight, eyesight, hole in needle, ring for hook. *v.t.* to look at, glance at. Various words prefixed by eye, e.g. **eye-ball, eyebrow, eyeglass, eyelash, eyelid, eyesight, eye-witness.**

Eyr'ie, *n.* (Eeer- or eye-) the nest of an eagle.

F

Fa'ble, *n.* legend, short story, esp. one with moral. **Fab'ulous,** *a.* legendary, incredible.

Fab'ric, *n.* woven material, structure, shell of building. **Fab'ricate,** *v.t.* to make, invent a tale or a lie. **Fab'ricator,** *n.* **Fabrica'tion,** *n.*

Facade' (Fass-), *n.* front of building.

Face, *n.* front part of head, the human features, expression, outward appearance; *sl.* impudence. *v.t. & i.* to turn toward, confront. **Fa'cial** (-shl), *a.* pertaining to the face.

Fac'et (Fass-), *n.* one of various surfaces of cut polished gem.

Face'tious (Fass-e-), *a.* lightly joking, not serious.

Fa'cia, Fa'scia (-shia), *n.* name-board over shop.

Fac'ile, *a.* easily done or performed, expert, smooth in manner. **Facil'itate,** *v.t.* to make easier. **Facil'ity,** *n.* freedom from difficulty. *n. pl.* means by which anything can be made easier or more comfortable. **Facilita'tion,** *n.*

Facsim'ile (Fak-sim-i-le), *n.* an exact reproduction or copy.

Fact, *n.* something actual or true. **Fact'ual,** *a.*

Fac'tion, *n.* small troublesome group of members within a larger polit. party. **Fac'tious,** *a.* troublesome.

Facti'tious, *a.* sham, artificial.

Fac'tor, *n.* cause of a given result; *math.* any of the numbers which when multiplied together produce a given result; an agent.

Fac'tory, *n.* industrial building where goods are manufactured.

Fac'ulty, *n.* ability to act or do, talent, mental or physical powers; university department.

Fad, *n.* a passing whim.

Fade, *v.t. & i.* to lose colour, grow old, wither.

Fail, *v.t. & i.* not to succeed, not to come up to expectation, to prove disloyal, be insufficient, to go bankrupt. **Fail'ure,** *n.* **Fail'ing,** *n.* defect, fault.

Faint, *v.i.* to lose consciousness, swoon. *a.* weak, timid, pale.

Fair, *a.* pleasing to the sight, without blemish, blonde, moderate, just, honest.

Fair, *n.* periodical market and entertainment.

Fair'y, *n.* elf, imaginary being with supernatural powers.

Faith, *n.* belief, trust, religion, confidence. **Faith'ful,** *a.* **Faith'less,** *a.*

Fake, *n.* not genuine, spurious. *v.t.* to pass off imitation as genuine thing, to conceal faults.

Fal'con (Faw-), *n.* swift bird of prey often used in sport. **Fal'coner,** *n.* expert who trains falcons for this. **Fal'conry,** *n.*

Fall (Fawl), *v.i.* to drop from a higher to lower place, to hang down, be overthrown or defeated, to happen. *n.*

Fall'acy, *n.* a faulty argument, wrong belief. **Falla'cious**, *a.* **Fall'ible**, *a.* liable to be wrong. **Fallibil'ity**, *n.*

Fall'ow, *n.* land ploughed up but left uncultivated in order to rest it. *a.*

False, *a.* untrue, dishonest, disloyal, artificial. **False'hood**, *n.* a lie. **Fal'sity**, *n.* an error, mistaken idea. **Fal'sify**, *v.t.* to make false, alter deceitfully.

Fal'ter (Fawl-), *v.t. & i.* to hesitate, waver.

Fame, *n.* renown, great and good reputation. **Fa'mous**, *a.* well-known, celebrated.

Famil'iar, *a.* well acquainted, intimate, informal, presumptuous. **Familiar'ity**, *n.* close acquaintance, offensive attempt at close relations. **Famil'iarize**, *v.t.* to become accustomed to, to make well known.

Fam'ily, *n.* group of closely related people, esp. parents & children.

Fam'ine (-in), *n.* great shortage of food, starvation. **Fam'ish**, *v.t. & i.* to starve, experience extreme hunger.

Fan, *n.* device for causing current of air, winnowing-instrument for sifting chaff from grain, blade of ship's screw, folding manual device for cooling person in hot weather. *sl.* an enthusiast, e.g. **film fan**. *v.t.* to cause air to move, to rouse, as of fire or temper.

Fanat'ic, *n.* person holding extreme and rigid views. **Fanat'icism**, *n.*

Fan'cy, *v.t.* to suppose, imagine, have a liking for. *n.* a particular taste or whim. *a.* affected, extravagant, ornate. **Fan'cier**, *n.* person taking special interest in something. **Fan'ciful**, *a.* unreal, imaginary.

Fan'fare, *n.* a flourish of trumpets.

Fang, *n.* long sharp tooth.

Fan'tasy, fanciful mental image, product of the imagination. **Fantas'tic**, *a.* unreal, grotesque.

Farce, *n.* play with grotesquely humorous and unlikely plot & situation, anything resembling this. **Far'cical**, *a.*

Fare, *n.* food, payment for journey as passenger. *v.i.* to get on, go, be treated.

Farm, *n.* area of land used for cultivation. *v.t. & i.* **Farm'er**, *n.* **Farri'er**, *n.* shoeing-smith.

Far'row (-ro), *n.* a litter of pigs. *v.t. & i.* to give birth to this.

Fas'cinate, *v.t.* to charm greatly, to render powerless by overwhelming attraction. **Fascina'tion**, *n.*

Fas'cism, *n.* extreme right-wing polit. movement advocating brutal methods and dictatorship. **Fas'cist**, *n.*

Fash'ion, *n.* manner, custom, style of dressing or behaving. *v.t.* to form, mould. **Fash'ionable**, *a.* of or following the prevailing style.

Fast, *a.* quick, rapid, firm, fixed, in advance of correct time, gay. **Fast'en**, *v.t. & i.* to make fast, secure, fix.

Fast, *v.i.* to abstain from food, esp. for relig. purposes in Lent.

Fastid'ious, *a.* difficult to please, of sensitive taste.

Fat, *a.* fleshy, bulky, containing much fat. *n.* solid oily animal substance. **Fatt'en,** *v.t.* & *i.* to put on weight, to bring to right condition as meat.

Fa'tal, *a.* causing death, disastrous. **Fatal'ity,** *n.* death from accident, calamity.

Fate, *n.* power beyond human control that is believed to determine course of events, person's lot or destiny. **Fa'talism,** *n.* resignation to external control of events.

Fa'ther (Fah-), *n.* male parent, head of family, founder, R.C. priest. *v.t.* to beget, originate, accept responsibility for. **Fatherhood,** *n.*

Fath'om, (-um), *naut.* measure equal to six feet. *v.t.* to ascertain depth of water, find meaning or reason of something. **Fathomless,** *a.* infinitely deep, too difficult to understand.

Fatigue' (-teeg), *n.* weariness, exhaustion ; soldier's chore. *v.t.* to tire completely.

Fat'uous, *a.* facetious, stupidly vain. **Fatu'ity,** *n.*

Fault, *n.* weakness, error, misdeed, *geol.* a break in rock-strata.

Fa'vour, *n.* an act of kindness, approval, partiality, badge. *v.t.* to approve, regard with favour or partiality, to oblige. **Fa'vourable,** *a.* auspicious, approving. **Fa'vourite,** *n.* person or object most liked, contestant, esp. race-horse, deemed to be most likely winner. *a.* preferred, best-liked. **Fa'vouritism,** *n.* undue partiality.

Fawn, *n.* young deer. *v.i.* to grovel, cringe.

Fear, *n.* dread, terror, awe. *v.t.* & *i.* to regard with dread, be afraid of. **Fear'ful,** *a.* terrible, causing dread. **Fear'some,** *a.* frightful, daunting.

Fea'sible, *a.* possible, practicable. **Feasibil'ity,** *n.*

Feast, *n.* a sumptuous meal, banquet. *v.t.* & *i.*

Feat, *n.* a courageous or skilful deed.

Feath'er (Feth-), *n.* bird's plume. *v.t.* & *i.* to cover or become covered with feathers.

Fea'ture, *n.* any part of the human face, a noticeable or characteristic part. *v.t.* to outline, portray, make prominent. **Featureless,** *a.* dull, characterless.

Feck'less, *a.* lacking in spirit, aimless.

Fec'und, *a.* fertile, fruitful. **Fecund'ity,** *n.*

Federa'tion, *n.* union of states or organizations with self-government over certain internal matters but submitting to central authority in others. **Fed'erate,** *v.i.* **Fed'eral,** *a.*

Fee, *n.* payment esp. for professional services. *v.t.*

Fee'ble, *a.* lacking strength, faint.

Feed, *v.t.* & *i.* to supply with or take food. *n.* animal fodder. **Food,** *n.* nourishment, sustenance.

Feel, *v.t.* & *i.* to be aware of, have sensation of something, examine by touch, to sympathize. **Feel'er,** *n.* organ of touch, antennum, tentative proposal. **Feel'ing,** *n.* a sensation of touch or contact, an emotion, attitude, conviction. *n. pl.*

Feign (Fane), *v.t.* & *i.* to pretend. **Feint** (Faint), *n.* a pretended blow or movement to conceal real intention.

Felic′itate, *v.t.* to congratulate. **Felicita′tions,** *n.pl.* congratulations. **Felic′ity,** *n.* great happiness, pleasant manner. **Felic′itous,** *a.* well-chosen, apt.

Fe′line, *a.* pertaining to cats.

Fell, *n.* a moorland hill.

Fell, *a.* savage, cruel.

Fell, *v.t.* to knock or cut down.

Fell′ow, *n.* companion, one of pair, a man, a member of certain societies. **Fellowship,** *n.* friendliness, companionship, postgraduate position in university.

Fel′on, *n.* criminal. **Fel′ony,** *n.* a serious crime.

Felt, *n.* material made of pressed wool.

Fe′male, *a.* pertaining to sex bearing young. *n.* **Fem′inine,** *a.* pertaining to women ; *gram.* of gender denoting female.

Fe′mur, *n.* the thigh bone. **Fem′oral,** *a.*

Fen, *n.* low marshy land.

Fence, *n.* a barrier between fields, private property. *v.t.* to enclose with a fence.

Fence, *v.i.* to practise the sport of sword-play.

Fence, *n. sl.* a receiver of stolen goods.

Fend, *v.t. & i.* repel, ward off, provide. **Fend′er,** *n.* fireguard, buffer to protect ship.

Fer′al (Feer-), *a.* wild, untamed.

Fermenta′tion, *n.* chemical change caused by yeast etc. **Fer′ment** (Fur-), *n.* substance causing this change. **Ferment′,** *v.t. & i.* **Ferment′ative,** *a.*

Fern (Furn), *n.* plant with feathery fronds.

Fero′cious, *a.* fierce, savage. **Feroc′ity,** *n.*

Ferr′y, *n.* boat or paddle-steamer for transporting across river or other stretch of water. *v.t. & i.*

Fer′tile (Fur-), *a.* fruitful, productive, abundant. **Fertil′ity,** *n.* **Fer′tilize,** *v.t.* to make productive, to enrich soil. **Fer′tilizer,** *n.* **Fertiliza′tion,** *n.*

Fer′vent, *a.* intense, ardent, vehement. **Fer′vour,** *n.* **Fer′vid,** *a.* passionate.

Festiv′ity, *n.* gaiety, celebration, feasting. **Fes′tive,** *a.* **Fes′tival,** *n.* a gay celebration.

Fes′ter, *v.t. & i.* to become sore, fill with pus, suppurate.

Festoon, *n.* a decorative chain of ribbons, flowers etc. *v.t.* decorate with this.

Fetch, *v.t. & i.* to go after and bring, be sold for, deal out blow. **Fetch′ing,** *a.* attractive.

Fête (Fate), *n.* an outdoor entertainment, a holiday, saint's day. *v.t.* to entertain as guest of honour.

Fe′tid, *a.* stinking.

Fet′ish, *n.* object supposed to be endowed with supernatural powers, object of obsessive devotion.

Fet′lock, *n.* projection on horse's leg, tuft of hair on this.

Fett′er, *n.* chain to hold legs of prisoner. *v.t.*

Fet′tle, *n.* good condition.

Feud (Fude), *n.* quarrel, esp. one of long-standing between clans or families, vendetta.

Feud′al, *a.* pertaining to mediaeval polit. & social system.

Fe′ver, *n.* illness characterized by rapid pulse and high temperature. *v.t.* to throw into a fever. **Fe′verish,** *a.*

Few (Fu), *a.* not many, small in number. *n.*

Fias′co, *n.* a complete failure.

Fi′bre (-ber), *n.* threadlike plant or animal tissue, raw material for spinning, character, quality. **Fi′brous,** *a.*

Fic′kle, *a.* unreliable, inconstant.

Fic′tion, *n.* not fact, a story, novel, untrue statement. **Fic′tional,** *a.* to do with stories. **Ficti′tious,** *a.* false, imaginary.

Fid′dle, *n.* a violin ; *naut.* a device to prevent dishes sliding from table in stormy weather. *v.i.* to play violin, to act in desultory way. *sl.* to engage in slightly unlawful act.

Fidel′ity, *n.* faithfulness.

Fidg′et, *v.i.* to keep moving restlessly, *n.* person who fidgets.

Field, *n.* a separate piece of farmland for cultivation or grazing, a scene of mil. operation. *v.t. & i.* in cricket etc. to stop and return the ball.

Fiend, *n.* devil, cruel person. **Fiend′ish,** *a.*

Fierce (Feerss), *a.* ferocious, savage.

Fi′ery, *a.* like, consisting of fire, flaming, angry.

Fight, *v.t. & i.* to strive against, combat, engage in war, box.

Fig′ment, *n.* invention, something imagined.

Fig′urative, *a.* metaphorical, not literal.

Fig′ure (-ger), shape, outline, body, diagram, illustration, personage, number, dance pattern. **Figure of speech,** *n.* metaphor, decorative or fanciful way of describing something.

Fig′ure, *v.t. & i.* to estimate, represent, calculate.

Fil′ament, *n.* fine thread or wire.

Filch, *v.t.* to pilfer.

File, *n.* folder or clip for keeping papers, documents, in. *v.t.* to keep or place in this.

File, *n.* rough-faced tool for smoothing or cutting *v.t.*

File, *n.* line of soldiers etc. moving one after another. *v.t. & i.* to move or march in single line.

Fil′ial, *a.* of or befitting a son or daughter.

Fil′igree, *n.* ornamental tracery in metal.

Fill, *v.t. & i.* to make or become full, to satisfy, discharge duty, occupy position, to stop up hole in tooth.

Fill′et, *n.* ribbon encircling hair.

Fill′et, *n.* boneless piece of fish or meat. *v.t.* to remove bones from.

Fill′y, *n.* young female horse.

Film, *n.* thin layer or coating, roll of celluloid for taking photographs. *v.t.* to take motion picture.

Fil′ter, *n.* material or device for straining off impurities or separate solid matter from liquid. *v.t. & i.*

Filth, *n.* unpleasant, foul matter, obscenity.

Fin, *n.* one of various projecting organs of fish enabling it to move & steer.

Fi′nal, *a.* coming at the end, conclusive. *n.* deciding bout in series of games. *n.pl.* final examinations. **Final′ity,** *n.* conclusiveness, completeness.

Fina′le (-li), *n.* final movement of symphony or other mus. composition.

Finance′, *n.* monetary resources, the control and direction of these. *v.t. & i.* to support project or person with money. **Finan′cial**, *a.* **Finan′cier**, *n.* expert in money matters.

Find (Fynd), *v.t.* to discover, come across, obtain, ascertain. *n.* worthwhile discovery.

Fine, *a.* of good quality, fair, sensitive, thin, excellent. **Fi′nery**, *n.* smart clothes or ornaments.

Fine, *n.* money exacted as penalty for minor offence. *v.t.* to punish by fining.

Finesse′, *n.* delicate cunning, subtlety. *v.t. & i.*

Fin′ger, *n.* digit of hand. *v.t. & i.* to touch or pick up with the fingers. **Fingerprint**, *n.* impression of lines of fingertips as means of identification of criminals.

Fin′ical, *a.* fussy.

Fin′ish, *v.t.* to complete, bring to an end, dispose of, kill. *n.* end of race, concluding part.

Fi′nite, *a.* having limits, not unbounded.

Fiord′, *n.* long narrow sea-inlet between high mountain slopes, esp. in Norway. Also as **Fjord**.

Fir, *n.* cone-bearing, evergreen, resinous tree.

Fire, *n.* flame, state of burning, conflagration, great heat, burning fuel, fervour, gunfire. *v.t. & i.* to set on fire, catch fire, excite, shoot. **Fire-** as part of many compound words, e.g. **Fire arm**, *n.* gun, pistol, etc. **Fire brigade**, **Fire-engine**, *n.* **Fire-damp**, *n.* inflammable gas occurring in coal-mines etc.

Fir′kin (Fur-), *n.* small tub for butter etc. measure of capacity of nine gallons.

Firm, *a.* fixed, unyielding, solid, stable, steady. *v.t.* to fix, make firm.

Firm, *n.* business company.

Firm′ament, *n.* the sky.

First, *a.* earliest in order or time, foremost in importance. *adv.*

Firth, *n.* an arm of the sea.

Fis′cal, *a.* relating to financial matters.

Fish, *n.* scaly, finned vertebrate breathing through gills and living in water. *v.t. & i.* to attempt to catch fish. **Fish′erman**, *n.* one who does this. **Fish′monger**, *n.* shopkeeper trading in fish. **Fish′ery**, *n.* the business of catching fish. **Fish′wife**, *n.* woman who hawks fish.

Fis′sile, *a.* capable of being split. **Fis′sion**, *n.* **Fis′sure** (Fishure), *n.* a narrowing opening, crack, cleft. **Fissip′arous**, *a.* propagating by fission.

Fist, *n.* the clenched hand.

Fis′tula, *n.* diseased opening, deep ulcer.

Fit, *n.* convulsive seizure, sudden illness. **Fit′ful**, *a.* changeable, restless.

Fit, *a.* proper, befitting, suitable, in healthy state. *v.t. & i.* to be of right size, to adjust, supply, make suitable. **Fit′ness**, *n.* rightness, good condition, qualification.

Fives, *n.* handball game played in enclosed court.

Fix, *v.t. & i.* to secure, make firm, fasten, arrange. *n.* an awkward predicament. **Fixa′tion**, *n.* obsessive state of mind. **Fix′ture**, *n.* something permanent.

Flabb'ergast, *v.t.* to astonish greatly.

Flabb'y, *a.* limp, feeble, loosely fat.

Flac'cid (Fla-sid), *a.* flabby.

Flag, *n.* a banner, ensign; paving-stone.

Flag, *v.i.* to falter, become tired, discouraged.

Flag'ellate (Flaj-), *v.t.* to whip. **Flagella'tion**, *n.*

Flag'on, *n.* large bottle or drinking-vessel.

Fla'grant, *a.* openly wicked, blatant.

Flail, *n.* a hinged implement for threshing.

Flair', *n.* instinctive ability, taste or skill.

Flake, *n.* a chip, small piece, fragment. *v.t. & i.* to crumble in flakes.

Flamboy'ant, *a.* showy, brilliant. **Flamboy'ance**, *n.*

Flame, *n.* burning gas or vapour, bright light, blaze, ardour ; *coll.* a sweetheart. *v.i.* to emit flames, burn brightly.

Flange, *n.* projecting rim on wheel to keep it on rail, projecting rim on pipe etc.

Flank, *n.* the side of anything, the part of an animal between ribs and hip. *v.t.* to be alongside, stand at side of.

Flann'el, *n.* soft loosely woven woollen cloth.

Flap, *n.* hinged piece attached to larger object. *v.t. & i.* to move to and fro like a flap, to flutter; *coll.* to panic.

Flare, *n.* sudden spasmodic blaze or light, a signal-light. *v.i.* to burst out suddenly and briefly, to lose temper.

Flash, *n.* a sudden brief burst of light or activity. **Flash-in-the-**

pan, *n.* misfire, project that fails after early promise. **Flash'y**, *a.* gaudy, showy.

Flask (Flahsk), *n.* small narrow often flat vessel for containing liquid; gunpowder container.

Flat, *a.* level, even, dull, out of tune.

Flat, *n.* an apartment on one floor.

Flatt'er, *v.t. & i.* to praise excessively and us. insincerely.

Flat'ulence, **Flat'ulency**, *n.* wind or gas in intestines; windy talk. **Flat'ulent**.

Flaunt, *v.t. & i.* to show off, display defiantly.

Fla'vour, *n.* characteristic taste or quality. *v.t.* to give flavour to, improve taste.

Flaw, *n.* a fault, defect. *v.t. & i.*

Flax, *n.* blue-flowered plant from whose stem fibres for linen are produced. **Flax'en**, *a.* of flax, pale yellow esp. of hair.

Flay, *v.t.* to skin.

Flea (Flee), *n.* small jumping insect that feeds on animal blood.

Fleck, *n.* speck, speckle, freckle. *v.t.* to mark with flecks.

Fledge, *v.t.* to acquire or furnish with feathers. **Fledgling**, **Fledge'ling**, *n.* young bird just starting to fly.

Flee, *v.t. & i.* to run away from, take flight.

Fleece, *n.* sheep's coat of wool. *v.t.* to shear wool, to rob.

Fleet, *n.* a large force of warships, an assembly of ships.

Fleet, *a.* swift, agile. *v.i.* to pass or move quickly. **Fleet-footed**, *a.* swift. **Fleet'ing**, *a.* passing quickly.

Flense, *v.t.* to flay & cut up, esp. of whale.

Flesh, *n.* meat, soft muscular animal tissue beneath skin or hide; the body, carnal appetites.

Flex, *v.t.* to bend or curve. *n.* insulated wire. **Flex'ible,** *a.* pliable, easily bent without breaking. **Flexibil'ity,** *n.*

Flick, *n.* a light quick stroke or blow. *v.t.*

Flick'er, *v.i.* to shine or burn in wavering manner, to flutter. *n.*

Flim'sy, *a.* fragile, unsubstantial. *n.* in R.N. a senior officer's report on junior.

Flinch, *v.i.* to falter in face of attack.

Fling, *v.t.* & *i.* to throw, cast, send out, rush about. *n.* a brief period of pleasure, a dance, a gibe.

Flint, *n.* hard kind of quartz, a piece of this. **Flintlock,** *n. arch.* gun fired by spark caused by striking flint & steel.

Flip, *v.t.* & *i.* to flick, strike lightly. *n.* a short trip in aircraft.

Flipp'ant, *a.* facetious, pert. **Flipp'ancy,** *n.*

Flipp'er, *n.* limb of aquatic animals e.g. seal.

Flipp'erty-gibbet, **Flibb'erty-gibbet,** *n.* capricious person.

Flirt, *v.t.* & *i.* to make love to insincerely, to move jerkily. *n.* a coquette, a sudden jerky movement. **Flirta'tion,** *n.* **Flirta'tious,** *a.* flighty.

Flit, *v.i.* to depart secretly, to dart.

Flitch, *n.* a side of bacon.

Fly, *v.t.* & *i.* to move through the air, to progress on wings, to go in aeroplane, go hurriedly. **Flight,** *n.* act of flying, journey in aircraft.

Float, *v.t.* & *i.* to swim in or be borne up on liquid, to be suspended or move in air, be borne along; to launch e.g. (in business) a company or rumour. *n.* small flat cart, cork for buoying up fishing-net etc., footlight. **Flota'tion,** *n.* the launching or financing of a project.

Flock, *n.* herd of sheep, crowd, tuft of wool, woollen refuse. *v.i.* to throng together.

Floe, *n.* large drifting sheet of ice.

Flog, *v.t.* to thrash. *sl.* to sell.

Flood (Flud), *n.* a large flow of water esp. in abnormal way, the ingoing tide, an inundation. *v.t.* & *i.* to overflow, submerge. **Flood-tide,** *n.* inflowing tide. **Flood-gates,** *n. pl.* sluices to control flow of water. **Flood'-lighting,** *n.* extensive use of electric lighting for outdoor arena etc.

Floor (Flore), *n.* bottom surface of room or building, rooms on same level. *v.t.* to cover with floor, to knock down, to defeat in argument.

Flop, *v.t.* & *i.* to collapse, to drop or let drop suddenly. *n. sl.* a failure.

Flor'a, *n.* the plants of a particular period or region, a catalogue of these. **Flor'al,** *a.* pertaining to flowers. **Flor'ist,** *n.* shopkeeper dealing in flowers. **Flor'iculture,** *n.* the cultivation of flowers. **Flores'cence,** *n.* the state or time of coming to flower.

Flor'id, *a.* flushed, bright in colour, showy.

Flor'in, *n.* a piece of money, esp. Brit. two shillings.

Floss, *n.* silky substance covering cocoon, strands of silk.

Flotill′a, *n.* fleet of small vessels, small fleet.

Flot′sam, *n.* remains of shipwreck or lost cargo floating in sea.

Flounce, *n.* ornamental gathered ruffle or addition to skirt. *v.i.* to trim with this.

Flounce, *v.i.* to go off abruptly or indignantly.

Flound′er, *v.i.* to struggle awkwardly.

Flound′er, *n.* a flat-fish.

Flour, *n.* fine meal of ground wheat etc.

Flour′ish (Flur-), *v.t. & i.* to grow, prosper, thrive, to brandish, a trumphant gesture, a mus. fanfare.

Flout, *v.t.* to defy, disdain, mock.

Flow (Flo), *v.i.* to move along easily, esp. of water, to pour out. *n.*

Flow′er (Flow-), *n.* blossom of plant, choicest part of anything. *v.t. & i.* to come to flower, to open, come to perfection. **Flow′ery,** *a.* full of flowers, ornamented.

Fluc′tuate, *v.i.* to function spasmodically, to change frequently, to rise and fall. **Fluctua′tion,** *n.*

Flue, *n.* pipe or passage for smoke etc. to escape.

Flu′ent (Floo-), *a.* moving smoothly, flowing, speaking with ease. **Flu′ency,** *n.*

Flu′id, *n.* a substance capable of flowing, i.e. liquid or gas. *a.* not solid. **Fluid′ity,** *n.*

Fluke, *n.* a successful but unintentional stroke, parasitic worm in sheep. *n. pl.* whale's tail.

Flunk′ey, *n.* footman. *sl.* cringing person.

Flu′or, *n.* calcium fluoride. **Fluores′cence,** *n.* property of converting invisible rays to visible light. **Fluores′cent,** *a.*

Flurry, *n.* sudden gust of wind, sudden burst of activity. *v.t.* confuse.

Flush, *v.t. & i.* to redden, glow, to cleanse with water, to startle birds etc. from cover. *n.* an abundance, a blush, a rush of water. *a. sl.* temporarily well-off; even or level with.

Flus′ter, *v.t. & i.* to confuse, agitate.

Flute, *n.* mus. wood-wind instrument. *v.t. & i.* to play on flute. **Flaut′ist** (Flaw-), *n.* flute-player.

Flute, *v.t. & i.* to make grooves in. **Flu′ting,** *n.* grooves.

Flutt′er, *v.t. & i.* to flit, fly or try to fly, flap wings. *n.* confusion, *sl.* a bet.

Flu′vial, *a.* pertaining to rivers.

Flux, *n.* a discharge of matter, e.g. blood, constant change or flow.

Fly, *v.t. & i.* to move through the air, to progress on wings, to go in aircraft, depart hurriedly. **Flight,** *n.* act of flying, journey in aircraft. **Fly at,** *v.t.* attack, rush at. **Fly out,** *v.t.* lose temper. **Flying Squad,** *n.* special mobile police force. **Fly,** *n.* various kinds of insect, esp. **house-fly,** *n.* a small horse-drawn vehicle.

Foal, *n.* the young of various equine animals. *v.t. & i.* to give birth to foal.

Foam, *n.* bubbles on surface of liquid produced by agitation or fermentation. *v.i.*

Fob, *v.t.* to put off, take in, cheat.

Fob, *n.* a small pocket for watch, ticket etc.

Fo'cus, *n.* point of convergence of rays of light etc. after refraction or reflection, adjustment of eye or lens for clearest image. *v.t. & i.* to adjust in order to get clearest image. **Fo'cal,** *a.* placed at a central point, relating to focus.

Focsle (Foke'sl), *n.* properly **Forecastle,** fore part of ship.

Fodd'er, *n.* food for cattle.

Foe, *n.* enemy.

Foe'tus, Fe'tus, *n.* fully developed embryo. **Foe'tal,** *n.*

Fog, *n.* thick haze or mist. *v.t.* to cover in fog, to obscure, perplex. **Fog-bank,** *n.* dense large cloud of fog. **Fog-horn,** *n.* warning siren used by ship in fog. **Fog-signal,** *n.* warning detonator used on railway in fog.

Fo'gey, *n.* odd old man.

Foi'ble, *n.* an oddity or weakness of character.

Foil, *n.* a fencing rapier. *v.t. & i.* to frustrate, baffle.

Foil, *n.* thin leaf or sheet of metal.

Foil, *n.* a contrast, metal used as backing to mirror or to show jewels to advantage.

Foist, *v.t.* to impose, palm off, introduce furtively.

Fold, *n.* a sheep-pen, a pleat or turning in material. *v.t. & i.* to enclose, to double, bend, crease.

Fold'er, *n.* a file, holder for papers.

Fo'liage, *n.* leaves, leafage.

Fo'lio, *n.* largest size of book, leaf or page number of book or MS., unit of length in printing.

Folk (Foke), *n.* a race or nation, people in general, kindred. **Folk-lore,** *n.* traditions, beliefs, customs, handed on from successive generations. **Folksong,** *n.* traditional song. **Folkdance,** *n.* traditional dance.

Foll'icle, *n.* tiny sac or cavity, seed-vessel.

Foll'ow, (-o), *v.t. & i.* to go or come after, to pursue, to copy, obey, practise. **Foll'ower,** *n.* disciple, adherent. **Foll'owing,** *n.* calling, profession, body of followers.

Foll'y, *n.* foolishness, a stupid action; a useless and extravagant building.

Foment', *v.t.* to apply hot med. lotion, to stir up. **Fomenta'tion,** *n.*

Fond, *a.* affectionate, devoted.

Fon'dle, *v.t. & i.* to caress, pet.

Font, *n.* vessel for holding holy water for baptism.

Food, *n.* nourishment, sustenance.

Fool, *n.* stupid person, jester, *v.t. & i.* to act foolishly, deceive, play tricks on. **Fool'ish,** *a.* **Fool'ery,** *n.* **Fool-hardy,** *a.* stupidly bold, rash. **Foolproof,** *a.* simple enough for anyone to work or understand.

Fools'cap, *n.* size of paper approx. seventeen by fourteen inches.

Foot, *n.* lowest part of leg on which humans and some other animals walk; a measure of length, twelve inches; the base or end of anything, the bottom. *v.t. & i.* to move by foot, pay a bill. **Foot-** as *pref.* to various self-explanatory words.

Fop, *n.* a dandy.

For, *prep.* in place of, because of, on account of, concerning.

For-, *pref.* meaning the opposite or negative of, bad effect, away, off or apart from, etc. e.g. **forbear, forgo, forswear, forbid.**

For'age, *n.* food for horses, esp. mil. *v.i.* to go in search of food.

For'ay, *n.* a raid for plunder. *v.i.*

For'bear, *n.* ancestor.

Forbear', *v.t. & i.* to refrain, be patient. **Forbearance,** *n.*

Forbid, *v.t.* to refuse permission, prohibit. **Forbidd'ing,** *a.* threatening, stern.

Force, *n.* power, strength, violence, compulsion, persuasion, mil. strength. *v.t.* to compel, break open, drive, encourage growth artificially. **For'cible,** *a.* **Force'ful,** *a.*

For'ceps, *n.* surgical or dental pincers.

Ford, *n.* shallow part of river which can be crossed on foot. *v.t. & i.* to wade across.

Fore- *pref.* meaning in front, beforehand, the front part, near or towards, anticipatory, e.g. **forebode, forecast, forearm, foreclose, forego, forehand, forestall, foreshadow,** etc.

Fore, *interj.* a warning cry in golf when making shot.

Fore-and-aft, *adv.* at bow and stern, lengthwise in ship.

For'eign, *a.* pertaining to another nation than one's own, introduced from outside, alien. **For'eigner,** *n.* an alien.

Foren'sic, *a.* pertaining to the courts of law or to public debate.

For'est, *n.* growth of trees covering large extent, sometimes moorland and trees, hunting-domain. **For'ester,** *n.* person who lives or works in forest. **For'estry,** *n.* the study and practice of cultivating trees for timber.

For'feit (-fit), *v.t.* to lose through default or neglect. *n.* penalty exacted for crime or neglect. **For'feiture,** *n.*

Forge, *v.t.* to fashion metal by hammering while it is soft from heat, to make a false imitation of. *n.* blacksmith's fire. **For'ger,** *n.* counterfeiter. **For'gery,** *n.* fraudulent imitation.

Forge, *v.i.* to proceed steadily.

Forget', *v.t. & i.* to fail to remember, omit.

Forgive', *v.t.* to pardon, to cease from reproaching.

Fork, *n.* pronged agricultural or gardening tool, pronged table implement, branch in road or river. *v.t. & i.* to use fork, to divide in a fork.

Forlorn', *a.* forsaken, miserable.

Form, *n.* the outward appearance or shape of anything, the human body, a manner of doing something, social behaviour, physical condition, a school class, a bench, a printed form for the inclusion of details, a hare's bed. *v.t. & i.* to shape, take shape, conceive, train. **Forma'tion,** *n.* forming, arrangement, shape. **For'-mative,** *a.*

For'mal, *a.* following set rules, ceremonious. **Formal'ity,** *n.* **Form'alism,** *n.* strict observance of conventions.

For'mat, *n.* size, shape and general presentation of a book.

For'mer, *a.* earlier, previous.

pron. former person or thing. For'merly, *adv.* in past time.

For'midable, *a.* hard to cope with, redoubtable.

Formula, *n.* specified way of doing something; *chem.* a rule or fact expressed in symbols. For'mulate, *v.t.* to put into a definite form, express in definite terms.

For'nicate, *v.i.* to partake in illicit sexual intercourse. Fornica'tion, *n.* Fornica'tor, *n.*

Forsake', *v.t.* to desert, abandon.

Forsooth', *adv. arch.* in truth, doubtless.

Forswear', *v.t.* to deny an oath, renounce.

Fort, *n.* strongly fortified building. For'tify, *v.t.* to strengthen or organize for defence. Fortifica'tion, *n.* organized system of defence. Fort'ress, *n.* a stronghold, fort.

For'titude, *n.* patient endurance in trouble or pain.

Fortnight, *n.* two weeks.

Fortu'itous, *a.* happening by chance, accidental.

For'tune, *n.* good or ill chance, luck, wealth. For'tunate, *a.* prosperous, lucky, favourable.

For'um, *n.* place for public discussion.

For'ward, *adv.* onward, ahead. *a.* in or towards the front. *v.t.* to help advance, promote.

Fosse, foss, *n.* trench or moat in front of fortification.

Foss'il, *n.* petrified plant or animal, part of this. *a.* Foss'ilize, *v.t. & i.* to turn into fossil. Fossiliza'tion, *n.*

Fos'ter, *v.t.* to nourish, encourage, rear. Foster-mother, *n.* woman bringing up children not her own.

Foul, *a.* offensive, disgusting, filthy. *v.t. & i.* to make filthy, pollute, become entangled with, tackle unfairly in sport. *n.* Foul play, *n.* murder, unsporting behaviour.

Foulard', *n.* thin silk material, neckerchief of silk.

Found, *v.t.* to originate, establish, base, rely. Founda'tion, *n.* base, fundamental part, endowed institution. Found'er, *n.* originator.

Found, *v.t.* to cast, form by moulding metal. Found'ry, *n.* workshop for casting metal.

Found'er, *v.t. & i.* to sink or cause to sink, esp. of ship. to break down.

Found'ling, *n.* abandoned child.

Fount, *n.* fountain, source, in printing, a set of type. Fount'ain, *n.* a spring of water, a source, an artificial spout of water.

Fowl, *n.* domestic cock or hen. Wildfowl, *n.* wild duck, geese, etc. than can be hunted. Fowl'er, *n. us* as Wildfowler, *n.* person who shoots wild duck etc. on marshes or inlets. Fowl'ing-piece, *n. arch.* a sporting gun.

Fox, *n.* wild animal of dog family with reddish coat and bushy tail. *v.t. & i.* to deceive, sham, as fox.

Foy'er, *n.* room in theatre where audience can go during interval.

Fracas' (Frak-ah), *n.* noisy squabble, disturbance.

Frac'tion, *n.* a part, a fragment, *math.* indicates number of equal parts of a whole. Frac'tional, *a.* of fractions, very small.

Frac′tious, *a.* peevishly unruly.

Frac′ture, *n.* breakage, esp. of bone. *v.t. & i.*

Frag′ile (-jyle), *a.* delicate, easily broken or damaged.

Frag′ment, *n.* an incomplete part, a piece broken off from larger body. **Fragmenta′tion**, *n.* **Frag′mentary**, *a.*

Fra′grant, *a.* pleasantly scented. **Fra′grance**, *n.*

Frail, *a.* delicate, weak in health, feeble. **Frail′ty**, *n.*

Frame, *v.t.* to enclose in a frame, to fashion, put together, express in words. *n.* a structure for enclosing or holding, a human body.

Fran′chise, *n.* citizenship, right to vote, exceptional right or privilege e.g. to run particular service.

Frank, *a.* honest, outspoken.

Frank, *n.* facility for passage of person or letter, mark signifying this. *v.t.* to mark with a frank giving free passage for letter etc.

Fran′tic, *a.* distracted, frenzied.

Frater′nal, *a.* pertaining to or like brothers. **Frater′nity**, *n.* brotherhood, also in rel. sense, a guild. **Frat′ernize**, *v.t. & i.* to associate as if with brothers. **Fraterniza′tion**, *n.* the act of doing this. **Frat′ricide**, *n.* the killing of one's own brother or sister.

Fraud, *n.* dishonest practice, criminal deceitfulness. **Fraud′ulence**, *n.* **Fraud′ulent**, *a.*

Fraught, *a.* us. as fraught with, laden, filled.

Fray, *n.* a brawl.

Fray, *v.t. & i.* to wear out, chafe.

Freak, *n.* an abnormal person or thing, a chance happening.

Frec′kle, *n.* brownish mark on skin. *v.t. & i.*

Free, *a.* possessing full personal liberty, unrestricted, unattached, without charge, generous, frank. *v.t.* to set at liberty, release. **Free′dom**, *n.* liberty.

Free′booter, *n.* a buccaneer, pirate.

Free′hold, *n.* complete ownership without restriction.

Free′lance, *n.* person working independently, esp. as writer or journalist.

Free′mason, *n.* member of ancient society practising mutual aid. **Freemasonry**, *n.*

Freethinker, *n.* person who forms religious opinions independently.

Freeze, *v.t. & i.* to become solid through intense cold, to chill, make rigid, rebuff. **Frost**, *n.* frozen particles of moisture, state of cold when temperature at or below freezing-point.

Freight (Frate), *n.* goods for transportation, cargo, hire of means of transport for carrying goods. **Freight′age**, *n.* charge for this.

French, *a.* pertaining to France. *n.* the language or people of France. **French leave**, *n. sl.* unauthorized absence. **French window**, *n.* glazed door us. opening on to garden.

Frenet′ic, *a.* frenzied, frantic.

Fren′zy, *n.* excited rage, uncontrollable temper. *v.t.*

Fre′quent, *a.* occurring often. **Frequent′**, *v.t.* to haunt, visit habitually. **Fre′quency**, *n.* the rate of occurrence.

Fres′co, *n.* painting made on

wall before plaster has dried.

Fresh, *a.* new, unsullied, newly arrived, additional, different, just gathered or killed. **Fresh'en,** *v.t. & i.* to make fresh, revive.

Fret, *v.t.* to design ornamentally, variegate. **Fret-saw,** *n.* fine-toothed saw for patterning wood. **Fretwork,** *n.*

Fret, *v.t. & i.* to vex, worry.

Fret, *n.* misty uncertain weather on the sea.

Fri'able, *a.* readily reduced to powder or crumbled.

Fri'ar, *n.* mendicant, wandering monk. **Fri'ary,** *n.* monastery of friars.

Fric'tion, *n.* rubbing of one body against another; *fig.* bad feeling, disagreement.

Friend (Frend), *n.* close companion, person bound to another by affection or esteem. **Friend'ship,** *n.*

Frieze (Freeze), *n.* ornamental band round room of wall; coarse woollen cloth.

Frig'ate, *n.* swift light warship.

Fright'en, *v.t.* to terrify, make afraid. **Fright,** *n.* fear. **Frightful,** *a.* hideous, horrible.

Frig'id (Frij-), *a.* stiff, extremely cold, dull. **Frigid'ity,** *n.*

Frill, *n.* ornamental edging on dress, fringe of hair. *v.t.*

Fringe, *n.* border or edging, outskirts, hair cut to hang over forehead. *v.t.*

Fripp'ery, *n.* vulgar finery.

Frisk, *v.t. & i.* to leap or run about joyfully; *sl.* to search person quickly for arms or smuggled goods.

Fritt'er, *n.* fried cake of batter.

Fritt'er, *v.t.* esp. as f. away, to waste.

Friv'olous, *a.* trivial, not serious. **Frivol'ity,** *n.* paltry, irresponsible behaviour.

Frock, *n.* woman's garment, priest's cassock.

Frog, *n.* tailless amphibious animal; ornamental fastening on uniform, belt-attachment for sword; horny growth in horse's hoof.

Frol'ic, *n.* a carefree game or activity. *v.i.*

Frond, *n.* leaf of fern etc.

Front (Frunt), *n.* the foremost part of anything, mil. firing-line, appearance, a polit. group in action. *v.t. & i.* to oppose, face. **Front'age,** *n.* land adjoining street, outlook. **Front'al,** *a.* of the front.

Front'ier, *n.* border between states.

Front'ispiece, *n.* illustration at beginning of book.

Froth, *n.* foam, scum on surface of liquid, mass of small bubbles, idle chatter. *v.t. & i.*

Fro'ward, *a.* disobedient, wilful.

Frown, *v.t. & i.* to wrinkle the brows in puzzlement or anger. *n.*

Frowz'y, *a.* stale-smelling, sluttish.

Fruc'tify, *v.t. & i.* to produce fruit, make fruitful. **Fructifica'tion,** *n.*

Fru'gal, *a.* sparing, abstemious in eating etc. **Frugal'ity,** *n.*

Fruit (Froot), *n.* the perfected seed and its surrounding substance produced by various plants; any produce or result. *v.i.* to bear fruit. **Frui'tion,** *n.* fulfilment, coming to fruit.

Frump, *n. sl.* dowdy old woman.

Frustrate', *v.t.* to baulk, baffle, thwart. **Frustra'tion,** *n.*

Fry, *n.* young fish.

Fry, *v.t. & i.* to cook with fat or oil.

Fud'dle, *v.t. & i.* to confuse or be confused with alcohol.

Fudge, *v.t. & i.* to do or perform badly, to botch. *n.* nonsense, a soft sweetmeat.

Fu'el, *n.* material used for supplying heat by combustion. *v.t. & i.* to supply with fuel.

Fug'gy, *a.* stuffy and hot, airless.

Fu'gitive, *n.* person who flees from danger or justice. *a.* fleeing from, not lasting long. **Fuga'cious,** *a.* elusive.

Fu'gleman, *n.* soldier standing in front of drilling squad to illustrate movements.

Fugue, *n. mus.* composition in which theme or themes are repeated.

Ful'crum, *n.* support on which a lever turns.

Fulfil', *v.t.* to complete or accomplish. **Fulfil'ment,** *n.*

Ful'gent (-jent), *a. poet.* brilliant, radiant. **Ful'gency,** *n.*

Full, *a.* replete, entire, completely filled, with no more empty space.

Ful'minate, *v.t. & i.* to explode, hold forth. **Fulmina'tion,** *n.*

Ful'some, *a.* effusive, excessive.

Fum'ble, *v.t. & i.* to grope, handle awkwardly.

Fume, *n.* vapour, gas, noxious exhalation. *v.t. & i.* to emit fumes, talk angrily. **Fu'migate,** *v.t.* to disinfect by fumes. **Fumiga'tion,** *n.*

Fun, *n.* harmless amusement.

Func'tion, *n.* the special purpose or duty of person or thing; a public ceremony. **Func'tional,** *a.* pertaining to usefulness without regard to aesthetic considerations. **Func'tionalism,** *n.* doctrine, esp. in architecture, based on this. **Func'tionary,** *n.* an official.

Fund, *n.* money, capital, collection. *n. pl.* financial resources.

Fundament'al, *a.* basic, essential. **Fundament'alist,** *n.* person believing in literal truth of Bible.

Fu'neral, *n.* ceremony of interment of dead person. **Fune'brial,** *a.* of a funeral. **Fune'real,** *a.* dismal, appropriate to a funeral.

Fun'gus, *n.* mould, mildew, mushroom, toadstool and similar plants. *pl.* **Fun'gi. Fun'goid,** *a.* like a fungus. **Fun'gicide,** (-ji-), *n.* anything capable of destroying fungi.

Funic'ular, *n.* esp. as **F.-railway,** cable railway for travelling up and down mountainside. *a.*

Funk, *n. sl.* fear, a coward. *v.t. & i.*

Funn'el, *n.* wide-mouthed, cone-shaped vessel with tube attached for transferring liquid, the smoke-vent of ship or railway-engine.

Fur, *n.* the soft hairy covering of certain animals, this treated and processed as woman's article of wear. **Furr'ier,** *n.* person who prepares and deals in furs.

Fur'bish, *v.t.* to renovate, clean up.

Furl, *v.t.* to roll up and secure, as of sail or flag.

Fur'long, *n.* linear measurement, two hundred & twenty yards.

Fur'lough (-lo), *n.* soldier's leave of absence.

Fur'nace (-nis), *n.* oven for achieving very great heat in various manufacturing processes.

Fur'nish, *v.t.* to fit out, esp. with furniture, to supply. **Fur'niture**, *n.* the fittings of a house, e.g. chairs, beds, tables etc.

Furore (Fure-), *n.* enthusiastic uproar.

Furr'ow, *n.* groove made in soil by plough, a cart-rut. *v.t.* to wrinkle, plough.

Fur'ther, *adv.* to or at greater distance, also, moreover. *a.* additional. *v.t.* to advance, promote. **Fur'therance**, *n.* help, advancement. **Fur'thermore**, *adv.* moreover, besides. **Fur'-thermost**, *a.* the most remote.

Fur'tive, *a.* secretive, stealthy.

Fu'ry, *n.* violent anger, violence. **Fu'rious**, *a.* very angry, violent.

Fus'cous, *a.* sombre, dark in colour.

Fuse, *v.t. & i.* to melt by heat, to join together. *n.* safety device in electricity, device for exploding bomb etc. **Fu'sion**, *n.* a joining together.

Fu'selage, *n.* the body of an aircraft.

Fuss, *n.* unnecessary bustle or worry. *v.t. & i*

Fus'tian, *n.* coarse cloth like corduroy, bombastic talk.

Fu'tile, *a.* useless, worthless, vain. **Futil'ity**, *n.*

Futtock', *n.* one of ship's middle timbers.

Fu'ture, *a.* yet to happen, of the time in which something will happen. *n.* time yet to come, subsequent happenings; *gram.* the future tense.

Fu'turism, *n.* modern art movement (*ca.* 1909-1914) characterized by admiration of speed, machines, and danger, and advocating the destruction of everything old. **Fu'turist**, *n.*

Fyl'fot (fil-), *n.* swastika, symbol of Hitlerism.

G

Gab, *n.* idle chatter, mouth. *v.i.* to talk loosely.

Gab'ardine, *n.* fine cloth resembling serge.

Gab'ble, *v.t. & i.* to jabber, talk fast. *n.*

Gab'erdine, *n.* long loose robe worn by Jews in past.

Ga'ble, *n.* triangular part of outer house-wall between apexes of roof.

Ga'by, *n.* dolt.

Gad, *v.t.* to go about for pleasure.

Gadg'et, *n.* device, contrivance.

Gae'lic (Gay-), *a.* pertaining to Celtic people of Sc. highlands. **Gael'** (Gale), *n.*

Gaff, *n.* hooked stick for landing large fish .*v.t.*

Gaffe, *n.* indiscreet remark.

Gaff'er, *n.* old man, foreman.

Gag, *n.* object put in mouth to hinder speech or keep mouth open during operation. *v.t. & i. n.* a joke, words interpolated by actor.

Ga-ga, *a. sl.* senile, daft.

Gage, *n.* pledge, promise, token of challenge.

Gai'ety, *n.* joyfulness, jollity. **Gay,** *a.*

Gain, *v.t. & i.* to derive advantage from, profit, obtain, win. *n.* profit, advantage.

Gainsay', *v.t.* to contradict.

Gait, *n.* style of moving.

Gait'er, *n.* leather covering for lower leg.

Ga'la (Gah-lah), *n.* a festive celebration, special performance.

Gal'axy, *n.* brilliant group, gathering of stars, the Milky Way.

Gale, *n.* a strong wind, storm.

Gall, *n.* bile of animals, bitterness.

Gall, *n.* sore caused by chafing. *v.t. & i.*

Gall'ant (Gal-), *a.* brave, chivalrous, courteous. *n.* a man with these qualities. **Gall'antry,** *n.*

Gall'eon, *n. arch.* large sailing vessel with three or four decks.

Gall'ery, *n.* long corridor, room for exhibiting pictures, balcony, topmost seats in theatre, underground passage.

Gall'ey, *n. arch.* single-decked vessel propelled by oars and sails.

Gall'ey, *n.* ship's kitchen; in printing, oblong tray for holding type.

Gall'on, *n.* liquid measure of four quarts.

Gall'op, *n.* swiftest pace of horse. *v.t. & i.* to ride at this.

Galore', *a.* abundant.

Gal'vanize, *v.t.* to coat with metal, to shock or rouse as if by electricity.

Gam'bit, *n.* opening in chess often with deliberate loss of piece; any opening move. *n.* a tentative project.

Gam'ble, *v.i.* to play for money, take risk. *n.* **Gam'bler,** *n.*

Gam'bol, *n.* a frolic. *v.i.*

Game, *n.* sport, play, amusement, set contest, part of a match; certain wild birds, fish and animals. *a.* plucky. *v.i.* to gamble.

Gamm'on, *n.* lower end of side of bacon; *coll.* nonsense.

Gam'ut, *n.* the major scale in mus., range of voice.

Gan'der, *n.* male goose.

Gang, *n.* band, us. in derogatory sense, mob, squad, body of workmen. **Gang'ster,** *n.* criminal.

Gan'grene, *n.* initial stage of mortification. **Gan'grenous,** *a.*

Gan'try, *n.* structure supporting railway signals, crane etc.

Gaol (Jale), *n.* prison. **Gaol'er,** *n.* prison-warder.

Gap, *n.* a breach, opening.

Gape, *v.i.* to open mouth wide, yawn. *n.*

Gar'age, *n.* building in which automobiles are kept or serviced. *v.t.* to put in g.

Garb, *n.* dress. *v.t.*

Garb'age, *n.* refuse, offal.

Gar'ble, *v.t.* to misrepresent, to mutilate verbally.

Gar'den, *n.* plot of land devoted to cultivation of flowers & vegetables. *v.i.* to work in this. **Gard'ener,** *n.*

Gargan'tuan, *a.* huge, gigantic.

Gar'gle, *v.t. & i.* to cleanse throat medically.

Garg'oyle, *n.* water-spout in gutter decorated with carving of head.

Gar'ish (Gare-), *a.* dazzling, gaudy.

Gar'land, *n.* crown of flowers or leaves. *v.t.*

Gar'ment, *n.* dress, piece of clothing.

Gar'ner, *v.t.* to collect, store, *n.* a granary.

Gar'net, *n.* semi-precious stone.

Gar'nish, *v.t.* to embellish, decorate. **Gar'niture,** *n.*

Garr'et, *n.* an attic, a small room in top of house.

Garr'ison, *n.* fortress in town manned by troops, these troops. *v.t.* to man a garrison.

Garr'ulous, *a.* talkative. **Garru'lity,** *n.*

Gar'ter, *n.* suspender for sock or stocking.

Gas, *n.* an airlike fluid, a combustible gaseous mixture used for providing heat and light. *v.t. & i.* to poison with gas; *sl.* to talk nonsense or volubly. **Gas'eous,** *a.* of or like gas.

Gash, *n.* gaping wound. *v.t.* to cut deeply.

Gas'ket, *n.* cord for furling ship's or yacht's sail, layer of material for sealing joint.

Gasp, *n.* a quick, convulsive breath. *v.i.*

Gas'tric, *a.* pertaining to the stomach. **Gastron'omy,** *n.* the art of good eating.

Gate, *n.* hinged barrier in opening in wall or fence. **Gateway,** *n.* **Gate-crash,** *v.t. & i.* to go to a party without being invited.

Gath'er, *v.t. & i.* to come or bring together, assemble, pick, collect, infer.

Gauche (Goshe), *a.* awkward. **Gau'cherie,** *n.* a clumsy or tactless act.

Gau'cho (Gow-), *n.* S. Amer. cowboy.

Gaud'y (Gawd-), *a.* tawdry, vulgarly gay. **Gaud,** *n.* a tawdry ornament.

Gauge (Gaje), *n.* a standard measurement, instrument for measuring, distance between railway rails. *v.t.* to judge, calculate, test.

Gau'ger, *n.* exciseman.

Gaunt (Gawnt), *a.* haggard.

Gaunt'let, *n.* glove with long wrist, steel glove.

Gauze (Gawz), *n.* thin transparent fabric of silk, cotton, wire etc.

Gav'el, *n.* mallet used by auctioneer or chairman for obtaining silence or finishing bidding.

Gaze, *v.i.* to look at steadily or fixedly. *n.*

Gazette', *n.* official journal for publication of government notices.

Gazetteer', *n.* dictionary of geographical names.

Gear, *n.* equipment, apparatus, device in engine for changing or transmitting power.

Gel'atine (Jel-), *n.* animal jelly obtained by rendering down bones, skin etc. **Gelat'inous,** *a.*

Geld (G-), *v.t.* to castrate a horse. **Gelding,** *n.* horse that has been castrated.

Gel'ignite (Jel-), *n.* nitro-glycerine explosive.

Gem (Jem), *n.* a jewel, precious stone, anything precious and brilliant. *v.t.* to deck with gems.

Gen'der (Jen-), *n. gram.* classification of noun by sex, masc., fem. or neut.

Gene (Jeen), *n.* hereditary factor in germ-cell.

Geneal'ogy, n. science of tracing descent of family. Geneal'ogist, n. specialist in this.

Gen'eral, a. universal, indefinite, unspecified, common. n. mil. officer ranking above colonel. General'ity, n. generalness. Gen'eralize, v.t. & i. to speak imprecisely or broadly, to draw general conclusions. Generaliza'tion, n.

Gen'erate, v.t. to bring into existence, produce. Genera'tion, n. the process of producing, people of same period, roughly thirty years. Gen'erative, a. productive, having power of producing. Gen'erator, n. begetter, apparatus by which power is produced.

Gen'erous, a. unselfish, liberal. Generos'ity, n.

Ge'nial, a. kindly, benign, clement. Genial'ity, n.

Gen'ital, a. pertaining to the generation of animals. n. pl. the organs of reproduction.

Gen'itive, n. gram. possessive case.

Ge'nius, n. remarkable intellectual ability.

Gen'ocide, n. mass race murder as practised by Nazis etc.

Genre, n. kind, style.

Genteel', a. fastidiously well-bred, now us. iron.

Gen'tile, n. person not of Jewish origin. a.

Gen'tle, a. mild, considerate, well-born, gradual, courteous. Gentil'ity, n. refinement, good behaviour. Gen'tleman, n. Gent'ry, n. now us. iron. upper class, esp. in country districts.

Gen'uflect, v.i. to bend the knee in respect or worship. Gen'uflexion, n.

Gen'uine, a. real, authentic, original, sincere.

Ge'nus, n. group of plants or animals with common characteristics but other differences, kind, order. pl. Gen'era. Gener'ic, a. pertaining to a genus or class. Genet'ics, n. science of origin & development of individuals & their inherited characteristics.

Geog'raphy, n. science of the earth's characteristics. Geog'rapher, n. person specializing in this. Geograph'ical, a.

Geol'ogy, n. science of the history and development of the earth's structure. Geol'ogist, n. specialist in this.

Geom'etry, n. branch of mathematics dealing with properties & measurements of angles, lines, surfaces and solids. Geometri'cian, n.

Germ, n. undeveloped beginning of plant or animal, microbe; fig. beginning of anything. Germ'icide, n. substance for destroying disease-carrying microbes. Ger'minate, v.t. & i. to grow or cause to grow, develop. Germina'tion. Ger'man, a. of same parents.

Germane', a. relevant, pertinent, connected with.

Gesta'tion, n. act or period of carrying young in womb.

Gestic'ulate, v.t. & i. to gesture expressively while talking. Gesticula'tion, n. Ges'ture, n. an expressive movement of hand or arm.

Get (Get), v.t. & i. to acquire, fetch, catch, become, reach. sl. inter. go away.

Get-up, *n.* style of dress, appearance.

Gey'ser (Geezer), *n.* natural hot spring discharging water or mud intermittently; an old-fashioned contrivance for heating bath-water.

Ghast'ly (-ah-), *a.* horrible, hideous.

Ghett'o, *n.* formerly part of town to which Jews were confined.

Ghost (Go-), *n.* phantom, spectre.

Ghoul (Gool), *n.* evil spirit in Oriental legends. **Ghoul'ish,** *a.*

Ghill'ie, *n.* Highland chief's servant, sportsman's attendant in Sc.

Gi'ant, *n.* in legend a man of supernatural size but human form, any very large person or thing. **Gigant'ic,** *a.* huge.

Gibb'er (Jib-), *v.i.* to speak quickly and incoherently. **Gibber'ish,** *n.* meaningless chatter.

Gibb'et, *n.* gallows on which body of dead criminal was exhibited.

Gibb'ous (Gib-), *a.* humped, of the moon between full and half-full.

Gibe (Jybe), *n.* a taunt, sneer. *v.t. & i.*

Gib'let (Jib-), *n.* esp. as *n. pl.* edible entrails of poultry.

Gidd'y (Gid-), *a.* dizzy, flighty.

Gift (G-), *n.* a present, something given.

Gift'ed *a.* talented, endowed with great ability.

Gig (G-), *n.* two-wheeled horse-drawn carriage, ship's boat for use of officers.

Gig'gle (Gig'l), *n.* a smothered, uncontrollable laugh. *v.i.*

Gild (G-), *v.t.* to coat with thin layer of gold, to gloss over,

conceal reality. **Gilt,** *a. & n.* gilded, gilding.

Gill (G-), *n.* fish's breathing-organ.

Gill (Jil), *n.* unit of liquid measure, a quarter of a pint.

Gim'bals (Gim-), *n. pl.* device for ensuring that compass etc. constantly level despite rolling of ship.

Gim'let (G-), *n.* small boring tool.

Gin (Jin), *n.* alcohol made from grain and flavoured with juniper berries.

Gin (Jin), *n.* a trap or snare; a machine for processing cotton fibre.

Gin'ger (Jin), *n.* tropical plant with sharp-tasting root used for flavouring; *coll.* energy, esp. as **Ginger-group** in polit.

Gin'gerly (Jin-), *adv.* timidly, cautiously.

Ging'ham (Ging'am), *n.* cotton dress for frocks.

Gip'sy, (Jip-), *n.* member of wandering dark-complexioned people probably originating in India.

Gird (Gurd), *v.t.* to encircle with a belt, to make ready, esp. for conflict. **Gir'dle,** *n.* a belt.

Gird'er (Gurd-), *n.* main supporting beam taking weight of bridge or other structure.

Girl (Gurl), *n.* female child, young woman. **Girl'hood,** *n.* **Girl'ish,** *n.*

Girth (Gurth), *n.* the measurement round a body, part of horse's harness to keep saddle in place.

Gist (Jist), *n.* the essential point of a matter or a story.

Give (Giv), *v.t.* to make a present, bestow freely, hand

over, devote, deliver, furnish,
utter, yield, perform etc.

Giz′zard, *n.* second stomach of
birds.

Gla′cier, *n.* vast mass of ice
moving slowly towards sea or
valley. **Gla′cial**, *a.* pertaining
to ice or the ice ages.

Glad, *a.* pleased, joyful. **Gladd′-
en**, *v.t. & i.*

Glade, *n.* long open clearing in
forest.

Glad′iator, *n.* orig. a professional fighter in Roman arena.
Gladiatori′al, *a.* to do with
professional combat.

Glam′our, *n.* alluring charm, us.
of a rather false kind. **Glam′-
orous**, *a.*

Glance, *n.* brief or hasty
sidelong look. *v.i.* to look at
cursorily, to hit lightly and
bounce off obliquely.

Gland, *n.* an organ which
processes substances in the
body. **Glan′dular**, *a.* pertaining
to glands. **Glan′ders**, *n.* feverish
contagious disease in horses
etc.

Glare, *n.* a dazzling light, hostile
look. *v.t. & i.* to shine in
dazzling manner, to gaze at
fiercely. **Glar′ing**, *a.* extremely
bright, very conspicuous.

Glass (Glahss), *n.* hard brittle
transparent substance made
from sand mixed with soda,
potash etc., any article made of
this. **Glaze**, *v.t. & i.* to provide
with glass, esp. in windows, to
become glassy, as with eyes.
Gla′zier, *n.* artisan who fits
window-glass. **Gla′zing**, *n.* the
trade or work of doing this.

Gleam, *n.* a small brief shaft of
light; *fig.* something resembling
this, e.g. gleam of hope. *v.i.* to

emit brief shaft of light,
twinkle.

Glean, *v.t. & i.* to gather corn
left after harvest, to obtain
knowledge here and there.

Glebe (Gleeb), *n. arch.* land
owned by parish church.

Glee, *n.* gaiety, merriment,
elation.

Glen, *n.* a coombe esp. in Sc.

Glib, *a.* speaking facilely but
insincerely.

Glide, *v.i.* to move along silently
and smoothly. **Gli′der**, *n.*
engineless aircraft.

Glim′mer, *n.* a feeble, flickering
light, a gleam. *v.i.*

Glimpse, *n.* a brief, hasty view.
v.t.

Glint, *n.* a brief flash. *v.i.* to
sparkle faintly.

Glis′ten (-sen), *v.i.* to gleam,
sparkle. **Glis′ter** (Glis-ter), *v.i.*

Glit′ter, *v.i.* to sparkle.

Gloam′ing, *n.* dusk.

Gloat (Glote), *v.i.* to gaze on in
spiteful triumph or greed.

Globe, *n.* a round object, a
sphere representing the earth,
the earth. **Glo′bal**, *a.* world-
wide. **Glob′ular**, *a.* round,
composed of drops or globe-
shaped particles. **Glob′ule**, *n.* a
very small globe-shaped particle.

Gloom, *n.* unhappiness, near
darkness.

Glor′y, *n.* splendour, distinction,
fame, honour. *v.i.* to exult.
Glor′ify, *v.t.* to worship, exalt,
give honour to. **Glor′ious**, *a.*
magnificent, splendid, praiseworthy.

Gloss, *n.* smooth shining coating. *v.t.* to render smooth, to
cover up imperfections. **Gloss′y**,
a. shiny.

Gloss'ary, *n.* explanatory notes at end of technical book.

Glottis, *n.* small opening in upper part of windpipe.

Glove (Gluv), *n.* a covering for the hand. **Glov'er**, *n.* maker or seller of gloves.

Glow (Glo), *v.i.* to emit heat and light without flame. *n.*

Glow'er (Glow-er), *v.i.* to scowl.

Glu'cose, *n.* form of natural sugar in fruit.

Glue (Gloo), *n.* coarse gelatine used for adhesive purposes. *v.t.* to join with this. **Glu'tinous**, *a.* sticky.

Glum, *a.* moody, sullen.

Glut'ton, *n.* greedy person. **Glut'tonous**, *a.*

Gnarl (Narl), *n.* a knot or twisted shape in wood. **Gnarled**, *a.* twisted, knotty.

Gnash (Nash), *v.t. & i.* to grind the teeth together.

Gnaw (Naw), *v.t.* to eat away gradually and repeatedly.

Gnome (Nome), *n.* underground elf.

Go, *v.i.* to move about, depart, travel, start, be, work, function, result, elapse, turn, etc.

Goad, *n.* sharp pointed stick for driving on cattle. *v.t.* to urge with a goad, urge into action persistently.

Goal, *n.* aim, purpose, a score at football etc.

Gob'ble, *v.t.* to eat and swallow greedily.

Gob'let, *n.* drinking vessel without handle.

Gob'lin, *n.* gnome, elf.

God, *n.* a deity, supernatural being worshipped by men, supreme being. **God'dess**, *n.* a female deity. **God'father**, *n.* man who accepts rel. responsibilities for someone else's child. **God'send**, *n.* good fortune, unexpected help. **God-forsaken**, *a.* abandoned, hopeless.

Goi'tre (Goy-ter), *n.* disease of thyroid gland in neck.

Gold, *n.* bright yellow precious metal used for coinage and jewellery, money, wealth. **Gol'den**, *a.*

Golf, *n.* game in which small ball is driven by club from hole to hole. *v.i.* **Gol'fer**, *n.*

Gon'dola, *n.* long narrow flat-bottomed decorated boat used esp. on canals of Venice. **Gon'dolier**, *n.* boatman of this.

Gong, *n.* round metal object struck with stick as summons to meal etc., an alarm-bell.

Good, *a.* fine in quality, efficient, virtuous, right, proper, sound. *n.* anything that is morally right, profit, advantage. **Goods**, *n. pl.* manufactured articles.

Gore, *n. iron.* or *arch.* blood.

Gore, *v.t.* to pierce esp. with horns.

Gorge, *n.* a deep narrow ravine, the throat. *v.t. & i.* to eat greedily.

Gor'geous (-jus), *a.* splendid, highly decorated.

Gos'ling, *n.* young goose.

Gos'pel, *n.* the history of the life and teachings of Christ, any trustworthy principle which is ardently believed in.

Goss'amer, *n.* light film of spider's web, any light gauzy material.

Goss'ip, *n.* idle, slightly slanderous talk about other people's affairs, person who makes a practice of this. *v.i.*

Gouge (Gowj), *n.* carpenter's

hollow chisel for making grooves. *v.t.* to use this, scoop out.

Gourd (Goord), *n.* trailing plant with large fleshy fruit, related to melon.

Gour'mand, (-mon), *n.* a greedy person. **Gour'met,** (-may), *n.* a person with good taste in food.

Gout (Gowt), *n.* inflammatory disease afflicting joints.

Gov'ern (Guv-), *v.t. & i.* to rule over, control, determine. **Gov'ernor,** *n.* **Gov'erness,** *n.* private woman tutor. **Gov'ernment,** *n.* authority or management, system of governing a country.

Gown, *n.* woman's dress, robe worn by judges, schoolmasters etc.

Grab, *v.t. & i.* to snatch, seize suddenly.

Grace, *n.* elegance of manner and movement, charm, kindness, prayer of thanks. *v.t.* to honour, favour. **Gra'cious,** *a.* courteous.

Grade, *n.* a step or degree, rank, position, division. *v.t.* to arrange according to quality. **Grada'tion,** *n.* gradual change. **Gra'dient,** *n.* even slope. **Grad'ual,** *a.* moving or changing by degrees.

Grad'uate, *n.* university student who has obtained degree. *v.t. & i.* **Gradua'tion,** *n.*

Graft (Grahft), *v.t.* to bind stem of one plant on to another for hybridization, to transplant living tissue onto another body. *n.*

Graft, *n.* corruption.

Grail (Grale), *n.* a cup, esp. as **Holy G,** cup celebrated in legend as being one Christ used at Last Supper.

Grain, *n.* seedlike fruit of cereal, small particle.

Grain, *n.* texture of wood, *fig.* the characteristics of a person.

Gram'mar, *n.* science dealing with forms of words and their inter-relation. **Gram'matical,** *a.* correct according to the rules of grammar.

Gran'ary, *n.* storehouse for grain.

Grand, *a.* splendid, magnificent, big, dignified.

Gran'deur (-dure), *n.* splendour, magnificence.

Grandil'oquent, *a.* pompous in speech. **Grandil'oquence,** *n.*

Gran'diose, *a.* ostentatious, imposing.

Grange, *n.* country house with farm attached.

Gran'ite (-it), *n.* hard durable crystalline rock. *a.*

Grant, *v.t. & i.* to allow, admit, bestow, give. *n.* a sum given officially.

Gran'ular, *a.* of or like grain or granules. **Gran'ulate,** *v.t. & i.* to form into grains. **Gran'ule,** *n.* a small grain.

Grape, *n.* the fruit of the vine. **Grape-shot,** *n. arch.* cluster of small iron shot.

Graph (Grahf), *n.* diagram illustrating relationship between different quantities or phenomena.

Graph'ic, *a.* pertaining to the art of drawing etc., illustrated, vivid.

Graph'ite, *n.* soft black carbon used in making pencils.

Grap'nel, *n.* small anchor with several hooks, grappling-iron.

Grap'ple, *v.t. & i.* to close in struggle with.

Grasp, *v.t. & i.* to seize, clutch,

understand. *n.* **Grasp'ing,** *a.* greedy.

Grass, *n.* herbage, pasture, *v.t.* to cover with grass.

Grate, *v.t. & i.* to break into fragments by rubbing, to cause a squeaking noise by rubbing, to cause irritation.

Grate, *n.* fireplace, fire-basket.

Grate'ful, *a.* thankful, appreciative, pleasant. **Grat'itude,** *n.*

Grat'ify, *v.t.* to please, delight, indulge. **Gratifica'tion,** *n.*

Gratu'itous, *a.* free, unasked. **Gratu'ity,** *n.* bounty, tip.

Grave, *n.* tomb, hole in ground for burying corpse. **Gravestone, Graveyard,** *n. n.*

Grave, *a.* solemn, serious. **Grav'ity,** *n.*

Grav'el, *n.* coarse pebbles, ground rock. *v.t.* to cover path with g.

Gr'aven, *a.* carved.

Grav'id, *a.* pregnant.

Grav'itate, *v.t. & i.* to be moved by gravity, to move towards, settle. **Gravita'tion,** *n.* force of gravity. **Grav'ity,** *n.* force which attracts all objects on or near earth towards it.

Gra'vy, *n.* meat juice, sauce.

Graze, *v.t. & i.* to eat grass, put out to pasture. **Gra'zier,** *n.* farmer who breeds cattle for market. **Gra'zing,** *n.* pasture.

Graze, *v.t. & i.* to scrape lightly. *n.* a slight abrasion.

Grease (Greece), *n.* thick oil, melted animal fat. *v.t.* to smear or lubricate with this. **Greas'y,** *a.* oily, slippery.

Great (Grate), *n.* big, grand, famous, extreme.

Greed, *n.* selfish desire.

Green, *a.* grass-coloured. *n.* colour between blue and yel-

low. *a.* unripe, inexperienced.

Greenhorn, *n.* a simpleton.

Greenhouse, *n.* glass-covered building for growing plants in.

Greensward, *n.* lawn, grass.

Greet, *v.t.* to welcome, receive warmly. **Greet'ing,** *n.* welcoming salute or message.

Gregar'ious, *a.* living in herds or flocks.

Gren'ade, *n.* bomb for throwing or shooting. **Gren'adier,** *n.* infantryman orig. armed with grenade.

Grey (Gray), *n.* colour obtained by blending black with white. *a.* dull, sombre.

Grid, *n.* grating, system of elec. supply.

Grid'dle, *n.* flat iron plate used for cooking scones etc.

Grid'iron, *n.* frame of iron bars for broiling meat and fish.

Grief (Greef), *n.* intense sorrow or trouble. **Griev'ance,** *n.* a hardship, complaint. **Griev'ous,** *a.* severe.

Grill, *n.* a gridiron, dish of meat or fish prepared on grill. *v.t.* to broil; *sl.* question closely. **Grill-room,** *n.*

Grille, *n.* protective bars over door or window.

Grim, *a.* stern, threatening.

Grim'ace, *n.* expression of disgust or annoyance. *v.i.*

Grime, *n.* dirt.

Grin, *n.* a wry or broad smile. *v.t. & i.*

Grind (Grine-), *v.t.* to crush into powder, sharpen, oppress, grate, study hard, turn handle. **Grindstone,** *n.* revolving stone for sharpening knives.

Grip, *v.t. & i.* to clasp, hold tightly. *n.* **Gripp'ing,** *a.* intensely interesting.

Grip, *n.* small hold-all for travelling.

Gripe, *v.t. & i.* to seize, esp. to cause pain in bowels.

Gris'ly (Griz-), *a.* gruesome, hideous.

Grist, *n.* corn to be ground.

Gris'tle (-s'l), *n.* cartilage, tough animal tissue.

Grit, *n.* particles of sand, any fine powdery hard substance; *coll.* courage. *v.t. & i.* to grind, esp. the teeth. **Griz'zle,** *v.i.* to complain in snivelling way. **Griz'zled,** (Griz'ld), *a.* grey-haired.

Groan (Grone), *n.* low moaning sound of pain or complaint. *v.t. & i.*

Gro'cer, *n.* dealer in domestic supplies. **Gro'ceries,** *n. pl.* the goods he deals in. **Gro'cery,** *n.* his shop.

Grog, *n.* rum and water. **Grogg'y,** *a.* affected by drink or blow, slightly unwell.

Groin, *n.* junction of thigh and body; in arch. curved ridge formed by intersecting arches.

Groom, *n.* man or boy in charge of horses. *v.t.* to tend horse.

Grooms'man, *n.* best man, bridegroom's companion.

Groove, *n.* a channel or furrow. *v.t.*

Grope, *v.t. & i.* to fumble for, search blindly.

Gross (Grose), *a.* fat, coarse, shameful, great.

Gro'tesque, *a.* fantastic, distorted, absurd.

Grot'to, *n.* picturesque cavern, often artificial.

Ground, *n.* the soil, the surface of the earth, bottom, foundation, basis, extent. *v.t. & i.* to fall to earth, to run ashore or strike seabed, to fail, to instruct basically. **Groundless,** *a.* without reason or foundation.

Grounds, *n. pl.* reasons.

Grounds, *n. pl.* dregs.

Group (Groop), *n.* cluster of things, collection of people. *v.t. & i.* to bring or assemble together.

Grouse, *v.i.* to grumble. *n.*

Grove, *n.* a small wood.

Grov'el, *v.i.* to cringe, humble oneself in cowardly way.

Grow (Gro), *v.t. & i.* to develop, expand, mature, arise, increae.

Growth (Groth), *n.* the process of growing or developing; a tumour.

Growl, *n.* subdued snarl. *v.t. & i.*

Grub, *v.t. & i.* to dig, root about, toil.

Grub, *n.* maggot, larva.

Grudge, *n.* ill-will, resentment, spite. *v.t. & i.* to envy, give or agree unwillingly.

Grue'some, *a.* grisly, ghastly.

Gruff, *a.* surly in manner.

Grum'ble, *v.i.* to complain.

Grum'py, *a.* surly, sulky.

Grunt, *n.* sound made by pig. sound resembling this. *v.i.*

Guarantee', *n.* warrant, statement that something is as represented or claimed, security for good faith. *v.t.* to promise, pledge. **Guarantor',** *n.* person who guarantees.

Guard, *n.* protector, superintendent, sentry. *v.t.* to look after, protect. **Guard'ian,** *n.* warden, person entrusted with care of someone else's child.

Guerill'a, *n.* partisan, unofficial soldier operating behind enemy lines.

Guess, *v.t. & i.* to surmise, form opinion without sure facts. *n.*

Guffaw′, *n.* loud harsh burst of laughter. *v.i.*

Guide, *n.* person who directs or leads, book of travel instructions. *v.t.* to lead or show the way. **Gui′dance**, *n.* direction, leadership.

Guild, *n.* craft association or brotherhood.

Guile, *n.* cunning.

Guillotine (-teen), *n.* machine for execution by beheading, esp. in France, machine for cutting thick quantities of paper.

Guilt, *n.* the fact of having committed a sin or crime. **Guilt′y**, *a.*

Guise, *n.* external appearance, likeness.

Gulf, *n.* large arm of the sea, an abyss.

Gull, *n.* large web-footed seabird, a dupe. *v.t.* to dupe, cheat.

Gull′et, *n.* food passage through throat.

Gull′ible, *a.* easily deceived. **Gullibil′ity**, *n.*

Gull′y, *n.* narrow ravine eroded by water.

Gulp, *v.t.* to swallow with difficulty or hastily. *n.*

Gum, *n.* flesh in which teeth are rooted.

Gum, *n.* glue. *v.t.* to fasten with gum.

Gump′tion, *n.* common sense, initiative.

Gun, *n.* fire-arm, cannon, rifle, pistol. **Gun** as part of various self-explanatory compounds, **gun-boat**, **gunman**, **gunshot** etc.

Gunn′ery, *n.* science and use of artillery. **Gunn′er**, *n.* serviceman skilled in gunnery.

Gun′wale (Gunnel), *n.* upper edge of boat's side.

Gur′gle, *n.* broken, bubbling sound as of liquid. *v.i.*

Gush, *n.* a sudden outflowing, an outburst. *v.i.* to flow out suddenly and copiously, to talk inanely.

Guss′et, *n.* tapering piece of material inserted into garment to enlarge it.

Gust, *n.* sudden violent rush of wind, an outburst, as of laughter.

Gust′o, *n.* zest, enjoyment.

Gut, *n.* intestine, narrow passage in waterway, catgut, as used for violin strings. *v.t.* to remove entrails from fish etc., to remove contents of by destruction. **Guts**, *n. pl. vulg.* courage.

Gutt′er, *n.* channel at roadside or under eaves of building for diversion of water.

Gutt′ural (Gutter-), *a.* pertaining to the throat, formed in the throat, harsh.

Guy (Gye), *n.* rope or wire for holding pole or crane etc. securely.

Guy, *n.* effigy, queer person. *v.t.* to make fun of.

Guz′zle, *v.t. & i.* to gorge, eat or drink greedily.

Gymkha′na (Jim-kah-), *n.* horse-riding display and competition.

Gymna′sium (Jim-), *n.* building or room for practising athletic exercises. **Gymnas′tic**, *a.* of exercise. *n. pl.* physical exercises. **Gym′nast**, *n.* person skilled in these.

Gynaecol′ogy (Gyne-), *n.* branch of medicine treating diseases of women. **Gynaecol′ogist**, *n.* medical expert in these.

Gyp′sum (Jip-), *n.* calcium

sulphate, used for making plaster of Paris.

Gyrate' (Jy-), *v.i.* to move in a spiral or circle. Gyra'tion, *n.* Gy'ratory, *a.* Gy'roscope, *n.* wheeled device revolving at high speed to maintain equilibrium. Gy'ro-compass, *n. naut.* compass equipped with gyroscope.

H

Hab'erdashery, *n.* small items of dress, socks, ties etc. Hab'erdasher, *n.* shopkeeper dealing in these.

Habil'iments, *n. pl.* attire, dress.

Hab'it, *n.* fixed characteristic action, settled practice. Hab'itual, *a.* usual, customary. Habit'uate, *v.t.* to accustom, get used to.

Habita'tion, *n.* a dwelling-place. Hab'itable, *a.* fit as this. Hab'itat, *n.* natural abode.

Hach'ure (Hash-), *n.* shading on map denoting hills. *v.t.*

Hack, *n.* hired riding-horse. *v.t. & i.* to hire out horse, ride horse.

Hack, *n.* drudge, esp. in lit. sense. Hack-work, *n.* ill-paid lit. drudgery.

Hack, *v.t. & i.* to kick, cut roughly, chop. Hack-saw, *n.*

Hac'kle, *n.* neck feathers of cockerel, dry fly for fishing.

Hack'ney, *n.* horse-drawn carriage for hire, cab.

Hack'neyed, *a.* commonplace, trite.

Haemoglo'bin, Hemo-, *n.* colouring matter of red blood corpuscles. Haemophil'ia, *n.* inherited and dangerous tendency to bleed. Haem'orrhage, *n.* serious escape of blood. Haem'orrhoids, *n.* piles.

Haft, *n.* handle esp. of cutting tool.

Hag, *n.* ugly old woman.

Hagg'ard, *n.* gaunt in appearance from worry.

Hagg'is, *n.* Sc. national dish based on sheep's offal boiled in stomach-bag.

Hag'gle, *v.i.* to wrangle, dispute price.

Hag'iology (Haj-), *n.* literature about saints, the study of this. Hag'iolatry, *n.* the worship of saints.

Hail, *n.* frozen vapour. *v.t. & i.* to fall as hail.

Hail, *v.t. & i.* to greet, salute, come from (as Hail from). *n.* a cry, *interj.* a greeting.

Hair, *n.* threadlike growth from head of human or forming part of animal's fur. Hair's-breadth, *n.* extremely small gap. Hair-splitting, *n.* quibbling, exaggerated distinction.

Hal'berd, *n. arch.* weapon combining spear and battleaxe.

Hal'cyon (-sion), *n.* mythical bird resembling the kingfisher reputed having power of calming the waves. *a.* calm, happy.

Hale, *a.* sound in health, robust.

Hale, *v.t.* to drag forcibly.

Half, (Hahf), *n.* one of two equal parts. *a. & adv.* **Half-** as part of various self-explanatory compounds, e.g. **half-breed, half-caste, half-hearted, half-witted,** etc.

Half-mast, *n.* position in which flag is flown in token of mourning.

Hall, *n.* large public assembly room, college, entrance-room to house, large house on estate.

Hall′mark, *n.* mark showing standard and particulars of gold and silver articles. *v.t.*

Hall′ow (Hal-o), *v.t.* to make sacred, reverence.

Hallucina′tion, *n.* a delusion, an imagined happening.

Ha′lo, *n.* luminous circle round sun or moon etc., fanciful ring of light round head of holy person in paintings.

Halt (Hawlt), *a.* crippled or lame. *v.i.* to limp.

Halt, *v.t. & i.* to come to a stop or cause to stop. *n.* a stopping-place.

Halt′er, *n.* head-rope for leading or tethering horse, a hangman's noose. *v.t.*

Hal′yard, Hall′iard, Haul′yard, *n. naut.* rope for manipulating sails etc.

Ham, *n.* back of thigh, this of pig prepared as food.

Ham, *n.* untalented actor.

Ham′let, *n.* a collection of houses in country.

Hamm′er, *n.* tool for driving in nails, device for firing gun. *v.t. & i.* to knock or beat as with a hammer.

Hamm′ock, *n.* sailor's swinging canvas bed, network bed for resting in garden.

Hamp′er, *n.* large wickerwork basket.

Hamp′er, *v.t.* to hinder, obstruct.

Ham′string, *n.* tendon at back of human knee, above and behind hock in animals. *v.t.* to lame by severing this.

Hand, *n.* arm below wrist, clock pointer, standard of measurement for horses (four inches), a round of cards, style of handwriting, assistance, control, etc. *v.t.* to pass, give with hand, hold out.

Hand′cuff, *n.* us. as *n. pl.* metal bracelets for restraining prisoner. **Hand′icap,** *n.* disadvantage, disablement, impediment. **Hand′icraft,** *n.* manual skill.

Hand′iwork, *n.* work done manually, work achieved by personal effort.

Hand′kerchief, *n.* square piece of cloth for blowing nose.

Han′dle, *n.* part of object by which it is held. *v.t.* to move, hold, touch by hand, deal with or in, manage.

Hand′some (Hansom), *a.* good-looking, generous.

Hang, *v.t. & i.* to suspend or be suspended, to execute or kill by suspending by neck, to fasten something so that it is suspended, to depend, to attach wallpaper.

Hang′ar, *n.* a building for housing aircraft.

Hang-dog, *a.* dejected, ashamed.

Hang′er-on, *n.* unwanted follower.

Hank, *n.* coil or skein.

Han′ker, *v.i.* to yearn or crave.

Han′som, *n.* two-wheeled horse-cab with outside seat for driver at rear.

Haphaz'ard, *a.* accidental, unintentional. *adv.* by chance.

Hap'less, *a.* unlucky.

Happ'en, *v.i.* to occur. **Hap,** *v.i.* to happen. **Hap'ly,** *adv.* perchance.

Happ'y, *a.* content, cheerful, fortunate. **Happy-go-lucky,** *a.* carefree.

Ha'raki'ri, *n.* Japanese method of committing suicide by disembowelment.

Harangue', *n.* a ranting speech. *v.t.*

Har'ass, *v.t.* torment, worry.

Harb'inger (-jer), *n.* herald, forerunner.

Harb'our, *n.* haven, shelter for ships. *v.t.* & *i.* to give or take shelter, to indulge.

Hard, *a.* firm, solid, harsh, severe, difficult to comprehend. *adv.* fast, strenuously. **Hard'en,** *v.t.* & *i.* to harden or make hard etc. **Hard'ship,** *n.* privation. **Hard'headed,** *a.* unsentimental. **Hard-hearted,** *a.* cruel, unfeeling. **Hard,** *n.* landing-beach. **Hard'y,** *a.* resolute, tough. **Hard'ihood,** *n.* audacity. **Hard'ly,** *adv.* scarcely.

Har'em (-eem), *n.* a Muslim's various wives and concubines, part of house where these are quartered.

Hark, *v.i.* to listen.

Harl'equin, *n.* buffoon, gaily dressed clown. **Harlequinade',** *n.* act in pantomime.

Harl'ot, *n.* a prostitute.

Harm, *n.* injury, damage. *v.t.*

Har'mony, *n.* *in mus.* combination of tones forming chords, concord, agreement. **Harmon'ic,** *a.* of or in harmony, concordant. **Harmo'nious,** *a.* in agreement. **Har'monize,** *v.t.*

& *i.* to arrange in mus. harmony, to perform in harmony.

Har'ness, *n.* equipment for controlling horse or attaching to vehicle. *v.t.* to put on harness, control.

Harp, *n.* a stringed mus. hand instrument. *v.i.* **Harp'er,** *n.* **Harp'ist,** *n.*

Harp, *v.i.* to keep returning tediously to a subject.

Harpoon', *n.* barbed missile with rope attached for killing whales. *v.t.* **Harpoon-gun,** *n.* gun used for projecting this. **Harpoon'er,** *n.*

Harp'sichord, *n.* old instrument similar to piano.

Harp'y, *n.* myth. monster part woman, part bird.

Har'quebus, (-kwi-) *n.* arch. kind of hand-gun.

Har'ridan, *n.* haggish, vicious old woman.

Har'row (-o), *n.* agric. instrument for raking soil or covering seeds. *v.t.*

Har'row, *v.t.* to distress deeply.

Har'ry, *v.t.* to pursue, plunder, worry. **Har'rier,** *n.* a hound for hunting the hare, species of falcon.

Harsh, *a.* rough, unkind, unpleasant to the feelings or senses.

Hart, *n.* a stag.

Harv'est, *n.* a ripe crop, the gathering of this. *v.t.* **Har'vester,** *n.* farmworker who gathers the crop, reaping-machine.

Hash, *v.t.* to chop into small pieces, to do a thing badly. *n.* a dish of meat & vegetables, a bungled affair.

Hash'eesh, Hash'ish, *n.* Indian hemp. us. as narcotic.

Hasp (Hahsp), *n.* metal clasp working in conjunction with staple to form fastening.

Has'sock, *n.* cushion for kneeling, esp. in church.

Hast'en (Has'n), *v.t.* & *i.* to hurry or cause to hurry. **Haste,** *n.* speed, rash action. **Ha'sty,** *a.* hurried, impetuous.

Hat, *n.* a covering for the head. **Hatt'er,** *n.* manufacturer of or dealer in men's hats.

Hatch, *n.* an opening in door or wall for serving, *naut.* an opening in ship's deck. **Hatchway,** *n.*

Hatch, *v.t.* & *i.* to incubate, bring or come out of egg. **Hatch'ery,** *n.* place where fish or hen eggs are hatched.

Hatch'et, *n.* small axe.

Hate, *v.t.* to detest, dislike extremely. *n.* **Hate'ful,** *n.* distasteful, abhorrent. **Ha'tred,** *n.* intense loathing.

Hau'berk (Haw-), *n.* mediaeval coat of chain mail.

Haugh'ty (Haw-), *a.* disdainful, arrogant. **Hau'teur,** *n.* arrogance.

Haul (Hawl), *v.t.* & *i.* to pull along forcibly, transport, change course, veer, as of wind. **Haul'age,** *n.* transporting. **Haul'ier,** *n.* professional transporter.

Haunch (Hawnch), *n.* hip and buttocks, leg and loin of meat.

Haunt (Hawnt), *n.* a place much visited. *v.t.* to visit persistently, hang about, esp. of ghost.

Have, *v.t.* & *i.* to own, possess, hold, be compelled to, to state, show, use.

Ha'ven, *n.* a harbour, sheltered place.

Hav'ersack, *n.* canvas bag with shoulder strap.

Hav'oc, *n.* ruin, devastation.

Haw, *n.* hawthorn berry, the hawthorn tree.

Hawk, *v.t.* to peddle goods. **Hawk'er,** *n.* travelling salesman.

Hawk, *n.* raptorial bird. *v.t.* & *i.* to hunt as a hawk or use hawk as in falconry.

Hawk, *v.i.* to clear the throat violently.

Haw'ser (-zer), *n.* cable used to moor or tow vessel.

Hay, *n.* grass mown and dried for fodder.

Haz'ard, *n.* danger, risk, chance, game of dice. *v.t.* to risk. **Haz'-ardous,** *a.*

Haze, *n.* mist, mental vagueness.

Ha'zel, *n.* light brown colour, nut-tree, its fruit.

Head (Hed), *n.* topmost part of body in man and most animals, containing brain and features, the upper part of anything, the position of chief or leader in institution or business etc. *v.t.* & *i.* to lead, govern, get in front of.

Head as qualifying part of various compounds, e.g. **Headache,** *n.* persistent pain in head, **Head-dress,** *n.* hat, covering for head, **Header,** *n.* a headfirst dive, **Headland,** *n.* a cape, **Headlight,** *n.* one of automobile's main lights, **Headline,** *n.* summary of news at top of newspaper article, **Headlong,** *adv.* rashly, out of control, **Headmaster,** *n.* principal of school, **Headquarters,** *n. pl.* place from which mil. operations are directed, **Headstrong,** *a.* obstinate, **Headwaters,** *n. pl.* source of a river, **Headway,** *n.* progress, onward motion.

Health (Helth), *n.* bodily and mental fitness; *n.* a toast wishing someone health and happiness. **Heal** (Heel), *v.t.* & . to restore to health, to become well again. **Health′iness,** *n.*

Heap, *n.* pile of things lying on top of each other, an untidy mass. *v.t.*

Hear, *v.t.* & *i.* to perceive by the ear, to listen, receive information, to try in court of law. **Hear′ing,** *n.* sense by which sound is perceived, attention, a chance to be heard. **Hear′say,** *n.* rumour.

Hearse (Herss), *n.* vehicle for carrying coffin to grave.

Heart (Hart), *n.* hollow organ in animals maintaining circulation of blood, the most essential part of anything, the interior, courage, sympathy, liking. **Heart′en,** *v.t.* to encourage. **Heart′felt,** *a.* sincere, earnest. **Heart′less,** *a.* callous, unfeeling.

Hearth (Harth), *n.* domestic fireplace.

Heat, *n.* warmth, high temperature, hotness, the sensation of feeling this, period of sexual activity in animals, eliminating bout in athletics, anger. *v.t.* & *i.* to make or become hot, to anger.

Heath, *n.* barren region covered with heather and other vegetation. **Heath′er** (heth-), *n.* small low-growing evergeen plant with mauve flowers growing on heath & moorland.

Hea′then, *n.* pagan, anyone not accepting conventional religions. **Heathendom,** *n.*

Heave, *v.t.* & *i.* to raise up with difficulty, to hurl ponderously, to swell, as of waves, to draw deep breath or sigh.

Heav′en (Hev-), *n.* the firmament, the legendary domain of God, any serene place.

Heav′y (Hev-), *a.* of considerable weight, ponderous, serious, oppressive.

Hebdom′adal, *a.* every week.

Hec′kle, *v.t.* to question persistently and hostilely, esp. at polit. meeting. **Heck′ler,** *n.*

Hec′tic, *a.* feverish, *coll.* exciting.

Hecto- *pref.* denoting one hundred and used in metric system.

Hec′tor, *v.t.* & *i.* to threaten, bully.

Hedge, *n.* fence of shrubs, small trees. *v.t.* to enclose with fence, beset.

Hedge, *v.i.* to ensure against losing by betting in various ways.

He′donism, *n.* doctrine that pleasure is the main purpose in life. **He′donist,** *n.*

Heed, *v.t.* to pay attention to. **Heed′ful,** *a.* **Heed′less,** *a.*

Heel, *v.t.* & *i.* of a ship, to tilt over on one side.

Heel, *n.* lower & back part of foot, corresponding part of sock, shoe, boot etc. *v.t.* to provide with a heel.

Heft′y, *a.* sturdy. **Heft,** *v.t.* to lift, heave.

Hegem′ony (Heg-), *n.* leadership.

Heif′er, (Hef-), *n.* young cow.

Height, *n.* overall length, altitude man′s stature, high position or importance. **Height'en,** *v.t.* to make higher, raise.

Hei'nous (Hay-), *a.* very wicked.

Heir (Air), *n.* person who legally inherits either title or property. **Heir'ess,** *n. fem.* **Heir-apparent,** *n.* next in royal line after monarch. **Heirloom,** *n.* possession passed on from generation to generation.

Helicop'ter, *n.* aircraft driven by horizontally revolving blades.

He'lio, *pref.* meaning sun, e.g. **Heliograph,** *n.* signalling device using reflected sun-rays. **Helioscope,** *n.* a kind of telescope. **Heliotherapy,** *n.* use of sun-rays for med. purposes.

He'lium, *n.* very light gas for inflating balloons.

Hell, *n.* legendary place to which wicked are supposed to be condemned after death.

Hellen'ic, *a.* to do with Greece, esp. ancient Greece and its culture. **Hell'enism,** *n.* the study and admiration of Greek culture.

Helm, *n.* ship's steering apparatus. **Helms'man,** *n.* steersman.

Hel'met, *n.* armoured headgear.

He'lot, *n.* member of lower orders in ancient Greece.

Help, *v.t. & i.* to give assistance to, aid, promote, support, serve.

Hel'ping, *n.* a portion of food.

Hel'te--skel'ter, *a. & adv.* pell-mell, in hurried confusion.

Helve, *n.* haft of axe.

Hem, *n.* edge of material doubled over and sewed to prevent wear. *v.t.* to sew like this, to surround.

Hem'isphere, *n.* a half sphere, esp. of the earth as divided by the equator.

Hemp, *n.* Indian plant from which hashish is made, also used for making rope and coarse material. **Hemp'en,** *n.*

Hen, *n.* female bird, female domestic fowl.

Hence, *adv.* for this reason, from this place or time. **Henceforward,** *adv.* **Henceforth,** *adv.* from this time on.

Hench'man, *n.* trusty follower or supporter.

Hen'pecked, *a.* of husband nagged by wife.

Hepta-, *pref.* meaning seven, e.g. **Hep'tachord,** *n.* seven-stringed instrument.

Hep'tagon, *n. geom.* seven-sided plane.

Hep'tarchy (-tarky), *n.* seven kingdoms of early England.

Hep'tateuch (-tuke), *n.* the first seven books of the Bible.

Her'ald, *n.* official who announces royal decrees etc., a messenger, forerunner. *v.t.* to proclaim. **Heral'dic,** *a.* pertaining to heraldry. **Her'aldry,** *n.* the study of armorial bearings.

Herb, (Hurb), *n.* plant with soft, juicy stem or aromatic properties, used in med. or cooking. **Herba'ceous,** *a.* planted with herbs, of herbs. **Herb'age,** *n.* greenstuff. **Herb'al,** *a.* **Herb'alist,** *n.* botanist expert in use of herbs as medicines. **Herbar'ium** (-bare-), *n.* collection of dried plants. **Herbiv'orous,** *a.* grass or plant eating, esp. of cattle etc.

Herd (Hurd), *n.* a flock of animals. *v.t. & i.* to drive along

in a herd, guard as a flock.
Herds'man, *n*.

Here (Hır), *adv*. in this place, in this direction. Hereabouts, *adv*. roughly in this place. Hereafter, *n*. future existence. Heretofore, *adv*. leg. form of formerly. Herewith *adv*. together with.

Hered'ity *n*. the passing on from different generations of physical or mental characteristics. Hered'itary, *a*.

Her'esy, *n*. an opinion contrary to the conventional, esp. in rel. Her'etic, *n*. person who holds such opinion. Heret'ical, *a*.

Her'itage, *n*. inheritance, something handed down from parent or other benefactor.

Hermaph'rodite, *n*. animal or plant possessing characteristics of both sexes.

Hermet'ic, *a*. completely airtight.

Her'mit (Hur-), *n. rel.* recluse. Her'mitage, *n*. his home or cell.

Hern'ia (Hurn-), *n*. a rupture.

He'ro, *n*. courageous man, central figure in story. Hero'ic, *a*. courageous, epic. Her'oine, *n. fem*.

Her'oin, *n*. sedative drug derived from morphine.

Hes'itate, *v.i*. to be uncertain, to falter, hold back. Hes'itant, *a*. Hes'itancy, *n*. Hesita'tion, *n*.

Het'erodox,*a*.heretical, unorthodox. Het'erodoxy, *n*.

Hetero-, *pref*. meaning other, different, e.g. Heterog'eneous (-oj-), *a*. unlike, composed of different kinds. Hetero-sexual, *a*. of or tending to opposite sexes.

Hew, *v.t. & i*. to cut into shape, to chop, hack at.

Hex'agon, *n*. plane with six sides and six angles. Hexag'onal, *a*.

Hexam'eter, *n*. line of verse with six metrical feet.

Hey'day (Hay-), *n*. peak of career, life etc.

Hia'tus (Hy-), *n*. a gap, a break in continuity.

Hi'bernate, *v.i*. to spend winter in state of torpor. Hiberna'tion, *n*.

Hide, *n*. skin of animal. *v.t*. to thrash. Hidebound,*a*.obstinate, narrow-minded.

Hide, *v.t. & i*. to conceal or be concealed.

Hid'eous, *a*. horrible to contemplate.

Hie (Hy), *v.t*. to hasten, go quickly.

Hi'erarchy (-arky), *n*. government by priests, the body of priests in general, *iron*. any governing body.

Hi'eroglyphics, *n. pl*. ancient picture writing.

Hig'gledy-pig'gledy, *a. & adv*. in a confused state.

High, *a*. far up, far above the ground, important, strong, shrill, main. *coll*. smelly, decomposing.

Highbrow', *a*. denoting detached intellectual quality.

High-falut'ing, *a*. pretentious.

High'wayman, *n*. bandit.

Hike, *v.t*. to walk for pleasure.

Hilar'ious (-läre-), *a*. boisterously gay. Hilar'ity, *n*.

Hill, *n*. elevated mass of land. Hill'ock, *n*. prominent mound. Hilly, *a*. steep.

Hilt, *n*. handle of dagger or sword.

Hind (Hynd), *n*. female deer; *arch*. a peasant.

Hind, *a*. at the rear. Hind'-

ermost, **Hindmost,** *a.* **Hind-quarters,** *n. pl.* rear part of animal.

Hin'der, *v.t.* to impede, delay, obstruct. **Hin'drance,** *n.*

Hinge, *n.* jointed device to enable door etc. to swing. *v.i.* to turn, depend on.

Hint, *n.* indirect suggestion. *v.t. & i.*

Hinterland', *n.* the interior of a country.

Hip, *n.* the broadening part of body below waist.

Hip, *n.* fruit of wild rose.

Hipp'odrome, *n.* properly a course for horse-racing, esp. trotting.

Hire, *v.t.* to employ or let out for payment. **Hire'ling,** *n.* employee in derogatory sense.

Hire-purchase, *n.* modern system for obtaining goods by easy payment.

Hir'sute (Hur-), *n.* hairy.

Hiss, *n.* sharp sibilant sound as of snake or disapproval. *v.t.*

His'tory, *n.* the study and written account of past events, a course of events. an eventful career. **Histor'ian,** *n.* expert who studies and writes about history. **Histor'ic,** *a.* famous in or connected with history. **Histor'ical,** *a.* pertaining to history, of accurate quality or fact regarding history.

Histrion'ic, *a.* pertaining to actors and the stage, affected.

Hit, *v.t. & i.* to strike, injure, collide with. *n.* a blow, a theatrical success.

Hitch. *n.* a sudden difficulty or setback, a kind of knot in rope. *v.t. & i.* to fasten, become entangled.

Hitch'hike, *v.i.* to solicit free ride in blatant fashion.

Hith'er, *adv.* here, to or towards this place.

Hitherto', *adv.* up to this time, until now.

Hive, *n.* bees' home, a sectional hutch or box for bees. *v.t. & i.* to place bees in hive, to enter a hive, live together.

Hoar'y, (Hore-) *a.* grey with age. **Hoar'frost,** *n.* white frost.

Hoard (Hord), *n.* a secret store. *v.t.* to lay up a stock furtively.

Hoard'ing (Hord-), *n.* large board for advertisements, wooden fencing round building operation.

Hoarse, *a.* husky, hoarse-sounding.

Hoax (Hokes), *n.* a mischievous fraud. *v.t.*

Hob, *n.* flat projection by hearth.

Hob'ble, *v.t. & i.* to limp, to restrict movement by tying legs. *n.* a limping movement.

Hob'bledehoy, *n.* country bumpkin.

Hobb'y, *n.* recreational pursuit.

Hock, *n.* joint in horse's etc. hind leg corresponding to ankle.

Hock, *n.* a white Rhenish wine.

Hock'ey, *n.* field game played with curved sticks and hard ball.

Ho'cus-po'cus, *n.* nonsense as blind for deception.

Hod, *n.* wooden trough with handle for carrying bricks etc.

Hoe, *n.* agric. or hort. implement for removing weeds, loosening soil. *v.t.*

Hog, *n.* domestic pig, first-year sheep, person with unpleasant habits.

Hogs'head, *n.* large wine cask,

liquid measure of $52\frac{1}{2}$ imp. gallons.

Hoist, *v.t.* to lift up, raise. *n.* a device for lifting.

Hoi'ty-toi'ty, *a.* petulant, haughty.

Ho'key-po'key, *n.* hocus-pocus, cheap ice-cream.

Hold (Holed), *v.t. & i.* to have in the hand, to grasp, seize, restrain, maintain opinion, conduct, occupy. *n.* grasp, possession.

Hold, *n.* ship's compartment below deck, esp. for cargo.

Hole, *n.* a cavity, a hollow. *v.t.* to make a hole in.

Hol'iday, *n.* a day or period free from work.

Holl'ow (-o), *n.* a cavity, a small coombe. *a.* with only a solid exterior, deep or dull in sound, insincere. *v.t.* to make hollow, scoop out.

Holm (Home), *n.* an islet.

Hol'ocaust (-kawst), *n.* utter destruction, esp. by fire.

Hol'ster, *n.* pistol case.

Holt, *n.* small wood by river.

Ho'ly, *a.* divine, sacred, devoted to the service or worship of God. **Ho'liness**, *n.* state of being holy, papal title.

Ho'lystone, *n.* sandstone for cleaning ship's deck.

Hom'age, *n.* respectful submission, acknowledgement of leader.

Home, *n.* a permanent residence. **Home'ly**, *a.* comfortable, ordinary, warmhearted.

Ho'meopathy, Homeop'athy, *n.* treatment of disease by drugs which in healthy person would produce symptoms similar to those of the disease in question. **Ho'meopathic**, *a.* **Ho'meopath**,

n. physician specializing in this.

Hom'icide, *n.* murder. **Hom'-icidal**, *a.*

Hom'ily, *n.* a private sermon, moral lecture.

Ho'mo-, *pref.* meaning same, e.g. **Homosexual**, *a. & n.*, **Homonym**, *n.* word spelt the same as another but with different meaning. **Homocentric**, *a.* having common centre.

Homoge'neous (-jen-), *a.* of similar kind, uniform. **Homogene'ity**, *n.* **Homo'genize**, *v.t.*

Hone, *n.* stone for sharpening. *v.i.*

Hon'est (on-), *a.* truthful, upright. **Hon'esty**, *n.*

Hon'ey (Hunni), *n.* sweet substance processed from nectar by bees. **Honeycomb**, *n.* wax structure in which bees store honey or keep eggs.

Hon'eymoon, *n.* wedding trip or holiday taken immediately after marriage.

Hon'our (On-er), *n.* great renown, high esteem, unsullied reputation, self-respect, eminent position. *n. pl.* mark or decoration of esteem, glory, academic distinction. *v.t.* to esteem highly, to accept and pay when due. **Hon'ourable**, *a.*

Hon'orary (on-), *a.* position or title conferred as honour only, unpaid. **Honora'rium**, *n.* courtesy fee.

Hood, *n.* a head-covering attached to coat or cloak, folding cover for motorcar or perambulator. *v.t.*

Hoo'doo, *n.* person or object causing ill-fortune. *v.t.* to cause ill-fortune.

Hood'wink, *v.t.* to mislead.

Hoof, *n.* foot of horse, antelope etc. *n. pl.* **Hoofs** or **hooves.**

Hook, *n.* a curved and sometimes barbed piece of metal or bone etc., for catching fish, lifting, crocheting, a sickle or other cutting implement. *v.t. & i.* to catch with a hook, to fasten.

Hook'er, *n.* small Dutch sailing-ship.

Hool'igan, *n.* young ruffian, stupid person delighting in violence. **Hool'iganism,** *n.*

Hoop, *n.* circular metal band for holding together cask etc., circular metal or wooden plaything, metal arch in croquet, device for expanding woman's skirt. *v.t.* to encircle, contain with a hoop.

Hoot, *n.* a shout, us. of derision, the sound of a motor-vehicle, the cry of an owl. *v.t. & i.*

Hop, *n.* vine whose flowers are used for flavouring beer.

Hop, *n.* a short sharp jump. *v.t. & i.* to move or jump one leg at a time.

Hope, *n.* expectation accompanied by desire, eager anticipation, confidence. *v.t. & i.*

Horde, *n.* a great multitude of a threatening kind.

Hori'zon, *n.* line at which earth and sky appear to meet, *fig.* extent of outlook. **Horizon'tal,** *a.* parallel to line of horizon, flat, level.

Hor'mone, *n.* internal secretion which activates organ n body.

Horn, *n.* long pointed hard growth on head of various animals, such as cow and sheep, anything made of this, a mus. wind instrument.

Horn'pipe, *n.* a sailor's dance.

Hor'oscope, *n.* person's future foretold by position of stars.

Horr'id, *a.* terrible, hideous. **Horr'ify,** *v.t.* fill with dread.

Horr'or, *n.* dread, extreme fear. **Horr'ible,** *a.* **Horrif'ic,** *a.* horrible in poet. or iron. sense.

Horse, *n.* domesticated quadruped used for riding or draught purposes. **Horseback,** *n.* **Horseman,** *n.*

Horse-power, *n.* unit of power, us. as 550 foot-pounds per second.

Hort'ative, Hort'atory *a.* serving to encourage or urge.

Hor'ticulture, *n.* gardening in an organized way. **Horticul'turist,** *n.* professional grower of flowers & vegetables.

Hose, *n. us.* as *n. pl.* (**Hose**), stocking, stockings. **Ho'siery,** *n.* socks, stockings. **Ho'sier,** *n.* shopkeeper selling these.

Hos'pice (-spiss), *n.* traveller's shelter maintained by monks.

Hos'pitable, *a.* generous in welcoming. **Hospital'ity,** *n.* friendly reception of guests.

Hos'pital, *n.* place for med. care and treatment of sick or injured.

Host, *n.* person who entertains guests, landlord of an inn. **Hos'tess,** *n.*

Host, *n.* a great throng, an army.

Host, *n.* consecrated bread in rel. communion.

Hos'tage, *n.* person left with enemy as pledge in temporary peace.

Hos'tel, *n.* hall of residence for undergraduates etc. **Hos'telry,** *n. arch.* for inn.

Hos'tile, *a.* of an enemy, unfriendly, warlike. **Hostil'ity,**

n. enmity. **Hostil′ities,** *n. pl.* acts of war.

Hot, *a.* heated, of high temperature, extremely warm, with spicy or biting flavour. Hot as part of various compounds, e.g. **Hot-bed,** *n.* forcing bed for plants, *coll.* place or group encouraging extreme behaviour. **Hot-head,** *n.* impetuous person. **Hot-house,** *n.* heated greenhouse.

Hotel′, *n.* large house for the reception of travellers.

Hott′entot, *n.* member of S. Afric. people, his language.

Hound, *n.* one of various breeds of hunting dog, a contemptible person. *v.t.* to pursue persistently, harry.

Hour (Owr), *n.* sixty minutes, the twenty-fourth part of a day, the time of day as registered by clocks, a particular or appointed time. *pl.* period of work or shop-opening. **Hour-glass,** *n.* an ancient device for measuring time.

Hou′ri (Hoor-), *n.* legendary beautiful woman in Muslim paradise.

House (Hows), *n.* a dwelling-place, building for particular purpose, a commercial firm, a polit. assembly. *v.t. & i.* (Howz) to provide accomodation for, to dwell in. **Household,** *n.* the general occupants of a house. **House′holder,** *n.* head of family or household.

Hov′el, *n.* a hut, a miserable dwelling.

Hov′er, *v.i.* to flutter over, lurk nearby.

How, *adv.* in what manner, to what extent, why, in what condition. **Howbe′it,** *adv. arch.* nevertheless. **Howev′er,** *adv.* in whatever manner. *conj.* nevertheless.

How′dah, *n.* seat with sides and sometimes canopy for riding on elephant.

How′itzer, *n.* light cannon for firing at steep angle.

Howl, *n.* long, wailing cry of wolf, dog, etc., a cry of distress or derision. *v.t. & i.*

Hub, *n.* central part of wheel, any centre of activity.

Hub′bub, *n.* tumult, din.

Huck′aback, *n.* coarse rough cloth for towelling.

Huck′ster, *n.* peddler, hawker.

Hud′dle, *v.t. & i.* to crowd together in fear or for warmth. *n.* a confused mass or group.

Hue, *n.* complexion, tint.

Hue, *n.* only as hue & cry, general outcry and pursuit.

Huff, *n.* a fit of crossness. *v.t. & i.* to offend or take offence, to capture piece in draughts as forfeit.

Hug, *n.* a strong embrace. *v.t.*

Huge, *a.* enormous, vast.

Hulk, *n.* wrecked or abandoned ship, any ungainly ponderous object or person. **Hulk′ing,** *a.* bulky, shambling.

Hull, *n.* frame of ship, outer skin or peel of fruit or vegetable.

Hum, *n.* a subdued murmur or buzz, a sound made through closed lips. *v.t. & i.*

Hu′man, *a.* characteristic of or pertaining to mankind. *n.* a human being. **Hu′mane,** *a.* kind, merciful, having civilized feelings. **Hu′manism,** *n.* liberal education, the condition of being human. **Human′ity,** *n.* mankind as a whole, kindness towards others. **Humanitar′ian,**

n. person devoted to the welfare of mankind. **Hu'manize,** *v.t.* & *i.* to make or become civilized.

Hum'ble, *a.* unassuming, not proud. *v.t.* to abase, humiliate, suppress one's pride. **Humil'ity,** *n.*

Hum'bug, *n.* a pompous fraud. *v.t.* to swindle.

Hum'drum, *a.* mundane, dull.

Hu'merus, *n.* bone between elbow & shoulder in man. **Hu'meral,** *a.*

Hu'mid, *a.* damp, moist. **Humid'ity,** *n.* the dampness in the air.

Humil'iate, *v.t.* to put to shame, humble, abase, wound the pride. **Humilia'tion,** *n.*

Humm'ock, *n.* a little hill, a mound.

Hu'mour, *n.* mood, temperament, state of mind, quality of being amusing or appreciating amusing things. *v.t.* to gratify, adapt to person's mood. **Humorist,** *n.* facetious or amusing person, light entertainer. **Hu'morous,** *a.*

Hump, *n.* a bulging lump, *coll.* feeling of vexation or depression.

Hu'mus, *n.* decayed vegetable matter.

Hunch, *v.t.* to round, esp. the shoulders. *n.* a hump, *sl.* a firm premonition.

Hun'dred, *n.* & *a.* cardinal number, ten times ten, formerly a division of a county. **Hundredfold,** *a.* & *adv.* & *n.* one hundred times as great. **Hun'dredweight,** *n.* one hundred & twelve pounds.

Hun'ger, *n.* desire or need for food, any strong need or desire. *v.i.* to have a need or longing for food. **Hung'ry,** *a.*

Hunk, *n.* a thick lump, esp. of meat or bread.

Hunt, *v.t.* & *i.* to pursue in order to kill or capture to search for. *n.* a pursuit of wild animals. **Hun'ter,** *n.* riding-horse used in hunting, person who hunts. **Hunts'man,** *n.* man in charge of pack of foxhounds.

Hur'dle, *n.* frame of interwoven branches as fences or obstacles in race.

Hur'dy-gur'dy, *n.* barrel-organ on wheels.

Hurl, *v.t.* to throw or fling violently.

Hur'ly-bur'ly, *n.* commotion, confusion.

Hurr'icane, *n.* violent tropical storm.

Hurr'y, *v.t.* & *i.* to increase speed, hasten, urge on.

Hurt, *v.t.* to injure, give pain or distress to. *n.* **Hurt'ful,** *a.* harmful.

Hur'tle, *v.t.* & *i.* to rush or throw swiftly or uncontrollably.

Hus'band (Huz), *n.* married man.

Hus'band, *v.t.* to manage economically.

Hus'bandry, *n.* agriculture.

Hush, *n.* a silence. *v.t.* & *i.* to make silent, become quiet.

Husk, *n.* pod or outer covering of pea or corn. *v.t.* to remove this.

Husk'y, *a.* dry and hoarse.

Hus'ky, *n.* Eskimo dog used for hauling sledge.

Hussar' (-zar), *n.* soldier of light cavalry regiment.

Huss'y, *n.* saucy girl, worthless woman.

Hust'ings, *n. pl.* polit. election campaign or platform.

Hus'tle (Hus'l), *v.t. & i.* to jostle, crowd roughly, hurry.

Hut, *n.* a small temporary dwelling, shed.

Hutch, *n.* coop for small animals.

Hy'brid, *n.* animal or plant resulting from crossing of two different species. *a.* **Hy'bridize,** *v.t.*

Hy'drant, *n.* water-connection to which hose can be attached.

Hy'draulic, *a.* worked by water-power, pertaining to liquids in motion. *n. pl.* science of water-power.

Hy'dro-, *pref.* meaning water, e.g. **Hydrophobia,** *n.* rabies; **Hydro-electric,** *a.* pertaining to electricity generated by water-power; **Hy'drogen,** *n.* colourless inflammable gas which with oxygen forms water; **Hydro'-pathy,** *n. med.* treatment by internal & external application of water, etc.

Hy'giene, *n.* principles of health, practice of sanitary methods. **Hygien'ic,** *a.* **Hy'gienist,** *n.* specialist in hygiene.

Hymene'al, *a.* pertaining to marriage.

Hymn (him), *n.* sacred rel. song. **Hym'nal,** *n.* book of hymns.

Hy'per, *pref.* meaning excessive, e.g. **Hyper-critical,** *a.* too critical, **Hyper-sensitive,** *a.* over-sensitive, **Hyperbole** (-boli), *n.* rhetorical statement, **Hyper-**

borean, *a.* of the extreme north, **Hyperphysical,** *a.* supernatural.

Hy'phen, *n.* punctuation dash joining compound words or dividing word into syllables. **Hy'phenate,** *v.t.*

Hyp'notism, *n.* method of inducing a condition similar to sleep in order to control person. **Hypno'sis,** *n.* **Hypnot'ic,** *a.* **Hyp'notist,** *n.* person with power of hypnotizing. **Hyp'-notize,** *v.t.*

Hypochon'dria (-kon-), *a.* morbid anxiety about one's health. **Hypochon'driac,** *n.* person suffering from this.

Hypoc'risy (Hippok-), *n.* insincerity, pretence of virtue one does not possess. **Hyp'ocrite,** *n.*

Hypoderm'ic, *a.* pertaining to tissues beneath outer skin, introduced under the skin.

Hypot'enuse, *n. geom.* side of right-angled triangle opposite the right-angle.

Hypoth'esis, *n.* unproved theory adopted as basis of argument. **Hypothet'ical,** *a.* suppositional.

Hysterec'tomy, *n.* the surgical removal of womb.

Hyste'ria, *n.* morbid nervous condition accompanied by uncontrollable excitement. **Hyster'ical,** *a.* **Hyster'ics,** *n. pl.* outburst of senseless excitement or weeping.

I, *pron.* first person sing., the speaker or writer.

Iamb'ic (I-), *n. & a.* metrical verse, pertaining to this.

Ibe'rian, *a.* relating to Spain and Portugal.

Ice, *n.* frozen water, a frozen dessert or confection.

Ice'berg, *n.* large mass of ice coming from glacier and floating in sea.

Ichthyol'ogy (Ik-thi-), *n.* the natural history of fish.

I'cicle, *n.* pendulous, tapering piece of ice.

Ic'ing, *n.* sugary coating for cake.

I'con, I'kon, *n.* a holy picture, esp. in Orthodox church. **Icon'oclast,** *n.* person who breaks icons for anti-rel. reasons, person who attacks beliefs in general. **Icon'oclasm,** *n.*

Id, *n.* in psycho-analysis, instinctive impulses.

Ide'a (I-de-), *n.* a mental conception, a notion, a plan.

Ide'al, *a.* existing in imagination only, unreal, perfect. *n.* anything or any person worthy to be imitated. **Ide'alism,** *n.* representation of things in perfect form. **Ide'alist,** *n.* person striving or wishing for perfect state. **Ide'alize,** *v.t.* to consider perfect in spite of reality.

Ident'ical, *a.* exactly the same. **Ident'ity,** *n.* sameness, individuality, personality. **Ident'ify,** *v.t.* to establish identity, treat or consider as the same. **Identifica'tion,** *n.*

Ides, *n. pl.* in ancient Roman calendar the 15th of March, May, July, October, and 13th of other months.

Id'iom, *n.* language, dialect, individual manner of expression. **Idiomat'ic,** *a.* colloquial.

Idiosyn'crasy, *n.* peculiarity or special characteristic of person. **Idiosyn'cratic,** *a.*

Id'iot, *n.* dolt, stupid person. **Id'iocy,** *n.* **Id'iotic,** *a.*

I'dle, *a.* lazy, not working, unused, pointless. *v.t. & i.* to do nothing, waste time. **I'dler,** *n.* lazy person. **I'dleness,** *n.*

I'dol, *n.* object of worship or devotion. **Idol'atry,** *n.* the heathen worship of images. **Idol'atrous,** *a.* characterized by excessive devotion or worship. **Idol'ater,** *n.* one who worships idols. **I'dolize,** *v.t.* worship excessively.

Id'yll, I'dyll, *n.* short *poet.* description of romantic or rural scene. **I'dyllic,** *a.* charmingly romantic.

If, *conj.* on the condition that, on the supposition that, whether.

Ig'loo, *n.* Eskimo's dome-shaped dwelling made of snow and ice blocks.

Ig'neous, *a.* pertaining to or like fire, formed by intense heat. **Ignite',** *v.t. & i.* to set on or take fire. **Igni'tion,** *n.* the act of doing this.

Igno'ble, *a.* degraded, mean.

Ig'nominy, *n.* shame, dishonour. **Ignomin'ious,** *a.* shameful, dishonourable.

Ig'norance, *n.* lack of knowledge. **Ignora'mus,** *n.* ignorant person. **Ig'norant,** *a.* uninformed, uncouth, wanting in knowledge. **Ignore',** *v.t.* to overlook intentionally.

Ilk, *n.* family, kind.

Ill, *a.* sick, unwell, evil, injurious. *adv. & n.* **Ill'ness,** *n.* bad health. **Ill'bred,** *a.* uncouth, badly brought up. **Ill-will,** *n.* animosity.

Ille'gal, *a.* against the law. **Ille'gality,** *n.* an unlawful act.

Illeg'ible (-lej-), *a.* difficult or impossible to be read. **Illeg'ibility,** *n.*

Illegit'imate, *a.* illegal, born of unmarried parents. **Illegit'imacy,** *n.*

Il- *pref.* signifying negation, e.g. **Illiberal,** *a.* not liberal; **Illimitable,** *a.* unlimited; **Illogical,** *a.* not logical; **Illiterate,** *a.* not literate; **Illicit,** *a.* not lawful.

Illu'minate, *v.t.* to give light to, make clear, decorate with colours, esp. ancient book. **Illumina'tion,** *n.* **Illu'minative,** *a.* **Illu'mine,** *v.t.* to light up.

Illu'sion, *n.* unreal or misleading appearance or belief. **Illu'sionist,** *n.* conjurer. **Illu'sory,** *a.* deceiving, false. **Illu'sive,** *a.*

Ill'ustrate, *v.t.* to make clear graphically, to show clearly. **Illustration,** *n.* pictorial ornament, graphic demonstration. **Ill'ustrative,** *a.* serving to make clear. **Ill'ustrator,** *n.* artist making illustrations for magazine or book.

Illus'trious, *a.* distinguished, eminent.

Im-, *pref.* form of in- used before words beginning with b, m & p, meaning against, without, or negative, e.g. **Immature',** *a.* not mature; **Immemorial,** *a.* beyond the reach of memory; **Immor'al,** *a.* unmoral, lacking in morals, **Immor'tal,** *a.* living forever; **Immov'able,** *a.* impossible to move; **Immo'bile,** *a.* motionless; **Immod'erate,** *a.* extreme, not moderate etc.

Im'age, *n.* a mental picture, a representation, a likeness, a statue. *v.t.* to represent, make likeness of. **Im'agery** (immij-ri), *n.* figurative description, fanciful language.

Imagina'tion, *n.* the power of forming mental pictures, crea-tive mental faculty. **Imag'ine** (-maj-), *v.t. & i.* to form a mental picture or idea. **Imag'inary,** *a.* unreal, existing only in the mind.

Im'becile, *a.* mentally defective. *n.* a feeble-minded person. **Imbecil'ity,** *n.*

Imbibe', *v.t.* to drink, absorb.

Imbrogl'io (-bro-lio), *n.* an involved or confused situation.

Imbue', *v.t.* to saturate, inspire.

Im'itate, *v.t.* to copy, mimic, use as pattern. **Imita'tion,** *n.* **Im'itative,** *a.* **Im'itator,** *n.*

Immac'ulate, *a.* faultless, unsullied.

Imm'anent, *a.* indwelling, inherent. **Imm'anence,** *n.*

Imme'diate, *a.* without delay, happening at once, forthwith, nearest, next. **Imme'diacy,** *n.*

Immense', *a.* enormous. **Immen'sity,** *n.*

Immerse', *v.t.* to plunge, dip into liquid, absorb in book or thought. **Immer'sion,** *n.*

Imm'igrate, *v.i.* to enter foreign country as settler. **Immigra'tion,** *n.* **Imm'igrant,** *n.*

Imm'inent, *a.* about to happen. **Imm'inence,** *n.*

Imm'olate, *v.t.* to offer as sacrifice. **Immola'tion,** *n.*

Immune', *a.* safe, protected against disease. **Immu'nity,** *n.* **Im'munize,** *v.t.* render safe esp. from disease by vaccination. **Immuniza'tion,** *n.*

Immure', *v.t.* to confine, imprison.

Immu'table, *a.* unchangeable. **Immutabil'ity,** *n.*

Imp, *n.* little demon, aggravating child.

Im'pact, *n.* collision, striking impression.

Impair', *v.t.* to harm, weaken quality. **Impair'ment**, *n.*

Impale', *v.t.* to pierce through, put to death by piercing with stake. **Impale'ment**, *n.*

Impart', *v.t.* to disclose information, tell.

Im'passe, *n.* deadlock, blind alley.

Impas'sioned, *a.* highly emotional.

Impass'ive, *a.* calm, unemotional. **Impass'ivity**, *n.*

Impa'tience, *n.* lack of patience or tolerance. **Impa'tient**, *a.* chafing at delay or frustration.

Impeach', *v.t.* to accuse of dereliction of duty or of treason. **Impeach'ment**, *n.*

Impecc'able, *a.* faultless.

Impecu'nious, *a.* lacking money, poor. **Impecunios'ity**, *n.*

Impede', *v.t.* to hinder, obstruct. **Imped'iment**, *n.* an obstruction, a defect in speech.

Impediment'a, *n. pl. iron.* mil. baggage and stores.

Impel', *v.t.* to drive forward, compel.

Impend', *v.i.* to be at hand, threaten, be imminent.

Imper'ative, *a.* necessary, peremptory, commanding, *n.* in gram. the mood expressing command.

Impe'rial, *a.* pertaining to an empire or emperor, regal. **Impe'rialism**, *n.* national policy aimed at extending territory. **Impe'rialist**, *n.*

Imper'il, *v.t.* to endanger.

Impe'rious, *a.* overbearing, arrogant.

Imper'ishable, *a.* indestructible.

Imper'sonal, *a.* unconnected with any particular person, without personal reference.

Imper'sonate, *v.t.* to play the part of somebody else, represent another character. **Impersona'tion**, *n.* **Imper'sonator**, *n.* actor who gives character sketches of others.

Impert'inent, *a.* rude, insolent. **Impert'inence**, *n.*

Impertur'bable, *a.* unruffled, calm. **Imperturbabil'ity**, *n.*

Imper'vious, *a.* impenetrable, resistant to penetration.

Impeti'go, *n.* contagious skin disease.

Impet'uosity, *n.* impulsiveness. **Impet'uous**, *a.*

Im'petus, *n.* force of momentum

Impi'ety, *n.* ungodliness, wicked act. **Imp'ious**, *a.*

Impinge', *v.i.* to come in contact with, encroach, touch on.

Implac'able, *a.* relentless, merciless. **Implacabil'ity**, *n.*

Im'plement, *n.* instrument, tool. *v.t.* to put into effect.

Im'plicate, *v.t.* to involve, imply. **Implica'tion**, *n.*

Implic'it, *a.* understood but not expressed, unquestioning.

Implore', *v.t.* to request urgently.

Imply', *v.t.* to suggest indirectly, hint, insinuate.

Impol'itic, *a.* injudicious, ill-advised.

Impon'derable, *a.* impossible to estimate by weight or significance. *n.* a questionable or unknown factor.

Import', *v.t.* to introduce from abroad, esp. commercially. *n. pl.* goods from foreign countries. **Importa'tion**, *n.* **Import'er**, *n.*

Import', *v.t. & i.* to be of consequence, to signify. **Import'ant**, *a.* momentous, significant. **Import'ance**, *n.*

Impor'tune, *v.t.* to ask insistently. **Impor'tunate**, *a.* pressing, persistent in asking.
Importu'nity, *n.*

Impose', *v.t. & i.* to obtrude,
make a nuisance of oneself, lay
a burden on, take advantage of
in selfish way. **Imposi'tion**, *n.*
a punishment, a burden such as
tax or punishment.

Impos'ing, *a.* impressive, dignified.

Impos'tor, *n.* swindler, person
pretending to be someone else
for fraudulent purposes. **Impos'-
ture**, *n.*

Im'potent, *a.* weak, powerless
physically or mentally. **Im'-
potence**, *n.*

Impound', *v.t.* to confiscate, shut
up straying cattle.

Impov'erish, *v.t.* to make poor,
use up resources of. **Impov'-
erishment**, *n.*

Impract'icable, *a.* of something
that cannot be put into effect.
Impract'ical, *a.*

Impreca'tion, *n.* a curse. **Im'-
precate**, *v.t.* to invoke evil.

Impreg'nable, *a.* unconquerable.
Impregnabil'ity, *n.*

Impreg'nate, *v.t.* to fertilize,
make pregnant, to fill, soak.
Impregna'tion, *n.*

Impresar'io, *n.* business organ-
izer of concerts, mus. tours
etc.

Impress', *v.t.* to affect pro-
foundly, to mark by applying
pressure, to imprint, fix deeply
on the mind. **Im'press**, *n.* mark
made by stamp or die. **Im-
pressibil'ity**, *n.* **Impres'sion**, *n.*
number of copies of a book
printed, a mental effect
produced from outside, a vague
idea or feeling **Impres'sion-**

-able, *a.* easily influenced or
taken in.

Impress', *v.t.* to force into mil.
or naval service, seize goods
for public use.

Impres'sionism, *n.* method of
painting producing beautiful
and moving general effect
without elaborating details.
Impres'sionist, *n.* artist of this
genre. **Impressionis'tic**, *a.*

Impress'ive, *a.* capable of inducing great feeling.

Imprint', *v.t.* to stamp, impress
on mind etc. **Im'print**, *n.* details
of publisher or printer of book.

Imprison', *v.t.* to put in gaol.
Impris'onment, *n.*

Impromp'tu, *a. & adv.* without
preparation, extempore. *n.*

Improp'er, *a.* incorrect, indecent.
Impropri'ety, *n.* improper act,
indecency, unbecomingness.

Improve, *v.t. & i.* to make or
become better, to increase in
quality.

Im'provise, *v.t.* to extemporize,
to implement without preparation. **Improvisa'tion**, *n.*

Im'pudent, *a.* cheeky, rude,
impertinent. **Im'pudence**, *n.*

Impugn (-pune), *v.t.* to attack as
false, call in question.

Im'pulse, *n.* a sudden unthinking
act or inclination, a driving
forward a sudden force impelling onward. **Impul'sion**, *n.* the
act of being driven forward.
Impul'sive, *a.* tending to act
without thought.

Impu'nity, *n.* freedom from
injury or punishment.

Impute', *v.t.* to attribute or
ascribe to. **Imputa'tion**, *n.*
accusation, charge.

In, *prep.* within the bounds of,
during at the time of, made of,

expressed in, dressed in, through, into etc.

In-, *pref.* denoting negative. In very many cases words beginning with this are the exact opposite of the simple word. It is therefore only necessary to look up the defininion of this to find the contrary meaning.

Inadvert'ent, *a.* unintentional, negligent. Inadvert'ence, *n.* careless oversight. Inadvert'ency, *n.*

Ina'lienable, *a.* incapable of being transferred or taken away. Ina'lienability, *n.*

Inane', *a.* senseless, pointless. Inan'ity, *n.* silliness.

Inani'tion, *n.* exhaustion from hunger.

Inaug'urate (-aw-), *v.t.* to install in office, to start formally, initiate. Inaug'ural, *a.* of or to do with a formal beginning or installation. Inaugura'tion, *n.*

Incal'culable, *a.* beyond estimation, immense.

Incandes'cent, *a.* glowing with heat, brilliant. Incandes'cence, *n.*

Incanta'tion, *n.* a ritual charm or spell, the reciting of this.

Incar'cerate, *v.t.* to immure, imprison. Incarcera'tion, *n.*

Incarn'ate, *v.t.* to embody or clothe with flesh. *a.* Incarna'tion, *n.* the assuming of bodily form, an ideal type.

Incen'diary, *n.* person who commits arson. *a.* pertaining to arson, inflammatory, provocative.

Incense', *v.t.* to anger.

In'cense, *n.* sweet-scented gum or spice burnt as part of rel. service.

Incen'tive, *n.* stimulus, encouragement through hope of reward. *a.*

Incep'tion, *n.* beginning, initial stage.

Incess'ant, *a.* constant, unceasing.

In'cest, *n.* sexual intercourse between categories of relations forbidden by law to marry. Incest'uous, *a.*

Inch, *n.* twelfth part of a foot. *v.t. & i.* as to inch along, move very slowly and cautiously.

Inch, *n.* small island, esp. in Sc.

In'choate, *a.* undeveloped.

In'cident, *n.* an unimportant event, occurrence. *a.* apt to happen, belonging. In'cidence, *n.* falling on, rate of happening. Inciden'tal, *a.* casual, happening in addition to main event. *n. pl.* small items.

Incin'erate, *v.t.* to destroy by fire. Incinera'tion, *n.* Incin'erator, *n.* container for burning rubbish in.

Incip'ient, *a.* beginning to be or appear.

Incise', *v.t.* to cut, engrave. Inci'sion, *n.* deep cut. Inci'sive, *a.* cutting, acute, of remark, comment etc.

Inci'sor, *n.* biting tooth.

Incite', *v.t.* to stir up, excite. Incite'ment, *n.*

Inclina'tion, *n.* a slanting position, slope, preference, tendency. Incline', *v.t. & i.* to tend towards, lean, slope. In'cline, *n.* a slope.

Include', *v.t.* to comprise as part of whole, to reckon in, contain. Inclu'sion, *n.* Inclu'sive, *a.*

Incog'nito, *a.* under false name, in disguise. *adv. & n.*

In'come, *n.* salary, wages, profits.

Incor'porate, *v.t.* to unite, combine into one body, include. **Incorpora'tion**, *n.*

Increase', *v.t. & i.* to make or become bigger, larger in number or quantity. **In'crease**, *n.* growth in size, intensity, etc.

In'crement, *n.* enlargement, increase, additional gain.

Incrim'inate, *v.t.* to charge with or involve in crime. **Incrim'inatory**, *a.* **Incrimina'tion**, *n.*

In'cubate, *v.t. & i.* to hatch out or brood eggs, to develop. **Incuba'tion**, *n.* **In'cubator**, *n.* apparatus for hatching eggs artificially or for special care of sickly or feeble newborn babies.

In'cubus, *n.* a nightmare.

In'culcate, *v.t.* to impress mentally by repetition. **Inculca'tion**, *n.*

Incum'bent, *n.* priest occupying benefice. *a.* resting on as duty.

Incur', *v.t.* to bring on oneself, become liable to.

Incur'sion, *n.* an invasion, intrusion.

Incur'able, *a.* incapable of being healed, hopelessly diseased or wicked.

Indebt'ed (-det-ed), *a.* owing money, under obligation.

Indeed', *adv.* in fact, in truth.

Indefat'igable, *a.* untiring, persevering.

Indefeas'ible, *a.* inalienable, incapable of being taken away, as right or title etc. **Indefeas'ibility**, *n.*

Indel'ible, *a.* permanent, incapable of being erased. **Indelibility**, *n.*

Indem'nify, *v.t.* to compensate for loss or damage. **Indemnifica'tion**, *n.* **Indem'nity**, *n.* esp. compensation paid by defeated country as part of peace terms.

Indent', *v.t.* to notch. **Indenta'tion**, *n.* notch or cut, in printing, space at commencement of line.

Indent', *v.t.* to order, make requisition. *n.* a requisition.

Inden'ture, *n.* formal agreement or contract.

In'dex, *n.* a sign, a forefinger, an alphabetical list of subjects in a book, list of books forbidden by R.C. church.

In'dicate, *v.t.* to point out, show. **Indica'tion**, *n.* a sign, suggestion. **Indic'ative**, *a.* suggesting; *gram.* mood of verb stating a fact. **In'dicator**, *n.* device for registering details.

Indict' (-dite), *v.t.* to accuse, charge. **Indict'ment** (-dite), *n.* a written charge. **Indict'able** (-dite-), *a.* liable to be charged.

Indiff'erent, *a.* uninterested, impartial, mediocre. **Indiff'erence**, *n.*

In'digence (-jence), *n.* poverty. **In'digent**, *a.* poor.

Indi'genous (-dij), *a.* native, produced or born in a country.

Indig'nant, *a.* experiencing anger or disapproval at wrongful treatment. **Indigna'tion**, *n.*

Indite', *v.t.* to put into words or writing.

Individ'ual, *a.* peculiar to one person or thing, distinctive. *n.* a separate person or thing. **Individ'ualism**, *n.* self-interest, selfishness, belief that good of individual is more important than that of society as a whole.

Individ'ualist, *n.* person who believes this.

In'dolent, *a.* lazy, idle. In'-dolence, *n.*

Indom'itable, *a.* stubborn, un-yielding.

In'door, *a.* inside a building, pertaining to the interior of a house. Indoors', *adv.* in or into a house.

Indorse', *v.t.* to approve. Indorse'-ment, *n.*

Indu'bitable, *a.* unquestion-able, undoubted.

Induce', *v.t.* prevail upon, per-suade. Induce'ment, *n.* per-suasion, incentive.

Induct', *v.t.* to install, introduce. Induc'tion, *n.* installation into office, the reaching of general conclusion from particular facts, electrification by proxim-ity to an already electrified body. Induc'tive, *a.*

Indue', *v.t.* to furnish, equip, endue.

Indulge', *v.t. & i.* to give way to, gratify desires, pander. Indul'-gence, *n* gratification, yielding to appetites. Indul'gent, *a.*

In'dustry, *n.* diligence, steady effort, manufacturing process-es. Indus'trial, *a.* pertaining to trade or industry. Indus'trious, *a.* hard-working. Industrial'ize, *v.t.* to introduce industries.

Inebria'tion, *n.* drunkenness. Ine'briate, *v.t.* to intoxicate. *a.* drunken person.

Ineff'able, *a.* beyond descrip-tion.

Inept', *a.* unsuitable, clumsy. Inept'itude, *n.*

Inert', *a.* lifeless. Iner'tia (-ur-sha), *n.* lifelessness.

Ines'timable, *a.* beyond value or price.

Inev'itable, *a.* unavoidable. In-evitabil'ity, *n.*

Inex'orable, *a.* unrelenting, im-placable.

In'famous, *n.* notorious, vil-lainous. In'famy, *n.*

In'fant, *n.* child, minor. In'-fancy, *n.* childhood. Infant'-icide, *n.* the murder of a new-born child, person who does this. In'fantile, *a.* childish, puerile.

In'fantry, *n.* foot soldiers.

Infatua'tion, *n.* extravagant af-fection. Infat'uate, *v.t.* to be seized with unreasoning pas-sion.

Infect', *v.t.* to affect with disease. Infec'tion, *n.* a catching dis-ease. Infec'tious, *a.*

Infer', *v.t.* to deduce, conclude. In'ference, *n.* a conclusion, deduction. Inferen'tial, *a.*

Infe'rior, *a.* lower in rank or quality. *n.* Inferior'ity, *n.*

Infern'al, *a.* devilish, outrage-ous. Infer'no, *n.* hell, a huge blaze.

Infest', *v.t.* to overrun, pester in great numbers. Infesta'tion, *n.*

In'fidel, *n.* rel. person who does not believe in one's own faith. *a.*

Infil'trate, *v.t. & i.* to filter through, enter hostile territory in small numbers, percolate. Infiltra'tion, *n.*

In'finite, *a.* unlimited, boundless. Infin'ity, *n.* space or time that has no limit. Infin'itude, *n.* boundlessness. Infin'itive, *a. & n. gram.* part of verb expressing general meaning.

Infinites'imal, *a.* infinitely small.

Infirm', *a.* weak or incapacitated through age.

Inflame', *v.t.* to set on fire, arouse, excite. Inflamm'able, *a.*

easily set alight, easily aroused. **Inflamm'atory,** *a.* tending to set alight or arouse.

Inflate', *v.t.* to distend with air or gas, artificially increase importance or price. **Infla'tion,** *n.* unhealthy state of nation's economy caused by people expecting too much for too little effort.

Inflec'tion, Inflex'ion, *n.* rise and fall in voice, *gram.* modification of form of words. **Inflect',** *v.t.* to vary thus, change tone of voice.

Inflict', *v.t.* to impose pain or punishment, cause by blow etc. **Inflic'tion,** *n.*

In'fluence, *n.* moral power or persuasion, any force affecting behaviour or course of events. *v.t.* **Influen'tial,** *a.*

Influen'za, *n.* severe infectious disease.

In'flux, *n.* an inflow, a pouring in.

Inform', *v.t. & i.* to provide knowledge or news, tell, give incriminating information against person. **Inform'ant,** *n.* person who imparts news or information. **Informa'tion,** *n.* news, knowledge of facts. **Inform'ative,** *a.* **Inform'er,** *n.* tale-teller.

Infra-, *pref.* meaning below, under, as in anat. terms, e.g. infrarenal, infrascapular, etc.

Infrac'tion, *n.* infringement, violation.

Infringe', *v.t.* to trespass, encroach, break law. **Infringe'-ment,** *n.*

Infu'riate, *v.t.* to anger greatly, enrage. **Infuria'tion,** *n.*

Infuse', *v.t.* to steep in liquid, to instil, pour in. **Infu'sion,** *n.*

Inge'nious, *a.* gifted, clever. **Ingenu'ity,** *n.* inventive cleverness.

Ingen'uous, *a.* open, innocent, guileless.

In'gle-nook, *n.* a chimney-corner with seat or ledge.

In'got, *n.* oblong mass of cast metal, esp. gold, steel etc.

Ingrained, *a.* inveterate, deeply founded.

Ingra'tiate, *v.t.* to get oneself into favour with.

Ingre'dient, *n.* part of a mixture or compound.

In'gress, *n.* access, means of entry.

Inhab'it, *v.t.* to occupy, live in. **Inhab'itable,** *a.* fit to be lived in. **Inhab'itant,** *n.*

Inhale', *v.t.* to breathe in. **Inha'-lant,** *n. med.* for inhaling. **Inhala'tion,** *n.*

Inher'ent, *a.* innate, inborn. **Inher'it,** *v.t. & i.* to derive from another generation, possessions, title, characteristics. **Inher'itance,** *n.* property or qualities handed down or inherited. **Inher'itor,** *n.* heir.

Inhib'it, *v.t.* to restrain, check. **Inhibi'tion,** *n.* in psycho-anal. an instinctive and morbid shrinking from certain actions. **Inhib'itory,** *a.* tending to have this effect.

Inhume', *v.t.* to inter, bury. **Inhuma'tion,** *n.*

Inim'ical, *a.* hostile, harmful.

Inim'itable, *a.* impossible to imitate, unique.

Iniq'uity, *n.* wickedness, injustice. **Iniq'uitous,** *a.*

Ini'tial, *a.* pertaining to the beginning. *n.* an initial letter. *v.t.* to sign or mark with initials.

Ini'tiate, v.t. to originate, set in motion, start, admit into special membership. Initia'tion, n.

Ini'tiative, n. an ability and readiness to take the lead.

Inject', v.t. to introduce forcibly, esp. of med. liquid. Injec'tion, n. med. dose introduced into body externally.

Injunc'tion, n. a legal order of restraint, a command.

In'jure, v.t. to harm, damage. Inju'rious, a. harmful. In'jury, n.

Ink, n. coloured fluid used for writing or drawing. v.t. to use ink.

Ink'ling, n. faint suggestion or suspicion.

In'land, n. the interior of a country or region. a. away from the coast, of some domestic aspects of country's economy.

In'lay, v.t. to decorate by inseting with pieces of wood, ivory etc.

In'let, n. creek, small arm of sea.

In'mate, n. an occupant of institution, etc.

In'most, a. deepest, most inward.

Inn, n. tavern, house for accommodation & refreshment of travellers. Inn'keeper, n. landlord of this.

Innate', a. inborn, natural.

Inn'er, a. & n. interior, internal.

Inn'ings, n.pl. division of cricket, baseball etc. during which one side is batting.

Inn'ocent, a. pure guiltless. n. Inn'ocence, n. purity, freedom from guilt.

Innoc'uous, a. harmless.

Innova'tion, n. a novelty, something new. Inn'ovate, v.t. to introduce new customs etc. Inn'ovator, n.

Innuen'do, n. a derogatory insinuation.

Innu'merable, a. without number.

Inoc'ulate, v.t. med. to protect against disease by deliberately introducing small number of germs of same disease. Inocula'tion, n.

Inord'inate, a. too much, excessive.

In'quest, n. official inquiry esp. into cause of person's death.

Inquire', Enquire', v.t. & i. to ask, seek information, seek information by questioning. Inqui'rer, n. Inqui'ry, n.

Inquisi'tion, n. a severe questioning or investigation, a R.C. tribunal in the past for suppressing independent thought. Inquis'itor, n. esp. a R.C. official conducting such an investigation. Inquisitor'ial, a.

Inquis'itive, a. very curious, prying.

In'road, n. an encroachment, an incursion.

Insane , a. mad. Insan'ity, n.

Insan'itary, a. harmful to the health, unhygienic.

Insa'tiable, a. impossible to satisfy, greedy. Insa'tiability, n.

Inscribe', v.t. to write, dedicate, engrave. Inscrip'tion, n. dedication.

Inscru'table, a. enigmatic, impossible to understand. Inscrutabil'ity, n.

In'sect, n. small invertebrate animal with six legs and us. two or four wings.

Insectiv'orous, a. insect-eating.

Insem'inate, v.t. to implant,

sow. **Insemina'tion,** *n.* impregna'tion.

Insen'sate, *a.* unfeeling, lacking sensibility.

Insert', *v.t.* to introduce or place between. **Inser'tion,** *n.*

In'set, *n.* something added, esp. page or drawing.

In'shore, *a. & adv.* near or toward the shore.

In'side, *a.* lying or being within, on the inside. *adv.* within. *n.* the interior; *sl.* the stomach, as the insides.

Insid'ious, *a.* treacherous, acting secretly or gradually.

In'sight, *n.* keen perception, mental awareness.

Insig'nia, *n. pl.* badges of honour or authority.

Insin'uate, *v.t.* to hint in slanderous manner, to penetrate by subtle means. **Insinua'tion,** *n.*

Insip'id, *a.* flavourless, dull. **Insipid'ity,** *n.*

Insist', *v.i.* to urge or ask repeatedly, to maintain. **Insist'ent,** *a.* **Insist'ence,** *n.*

In'sola'tion, *n.* treatment by exposure to sun's rays. **In'solate,** *v.t.*

In'solence, *n.* contemptuous rudeness. **In'solent,** *a.*

Insol'uble, *a.* that cannot be solved or dissolved. **Insolubil'ity,** *n.*

Insol'vent, *a.* unable to settle debts, bankrupt. *n.* such a person. **Insol'vency,** *n.*

Insom'nia, *n.* sleeplessness.

Inspect', *v.t.* to examine in detail, review, survey. **Inspec'tion,** *n.* **Inspec'tor,** *n.*

Inspire', *v.t.* to stimulate to better and greater action, to inhale. **Inspira'tion,** *n.* creative impulse or influence.

Install', *v.t.* to put in position or office. **Installa'tion,** *n.*

Instal'ment (-stawl-), *n.* one of several parts produced as series, part of larger sum paid at intervals.

In'stance, *n.* an example, suggestion, request. *v.t.* to cite as an instance or example.

In'stant, *a.* urgent, pressing. *n.* a point of time, a moment. **Instanta'neous,** *a.* happening at once.

Instead', *adv.* in the place of.

In'step, *n.* upper arched surface of human foot between toes & ankle.

In'stigate, *v.t.* to urge on, to cause to happen. **Instiga'tion,** *n.* **In'stigator,** *n.*

Instil', *v.t.* to imbue, infuse, introduce liquid by drops. **Instilla'tion,** *n.*

In'stinct, *n.* natural inborn impulse, intuition. *a.* charged with life. **Instinct'ive,** *a.*

In'stitute, *v.t.* to set up, establish, found. *n.* an establishment for education etc. **Institu'tion,** *n.* an established practice, a society for promoting some social activity, the building it uses. **Institu'tional,** *a.*

Instruct', *v.t.* to teach, educate, train. **Instruc'tion,** *n.* training, teaching. **Instruc'tive,** *a.* informative. **Instruc'tor,** *n.*

In'strument, *n.* a tool or implement, a mus. device, a legal document, a person exploited or employed by someone else. **Instrument'al,** *a.* **Instrumental'ist,** *n.* mus. performer. **Instrumenta'tion,** *n.* arrangement of mus. for instruments.

In'sular, *a.* narrow-minded, pertaining to an island. **Insular'ity,** *n.*

In'sulate, *v.t.* to keep apart, to make safe from electricity, heat. **Insula'tion. In'sulator,** *n.* mate rial or device that does not conduct electricity.

In'sulin, *n. med.* preparation from pancreas of sheep etc. for treatment of diabetes.

Insult', *v.t.* to be deliberately rude or abusive. **In'sult,** *n.*

Insu'perable, *a.* too difficult to overcome.

Insur'ance, *n.* (-shure-) business system whereby losses by fire or theft etc. are made good by company to whom regular premium is paid by person wishing to be so protected. **Insure',** *v.t.* to protect against loss or damage, to make sure.

Insurg'ent, *n.* a rebel. *a.* rebellious. **Insur'gence,** *n.*

Insurrec'tion, *n.* revolt, mutiny.

Intact', *a.* complete, undamaged.

In'teger (-jer), *n.* a whole number. **In'tegral** (-grl), *a.* making a whole, complete.

In'tegrate, *v.t.* to make complete or one. **Integra'tion,** *n.*

Integ'rity, *n.* honesty, uprightness.

Integ'ument, *n.* skin, covering.

In'tellect, *n.* mental power, ability to reason. **Intellec'tual,** *a.* pertaining to this. *n.* a person with cultivated mind. **Intellectual'ity,** *n.*

Intell'igence, *n.* aptitude to understand, news, information. **Intell'igent,** *a.* **Intell'igible,** *a.* comprehensible.

Intelligent'zia, *n.* intellectual or well educated people.

Intense', *a.* extreme, acute. **Intens'ify,** *v.t.* to increase in degree or intensity. **Intensifica'tion,** *n.* **Intens'ity,** *n.* degree, extremity. **Intens'ive,** *a.* concentrated.

Inten'tion, *n.* purpose, design. **Inten'tional,** *a.* purposely, deliberately. **Intent',** *n.* aim, purpose. *a.* concentrated. **Intend',** *v.t.* to mean, to plan.

Inter', *v.t.* to bury. **Inter'ment,** *n.*

In'ter-, *pref.* meaning among, between, together, one with another, etc. e.g. **Interact,** *v.i.,* **Interchange,** *v.t. & i.* **Interleave,** *v.t.,* **Intermarry,** *v.i.,* **International,** *a.* etc.

Intercede', *v.i.* to plead for another person. **Interces'sion,** *n.* **Intercess'or,** *n.*

Intercept', *v.t.* to cease or stop in transit. **Intercep'tion,** *n.*

In'tercourse, *n.* conversation, communication, connection.

Interdict', *v.t.* to forbid, prohibit. **In'terdict,** *n.* **Interdic'tion,** *n.* **Interdict'ory,** *n.*

In'terest, *n.* attention, curiosity, a matter arousing this, payment for use of borrowed money, a right, a share. *v.t.* to cause interest, engage attention or sympathy.

Interfere', *v.i.* to intervene, meddle. **Interfer'ence,** *n.*

In'terim, *n.* the meantime. *a.* of an interval.

Inte'rior, *a.* inner, internal. *n.* the inside. inland.

Interject', *v.t.* to interpose a remark. **Interjec'tion,** *n.*

Interloc'utor, *n.* a questioner in conversation.

In'terloper, *n.* an intruder.

Interme'diary, *n.* a mediator.

Interme'diate, *a.* intervening, coming between.

Interm'inable, *a.* never-ending, boring.

Intern', *v.t.* to confine within limits, esp. of civilian living in hostile territory at outbreak of war. **Intern'ment,** *n.*

Inter'nal, *a.* pertaining to the inside.

Interne'cine, *a.* mutually destructive.

Inter'polate, *v.t.* to introduce new or unauthorized matter. **Interpola'tion,** *n.*

Inter'pret, *v.t.* to translate verbally from foreign language, to explain. **Inter'preter,** *n.* **Interpreta'tion,** *n.*

Interreg'num, *n.* an interruption between successive reigns or governments.

Inter'rogate, *v.t.* to question severely. **Interroga'tion,** *n.* examination by questioning. **Interrog'ative,** *a.* questioning. *n.* a word which puts a question. **Inter'rogator,** *n.*

Interrupt', *v.t.* to break into or hinder a conversation. **Interrup'tion,** *n.* a break in continuity.

Intersec'tion, *n.* a crossing of two lines. **Intersect',** *v.t. & i.* to cut across.

Intersperse', *v.t.* to put in here and there. **Intersper'sion,** *n.*

In'terval, *n.* a space or time between two passages or actions.

Intervene', *v.i.* to interfere, come between. **Interven'tion,** *n.*

In'terview, *v.t.* to question in order to obtain information or assess qualifications. *n.*

Intest'ate, *a.* dying without having made a will.

Intest'ine, *n.* esp. as *n. pl.* the bowels. **Intest'inal,** *a.*

In'timate, *a.* close, familiar. *n.* a close friend. **In'timacy,** *n.*

In'timate, *v.t.* to suggest, make known. **Intima'tion,** *n.* announcement, a hint.

Intim'idate, *v.t.* to frighten, cow by threats. **Intimida'tion,** *n.* **Intim'idator,** *n.*

Intona'tion, *n.* accent, modulation of voice. **Intone',** *v.t. & i.* to chant, recite in singing tone.

Intoxica'tion, *n.* drunkenness. **Intox'icate,** *v.t.* to make drunk, *fig.* to elate, excite. **Intox'icant,** *n.* alcohol.

In'tra-, *pref.* meaning within, inside.

Intract'able, *a.* unmanageable, obstinate. **Intractabil'ity,** *n.*

Intrep'id, *a.* fearless, bold. **Intrepid'ity,** *n.*

In'tricate, *a.* complicated. **In'-tricacy,** *n.*

Intrigue', *v.t. & i.* to plot in secret, to arouse interest. *n.* a plot, clandestine love affair.

Intrin'sic, *a.* inherent, essential.

In'troduce, *v.t.* to make known, bring into, present, put into. **Introduc'tion,** *n.* **Introduct'ory,** *a.*

Introspec'tion, *n.* the process or tendency of examining one's own thoughts. **Introspec'tive,** *a.* subjective, turning inward.

In'trovert, *n. & a.* introspective, introspective person, with morbid tendency to self-interest.

Intrude', *v.t. & i.* to trespass, encroach, enter uninvited. **Intru'der,** *n.* **Intru'sion,** *n.* **Intru'sive,** *a.*

Intui'tion, *n.* instinct, insight. **Intu'itive,** *a.*

Inunda'tion, *n.* a flood. In'-undate, *v.t.* to overwhelm, flood.

Inure', *v.t.* to accustom, toughen.

Invade', *v.t.* to enter or assail in hostile manner. Inva'der, *n.* Inva'sion, *n.*

Invalid', *n.* sick person. *a.* sick. *v.t. & i.* to send away or dismiss because of sickness.

Inval'id, *a.* not valid, valueless. Inval'idate, *v.t.* to render or declare invalid.

Inval'uable, *a.* beyond price.

Invec'tive, *n.* abusive speech.

Inveigh' (-vay), *v.i.* to revile, speak bitterly against.

Invei'gle (-vay-), *v.t.* to lure, persuade by flattery.

Invent', *v.t.* to originate, devise something completely new. Inven'tion, *n.* Invent'ive, *a.* creative in original way. Inven'tor, *n.*

In'ventory, *n.* a detailed list of articles.

Invert', *v.t.* to reverse position or order of. In'verse, *a.* reversed or opposite in position or tendency. Inver'sion, *n.*

Inver'tebrate, *n.* an animal without backbone. *a.*

Invest', *v.t. & i.* to put into, to establish in office, to dispose of money for profit. Invest'ment, *n.* money invested for profit, stocks and shares bought with this.

Investiga'tion, *n.* a thorough inquiry or examination. Invest'igate, *v.t.* Invest'igator, *n.*

Invest'iture, *n.* ceremony of awarding person title or installing in office.

Invet'erate, *a.* deep-rooted, habitual. Invet'eracy, *n.*

Invid'ious, *a.* likely to provoke offence.

Invig'orate, *v.t.* to revive, stimulate.

Invin'cible, *a.* unconquerable. Invincibil'ity, *n.*

Invi'olate, *a.* unbroken, unsullied. Invi'olable, *a.* immune from harm.

Invite', *v.t.* to request courteously, to offer to entertain. Invita'tion, *n.*

In'voice, *n.* notification of goods sent and prices of these. *v.t.* to send this out.

Invoca'tion, *n.* a prayer, supplication; a summoning. *v.t.*

Involve', *v.t.* to implicate, entangle, entail. Involvement', *n.*

Ir-, *pref.* meaning negative and used before words beginning with r, the meaning of which can be obtained by consulting main or simple word and adding negative sense where necessary.

Ire, *n.* anger. Iras'cible, *a.* tending to anger, easily angered. Irascibil'ity, *n.*

Irides'cent, *a.* shimmering, rainbow-coloured. Irides'-cence, *n.*

I'ris, *n.* coloured membrane of eye encircling pupil.

Irk (Urk), *v.t.* to annoy, weary. Irk'some, *a.* tedious.

I'ron, *n.* firm, hard, common metal, basis of steel, implement for smoothing laundry. *v.t.* to use this. *a.* made of iron, hard, firm, adamant.

I'rony, *n.* conveying opposite meaning, sarcastic humour. Iron'ical, *a.*

Irra'diate, *v.t.* to brighten, cast light upon.

Irreden'tist, *n.* advocate of

seizure of outlying regions of similar linguistic characteristics by home country.

Irr′igate, *v.t.* to supply with water for cultivation. **Irriga′tion**, *n.*

Irr′itate, *v.t.* to annoy, chafe, inflame. **Irrita′tion**, *n.* **Irr′itant**, *n.* thing causing irritation. **Irr′itable**, *a.* annoyed, easily annoyed.

Irrup′tion, *n.* a sudden invasion, a sudden bursting in.

Is′lam, *n.* the Mohammedan rel., the entire body of countries & people believing in this. **Islam′ic**, *a.*

I′sland (I-land), *n.* piece of land surrounded by water, any place resembling this. **I′slander**, *n.* inhabitant of an island. **Isle** (Ile), *n.* a small island, *poet.* **I′slet** (I-let), *n.* a small island.

I′sobar, *n.* chartline linking places at which barometric pressure is same. **Iso-** as *pref.* in general meaning equal, e.g. **Isotherm**, chartline linking places at which temperature is same; **Isometric**, *a.* of equal measure. **Isos′celes** (-leez), *a.* having two sides equal.

I′solate, *v.t.* to place alone. **Isola′tion**, *n.* separation from everyone else, solitude.

I′sotope, *n.* element similar to another in chem. properties but of different atomic weight.

Iss′ue, *n.* an outlet, production, edition, offspring. *v.t. & i.* to come out of, to publish, to arise.

Isth′mus (Iss-mus), *n.* a neck of land connecting two larger land-masses.

Ital′ic, *n.* a sloping kind of print. *a.* **Ital′icize**, *v.t.*

Itch, *n.* an irritation of the skin, *coll.* a keen desire. *v.t.* to experience irritation of the skin.

I′tem, *n.* a separate, small article or entry. **I′temize**, *v.t.* to state or enter in detail.

Itin′erant, *a.* travelling from place to place. **Itin′erary**, *n.* a schedule for a journey, record of this.

I′vory, *n.* hard white substance forming tusks of elephants and walruses, anything made from this. *a.*

J

Jab, *v.t. & i.* to stab or poke sharply. *n.*

Jabb′er, *v.t. & i.* to talk incoherently, gabble. *n.*

Jack, *n.* device for lifting or raising, knave at cards. *v.t.* to raise by means of jack.

Jack′anapes, *n.* impertinent child or person.

Jack′ass, *n.* silly person.

Jack′boot, *n.* long heavy boot reaching above knee.

Jack′et, *n.* outer garment with sleeves, covering for book.

Jade, *n.* hard semi-precious stone.

Jade, *n.* worthless woman.

Jade, *v.t.* to weary.

Jag, *n.* sharp projection, ragged edge. **Jagg'ed,** *a.*

Jail, *n.* prison, gaol.

Jam, *v.t. & i.* to press or squeeze in tightly, pack closely, smear with jam, crush, become unworkable. *n.* preserve made with sugar and fruit.

Jamb (Jam), *n.* side-piece of door or window.

Jamboree', *n.* celebration, rally.

Jan'gle, *v.t. & i.* to sound harshly, esp. when out of tune. *n.*

Jan'itor, *n.* caretaker, door-keeper.

Jan'uary, *n.* first month of year.

Japan', *n.* a glossy lacquer. *v.t.* to coat with this.

Jape, *n. & v.i.* jest.

Jar, *n.* broadmouthed glass vessel.

Jar, *v.t. & i.* to shake, make a harsh grating sound.

Jar'gon, *n.* incomprehensible talk, specialized professional talk.

Jas'per, *n.* semi-precious stone.

Jaun'dice (Jawn-dis), *n.* disease caused by excess of bile. **Jaundic'ed,** *a.* prejudiced, sour.

Jaunt, *n.* a short pleasure trip. *v.i.*

Jaun'ty, *a.* carefree.

Jav'elin, *n.* short light throwing spear.

Jaw, *n.* bone in which teeth are set. *v.t. & i. sl.* to talk at length.

Jazz, *n.* syncopated dance mus. largely of Negro & Afric. origin. *v.t. & i.*

Jeal'ous (Jel-), *a.* envious, suspiciously fearful. **Jeal'ousy,** *n.*

Jeer, *v.t. & i.* to ridicule, mock.

Jejune', *a.* meagre, uninteresting.

Jell'y, *n.* fruit- or meat-juice solidified by boiling and cooling.

Jemm'y, *n.* housebreaker's crowbar for forcing door or window.

Jeop'ardy (Jep-), *n.* peril. **Jeop'ardize,** *v.t.* to endanger.

Jerk, *v.t. & i.* to push or move abruptly. *n.* a sudden push or movement. **Jerk'ily,** *adv.*

Jer'kin, *n.* close-fitting, sleeveless jacket.

Jer'sey (-ze), *n.* knitted jumper or sweater.

Jest, *n.* a joke. *v.i.* **Jes'ter,** *n.* one who makes jokes, court fool.

Jet, *n.* a strong stream of liquid coming from hose etc. *v.t. & i.* to spout out in a jet.

Jet, *n.* hard black mineral, deep glossy black colour.

Jett'ison, *v.t.* to throw cargo overboard to lighten ship in danger. **Jet'sam,** *n.* cargo jettisoned & later washed ashore.

Jett'y, *n.* landing-stage.

Jew'el, *n.* precious stone or gem used as ornament. **Jew'eller,** *n.* maker or dealer in gems. **Jewel'ry,** *n.*

Jib, *n.* sailing-vessel's triangular sail at bow.

Jib, *v.i.* to object, refuse to go on.

Jig, *n.* an informal lively dance. *v.i.* to dance briskly, move jerkily.

Jilt, *v.t.* to discard a sweetheart. *n.* person who does this.

Jin'gle, *v.t. & i.* to make a slight tinkling noise, to cause coins or bells to make such a sound. *n.* a catchy tune or rhyme.

Jin'go, *n.* truculent patriot. **Jin'goism,** *n.* warmongering.

Job, *n.* a task, a piece of work, occupation. *v.t. & i.* to work casually, work as stockbroker. **Jobb'ery,** *n.* dubious business.

Joc'key, *n.* professional horseman riding in races. *v.t.* to manoeuvre for position or advantage.

Jocose', *a.* merry, humorous. **Joc'ular,** *a.* affable, joking. **Jocular'ity,** *n.*

Joc'und, *a.* jovial, merry. **Jocund'ity,** *n.*

Jog, *v.t. & i.* to shake slightly, move at slow pace, remind, as of memory. **Jog-trot,** *n.* easygoing gait.

Jog'gle, *v.t. & i.* to shake or move jerkily.

Join, *v.t. & i.* to connect, bring together, fasten, unite. *n.* a connection or joining together. **Join'er,** *n.* carpenter. **Join'ery,** *n.* carpentry.

Joint, *n.* place or point where two things are united, a bone with meat. *v.t.* to connect by joint, to sever at joint. **Joint'ly,** *adv.* together.

Joist, *n.* beam for supporting floor or ceiling.

Joke, *n.* a jest, something done or said for amusement. *v.i.* **Jo'ker,** *n.* jester, special card in pack.

Joll'y, *a.* merry, light-hearted. **Joll'ity,** *n.* **Jollifica'tion,** *n. iron.*

Jolt, *ż.t. & i.* to move or shake with sudden jerks. *n.*

Jos'tle (Jos'l), *v.t.* to push against roughly.

Jot, *v.t.* to make a note, write down briefly.

Jot, *n.* small quantity.

Jour'nal (Jur-), *n.* a daily record, a daily newspaper. **Jour'-** nalism, *n.* the occupation of writing or editing a newspaper. **Jour'nalist,** *n.* newspaper writer. **Journalese',** *n.* worthless writing.

Jour'ney (Jur-), *n.* a going from one place to another, a long trip. *v.i.* to travel.

Jour'neyman, *n.* artisan, workman.

Joust (Jowst), *n.* armed combat between mounted knights, part of a tournament. *v.i.* to partake in combat or dispute.

Jo'vial, *n.* merry, warmspirited. **Jovial'ity,** *n.*

Jowl, *n.* jaw, cheek.

Joy, *n.* gladness, happiness. **Joy'ful,** *a.* **Joy'ous,** *n.*

Joy'less, *a.* sad.

Jubila'tion, *n.* exultation. **Ju'bilant,** *a.*

Ju'bilee, *n.* special celebration, esp. fiftieth anniversary.

Judge, *n.* legal officer who presides over lawsuits, person deciding on relative merits or skill of others, an umpire, referee. *v.t. & i.* to act as judge, to try, estimate. **Judg'ment,** *n.* the decision of a court, discernment, arbitration.

Judi'cial, *a.* pertaining to judgment, considered, impartial. **Judi'ciary,** *n.* the system of lawcourts in a country, the officials of this.

Judi'cious, *a.* wise, sensible.

Ju'do, *n.* advanced stage of ju-jitsu, skilled unarmed selfdefence.

Jug, *n.* vessel with handle, for holding liquids.

Jug'gle, *v.t. & i.* to play conjuring tricks, exercise sleight of hand, defraud. **Jug'gler,** *n.* **Jug'glery,** *n.*

Jug'ular, *a.* pertaining to throat or neck.

Ju-jit'su, *n.* skilled unarmed self-defence.

Ju-ju, *n.* a fetish, powerful primitive Afric. or W.I. charm.

July', *n.* seventh month of year.

Jum'ble, *n.* disorder, muddle. *v.t. & i.*

Jump, *v.t. & i.* to leap or bound into the air to leap over an obstacle, to start nervously. *n.* a leap, sudden upward movement.

Jum'per, *n.* woollen jersey, seaman's loose outer garment.

Junc'tion, *n.* meeting-place. joining, railway station where different lines meet.

Junc'ture, *n.* point or time at which things or events meet or happen.

June, *n.* the sixth month of year.

Jun'gle, *n.* tropical land with dense undergrowth and trees.

Jun'ior, *a.* younger, lower in rank or position. *n.* a younger person, a son.

Junk, *n.* Chinese sailing vessel with flat bottom & high stern.

Junk, *n.* worthless stuff.

Junk'et, *n.* curdled milk. *v.i.* to feast.

Jurid'ical, *a.* pertaining to legal proceedings. **Juris'diction**, *n.* limits of authority, administration of justice. **Jurispru'dence**, *n.* the science and practice of law.

Ju'ry, *n.* body of citizens, us. twelve in number, selected to assess lawsuit. **Ju'ror**, **Jur'y-man**, *n.* member of this.

Ju'ry-mast, *n.* temporary mast.

Just, *a.* fair, honest, equitable, exact.

Jus'tice, *n.* the principle of dealing fairly, of treating according to the law.

Just'ify, *v.t. & i.* to show or prove to be right, to defend, vindicate, give reasons for. **Justifi'able**, *a.* **Justifica'tion**, *n.* sufficient reason.

Jut, *v.i.* to project, stick out.

Jute, *n.* plant fibre used in manufacturing rope and sacks etc.

Ju'venile, *a.* youthful, pertaining to the young. **Juvenil'ity**, *n.* **Juven'ilia**, *n. pl.* lit. works perpetrated in author's youth.

Juxtapose', *v.t.* to place side by side. **Juxtaposi'tion**, *n.* the condition of being placed side by side.

K

Kaleid'oscope (-ide-), *n.* optical device for showing variety of beautiful patterns. **Kaleido-scop'ic**, *a.* changing rapidly and beautifully.

Ka'olin (Kay-), *n.* fine white clay used for making porcelain.

Ka'pok (Kay-), *n.* fruit-pod fibres from tropical tree used for stuffing-material.

Kar'ma, *n.* Buddhist conception of individual's total actions in all stages of existence.

Kay'ak (Ky-), *n.* Eskimo canoe.

Kedge, *n.* light anchor.
Kedg'eree, *n.* dish made of eggs, fish and rice.
Keel, *n.* wooden or steel plate forming main foundation of ship. **Keel'son,** *n.* strengthening beam fastened to keel. **Keelhaul,** *v.t. arch.* to drag seaman under ship's keel as punishment.
Keen, *a.* sharp, enthusiastic.
Keen, *n.* a mourning song. *v.t. & i.*
Keep, *n.* fortified tower, main part of castle.
Keep, *v.t. & i.* to retain, take care of, observe as festival, to preserve, maintain, remain, continue. **Keep'er,** *n.* warden, guard. **Keep'ing,** *n.* custody, possession. **Keep'sake,** *n.* souvenir, memento.
Keg, *n.* small tub or cask.
Kelp, *n.* seaweed from which iodine is obtained.
Ken, *n.* extent of knowledge or acquaintance. *v.t.* Sc. to know.
Kenn'el, *n.* place for keeping dogs. *v.t. & i.* to keep in kennel, confine.
Kerb, *n.* stone border.
Ker'chief, *n.* cloth worn as woman's head-covering.
Kerm'es (-iz), *n.* pregnant female insect, dye made from this.
Kerm'ess, *n.* a Dutch or Flemish fair.
Kern (Kurn), *n. arch.* Ir. peasant.
Kern'el, *n.* soft inner part of nut, essential part of anything.
Ker'osene, *n.* paraffin, lamp-oil.
Kers'ey, *n.* coarse ribbed woollen material.
Ketch, *n.* two-masted sailing-vessel rigged fore-and-aft.
Ketch'up, *n.* spicy sauce.

Ket'tle, *n.* utensil with spout and handle for boiling water.
Ket'tledrum, *n.* drum made of parchment stretched over hollow hemisphere of brass or copper.
Key (Kee), *n.* instrument for winding clock, turning lock, anything that facilitates entrance or control, in *mus.* system of notes related to each other. *v.t.* to control pitch of, to make tense, esp. as to key up. **Keyboard,** *n.* row of keys on piano or organ. **Key-note,** *n.* in *mus.* first note of scale. **Key-stone,** *n.* central stone supporting arch, central principle of anything.
Key, *n.* small reef or island.
Kha'ki (-ah-), *n.* uniform of dull olive-green colour. *a.*
Kick, *v.t. & i.* to hit or strike at with foot or hoof. *n.* a blow with foot or hoof, the recoil of a gun.
Kid, *n.* a young goat, *coll.* a child, soft leather.
Kid, *v.t. sl.* to deceive.
Kid'nap, *v.t.* to abduct, carry away forcibly. **Kid'napper,** *n.*
Kid'ney, *n.* one of two glandular organs in humans & animals which separate urine from the blood. *Coll.* sort, character.
Kill, *v.t.* to slay, destroy, put to death. **Kill'er,** *n.* **Kill,** *n.* the act of killing, esp. in hunting.
Kilo-, *pref.* meaning one thousand and used in metric system.
Kilt, *n.* properly as *n. pl.* short pleated tartan skirt worn by Highlanders of Sc.
Kimo'no, *n.* loose outer garment worn by Jap.
Kin, *n.* kindred, relatives. **Kins'-man,** *n.* close relation, one of

same clan. **Kins'folk,** *n.* relations.

Kind (Kynd), *n.* sort, variety, species.

Kind, *a.* generous, warm-hearted. **Kind'liness,** *n.* goodness, benevolence. **Kind'ly,** *a.* genial. **Kind-hearted,** *a.*

Kin'dergarten, *n.* school for children below normal school age.

Kin'dle, *v.t. & i.* to set fire to, catch fire, excite. **Kind'ling** (Kin-), *n.* dry wood or other material for starting fire.

Kin'dred, *n.* relations.

Kine, *n. pl. arch.* cattle.

King, *n.* male sovereign or ruler, principal man in chess, a card bearing picture of king. **King'dom,** *n.* a state ruled over by monarchy.

Kink, *n.* a twist, a whim, a flaw in character.

Kiosk (Kee-), *n.* a small open structure for selling newspapers etc., a small pavilion.

Kip, *n.* hide of young animal.

Kipp'er, *n.* herring cured by salting & smoking. *v.t.*

Kirk, *n. Sc.* church.

Kir'tle (Kur-), *n. arch.* woman's skirt or petticoat, man's tunic.

Kiss, *v.t. & i.* to touch or caress other person's lips with one's own as sign of greeting or affection. *n.*

Kit, *n.* clothes, outfit, equipment.

Kitch'en, *n.* room in which cooking is done.

Kite, *n.* light wooden frame covered with paper for flying in air while attached to cord, a bird of prey.

Kith, *n.* friends, acquaintances, relations, us. only as k. & kin.

Kitt'en, *n.* a young cat.

Kleptoma'nia, *n.* irresistible impulse to thieve. **Kleptoma'niac,** *n.* person affected by this.

Knack (Nack), *n.* adroitness, skill, flair.

Knack'er (Nack-), *n.* dealer in aged horses for slaughtering as meat.

Knap'sack (Nap-), *n.* haversack.

Knave (Nave), *n.* rascal, cheat, the jack in cards. **Kna'very,** *n.* dishonesty. **Kna'vish,** *a.* deceitful.

Knead (Need), *v.t.* to press and mix with the hands, esp. dough.

Knee (Nee), *n.* in human body, joint between thigh and lower leg, part of trousers etc. covering this. **Knee-cap,** *n.* movable bone protecting knee. **Kneel** (Neel), *v.i.* to go down on bent knees.

Knell (Nel), *n.* the tolling of a funeral bell, any dismal portent. *v.i.*

Knick'erbockers (Nick-), *n. pl.* loose-fitting breeches tucked in stocking at knee.

Knick'-Knack (Nik-Nak), *n.* trifling ornament, trinket.

Knife (Nife), *n.* sharp-edged cutting implement with handle. *v.t.* to cut or stab with knife.

Knight (Nite), *n. med.* mounted warrior, now lowest form of titled person, possessing right to title of Sir preceding name, a chessman. *v.t.* to dub a person knight. **Knight'hood,** *n.* rank or dignity of being a knight.

Knit (Nit), *v.t. & i.* to make garment or other article by interweaving strands of wool by means of needles, to unite closely in any way, to bring together, wrinkle esp. the brows.

Knob (Nob), *n.* round handle, round protruberance, door-handle. **Knobb'ly**, *a.* uneven, covered in knobs. **Knob'kerry**, *n.* stick with knobbed head, S. Afric. weapon.

Knock (Nok), *v.t. & i.* to strike, collide with lightly, rap. *sl.* to criticize. **Knock'-out**, *n.* blow that stuns boxer. **Knock-about**, *n.* easy-going comedy. **Knock off**, *v.t. & i. coll.* to stop work.

Knoll (Nol), *n.* rounded hillock.

Knot (Not), *n.* an interwining of ropes or cords for fastening securely, a flawed lump in the grain of wood, a cluster. **Knott'y**, *a.* full of knots, difficult to solve.

Knot, *n. naut.* measure of speed, one naut. mile or 6080 feet per hour.

Knout (Nowt), *n.* whip used in Tsarist Russia.

Know (No), *v.t. & i.* to have knowledge, be acquainted, understand, be certain. **Know'-ing**, *a.* shrewd. **Know'ledge** (Nol-), *n.* learning, comprehension of a subject, facts acquired, experience. **Know'ledgeable**, *a.* well informed, intelligent.

Knuck'le (Nuk-), *n.* finger-joint. *v.t. & i.* to rap with knuckles, as knuckle down, to submit. **Knuckleduster**, *n.* thuggish device for increasing power of blow from fist.

Knur (Nur), **Knurl** (Nurl), *n.* a knot, hard lump.

Knur (Nur), *n.* wooden ball in north country game of **knur-and-spell.**

Koran (-ahn), *n.* sacred Mohammedan book. **Koran'ic**, *a.*

Ko'sher, *a.* food clean according to requirements of Jewish rel. law.

Kowtow', *n.* deep obeisance, orig. Chinese. *v.i.* to show excessive deference.

Kraal (Krahl), *n.* S. Afric. village of huts.

Ku'dos, *n.* credit, advantage.

Kuk'ri, *n.* (Koo-) curved knife widening at point used by Gurkhas of Nepal.

Kyle, *n.* Sc. arm of sea, strait.

L

Laag'er (Lahg-), *n.* camp protected by wagons, encampment. *v.t. & i.* to encamp. esp. when with vehicles.

Labefac'tion (Laby-), *n.* collapse, shaking.

La'bel, *n.* tag attached to luggage or parcel giving address or other details. *v.t.* tie or gum on a label.

La'bial, *a.* pertaining to the lips. *n.* a sound or letter produced by lips, e.g. p, b, f, etc.

La'bour, *n.* physical or mental toil, an arduous task, pains of childbirth, the whole body of working-people. *v.t. & i.* to toil, to act or move with difficulty, to toss about, as of a ship, to strive, to emphasize

La'bourer, *n.* manual workman.

Labor'ious, *a.* hard-working, ponderous.

Lab'oratory, *n.* scientific workroom.

Lab'yrinth (Lab-irr-), *n.* a confused network of passages. **Labyrin'thine,** *a.* intricate, bewildering.

Lace, *n.* decorative work of silk or cotton in open pattern, a cord for fastening shoe or dress etc. *v.t. & i.* to fasten or be fastened with laces. *coll.* to flavour with alcohol.

Lac'erate, *v.t.* to mangle, tear. **Lacera'tion,** *n.*

Lach'rymal (Lak-ri-), *a.* pertaining to tears. **Lach'rymose,** *a.* tearful.

Lack, *v.t. & i.* to have need of, be without. *n.* need, shortcoming.

Lackadai'sical, *a.* listless, indifferent.

Lack'ey, *n.* formerly a footman, now *iron.* a toady.

Laconic', *a.* terse.

Lac'quer, (-ker) *n.* transparent varnish. *v.t.* to paint with this.

Lacrosse' (Lah-), *n.* field game played with rackets & ball and orig. by Red Indians.

Lac'tic, *a.* pertaining to milk. **Lacta'tion,** *n.* secretion or yield of milk. **Lactif'erous,** *e.* yielding milk.

Lacu'na, *n.* a hiatus, blank, missing part.

Lacus'trine, *a.* of lakes.

Lad, *n.* a boy, youth.

Ladd'er, *n.* portable frame of uprights joined by number of bars for climbing, a flaw in stocking. *v.i.* to develop such a flaw.

Lade, *v.t.* to load cargo aboard ship. **La'ding,** *n.* cargo, act of loading this.

La'den, *a.* weighed down, burdened.

La'dle, *n.* large long-handled spoon for dipping. *v.t.*

La'dy, *n.* a gentlewoman, title of wife of ennobled man.

Lag, *v.i.* to dawdle, fall behind. **Lagg'ard,** *n.* backward person.

Lagoon', *n.* shallow lake near or connected with the sea.

Lair (Lare), *n.* animal's den.

Laird, *n.* Sc. squire.

La'ity, *n.* ordinary people outside a profession, esp. people as distinct from priests. **La'ic,** *a.* of the laity, secular.

Lay, *a.* to do with the laity, non-professional. **Lay'man,** *n.*

Lake, *n.* large body of water surrounded by land.

Lake, *n.* crimson pigment.

Lalla'tion, *n.* pronunciation of r as l.

Lam, *v.t. & i. sl.* to punch or strike.

La'ma (Lah-mah), *n.* Buddhist priest in Tibet and Mongolia. **Lamas'ery,** *n.* monastery of lamas.

Lamb, *n.* young sheep. *v.i.* to bring forth lamb.

Lam'baste, *v.t.* to thrash.

Lam'bent, *a.* gently glowing, flickering.

Lame, *a.* crippled in leg or foot, feeble, esp. of excuse. *v.t.* to make lame, cripple.

Lament', *v.t. & i.* to mourn, regret deeply. **Lamenta'tion,** *n.* deep expression of sorrow. **Lam'entable,** *a.* deplorable.

Lam'ina, *n.* a thin plate or layer. **Lam'inate,** *v.t. & i.* to split into layers, cover with thin plates. **Lamina'tion,** *n.*

Lamp, *n.* apparatus for providing light.

Lam′poon, *n.* a satire against a particular person. *v.t.*

Lance (Lahnce), *n.* fighting spear carried by horseman. **Lan′cer,** *n.* cavalryman armed with this. **Lan′cers,** *n. pl.* a quadrille.

Lan′cet, *n.* surg. knife.

Land, *n.* the solid part of the earth's surface as opposed to sea, property, country, region, ground. *v.t. & i.* to come to land, descend or disembark on land, to end up in, to win or catch.

Land as part of various compounds, e.g. **Landfall,** *n. naut.* approach to land for first time during voyage; **Landlord,** *n.* landed proprietor, keeper of inn etc. **Landlady,** *n.* keeper of boarding-house. **Landlubber,** *n.* sailor's derisive term for person living on land. **Landmark,** *n.* prominent feature. **Landscape,** *n.* the scenery of the countryside.

Lane, *n.* a narrow street or country pathway.

Lan′guage (-gwij), *n.* means of verbal communication or expression, human speech, style of writing or speaking.

Lan′guid, *a.* listless, dull, bored. **Lan′guor** (-ger), *n.* lack of energy, dreaminess. **Lan′guish,** *v.i.* to pine, grow lifeless. **Lan′guorous,** *a.* (-ger-).

Lank, *a.* tall and thin. **Lank′y,** *a.*

Lan′olin, *n.* greasy extract from sheep's wool used in making ointments.

Lan′tern, *n.* metal case containing oil-wick or candle and with transparent panes of glass or horn. **Lant′horn,** *n. arch.* form.

Lan′yard, *n. naut.* short rope or cord for securing.

Lap, *n.* knees of seated person. **Lap′dog,** *n.* pet dog small enough to be held on the lap.

Lap, *n.* one complete length of a race-track. *v.t. & i.* in athletics to outpace another competitor to the extent of a whole lap.

Lap, *v.t. & i.* to take up with the tongue, to splash against, to surround.

Lapel′, *n.* turned back part of coat collar.

Lap′idary, *a.* pertaining to precious stones. *n.* a dealer, collector or craftsman in gems.

Lapse, *n.* a falling back, a mistake, failure. *v.i.* to fall back, fall into disuse, revert.

Lar′board, *a. & n. arch.* form for port side of ship.

Lar′ceny, *n.* theft. **Lar′cenous,** *a.*

Lard, *n.* melted pig's fat used in cooking. *v.t.* to smear with this.

Lard′er, *n.* pantry, storeroom for provisions.

Large, *a.* big, extensive, numerous. **Large′ly,** *adv.* to a considerable extent, broadly.

Lar′gesse, *n. arch. & iron.* money or favours scattered at random.

Lar′go, *a., adv. & n. mus.* slow, dignified, movement like this.

Lar′iat, *n.* lasso, tethering-rope.

Lark, *n.* a light-hearted adventure. *v.i.* to frolic.

Lar′va, *n.* insect in caterpillar form, between egg and pupa. **Lar′val,** *a.*

Lar′ynx, *n.* upper end of windpipe holding vocal cords. **Laringy′tis** (-jy-), *n.* inflamed condition of this.

Lasciv'ious (Las-siv-), *a.* sensual, lustful.

Lash, *v.t.* to thrash or fasten with rope. *n.* a whip for flogging.

Lass, *n.* a girl, young woman.

Lass'itude, *n.* exhaustion, indifference.

Lass'o (-soo), *n.* a noosed rope for catching animals. *v.t.*

Last, *n.* cobbler's foot-shaped model for shaping or repairing footwear.

Latch, *n.* device for securing door or gate. *v.t. & i.* to fasten with a latch.

Lat'chet, *n. arch.* shoe-fastening.

Late, *a.* after the right or usual time, tardy, of recent date or occurrence, lately dead. *adv.* at an advanced hour of night, behindhand. Last, *a., adv. & n.* arriving after everyone else, coming at the end in rank or order, the least likely, finally. *v.i.* to endure or wear for a long time. Last'ing, *a.* enduring, wearing a long time.

Lateen', *a. us.* as lateen sail, triangular sail on oblique yard.

La'tent, *a.* present but concealed & inactive.

Lat'eral, *a.* pertaining to the side.

Lath (Lahth), *n.* narrow strip of wood.

Lathe, *n.* machine for turning and shaping wood or metal etc.

Lath'er, *n.* froth caused by mixing soap & water. *v.i.*

Lat'in, *n.* the language of ancient Rome. *a.* pertaining to this or countries whose language is based on this. *n.* a person native of such a country.

Lat'itude, *n.* distance *n.* or *s.* of equator as measured in degrees, a region.

Lat'itude, *n.* range, scope, freedom from restriction.

Latitudinar'ian, *n.* person of liberal outlook, one claiming freedom of thought. Latitudinar'ianism, *n.*

Latrine' (-treen), *n.* lavatory in barracks etc.

Latt'er, *a.* the more recent, later.

Latt'ice (-iss), *n.* screen or other structure formed of laths crossed at right-angles, window with panes set in crossed leadwork. Lattice-work, *n.*

Laud, *v.t.* to glorify, praise. *n.* a song of praise. Laud'able, *a.* praiseworthy. Laud'atory, *a.* expressing praise.

Laud'anum, *n.* tincture of opium.

Laugh (Lahf), *v.i. & i.* to express amusement, scorn, happiness. *n.* the act or sound of laughing. Laugh'able, *a.* amusing, ridiculous. Laugh'ter, *n.* the act or sound of laughing. Laughingstock, *n.* person who makes himself ridiculous.

Launch, *v.t. & i.* to set afloat, to start on career, put project into effect.

Launch, *n.* large motor-boat for pleasure, warship's largest motorboat.

Laun'dry, *n.* place for washing clothes, act of doing this, garments sent to be washed. Laun'dress, *n.* woman who washes clothes. Laun'der, *v.t.* to wash and iron clothes.

Lau'reate, *a.* crowned with laurel, esp. as Poet Laureate, poet appointed by monarch in recognition of excellence.

Lau'reateship, *n.* an acad. prize.

La'va (Lah-), *n.* molten rock ejected by volcano.

Lav'atory, *n. prop.* room for washing hands, us. a water-closet.

Lave, *v.t. arch.* to wash.

Lav'ish, *a.* liberal, generous, excessive. *v.t.* to give or spend excessively.

Law, *n.* an established rule of action on which a society is established, a set of accepted rules, a general principle. **Law'-ful,** *a.* legal, permitted. **Law'-less,** *a.* undisciplined, criminal. **Law'-abiding,** *a.* responsible, accepting the rules of society. **Law'suit,** *n.* legal process. **Law'yer,** *n.* professional practitioner of the law.

Lawn, *n.* a formal, cared-for stretch of grass in garden.

Lawn, *n.* very fine linen.

Lax, *a.* negligent, careless. **Lax'ity,** *n.* looseness, negligence.

Lax'ative, *n. med.* for loosening the bowels. *a.*

Lay, *n.* short narrative song or poem.

Lay, *v.t.* to put or place, to bring down, impose, reduce.

Lay, *v.i.* to produce eggs, to wager.

Lay'er, *n.* a thickness, a stratum, a coating.

Layette', *n.* set of clothes for baby.

Lay figure, *n.* artist's dummy model, unimportant character.

Laz'ar, *n. arch.* a leper. **Lazarett'o,** *n.* a hospital for lepers.

La'zy, *a.* work-shy, idle. **Laze,** *v.i.* to idle.

Lea (Lee), *n. poet.* stretch of meadow or grassland.

Lead (Led), *n.* heavy malleable base metal, lead weight attached to cord for taking depths of sea, thin stick of graphite in pencil. *n. pl.* thin lead strip used in printing, roof of e.g. church protected by lead.

Lead (Leed), *v.t. & i.* to guide, conduct, influence, to be in front of. *n.* being in front, example. **Lead'er,** *n.* person occupying or taking chief place, one who shows the way, main editorial article in newspaper (short for leading article). **Lead'ership,** *n.* position or quality of leading.

Lead (Leed), *n.* channel through ice, elec. connection.

Leaf, *n.* blade on stem or branch of plant, sheet of book, thin beaten metal, esp. gold. *v.t. & i.* to produce leaves, to thumb through paper or pages of book.

Leaf'let, *n.* printed circular or handbill.

League, *n. arch.* measure of distance, approx. 3 miles.

League, *n.* a combination of sporting clubs, a federation of organizations or states. *v.t. & i.* to unite for common objects.

Leak, *n.* a fault or hole admitting liquid or gas or allowing it to escape. *v.i.* **Leak'age,** *n.* an escape of gas or fluid.

Leal, *a. poet.* honest, loyal.

Lean, *v.t. & i.* to incline, bend from upright position, to place in sloping position.

Lean, *a.* not fat, meagre, thin. *n.* the non-fatty part of meat., consisting of muscular tissue.

Leap, *v.t. & i.* to jump or bound, vault. *n.*

Learn, *v.t. & i.* to acquire knowledge or skill from studying or practising, to find out, obtain information. **Learn'ed,** *a.* very knowledgeable, wise. **Learn'ing,** *n.* acquired knowledge.

Lease, *n.* legal contract for the renting of property for stipulated number of years. *v.t.* to grant or take possession thus. **Lease'hold,** *a.* of property not sold outright or freehold.

Leash, *n.* thong or chain for controlling dog etc. *v.t.* to hold in check with a leash.

Leath'er (Leth-), *n.* prepared skin of animal. **Leath'ern,** *n.* **Leath'ery,** *a.* of or like leather, tough.

Leave, *v.t. & i.* to depart, allow to remain behind, deliver, stop, bequeath. *n.* permission, farewell, holiday from duty.

Leav'en (Lev-), *n.* substance added to induce fermentation, yeast. *v.t.* to modify, lighten, cause fermentation.

Lech'erous, *a.* lustful, lascivious. **Lech'er,** *n.* lustful or lewd man. *v.i.* to fornicate. **Lech'ery,** *n.*

Lec'tern, *n.* reading or song desk in church.

Lec'ture, *n.* a formal address of instruction, *coll.* a reproof. *v.t. & i.* **Lec'turer,** *n.* **Lect'ureship,** *n.* academic position.

Ledge, *n.* narrow flat projection, a shelf.

Ledg'er, *n.* book for keeping accounts.

Lee, *n.* protected side away from wind. **Lee'ward** (Loo-ard), *n.* on the sheltered side. **Leeway,** *n.* progress of ship as blown by wind, forward progress in general.

Leech, *n.* bloodsucking aquatic worm, *iron.* a doctor. *v.t. med.* to draw blood from with leeches.

Leer, *n.* a lewd or malignant glance. *v.t.*

Lees, *n. pl.* dregs of wine, sediment of any liquor.

Leet, *n.* ancient local court with special functions.

Left, *a. & n.* pertaining to the side of person or thing which is westward when he or it faces the N., in polit., radical.

Leg, *n.* one of limbs used for animal locomotion, anything resembling a leg, e.g. **table-l,.** **chair-l.,** part of garment worn over legs.

Leg'acy, *n.* a gift bequeathed in person's will. **Legatee',** *n.* person who receives this.

Le'gal, *a.* pertaining to or permitted by the law. **Legal'ity,** *n.* state of being legal or lawful. **Le'galize,** *v.t.* to make lawful. **Legalisa'tion,** *n.* the process of doing this.

Leg'ate, *n.* a papal representative.

Lega'tion, *n.* diplomatic mission or residence.

Lega'to (-ah-), *a., adv. & n. mus.* smoothly, unbroken.

Leg'end (-jend), *n.* traditional story of romantic kind, title or inscription. **Leg'endary,** *a.* mythical, not historical.

Leg'erdemain (Lej-), *n.* sleight of hand, deception.

Leg'ible (Lej-), *a.* easily read, capable of being read. **Legibil'ity,** *n.*

Le'gion (Leej-), *n.* division of Roman army between three &

six thousand men, any large force, an association. **Le'gionary,** n. soldier in a legion.

Leg'islate (Lej-), v.i. to enact laws. **Legisla'tion,** n. **Leg'islative,** a. to do with the passing of laws. **Leg'islator,** n. one who passes or frames laws. **Leg'islature,** n. law-making body, parliament.

Legit'imate, a. lawful. **Legit'imacy,** n. condition of lawfulness. **Legit'imize,** v.t. to make lawful.

Legu'minous (Leg-), a. of plants bearing pods, esp. bean and pea.

Lei'sure (Lezh'er), n. spare time, time not taken up by work.

Lend, v.t. & i. to allow use of temporarily, to make a loan, to give.

Length, n. extent, measurement from end to end, duration, a specified measurement. **Length'en,** v.t. & i. to make or become longer. **Length'wise,** a. & adv. in the direction of the length or in the direction from end to end.

Le'niency, n. tolerance, mildness. **Le'nient,** a.

Lens, n. (Lenz) curved piece of glass for concentrating or adjusting light-rays. pl. **Lenses.**

Le'onine, a. pertaining to the lion, majestic.

Lepidop'tera, n. pl. order of insects including butterflies and moths.

Lep'rosy, n. distressing disease causing gradual eating away of skin. **Lep'er,** n. person suffering from this. **Lep'rous,** a.

Les'bian, n. woman with homosexual tendencies. **Les'bianism,** n.

Lese-maj'esty (Layz-mazhestay), n. treason.

Le'sion, n. damage, injury; med. change in texture or working of organs.

Less, a. not so much. **Less'en,** v.t. to diminish. **Less'er,** a. smaller. n. the smaller of two.

Less'on, n. a period of instruction, something learnt or taught, a reading from the Bible.

Lest, conj. for fear that, in case.

Let, v.t. & i. to allow, to rent.

Let, n. arch. a hindrance, esp. as without let or hindrance, i.e. unimpeded; in certain games when ball strikes net during service.

Le'thal, a. deadly, fatal.

Leth'argy, n. listlessness, unnatural drowsiness. **Lethar'gic,** a. sluggish.

Lett'er, n. alphabetical symbol, a written communication. **Letters,** n. pl. literature, learning.

Leuke'mia, n. serious disease characterized by excess of white blood cells.

Lev'ee, n. official reception by royalty or important dignitary.

Lev'el, a. of unbroken horizontal surface, even, equal, smooth, steady. n. a flat place, an instrument for testing levelness. v.t. to make flat, to bring to an equal position, to aim a gun, to destroy right to the ground.

Level-headed, a. cool, unexcitable. **Level-best,** n. one's utmost.

Levell'er, n. member of 17th cent. polit. movement wishing to achieve absolute social equality.

Le'ver, n. bar used for prising up or moving heavy object using other object as fulcrum; the operating arm of a machine. Le'verage, n.

Levi'athan, n. Bib. sea-monster.

Lev'ity, n. misplaced frivolity.

Lev'y, v.t. & i. to raise or collect taxes or fighting men by authority. n. the act of doing this.

Lewd, a. vulgar, indecent.

Lex'icon, n. a dictionary, esp. of ancient language. Lexicog'-raphy, n. the work of compiling this. Lexicog'rapher, n.

Li'able, a. answerable for, legally responsible for, open to. Liabil'ity, n.

Liai'son (Lee-a-), n. a connection, a clandestine attachment, in gram. the sounding of an otherwise mute final consonant with vowel at beginning of following word.

Li'ar, n. untruthful person. Lie, an untruthful statement. v.i.

Liba'tion, n. rel. the offering of a drink to the gods, iron. a drink.

Li'bel, n. defamatory statement calculated to damage another person's reputation. v.t. to publish such a statement. Li'-bellous, a.

Lib'eral, a. generous, abundant, to do with polit. party favouring progressive and democratic policies. n. member of this. Lib'eralism, n. principles of this party. Liberal'ity, n. generousness, broadmindedness. Lib'eralize, v.t.

Lib'ertine, n. a dissolute person.

Lib'erty, n. freedom, independence, right to do as one pleases within the laws and interests of society. Lib'erate, v.t. to release, set free. Libera'tion, n.

state of being set free. Lib'-erator, Libertar'ian, n. fanatical advocate of liberty.

Libi'do (-be-doh), n. in psychoanal. sexual urge, procreative urge.

Libid'inous, a. lustful.

Li'brary, n. a collection of books, the room or building in which this is kept. Librar'ian, n. person who looks after collection of books.

Librett'o, n. dialogue and songs for opera or mus. play. Librett'ist, n. writer of these.

Li'cence, n. official sanction, permit, unrestricted liberty. v.t. to grant permission formally. Licensee, n. person granted licence, i.e. of public-house. Licent'iate, n. person granted certificate of qualification to practise profession.

Licen'tious, a. unrestrained in sexual matters.

Li'chen (Liken), n. flowerless, leafless plant growing on rocks etc.

Lick, v.t. to pass the tongue over, touch lightly. n.

Lid, n. movable cover for box, skin protecting the eye.

Li'do (Lee-), n. bathing-beach.

Lie, v.i. to recline in a horizontal position, to be situated. n. manner, direction or position in which a thing is situated.

Lief (Leef), adv. arch. or iron. willingly.

Liege (Leej), a. entitled to or bound to give allegiance. n. superior, lord, sworn follower.

Li'en (Lee-en), n. legal right to take possession of someone else's property until disputed debt is paid.

Lieuten'ant (Lef- or Let-), n.

naval or mil. rank, a deputy or assistant.

Life, *n.* animate existence, vital quality distinguishing animals & plants from inanimate things such as rocks, soil, water; existence, human affairs, living beings in general, mode of living, energy, duration of a being's existence. **Live,** (Liv) *v.t. & i.* to have life, to exist, dwell, to earn livelihood. **Live** (Lyve), *a.* having life, alive, actual. **Liv'en** (Ly-), *v.t. & i.* to put life into, make or become brisk or cheerful. **Live'lihood,** *n.* means by which person subsists, regular work. **Live'-liness,** *n.* vigour, cheerfulness. **Live'long** (Liv-), *a.* entire, whole length of.

Lift, *v.t. & i.* to raise up, to rise, to take up. *n.* an elevator.

Lig'ament, *n.* tough fibrous tissue connecting joints of animal or human body.

Lig'ature, *n.* bandage to stop serious bleeding.

Light, *n.* illumination which makes sight possible, brightness, something that induces mental clarity, the condition of being visible. *a.* clear, not dark, shining, pale in hue. *v.t. & i.* to make visible, to become bright, to set on fire, cause lamp to function. **Light'en,** *v.t. & i.* to make or become clear.

Light, *a.* of small weight, not heavy, easy to bear or do, agile, cheerful, frivolous, small in quantity, not burdened. **Light'en,** *v.t.* to make less in weight, easier to bear.

Ligh'ter, *n.* barge for loading or unloading vessel anchored off port.

Light'house, *n.* warning beacon for ships at top of tall building or structure. **Light'ship,** *n.* anchored ship with warning beacon.

Light'ning, *n.* flash of electricity during thunderstorm.

Lig'neous, *a.* pertaining to wood.

Lig'nite, *n.* brown soft coal.

Like, *v.t. & i.* to have a taste or affection for, find pleasant, enjoy, prefer. **Like'able,** *a.*

Like, *a.* similar, characteristic of, in a mood for. *prep.* in the manner of. *n.* equal, counterpart.

Like'ly, *a.* probable, promising. **Like'lihood,** *n.* probability.

Lilt, *n.* song with gay rhythm. *v.t. & i.*

Limb (Lim), *n.* arm or leg, anything resembling these, branch of tree.

Lim'ber, *a.* lithe, flexible. *v.t. & i.* esp. as **l. up,** make or become more supple.

Lim'bo, *n. myth. rel.* place between heaven and hell.

Lime, *n.* white alkaline substance obtained by burning limestone and used in making mortar, cement etc. *v.t.* to spread land with lime to freshen grass. **Lime'stone,** *n.* a kind of rock.

Lime'light, *n.* prominent publicity.

Lim'erick, *n.* nonsensical rhyme of five lines.

Lim'it, *n.* border, utmost extent. *v.t.* to confine, keep within certain bounds. **Limita'tion,** *n.* restriction.

Limn (Lim), *v.t.* to draw, portray.

Lim'ousine (-zeen), *n.* large luxurious automobile.

Limp, *v.i.* to walk in crippled fashion. *n.*

Limp, *a.* flaccid, not stiff.

Limp′id, *a.* sparklingly transparent. Limpid′ity, *n.*

Li′nage, *n.* number of lines in newspaper article; payment for it.

Linch′pin, *n.* iron pin in axle to keep wheel in place.

Line, *n.* a length of wire or cord stretched between poles, a thin long mark, a boundary, a course of action, a row, a set of words, a wrinkle, a series. *v.t.* to mark with a line.

Lin′eage (Lin-e-ij), *n.* line of descent in family. Lin′eal (Lin-e-al), *a.* pertaining to this.

Lin′eament (Lin-e-a-), *n.* or as *n. pl.* the features.

Lin′ear, *a.* esp. as l. measurement, measurement, measurement by length.

Lin′en, *n.* thread spun from flax and material made from this.

Li′ner, *n.* large passenger ship.

Lin′ger, *v.i.* to loiter, delay.

Lin′gual (-gwal), *a.* pertaining to the tongue or language. Ling′uist (-gwist), *n.* person skilled in languages. Ling′uistic, *a.* to do with languages.

Lin′iment, *n. med.* embrocation for rubbing limbs.

Link, *n.* a connection, single ring in chain. *v.t. & i.* to join up, connect.

Link, *n.* one link in surveyor's measuring chain, a hundredth part of this equalling 7.92 in.

Links, *n. pl.* a golf course.

Lino′leum (Lin-o-), *n.* floor coveringmade from canvas strengthened with hardened linseed oil and ground cork.

Li′notype, *n.* in printing, kind of typesetting machine casting each line in one piece.

Lin′seed, *n.* flax seed.

Lint, *n.* linen dressing for wounds.

Lint′el, *n.* horizontal piece of timber or stone above door or window.

Li′on, *n.* large mammal of cat family, *fig.* an important person. Li′onize, *v.t. & i.* to treat person as very important.

Lip, *n.* border of mouth, rim of drinking-vessel.

Liq′uid (-kwid), *a.* fluid, not solid, flowing freely, unsettled. *n.* a fluid substance. Liq′uefy, *v.t. & i.* to turn into or become liquid. Liquefac′tion, *n.* action of changing from solid or gas into liquid form.

Liq′uidate, *v.t.* to settle business or personal affairs by changing property into cash us. to pay debts. Liquida′tion, *n.*

Liq′uidate, *v.t.* euphemism for getting rid of, killing, esp. in polit. sense.

Liq′uor, *n.* strong alcohol. Liqueur′ (Lik-cure), *n.* specially flavour alcohol taken after meal with coffee.

Liq′uorice (-iss), *n.* black substance made from root of plant of same name and used in med. or sorts of sweet.

Lisp, *v.t. & i.* to pronounce defectively or affectedly, esp. turning s into th. *n.*

Liss′om, *a.* nimble, graceful, lithe.

List, *n.* catalogue, register, roll of names or items. *v.t.* to make such.

List, *v.i.* to lean over to one side, esp. of ship. *n.*

List, *n. arch. v.t. & i.* to hear, listen.

List'en (Lis'n), *v.t. & i.* to hearken, give ear to, attend.

List'less, *a.* spiritless, indifferent.

Lit'any, *n.* form of short prayers with responses.

Lit'eral, *a.* exact, unexaggerated.

Lit'erate, *a.* educated, able to read and write. Lit'eracy, *a.*

Lit'erature, *n.* books and writings in general of a high quality.

Lit'erary, *a.* pertaining to books and authors.

Lithe, *a.* agile, lissom.

Lithog'raphy, *n.* method of drawing on stone and printing impressions on it. Lith'ograph, *n.* a picture made by this process. Lithog'rapher, *n.*

Litiga'tion, *n.* the process of embarking on a lawsuit. Lit'-igant, *n.* person who does this. Lit'igate, *v.i.* to go to law. Liti'gious (-je-us), *a.* inclined to go to law.

Lit'mus, *n.* esp. as l.-paper, impregnated with blue dye obtained from kind of lichen and used in chem.

Li'totes (-to-tiz), *n.* ironical understatement.

Litt'er, *n.* brood of young pigs, dogs etc. *v.t.* to give birth to these.

Litt'er, *n.* covered couch or bed carried by means of poles.

Litt'er, *n.* untidy unnecessary rubbish, refuse. Litt'er-lout, *n.* thoughtless and selfish person who leaves rubbish.

Lit'tle, *a.* small, insignificant. *n.* a small quantity. *adv.* in small degree.

Litt'oral, *a.* pertaining to the sea-shore.

Lit'urgy, *n.* set form of Christian service in some churches. Litur'gical, *a.*

Liv'ing, *n.* a church appointment.

Live'stock, *n.* farm animals.

Liv'er, *n.* bile-producing glandular organ in abdomen.

Liv'ery, *n.* private uniform worn by servants or members of City guild, a stable for boarding or hiring horses.

Liv'id, *a.* discoloured, black and blue.

Load, *v.t. & i.* to place cargo in ship, vehicle, burden, animal or person, weigh down, take cargo on board. *n.* a burden, cargo, heavy weight.

Load, *v.t. & i.* to charge a gun. *n.*

Load'stone, Lode'stone, *n.* a magnetic iron ore with great powers of attraction.

Loaf, *n.* a shaped mass of bread, cone-shaped piece of sugar.

Loaf, *v.t. & i.* to laze. Loaf'er, *n.* idler.

Loam, *n.* rich fertile soil.

Loan, *v.t.* to lend. *n.*

Loath, loth, *a.* reluctant, unwilling.

Loathe, *v.t.* to dislike intensely, regard with disgust. Loath'ing, *n.* strong disgust. Loath'some, *a.* detestable.

Lob, *v.t. & i.* to pitch, throw or hit ball gently. *n.*

Lobb'y, *n.* hall or vestibule. *v.i.* to approach M.P.s on a particular subject in lobby of parliament.

Lobe, *n.* lower pendulous part of ear, any similar projection.

Local'ity, *n.* a district, neighbourhood. Lo'cal, *a.* pertaining to this. Lo'calize, *v.t.* to confine or restrict to a particular place.

Loca'tion, *n.* a position or situation, in cinematography an outdoor place where film is made.

Loc'ative, *a. & n.* gram. case indicating place where.

Loch (Lokh), *n.* Sc. a lake.

Lock, *n.* a device for fastening door or lid, firing mechanism in gun, compartment between sluice-gates in canal or river for passing vessels from one level to another. *v.t. & i.* to fasten with a lock, to become entwined, grapple. **Lock'smith,** *n.* maker of locks.

Lock, *n.* a curl of hair or wool.

Lock'er, *n.* small private cupboard.

Lock'et, *n.* small ornamental pendant containing miniature portrait.

Lock'-jaw, *n.* kind of tetanus characterized by jaws becoming locked.

Locomo'tion, *n.* the act of moving, power to move from place to place. **Locomo'tive,** *a.* possessing this power. *n.* a railway engine.

Locu'tion, *n.* mode of expression, a phrase.

Lodge, *v.t. & i.* to provide with or find temporary accommodation, to come to rest in. *n.* a small house, a gardener's or gatekeeper's cottage, branch of certain societies. **Lodg'er,** *n.* person who pays for board or lodging in someone else's house. **Lodg'ing,** *n.* or as *n. pl.* the place he occupies. **Lodge'-ment,** *n.* a temporary foothold, the depositing or registering of a complaint etc.

Loft, *n.* an attic, room immediately under roof, upper floor.

Lof'ty, *a.* high, dignified, haughty. **Lof'tiness,** *n.*

Log, *n.* lump of wood, felled tree.

Log, *n.* ship's daily record, device for measuring ship's speed. *v.t.* to enter item in ship's record.

Log'arithm (-ah-), *n.* a figure indicating how many times a number needs to be multiplied by itself to produce a given number.

Log'gerhead, *n.* esp. as *n. pl.* in disagreement, quarrelling.

Log'ic (Loj-), *n.* correct or rational reasoning, the science of this. **Log'ical,** *a.* reasonable. **Logic'ian,** *n.* person skilled in logic.

Loin, *n.* part of body between thighs and belly, a special cut of meat.

Loi'ter, *v.i.* to hang about idly, delay on way. **Loi'terer.**

Loll, *v.t. & i.* to sprawl at ease, to hang out loosely, as of tongue.

Lone, *a.* solitary. **Lone'liness,** *n.* solitude. **Lone'some,** *a. sl.* depressed and solitary.

Long, *a.* stretching a long way, extended, not short. *adv.* for a long time, to a great extent or length. **Length,** *n.* the condition of being long.

Long, *v.i.* to yearn, desire something greatly. **Long'ing,** *n.*

Longev'ity (-jev-), *n.* great span of life.

Lon'gitude (Lonj-), *n.* distance east or west measured in degrees from meridian of Greenwich. **Lon'gitudinal,** *a.* lying longways.

relating to this, running lengthwise.

Look, *v.t. & i.* to regard with the eyes, to appear, to show by expression, to take care of as **look after,** to expect as **look forward,** to examine as **look over,** to keep watch as **look out.**

Look'er-on, *n.* bystander.

Look'ing-glass, *n.* a mirror.

Loom, *n.* machine for weaving cloth.

Loom, *v.i.* to appear in view bulkily or obscurely.

Loop, *n.* a doubled end of rope or string, a noose, a circular turn or bend. *v.t. & i.*

Loop'hole, *n.* firing-slit in wall of fortification, a narrow way of escape.

Loose (Looss), *a.* not fast, free, general, imprecise, lax. *v.t.* to set free, unbind. **Loos'en,** *v.t. & i.* to make or allow to become less firm or restricted.

Loot, *v.t. & i.* to pillage, plunder. *n.*

Lop, *v.t.* to cut off, trim.

Lope, *n.* a leisurely swinging gait. *v.i.*

Lop'sided, *a.* heavier or bigger on one side than the other, unbalanced.

Loqua'cious (-kway-), *a.* talkative. **Loquac'ity,** *n.*

Lord, *n.* ruler, master, nobleman, God. *v.i.* to rule over.

Lore, *n.* knowledge, particularly a special body of knowledge or facts, e.g. folk-lore.

Lor'gnette (Lorn-yet), *n.* esp. as *n. pl.* eyeglasses with handle.

Lorn, *a. poet.* forlorn, solitary.

Lose (Looz), *v.t. & i.* no longer to have, to fail to keep or maintain, to waste, to stray from path, to fail. **Los'er**

(Looz-er), *n.* person who is defeated or who fails to keep.

Los'ings, *n. pl.* e.g. money that has been lost. **Loss,** *n.* condition or fact of being lost, opposite of profit, bereavement, defeat.

Lot, *n.* person's fate or destiny, share, way of deciding share or choice, a group or collection of things, an item or items in auction sale.

Lo'tion, *n. med.* preparation for skin treatment.

Lott'ery, *n.* game of chance decided by drawing numbers.

Loud, *a.* noisy, at the top of the voice, not silent, clamorous, vehement. **Loud'ness,** *n.*

Lounge, *v.i.* to sprawl, act in lazy fashion. *n.* a room for casual use.

Lour, *v.i.* to give threatening or gloomy appearance. *n.* a baleful look.

Louse (Lowss), *n. pl.* lice, various kinds of insect.

Lout, *n.* uncouth person, oaf. **Lout'ish,** *a.*

Love (Luv), *n.* deep and tender affection, passionate devotion. *v.t.* to harbour deep affection or passion for, to take delight in. **Lov'er,** *n.* sweetheart. **Love'liness,** *n.* beauty. **Lov'able,** *a.* worthy of love, pleasant.

Low (Lo), *a.* far down, deep, soft in tone, cheap, slow, vulgar, not high, base

Low, *n.* the cry of a cow. *v.i.* to moo.

Low'er, *v.t. & i.* to bring further down, to allow to fall, to decrease, weaken, humble.

Loy'alty, *n.* fidelity, devotion. **Loy'al,** *a.* **Loy'alist,** *n.* person supporting established authority as against rebels.

Loz'enge, *n.* diamond-shaped figure, *med.* dose in capsule.

Lubb'er, *n.* lout.

Lu'bricant, *n.* oily or greasy substance for facilitating action of machine. Lu'bricate, *v.t.* to apply this. Lubrica'tion, *n.*

Lu'cent, *a.* radiant, shining clearly.

Lu'cid, *a.* clear, easily understood. Lucid'ity, *n.*

Luck, *n.* good or bad fortune, chance. Luck'less, *a.* unfortunate.

Lu'crative, *a.* profitable financially.

Lucubra'tion, *n.* sedulous study.

Lu'dicrous, *a.* laughable, ridiculous.

Luff, *v.i.* to sail closer to the wind.

Lug, *v.t.* to carry or drag with difficulty.

Lugg'age, *n.* baggage, suit-cases.

Lugg'er, *n.* sailing-vessel with square sails set obliquely.

Luke'warm, *a.* tepid, half-hearted.

Lull, *n.* an interval, temporary calm. *v.t. & i.* to make or become calm.

Lull'aby (-bye), *n.* a song to lull children to sleep.

Lumba'go, *n.* rheumatism of the back and loins. Lum'bar, *a.* pertaining to the loins.

Lumber, *n.* sawn timber, useless material or things. *v.t. & i.* to fell and prepare timber, to clutter up.

Lum'ber, *v.i.* to move clumsily.

Lu'minous, *a.* radiant, shining. Lu'minary, *n.* radiant body, *iron.* prominent person in certain activity.

Lump, *n.* protuberance, shapeless mass. *v.t. & i.* to bring together indiscriminately, shape or form into a mass. Lump'ish, *n.* dull, ponderous.

Lu'nar, *a.* pertaining to the moon. Lu'nacy, *n.* insanity influenced by moon, madness in general. Lu'natic, *a.* pertaining to insanity, absurd. *n.* a mad person.

Lunch, *n.* midday meal. *v.i.* to eat this. Lun'cheon, *n.* the same in more formal sense.

Lung, *n.* one of two organs of breathing.

Lunge, *v.i.* to plunge forward, to thrust at suddenly. *n.* a sudden forward movement or attack.

Lurch, *n.* an abrupt sideways or staggering movement. *v.i.*

Lurch, *n.* difficult situation. us. only as leave in the lurch, to desert at critical moment.

Lurch'er, *n.* mongrel dog often used by poachers.

Lure, *n.* a decoy, bait, attraction. *v.t.*

Lu'rid, *a.* ghastly, glaring, shining violently or unnaturally.

Lurk, *v.i.* to be hidden, to hang about furtively.

Lusc'ious (Lush'us), *a.* juicily sweet.

Lush, *a.* abundant, verdant.

Lust, *n.* strong sinful desire. *v.i.* Lust'ful, *a.*

Lus'tre, *n.* a brilliant surface, a radiance. Lus'trous, *a.* gleaming, brilliant.

Lus'ty, *a.* healthy and vigorous.

Lute, *n.* a stringed mus. instrument resembling guitar.

Luxu'riant (Luk-zure-), *a.* prolific, growing abundantly. Luxu'riate, *v.i.* to grow abundantly, to enjoy oneself richly.

Luxu′rious, *a.* tending to voluptuousness, extremely comfortable. **Lux′ury,** *n.* sumptuous but unnecessary condition or appurtenances, indulgence in such.

Lye, *n.* an alkaline detergent.

Lymph, *n.* colourless fluid from animal organs. **Lymphat′ic,** *a.* pertaining to this, *fig.* sluggish.

Lynch, *v.t.* to put to death at instance of self-appointed, illegal court.

Lyre, *n. mus.* harplike instrument.

Lyr′ic (Lir-), *n.* short mus. poem, orig. sung to the lyre, now a song esp. in mus. comedy. *a.* pertaining to song. **Lyr′ical,** *a.*

M

Maca′bre (-kahbr), *a.* gruesome, horrific.

Macad′am, *n.* method of making roads with successive layers of graded tightly packed stones.

Mace, *n.* med. spiked clubbing weapon, symbolic staff resembling this.

Mace, *n.* spice made from dried outer skin of nutmeg.

Machina′tion (Mak-), *n.* us. *n. pl.* a dastardly scheme.

Machine′ (-sheen), *n.* apparatus for producing power, an engine, a vehicle. **Machi′nery,** *n.* the parts of an engine or machine, the means by which anything is motivated or set going.

Mac′rocosm, *n.* the entire world, the universe.

Ma′cron, *n.* dashlike mark placed over vowel to denote that it is long in quality.

Mad, *a.* insane, crazy, rash, rabid. **Madd′en,** *v.t. & i.* to make or become mad. **Mad′house,** *n.* lunatic asylum. **Mad′ness,** *n.* lunacy, foolishness.

Mad′am, *n.* form of polite address to woman.

Mad′rigal, *n.* love poem set to music.

Mag′azine (-zeen), *n.* periodical publication containing short stories or articles.

Mag′azine, *n.* a storehouse for armaments and explosives, cartridge chamber of gun.

Magg′ot, *n.* grub, a persistent notion.

Ma′gi (-ji), *n. pl. bib.* the three wise men who brought gifts to Jesus. *sing.* **Magus.**

Mag′ic (Maj-), *n.* pretended or inexplicable ability to summon or control supernatural phenomena, witchcraft. *a.* **Mag′ical,** *a.* pertaining to magic. **Magic′ian,** *n.* sorcerer, person claiming to have occult powers.

Mag′istrate (-jis-), *n.* minor local judge. **Magiste′rial,** *a.* pertaining to this, dignified.

Magnanim′ity, *n.* greatness of mind or heart, noble generosity. **Magnan′imous,** *a.*

Mag′nate, *n.* person of importance and influence esp. in industry.

Magne′sia, *n. med.* white, flavourless powder.

Magne'sium, *n.* metallic element that burns with brilliant light.

Mag'net, *n.* loadstone, piece of iron ore with great attractive properties, curved piece of iron or steel artificially magnetized, any person or thing with powerful attractive qualities. **Magnet'ic,** *a.* **Mag'netism,** *n.* properties of a magnet. **Mag'netize,** *v.t.* to endue with magnetic qualities, to attract irresistibly.

Magne'to, *n.* apparatus for ignition in petrol engine.

Magnif'icent, *a.* splendid, majestic, fine. **Magnif'icence,** *n.*

Mag'nify (-fye), *v.t.* to exaggerate, cause to seem greater, as with microscope. **Magnifica'tion,** *n.* the state of being made greater or larger.

Mag'nitude, *n.* greatness, importance, extent.

Maid (Made), *n.* a girl, a female servant. **Maid'en,** *n.* girl or unmarried young woman. **Maid'enly,** *a.* seemly to a girl, modest. **Maidenhood,** *n.* the condition of being a maiden.

Mail (Male), *n.* protective body armour.

Mail, *n.* articles sent and delivered by post. *v.t.* to send by post.

Maim (Mame), *v.t.* to injure seriously, cripple.

Main, *a.* principal, chief, foremost.

Main, *n. arch.* or *poet.* the open sea.

Maintain', *v.t.* to keep in good condition, to uphold, assert, support. **Main'tenance,** *n.* the act of supporting, the means of this, general means of subsistence or keeping in good order.

Mai'sonette (May-zon-et), *n.* part of a house let separately.

Maize, *n.* Indian corn.

Maj'esty, *n.* royal power or state, dignity, title of a monarch. **Majes'tic, majes'tical,** *a.* stately, magnificent.

Ma'jor, *a.* higher in rank or position, greater in extent. *n.* a mil. rank above captain. **Major'ity,** *n.* the greater number out of two parts of a whole, the state of becoming a major, full legal age.

Major-domo, *n.* chamberlain, head official in a royal or important household.

Make, *v.t. & i.* to construct, build, put together, obtain, gain, force, perform, prepare, put in office. *n.* brand, style. **Make-believe,** *n.* pretence, **Make-shift,** *n. & a.* of something improvised, temporary.

Mal-, *pref.* meaning ill, bad, wrong, e.g. **Maltreat,** *v.t.* to treat badly, **Maladjusted,** *a.* faultily adjusted, **Maladministration,** *a.* corrupt or bad management, **Maladroit,** *a.* clumsy etc.

Mal'ady, *n.* an illness or disease.

Malar'ia (-lare-), *n.* recurrent tropical disease caused by parasite introduced into bloodstream by mosquito bite. **Malar'ial,** *a.*

Male, *a.* masculine, pertaining to the sex that begets progeny. *n.* a member of this sex.

Mal'ediction, *n.* a curse.

Mal'efactor, *n.* a criminal, wrong-doer. **Mal'efaction,** *n.*

Malev'olence, *n.* evil spite. **Malev'olent,** *a.*

Malfea'sance, *n.* official mis-conduct.

Mal'ice, *n.* evil spite, ill-will. Malic'ious, *a.*

Mal'ign (-ine), *v.t.* to slander. *a.* malicious, abusive.

Malig'nant, *a.* showing great ill-will, virulent. Malig'-nity, *n.* Malig'nancy, *n.* fatal quality, ill-will.

Malin'ger, *v.i.* to pretend to be sick in order to evade work or duty. Malin'gerer, *n.*

Mall'ard (Mal-), *n.* male wild duck.

Mall'eable (Mal-), *a.* pliable, able to be hammered without breaking.

Mall'et (Mal-), *n.* wooden-headed hammer, stick with right-angled cylindrical head used in croquet, polo etc.

Malt, *n.* barley prepared for brewing. *a.* Malt'ster, *n.* person who makes malt.

Mamm'al, *n.* class of animals secreting milk for nourishment of young. Mamm'ary, *a.* per-taining to the milk glands.

Mamm'oth, *n.* huge prehist. elephant. *a.* immense.

Man, *n.* a male human being, the human race in general, an upright person, a servant, a husband, a piece in chess. *v.t.* to equip with a crew, to prepare oneself for danger etc. Man'ful, *a.* sturdy, courageous. Man'-hood, *n.* men in general, the condition of being a man, courage, uprightness. Man'-kind, *n.* the human race in general. Man'ly, *a.* dignified, frank. Man-handle, *v.t.* & *i.* to seize forcibly, treat roughly. Man-o'-war, *n.* warship. Man-slaughter, *n.* the illegal but unintentional killing of a human-being.

Man'acle, *n.* us. as *n. pl.* fetters, handcuffs. *v.t.*

Man'age, *v.t.* to conduct, regulate, superintend, contrive. Man'ageable, *a.* Man'agement, *n.* the act or skill of controlling or directing. Man'ager, *n.* person in charge of a business etc.

Man'date, *n.* official command, authoritative instructions. Man'datory, *a.* pertaining to this, obligatory.

Man'dible, *n.* lower part of jaw or beak.

Mane, *n.* long thick hair on neck of horse or lion etc.

Mange, *n.* contagious skin dis-ease among animals. Mang'y, *a.*

Man'ger (-jer), *n.* raised eating-trough for cows or horses.

Man'gle, *n.* machine with twin rollers for smoothing laundry. *v.t.*

Man'gle, *v.t.* to hack to pieces, mutilate.

Ma'nia, *n.* madness, frenzy, craze. Ma'niac, *n.* madman. *a.* affected with madness. Mani'-acal, *a.*

Man'icure, *n.* the care of the hands. *v.t.* Man'icurist, *n.* professional expert in this.

Man'ifest, *a.* evident, plain. *v.t.* to make plain. *n.* list of a ship's cargo. Manifesta'tion, *n.* a disclosure, a revelation. Man'-ifesto, *n.* a statement of polit. policy or aims.

Man'ifold, *a.* numerous, various in kind or quality.

Man'ikin, *n.* a dwarf, very small person.

Manip'ulate, *v.t.* to manage

skilfully, operate, control dextrously. Manipula'tion, n.

Mann'equin (-e-kin), n. woman employed to display dresses.

Mann'er, n. style, sort, way in which something is done. n. pl. social behaviour, courtesy. Mann'erism, n. habitual and particular way of behaving, affectation.

Manoeu'vre (-oover), n. mil. movement or operation. v.t. & i. to carry this out, to move or act in order to obtain best advantage.

Man'or, n. landed country house. Manor'ial, a.

Manse, n. Sc. minister's residence, parsonage.

Man'sion, n. large dwelling-house.

Man'tel, n. frame of wood or stone etc. around fireplace. Mantelpiece, n. shelf above fireplace.

Man'tle, n. sleeveless cloak, covering for gas-flame to provide incandescent light.

Man'tle, v.i. to blush.

Man'ual, a. pertaining to the hands. n. a handbook of instructions.

Man'ufacture, v.t. to make, esp. industrially. n. Manufac'turer, n. industrialist owning factory.

Manure', n. animal dung, fertilizer. v.t. to spread soil with this.

Man'uscript, n. lit. work written by hand, the original work of a book or story etc.

Man'y, a. numerous. n. a large number.

Map, n. a chart, a flat representation of the earth or a particular region. v.t. to make a map, show or plan in detail..

Mar, v.t. to spoil, disfigure.

Mar'athon, n. a long distance race.

Maraud'er, n. intruder in search of plunder. Maraud' (-rawd), v.t. & i. to go raiding for plunder.

Mar'ble, n. hard smooth gleaming limestone. a. of this, fig. aloof, cold.

March, n. a frontier region, border.

March, n. a regular pace or manner of walking, a distance covered in this manner, regular onward progress. v.t. & i. to walk or cause to walk in regular manner.

March, n. mus. composition for marching to.

March, n. the third month of the year.

Mare, n. female of horse family.

Mar'gin, n. an edge, a surrounding, unused column at side of page, amount of money or time to spare. Mar'ginal (-jin-), a. pertaining to a margin, of a very small amount or quantity.

Marine' (-reen), a. pertaining to the sea or shipping. n. seago ng soldier, the entire shipping of a country, esp. as merchant marine. Mar'iner, n. seaman. Mar'itime, a. pertaining to the sea, sea commerce and navigation.

Mar'ital, a. pertaining to marriage or husband.

Mark, n. a visible sign, blemish, a target, a distinctive feature, a trade brand, an eminent position, a symbol indicating a grade or quality in lessons. v.t. & i. to identify with a sign, to indicate, to select, define, adjudge quality, observe.

Marked, *a.* conspicuous.

Mark'er, *n.* person who keeps score at billiards.

Mark'et, *n.* trading centre for buying and selling, the general scope for selling goods. *v.t.* to sell, put on market.

Marl, *n.* clay rich in lime used as fertilizer.

Mar'line (-lin), *n. naut.* two-stranded cord for binding ends of rope. **Marline-spike,** *n.* pointed tool used with this.

Maroon', *n.* signal-detonator, dark brownish-red colour.

Maroon', *n.* formerly runaway slave, a person castaway on an island. **Maroon',** *v.t.* to abandon in a desolate place.

Marque (Mark), *n.* hist. seizure of enemy ships by special licence, esp. as letters of m., privateer's authority to act as warship.

Marquee' (-kee), *n.* a large tent.

Mar'quetry (-ket-), *n.* inlaid work on floors or furniture.

Mar'quis, Mar'quess, *n.* nobleman ranking below duke and above earl. **Mar'chioness,** *n.* wife of marquis.

Mar'row (-ro), *n.* fatty material filling hollow of bones, *fig.* the central part of anything.

Marr'y, *v.t. & i.* to join or take in wedlock, become husband and wife. **Marr'iage,** *n.* the legal ceremony of this.

Marsh, *n.* swampy ground.

Marsh'al, *n.* a royal official, a mil. officer of highest rank. *v.t.* to bring together in organized way, to arrange in order.

Marsu'pial, *a. & n.* of class of animals carrying their young in pouch until fully developed.

Mart, *n.* a market-place.

Mar'tial, *a.* warlike, pertaining to war.

Martinet, *n.* severe authoritarian.

Mar'tyr (-ter), *n.* person who allows himself to be killed or tortured rather than renounce his faith. *v.t.* to persecute because of faith. **Mar'tyrdom,** *n.*

Mar'vel, *n.* a wonder, something astonishing. *v.i.* to be astonished at, struck with wonder. **Mar'vellous,** *a.*

Mas'cot, *n.* a person or object reputed to bring good luck.

Mas'culine (-lin), *a.* pertaining to the male sex, manly, sturdy, in gram. of male gender.

Mash, *n.* warm mixture of bran and water as feed for animals and poultry. *v.t.* to mix into a mash, pulp.

Mask (Mahsk), *n.* covering for the face as disguise or protection. *v.t.*

Mas'ochist, *n.* person deriving perverted pleasure from being maltreated. **Mas'ochism,** *n.*

Ma'son, *n.* craftsman in stone. **Ma'sonry,** *n.* his work, stonework.

Mason'ic, *a.* pertaining to freemasonry, a mutual aid society formerly secret.

Masque, *n. arch.* a pageant of mus., poetry, drama.

Mas'querade, *n.* masked or fancy dress ball. *v.i.* to dress up in disguise.

Mass, *n.* heap or compact collection of material, large amount. as *n. pl.* esp. the Masses, people in general. **Mass'ive,** *n.* large and ponderous.

Mass, *n. rel.* celebration of the Eucharist.

Mass´acre (-ker), *n.* wholesale brutal killing. *v.t.*

Mass´age (-ahzh), *n. med.* treatment of body and limbs by rubbing and working muscles with the hands. *v.t.* **Mass´eur,** *n.* **Mass´euse,** *n. fem.* skilled person performing massage.

Mast (Mahst), *n.* spar or pole for supporting rigging in ship.

Mast, *n.* fruit of oak and beech, esp. when used as food for pigs.

Mast´er, *n.* head of a family, person who employs others, captain of a merchant ship, male schoolteacher, person in command, acknowledged expert. *v.t.* to overcome or subdue. **Mast´erful,** *a.* domineering. **Mast´erly,** *a.* expert. **Mast´ery,** *n.* dominion, supremacy.

Mas´terpiece, *n.* esp. a work of art or lit. of eminent quality.

Mas´tic, *n.* resinous gum used as basis for varnish.

Mas´ticate, *v.t.* to chew. **Mastica´tion,** *n.*

Mat, *n.* small thick piece of material for wiping footwear on, piece of fabric placed under dishes to protect table.

Mat, *v.t. & i.* to become tangled or stuck together. *n.*

Mat, *a.* dull, lustreless. *n.* a surface with dull or unpolished finish.

Mat´ador, *n.* man whose job it is to kill the bull in bull-fighting.

Match, *n.* an equal, anything or anyone exactly alike another, persons suitable to each other in marriage, a sporting contest. *v.t. & i.* compete with, marry, to tally, correspond with. **Match´less,** *n.* peerless. **Matchmaker,** *n.* woman who endeav-

ours to bring man and woman together in marriage.

Match, *n.* thin short stick of wood tipped with combustible material that takes fire when rubbed against rough surface. **Match´lock,** *n. arch.* form of gun set off by match or fuse.

Mate, *n.* companion, partner, merchant ship's officer next to captain in rank. *v.i.* to pair for breeding purposes.

Mate, *n. & v.t.* decisive move in chess, esp. as **Checkmate,** signifying defeat of opponent.

Mate´rial, *n.* matter or substance. *a.* actual, substantial, bodily, physical, not spiritual. **Mate´rialism,** *n.* doctrine that matter is the only reality as opposed to spiritual things. **Mate´rialist,** *n.* one who believes this, one who pays excessive attention to worldly possessions. **Mate´rialize,** *v.t. & i.* to make or become actual.

Mater´nal, *a.* pertaining to motherhood. **Mater´nity,** *n.* the condition of being a mother, motherhood.

Mathemat´ics, *n. pl.* but used as *n. sing.* science treating of quantities. **Mathemat´ical,** *a.* **Mathemati´cian,** *n.*

Mat´inée (-nay), *n.* theatrical or other performance taking place in afternoon.

Ma´tins, *n. pl. rel.* morning service.

Ma´triarch, *n.* female head of family or society. **Ma´triarchy,** *n.* society ruled by women.

Mat´ricide, *n.* the crime of killing one's own mother, person who commits this. **Matrici´dal,** *a.*

Matric´ulate, *v.t. & i.* to register

or be admitted as university student. **Matricula'tion,** *n.*

Mat'rimony, *n.* marriage. **Mat'-rimonial,** *a.*

Ma'trix, *n.* womb, mould for casting type.

Ma'tron, *n.* older married woman, chief nurse in hospital etc. **Ma'tronly,** *n.* sedate, dignified.

Matt'er, *n.* substance, pus, general contents, affair, business, concern. *v.i.* to be of concern or importance.

Matt'ress, *n.* stuffed canvas or cloth bag used as basis for bed.

Mature', *v.t. & i.* to develop fully, ripen, to bring to completion, perfect. *a.* **Matu'rity,** *n.* ripeness, full development or growth.

Maud'lin, *a.* tipsily sentimental.

Maul, *v.t.* to treat viciously or brutally. *n.* a rough mêlée.

Maund'er, *v.i.* to speak or act in aimless fashion.

Mausole'um, *n.* splendid ornate tomb in building.

Mauve, *n.* soft purple or lilac colour.

Maw, *n.* crop of bird, stomach of animal.

Mawk'ish, *a.* sickening, excessively sentimental.

Max'illary, *a.* pertaining to the jaw.

Max'im, *n.* an adage, a concisely expressed truth.

Max'imum, *n.* greatest possible number, quantity, quality. *a.*

May, *n.* the fifth month of the year.

May'hem, *n.* the deliberate and criminal wounding of a person.

May'or, *n.* head official and magistrate of municipality.

May'oral, *a.* **May'oralty,** *n.* his office or term of office.

Maze, *n.* a labyrinth, a confused state of mind.

Mead, *n.* alcoholic liquor based on fermented honey.

Mead'ow (Med-), *n.* a field of pasture. **Mead,** *n. poet.*

Mea'gre, *a.* scanty, sparse, thin.

Meal, *n.* food taken at a set time, ground corn.

Mean, *a.* ungenerous, narrow-minded, ill-disposed.

Mean, *v.t.* to signify, intend, designate. **Mean'ing,** *n.* the sense, explanation.

Mean, *a.* average, intermediate, in between. **Mean'time,** *n.* the interval between two happenings. **Mean'while,** *n. & adv.*

Meand'er (Me-an-), *v.i.* to wander at random, to flow sinuously.

Mea'sles (Meez'ls), *n. pl.* as *sing.* contagious disease characterized by fever & itching skin.

Meas'ure (Mezh-), *n.* size, quantity, capacity, unit of measurement, device for measuring, in mus. the time of a composition, *poet.* a rhythm, a course of action, an amount. *v.t. & i.* to determine size etc., to extend to or be of certain length. **Meas'urable,** *a.* **Meas'-ured,** *a.* thoughtfully considered, stately. **Meas'ureless,** *a.* infinite. **Meas'urement,** *n.* system of measuring, act of ascertaining dimensions, size or quantity.

Meat, *n.* the flesh of animals used as food, food in general.

Mechan'ics (-kan-), *n. pl.* used as *sing.* the science of machinery. **Mechan'ic,** *n.* skilled workman tending machinery. **Mechan'-ical,** *a.* pertaining to mechanics, powered by machinery. **Mech'-anize**, v.t. to make mechanical, use mechanical power instead of manual. **Mechaniza'tion**, n.

Med'al, n. metal disc or similar shape commemorating courageous action or historic event.

Medall'ion, n. large medal, ornamented tablet or panel.

Mediae'val (Meddi-e-val), a. pertaining to the Middle Ages.

Me'dian, a. in the middle. n. point or number in this position. **Me'dial**, a.

Me'diate, v.t. & i. to act as peacemaker between disputants. **Media'tion**, n. **Me'diator**, n. person who tries to bring quarrelling parties together.

Medic'ament, n. a medicine.

Med'icine (-sin), n. science of treating diseases & ailments, a curative remedy. **Med'ical**, a. **Med'icated**, a. containing medicine. **Medic'inal**, a. possessing power to cure.

Me'diocre, a. commonplace, of average quality. **Medioc'rity**, n.

Medita'tion, n. serious thought. **Med'itate**, v.t. & i. **Med'-itative**, a.

Me'dium, n. average or middle quality, means, agency, person claiming occult or spiritualistic powers. a. moderate, average.

Med'ley, n. a miscellany, mus. a composition made up of selections from other works.

Meed, n. reward.

Meek, a. humble.

Meet, a. fitting, proper.

Meet, v.t. & i. to encounter, join, oppose in combat, satisfy, come together. **Meet'ing**, n. a coming together, an assembly.

Mel'ancholy (-koli), n. sadness, gloomy state. a. mournful.

Melée (Mel-lay), n. a confused struggle or fight.

Mellif'luous, a. smoothly flowing, esp. of voice.

Mell'ow (-o), a. mature, soft, ripe. v.t. & i. to make or grow tolerant, ripe.

Mel'ody, n. song or tune, harmonious arrangement of sounds. **Melo'dious**, a. pleasantly tuneful.

Mel'odrama, n. (-drah-) exciting, emotional, romantic play, iron. any event resembling this. **Mel'odramatic**, a.

Melt, v.t. & i. to dissolve, change from solid to liquid by action of heat, to soften, diminish.

Mem'ber, n. a limb, any part of a whole, person belonging to club or association. **Mem'-bership**, n. condition of being a member of organization, collectively members of such.

Mem'brane, n. tissue connecting or protecting other parts of animal body. **Mem'branous**, a.

Mem'oir (-war), n. record of events written from personal experience, autobiography, biography.

Mem'orable, a. noteworthy, likely to be remembered.

Mem'orandum, n. a note to remind, a report.

Memor'ial, n. an event or thing to perpetuate the memory of a person or historic occurrence.

Mem'ory, n. the power or ability to retain image or details of past happenings or people in the mind, recollection, reminiscence. **Mem'-orize**, v.t. to retain as a memory.

Men'ace, n. a threatened danger. v.t. to threaten.

Menag'erie (-aj-), *n.* a collection of wild animals kept in cages, a zoo.

Mend, *v.t. & i.* to repair, grow better, improve.

Menda'cious, *a.* tending to lie. **Mendac'ity,** *n.* untruthfulness.

Me'nial, *n.* a domestic servant. *a.* pertaining to or suitable for this.

Mental'ity, *n.* the intellect, the mind. **Men'tal,** *a.* pertaining to the intellect. *sl.* daft.

Men'tion, *v.t.* to refer to, speak of by name. **Men'tionable,** *a.*

Men'tor, *n.* teacher, adviser.

Mer'cantile (Mur-), *a.* pertaining to trade or merchants.

Mer'cenary, *a.* acting only for gain, avaricious. *n.* volunteer soldier fighting for another country.

Mer'chant, *n.* trader, commercial dealer. **Mer'chandise,** *n.* commercial goods & articles.

Mer'chantman, *n.* cargo ship. **Merchant Marine,** *n.* all the cargo ships of a nation.

Mer'cury, *n.* quicksilver, liquid metal used in thermometers etc. **Mercu'rial,** *a.* pertaining to this, lively, changeable.

Mer'cy, *n.* readiness to forgive or show leniency, an act of kindness. **Mer'ciful,** *a.* **Mer'ciless,** *a.* pitiless, cruel.

Mere (Meer), *n.* shallow lake.

Mere, *a.* nothing but, simple. **Mere'ly,** *adv.* simply, only.

Meretric'ious (Mer-i-), *a.* alluring in a flashy or false way.

Merge (Murj), *v.t. & i.* to combine, blend, join. **Mer'ger,** *n.* a combination, a joining together into one.

Merid'ian, *n.* the highest point, highest altitude of sun or stars, line from N. to S. poles on which noon is simultaneous. *a.* relating to this.

Mer'it, *n.* worth, excellence. *v.t.* to deserve. **Meritor'ious,** *a.* praiseworthy.

Mer'maid, *n.* legendary sea-creature with body of woman & tail of fish. **Mer'man,** *n.*

Mer'riment, *n.* jollity, gaiety. **Merr'y,** *a.*

Mesh, *n.* one of the spaces between cords of net, the interlocking of gears in a machine. *v.t. & i.* to catch or become entangled, to fit together as in gears.

Mes'merize, *v.t.* to hypnotize, fascinate. **Mes'merism,** *n.*

Mess, *n.* a muddle, dirty confusion. *v.t. & i.* to make this, to act idly, esp. as mess about.

Mess, *n.* a meal, a place where meals are taken collectively, esp. in navy or army. *v.t. & i.* to provide food, eat together.

Mess'age, *n.* a written or verbal communication. **Mess'enger,** *n.* person who carries this.

Metab'olism, *n.* process by which food is changed into living matter in organic body. **Metabol'ic,** *a.*

Met'al, *n.* hard chem. element solid, heavy and shining in character, such as gold, copper, iron, tin etc., crushed stone for roadmaking. *a.* **Metall'ic,** *a.* pertaining to metal, having the quality of metal. **Met'allurgy,** *n.* the craft of processing metals. **Met'allurgist,** *n.* expert in this.

Met'amorphose, *v.t.* to change into completely different form, to transmute.

Met'amorphosis, n. transformation.

Met'aphor, n. figure of speech, fanciful application of descriptive term to object to which it is not lit. suitable. Met'aphorical, a.

Met'aphysics, n. the philosophy of being and knowing. Met'aphysical, a. pertaining to this, of the supernatural, abstract.

Mete (meet), v.t. to apportion, measure.

Me'teor, n. a shooting star, mass of burning matter falling through sky. Meteor'ic, a. brilliant but brief. Me'teorite, n. a meteor fallen to earth.

Meteorol'ogy, (-ji), n. the science of weather. Meteorol'ogist, n. expert in this. Meteorolog'ical, a.

Me'ter, n. apparatus for measuring or recording.

Meth'od, n. way of doing or performing something. Method'ical, a. orderly, systematic.

Metic'ulous, a. sedulously careful, fussy over details.

Me'tre, n. standard unit of length in metric system, 39.37 ins.

Met'ronome, n. mus. instrument which beats time at necessary pace for practice.

Metrop'olis, n. chief city of a country or region. Metropol'itan, a. of this. n. an archbishop.

Met'tle, n. courage, spirit. Met'tlesome, a. spirited.

Mew, v.t. to confine in a cage, esp. of falcon. Mews, n. pl. stabling and hawkhouses combined round open yard.

Mez'zo (Metzo), a. mus. moderate, moderately soft. M.-soprano.

Mez'zotint, n. engraving process whereby light effects are produced by scraping roughened surface.

Mias'ma, n. noxious emanations from marshland.

Mi'ca, n. silicate mineral separable into thin transparent scales or plates.

Mi'crobe, n. tiny living organism that can only be seen under microscope.

Mi'crocosm, n. a miniature world, any miniature representation.

Mi'crophone, n. apparatus for strengthening sound waves.

Mi'croscope, n. optical instrument for enlarging image of very small objects. Microscop'ic, a. so small as to be only visible through microscope.

Mid, a. middle. Mid'dle, a. intermediate, halfway. n. the centre, a point equidistant from two others in a straight line. Mid-day, n. noontide. Various self-explanatory words prefixed by Mid.

Midge, n. very small insect, gnat, small person.

Midg'et, n. abnormally small but normally built person. a.

Mid'wife, n. woman skilled in assisting at childbirth. Mid'wifery (-wiff-), n.

Might, n. power, strength. Might'y, a. massive, powerful.

Mi'graine, n. very painful & severe headache.

Mi'grate, v.i. to move from one country to another and settle there, to travel seasonally according to climate. Mi'grant, *a.* & *n.* **Migra'tion**, *n.* **Mi'-gratory**, *a.*

Milch, *a.* giving milk, esp. of cow.

Mild (Myld), *a.* kind, gentle, clement.

Mil'dew, *n.* tiny fungus attacking plants or growing on decaying matter. *v.i.* to be affected by mildew.

Mile, *n.* a measure of length of 1760 yards. **Mile'age**, *n.* distance covered, an allowance for travelling expenses.

Mil'itary, *a.* relating to armed forces or war. *n.* an army, armed forces. **Mil'itant**, *a.* aggressive, warlike. *n.* person who fights, a person ready to act violently in promoting a cause. **Mil'itarism**, *n.* outlook which regards force as a conclusive remedy. **Mili'tia**, *n.* citizen army as auxiliary to regular force.

Mil'itate, *v.t.* to work against, tell against, as of force or argument.

Milk, *n.* white fluid secreted by female mammals as food for their young. *v.t.* to draw milk from.

Mill, *n.* a machine for grinding, the building that houses this. *v.t.* & *i.* to grind in a mill, to circle round in confusion. **Mill'er**, *n.* person who grinds corn. **Mill'wright**, *n.* builder of mills, mechanic repairing mills.

Mill'iner, *n.* person who makes or sells women's hats. **Mill'inery**, *n.* women's hats, trade in these.

Mill'ion, *n.* one thousand thousand. **Millionaire**, *n.* person owning a million pounds or great wealth in general.

Mime, *v.i.* to imitate or act in dumbshow. **Mim'ic**, *n.* person who imitates. *a.* sham, imitative. **Mim'icry**, *n.*

Minaret' (Min-), *n.* tower of Moslem mosque from which priest summons people to prayer.

Mince, *v.t.* to chop up finely.

Mince, *v.t.* & *i.* to gloss over, to walk or talk artificially. **Min'cing**, *a.* affected.

Mind, *n.* the intellect, consciousness, memory, thoughts, opinions. *v.t.* & *i.* to pay attention to, object, take care of, feel annoyance. **Mind'ful**, *a.* heedful. **Mind'less**, *a.* thoughtless, careless, disregarding.

Mine, *n.* underground excavation for obtaining minerals, excavation with explosive charge under enemy fortification, explosive charge in floating container to damage enemy ships. *v.t.* & *i.* to make or work in a mine, to blow up by mine. **Mi'ner**, *n.* **Mineshaft'**, *n.*

Min'eral, *n.* inorganic substance, substance obtained from mining, ore. *a.* **Mineral'ogy**, *n.* the science of minerals. **Mineral'ogist**, *n.*

Min'gle, *v.t.* & *i.* to associate, blend.

Min'iature, *n.* very small painting, us. as portrait, small model of any sort. *a.* on a small scale.

Min'imize, *v.t.* to reduce to smallest possible quantity or quality. **Min'imal**, *a.* very small. **Min'imum**, *n.* the smallest quantity.

Min'ion, *n.* follower, servant in derogatory meaning.

Min'ister, *n.* head of a government department, diplomatic representative, clergyman. *v.i.* to serve as priest, to attend to others' needs. **Minister'ial**, *a.* relating to the office or function of a minister. **Ministra'tion**, *n.* the act of serving or ministering. **Min'istrant**, *a.* person who gives aid. **Min'istry**, *n.* a government department, a priest's office or duty, church officials in general.

Mi'nor, *n.* person not yet of full legal age, i.e. twenty-one. *a.* lesser, unimportant. **Minor'ity**, *n.* smaller number or part, condition of being under age.

Min'ster, *n.* church of a monastery, sometimes a cathedral.

Min'strel, *n.* mediaeval singer and musician. **Min'strelsy**, *n.* company of minstrels, their art, a collection of ballads.

Mint, *n.* official place where state's money is made, a lot, esp. of money. *v.t.* to coin money.

Min'uet, *n.* old-fashioned stately dance, the mus. for it.

Mi'nus, *a.* sign of subtraction, *a.* negative.

Min'ute (-it), *n.* one sixtieth part of an hour or a degree, a brief official memorandum. *n. pl.* written record of decisions taken at committee meeting.

Mi'nute, *a.* tiny, detailed.

Minx, *n.* hussy.

Mir'acle, *n.* supernatural or inexplicable happening, something brought about by faith. **Mirac'ulous**, *a.* marvellous.

Mirage' (-rahzh), *n.* visual illusion caused by atmospheric conditions.

Mire, *n.* muddy, boggy place. *v.t. & i.* to get stuck in mud, become muddied.

Mirr'or, *n.* looking glass, anything that reflects a likeness. *v.t.* to reflect.

Mirth (Murth), *n.* merriment, laughter. **Mirth'ful**, *a.* jolly. **Mirth'less**, *a.* gloomy.

Mis-, *pref.* meaning bad or badly, wrong or wrongly. The meaning of all such words can be found by referring to the definition of the main word and qualifying with the sense here explained.

Mis'anthrope, *n.* person who hates mankind. **Misanthrop'ic**, *a.*

Miscarr'y, *v.i.* to give birth prematurely, to fail. **Miscarr'iage**, *n.* premature birth.

Miscell'any, *n.* a collection of various lit. or mus. pieces, an assortment. **Miscella'neous**, *a.*

Mis'chief, *n.* annoying or harmful behaviour, misfortune, injury. **Mis'chievous**, *a.* irritating, wilful.

Mis'creant, *n.* wrongdoer.

Mi'ser, *n.* avaricious person who gloats over his wealth.

Mis'erable, *a.* wretched, poor, mean, unhappy. **Mis'ery**, *n.*

Misno'mer, *n.* incorrect name or term.

Misog'ynist (-oj-i-), *n.* man who hates women. **Misog'yny**, *n.*

Miss, *v.t. & i.* to fail to catch or hit, fail to attend, to escape or avoid, to feel the absence of, *n.*

Miss, *n.* title for unmarried woman or girl.

Miss'al, *n.* book of prayers and devotions.

Miss'ile, *n.* a throwing or hurling weapon.

Mis'sion, *n.* a vocation, a special trust or duty. **Miss'ionary**, *n.* priest or layman who propagates the gospel, esp. abroad. *a.*

Miss'ive, *n.* a letter.

Mist, *n.* visible water vapour, haze in atmosphere. *v.i.*

Mistake', *n.* a fault, an error. *v.t. & i.* to make an error, to fail to understand, to mis-identify. **Mistak'able**, *a.* **Mistak'en**, *a.* wrong, misunderstood, mis-identified.

Mis'tress, *n.* woman head of family, female employer, female school-teacher, lover.

Mite, *n.* microscopic insect, very small object or child.

Mit'igate, *v.t.* to relieve, lessen, soften. **Mitiga'tion**, *n.*

Mi'tre, *n.* ornate hat worn by bishop or arch-b.

Mi'tre, *v.t.* in joinery to make special joint at corner of picture frame etc.

Mitt'en, *n.* fingerless glove, glove covering four fingers together and thumb separately.

Mix, *v.t. & i.* to associate, blend, confuse. **Mix'ture**, *n.*

Mizz'en, *n.* lowest square sail of full-rigged sailing-ship. **Mizzen-mast**, aftermost mast in this.

Mnemon'ic (Nem-), *a.* pertaining to the memory, helping the memory.

Moan, *n.* a subdued sound of distress. *v.t. & i.*

Moat, *n.* protective ditch round fortification.

Mob, *n.* rabble, riotous throng. *v.t.* to attack in a crowd, to jostle round.

Mo'bile, *a.* moving easily. **Mobil'ity**, *n.*

Mo'bilize, *v.t.* to call up mil. reserves and forces on threat of war. **Mobiliza'tion**, *n.*

Mocc'asin, *n.* Amer. Indian's deerskin leather shoe.

Mock, *v.t.* to ridicule, make fun of, imitate derisively. **Mock'-ery**, *n.* ridicule, a feeble imita-tion.

Mode, n. manner, method, custom.

Mod'el, *n.* pattern, miniature representation, something worthy or suitable to be copied, person employed to pose for artist or to exhibit new fashions in clothes. *v.t.* to form from model, to exhibit clothes. *a.* exemplary.

Modera'tion, *n.* the avoidance of extremes, restraint. **Mod'erate**, *a.* restrained, not intense. **Moderate**, *v.t. & i.* to make or become less extreme.

Mod'erator, *n.* Presbyterian church official.

Mod'ern, *a.* pertaining to the present, up to date, newly developed. **Mod'ernism**, *n.* modern methods or outlook. **Mod'ernist**, *n.* **Modern'ity**, *n.* condition of being modern or of the present. **Mod'ernize**, *v.t.* to adopt new, more efficient methods. **Moderniza'tion**, *n.*

Mod'esty, *n.* decorum, humility, chastity. **Mod'est**, *a.* virtuous, not boastful.

Mod'icum, *n.* a small amount.

Mod'ify, *v.t.* to adjust or alter slightly. **Modifica'tion**, *n.*

Mod'ulate, *v.t. & i.* to adjust, regulate, change tone, *mus.* to change key. **Modula'tion**, *n.*

Mohamm'edan, *a.* a follower of Mahomet. *a.* pertaining to the rel. founded by him. **Mohamm'-edanism**, *n.* rel. founded by Mahomet, Islam.

Moist, *a.* slightly wet, damp.

Moist'en (mois'n), v.t. & i. to make or become damp. Moist'ure, n. moderate amount of dampness.

Mo'lar, n. grinding tooth. a.

Molass'es, n.pl. as n. syrup obtained from the processing of sugar.

Mole, n. small dark blemish on skin.

Mole, n. breakwater protecting harbour.

Mol'ecule, n. smallest part into which substance can be split without losing identity or characteristics. Molec'ular, a.

Molest', v.t. to pester, annoy. Molesta'tion, n.

Moll'ify, v.t. to appease, soften. Mollifica'tion, n.

Moll'usc, n. soft-bodied and us. hard-shelled animal. e.g. oyster, snail.

Mo'ment, n. a very short space of time, the immediate present. Mo'mentary, a. very brief as a moment.

Moment'ous, a. of great importance.

Moment'um, n. impetus.

Mon'arch (-ark), n. sovereign ruler, king or queen. Mon'archy, n. system of government with sovereign as head. Mon'archist, n. supporter of this principle.

Mon'astery, n. building occupied by celibate order of monks. Monas'tic, a. pertaining to this, secluded, frugal. Monas'ticism, n.

Mon'ey (Mun-), n. coin, currency, means of exchange. Mon'etary, a. to do with money, financial.

Mon'grel (Mun-), n. a hybrid. a.

Mon'itor, n. senior pupil in school with certain authority, slow, heavily armoured, heavily armed battleship for use as floating gun-battery, counsellor.

Monk (Munk), n. member of monastic order.

Mon'o-, pref. meaning one or single, e.g. Monochrome, n. painting in single colour; Monog'amy, n. convention of being married to only one spouse at a time; Mon'ograph, n. academic treatise on one particular subject; Mon'osyllable, n. word consisting of one syllable etc.

Monop'olize, v.t. to obtain or seize exclusive ownership or production. Monop'oly, n. exclusive possession or control. Monop'olist, n.

Monot'onous, a. tiresomely unvaried, dull. Monot'ony, n. Mon'otone, n. dull unvarying style.

Mon'soon, n. periodic winds in Indian Ocean bringing long, heavy rainfall.

Mon'ster, n. an abnormal creature, a fabulous animal, a cruel person. Mon'strous, a. huge, extremely wicked. Monstros'ity, n. anything misshapen or hideous.

Montage' (-tahzh), n. the cutting and editing of a moving film.

Month (Munth), n. one of twelve parts into which year is divided, a calendar month; lunar month, period of moon's revolution. Month'ly, a. occuring, payable, appearing once a month. n. a magazine that appears once a month.

Mon'ument, n. a work or erection to commemorate an event

or person. **Monument'al,** *a.*
pertaining to this, vast, enduring.

Mood, *n.* state of mind. **Mood'y,**
a. sulky.

Mood, *n.* gram. form of verb
showing mode of action.

Moon, *n.* satellite of the earth or
any planet. **Moonlight, Moon-
beam,** *nn.* **Moonstruck,** *a.* mad,
daft.

Moor, n. barren countryside
with rocks and heather.

Moor, *n.* Saracen, esp. of
Muslim invader of Spain in
mediaeval times. **Moor'ish,** *a.*
of the style of the Moors, esp.
in arch.

Moor, *v.t. & i.* to secure vessel by
rope or cable. **Moor'ing,** moorings, *n., n.pl.* place or buoy
where vessel is secured, ropes
for doing this.

Moot, *v.t.* to put forward for
discussion. *a.* arguable.

Mop, *n.* loose, floppy bundle of
rags or cloth on handle for
cleaning floors etc. *v.t.* to clean
with this, to wipe up moisture.

Mope, *v.i.* to be dispirited.

Mo'raine, *n.* glacial deposit.

Mor'al, *a.* ethical, pertaining to
right and wrong, virtuous. *n.*
ethical point of a story or
event. **Morals,** *n. pl.* accepted
social behaviour. **Moral'ity,** *n.*
irreproachable ethical conduct,
moral goodness. **Mor'alize,** *v.t.
& i.* to improve morally, to
expound moral principles.

Morale' (-ahl), *n.* confidence,
discipline, esp. in face of
difficulties.

Morass', *n.* soft, swampy
ground.

Morator'ium, *n.* official suspension of debts.

Mor'bid, *a.* of or indicating
disease, sickly, unwholesome.

Mor'dant, *a.* biting, incisive.

More, *a.* greater in number or
content, additional, in excess
of, again. *n.*

Morganat'ic, *a.* esp. as **m.
marriage,** marriage between
royal person and someone of
lesser rank.

Morgue (Morg), *n.* public
mortuary.

Mor'ibund, *a.* approaching
death.

Mor'ning, *n. & a.* beginning of
daytime. **Morn,** *n. poet.* dawn,
daybreak.

Mor'on, *n.* mentally backward
person. **Mo'ronic,** *a.*

Morose', *a.* sullen.

Mor'phine (-feen), *n.* pain-kil-
ling drug derived from opium.

Morr'ow (-o), *n.* the following
day.

Morse, *n.* esp. as **m. code,**
system of sending messages by
radio telegraphy.

Mor'sel *n.* a small piece of food.

Mor'tal, *n.* a human being esp.
in sense of being subject to
death. *a.* fatal, deadly, extreme,
pertaining to humans. **Mortal'-
ity,** *n.* death rate, death.

Mor'tar, *n.* building cement for
joining bricks, a kind o annon
for steep firing, a vessel for
grinding substances in.

Mort'gage (Mor-gij), *n.* the
making over of property as
security for sum borrowed.
v.t. **Mort'gagee** (Morgaji), *n.*
person lending money on this
basis. **Mort'gagor** (-ga-jor), *n.*
person making over property
as security.

Mor'tify, *v.t.* to humiliate,
embarrass, restrain by self-

denial. **Mortifica′tion,** *n.* shame, chagrin.

Mor′tify, *v.i.* to be affected by gangrene. **Mortifica′tion,** *n.*

Mort′uary, *n.* building where dead bodies are retained until identified or claimed.

Mosa′ic, *n.* decorative design made with variegated pieces of stone fitted together. *a.*

Mos′lem, Mus′lim, *n.* Mohammedan. *a.*

Mosque, *n.* Moslem place of worship.

Mote, *n.* tiny particle.

Moth′er, *n.* female parent, head of convent. *a.* native, inborn. *v.t.* to care for as a mother. **Motherhood,** *n.* state of being a mother. **Motherly,** *a.* kindly. **Mother-in-law,** *n.* mother of one's spouse. **Mother tongue,** *n.* one's native tongue.

Mo′tif, *n.* main idea or theme.

Mo′tion, n. the act of moving, movement, a gesture, a formal proposal, legal application. *v.t & i.* to gesture, indicate by manual sign. **Mo′tionless,** *a.* unmoving. **Mo′tive,** *a.* causing motion.

Mo′tivate, *v.t.* to provide reason for, to induce, give impulse for. **Motiva′tion,** *n.* **Mo′tive,** *n.* essential reason for any action.

Mot′ley, *a.* composed of varying colours, variegated. *n.* a multicoloured dress etc.

Mo′tor, *n.* engine with power of propelling or energizing, a **Motor-car.** *a.* pertaining to motors. *v.i.* to travel by motor-car. **Mo′torist,** *n.* person who drives motor-car.

Mot′tle, *v.t.* to mark with spots or blotches, esp. as **Mottled,** *a.*

Mott′o, *n.* concise phrase or single word expressing essential principle esp. as inscribed on heraldic emblem.

Mould (Moled), *n.* rich soil composed of compost or decayed matter.

Mould, *n.* fungoid growth caused by dampness. **Mould′y,** *a.* rotten. **Mould′er,** *v.i.* to crumble, decay.

Mould, *n.* pattern matrix, form. *v.t.* to shape, cast.

Moult, *v.t. & i.* to shed or change feathers or hair.

Mound (Mownd), *n.* small hill, heap of material.

Mount, *v.t. & i.* to get up on, esp. horse, to climb, to establish for use, to increase, rise steeply. *n.* a horse, a mountain.

Mount′ain, *n.* a tall natural elevation. **Mountaineer′,** *n.* climber of mountains. **Mount′ainous,** *a.* full of mountains, very high and steep.

Moun′tebank, *n.* charlatan, jester, ludicrous person.

Mourn (Morn), *v.t. & i.* to grieve over, sorrow for. **Mourn′er,** *n.* person who laments death of another. **Mourn′ing,** *n.* grief, black clothes worn at funeral or during period of mourning.

Moustache′ (Mus-tahsh), *n.* hair allowed to grow on man's upper lip.

Mouth, *n.* (Mowth) opening in animal head for eating or uttering sounds, the cavity containing tongue and teeth, any opening, the estuary of a river, entrance to harbour etc. *v.t. & i.* to eat, to grimace, to speak in distorted fa on.

Move (Moov), *v.t. & i.* to change position, to go on, to shake, provoke, affect, to act. *n.* a movement. **Mov'able,** *a.* **Move'-ment,** *n.* the act of changing place, a stirring, mechanism, division of mus. composition. **Mov'ing,** *a.* affecting, stirring the feelings.

Mow (mo), *v.t.* to cut grass, cut down. *n.* a gathering of hay, place for storing this.

Muck, *n.* filth.

Mu'cus, *n.* viscous secretion in mucous membrane. **Mu'cous,** *a.* pertaining to this. **Mucous membrane,** *n.* moist lining of various passages of body.

Mud, *n.* soft wet soil.

Mud'dle, *n.* a confused state, bewilderment. *v.t.* & *i.*

Muf'fle, *v.t.* to deaden sound by covering up source of noise, to wrap up closely. **Muf'fler,** *n.* scarf.

Muf'ti, *n.* civilian clothes worn by servicemen off duty.

Muf'ti, *n.* Muslim priest of high rank.

Mug, *n.* drinking vessel.

Mug, *n. sl.* stupid person.

Mugg'y, *a.* damp and close.

Mulatt'o, *n.* offspring of white and black parents.

Mulch, *n.* composted garden material to enrich soil round plants. *v.t.* to spread with this.

Mulct, *v.t.* to punish by fining. *n.* a fine.

Mule, *n.* hybrid of horse and donkey, *coll.* a stubborn person. **Mu'leteer,** *n.* mule driver. **Mu'lish,** *a.* sullenly obstinate.

Mull, *v.t.* to warm wine or ale and flavour with sugar and spice.

Mull, *v.i. coll.* to ponder over.

Mull'ion, *n.* upright bar dividing panes in window

Mul'ti- *pref.* meaning many, e.g. **Multitude,** *n.* a great number. **Multitu'dinous,** *a.* in great numbers. **Mul'tiplex,** *a.* manifold. **Multifar'ious,** *a.* in great variety.

Mul'tiple, *n.* quantity or number containing another an exact number of times. *a.* repeated many times, possessing many parts. **Mul'tiply,** *v.t.* & *i.* to increase, to determine product of repeating a number a certain number of times. **Multiplica'-tion,** *n.* process of multiplying, increase. **Multiplic'ity,** *n.* a great many, many variations

Mum, *a.* silent.

Mum'ble, *v.t.* & *i.* to mutter, talk indistinctly.

Mumm'er, *n.* actor in dumb-show. **Mumm'ery,** *n.* dumb-show, nonsense.

Mumm'y, *n.* dead human body embalmed in special manner. **Mumm'ify,** *v.t.* to preserve corpse esp. as done in Ancient Egyp. times.

Mumps, *n. pl.* as *n.* contagious disease characterized by painful swellings.

Munch (Munsh), *v.t.* & *i.* to chew steadily and crisply.

Mun'dane, *a.* worldly, ordinary.

Municipal'ity, *n.* city or town with right of self-government in local affairs. **Munic'ipal,** *a.* pertaining to this.

Munif'icence, *n.* splendid generosity. **Munif'icent,** *a.*

Mu'niment, *n.* esp. in *pl.* legal documents as evidence of right or title.

Muni'tions, *n. pl.* ammunition, general mil. offensive stores.

Mu'ral, *a.* pertaining to a wall.

n. a wall-painting, esp. as
mural painting.

Mur'der, *n.* the criminal and
intentional killing of another
human being. *v.t.* to kill
deliberately. **Mur'derer,** *n.*

Murk, *n.* gloomy darkness.

Mur'mur, *n.* subdued speech or
sound. *v.t. & i.* to speak softly,
make a low continuous sound.
Murmur'ous, *a.*

Murr'ain, *n. arch.* term for
foot-and-mouth disease. *interj.*
a malediction.

Mus'cle (Mussel), *n.* fibrous
tissue in body which produces
and controls movement of
limbs etc. **Mus'cular,** *a.* physically strong.

Muse, *v.i.* to meditate, ponder.

Muse (Muze), *n.* poetic inspiration, one of the nine goddesses
of the arts.

Mush'room, *n.* an edible fungus.

Mu'sic (-zik), *n.* the art of
combining sounds harmoni-
ously and melodiously, the laws
limiting and controlling this,
any mus. composition. **Mu'-
sical,** *a.* pertaining to music,
adept at mus. **Music'ian,** *n.*
skilled performer at music.

Musk, *n.* scent based on secretion in gland of male musk-
deer.

Musk'et, *n. arch.* smooth-bore
gun used by infantry. **Musk'-
eteer',** *n.* **Musk'etry,** *n.* small
arms, their use and practice.

Muslim, Moslem, *n.* Mohammedan. *a.*

Mus'lin, *n.* fine soft material of
cotton. *a.*

Muss'el, *n.* bivalve shellfish.

Mus'sulman, *n.* a Mohammedan.

Must, *aux. v.* to be obliged to,
be certain to.

Must, *n.* **Musth,** *n.* uncontrollable bout of frenzy experienced
by male elephants.

Must, *n.* new wine, esp. before
fermentation.

Must, *n.* mould. **Must'y,** *a.*
mouldy, decaying.

Mus'tang, *n.* semi-wild Amer.
horse.

Must'ard, *n.* condiment made
from powdered seeds of m.-
plant.

Must'er, *n.* an assembly of
troops, a collection. *v.t. & i.*
to assemble on parade.

Mu'table, *a.* changeable. **Muta'-
tion,** *n.* alteration, deviation in
characteristics of species.

Mute, *a.* silent, dumb. *n.* a dumb
person, a paid mourner.

Mu'tilate, *v.t.* to maim, disfigure, damage. **Mutila'tion,** *n.*

Mu'tiny, *n.* rebellion by troops
or seamen. *v.i.* **Mu'tinous,** *a.*
insubordinate. **Mutineer',** *n.*

Mutt'er, *v.t.* to speak indistinctly, mumble, *n.*

Mutt'on, *n.* flesh of sheep.

Mu'tual, *a.* reciprocal, inter-
changed.

Muz'zle, *n.* snout of animal,
device to prevent dog biting,
mouth of firearm. *v.t.* to stifle
utterance, put muzzle on to
prevent biting.

Mycol'ogy, *n.* science and study
of fungi. **Myco'sis,** *n.* disease
caused by certain fungi.

Myo'pia, *n.* chronic short sight.
Myo'pic, *a.* short-sighted.

Myr'iad (Mir-), *n.* a huge
number. *a.* innumerable.

Myr'midon (Mur-midd-), *n.*
ruffianly follower.

Mys'tery (Miss-), *n.* something
inexplicable or secret, mediaeval rel. play. **Myste'rious,** *a.*

puzzling, of hidden mean-
ing, wrapt in or full of
mystery.
Mys'tic, *a.* containing a hidden
or supernatural meaning. *n.*
person seeking direct spiritual
contact with God. **Myst'ical**, *a.*
Myst'icism, *n.* belief that communication with deity can
come about through profound
meditation.

Myst'ify, *v.t.* to bewilder, puzzle,
dupe. **Mystifica'tion**, *n.*
Myth (Mith), *n.* legend often
embodying primitive beliefs of
a people about their origins,
fables of folk-heroes. **Mythol'-
ogy**, *n.* collection of myths, the
study of these. **Mythol'ogist**, *n.*
person who studies these.
Myth'ical, *a.* not factual,
legendary.

N

Nab, *v.t.* to seize suddenly.
Na'bob, *n. arch.* governor of
Indian province during Mogul
empire, wealthy and powerful
person.
Na'dir, *n.* lowest point, time of
lowest fortune.
Nag, *n.* a worn-out horse.
Nag, *v.t. & i.* to pester, torment
insistently.
Nai'ad (Ny-), *n.* water-nymph.
Nail, *n.* horny covering at tip
of finger or toe, tapering piece
of metal for fastening woodwork etc. *v.t.* to fasten with
a nail.
Naive' (Ny-eev), *a.* excessively
simple, unaffected. **Naiv'ety**, *n.*
Na'ked, *a.* nude, uncovered.
Name, *n.* word by which person
or object is known, reputation,
fame. *v.t.* to give a name to, to
refer to by name, mention.
Name'ly, *adv.* that is to say, to
state more specifically. **Name'-
sake**, *n.* person bearing same
name as another.
Nap, *n.* a short light sleep, doze.
v i.

Nap, *n.* pile on surface of mater-
ial, soft short surface.
Nap, *n.* a card game.
Nape, *n.* the back of the neck.
Na'pery, *n.* table linen.
Naph'tha, *n.* inflammable liquid
obtained from petroleum, coal,
etc.
Nap'kin, *n.* a serviette, a small
towel.
Narcot'ic, *n.* drug inducing sleep
or deadening pain. **Narco'sis**, *n.*
effect of such a drug.
Nark, *n. sl.* police informer.
Narrate', *v.t.* relate, recount.
Narra'tion, *n.* the act of
recounting. **Narr'ative**, *n.* story.
a. **Narra'tor**, *n.* person who
tells a story or recounts an
event.
Narr'ow (-o), *a.* of little breadth
or width, unimaginative, restricted .*n.* esp. *n. pl.* narrow
passage in waterway. *v.i.* to
become narrow or narrower.
Na'sal, (-zal) *a.* pertaining to
the nose.
Na'scent, *a.* just beginning,
undeveloped.

Nas'ty, *a.* disgusting, unpleasant.

Na'tal, *a.* pertaining to birth.

Nata'tion, *n.* swimming.

Na'tion, *n.* a people organized as a state and having common interests and characteristics. Nat'ional (Nash-on-), *a.* pertaining to a nation. National'ity, *n.* national identity, qualification to be citizen of particular country. Nat'ionalism, *n.* extreme and narrow-minded patriotism. Nat'ionalist, *n.* person who believes in this. Nat'ionalize, *v.t.* to put basic industries under control of the state. Nationaliza'tion, *n.* the act of doing this.

Na'tive, *n.* person born in certain country or region. *a.* born in or belonging to such.

Nativ'ity, *n.* birth, esp. as the N., the birth of Christ.

Natt'y, *a.* dapper, smart.

Na'ture, *n.* the physical world in its entirety, all the phenomena existing in it, the essential character of anything, kind or quality. Nat'ural, *a.* pertaining to nature, of anything happening normally, unaffected, innate, inborn. Natural history, *n.* the study of natural phenomena. Nat'uralist, *n.* student of nature.

Nat'uralize, *v.t.* to accept a foreigner as citizen of country, to introduce and cultivate some foreign phenomenon. Naturaliza'tion, *n.* the act of doing this.

Naught (Nawt), *n.* nothing, symbol representing this.

Naught'y (Nawt-), *a.* mischievous, ill-behaved.

Nau'sea (Naw-zi-a), *n.* sickness, loathing. Nau'seate, *v.t.* to sicken, disgust. Nau'seous, *a.* causing sickness or disgust.

Naut'ical, *a.* maritime, pertaining to ships and sailors.

Nave, *n.* main body of church lengthways from inner door to chancel.

Na'vel, *n.* small depression on surface of belly left by cutting of umbilical cord.

Naviga'tion, *n.* the skill and science of finding way across unmarked land or sea by means of nautical astronomy. Nav'igator, *n.* person skilled in navigation, formerly workman employed on construction of canals, now navvy. Nav'igable, *a.* of river etc. able to be penetrated by ship. Nav'igate, *v.t. & i.* to steer by compass bearing, to sail.

Na'vy, *n.* a nation's warships and seamen. Na'val, *a.*

Neap, esp. as neap tide, *n.* tide coinciding with first and third quarters of moon when high-water level is at lowest.

Near, *a., adv. & prep.* close, not far away, direct, almost, closely related, mean, of the left-hand side. *v.t. & i.* to come close to. Near-sighted, *a.* short-sighted. Near'ly, *adv.* almost, all but.

Neat, *n. pl. arch.* cattle. Neatherd, *n.*

Neat, *a.* tidy, smart, skilful. *sl.* undiluted.

Neb'ulous, *a.* vague, indistinct. Neb'ula, *n.* group of stars so distant as to be seen only hazily. Neb'ular, *a.*

Necess'ity, (Ness-), *n.* something urgently needed or required, an essential want, factor obliging one to behave in certain

way. **Nec'essary,** *a.* essential,
indispensable. **Necess'itate,** *v.t.*
to make unavoidable or obligatory.

Neck, *n.* part of body linking
head with shoulders, narrow
strip of land, tube-shaped top
of bottle etc.

Nec'romancer, *n.* magician.
Nec'romancy, *n.* the pretended
art of communicating with the
dead.

Necroph'agous, *a.* carrion-eating.

Necrop'olis, *n.* a cemetery.

Nec'tar, *n.* sweet fluid found in
plants and used by bees as
basis of honey, *myth.* the drink
of the gods.

Née (Nay), *a.* born, esp. used to
indicate married woman's
maiden name.

Need, *n.* a necessity, lack, indigence. *v.t.* to require, want.
Need'ful, *a.* necessary. **Need'-
less,** *a.* **Need'y,** *a.* poverty-
stricken.

Need'le, *n.* sharp thin implement
used for sewing and knitting,
anything resembling this.

Nefar'ious, *a.* extremely wicked.

Nega'tion, *n.* a denial, a contradiction. **Neg'ative,** *a.* expressing this, opposite of positive.
n. a refusal, denial, minus
quantity, photographic plate
with image. *v.t.* to contradict,
disprove, counteract.

Neglect', *n.* lack of attention,
carelessness. *v.t.* to disregard,
fail to pay proper attention to,
abandon. **Neglect'ful,** *a.* **Neg'-
ligence,** *n.* heedlessness, lack of
proper care. **Neg'ligent,** *a,*
careless, inattentive. **Neg'-
ligible,** *a.* unimportant.

Nego'tiate, *v.t. & i.* to arrange
by discussion, to bargain with,

get over. **Nego'tiable,** *a.* convertible into cash. **Negotia'-
tion,** *n.* **Negotia'tor,** *n.*

Ne'gro, *n.* person belonging to
or originating from one of
dark-skinned peoples of Africa.
Ne'groid, *a.* pertaining to this.

Neigh (Nay), *n.* the cry of a
horse. *v.i.*

Neigh'bour, *n.* person living
close to one, any fellow human.
Neigh'bourhood, *n.* locality,
vicinity. **Neigh'bouring,** *a.*
adjoining. **Neigh'bourly,** *a.*
friendly, helpful.

Nei'ther (Ny-), *pron., a., conj.*
not one nor the other, nor, nor
yet.

Nem'esis, *n.* retribution.

Ne'o-, *pref.* meaning new or
recent, e.g. **Neolithic,** *a.* of
later Stone Age, **Neophyte,** *n.*
a novice, **Neoteric,** *a.* modern.

Ne'on, *n.* gaseous element in
Earth's atmosphere.

Neph'ew, *n.* son of one's brother
or sister.

Nerve, (Nurv) *n.* fibre transmitting impulses between brain and
body, vital sinew, boldness.
Nerve'less, *a.* lifeless, supine.
Ner'vous, *a.* timid, easily
frightened.

Nest, *n.* structure made by bird
for laying eggs in, any snug
place. *v.t.* to make a nest.
Nest'ling, *n.* young bird just
out of egg.

Nes'tle (Nessel), *v.t. & i.* to
snuggle down, rest cosily and
safely, cuddle.

Net, *n.* fabric constructed of
lengths of cord etc. knotted
together at right angles to form
interstices, any such openwork.
v.t. & i. to catch in a net, to
protect or cover with a net.

Net, *a.* left after deduction of expenses or allowance for waste.

Neth'er, *a.* situated beneath, lower.

Neu'ral (Nu-), *a.* pertaining to the nerves. **Neurasthe'nia,** *n.* debility of the nerves. **Neural'gia,** *n.* sharp nervous pain. **Neu'ritis,** *n.* inflammation of the nerves. **Neurol'ogy,** *n.* science and treatment of nerves. **Neurol'ogist,** *n.* **Neuro'sis,** *n.* nervous disorder. **Neurot'ic,** *a.* highly strung. *n.* person morbidly sensitive or nervously deranged.

Neu'ter, *a.* without sex, *gram.* neither masc. nor fem. *n.* sexless organism.

Neu'tral, *a.* impartial, indifferent. *n.* person or country not taking sides in war or dispute between others. **Neutral'ity,** *n.* the state of being neutral or indifferent. **Neu'tralize,** *v.t.* to make inactive, counteract. **Neutraliza'tion,** *n.*

Nev'er, *adv.* not at any time, not at all. **Nevermore,** *adv.* never again. **Nevertheless,** *adv.* & *conj.* inspite of, however.

New, *a.* fresh, just made or developed, modern. **News,** *n. pl.* as *sing.* fresh information of current events, tidings.

New'el, *n.* post supporting banister at top or bottom.

Nib, *n.* sharp point, end of pen.

Nibb'le, *v.t. & i.* to take a small bite, to eat steadily and delicately, *n.*

Nice, *a.* pleasant, exact, well-behaved, amiable. **Ni'cety,** *n.* accuracy, precision, a subtle detail.

Niche (Nich), *n.* small recess, ledge.

Nick, *n.* a small incision, notch, the precise or critical moment. *v.t.* to make small incision in.

Nick'el, *n.* silvery white metal.

Nick'name, *n.* affectionate or derisive term added to person's real name. *v.t.*

Nic'otine, *n.* poisonous substance in tobacco.

Niece (neess), *n.* daughter of one's brother or sister.

Nigg'ardly, *a.* mean, stingy. **Nigg'ard,** *n.* miser. **Nigg'ling,** *a.* fussy, finicky. **Nigg'le,** *v.i.*

Nigh (Ny), *a., adv. prep.* close in time or place, almost, close to.

Night, *n.* end of day, darkness, period from sunset to sunrise.

Nightmare', *n.* horrifying dream, any horrifying experience.

Ni'hilism, *n.* polit. doctrine akin to anarchism. **Ni'hilist,** *n.*

Nil, *n.* nothing, nought.

Nim'ble, *a.* agile.

Nim'bus, *n.* halo, bright cloud, rain-cloud.

Nim'rod, *n.* great hunter.

Nin'compoop, *n.* idiot.

Ninn'y, *n.* dunce.

Nip, *v.t.* to clip, pinch, cut off closely. *n.* a pinch, a tot of alcohol. **Nipp'y,** *a.* quick, cold.

Nipp'le, *n.* part of breast through which milk is drawn.

Nit, *n.* egg or young of parasitic insect.

Ni'tre, *n.* potassium nitrate.

Ni'trogen, *n.* gas from which four-fifths of volume of air is composed. **Nitrog'enous (-oj-),** *a.* containing nitrogen.

No, *n. adv. & a.* a negative, a denial, not, not at all.

Noth'ing (Nuth-), *n.* not anything.

No'body, *n*. not anybody, person of no account.

No'ble, *a*. of high principle, eminent, aristocratic, of fine character. *n*. member of the nobility. No'bleman, *n*. high titled person. Nobil'ity, *n*. noble rank or character, the class of nobles.

Noctur'nal, *a*. pertaining to the night, emerging at night.

Noc'turne, *n*. pleasantly languorous mus.

Nod, *v.t. & i*. to incline the head slightly in acknowledgement or recognition, to let head bend forward sleepily. *n*.

Node, *n*. swelling, knot. Nod'ule, *n*. small knot or tumour.

Nogg'in, *n*. a small mug or liquid measure.

Noise, *n*. unpleasant sound, clamour. *v.t*. to spread rumour.

Noi'some, *a*. offensive to the smell.

No'mad, Nom'ad, *n*. member of wandering tribe herding their animals according to the seasons. Nomad'ic, *a*.

No'menclature, *n*. system of names, catalogue.

Nom'inal, *a*. existing in name only, unsubstantial.

Nom'inate, *v.t*. to name or propose person as candidate. Nomina'tion, *n*. Nom'inator, *n*. person who proposes another as candidate. Nominee', *n*. person proposed.

Non-, *pref*. implying neg. and making sense of compound clear when meaning of main word is known.

Non'age, *n*. condition of being under legal majority.

Nonagenar'ian, *n*. person ninety years old or in his nineties.

Non'chalance, *n*. jauntiness, unconcern. Non'chalant, *a*.

Non'descript, *a*. undistinguished, ordinary.

Nook, *n*. a niche, a sheltered place.

Noon, *n*. midday. Noonday, Noontide, *nn*.

Noose (Nooss), *n*. a loop as in a lasso. *v.t*. to catch in this.

Nor'mal, *a*. regular, according to standard or convention, average. Normal'ity, *a*. Norm, *n*. pattern, standard.

North, *n*. point opposite sun at noon in northern hemisphere, point to left of person facing sunrise, region situated further north than another, one of four points of compass. Nor'therly, *a*. Nor'thern, *a*. Nor'therner, *n*. person living in a northern region. Nor'dic, *a*. pertaining to people of Scandinavian or northern ethnog. type. Norse'-man, *n*. *hist*. a Northman, a Scandinavian Viking.

Nose, *n*. part of head containing nostril, organ of smell, inlet and outlet for breath, any forward projection. *v.t. & i*. to touch with nose, smell. Nos'-tril, *n*. one of two openings in nose.

Nostal'gia, *n*. a yearning for time or place out of reach. Nostal'-gic, *a*.

Nos'trum, *n*. fraudulent remedy.

No'table, *a*. remarkable, worthy of attention. Notabil'-ity, *n*. a well-known person. Note'worthy, *a*. unusual, worth remembering.

No'tary, *n*. lawyer specializing in deeds and contracts etc.

Note, *n*. a brief letter, a mus. symbol, reputation, notice, attention. *v.t.* to make a note of, record. **Nota'tion,** *n.* system of signs or symbols, act of noting. **No'ted,** *n.* taken note of, famous.

No'tice, (-tiss) *n.* warning, attention, official proclamation or announcement, poster giving details. *v.t.* to perceive, mention. **No'ticeable,** *a.* prominent, remarkable. **No'tify,** *v.t.* to inform, make known. **Notifi'able,** *a.* of something that must be notified to authorities. **Notifica'tion,** *n.*

No'tion, *n.* an idea, an inclination, a whim.

Notori'ety, *n.* condition of being known in derogatory way. **Notor'ious,** *a.* ill-famed.

Notwithstand'ing, *prep. & adv.* in spite of, nevertheless, all the same.

Nought (Nawt), *n.* nothing, zero, symbol representing nothing.

Noun (Nown), *n. gram.* substantive, word indicating person, object, idea.

Nour'ish (Nurrish), *v.t.* to feed, foster. **Nour'ishment,** *n.* sustenance.

Nov'el, *n.* a work of fiction, romance. *a.* new, unusual. **Nov'elist,** *n.* writer of novels. **Nov'elty,** *n.* new gadget, innovation.

Novem'ber, *n.* the eleventh month of the year.

Nov'ice, *n.* beginner, neophyte, applicant to join rel. order. **Novit'iate,** *n.* probation, trial period.

Now, *adv. & conj.* at the present time, as, because.

Nox'ious, *a.* deadly, injurious.

Noz'zle, *n.* spout of hose, mouthpiece.

Nu'ance, *n.* subtle difference in meaning.

Nu'bile, *a.* marriageable, esp. of girl.

Nu'cleus, *a.* central part of atom, head of comet. **Nu'clear,** *a.* pertaining to this.

Nude, *a.* naked, unclothed. **Nu'dity,** *n.* **Nu'dist,** *n.* person who believes in living naked.

Nudge, *v.t.* to jog, push lightly in order to draw attention. *n.*

Nu'gatory, *a.* negligible, worthless.

Nugg'et, *n.* lump of mineral, esp. gold.

Nui'sance (New-), *n.* offensive or annoying behaviour, anything disagreeable.

Null'ify, *v.t.* to render inoperative, make ineffective. **Nullifica'tion,** *n.* **Null,** *a.* void, ineffective.

Numb (Num), *v.t.* to deprive of feeling. *a.* **Numb'skull,** *n.* dolt.

Num'ber, *n.* a total of things or persons, a figure representing a number or total, part of a regular series, a song, *gram.* word-form denoting *sing.* or *pl. v.t.* to count, give numbers to. **Numberless,** *a.* too many to count.

Nu'meral, *n.* a symbol expressing a number. **Numer'ical,** *a.* pertaining to numbers. **Nu'merate,** *v.t.* to count or number. **Numera'tion,** *n.* **Nu'merator,** *n.* upper number in fraction indicating how much of whole. **Nu'merous,** *a.* many.

Numismat'ics, *n. pl.* science or study of coins and medals. **Numis'matist,** *n.*

Nun, *n.* woman living in convent and accepting rel. vows of self-denial. **Nunn'ery,** *n.* convent.

Nup'tial, *a.* pertaining to marriage. *n. pl.* wedding ceremony.

Nurse, *n.* person skilled in tending the sick or children. *v.t. & i.* to tend, care for, cultivate. **Nurs'ery,** *n.* children's room.

Nurs'ery, *n.* greenhouse or garden for cultivating plants. **Nurseryman,** *n.* skilled horticulturalist.

Nur'ture, *n.* sustenance, encouragement of development. *v.t.* to rear, feed.

Nut, *n.* fruit of certain trees encased in hard shell.

Nu'triment, *n.* food, nourishment. **Nu'trient,** *a.* sustaining, encouraging growth, *n.* food. **Nutri'tion,** *n.* food, the process of assimilating food. **Nutrit'ious,** *a.* nourishing. **Nu'tritive,** *a.* serving as food.

Nuz'zle (Nuzzel), *v.i.* to push nose against affectionately.

Ny'lon, *n.* synthetic substance, also as substitute for silk.

Nymph, *n.* legendary minor woodland goddess.

Nym'phomania (Nim-), *n.* overdeveloped sexual desire in women.

O

Oaf, *n. arch.* a changeling left by fairies, us. an idiot.

Oa'kum (Okum), *n.* fibre obtained from frayed rope and used for caulking.

Oar(ore),*n.*long pole with flat blade for propelling rowing boat.

Oa'sis (O-a-), *n.* fertile place in desert. *pl.* **Oases.**

Oath, *n.* a solemn promise to speak truth or keep faith, an imprecation, profanity.

Ob'duracy, *n.* stubbornness, unyieldingness. *a.*

Obe'dience, *n.* compliance, submission to another's control or order. **Obe'dient,** *a.*

Obei'sance (-bay-), *n.* gesture of respect or submission.

Ob'elisk, *n.* tapering four-sided stone shaft with pointed top, in printing a mark of reference.

Obes'ity, *n.* corpulence. **Obese',** *a.*

Obey' (-bay), *v.t. & i.* to do as ordered, to submit to authority.

Obit'uary, *n.* short biographical note about person at time of death.

Object', *v.t. & i.* to oppose, express disagreement with, protest, put forward as reason against. **Objec'tion,** *n.* **Objec'tionable,** *a.* unpleasant, open to objection. **Objec'tor,** *n.*

Ob'ject, *n.* anything tangible, a person, thing, a purpose, *gram.* word or clause governed by verb.

Ob'jurgate, *v.t.* to chide. **Objurga'tion,** *n.*

Oblate', *a.* of spheroid, flattened at poles.

Obla′tion, *n.* a sacrifice or offering.

Oblige′, *v.t.* to compel, constrain, to do a favour. **Obliga′tion,** *n.* a promise, a compulsion to act or reciprocate, debt of gratitude. **Oblig′atory,** *a.* compulsory, binding. **Obli′ging,** *a.* helpful.

Oblique′ (-bleek), *a.* slanting, allusive. **Obliq′uity,** *n.* deviation from vert. or horiz., crookedness of thought.

Oblit′erate, *v.t.* to wipe out, destroy. **Oblitera′tion,** *n.*

Obliv′ion, *n.* state of forgetfulness, or being forgotten. **Obliv′ious,** *a.* disregarding, unaware.

Ob′long, *n.* rectangle with two opposite sides longer than other two. *a.*

Ob′loquy (-kwi), *n.* dishonour, scandal.

Obnox′ious, *a.* objectionable.

O′boe (-bo), *n.* mus. wood-wind instrument.

Obscene′, *a.* offensive to modesty. **Obscen′ity,** *n.* lewdness.

Obscure′, *a.* dim, vague, undistinguished. *v.t.* to hide from view, render difficult to understand. **Obscu′rity,** *n.* **Obscu′rantist,** *n.* person who tries to hinder progress.

Ob′sequies, *n. pl.* funeral ceremony.

Obse′quious, *a.* toadying, cringing.

Observe′, *v.t. & i.* to regard, remark, study, commemorate, comment. **Observ′ant,** *a.* keenly perceptive, watchful. **Observ′ance,** *n.* the act of keeping or commemorating. **Observa′tion,** *n.* a remark, keen attention or watchfulness. **Observ′atory,** *n.*

place with telescope for observing heavenly bodies. **Observ′er,** *n.* one who observes or watches.

Obsess′, *v.t.* to preoccupy one's thoughts excessively. **Obses′sion,** *n.* a fixed idea.

Obsid′ian, *n.* dark-coloured glassy volcanic rock.

Ob′solete, *a.* antiquated, gone out of use. **Obsoles′cent,** *a.* **Obsoles′cence,** *n.*

Ob′stacle, *n.* a hindrance, impediment.

Obstet′ric, *a.* esp. as **Obstetrics,** *n. pl.* science of midwifery. **Obstetri′cian,** *n. med.* expert in this.

Ob′stinate, *a.* self-willed, stubborn. **Ob′stinacy,** *n.*

Obstrep′erous, *a.* unruly, turbulent.

Obstruct′, *v.t.* to impede, get in way of. **Obstruc′tion,** *n.* obstacle. **Obstruc′tive,** *a.* tending to impede or hinder.

Obtain′, *v.t. & i.* to gain possession of, to be valid. **Obtain′able,** *a.*

Obtrude′, *v.t. & i.* to intrude, enter uninvited, thrust oneself or one's opinions forward. **Obtru′sion,** *n.* **Obtru′sive,** *a.*

Obtuse′, *a.* blunt, stupid, *geom.* greater than a right angle.

Ob′verse, *n.* front surface of coin or medal etc.

Ob′viate, *v.t.* to preclude, remove.

Ob′vious, *a.* evident, plain.

Occa′sion, *n.* a particular happening, an occurrence, an opportunity, need. *v.t.* to give rise to, cause. **Occa′sional,** *a.* occurring irregularly.

Oc′cident (oksi-), *n.* the western part of the world. **Occident′al,** *a.*

Oc'ciput, *n.* back of the head.

Occult', *a.* secret, supernatural.

Occ'upy, *v.t.* to take possession of, to inhabit, employ, fill, hold. **Occ'upancy,** *n.* act of holding or dwelling in. **Occ'upant,** person who dwells in house or is using room. **Occupa'tion,** *n.* act of occupying, employment.

Occur', *v.i.* to happen, exist, come to mind. **Occurr'ence,** *n.* a happening, an incident.

O'cean (o-shun), *n.* great expanse of sea. the sea in general. **Ocean'ic,** *a.* of the sea, occurring in the sea. **Oceanog'raphy,** *n.* study of the oceans and their phenomena.

Oc'tagon, *n. geom.* figure with eight angles and sides. **Octag'onal,** *a.*

Oc'tave, *n. mus.* interval of eight steps, eighth note in scale.

Octa'vo, *n.* size of page or book resulting from folding paper into eight leaves.

Octo'ber, *n.* the tenth month of year, orig. the eighth.

Octogena'rian, *n.* person aged between eighty and ninety.

Oc'ular, *a.* pertaining to the eyes and eyesight, visual. **Oc'ulist,** *n.* eye specialist.

Odd, *a.* strange, uneven, alone, extra. **Odd'ity,** *n.* queer person or thing. **Odds,** *n. pl.* superiority, adjustment in betting according to quality e.g. of horses.

Ode, *n.* lyric poem of lofty character.

O'dious, *a.* offensive, detestable. **O'dium,** *n.* blame, reproach.

O'dour (-der), *n.* perfume, smell. **Odorif'erous,** *a. iron.* fragrant.

O'dorous, *a.* emitting a scent or smell.

Of (ov), *prep.* from, by, in, related to, belonging to.

Off, *a., adv. & prep.* away, disconnected, distant, away from, on the right-hand side.

Off'al, *n.* refuse from slaughtered animal.

Offend', *v.t. & i.* to annoy, displease, commit sin. **Offence',** *n.* **Offender',** *n.* **Offen'sive,** *a.* objectionable, aggressive. *n.* aggressive attitude or position.

Off'er, *v.t. & i.* to put forward for acceptance or refusal, to propose, attempt, arise. *n.* a price bid or proposed. **Off'ering,** *n.* a thing put forward as a gift.

Off'ertory, *n.* church collection, mus. played while this is made.

Off'ice, *n.* a bureau, a place for doing clerical work, an administrative room, an administrative position, a function. *n. pl.* lavatories etc. attached to house.

Off'icer, *n.* person commissioned to take command in various ranks of armed forces, person elected or appointed to do public work or duties.

Offi'cial *a.* authoritative. *n.* an appointed person in charge of some office or function. **Offi'ciate,** *v.i.* to take part in the performance of official duties. **Offi'cious,** *a.* pompous, unduly interfering.

Of'ten, *adv.* frequently. **Oft,** *adv. poet.*

O'gle, *v.t. & i.* to flirt with the eyes.

O'gre, *n.* hideous giant.

Ohm (ome), *n.* unit of the resistance of an elec. current.

Oil, *n.* light inflammable greasy or fatty substance derived from minerals and also plants and animals. *v.t.* to lubricate or treat with oil.

Oint'ment, *n.* unguent for medical or beauty treatment of skin.

Old (ole-), *a.* having lived for a long time, ancient, out of date.

Oleag'inous (oli-aj-), *a.* containing properties of or producing oil.

Olfac'tory, *a.* pertaining to smell.

Ol'igarchy (-garki-), *n.* government of state by small group, such a group. **Ol'igarch,** *n.* a member of this.

Om'elette, *n.* eggs beaten up, formed into long flat folded shape with herbs or other ingredients and fried lightly.

Omen, *n.* an augury.

Om'inous, *a.* threatening, foreshadowing disaster.

Omis'sion, *n.* a thing left out, an action not carried out. **Omit',** *v.t.* to leave out, fail to insert.

Om'nibus, *n.* large motor-vehicle for public transport. *a.* all-inclusive.

Omnip'otence, *n.* absolute power. **Omnip'otent,** *a.*

Omnipres'ence, *n.* the state or power of being everywhere at same time. **Omnipres'ent,** *a.*

Omnis'cience, *a.* absolute knowledge. **Omnis'cient,** *a.*

Omniv'orous, *a.* feeding upon everything.

On, *prep. & adv.* upon, along or by, in condition of, in direction of, at time of, forward, longer, in progress etc.

Once (wunss), *adv.* at one time, one time only, ever.

One (wun), *n., pron. & a.* the first number in counting, a single thing or person, the same.

On'erous, *a.* arduous, difficult. **O'nus,** *n.* burden.

On'looker, *n.* casual spectator.

On'ly (o-), *a. & adv. & conj.* single, sole, merely, no more than, but.

Onomatopoe'ic (pe-ic), *a.* of word whose sound suggests its sense.

On'set, *n.* the early stages, an attack.

On'slaught, *n.* a furious assault.

On'ward, *a. & adv.* advancing, forward.

On'yx (-iks), *n.* kind of quartz.

Ooze, *n.* slimy mud, thick liquid. *v.i.* to flow sluggishly.

O'pal, *n.* quartz-like stone with constantly changing colours. **Opales'cent,** *a.*

Opaque, *a.* not transparent, dull of surface. **Opac'ity,** *n.*

O'pen, *a.* not shut, free of access, frank, blatant, uncovered, vacant, unconcealed. *v.t. & i.* to unblock, unclose, start, unfold. Various compounds with open, e.g. **Open-hearted,** *a.* generous, **Open-minded,** *a.* impartial, etc.

Op'era, *n.* drama set to mus. **Operat'ic,** *a.*

Opera'tion, *n.* action, manner in which something works, mil. manoeuvre or action, surgical treatment. **Op'erate,** *v.t. & i.* to work, act, perform an operation, manage. **Op'erative,** *a.* in effect, working. **Op'erator,** *n.* person who tends machine, performs work of mechanical kind.

Ophthal'mia, *n.* inflammation of eye and its membranes. **Ophthal'mic,** *a.* pertaining to the eyes.

O'piate, *n.* tranquillizing drug. *a.* soothing.

Opin'ion, *n.* belief, estimation. **Opine',** *v.t. & i.* to give an opinion, suppose. **Opin'-ionated,** *a.* conceited or obstinate in one's opinions.

O'pium, *n.* narcotic obtained from certain kinds of poppy.

Opportu'nity, *n.* convenient or favourable time or occasion. **Opp'ortunist,** *n.* person who seizes opportunity selfishly without regard to others. **Opp'-ortunism,** *n.* **Opp'ortune,** *a.* suitable, convenient.

Oppose', *v.t.* to resist, withstand, object. **Oppo'nent,** *n.* one who opposes, foe. **Oppo'-ser,** *n.* one who opposes a proposal. **Opposi'tion,** *n.* resistance, polit. party out of power.

Opp'osite (-zit), *a.* completely different, contrary, facing.

Oppress', *v.t.* to crush, rule cruelly, tyrannize. **Oppres'sor,** *n.* tyrant. **Oppres'sion,** *n.* heaviness of feeling, tyranny. **Oppress'ive,** *a.* heavy, overpowering.

Oppro'brium, *n.* dishonour. **Oppro'brious,** *a.* disgraceful, reproachful.

Op'tic, *a.* pertaining to the eye and eyesight. *n. pl.* science of light and vision. **Op'tical,** *a.* **Optic'ian,** *n.* person making or selling optical lenses etc.

Op'timism, *n.* tendency to expect the best to happen, belief that good eventually prevails. **Op'timist,** *n.* **Optimist'ic,** *a.* hopeful, cheerful.

Op'tion, *n.* preference, power of choosing. **Op'tional,** *a.* open to choice.

Op'ulence, *n.* great wealth. **Op'ulent,** *a.*

O'pus, *n.* a work, esp. in mus.

Or, *conj.* connecting word between alternatives, otherwise.

Or'acle, *n.* supernatural revelation, infallible advice or adviser. **Orac'ular,** *a.* solemnly prophetic, portentous.

Or'al, *a.* spoken, verbal, pertaining to the mouth.

Orator'io, *n.* sacred dramatic poem set to mus.

Or'atory, *n.* the skill and practice of public speaking. **Ora'-tion,** *n.* a public speech or declamation. **Or'ator,** *n.* eloquent public speaker. **Orator'-ical,** *a.*

Or'atory, *n.* small chapel for private devotions.

Orb, *n.* a sphere, globe.

Or'bit, *n.* path of heavenly body round another, course of action, eye-socket.

Or'chard, *n.* place for growing fruit-trees.

Or'chestra (-kes-), *n.* collection of mus. instrumentalists playing in unison. **Orches'tral,** *a.* **Orchestra'tion,** *n.* the arrangement of mus. for playing by orchestra.

Ordain', *v.t.* to decree, order, to admit novice to priesthood. **Ordina'tion,** *n.*

Or'deal, *n.* a difficult or painful experience or test.

Or'der, *n.* a command, a succession, an established arrangement, proper condition, a rank or degree, a medal or decoration. *v.t.* to command, send for, arrange. **Or'derly**, *a.* properly arranged, well-behaved. *n.* a mil. attendant or messenger. **Or'dinal**, *a. & n.* number or of number indicating position in order or series.

Ord'inance, *n.* a decree, authoritative command.

Ordi'nary, *a.* usual, regular, normal.

Ord'nance, *n.* heavy artillery and equipment for this. **O. survey**, *n.* the official mapping of Great Britain.

Ore, *n.* metal-producing mineral.

Or'gan, *n.* working part of animal body for special purpose, large mus. wind-instrument with series of pipes powered by bellows and played by keyboard, a newspaper or other means of expression. **Organ'ic**, *a.* pertaining to the organs of the body.

Or'ganism, *n.* a living co-ordinated being. **Organ'ic**, *a.* pertaining to a living thing or once-living thing, basic.

Or'ganize, *v.t.* to co-ordinate into working whole, arrange methodically. **Organiza'tion**, *n.* the act of co-ordinating, a co-ordinated working body.

Or'gasm, *n.* frenzied sexual excitement.

Or'gy (-ji), *n.* a drunken revel. **Orgias'tic**, *a.* of the nature of this.

Or'iel, *n.* projecting window supported by stones at rt. angles to wall.

Or'ient, *n.* the Eastern part of the world, the east. *v.t.* to fix bearings in relation to the east.

Orien'tal, *a.* pertaining to the east. **Or'ientate**, *v.t.* to establish in proper relation. **Orienta'tion**, *n.*

Or'ifice (-fis), *n.* a mouth or opening.

Or'igin, *n.* beginning, birth, source. **Or'iginal**, *a.* earliest, first in kind, inventive, novel, uninfluenced by anything else. **Original'ity**, *n.* condition of being new, ability to form one's own thoughts or actions. **Ori'ginate**, *v.t. & i.* to initiate, create, come into being.

Or'ison, *n.* esp. as *n. pl.* prayers.

Or'nament, *n.* an adornment, decoration. *v.t.* to decorate. **Ornament'al**, *a.* **Ornamenta'tion**, *n.* act of adorning, decorations. **Ornate'**, *a.* lavishly decorated.

Ornithol'ogy, *n.* the study of birds. **Ornitholog'ical**, *a.* **Ornitholo'gist**, *n.* person who studies birds.

Or'otund, *a.* verbally pompous.

Or'phan, *n.* child one or both of whose parents is or are dead. *v.t.* **Or'phanage**, *n.* institution for orphans.

Or'thodox, *a.* conventional. **Or'thodoxy**, *n.*

Orthog'raphy, *n.* science of spelling.

Orthopae'dic, *a.* pertaining to the curing of esp. infantile deformities. *n. pl.* as *n.* the science of this.

Os'cillate, *v.i.* to swing backwards and forwards, to vary constantly. **Oscilla'tion**, *n.*

Oss'eous, *a.* bony, of bone. **Ossifica'tion**, *n.* the condition of changing or being changed into bone. **Oss'ify**, *v.t. & i.* to change or be changed into bone.

Osten'sible, *a.* apparent, pretended.

Ostenta'tion, *n.* conceited display. Ostenta'tious.

Osteop'athy, *n.* manipulative med. or surgery. Os'teopath, *n.* med. practitioner of this.

Os'tler (Ossler), *n. arch.* groom employed by inn.

Os'tracize, *v.t.* to banish from society. Os'tracism, *n.* exclusion from social intercourse.

Oth'er (Uth-), *a., n., & pron.* different, not the same, opposite, alternating, someone else. Otherwise, *adv., a. & conj.* in a different way, if not, else.

O'tiose, *a.* lazy, futile.

Oust, *v.t.* to drive or turn out.

Out, *adv. a., prep. & n.* not in, away, not in position, incorrect, not at home, not burning, in the open, revealed.

Out-, *pref.* meaning more, longer, outside, beyond, in excess.

Out'cast, *n.* ostracized person.

Out'crop, *n.* esp. in geol. a layer of rock showing on surface.

Out'law, *n.* banished felon.

Outrage, *n.* vile behaviour *v.t.* to abuse, offend grossly. Outra'geous, *a.* atrocious.

Out'rigger, *n.* sailing boat with horizontal balancing frame.

Out'right, *a. & adv.* straightfoward, all at once.

O'val, *a.* shaped like an egg. *n.*

O'vary, *n.* organ in which egg cells are formed in female.

Ova'tion, *n.* sustained applause.

Ov'en, *n.* enclosed place over or alongside fire for baking.

O'ver, *prep. & adv.* above in position, across, beyond, too much, finished, more than.

O'ver, *n.* in cricket series of six balls bowled from each end of wicket in turn.

O'ver-, *pref.* meaning excessive, across, beyond, further than. Words prefixed with this are self-explanatory when meaning of main word is known.

O'vert, *a.* open, unconcealed.

O'verture, *n.* mus. prelude or introduction.

Overween'ing, *a.* arrogant, conceited.

Overwhelm', *v.t.* to submerge, overpower.

Overwrought', *a.* nervously overstrung.

O'vine, *a.* pertaining to sheep.

Owe (O), *v.t. & i.* to be indebted for, be in debt. Ow'ing (O-ing), *a.* due as debt.

Ow'ing (O-ing), *a.* esp. as owing to, because of.

Own (Oan) *v.t. & i.* to possess, acknowledge. *a.* belonging to, possessed by.

Ox, *n.* castrated bull. *pl.* Oxen.

Oxal'ic, *a.* esp. as O. acid, acid made from wood-sorrel.

Ox'ygen (-i-jen), *n.* gas forming part of atmosphere and necessary for life. Ox'ide, *n.* compound of this and another element. Ox'idize, *v.t. & i.* to combine or be combined with oxygen, to rust through such action.

Oy'ster, *n.* bivalve mollusc prized as food.

O'zone, *n.* condensed form of oxygen, *fig.* invigorating air, esp. at the seaside or in the mountains.

P

Pace, *n.* a regular step, length of this, speed or manner of walking. *v.t. & i.* to measure by pacing, to keep speed for in running or walking.

Pach'yderm (Pak-i-), *n.* thick-skinned quadruped such as elephant.

Pac'ify, *v.t.* to make tranquil, calm. **Pacifica'tion,** *n.* the act of making calm or peaceful. **Pacif'ic** *a.* calm, peaceful. **Pacif'ism,** *n.* belief that international disputes can and should be settled without resort to war. **Pac'ifist,** *n.* believer in this.

Pack, *n.* a bundle or set, a herd of animals, gathering of people, area of drifting ice. *v.t.* to put together compactly, to stow things in suitcase, to press together. **Pack'age,** *n.* a bundle or parcel. **Pack'et,** *n.* a small bundle, ship carrying mails. **Pack'ing,** *n.* protective material round articles packed.

Pact, *n.* an agreement.

Pad, *v.t. & i.* to walk slowly and silently, to protect with layer of material. *n.* a block of writing-paper, an animal's paw. **Padd'ing,** *n.* protective material, in lit. worthless material to fill out space.

Pad'dle, *n.* short, broad-bladed oar for canoeing, board forming part of paddle-wheel. *v.t.* to propel with a paddle, to wade foot-deep in water.

Padd'ock, *n.* small enclosed pasture for horses, race-course enclosure.

Padd'y, *n.* esp. as **p.-field,** *n.* rice-field.

Pad'lock, *n.* detachable lock. *v.t.* to fasten with this.

Pa'dre (Pah-dray), *n.* mil. or naval chaplain.

Pae'an (Pe-), *n.* song of praise.

Pa'gan, *n.* person with primitive rel. beliefs, heathen. *a.* **Pa'ganism,** *n.*

Page, *n.* one face of the leaf of a book etc. **Pag'inate** (Paj-), *v.t.* to number pages of. **Pagina'tion,** *n.*

Page, *n.* boy messenger, *arch.* a knight's or monarch's attendant.

Pag'eant (Paj-ant), *n.* brilliant display, costumed representation of historic events. **Pag'eantry,** *n.*

Pago'da, *n.* sacred ornamented oriental tower.

Pail, *n.* a bucket.

Pain, *n.* physical or mental suffering, formerly penalty or punishment. *v.t.* to cause suffering or distress. **Pain'ful,** *a.* **Pain'less,** *a.* **Pains,** *n. pl.* diligence. **Pains'taking,** *a.* industrious, careful.

Paint, *v.t. & i.* to decorate in colour, to depict in colour.

Paint'er, *n.* house-decorator, artist. **Paint'ing,** *n.* the art or work of painting in colour, a picture in colours.

Paint'er, *n.* rope for mooring boat.

Pair, *n.* a set of two, a couple. *v.t. & i.* to join in pairs.

Pal'ace, *n.* sumptuous building, residence of sovereign or ecclesiast. **Pala'tial,** *a.* magnificent, like a palace.

Pal'adin, *n.* mediaeval knight, esp. one of Charlemagne's followers.

Palanquin' (-kin), *n.* an ornate litter or bed carried on poles held on servants' shoulders.

Pal'atine, *a.* possessing restricted royal privileges.

Pal'ate, *n.* roof of mouth in which sense of taste is situated. **Pal'atable,** *a.* agreeable to the taste, acceptable.

Pala'ver (-ah-), *n.* a wordy discussion. *v.i.*

Pale, *a.* lacking in colour, wan. *v.i.* **Pall'or** (Pal-er), *n.* lack of colour, esp. of face.

Pale, *n.* a stockade, a boundary esp. when surrounded by foe.

Pal'eography, Palaeography, *n.* the scientific study of ancient writings.

Pal'ette, *n.* oval or oblong board with thumbhole used by artist to work colours.

Pal'frey, *n. arch.* a saddle-horse for lady or child.

Palimp'sest, *n.* manuscript overwritten with fresh material.

Palisade', *n.* fortified stockade.

Pall (Pawl), *n.* velvet cloth for covering coffin, any thick covering, cloud of smoke.

Pall, *v.i.* to lose ability to interest.

Pall'iate (Pal-), *v.t.* to mitigate, extenuate. **Pallia'tion,** *n.* **Pall'iative,** *n. & a.* tending to relieve or lessen.

Palm (-ahm), *n.* main inner surface of human hand. *v.t.* to conceal fraudulently in hand. **Palm'istry,** *n.* alleged skill to tell person's fortune through lines on palm. **Palm'ist,** *n.*

Palm, *n.* tropical tree with handsome leaves, hence **Palm'er,** *n. arch.* pilgrim returning from Holy Land with palm branch. **Palm'y,** *a.* flourishing, as of a palm.

Pal'pable, *a.* evident, tangible.

Pal'pitate, *v.i.* to throb rapidly, flutter. **Palpita'tion,** *n.*

Pal'sy (Pawl-), *n.* paralysis. *v.t.*

Pal'ter (Pawl-), *v.t.* to act furtively or deceitfully, haggle. **Pal'try,** *a.* petty, contemptible.

Pam'per, *v.t.* to spoil, coddle.

Pamph'let, *n.* booklet. **Pamphleteer',** *n.* writer of pamphlets, esp. polit.

Pan, *n.* shallow household dish. *v.t.* esp. in gold-mining, to wash out gravel from gold.

Panace'a, *n.* an all-embracing remedy.

Panache' (-ash), *n.* plume on helmet, *fig.* swagger, dash.

Pan'creas (-cre-as), *n.* intestinal organ used in process of digestion.

Pandemo'nium, *n.* uproar, disorder.

Pan'der, *v.t.* to procure, gratify base desires. *n.*

Pane, *n.* piece of glass for window.

Panegyr'ic (Pan-i-jir), *n.* fulsome praise formally delivered.

Pan'el, *n.* section or division of surface such as door, thin boarding mounted on wall, a body of experts.

Pang, *n.* sudden pain or emotion.

Pan'ic, sudden uncontrollable fear or dread. **Panic-stricken,** *a.* excessively frightened.

Pann'ier, *n.* wicker basket carried by pack-animal.

Pan'oply, *n.* complete suit of armour, brilliant array.

Panora'ma (-rah-), *n.* picture providing a view all round. **Panoram'ic,** *a.*

Pant, *v.t. & i.* to gasp, draw breath rapidly, utter breathlessly.

Pan'theism, *n.* doctrine that God and the universe are all one. **Pan'theist,** *n.* believer in this.

Pan'tomime, *n.* dumbshow, comic entertainment.

Pan'try, *n.* storeroom for food.

Pap, *n.* semi-liquid food for babies.

Pa'per, *n.* material processed from rags or wood-pulp and used for printing, writing, packaging etc.

Papy'rus (Pap-i-), *n.* Ancient Egypt. paper made from pith of reed.

Par, *n.* normal value, equality. **Par'ity,** *n.* equality.

Par'able, *n.* story used to illustrate moral.

Parab'ola, *n.* symmetrical curve. **Parabol'ic,** *a.*

Parachute' (-shute), *n.* device to enable person to float down to earth from aeroplane. **Parachut'ist, Paratrooper',** *nn.*

Parade', *n.* formal mil. muster or review, an ostentatious display. *v.t. & i.*

Par'adise (-dice), *n.* place or state of bliss, heaven.

Par'adox, *n.* superficially contradictory but actually true statement or happening. **Paradox'ical,** *a.*

Par'affin, *n.* oil obtained from shale or wood.

Par'agon, *n.* model of virtue.

Par'agraph, *n.* subdivision in page of book or magazine. *v.t.* to divide in paragraphs.

Par'allel, *a. & n.* line equidistant from another throughout its length, something similar to or comparable with another. **Parallel'ogram,** *n.* four-sided plane figure whose opposite sides are parallel.

Paral'ysis, *n.* loss of power to move. **Par'alyze,** *v.t.* **Paralyt'-ic,** *n.* person affected with paralysis. *a.*

Par'amount, *a.* supreme, dominant.

Par'amour, *n.* mistress, illicit lover.

Par'apet, *n.* low wall along edge of roof etc., protective addition to top of trench or fortification.

Parapherna'lia, *n. pl.* various articles of equipment.

Par'aphrase, *n.* a different rendering of the same lit. substance. *v.t.*

Par'asite, *n.* animal or plant living on and at the expense of another. **Parasit'ic,** *a.*

Parasol', *n.* sunshade.

Par'avane, *n.* device towed underwater to cut moorings of submerged mines.

Par'boil, *v.t.* to boil partially.

Par'cel, *n.* package, neat bundle, plot of land for sale. *v.t.* to pack in a parcel, apportion.

Parch, *v.t. & i.* to dry up, become dry.

Parch'ment, *n.* skin of sheep

prepared as writing-material.

Pard'on, *v.t.* to forgive. *n.* **Par'-donable**, *a.* excusable.

Pare, *v.t.* to cut off surface, trim carefully. **Par'ing**, *n.*

Par'ent, *n.* father or mother. **Parent'al**, *a.* **Par'enthood**, *n.* state of being parent.

Par'entage, *n.* ancestry.

Paren'thesis, *n.* word or clause inserted in brackets or otherwise in sentence to which it is not essential. *pl.* **Paren'theses**. **Parenthet'ical**, *a.*

Par'iah, *n.* an outcast.

Par'ish, *n.* ecclesiastical district, small administrative unit us. embracing one village. **Parish'ioner**, *n.* member of this.

Park, *n.* ornamental private or public grounds with trees and lawns.

Park, *v.t.* to place and leave motor-vehicle temporarily.

Par'lance, *n.* manner of speaking.

Par'ley, *v.i.* to discuss, esp. terms with enemy. *n.*

Parl'iament, *n.* supreme democratic legislative assembly. **Parliament'ary**, *a.* **Parliamenta'-rian**, *n.* supporter of system of parliamentary government.

Parl'our, *n.* a sitting-room, reception-room.

Par'lous, *a.* perilous, fraught with difficulty.

Paro'chial (-ki-al), *a.* pertaining to a parish, petty. **Paro'-chialism**, *n.* petty-mindedness.

Par'ody, *n.* satirical imitation, travesty. *v.t.*

Parole', *n.* word of honour given by prisoner of war not to escape if allowed limited freedom.

Par'oxysm, *n.* sudden violent seizure.

Par'quet (-kay), *n.* flooring of patterned, fitted wooden blocks. **Par'quetry**, *n.*

Parr'icide, *n.* the murder or murderer of parent or close kindred.

Parr'y, *v.t.* to ward off, esp. a blow.

Par'simony, *n.* excessive meanness. **Parsimo'nious**, *a.*

Par'son, *n.* clergyman in charge of parish church. **Par'sonage**, *n.* his dwelling.

Part, *n.* a share, a portion, duty, actor's role. *v.t. & i.* to divide, separate, split up. **Partake'**, *v.t. & i.* to join in, to receive a portion of.

Par'terre (-tare), *n.* theatre pit, ornamental series of flower beds.

Par'tial, *a.* having a liking for, prejudiced, incomplete. **Partial'ity**, *n.* a liking, favouritism.

Partic'ipate, *v.t. & i.* to take part in, share in. **Partic'ipant**, *n.* person who takes part. **Participa'tion**, *n.*

Part'iciple, *n.* adjectival part of verb.

Part'icle, *n.* tiny piece, grain.

Partic'ular, *a.* special, distinct from others, fussy. *n.* a detail. **Partic'ularity**, *n.* a peculiarity, carefulness. **Partic'ularize**, *v.t.* to be specific, give details.

Partisan', *n.* devoted follower. *a.* prejudiced.

Parti'tion, *n.* a light dividing wall, the act of dividing up. *v.t.* to divide into parts.

Part'ner, *n.* companion, husband or wife, person one dances or plays game with, fellow-member of a business. **Part'-**

nership, *n.* business association.

Parturi'tion, *n.* childbirth.

Part'y, *n.* polit. organization, social gathering for pleasure.

Par'venu, *n.* odious person with newly acquired money or power.

Pass, *v.t. & i.* to proceed from one place to another, to move freely, to elapse, meet without stopping, to happen, to be successful in examination, to give judgement. *n.* a permit to pass, a narrow connection across or between mountains, a poor condition. Pass'able, *a.* moderately good, able to be passed or travelled over.

Pass'age, *n.* a voyage by ship, part of a book, conflict, corridor, enactment, right to travel.

Pass'enger, *n.* person going on a passage or journey.

Pas'sion, *n.* intense emotion, esp. of love. Pas'sionate, *a.* ardent, intense, swayed by strong emotion.

Pass'ive, *a.* submissive, inert. *n. gram.* indicating state of being acted upon. Passiv'ity, *n.*

Pass'over, *n.* Jewish feast commemorating the sparing of Jewish houses when Egyptians' firstborn were slain.

Pass'port, *n.* official document giving right to travel abroad.

Pass'word, *n.* watchword, response given to sentinel's challenge.

Past, *n.* previous history or life, time gone by. *a., adv. & prep.* gone by, beyond, by.

Paste, *n.* adhesive, dough ready for baking as pastry, preparation made of fish etc., fine glass substance used as imitation jewels. *v.t.* to stick with paste.

Pas'tel, *n.* coloured crayon, a picture drawn with crayon.

Pas'teurize (-ter-), *v.t.* to heat esp. milk sufficiently to kill germs. Pasteuriza'tion, *n.*

Pasti'che (-teesh), *n.* picture or mus. composed from various sources.

Pas'time, *n.* recreation, hobby.

Pas'tor, *n.* clergyman. Past'oral, *a.* pertaining to pastor or his duties. Past'orate, *n.* his office.

Past'oral, *a.* pertaining to shepherds. *n.* a poem or play depicting rural life.

Pa'stry, *n.* tarts or pies enclosed or covered with crust of baked dough.

Past'ure, *n.* field or land for grazing cattle and sheep. *v.t. & i.* to put out to feed on grass. Past'urage, *n.* land used for grazing animals.

Pas'ty, *n.* small pie full of chopped meat.

Pat, *n.* a gentle affectionate blow, a small shape of butter etc. *v.t.* to touch gently, stroke.

Patch (Pach), *n.* a small piece of material or ground, a covering put over a hole or weak place, a splash of colour. *v.t.* to mend or strengthen with a patch. Patch'work, *n.* rug or quilt etc. made of variegated left-over material. Patch'y, *a.* indifferent.

Pate, *n.* the head or crown of the head.

Pa'tent, *n.* official protection for invention to prevent anyone but inventor or owner using it. *a.* protected thus, plain, open. *v.t.* to protect by patent.

Pater'nal, *a.* pertaining or

related to a father. **Pater′nity,** *n.* fatherhood. **Pater′nalism,** *n.* condescending form of ruling.

Path (-ahth), *n.* a footway, track.

Pathol′ogy, *n.* scientific study of diseases. **Patholog′ical,** *a.* pertaining to this, of the nature of disease. **Pathol′ogist,** *n.*

Pa′thos, *n.* quality inducing sympathy or pity. **Pathet′ic,** *a.* pitiful.

Pa′tient, *n.* person being treated by doctor. *a.* enduring hardship or suffering uncomplainingly. **Pa′tience,** *n.* forbearance, resignation.

Pat′ina, *n.* incrustation on old bronze etc.

Pat′io, *n.* uncovered courtyard surrounded by buildings.

Pat′ois (-twah), *n.* regional language or dialect.

Pa′triarch (-ark), *n.* founder or ruler of family, any respected old man. **Pa′triarchal,** *a.*

Patri′cian, *n.* orig. a member of ancient Roman nobility, any person of distinguished birth and character. *a.*

Pat′rimony, *n.* property inherited from father or other ancestors.

Pat′riot, *n.* person who loves his country both in peace & war. **Patriot′ic,** *a.* **Pat′riotism,** *n.*

Patrol′ (-ole), *v.t.* to move about on guard. *n.* body of soldiers, policeman, etc. patrolling.

Pa′tron, *n.* guardian or protector, person who encourages artist etc. or helps any commendable activity. **Pat′ronage,** *n.* **Pat′ronize,** *v.t.* to support, regard with condescension, to deal at a shop.

Patronym′ic, *n.* surname.

Patt′er, *v.t.* to run with quick light steps. *n.* the sound of these. small talk.

Patt′ern, *n.* an example or model, a design or figure.

Pau′city, *n.* meagreness, smallness of quantity.

Paunch, *n.* the belly.

Pau′per, *n.* a very poor person. **Pau′perism,** *n.* **Pau′perize,** *v.t.* to reduce to utter poverty.

Pause, *n.* a short interval or break. *v.i.* to wait briefly.

Pave, *v.t.* to make a regular surface on road or street, to prepare the way. **Pave′ment,** *n.* footpath at side of street.

Pavil′ion, *n.* building for spectators and sportsmen at cricket-match etc.

Paw, *n.* an animal's foot, esp. one with claws. *v.t.* & *i.* to touch or scrape with paw.

Pawn, *v.t.* to leave something as security for money borrowed. **Pawn′broker,** *n.* tradesman accepting goods as security for loan.

Pawn, *n.* chessman of lowest value, any unimportant person in a scheme.

Pay, *v.t.* & *i.* to hand over money for goods or services, to be profitable. *n.* wages. **Pay′ment,** *n.* act of paying.

Peace, n. tranquillity, freedom from violence. **Peace′able,** *a.* calm, law-abiding. **Peace′ful,** *a.* **Peace′maker,** *n.* mediator.

Peach, *v.i.* & *sl.* to inform against.

Peak, *n.* a pointed end, the top of a mountain, the highest point of anything.

Peal, *v.t.* & *i.* to emit loud sonorous sound. *n.* sound of bells, clap of thunder.

Pearl (Purl), *n.* white concretion

found in oyster etc. and regarded as precious gem.

Peas'ant (Pez-), *n.* farm labourer, us. in arch. sense. *a.* **Peas'antry,** *n.* peasants, small farmers collectively.

Peat, *n.* decayed vegetable matter used as fuel.

Peb'ble, *n.* small smooth round stone.

Peccadill'o, *n.* a trifling offence.

Peck, *v.t. & i.* to strike or pick up with beak. *n.*

Peck, *n.* measure of capacity equalling two gallons.

Pec'toral, *a.* pertaining to the breast.

Pecula'tion, *n.* embezzlement. **Pec'ulate,** *v.t. & i.* to embezzle.

Pecu'liar, *a.* individual, particular, odd. **Peculiar'ity,** *n.* a characteristic, an oddity.

Pecu'niary, *a.* pertaining to money.

Ped'agogy (-goji), *n.* science & practice of education. **Ped'agogue,** *n.* teacher.

Ped'al, *a.* of or operated by foot. *n.* device for producing energy or motion by foot. *v.i.*

Ped'ant, *n.* person who is sedulously learned. **Pedant'ic,** *a.* fussy about academic details. **Ped'antry,** *n.* unnecessary display of knowledge or insistence on details.

Ped'dle, *v.t.* to hawk goods. **Pedd'ler, Ped'lar,** *n.*

Ped'estal, *n.* base of a column or statue.

Pedes'trian, *n.* person who goes on foot *a.* slow-moving, uninteresting *n.* **Pedes'trianism,** *n.*

Pediat'rics, Paediat'rics, *n. pl.* as *n.* study of infantile diseases. **Pediatric'ian,** *n.* expert in this.

Ped'icure, *n.* chiropody, chiropodist.

Ped'igree, *n.* ancestry, official record of descent.

Ped'iment, *n.* triangular space or decoration over door or window.

Peel, *n.* skin of fruit. *v.t. & i.* to cut off skin, take off in strips.

Peer, *n.* an equal, a nobleman. **Peer'age,** *n.* the rank or dignity of being a peer, the whole body of peers collectively. **Peer'less,** *a.* matchless.

Peer, *v.i.* to look closely or narrowly.

Peev'ish, *a.* petulant, irritable.

Pell-mell', *adv. a.* headlong, in confusion.

Pellu'cid, *a.* transparent, clear.

Pel'met, *n.* strip of material to conceal top of curtains.

Pelt, *n.* an animal's fur or skin.

Pelt, *v.t. & i.* to hurl things at rapidly & repeatedly, to fall heavily as of rain.

Pel'vis, *n. anat.* bone-structure supporting spine & linking legs to this.

Pen, *n.* a writing-instrument. *v.t.* to write.

Pen, *n.* small enclosure for animals. *v.t.*

Pen'alty, *n.* a legal punishment. **Pe'nal,** *a.* pertaining to this. **Pe'nalize,** *v.t.* to inflict punishment on.

Pen'ance, *n.* act of atoning for a sin.

Pen'chant (-shant), *n.* leaning, taste, liking.

Pen'cil, *n.* dry writing or drawing instrument. *v.t.*

Pend'ant, *n.* an ornament hung round the neck. **Pend'ent,** *a.* hanging, suspended.

Pen'ding, *a. & prep.* unfinished, during, until.

Pend'ulum, *n.* weight suspended so that it swings from side to side, esp. to regulate clock. **Pend'ulous**, *a.* swaying.

Pen'etrate, *v.t. & i.* to pass through, enter into, pierce. **Penetra'tion**, *n.*

Penin'sula, *n.* piece of land almost entirely surrounded by water. **Penin'sular**, *a.*

Pen'itence, *n.* remorse, repentance. **Pen'itent**, *a.* **Peniten'tial**, *a.* **Peniten'tiary**, *a.* pertaining to penitence. *n.* a prison.

Penn'ant, *n.* long narrow flag worn at masthead of ship.

Pen'sion, *n.* payment to retired person. *v.t.* **Pen'sioner**, *n.* retired person living on pension.

Pen'sive, *a.* meditative.

Pent, *a.* shut up, confined.

Pent'a-, *pref.* meaning five and used in various compounds, *e.g.* **Pentagon**, *n.* a five-sided, five-angled plane, **Pentateuch**, *n.* the first five books of the Bible, **Pentathlon**, *n.* athletic contest comprising five events.

Pent'house, *n.* apartment on top of main building.

Penul'timate, *a.* last but one.

Pen'ury, *n.* utter poverty. **Penu'-rious**, *a.* poor, miserly.

Peo'ple (Pe-), *n.* human beings in general, *a.* community of these, a nation. *v.t.* to populate.

Per- (Pur-), *pref.* meaning through or thoroughly. Where necessary reference to the main word should be made.

Perceive', *v.t.* to discern, become aware of. **Percep'tible**, *a.* discernible, noticeable. **Percep'-tion**, *n.* understanding, power

of perceiving. **Percip'ient**, *a.* aware, perceiving.

Per'colate, *v.t. & i.* to trickle or filter through. **Percola'tion**, *n.* **Per'colator**, *n.* apparatus for filtering, e.g. coffee.

Percus'sion, *n.* violent collision, shock or sound waves caused by this, mus. instruments such as drums played by striking.

Perdi'tion, *n.* utter ruin or damnation.

Per'egrinate, *v.i.* to roam about from place to place. **Peregrina'-tion**, *n.*

Perempt'ory, *n.* brusque, authoritative, imperious.

Perenn'ial, *a.* enduring, living several years, esp. botan. *n.* such a plant.

Per'fect, *a.* complete, unsullied. *n. & a. gram.* tense indicating completed action. **Perfect'**, *v.t.* to make complete or as good as possible. **Perfec'tion**, *n.* completeness, perfect state.

Per'fidy, *n.* treachery. **Perfid'-ious**, *a.*

Per'forate, *v.t.* to pierce with holes. **Perfora'tion**, *n.*

Perforce', *adv.* necessarily.

Perform', *v.t. & i.* to carry out a duty or task, to play or act in public. **Perform'ance**, *n.* the execution of a deed, a feat, a public exposition of one's talent. **Perform'er**, *n.*

Per'fume, *n.* fragrant scent. **Perfume'**, *v.t.* to scent.

Perfunct'ory, *a.* superficial, cursory.

Per'gola, *n.* an arbour.

Perhaps', *adv.* possibly.

Per'il, *n.* danger. **Per'ilous**, *a.* hazardous.

Perim'eter, *n.* an outer boundary.

Pe'riod, *n.* a space of time, *gram.* a complete sentence, a full stop. Period'ic, *a.* happening at intervals. Period'ical, *a.* pertaining to intervals of time. *n.* a periodical publication.

Peripatet'ic, *a.* itinerant, walking about.

Periph'ery, *n.* boundary, circumference.

Per'iscope, *n.* vertical and movable tube equipped with lenses and mirrors to enable submarine officer to watch surface activity when vessel is submerged.

Per'ish, *v.i.* to die. Per'ishable, *a.* liable to perish, esp. by decaying.

Peritoni'tis, *n.* inflammation of lining of stomach.

Per'jury, *n.* the breaking of a solemn oath, lying under oath. Per'jure, *v.t.* & i.

Perk, *v.t.* & i. to jerk up quickly, esp. head, to cheer up. Perk'y, *a.* cheerful.

Perks, *n. pl. sl.* short for perquisites.

Per'manent, *a.* perpetual, everlasting. Per'manence, *n.*

Per'meate, *v.t.* to saturate, pervade, pass through. Per'meable, *a.*

Permit', *v.t.* to sanction, allow. Per'mit, *n.* official pass. Permis'sion, *n.* consent. Permiss'ible, *a.* allowable. Permiss'ive, *a.* granting consent.

Permute', *v.t.* to change order of. Permuta'tion, *n.* variation of arrangement, esp. of numbers.

Pernic'ious, *a.* injurious, harmful, destructive, likely to cause damage.

Perora'tion, *n.* the climax of a speech.

Perpendic'ular, *a.* vertical, upright. *n. archit.* style with this characteristic.

Per'petrate, *v.t.* to commit, cause, esp. in derogatory sense. Perpetra'tion, *n.* Per'petrator, *n.*

Perpet'uate, *v.t.* to continue endlessly, to make everlasting. Perpet'ual, *a.* everlasting. Perpetu'ity, *n.* quality of being everlasting.

Perplex', *v.t.* to mystify, confuse. Perplex'ity, *n.* bewilderment, confusion of mind.

Per'quisite, *n.* petty right or payment connected with job apart from ordinary payment.

Per'secute, *v.t.* to oppress, illtreat. Persecu'tion, *n.* Per'secutor, *n.* tormentor.

Persevere', *v.i.* to keep up effort, work earnestly in spite of difficulties. Persever'ance, *n.*

Per'siflage, *n.* bantering talk.

Persist', *v.i.* to continue insistently or obstinately. Persis'tent, *a.* Persist'ence, *n.*

Per'son, *n.* a human being, physical appearance or presence, *gram.* one of three classes of personal pron. indicating person speaking, spoken to or of. Per'sonal, *a.* relating to a person, individual, one's own. Personal'ity, *n.* individuality, an outstanding person. Per'sonalty, *n.* personal estate esp. in connection with will. Per'sonable, *a.* attractive in appearance. Per'sonage, *n. iron.* an important person. Person'ify, *v.t.* to be typical of, to regard or represent as a person. Personifica'tion, *n.* the embodiment. **Personnel'**, *n*. persons collectively when employed as staff.

Perspect'ive, *n*. the correct relationship of things in drawing, an all-embracing view.

Perspicac'ity, *n*. discernment, quickness of comprehension. **Perspica'cious**, *a*.

Perspicu'ity, *n*. clarity of expression or thought. **Perspic'uous**, *a*. easily understood, well expressed.

Perspire', *v.i.* to sweat. **Perspira'tion**, *n*.

Persuade' (-swade), *v.t.* to convince by reason. **Persua'sion**, *n*. act or power of persuading, conviction. **Persua'sive**, *a*.

Pert, *a*. cheeky, forward in manner.

Pertain', *v.i.* to belong, to apply to, relate or refer to. **Per'tinent**, *a*. appropriate, related to a subject. **Pert'inence**, *n*.

Pertinac'ity, *n*. obstinate perseverance. **Pertina'cious**, *a*. persistent, dogged.

Perturb', *v.t.* to disturb, disquiet. **Perturba'tion**, *n*.

Peruse' (Per-ooz), *v.t.* to read attentively. **Peru'sal**, *n*.

Pervade', *v.t.* to spread throughout, permeate. **Perva'sion**, *n*. **Perva'sive**, *a*.

Perverse', *a*. obstinately wicked or difficult. **Pervers'ity**, *n*.

Pervert', *v.t.* to deviate from proper use, to lead astray. **Per'vert**, *n*. person who acts abnormally or gives up faith. **Perver'sion**, *n*. corruption, wrongful action. **Perver'sive**, *a*. tending to lead astray.

Pess'imism, *n*. tendency to expect the worst. **Pess'imist**, *n*. **Pess'imistic**, *a*.

Pest, *n*. the plague, a constant annoyance. **Pestif'erous**, *a*. bearing plague, *coll*. annoying. **Pes'tilence**, *n*. plague, pest. **Pestilen'tial**, *a*. pertaining to a plague, vexatious. **Pest'ilent**, *a*. deadly, corrupting, mischievous. **Pest'er**, *v.t.* to annoy continually.

Pes'tle (Pess'l), *n*. implement for pounding substances in a mortar.

Pet, *n*. a tame animal, favourite child. *v.t.* to fondle, make much of.

Pet, *n*. peevishness.

Pet'al, *n*. coloured leaf of flower.

Pe'ter, *v.i.* only as peter out, come gradually to an end.

Peti'tion, *n*. an earnest entreaty esp. in writing. *v.t.* to request earnestly. **Peti'tioner**, *n*.person presenting a petition.

Pet'rify, *v.t.* to transform into stone, *coll*. to strike motionless with terror. **Petrifac'tion**, *n*.

Petro'leum, *n*. mineral oil. **Pet'rol**, *n*. this refined.

Pettifogg'ing, *a*. quibbling over details.

Pett'y, *a*. trifling, narrowminded, small.

Pet'ulant, *a*. irritable. **Pet'ulance**, *n*.

Pew, *n*. a bench in church.

Pew'ter, *n*. alloy of tin and lead, utensils made of this.

Phal'anx, *n*. compact formation of soldiers.

Phan'tasm, *n*. phantom, ghostly vision. **Phantas'mal**, *a*. **Phantasmagor'ic**, *a*.

Phan'tom, *n*. a ghost, an apparition.

Pharisa'ical, *a*. hypocritical.

Phar'macy, *n*. the preparation

of medicines, a chemist's shop.
Phar'macist, *n.* person skilled in preparation of medicines. **Pharmaceut'ic** (-sutic), *a.* pertaining to pharmacy.

Phase, *n.* aspect of moon, stage or period in development.

Phenom'enon, *n.* any natural happening, something remarkable. *pl.* phenomena. **Phenom'enal**, *a.* remarkable.

Phi'al, *n.* small bottle for medicines.

Phil'anthropy, *n.* love of mankind, great generosity. **Philanthrop'ic**, *a.* **Philan'thropist**, *n.* rich man who gives away wealth for general good.

Philat'ely, *n.* the methodical collecting of postage-stamps. **Philatel'ic**, *a.* **Philat'elist**, *n.* stamp-collector.

Phil'harmonic, *a.* devoted to music.

Phil'ology, *n.* scientific study of languages and their origins. **Philolo'gical**, *a.* **Philol'ogist**, *n.*

Philos'ophy, *n.* the study and exposition of wisdom, study of ultimate reality, a system for social and individual behaviour. **Philos'opher**, *n* exponent of these. **Philosoph'ical**, *a.* wise, reasoned. **Philos'ophize**. *v.i.* to reason, search out the truth of the nature of life.

Phil'tre, *n. arch.* a love-potion.

Phlegm (Flem), *n.* bronchial mucus, calmness, indifference. **Phlegmat'ic** (Fleg-), *a.* calm, unemotional.

Pho'bia. *n.* morbid dread.

Phonet'ic, *a.* pertaining to vocal sounds. *n. pl.* as *n.* science of vocal sounds.

Pho'nograph, *n.* early form of gramophone.

Phos'phorus, *n.* non-metallic, inflammable, luminous element. **Phosphores'cent**, *a.* luminous in the dark like phosphorus. **Phosphores'cence**, *n.*

Photog'raphy, *n.* process of making pictures or images through action of light on sensitized material. **Pho'tograph**, *n.* picture so obtained. *v.t.* to make a photograph. **Photog'rapher**, *n.* person using camera to make photograph. **Photograph'ic**, *a.*

Phrase, *n.* coherent group of words, concise expression. *v.t.* to put into words. **Phraseol'ogy**, *n.* method of expression, arrangement of words.

Phrenol'ogy, *n.* method of estimating intellectual qualities & character by studying shape of skull. **Phrenol'ogist**, *n.* person skilled in this.

Phys'ic (Fiz-), *n. arch.* medicine. *v.t.* to treat with medicine. **Physi'cian**, *n.* medical doctor.

Phys'ics, *n.* science dealing with matter and energy. **Phys'icist**, *n.* specialist in this. **Phys'ical**, *a.* to do with matter or the body, pertaining to natural science.

Phys'iognomy (Fiz-i-on-), *n.* the face, the skill of estimating character from the face.

Physiog'raphy, *n.* physical geography.

Physiol'ogy *n.* (-ji) scientific study of functions of living things and their organs etc.

Physique' (Fiz-eek), *n.* structure and organization of the human body.

Pian'o, *n.* **Pian'oforte**, *n. mus.* keyboard instrument. **Pian'o**, *a. & adv.* soft, softly. **Pian'ist**, *n.* person who plays the piano.

Picaresque', *a.* of fiction that romanticizes criminals.

Picc'olo, n. *mus.* small instrument resembling flute.

Pick, *n.* the best of something, choice. *v.t.* to gather, scratch, pluck, choose, bring, about. **Pick'ings**, *n. pl.* gleanings.

Pick, *n.* heavy tool with two-pointed head for breaking up ground. **Pick-axe**, *n.* the same.

Pick'et, *n.* strikers posted at factory gates etc. to persuade comrades not to work, military guard, pointed stake. *v.t.*

Pic'kle, *n.* esp. as *n. pl.* vegetables preserved in vinegar, a difficult situation. *v.t.* to preserve in vinegar.

Pic'nic, *n.* trip to countryside or sea with outdoor meal. *v.i.* **Pic'nicker**, *n.*

Pic'ture, *n.* a scene or portrait painted, drawn or photographed. *v.t.* to imagine, make a likeness of. **Pictor'ial**, *a.* pertaining to pictures. *n.* an illustrated magazine. **Picturesque'**, *a.* mawkishly charming.

Pie, *n.* meat or fruit dish covered with pastry.

Pie'bald, *a.* having patches of black and white. *n.* a horse so marked.

Piece (Peess), *n.* a bit or fragment taken or broken from whole, a separate composition, a unit, a coin, an action. *v.t.* to join together. **Piecemeal**, *adv.* bit by bit. **Piecework**, *n.* work paid for by amount done not by time.

Pier (Peer), *n.* pillar supporting bridge, construction built from shore some distance into sea and used as landing-stage and pleasure promenade.

Pierce, *v.t.* to perforate, make a hole in, to penetrate.

Pi'ety, *n.* devoutness, reverence. **Pi'ous**, *a.*

Pig'ment, *n.* colouring matter. **Pigmenta'tion**, *n.*

Pike, *n. arch.* spearlike weapon. **Pike'staff**, *n.*

Pilas'ter, *n.* rectangular column attached to wall.

Pile (Pyle), *n.* mass or heap, large quantity. *v.t. & i.* to make a heap, to load up, accumulate.

Pile, *n.* timber, metal or concrete column driven into damp ground as foundation of bridge or building. **Pile-driver**, *n.* machine for setting piles.

Pile, *n.* nap on cloth or carpet.

Pil'fer, *v.t. & i.* to thieve in petty way. **Pil'ferage**, *n.*

Pil'grim, *n.* devout person visiting shrine. **Pil'grimage**, *n.* his journey.

Pill, *n.* medicine contained in small ball of substance.

Pill'age, *v.t. & i.* to plunder, despoil. n.

Pill'ar, *n.* a supporting column.

Pill'ion (Pilyun), *n.* seat for passenger behind horse-rider, motorcyclist etc.

Pill'ory, *n. arch.* punishment where y offender was secured by hands and neck in wooden frame and exposed to public ridicule and abuse. *v.t.* to expose to public ridicule.

Pill'ow, *n.* linen cushion stuffed with feathers as support for head of person in bed. *v.t.* to place on or support with pillow.

Pi'lot, *n.* marine officer steering ship through difficult local waters of which he has special knowledge, officer in charge of aircraft. *v.t.* to steer, guide, esp. through difficult conditions.

Pim'ple, *n.* spot, inflamed swelling.

Pin, *n.* short sharp stiff piece of wire for fastening material together, a bolt or peg, a roller. *v.t.* to fasten with a pin, to hold down. **Pinpoint,** *v.t.* to fix or ascertain a position with exactitude.

Pince'-nez (Panse-nay), *n.* spectacles held in place by spring or clip on bridge of nose.

Pin'cers, pin'chers, *n.* gripping tool.

Pinch, *v.t.* to to squeeze or nip. *n.* a nip, a tiny amount, economic pressure.

Pine, *v.i.* to languish, become weak through grief.

Pin'ion, *n.* a bird's wing. *v.t.* to clip ends of wings to prevent flight, to hold by the wings or arms.

Pink, *n.* very faint red, good condition.

Pink, *v.t. arch.* to pierce with a sword.

Pinn'ace, *n.* ship's tender, *arch.* small two-masted vessel.

Pinn'acle, *n.* pointed tower, highest point of career etc, pointed peak of mountain.

Pinn'ate, *a.* with identical parts on either side of axis, as in leaf or feather.

Pi'oneer, *n.* innovator, explorer, person who goes in advance to clear or prepare way for others. *v.t.*

Pip, *n.* small seed of fruit.

Pip, *n.* poultry disease, *sl.* depression.

Pipe, *n.* implement for smoking tobacco, long hollow tube for conveying liquid or gas, a mus. wind instrument, a thin high call. *v.t. & i.* to convey through pipe, play on pipe, cry in shrill fashion. **Pi'per,** *n.* person who plays pipe, esp. bagpipes. **Pi'ping,** *n.*

Pip'kin, *n.* small earthenware jar.

Pipp'in, *n.* kind of apple.

Pi'quant (Pe-kant), *a.* pungent, tart.

Pique (Peek), *n.* vexation. *v.t.*

Pi'racy, *n.* armed robbery at sea, lit. or mus. plagiarism. **Pi'rate,** *n.* sea-robber, the ship he sails in. *v.t. & i.* **Pirat'ical,** *a.*

Pirouette', *v.i.* in ballet-dancing to spin rapidly on the toes in one place. *n.*

Pis'catory, *a.* pertaining to fishes and fishing. **Piscator'ial,** *a.*

Pis'til, *n. bot.* female seed-bearing flower-organ.

Pis'tol, *n.* small hand-gun. *v.t.* to use this.

Pis'ton, *n.* tightly fitting disc or cylinder sliding up and down within larger cylinder.

Pit, *n.* a mine-shaft, a cavity or depression, part of theatre auditorium. *v.t.* to mark or scar.

Pit, *v.t.* to set against.

Pitch, *n.* black viscous substance obtained from tar or turpentine.

Pitch, *v.t. & i.* to set up in position, to hurl, to fall headlong, plunge. *n.* mus. tone, wicket prepared for cricket.

Pitch'er, *n.* large jug.

Pith, *n.* essence, gist, central substance of stem. **Pith'y,** *a.* concise.

Pitt'ance, *n*. a meagre allowance.
Pitu'itary, *a*. of or secreting mucus.
Pit'y, *n*. compassion, sympathy with others' distress, mercy, anything regrettable. *v.t.* **Pit'-eous**, *a*. evoking pity. **Pit'iable**, *a*. **Pit'iful**, *a*. miserable. **Pit'-iless**, *a*. merciless.
Piv'ot, *n*. fixed shaft on which object turns, *fig*. anything on which matter of importance depends. *v.t. & i*. to turn or place on a pivot. **Piv'otal**, *a*.
Pix'ie, *n*. an elf.
Plac'ard, *n*. an advertising poster. *v.t.*
Plac'ate, *v.t.* to appease, calm.
Place, *n*. a specific locality, a public square, a situation, an appointment, a position in a contest, a building. *v.t.* to put, to appoint, to identify.
Placid'ity, *n*. serenity. **Plac'id**, *a*. serene.
Pla'giarize (Pla-gi-), *v.t. & i*. to infringe another's copyright. **Pla'giarism**, *n*. **Pla'giarist**, *n*.
Plague, **n**. pestilence, bubonic plague, dangerous epidemic. *v.t.* to afflict with plague, to torment.
Plaid (Plad), *n*. tartan cloth used by Sc. Highlanders.
Plain, *a*. clear, straightforward, level, unadorned, unsweetened. *n*. flat open tract of land.
Plaint, *n*. a complaint, a lamentation. **Plain'tive**, *a*. mournful.
Plain'tiff, *n*. person bringing action in law-court.
Plait (Plat), *n*. braid of hair, straw etc. *v.t.* to form into plaits.
Plan, *n*. scheme, project, a diagram. *v.t. & i*.
Plane, *n*. a carpenter's tool for smoothing wood, a flat surface. *a*. flat. *v.t. & i*. to use a plane, make smooth.
Plan'et, *n*. heavenly body revolving round sun. **Planetar'ium**, *n*. hall with apparatus in ceiling for illustrating the movements of heavenly bodies. **Plan'etary**, *a*. pertaining to the planets.
Plank, *n*. long sawn board of timber. *v.t.* to cover with planks, to put down.
Plant, *n*. vegetable organism, industrial equipment, *sl*. a swindle, false clues deliberately left. *v.t.* to set in soil for growth, to introduce.
Planta'tion, *n*. estate for specialized cultivation, a settlement. **Plan'ter**, *n*. overseer or owner of plantation.
Plaque, *n*. ornamental commemorative tablet.
Plas'ma, *n*. colourless liquid part of blood, lymph, milk etc.
Plas'ter, *n*. lime, sand and water mixed together to form coating for walls, *med*. adhesive protective material. *v.t.* to cover with either of these.
Plas'tic, *a*. capable of being shaped, pliant, of synthetic material. *n*. **Plastic surgery**, *n*. restoration of injured flesh by grafting on living tissue.
Plate, *n*. a shallow eating dish, a thin flat piece of metal or glass, sensitized photographic glass, book illustration, strip of metal for inscription of name etc. *v.t.* to cover with sheets of metal.
Plateau' (-o), *n*. high flat land.
Plat'form, *n*. raised structure for speaking from, stage for boarding train, *fig*. polit. party's policy.

Plat′inum, *n.* heavy grey malleable valuable metal. *a.*

Plat′itude, *n.* trite, obvious remark. **Platitu′dinous,** *a.* dull in style.

Platon′ic, *a.* pertaining to the philosophy of Plato, us. in reference to purely spiritual love as opposed to sexual.

Platoon′, *n. mil.* subdivision of company, half a company.

Platt′er, *n.* large flat plate or dish.

Plau′dit (Plaw-), *n.* esp. as *n. pl.* great applause.

Plau′sible, *a.* specious, persuasive. **Plausibil′ity,** *n.*

Play, *v.t. & i.* to take part in sport, to act for pleasure, to perform on a mus. instrument, to frivol, to take part in a theatrical piece, to use. *n.* the action of a game, a frolic, a theatrical drama, a movement. **Playwright,** *n.* dramatist.

Plea, *n.* an excuse, entreaty.

Plead, *v.t. & i.* to beg, to present a case in lawcourt, to urge. **Plead′ing,** *n.* esp. as *n. pl.* legal statements in court.

Pleas′ure, *n.* delight, enjoyment, satisfaction. **Please,** *v.t. & i.* to give this. **Pleas′ing,** *a.* **Pleas′urable,** *a.* gratifying. **Pleas′ant** (Plez-), *a.* agreeable. **Pleas′antry,** *n.* verbal playfulness.

Pleat, *n.* a fold in cloth or material. *v.t.*

Plebe′ian *a.* pertaining to the common people, vulgar.

Pleb′iscite, *n.* a direct vote by whole population on particular issue.

Pledge, *n.* a security, a bond, word of honour, toast. *v.t.*

Ple′nary, *a.* full, unlimited, esp. as **Plenary powers.**

Plenipoten′tiary, *a.* having complete power. *n.* diplomatic representative with full powers.

Plen′itude, *n.* abundance. **Plen′teous,** *a.* abundant. **Plen′tiful,** *a.* ample, sufficient. **Plen′ty,** *n.* a sufficiency.

Pleth′ora, *n.* an overabundance.

Pleur′isy (Ploor-), *n.* inflammation of membrane covering lungs.

Plex′us, *n.* network of veins or nerves.

Pli′able, *a.* easily bent or moulded, submissive. **Pliabil′ity,** *n.* **Pli′ant,** *a.* easily influenced.

Pli′ers, *n. pl.* small gripping tool, pincers.

Plight, *n.* a predicament.

Plight, *v.t.* to pledge, promise.

Plinth, *n.* foot of column or pedestal.

Plod, *v.t. & i.* to trudge, walk wearily or heavily. *n.* **Plod′der** *n.* earnest but backward person.

Plot, *n.* a secret scheme, a piece of land, the essential story in work of fiction, a chart. *v.t. & i.* to conspire, work out course.

Plough (Plow), *n. agric.* implement for turning up soil. *v.t. & i.* to make furrows, to proceed clumsily. **Plough-share,** *n.* blade of plough.

Ploy, *n.* a scheme, escapade.

Pluck, *v.t. & i.* to strip feathers from, pull sharply. *n.* courage, animal offal. **Pluck′y,** *a.* brave.

Plug, *n.* small object to stop hole or leak, elec. connection, water-closet connection. *v.t. & i.* to stop a leak, make elec. connection, to advertise by reiteration.

Plum, *n.* stone fruit from tree of

same name, an enviable position.

Plu'mage, *n.* bird's feathers.

Plume, *n.* long ornamental feather.

Plumb (Plum), *n.* sounding-lead, small weight on cord for estimating vertical. *a.* absolutely straight or correct. *v.t.* to ascertain depth or vertical. **Plumb-line**, *n.*

Plum'ber (Plummer), *n.* artisan specializing in water-fittings. **Plum'bing**, *n.*

Plump, *a.* well-fleshed. *v.t. & i.* to make or grow chubby, fat.

Plump, *v.t. & i.* to fall or drop heavily, to come out in support of. *a.* abruptly, heavily.

Plun'der, *v.t. & i.* to rob violently, loot. *n.* booty.

Plunge, *v.t. & i.* to dive, hurl oneself into, leap. *n.*

Plu'perfect, *a. & n. gram.* tense of verb indicating action completed before another.

Plur'al (Ploor-), *a.* consisting or denoting more than one. **Plural'ity**, *n.* state of being plural, large number, practice of holding two positions simultaneously.

Plus, *a.* in addition, to be added. *n.* an addition, symbol representing this.

Plush, *n.* fabric resembling velvet.

Plutoc'racy, *n.* government by the wealthy, the rich as a class. **Plu'tocrat**, *n.* person whose wealth gives him power.

Pluton'ium, *n.* (-tone-) radioactive element derived from uranium.

Plu'vial, *a.* of rain, caused by rain.

Ply, *v.t. & i.* to work or use, to run to and fro, to urge or give persistently, **p. for hire** or **p. with liquor.**

Ply, *n.* a fold or thickness, esp. as **Plywood**, *n.* thin boarding composed of several thicknesses.

Pneumat'ic (Nu-), *a.* pertaining to air, filled with air, worked by air pressure.

Pneumo'nia, *n.* inflammation of the lungs.

Poach, *v.t. & i.* to cook shelled egg in boiling water, to take game illegally, to trample ground into mire. **Poach'er**, *n.* trespasser in search of game.

Pock, *n.* eruptive spot in smallpox, scar left by this.

Pock'et, *n.* small pouch in clothes, a cavity, a bag of air or water separate from surrounding substance. *v.t.* to put into a pocket, to seize esp. illegally.

Pod, *n.* seed-vessel of pea, etc.

Po'em, *n.* a composition in verse. **Po'esy**, *n.* poetry. **Po'et**, *n.* writer of poetry, **Po'etry**, *n.* the art of writing verse. **Po'etic**, *a.* romantically expressed, written in poetry. **Po'etaster**, *n. iron.* mediocre versifier.

Pog'rom, *n.* organized massacre esp. of Jews and as practised by Tsarist regime and Nazis.

Poign'ant (Poin-), *a.* painfully acute, moving. **Poign'ancy**, *n.*

Point, *n.* a specific place or time, a juncture, a sharp end, a purpose, a relevancy, a feature or characteristic, a dot, a headland. *v.t. & i.* to sharpen, to indicate direction, to draw attention, to show position. **Point'ed**, *a.* direct, sharp. **Point'er**, *n.* an indication, thing for indicating, kind of game-dog.

Poin'tillism(Pwan-), n. method of painting in dots. Poin'tillist, n.

Poise, v.t. & i. to balance, hold or place steadily. n. stance, carriage.

Poi'son (-zn), n. deadly substance. v.t. to administer poison, to corrupt, spoil. Poi'sonous, a. deadly, harmful.

Poke, v.t. & i. to push or thrust with pointed or other object, make hole in by this, to interfere. n. a bonnet, a sack. Po'ker, n. implement for stirring fire, a card-game for money. Pok'y, a. restricted, mean, esp. of place.

Pole, n. a long round staff, a measure of length of $5^1/_2$ yards.

Pole, n. either end of earth's or other sphere's axis, magnetic terminal. Po'lar, a. pertaining to the earth's axes. Polar'ity, n. tendency of magnet to point to north. Po'larize, v.t. to give polarity to, modify radiation in light or heat and induce conformation of its vibrations. Polariza'tion, n.

Pole'axe, n. instrument for slaughtering animals, mediaeval weapon. v.t.

Polem'ic, Polem'ical, a. pertaining to argument or controversy. Polem'ics, n. pl. as n. the art of controversy.

Police' (-leece), n. branch of administration responsible for maintaining law and order, the personnel of this. v.t. to keep order with police, to patrol.

Pol'icy, n. a course of action, polit. intentions, a contract of insurance. Pol'itic, a. prudent, discreet. n. pl. as n. the

science of government. Politi'cian, n. person working in politics. Polit'ical, a. pertaining to politics. Pol'ity, n. constitution, organized government.

Poliomyeli'tis, (Polio-myelly-), n. infantile paralysis.

Pol'ish, v.t. & i. to make smooth and shiny, to improve. n. material for polishing, elegant finish.

Pol'ka, n. a lively dance, mus. for this.

Poll (Pole), n. arch. for top of head, the hair. v.t. & i. to trim top, esp. of trees, horns of cattle etc.

Poll (Pole), n. an election, the collective body of voters. v.t. to cast votes, receive votes.

Poll'en, n. fertilizing element in plants. Poll'inate, v.t. to fertilize. Pollina'tion, n.

Pollute', v.t. to make filthy, defile. Pollu'tion, n.

Po'lo, n. hockey on horseback.

Poltroon', n. cowardly fool.

Pol'y, pref. meaning many, as in Polyandry, n. practice of having more than one husband, Polygamy, n. practice of having more than one wife. Polyglot, a. containing or speaking several languages. Pol'ygon, n. plane figure with five or more sides. Polysyllable, n. word with several syllables, etc.

Pol'yp, (-ip), n. tiny marine animal.

Pomade', n. scented ointment for head-treatment.

Pomm'el, n. rounded top of sword handle, front of saddle.

Pomp, n. splendour. Pomp'ous, a. self-important, pretentious. Pompos'ity, n.

Pond, n. a small lake or pool.

Pon'der, *v.t.* & *i.* to meditate, reflect.

Pond'erous, *a.* clumsily heavy.

Pon'tiff, *n.* the pope, a bishop. Pontif'ical, *a.* Pontif'icate, *n. v.i. coll.* to talk pompously.

Pontoon', *n.* a temporary bridge made of flat-bottomed boats, a landing-stage resembling raft.

Po'ny, *n.* a small horse of not more than 13 hands, *sl.* £25.

Poo'dle, *n.* curly haired dog.

Pool, *n.* a pond, a puddle of liquid.

Pool, *n.* a business combine, a store of material, stakes in games of chance. *v.t.* to put into common fund.

Poop, *n.* stern of ship, raised deck on this.

Poor, *a.* needy, feeble in quality, pitiable. Poor'ly, *a.* ailing.

Pope, *n.* pontiff, head of R.C. church. Po'pery, *n.* the papal system in derogatory sense.

Pop'injay, *n.* a conceited fool.

Pop'ulace, *n.* people in general. Pop'ulation, *n.* the entire number of inhabitants. Pop'ulate, *v.t.* to fill with people. Pop'ulous, *a.* thickly inhabited.

Pop'ular, *a.* well-liked generally. Popular'ity, *n.* condition of being well-liked. Pop'ularize, *v.t.* to make popular. Populariza'tion, *n.*

Por'celain, *n.* fine glazed earthenware. *a.*

Porch, *n.* projecting roof and walls to protect doorway.

Pore, *n.* tiny hole in skin or material. Por'ous, *a.* having pores and thus permeable by liquid.

Pore, *v.i.* to study closely.

Pork, *n.* flesh of pig. Pork'er, *n.* pig bred for food. Por'cine (-seen), *a.* relating to pigs.

Pornog'raphy, *n.* obscene writing or illustrations. Pornog'rapher, *n.* Pornograph'ic, *a.*

Port, *n.* fortified red wine.

Port, *n.* a harbour, town with large harbour, left side of ship facing bows, a loophole, a ship's window esp. as port-hole.

Port'able, *a.* capable of being carried esp. by hand.

Port'age, *n.* the act of transporting, esp. overland at unnavigable stretches of water.

Por'tal, *n.* doorway, entrance. Portcull'is, *n.* mediaeval protective grating over gateway of castle.

Portend', *v.t.* to foreshadow, give warning of. Por'tent, *n.* omen. Porten'tous, *a.* threatening, significant.

Por'ter, *n.* door-keeper, janitor, person who carries luggage at railway-stations.

Port'er, *n.* dark brown bitter beer.

Portfo'lio, *n.* brief-case for carrying documents, office of government minister.

Port'ico, *n.* a colonnade, a columned porch.

Por'tion, *n.* a share, a part, lot, fate, dowry. *v.t.* to allot, share out in portions.

Port'ly, *a.* stout but dignified.

Portman'teau (-to), *n.* large suitcase.

Por'trait, *n.* a painted or drawn likeness of a person. Por'traiture, *n.* the skill of painting portraits. Portray', *v.t.* to paint or draw a likeness, to represent, play a part. Portray'al, *n.*

Pose, *v.t.* & *i.* to take up or place in an attitude, to lay false claim to being something or someone. *n.* an attitude. **Poseur'** (-zer), *n.* pretentious person.

Pose, *v.t.* to put a difficult question or problem. **Po'ser,** *n.* a difficult problem.

Posi'tion, *n.* place or manner in which thing or person is situated, a job, rank, attitude.

Pos'itive, *a.* confident, definite, undoubted, clearly defined or stated, not negative, *n.* a plus quantity, a developed photograph, positive adjective in gram.

Pos'itivism, *n.* phil. & rel. doctrine based on recognition only of positive facts and observable phenomena.

Poss'e (Poss-ee), *n.* body of armed men.

Possess', *v.t.* to own, control. **Posses'sion,** *n.* a belonging, the fact of owning. **Possess'ive,** *a.* eager or tending to possess, in gram. indicating possession. **Possess'or,** *n.*

Poss'ible, *a.* capable of happening or being achieved. *n.* **Possibil'ity,** n. anything likely to happen, a contingency.

Po'st, *n.* vertical pole as part of fence, support for wires etc.

Po'st, *n.* a position of trust, an office or duty, the official postal system. *v.t. & i.* to put in a particular position, to make known by printed announcement, to send by mail. **Po'stal,** *a.* pertaining to the official mail. **Po'stage,** *n.* charge for sending by mail.

Post-, *pref.* meaning behind or after e.g. **post-graduate,** *n.* university student continuing studies after graduation. **Pos'-thumous,** *a.* born after death of father, published after death of author. **Post-meridiem,** *n.* afternoon. **Post-mortem,** *n.* examination after death etc.

Po'ster, *n.* placard.

Poste'rior, *n.* the rump. *a.* later, hinder.

Poster'ity, *n.* following generations, the human future.

Postpone', *v.t.* to put off to a later date, defer. **Postpone'-ment, n.**

Pos'tulate, *v.t. & i.* to assume as self-evident, to take for granted. *n.*

Pos'ture, *n.* attitude, carriage. *v.t. & i.* to strike a pose.

Po'sy, *n.* a bunch of flowers.

Po'tent, *a.* powerful. **Po'tency,** *n.* **Po'tentate,** *n.* all-powerful ruler. **Poten'tial,** *a. & n.* latent or latent power, possible or possibility.

Po'tion, *n.* a dose of medicine.

Pott'er, *v.i.* to work or walk in desultory fashion.

Pott'ery, *n.* earthenware utensils, place where these are made. **Pott'er,** *n.* expert craftsman in pottery.

Pouch, *n.* a small bag, marsupial's sac in front of body for carrying young. *v.t.* to put into a pouch.

Poultice (Pole-tis) *n.* hot med. application for treating sore. *v.t.* to apply this.

Poul'try (Pole-) *n.* domestic fowls. **Poult'erer,** *n.* shopkeeper who sells poultry.

Pounce (Pownce) *v.i.* to spring or swoop suddenly. *n.*

Pound, **n.** public enclosure for stray animals.

Pound, *v.t. & i.* to beat, crush to powder, run with heavy footsteps.

Pound, *n.* a measure of weight equalling sixteen ounces avdp. or of troy twelve ounces, British standard of money as p. sterling.

Pour (Poor) *v.t. & i.* to flow or cause to flow, to discharge or utter freely, to descend thickly as rain.

Pout, *v.t. & i.* to grimace by protruding lips.

Pov'erty, *n.* extreme need, indigence. **Poverty-stricken,** *a.* utterly needy.

Pow'der, *n.* substance broken up into fine particles or dust. *v.t. & i.* to pulverize, sprinkle with powder, crumble.

Pow'er, *n.* strength, authority, force, ability to act, a great influence, a great nation. **Pow'-erful,** *a.* **Pow'erless,** *a.*

Prac'tice, *n.* a custom, accepted procedure, repeated exercise of a skill. **Prac'tise** (-tiss) *v.t. & i.* to do something habitually, to exercise, to work in specialized job. **Prac'tised,** *a.* expert. **Practi'tioner,** *n.* person who practises a profession e.g. law or med. **Prac'tical,** *a.* pertaining to action. **Prac'ticable,** *a.* capable of being put into practice, feasible.

Pragmat'ic, *a.* practical, dogmatic, relating to commonplace matters. **Prag'matism,** *n.* the evaluation of something by its consequences.

Prair'ie, *n.* extensive undulating treeless grassland.

Praise, *v.t.* to commend, laud, glorify. *n.* **Praiseworthy,** *a.*

Prance (Prahnce) *v.i.* to move with bounding motion, of horse to rise up on hindlegs.

Prank, *n.* a mischievous joke.

Prate, *v.i.* to chatter boastfully.

Prat'tle, *v.t. & i.* to babble, talk idly. *n.* **Prat'tler,** *n.*

Pray, *v.t. & i.* to offer prayer to God, to request urgently. **Pray'er** (Prare) *n.* an entreaty esp. to God.

Pre-, *pref.* meaning beforehand, before.

Preach, *v.t. & i.* to talk instructively esp. about rel. **Preach'er,** *n.*

Pream'ble (Pre-am-) *n.* an introduction to speech or writing.

Preb'end, n. stipend of canon or other member of cathedral chapter. **Preb'endary,** *n.* holder of this, his title.

Precar'ious (-care-) *a.* insecure, dangerous.

Precau'tion (-kaw-) *n.* prudent measure taken beforehand. **Precau'tionary,** *a.*

Precede', *v.t. & i.* to go in front of in order, rank, time etc. **Prec'edence,** *n.* **Prec'edent,** *n.* past happening or case as example or rule. **Prece'ding,** *a.* previous, prior.

Precep'tor, *n.* a teacher. **Pre'-cept,** *n.* an order, a maxim.

Pre'cinct (-sinkt), *n.* enclosed space adjoining building *esp.* as *n. pl.* ground attached to church etc.

Prec'ious, *a.* greatly esteemed, of great value, *coll.* affected, mannered, extreme. **Precios'ity,** *n.* excessive refinement, esp. in cultural matters.

Prec'ipice (-pis), *n.* almost vertical rockface or cliff. **Precip'itous,** *a.* very steep, sheer.

Precip'itate, *v.t.* to rush or throw headlong, to condense. *a.*

hasty. *n.* in chem. a body precipitated from solution. **Precipita'tion,** *n.* condensed moisture as rain or snow.

Pre'cis (Pra'see) *n.* a summary.

Precise', *a.* accurate, exact. **Preci'sion,** *n.* accuracy.

Preclude', *v.t.* to prevent, render impossible. **Preclu'sion,** *n.*

Preco'cious, *a.* excessively mentally developed in relation to age. **Precoc'ity,** *n.*

Precur'sor, *n.* a forerunner, person heralding another's coming.

Pred'atory, *a.* of animal living by preying on others. **Preda'-cious,** *a.*

Pre'decessor, *n.* previous holder of office.

Predic'ament, *n.* a difficult or distressing situation.

Pred'icate, *v.t.* to assert, declare. *n. gram.* what is said of the subject.

Predict', *v.t.* to foretell. **Predic'-tion,** *n.*

Predilec'tion, *n.* a partiality.

Pre-emp'tive, *a.* of a high bid made to forestall others. **Pre-emption,** *n.* **Pre-empt,** *v.t.*

Preen, *v.t.* to arrange feathers, to groom oneself.

Pref'ace, *n.* introduction to book. *v.t.* to introduce in this manner. **Pref'atory,** *a.*

Pre'fect, *n.* orig. a Roman official, now a senior pupil with limited authority.

Prefer', *v.t.* to favour, like better. **Pref'erable,** *a.* more desirable. **Pref'erence,** *n.* a choice, the fact of liking better. **Preferen'tial,** *a.* manifesting a preference. **Prefer'ment,** *n.* promotion, esp. eccl.

Pre'fix, *n.* verbal element preceding main word to modify or qualify meaning. **Prefix',** *v.t.*

Preg'nant, *a.* gravid, with child, full of meaning. **Preg'nancy,** *n.*

Prehen'sile, *a.* capable of grasping.

Prehistor'ic, *a.* of time before written or recorded history.

Prej'udice, *n.* unfavourable or partial opinion formed without proper judgement. *v.t.* to injure by this. **Prejudi'cial,** *a.*

Prel'ate, *n.* high-ranking priest. **Prel'acy,** *n.*

Prelim'inary, *a. & n.* preparatory, introductory.

Prel'ude, *n.* a mus. introduction, a preface. *v.t. & i.* to introduce or precede.

Premature', *a.* untimely, too soon.

Prem'ier, *a.* chief, foremost. *n.* prime minister.

Prem'ise, *n.* previous statement from which inference is drawn, basis for statement. *v.t.* to introduce or base argument. *n. pl.* building and surroundings.

Pre'mium, *n.* a reward, bonus, regular payment for insurance policy, fee for being articled or apprenticed.

Premoni'tion, *n.* a foreboding, a presentiment.

Pre-occ'upy, *v.t.* to engage the mind completely.

Prepare', *v.t. & i.* to make something ready for use, get into suitable condition for, equip. **Prepara'tion,** *n.* act of making ready. **Prepar'atory,** *a.* **Prepar'edness,** *n.* state of being ready.

Prepon'derate, *v.i.* to exceed in number or weight. **Prepon'der-**

ant, *a.* outweighing. **Prepon'-derance,** *n.*

Preposi tion, *n. gram.* part of speech showing relation between n. & pron. it governs and other word.

Prepos'terous, *a.* absurd, contrary to common sense.

Prerog'ative, *n.* a peculiar right or privilege attached to certain position.

Pres'age, *n.* a foreboding, an omen. **Presage',** *v.t.*

Pres'byter (-bitt-), *n.* an elder in the Presbyterian church, a priest. **Presbyte'rian,** *a.* of church ruled over by council of elders. *n.* member of this church.

Pres'cience (Presh-), *n.* foreknowledge. **Pres'cient,** *a.*

Prescribe', *v.t. & i.* to advise med. remedy, to suggest, to direct for curative purposes. **Prescrip'tion,** *n.* a written med. remedy.

Pres'ence, *n.* being present, place where person is, carriage, appearance, nearness.

Pres'ent, *a.* being in a place personally, of the existing time. *n.* the time now passing.

Present', *v.t.* to give, submit, introduce socially, to exhibit, come forward, hold in position. **Pres'ent,** *n.* a gift. **Present'able,** *a.* fit to be introduced, proper in appearance. **Presenta'tion,** *n.* the act of presenting, the showing of a play etc.

Present'iment, *n.* a foreboding, a sense of approaching misfortune.

Preserve' (-zurv), *v.t.* to protect from spoiling or harm, to maintain. *n.* esp. as *n. pl.* fruit etc. preserved with sugar.

Preserva'tion, *n.* the act of preserving from injury or destruction. **Preser'vative,** *n. & a.* substance for or means of preserving.

Preside, *v.i.* to control, act as chairman. **Pres'idency,** *n.* office of a president. **Pres'ident,** *n.* chief executive of a republic, head of business corporation, association etc. **Presiden'tial,** *a.*

Press, *v.t. & i.* to compress, push, squeeze, urge, impose, weigh heavily on, smooth by ironing, hurry. *n.* a great crowd, newspapers and their journalists, a printing machine. **Press'-ing,** *a.* urgent.

Pres'sure, *n.* a great pressing on, extreme persuasion, weight of influence, force.

Prestidig'itator (-dij-), *n.* a juggler.

Prestige', *n.* influence, reputation.

Presume', *v.t. & i.* to take for granted, suppose, take liberties. **Presu'mable,** *a.* possible to expect. **Presump'tion,** *n.* reasonable probability, impudent assurance. **Presump'tive,** *a.* reasonably probable. **Presump'-tuous,** *a.*

Pretend', *v.t. & i.* to feign, make believe, make false claim. **Preten'der,** *n.* one who makes false claim. **Pretence',** *n.* **Preten'sion,** *n.* **Preten'tious,** *a.* ostentatious.

Pret'erite (-it), *a. & n. gram.* indicating past action.

Pre'text, *n.* a false excuse.

Prett'y, *a.* attractive to look at.

Prevail', *v.i.* to triumph, to be prevalent, persuade. **Prev'-alence,** *n.* a frequent occurrence or practice. **Prev'alent,** *a.* widespread.

Prevar'icate, *v.i.* to lie, equivocate. **Prevarica'tion,** *n.*

Prevent', *v.t.* to impede, stop from occurring or doing. **Preven'tion,** *n.* **Preven'tive,** *a.* serving to obstruct or deter.

Pre'vious, *a.* preceding, former.

Prey (Pray), *v.i.* to seize for food, to afflict. *n.* quarry, victim.

Price, *n.* cost, value, expense. **Price'less,** *a.* beyond value.

Prick, *v.t. & i.* to mark or pierce with pointed object, to sting, raise, spur. *n.*

Pric'kle, *n.* stinging feeling, small sharp point. *v.t. & i.* to feel or give prickly feeling. **Pric'kly,** *a.* thorny, tingling.

Pride, *n.* great self-opinion, self-dignity, arrogance. *v.t.* flatter oneself, be proud of.

Priest (Preest), *n.* person who performs rel. rites, clergyman. **Priest'hood,** *n.* the collective body of priests.

Prig, *n.* self-satisfied person. **Prigg'ish,** *a.*

Prim, *a.* prudish, very proper.

Pri'macy, *n.* office of archbishop, condition of being first in rank. **Pri'mate,** *n.* archbishop.

Pri'mary, *a.* basic, chief, original, first in time. *n.* primary colour, bird's large flight feather. **Pri'mal,** *a.* first, of the earliest age.

Prime, *a.* chief, principal. *n.* the best. **Pri'mer,** *n.* young child's schoolbook.

Prime, *v.t.* to load a gun, prepare a pump for action, impart information or instructions to, prepare (wood) for paint with preliminary compound.

Prime'val, *a.* pertaining to the earth's earliest history.

Prim'itive, *a.* crude, undeveloped.

Primogen'iture (-jen-), *n.* state of being first-born in a family, in some countries legal right of first-born to inherit all family property.

Prince, *n.* son of a monarch, close male relation of royal family, petty ruler. **Prince'dom,** *n.* **Prince'ly,** *a.* **Prin'cess,** *n.* **Principal'ity,** *n.* a prince's domain.

Prin'cipal, *a.* chief in rank, first in importance. *n.* head person, person represented by an agent.

Prin'ciple, *n.* motive, impulse, moral rule of action.

Print, *v.t. & i.* to produce lettering by means of type, to impress, reproduce photographically, publish. *n.* any reading matter produced by type, a mark, impression. **Prin'ter,** *n.* craftsman skilled in making and setting type. **Print'ing,** *n.* the setting of type, reading-matter in type.

Pri'or, *a.* preceding in time or importance. **Prior'ity,** *n.* precedence, condition of being first.

Pri'or, *n.* monastic superior. **Pri'ory,** *n.* small monastery ruled by prior.

Prism, *n.* solid with ends parallel and equal and whose sides form parallelograms, transparent body of this form which refracts light. **Prismat'ic,** *a.* pertaining to a prism, of spectrum formed by prism.

Pris'on, *n.* a gaol, a place for confining offenders. **Pris'oner,** *n.* person kept in prison.

Pris'tine (-teen), *a.* primitive, belonging to the past.

Pri'vate, *a.* not public, personal, confidential, pertaining to person's own affairs. **Pri'vacy,** *n.* condition of being private or undisturbed, seclusion.

Privateer', *n. hist.* a private ship permitted by special licence to act as warship.

Priva'tion, *n.* deprivation, need.

Priv'ilege, *n.* special right or favour. *v.t.*

Priv'y, *a.* confidential, secret, personal.

Prize, *n.* reward for good work or conduct, worthwhile aim, captured enemy ship. *a.* of excellent quality, prize-winning. *v.t.* to value greatly.

Pro, *adv.* in favour of.

Prob'able, *a.* likely, anticipated. **Probabil'ity,** *n.* likelihood.

Pro'bate, *n.* official sanction for executing of will.

Proba'tion, *n.* period of testing person's skill or good faith. **Proba'tioner,** *n.* person undergoing probation, esp. as young offender or hospital nurse in training.

Probe, *v.t.* to enquire into or examine closely. *n.* surg. instrument for examining wound.

Pro'bity, *n.* rectitude, honesty.

Prob'lem, *n.* a subject difficult to understand, in math. proposition requiring explanation. **Problemat'ic, problemat'ical,** *a.*

Probos'cis (-boss-is), *n.* a long snout, e.g. elephant's trunk.

Proceed', *v.i.* to go on, to progress, carry on. **Proce'dure,** *n.* a proceeding, a course of action, a manner of acting. **Procee'ding,** *n.* esp. as *n. pl.* the records or action in law or at a business meeting. **Pro'ceeds,** *n. pl.* esp. profits from an action.

Pro'cess, *n.* a series of actions, a continuous action, a method of operating, a summons or writ. *v.t.* to treat, work on.

Proces'sion, *n.* a ceremonial parade. **Proces'sional,** *a.* relating to this. *n.* church hymn.

Proclaim', *v.t.* to announce publicly, declare. **Proclama'tion,** *n.* official announcement.

Procras'tinate, *v.i.* to delay through laziness. **Procrastina'tion,** *n.*

Proc'tor, *n.* university disciplinary official.

Procure', *v.t.* to obtain, bring about. **Procur'able,** *a.* **Proc'urator,** *n.* legal agent.

Prod'igal, *a.* wasteful. *n.* a spendthrift. **Prodigal'ity,** *n.* improvidence, extravagance.

Prod'igy (-ji), *n.* extremely remarkable person or happening, precocious child. **Prodig'ious** (-dij-), *a.* huge, astonishing.

Produce', *v.t.* to bring forth, grow, make, to present, cause. **Prod'uce,** *n.* esp. what is cultivated. **Produ'cer,** *n.* grower or manufacturer, person who puts on a play. **Prod'uct,** *n.* anything resulting from cultivation, effort, thought etc. **Produc'tion,** *n.* the act or result of producing. **Produc'tive,** *a.* tending to produce. **Productiv'ity,** *n.*

Pro'em, *n.* a foreword.

Profane', *v.t.* to desecrate, treat irreverently. *a.* not sacred. **Profan'ity,** *n.* blasphemous conduct.

Profess', *v.t. & i.* to avow,

declare, claim. **Profes'sion,** *n.* a declaration, a job with special qualifications, the body of people working in a specific kind of job. **Profes'sional,** *a.* expert, not amateur, working for pay as opposed to pleasure. **Profess'or,** *n.* university teacher, head of university faculty. **Professor'ial,** *a.*

Proff'er, *v.t.* to offer.

Profic'iency, *n.* skill. **Profic'ient,** *a.* expert, skilled.

Pro'file, *n.* side view of face or other object, outline.

Prof'it, *n.* gain made from successful project, advantage, benefit. *v.t.* **Prof'itable,** *a.* **Profiteer',** *n.* greedy person who makes unreasonable profit.

Prof'ligate, *a.* dissolute, depraved. **Prof'ligacy,** *n.*

Profound', *a.* deep, intense, learned, solemn. **Profun'dity,** *n.*

Profuse', *a.* copious, abundant. **Profu'sion,** *n.*

Prog'eny (Proj-), *n.* children, descendants. **Progen'itor,** *n.* forefather.

Prognos'ticate, *v.t.* to foretell. **Prognostica'tion,** *n.* a prediction.

Pro'gramme, *n.* a plan of action, particulars of concert or play.

Progress', *v.i.* to move on, to improve, develop. **Pro'gress,** *n.* improvement, advancement, a forward movement. **Progres'sion,** *n.* **Progres'sive,** *a.* moving on regularly, having liberal ideas.

Prohib'it, *v.t.* to forbid. **Prohibi'tion,** *n.* the act of forbidding, esp. the selling of alcohol. **Prohib'itive,** *a.* tending to prohibit, esp. of very high prices.

Proj'ect, *n.* a scheme, plan. **Project',** *v.t.* & *i.* to hurl, fire, cast, jut out. **Projec'tile,** *n.* something fired or thrown. **Projec'tion,** *n.* something that obtrudes, the act of firing or throwing. **Projec'tor,** *n.* apparatus for showing films.

Proletar'iat, *n.* the working-classes. **Proletar'ian,** *n.* & *a.* a member of this, to do with this, dull, humdrum.

Prolif'ic, *a.* abundant fertile.

Pro'lix, *a.* tiresome, boring. **Prolix'ity,** *n.* tediousness of speech or style.

Pro'logue, *n.* introduction to poem or play.

Promenade (-ahd), *n.* an esplanade, *iron.* a walk for pleasure. *v.i.*

Prom'inent, *a.* conspicuous, eminent. **Prom'inence,** *n.* a noticeable feature, the condition of being well-known.

Promis'cuous (-misk-), *a.* indiscriminate, loose in morals. **Promiscu'ity,** *n.*

Prom'ise, *n.* a pledge, grounds for optimism. *v.t.* to give one's word, to hold out expectation of satisfaction or success. **Prom'ising,** *a.* likely to succeed or prove satisfactory.

Prom'issory, *a.* esp. as **p. note,** promise to pay.

Prom'ontory, *n.* headland, prominent geog. feature.

Promote', *v.t.* to inaugurate, raise in rank, to support. **Promo'tion,** *n.* advancement in position, the supporting of a cause. **Promo'ter,** *n.* patron, entertainment manager.

Prompt, *a.* ready, quick, on time,

alert. *v.t.* to stir into action, to suggest, to remind person forgetting acts or thoughts. **Promp'titude,** *n.* punctuality, readiness to act.

Prom'ulgate, *v.t.* to proclaim officially. **Promulga'tion,** *n.*

Prone, *a.* lying face downward, liable to.

Prong, *n.* sharp end of fork or horn.

Pro'noun, *n. gram.* word used in place of noun.

Pronounce', *v.t. & i.* to utter, enunciate, declare formally. **Pronounced',** *a.* marked, emphatic. **Pronounce'ment,** *n.* formal declaration. **Pronuncia'tion,** *n.* the way in which word should be spoken.

Proof, *n.* conclusive evidence, standard strength in alcohol etc., demonstration that something is true, a test, a preliminary printing so that corrections can be made, esp. as *n. pl. a.* resistant, treated against various contingencies.

Propagan'da, *n.* the dissemination of particular opinions or beliefs. **Propagan'dist,** *n.*

Prop'agate, *v.t. & i.* to spread abroad, cause to increase, multiply. **Propaga'tion,** *n.*

Propel', *v.t.* to urge or drive forward. **Propell'er,** *n.* bladed device through which engine-power passes to make ship etc. progress.

Propen'sity, *n.* a tendency or inclination.

Prop'er, *a.* right, fitting, decent, characteristic, real.

Prop'erty, *n.* possessions, anything owned, an attribute.

Proph'esy, *v.t.* to foretell, predict. **Proph'ecy,** *n.* **Proph'et,**

n. a forecaster, esp. in Bib. sense. **Prophet'ic,** *a.* predictive.

Prophylac'tic (Proffil-), *a. & n.* med. preventing disease.

Propin'quity, *n.* proximity, nearness.

Propit'iate, *v.t.* to appease. **Propitia'tion,** *n.* **Propi'tiatory,** *a.*

Propi'tious, *a.* auspicious, favourable.

Propor'tion, *n.* a part of, a ratio. **Propor'tional,** *a.* relative, in ratio. **Propor'tionate,** *a.* commensurate.

Propose', *v.t. & i.* to suggest, nominate, ask for hand in marriage. **Propo'sal,** *n.* the act of suggesting, a marriage-offer. **Proposi'tion,** *n.* a proposal, a suggestion for consideration, *math.* a problem.

Propound', *v.t.* to put forward for discussion.

Propri'etor, *n.* an owner of property, **Propri'etary,** *a.* of a proprietor, associated with an owner.

Propri'ety, *n.* proper conduct.

Prorogue', *v.t. & i.* to bring parliamentary session to an end without customary dissolution.

Proscribe', *v.t.* to banish, outlaw, prohibit. **Proscrip'tion,** *n.*

Prose, *n.* written or spoken language without metre. **Prosa'ic,** *a.* humdrum, dull.

Pros'ecute, *v.t. & i.* to bring before a court of law, to carry out an activity diligently. **Prosecu'tion,** *n.* the bringing of a lawsuit, the lawyer or party who prosecutes, the carrying out of something. **Pros'ecutor,** *n.* barrister who conducts prosecution, person who does this.

Pros'elyte, *n.* a convert, esp. rel. **Pros'elytize** (-it-yze), *v.t.* to seek to convert.

Pros'ody, *n.* principles of versification.

Prospect', *v.t. & i.* to search, esp. for gold etc. **Pros'pect,** *n.* a view, an outlook. **Prospec'tive,** *a.* anticipated, coming in the future. **Prospec'tor,** *n.* person examining territory for gold etc. **Prospec'tus,** *n.* explanation of proposed scheme.

Pros'per, *v.i.* to flourish, make good. **Prosper'ity,** *n.* success, well-being. **Pros'perous,** *a.*

Pros'titute, *n.* a whore. *v.t.* to sell oneself unworthily. **Prostitu'tion,** *n.*

Pros'trate, *a.* prone, overcome. **Prostrate',** *v.t.* to overwhelm, lay person down, cast oneself down. **Prostra'tion,** *n.*

Protag'onist, *n.* chief actor in drama.

Pro'tean (-te-an), *a.* variable, of many parts.

Protect', *v.t.* to guard, preserve, shield, defend. **Protec'tion,** *n.* means of protecting. **Protec'tive,** *a.* **Protec'tionism,** *n.* polit. doctrine of safeguarding home industries by heavy import-duty. **Protect'or,** *n.* champion, person who protects. **Protect'orate,** *n.* the protection of an undeveloped region or country by a stronger country which does not actually own it, the regime set up under the Cromwellians. **Prot'égé** (-ezhay), *n. lit.* one protected, person whose interests are encouraged by another.

Pro'tein (-teen). *n.* essential part or constituent of food.

Protest', *v.i.* to object to, to declare formally against. **Pro'test,** *n.* an objection. **Protesta'tion,** *n.* an affirmation, declaration. **Prot'estant,** *n. lit.* one who protests against R.C. church and therefore belongs to denomination separated from this. **Prot'estantism,** *n.* doctrine of this church.

Proto-, *pref.* meaning first, original, primitive, e.g. **Protoplasm,** *n.* essential living matter. **Prototype,** *n.* an original type. **Protozo'on,** *n.* most primitive kind of animal life.

Pro'tocol, *n.* system of diplomatic etiquette, draft agreement.

Protract', *v.t.* to prolong, draw to scale. **Protrac'tion,** *n.*

Protrac'tor, *n.* instrument for measuring & drawing angles.

Protrude', *v.t. & i.* to project, stick out. **Protru'sion,** *n.*

Protu'berance, *n.* a bulge. **Protu'berant,** *a.*

Proud, *a.* arrogant, manifesting self-pride, dignified.

Prove (Proov), *v.t. & i.* to show by evidence, to eventuate, show or accept as genuine.

Prov'enance, *n.* place of origin.

Prov'ender, *n.* fodder, foodstuffs.

Prov'erb, *n.* adage, maxim, moral expressed concisely.

Provide', *v.t. & i.* to supply, furnish with, equip, make arrangements for. **Provi'sion,** *v.t.* to supply, esp. with food. *n. pl.* foodstuffs.

Provi'ded. *conj.* on condition that.

Prov'idence, *n.* prudence, foresight, divine concern. **Providen'tial,** *a.* fortunate esp. by divine intervention.

Prov'ident, *a.* far-sighted, thrifty.

Prov'ince, *n.* division of a country, regions beyond the metropolis. Provin'cial, *a.* pertaining to the provinces, dull, limited in outlook. Provin'cialism, *n.*

Provi'sional, *a.* conditional, temporary. Provi'so, *n.* a conditional clause.

Provoke', *v.t.* to give rise to, to incite, anger. Provoca'tion, *n.* Provoc'ative, *a.*

Prov'ost, *n.* head of college or rel. order, Sc. mayor.

Prow, *n.* the bows of a ship.

Prow'ess, *n.* bold accomplishment.

Prowl, *v.t. & i.* to roam or lurk stealthily. *n.*

Prox'imity, *n.* closeness.

Prox'y, *n.* person authorized to act for another.

Prude, *n.* excessively prim person. Pru'dish. Pru'dery, *n.*

Pru'dent, *a.* cautious, wary. Pru'dence, *n.* Pruden'tial, *a.* sound in judgement.

Pru'rience, *n.* indulgence in lewd matters. Pru'rient, *a.*

Pry, *v.i.* to peer or interfere inquisitively.

Psalm (Sahm), *n.* sacred song from Bible. Psalm'ist, *n.* the writer of the Psalms.

Psal'ter (Sawl-), *n.* the Book of Psalms.

Psal'tery, *n.* Bib. stringed mus. instrument.

Pseu'do, *a.* false, sham.

Pseu'donym (Su-), *n.* false name, pen-name. Pseudon'ymous, *a.* written under an assumed name.

Psychi'atry (-ky-), *n.* the study and treatment of mental disorders. Psychi'atrist, *n.*

Psy'chic (Sy-kik), *a.* spiritual, pertaining to the soul or mind *n.* a medium.

Psy'cho-, *pref.* meaning soul or mind and used in various compounds, e.g. Psycho-analysis, *n.* the study of the mind as divided into the conscious and subconscious. Psychology, *n.* scientific study of the mind. Psychosomatic, *a.* of diseases caused or precipitated by an emotional defect etc.

Pto'maine (To-), *n.* poisonous substance in decaying organic matter.

Pu'berty, *n.* the age at which children reach sexual maturity.

Pub'lic, *a.* pertaining to the community in general, not private, openly known, owned by the public. *n.* people collectively. Pub'lican, *n.* landlord of an inn or public-house.

Pub'licize, *v.t.* to make known publicly, advertize. Pub'licist, *n.* person who writes on subjects of polit. & international interest. Public'ity, *n.* propaganda, advertising.

Pub'lish, *v.t.* to make widely known, to organize the process of issuing books etc. Pub'lisher, *n.* person engaged in the making and issuing of books.

Puck, *n.* hard rubber disk used in ice-hockey, traditional fairy.

Puck'er, *v.t. & i.* to wrinkle.

Pudd'ing (Pood-), *n.* food enclosed in flour mixture and cooked.

Pu'erile, *a* trivial, childish. Puerility, *n.*

Pu'gilist (-jil-), *n.* prize-fighter. Pu'gilism, *n.* prize-fighting. Pugilist'ic, *a.*

Pugnac'ity, *n.* tendency to fight. Pugna'cious, *a.*

Pul'monary, *a.* pertaining to the lungs.

Pul'pit (Pull-), *n.* raised enclosed platform for preacher.

Pulse, *n.* throbbing in artery caused by blood being pumped through. Pulsate', *v.i.* to throb as a pulse. Pulsa'tion, *n.*

Pul'verize, *v.t.* to grind to powder, destroy, beat. Pulveriza'tion, *n.*

Pum'ice (-miss), *n.* esp. as p. stone, light spongy lava used for cleaning purposes.

Pumm'el, Pomm'el, *v.t.* to beat with the fists.

Pump, *n.* apparatus for bringing water to surface, getting rid of water. *v.t. & i.* to work a pump or like a pump, *coll.* to get information from indirectly.

Pun, *n.* a play upon words.

Punch, *n.* a blow with the fist. *v.t.*

Punch, *n.* a tool or machine for making holes, indenting etc. *v.t.*

Punch, *n.* an alcoholic mixture flavoured with fruit juice or sugar.

Pun'cheon (-shun), *n.* large cask.

Punctil'ious, *a.* very particular in conduct etc.

Punc'tual, *a.* on time. Punctual'ity, *n.* promptness.

Punc'tuate, *v.t.* to make writing intelligible by dividing into sections by means of punctuation marks, to interrupt. Punctua'tion, *n.* the marking off in printing or writing of phrases, clauses, sentences etc.

Punc'ture, *v.t.* to pierce, make a hole in, deflate. *n.* deflation of balloon or tyre through hole in fabric.

Pun'dit, *n.* in India, a learned teacher, *iron.* learned authority.

Pun'gent (-jent), *a.* sharp, mordant. Pun'gency, *n.*

Pun'ish, *v.t.* to chastise, inflict penalty on for wrong-doing. Pun'ishable, *a.* Pun'ishment, *n.*

Pu'nitive, *a.* pertaining to punishment, intending to punish.

Punt, *n.* long flat-bottomed, square-ended pleasure boat propelled by pole. *v.t.*

Punt, *v.t.* to kick a ball long and high, to gamble on horses. Punt'er, *n.*

Pu'ny, *a.* feeble, undersized.

Pu'pa, *n.* chrysalis. Pu'pal, *a.*

Pu'pil, *n.* scholar, person receiving instruction.

Pu'pil, *n.* opening in iris of eye.

Pupp'et, *n.* miniature figure worked by wires or on gloves, person under control of someone else in spite of superficial independence.

Pupp'y, *n.* young dog.

Pur'blind, *a.* half-blind, stupid.

Pur'chase, *v.t.* to buy. *n.* the act of buying, something bought, a firm grasp. Pur'chaser, *n.* buyer.

Pure, *a.* unspoilt, unblemished, innocent, chaste. Pu'rify, *v.t. & i.* to make pure. Purifica'tion, *n.* Pu'rity, *n.*

Purge, *v.t.* to cleanse, now *polit.* to eliminate. *n.* a med. for cleansing the bowels, a medicine. Pur'gative, *n.* med. for purging.

Pur'gatory, *n. myth.* probationary state before admission into heaven. Purgator'ial, *a.*

Pu'rist, *n.* person paying sedulous attention to lit. style etc. Pu'rism, *n.*

Pu'ritan, *n.* bigoted person, one with harsh attitude to pleasure, extreme Protestant. **Pu'ritanical,** *a.* intolerant.

Purloin', *v.t.* to make off with, filch.

Pur'ple, *a. & n.* colour made from mixing red and blue, *fig.* royal power.

Purport', *v.t.* to profess, seem to mean. **Pur'port,** *n.* meaning or pretended meaning.

Pur'pose (-pus), *n.* intention, object, point. *v.t.* to intend. **Pur'posely,** *adv.* intentionally.

Purse, *n.* small pouch for money, *fig.* money. *v.t.* to close up as with a purse, to pucker.

Pur'ser, *n.* ship's accountant officer.

Pursue', *v.t.* to chase follow insistently, engage in. **Pursu'ance,** *n.* the act of pursuing or carrying out. **Pursu'ant,** *a.* pursuing, accordingly. **Pursu'er,** *n.* **Pursuit'** (-sute), *n.* a persistent chasing, hunt, an occupation.

Pusillan'imous (Pew-), *a.* timid, mean-spirited. **Pusillanim'ity,** *n.*

Puta'tive, *a.* supposed, reputed.

Pu'trid, *a.* decomposing. **Pu'trefy,** *v.t. & i.* to decompose.

Putrefac'tion, *n.* **Putres'cent,** *a.* in the process of decomposing.

Pyg'my, *n.* a dwarf, member of a dwarf Afric. race.

Pyja'mas (-jah-), *n. pl.* sleeping-suit.

Py'lon, *n.* tower used for supporting elec. cables, *arch.* gateway of Egypt. temple.

Pyorrhoe'a (-re-ah), *n.* disease of gums.

Pyr'amid, *n.* gigantic ancient Egyp. structure us. on square base with sloping sides meeting at apex, any shape resembling this. **Pyram'idal,** *a.*

Pyre, *n.* pile of inflammable material for ceremonial burning of corpse.

Py'ro-, *pref.* meaning fire and making various compounds, e.g. **Pyrotechnics,** *n. pl.* firework display or something resembling this, **Pyromania,** *n.* irresistible impulse to set fire.

Pyrr'hic, *a.* esp. as **P.-victory,** victory gained at excessive cost.

Pyx (Piks), *n.* container for consecrated bread, box in Royal Mint for sample coins which are tested at annual ceremony.

Q

Quack, *n.* sound made by duck, bogus med. practitioner. *v.i.*

Quad'rangle (Kwod-), *n.* four-sided plane, four-sided courtyard. **Quadrang'ular,** *a.*

Quad'rant, *n.* one-fourth of circumference of circle, instrument for measuring altitudes.

Quad'rate, *v.t. & i.* to square, to conform or cause to conform. **Quadrat'ic,** *a.* in math. containing a square.

Quadrilat'eral, *a.* four-sided.

Quadri-, *pref.* denoting four and used in various compounds & words e.g. **quadricentennial,** *a.*

of every four hundred years,
Quadruped, *n.* four-footed
animal, quadruple, *a.* four-fold,
etc.

Quaff (Kwof), *v.t. & i.* to drink
deeply.

Quag'mire, *n.* a quaking bog.

Quail, *v.i.* to flinch.

Quaint, *a.* attractively or mawkishly odd.

Quake, *v.i.* to tremble from
fear.

Qua'ker, *n.* nickname for
member of Society of Friends.

Qual'ify, *v.t. & i.* to moderate,
to become fit for post.
Qualifica'tion, *n.* skill or knowledge etc. that makes person
fit or competent for office, a
restriction or moderation.

Qual'ity, *n.* a characteristic, an
attribute, a degree of excellence, *iron.* the gentry. **Qual'-**
itative, *a.* pertaining to quality.

Qualm (Kwahm), *n.* uneasiness,
doubt, feeling of sickness or
fear.

Quandar'y (Kwon-), *n.* per-
plexing doubt or situation.

Quan'tity, *n.* a number or
amount. **Quan'titative,** *a.*

Quar'antine (-teen), *n.* state of
isolation to prevent spread of
disease. *v.t.*

Quarr'el, *n.* a bitter dispute, a
falling-out of friends, *arch.* a
crossbow bolt. *v.i.* to fight, fall
out, dispute. **Quarrelsome,** *a.*

Quarr'y, *n.* prey, hunted thing.

Quarr'y, *n.* surface excavation
for obtaining stone etc. *v.t. & i.*

Quart, *n.* measure of capacity,
two pints.

Quart'er, *n.* a fourth part, a district of town. as *n. pl.* lodgings.
v.t. to divide into quarters.

Quart'er, *n.* mercy, esp. arch. in
battle.

Quart'erdeck, *n.* upper deck at
stern of ship for use of officers.

Quart'erly, *a. & adv.* happening or falling due every three
months. **Quart'ermaster,** *n. mil.*
officer in charge of supplies, in
navy a steersman.

Quartet', *n.* set of four people,
esp. four musicians, mus. for
four instruments.

Quart'o, *n.* size of paper obtained by folding sheet twice,
giving four leaves.

Quartz, *n.* very common hard
mineral, sometimes with gold.

Quash, *v.t. leg.* to set aside a
judgement, declare void, subdue.

Qua'si (Kway-), *conj. & pref.* as
it were, almost seemingly.

Quat'rain, *n.* four line stanza.

Qua'ver, *v.t. & i.* to shake, speak
in trembling voice. *n.* a trembling tone, in mus. half a
crotchet.

Quay (Kee), *n.* pier, landing-
stage.

Quea'sy (Kweezy), *a.* squeamish,
feeling sick.

Queen, *n.* female sovereign, wife
of king, chessman, most important bee in hive, court card
etc. **Queen'ly,** *a.* stately.

Queer, *a.* abnormal, strange,
odd.

Quell, *v.t.* to subdue.

Quench, *v.t.* to satisfy thirst, put
out flames.

Quer'ulous, *a.* peevish, whining.

Que'ry, *n.* a question, question-
mark. *v.t.* to question, call in
doubt.

Quest, *n.* a search, esp. in
romantic sense.

Ques'tion (Kwes-chun), *n.* the

act of inquiring or querying, a matter under discussion. *v.t.* to interrogate, dispute. **Ques'-tionable**, *a.* open to doubt. **Questionnaire'**, *n.* an interrogation in printed form.

Queue (Kew), *n.* a pig-tail, a line of people etc. awaiting their turn. *v.t. & i.* to wait in a queue.

Quib'ble, *v.i.* to equivocate, to argue pettily. *n.*

Quick, *a.* swift, nimble. *n.* living flesh. **Quick'en**, *v.t. & i.* to hasten, instil life into.

Quid'nunc, *n.* nosey-parker.

Quies'cent (Kwi-es-), *a.* tranquil, still. **Quies'cence**, *n.*

Qui'et, *a.* silent, undisturbed. *n.*, *v.t. & i.* **Qui'etude**, *n.* tranquillity.

Quie'tus (Kwy-e-), *n.* final blow, death, final settlement of debt.

Quill, *n.* large feather used as pen, long sharp spine.

Quilt, *n.* padded covering for bed.

Quinine' (-een), *n.* bitter drug formerly used for treating malaria.

Quinquenn'ial, *a.* happening every five years, lasting same.

Quin'sy, *n.* inflammation of throat and tonsils.

Quintess'ence, *n.* pure essence, perfect example. **Quintessen'-tial**, *a.*

Quintet', *n.* mus. for five voices or players, these performers.

Quin'tuplet (tupe-), *n.* one of five babies born at one birth.

Quip, *n.* a humorous or mordant remark.

Quire, *n.* 24 sheets of paper of uniform size.

Quirk, *n.* a quip, a mannerism, a twist of the pen.

Quis'ling, *n.* traitor who collaborates with enemy occupation forces.

Quit, *v.t.* to leave job or tenancy. *a.* free, rid of *n. pl.* even through payment or retaliation. **Quitt'ance**, *n.* discharge of a debt or obligation.

Quite, *a.* totally, entirely.

Quiv'er, *v.i.* to tremble, esp. from cold or fear. *n.* a tremulous movement, a sheath for arrows.

Quixot'ic (Kwiks-), *a.* extravagantly chivalrous.

Quiz, *v.t.* to cast an eye over, tease. **Quizz'ical**, *a.* comical, teasing.

Quiz, *n.* a game of question and answer entailing general knowledge.

Quoin (Koin), *n.* in architect. a cornerstone.

Quoit (Koit), *n.* iron or rubber ring in game of throwing. **Quoits**, this game.

Quon'dam, *a.* former, one-time.

Quor'um, *n.* minimum number of people required before assembly or committee can function.

Quo'ta, *n.* share to be contributed or received.

Quote, *v.t. & i.* to repeat somebody else's writings or remarks, to give an estimate in price. **Quota'tion**, *n.* a passage quoted, an estimate of price.

Quoth, *v.t. arch.* or *iron.* said, spoke.

Quotid'ian, *a.* daily, commonplace.

Quo'tient, *n.* result obtained by dividing one number by another.

R

Rabb'i (-by), *n.* ordained Jewish doctor of rel. law. **Rabb'inate,** *n.* his office, rabbis collectively. **Rabbin'ical,** *a.*

Rab'ble, *n.* disorderly mob.

Rab'id, *a.* infected with rabies, unreasonably furious, fanatical. **Ra'bies,** *n.* hydrophobia.

Race, *n.* group of people linked by common descent or united by language etc., a sub-division of the one human race, a breed of animals. **Ra'cialism,** *n.* bigoted policy advocating segregation of races.

Race, *n.* competition in speed, a fast concentrated current of water, a career, life. *v.t. & i.* to run swiftly, to engage in speed competition, to enter for a race. **Ra'cy,** *a.* exciting, distinctively flavoured.

Ra'ceme (seem), *n.* bot. flower-cluster in which separate flowers occur at intervals on stalk.

Rack, *n.* wooden framework or stand for objects, mediaeval instrument of torture for stretching person's limbs, toothed bar working in con-junction with cog-wheel. *v.t.* to torture on the rack, to extort, think hard, esp. as **rack one's brains.**

Rack, *n.* scudding clouds, de-struction, esp. as rack and ruin.

Rack'et, *n.* loud discordant noise, a swindle. *v.i.* **Racketeer',** *n.* gangster specializing in extorting protection money.

Rack'et, *n.* round-headed bat with crosswork of gut for tennis etc.

Ra'dar, *n.* use of high frequency radio waves for range and direction finding in ships and aircraft.

Ra'diance, *n.* brilliancy. **Ra'-diate,** *v.i.* to send out light or heat, spread generally. **Radia'-tion,** *n.* act of emitting rays, rays emitted by radio-active matter. **Ra'diant,** *a.* glowing, brilliant. **Ra'diator,** *n.* ap-paratus for spreading heat, cooling device in motor-car engine.

Rad'ical, *a.* fundamental, es-sential, advocating reform. *n. polit.* in favour of speedy reform or advance. **Rad'-icalism,** *n.* a polit. doctrine.

Ra'dio, *n.* wireless communica-tion.

Ra'dio-, *pref.* denoting of rays or radiation and of radium. esp. e.g. **Radio-active,** *a.* send-ing out invisible harmful rays as from radium and uranium etc. **Radio-therapy,** *n.* med. treatment by X-rays.

Ra'dium, *n.* metal resembling barium and used in producing X-rays.

Ra'dius, *n.* a straight line from

the centre of a circle to its circumference. **Ra'dial,** *a.* pertaining to radius.

Raff'ish, *a.* disreputable.

Raf'fle, *n.* a lottery. *v.t.*

Raft (Rahft), *n.* floating framework of timber, supplementary lifeboat in form of floating platform.

Raft'er (Rahf-), *n.* supporting beam in roof.

Rag, *n.* piece of cloth, tatter, a student street-performance for charity. *v.t.* to tease. **Rag'-amuffin,** *n.* unkempt boy in tattered clothes.

Rage, *n.* extreme anger. *v.t.* to give vent to furious anger, to storm.

Raid, *n.* a hostile incursion, a sudden descent. *v.t.*

Rail, *n.* bar of wood or metal between posts, steel bar as part of railway track. *v.t.* to enclose with rails, to send by rail.

Rail, *v.i.* to speak angrily or contemptuously.

Raill'ery, *n.* good-natured ridicule.

Rail'way, *n.* track for locomotives, organized system of train-transport. **Rail'road,** *n.*

Rai'ment, *n.* dress, clothing.

Rain, *n.* water falling in drops condensed from moisture in atmosphere, anything resembling this. *v.t. & i.* to fall as rain or like rain. **Rain'bow** *n.* arc of prismatic colours formed by reflection of sun's rays from falling rain.

Raise, *v.t.* to lift up, set up, cultivate, collect, stir up, elevate in rank or position.

Rake, *n.* agric. or hort. implement for loosening soil, gathering up. *v.t. & i.*

Rake, *n.* a dissolute person.

Rake, *n.* a slant. *v.t. & i.* to slant or caused to slant, to fire along the length of something. **Ra'kish,** *a.* fast-looking.

Rall'y, *v.t. & i.* to encourage after set-back, to muster, recover. *n.* a recovery, a special meeting, long bout of play in tennis.

Ram, *n.* male sheep, an instrument for battering, *hist.* a warship with special projecting underwater beak for ramming. *v.t.* to collide against deliberately, to thrust material in tight.

Ram'ble, *v.i.* to wander aimlessly, talk incoherently. *n.* a walk for pleasure.

Ram'ify, *v.i.* to divide into branches, subdivide. **Ramifica'-tion,** *n.*

Ramp, *n.* a graduated slope for going from one level to another.

Ram'page, *v.i.* to go about in fury. *n.* furious anger or excitement.

Ram'pant, *a.* rearing up on hind legs, esp. in heraldry, rampaging, uncontrolled. **Ramp,** *v.i.* to rear up on hind legs, to rage about.

Ram'part, *n.* top of fortified wall.

Ram'rod, *n.* rod for cleaning inside of gun-barrel or *arch.* for ramming home charge in muzzle-loader.

Ram'shackle, *a.* derelict.

Ranch, *n.* large Amer. cattle or horse farm. *v.i.*

Ran'cid, *a.* tainted, putrid.

Ran'cour, *n.* bitter hate, resentment. **Ran'corous,** *a.*

Ran'dom, *a.* haphazard.

Range, *v.t. & i.* to roam widely,

arrange in order, estimate distance, side with, vary, extend. *n.* a chain of mountains, an extent or limit, distance gun can fire, a place for practising shooting, a cooking stove. **Ran'ger,** *n.* a warden.

Rank, *n.* social or official position, mil. grade, line of troops, row or series of anything, high quality. *v.t. & i.* to classify, place in order, estimate quality.

Rank, *a.* rancid, coarse, extreme.

Ran'kle, *v.i.* to caused resentment, to fester.

Ran'sack, *v.t.* to search thoroughly and violently, to plunder.

Ran'som, *n.* payment made for release of captured enemy or kidnapped person. *v.t.* to release after payment of ransom.

Rant, *v.i.* to talk furiously and stupidly. *n.*

Rap, *v.t. & i.* to strike sharply but lightly.

Rap, *n.* a thing of small worth.

Rapa'cious, *a.* greedy, avaricious, grasping. **Rapac'ity,** *n.*

Rape, *v.t.* to ravish, seize by force. *n.* **Rap'ine,** *n.* pillage.

Rap'id, *a.* swift. *n. pl.* place in river where water flows rapidly and dangerously over rocks. **Rapid'ity,** *n.*

Ra'pier, *n.* light slender sword.

Rapscall'ion, *n.* a light-hearted rogue.

Rap'ture, *n.* ecstasy, great joy. **Rap'turous,** *a.* **Rapt,** *a.* entranced, absorbed.

Rare, *a.* very unusual, scarce. **Rar'ity,** *n.*

Rare, *a. coll.* undercooked, esp. of meat.

Rar'efy, *v.t. & i.* to refine, make or become less dense. **Rarefac'tion,** *n.*

Ras'cal, *n.* rogue, scamp.

Rash, *a.* impetuous, done without thought.

Rash, *n.* an eruption on the skin.

Rash'er, *n.* thin slice of bacon.

Rasp, *v.t. & i.* to abrade, scrape, irritate, make harsh noise. *n.* a filing tool.

Ratch'et, *n.* catch or brake to control toothed wheel or cog.

Rate, *n.* standard of reckoning, fixed charge, speed, degree. *n. pl.* local taxes *v.t. & i.* to estimate, fix value. **Rate'able,** *a.*

Rate, *v.t. & i.* to scold. **Ra'ting,** *n.*

Rath'er, *adv.* to a greater degree, more willingly, instead, on the contrary, somewhat.

Rat'ify, *v.t.* to make official, approve. **Ratifica'tion,** *n.*

Ra'ting, *n.* a naval seaman.

Ra'tio, *n.* proportion, relation in degree or quantity.

Rat'ion, (Rash-un), *n.* a fixed allowance esp. of food. *v.t.*

Rat'ional, *a.* based on reason, possessing the power of reasoned thought. **Rationalism,** *n.* the regarding of reason as the only basis for thought or action. **Rat'ionalist,** *n.* **Rat'ionalize,** *v.t.* to act according to reason, to explain esp. to explain away by reason. **Rational'ity,** *n.*

Rauc'ous, *a.* discordant, harsh.

Rav'age, *v.t.* to devastate, overrun. **Rav'en,** *v.t. & i.* to overrun or harry for food. **Rav'enous,** *a.* extremely hungry.

Rave, *v.i.* to speak or act dementedly, *coll.* to enthuse.

Ravine' (-een), *n.* a gully, a gorge.

Rav'ish, *v.t.* to enrapture, rape,

carry off. **Rav'ishing,** *a.* very attractive. **Rav'ishment,** *n.*

Raw, *a.* uncooked, untreated, inexperienced.

Ray, *n.* a beam, line of light. **Ra'dial,** *a.* pertaining to rays.

Raze, *v.t.* to obliterate.

Ra'zor, *n.* implement for shaving.

Reach, *v.t. & i.* to arrive at, attain, stretch out, make contact with. *n.* scope, extent, stretch of a river.

React' (Re-), *v.i.* to respond to another action, to rebound. **Reac'tion,** *n.* **Reac'tionary,** *n.* polit. person who wishes to retard progress. *a.* **React'or,** *n.* plant for generating power by nuclear fission. **Rea'gent** (Re-aj-), *n.* chemical substance reacting in certain way under certain conditions.

Read, *v.t. & i.* to peruse written or printed matter, to learn or understand by reading. **Read'-able,** *a.* legible, comprehensible by reading, interesting enough to read. **Read'er,** *n.* one who reads, a school-book for reading.

Read'y (Red-), *a.* prepared, willing.

Real (Re-), *a.* actual, existing, true. **Re'alism,** *n.* esp. in art and lit. the representation of subjects as they actually are. **Re'alist,** *n.* rationalist, unromantic person. **Realist'ic,** *a.* resembling life, unadorned. **Real'ity** (Re-al-), *n.* actuality.

Re'alize, *v.t.* to make real or possible, to gain as profit, to turn property into cash, to understand. **Realiza'tion,** *n.*

Realm (Relm), *n.* kingdom, domain.

Ream (Reem), *n.* twenty quires or about 480 sheets of paper.

Reap, *v.t. & i.* to cut, esp. a crop, to gain a benefit.

Rear, *n.* the hind part. *a.*

Rear, *v.t. & i.* to prance on hindlegs, to raise or lift up, to bring up, cultivate.

Rea'son, (Reezn), *n.* intellectual faculty, common sense, motive, cause. *v.t. & i.* to persuade by reason, to think something out. **Rea'sonable,** *a.* moderate, sensible.

Re'bate, *n.* a discount.

Rebel', *v.i.* to revolt, resist authority. **Reb'el,** *n.* person who does this. **Rebell'ion,** *n.* organized revolt. **Rebell'ious,** *a.*

Rebuff', *v.t.* to repulse, snub. *n.*

Rebuke', *v.t.* to chide, reprimand. *n.*

Rebut', *v.t.* to refute, oppose. **Rebutt'al,** *n.*

Recal'citrant, *a.* stubbornly disobedient. **Recal'citrance,** *n.*

Recant', *v.t. & i.* to abjure, revoke previous statement. **Recanta'tion,** *n.*

Recede', *v.i.* to move back, withdraw. **Reces'sion,** *n.* a withdrawal. **Reces'sional,** *n.* church hymn sung while priests are withdrawing. **Recess'ive,** *a.* tending to recede.

Receipt (-seet), *n.* official acknowledgement of payment, *arch.* a recipe.

Receive', *v.t. & i.* to obtain from someone else, to greet, experience. **Recei'ver,** *n.* person who receives, part of telephone, official in charge of bankruptcy case.

Re'cent, *a.* new, fresh, just happened.

Recep'tacle, *n.* holder, container.

Recep'tion, *n.* the act or manner or receiving, formal welcome.

Recep'tive, *a.* open to ideas, quick to comprehend.

Recess', *n.* an alcove, niche in wall, hollow, an official collective holiday as of parliament.

Rec'ipe (Ress-i-pe), *n.* detailed directions for cooking, *fig.* instructions or means of accomplishing something.

Recip'ient, *n.* person who receives. *a.* pertaining to receiving.

Recip'rocate, *v.t. & i.* to return, give and take, interchange. **Recip'rocal,** *a.* **Reciproca'tion,** *n.* **Reciproc'ity** (-prossi-), *n.*

Recite', *v.t. & i.* to recount, declaim aloud. **Reci'tal,** *n.* a performance for entertainment, a recounting. **Recita'tion,** *n.* a saying aloud from memory. **Recita'tive,** *n.* mus. narrative in opera etc.

Reck'less, *a* foolhardy.

Reck'on, *v.t. & t.* to calculate, consider. **Reck'oning,** *n.* a calculation, a determination of position, esp. a ship.

Reclama'tion, *n.* esp. the restoration of abandoned or poor land. **Reclaim'**, *v.t. & i.*

Recline', *v.t. & i.* to lie full length.

Rec'luse, *n.* hermit, person who deliberately lives alone.

Recog'nizance, *n.* legal pledge.

Rec'ognize, *v.t.* to identify, acknowledge acquaintance, admit. **Recogni'tion,** *n.* **Rec'ognizable,** *a.*

Recoil', *v.i.* to draw back from, rebound, spring back. *n.* the kick of a gun.

Recollect', *v.t.* to remember. **Recollec'tion,** *n.*

Recommend', *v.t.* to advise, entrust, speak or write of favourably. **Recommenda'tion,** *n.*

Rec'ompense, *v.t.* to reward, give in place of. *n.*

Rec'oncile, *v.t.* to bring back to friendship, resign to, make compatible, compose a quarrel. **Reconcilia'tion,** *n.*

Rec'ondite, *a.* abstruse.

Recon'naissance, *n.* a survey of enemy or unknown territory. **Reconnoi'tre,** *v.t. & i.*

Record', *v.t.* to register, write down. **Rec'ord,** *n.* something recorded, a report, a best known performance, a device for recording mus. etc. *a.* best known, most remarkable. **Recor'der,** *n.* a kind of judge, a mus. instrument. **Record'ing,** *n.* act of recording for gramophone or radio.

Recount', *v.t.* to describe in detail.

Recoup', *v.t.* to regain esp. loss.

Recourse', *n.* an expedient, a resorting to for help.

Recov'er, *v.t. & i.* to regain, get better. **Recov'ery,** *n.*

Rec'reant, *a. & n.* faithless person.

Recrea'tion, *n.* sport, pastime, activity other than work.

Recrimina'tion, *n.* countercharge, counter accusation. *v.i.* **Recrim'inatory,** *a.*

Recrudes'cence, *n.* a renewal esp. e.g. of disease.

Recruit' (-kroot), *n.* a new member, a newly enlisted serviceman. *v.t. & i.* to enlist, to gather one's strength. **Recruit'ment,** *n.*

Rec'tangle, *n.* four-sided figure with four right-angles. **Rectang'ular,** *a.*

Rec'tify, *v.t.* to put right, correct. **Rectifica'tion**, *n.*

Rec'titude, *n.* correctness of thought or action integrity.

Rec'tor, *n.* parish priest, head of college. **Rec'tory**, *n.* rector's dwelling.

Rec'tum, *n.* lower end of great intestine.

Recum'bent, *a.* reclining.

Recu'perate, *v.t. & i.* to recover health. **Recupera'tion**, *n.* **Recu'perative**, *a.*

Recur', *v.i.* to happen again, to go back. **Recurr'ence**, *n.* **Recurr'ent**, *a.* returning at intervals.

Red, *a.* of colour like that of blood, primary colour of shades ranging from orange to crimson. **Redd'en**, *v.t.* to make red, blush. **Red-handed**, *a.* caught in the act.

Redeem', *v.t.* to regain something by discharging debt, to rescue. **Redeem'er**, *n.* **Redemp'tion**, *n.*

Red'olent, *a.* pleasantly reminiscent, esp. through fragrance. **Red'olence**, *n.*

Redoubt', *n.* supplementary fortification.

Redoubt'able, *a.* formidable.

Redound', *v.i.* to react, to recoil.

Reduce', *v.t.* to decrease, become or make small in size or quantity, lower, subdue, restore. **Reduc'tion**, *n.* a diminution.

Redun'dant, *a.* unnecessary, superfluous. **Redun'dancy**, *n.*

Reef, *n.* shelf of rock or sand near surface.

Reef, *n.* part of sail able to be rolled up. *v.t.* to roll up and secure sail.

Reek, *n.* an unpleasant smell. *v.i.*

Reel, *n.* device for winding fishing-line etc., strip of film. *v.t.* to wind on a reel.

Reel, *v.i.* to stagger.

Reel, *n.* Sc. dance.

Refec'tory, *n.* communal dining-room.

Refer' (-fur), *v.t. & i.* to mention, allude, consult, call attention, direct elsewhere. **Ref'erence**, *n.* the act of referring, a source consulted, an allusion, a recommendation.

Referee', *n.* an umpire, an adjudicator. *v.t. & i.* to arbitrate.

Referen'dum, *n.* a plebiscite.

Refine', *v.t.* to make fine or pure, remove blemishes. **Refine'ment**, *n.* freedom from blemishes, well-mannered.

Reflect', *v.t. & i.* to throw back light or heat etc., to give image of as in mirror, to meditate, to redound on. **Reflec'tion**, *n.* an image, careful thought, criticism. **Reflec'tive**, *a.* thoughtful.

Re'flex, *n. psycho-anal.* automatic reaction, a reflection or image.

Reform', *v.t. & i.* to improve, make progressive adjustment to polit. system, mend one's ways, rectify. **Reforma'tion**, *n.* the act of reforming, a rel. movement to eliminate abuses of the church, the establishment of Protestantism.

Refor'matory, *n.* a school for delinquents.

Refract', *v.t.* to bend rays from straight line. **Refrac'tive**, *a.* **Refrac'tion**, *n.*

Refrac'tory, *a.* wilfully disobedient, recalcitrant.

Refrain', *v.i.* to desist from.

Refrain', *n.* recurrent theme or words in song.

Refresh'ment, *n.* food or drink, stimulus. **Refresh'**, *v.t.* to give refreshment to, to invigorate.

Refrig'erate (-frij-), *v.t.* to cool or freeze in order to preserve. **Refrig'erator**, *n.* machine for doing this.

Ref'uge, *n.* protection, shelter. **Refugee'**, *n.* person fleeing from persecution or disaster.

Reful'gent, *a.* splendid, bright, shining. **Reful'gence**, *n.*

Refund', *v.t.* to pay back, compensate. **Re'fund**, *n.* rebate.

Refuse', *v.t. & i.* to decline to do, be unwilling to accept. **Refu'sal**, *n.*

Ref'use, *n.* rubbish, garbage, waste household matter.

Refute', *v.t.* to deny, disprove. **Refuta'tion**, *n.*

Re'gal, *a.* kingly, royal. **Reg'nal**, *a.* pertaining to the reign of a sovereign.

Regale', *v.t.* to give refreshment to sumptuously.

Regard', to look at, contemplate, relate to. *n.* a look, esteem. *n. pl.* greetings.

Regatt'a, *n.* an organized water-festival.

Re'gent, *n.* person appointed to govern during infancy or incapacity of sovereign. **Re'gency**, *n.*

Reg'icide, *n.* the murder or murderer of a king.

Regime' (Ray-jheem), *n.* a system of government, an organized way of living. **Reg'imen**, *n.* a system of diet, control.

Reg'iment, *n.* organized body of soldiers commanded by colonel. **Regimen'tal**, *a.* **Reg'-**iment, *v.t.* to rule by force. **Regimenta'tion**, *n.*

Re'gion (-jun), *n.* a district, territory with more or less distinct characteristics. **Re'gional**, *a.*

Reg'ister, *n.* an official record, range of voice or instrument, apparatus for registering. *v.t.* to record. **Registrar'**, *n.* official recorder, university official. **Reg'istry**, *n.* place or office where registers are kept. **Registra'tion**, *n.*

Regress', *v.i.* to return, go back. *n.* a going back, a deterioration. **Regres'sion**, *n.* **Regres'sive**, *a.*

Regret', *v.i.* to deplore, be distressed about. *n.* **Regret'ful**, *a.* **Regrett'able**, *a.* deplorable.

Reg'ular, *a.* occurring at fixed intervals, consistent, in order, normal, belonging to professional army. *n.* professional soldier. **Regular'ity**, *n.* **Regular'ize**, *v.t.* to make regular. **Regulariza'tion**, *n.*

Reg'ulate, *v.t.* to adjust, to rule. **Regula'tion**, *n.* an official rule. **Reg'ulator**, *n.* mechanical device, person who governs in accordance with regulations.

Regur'gitate, *v.t. & i.* to bring up deliberately from stomach, to cast up again. **Regurgita'tion**, *n.*

Rehabil'itate, *v.t.* to restore to former position or condition. **Rehabilita'tion**, *n.*

Rehearse' (-herse), *v.t.* to practise, narrate. **Rehears'al**, *n.* practice in preparation for performance.

Reign (Rain), *n.* royal power or rule, period of this. *v.i.*

Reimburse' (Re-im-), *v.t.* to indemnify, repay. **Reimburse'-ment**, *n.*

Rein (Rain), *n.* leather strap controlling horse. *v.t.*

Reit'erate (Re-it-), *v.t.* to repeat frequently. **Reitera'tion**, *n.*

Reject', *v.t.* to decline to have, refuse to take. **Rejec'tion**, *n.*

Rejoice', *v.t. & i.* to gladden, become joyful.

Rejoin'der, *n.* a retort. **Rejoin'**, *v.i.*

Reju'venate, *v.t.* to renew youth of. **Rejuvena'tion**, *n.*

Relapse', *n.* a deterioration, a falling back. *v.*

Relate', *v.t. & i.* to connect or be connected with, to narrate. **Rela'tion**, *n.* a connection, a relative. *n. pl.* contacts, state of affairs. **Rel'ative**, *n.* person connected by ancestry or marriage. *a.* comparative, pertaining to. **Relativ'ity**, *n.* philos. doctrine that space-time is a fourth dimension.

Relax', *v.t. & i.* to slacken, ease off, rest. **Relaxa'tion**, *n.*

Relay', *v.t.* to pass on by successive means. **Re'lay**, *n.* new supply of men or horses to take up running from others.

Release', *v.t.* to liberate, to put into public circulation, let go. *n.*

Rel'egate, *v.t.* to banish, dismiss, transfer to lower grade. **Relega'tion**, *n.*

Relent', *v.i.* to show mercy, become less severe. **Relent'less**, *a.* unmerciful.

Rel'evant, *a.* pertinent, having reference to, appropriate. **Rel'-evance**, *n.* **Rel'evancy**, *n.*

Reli'able, *a.* dependable. **Reliabil'ity**, *n.*

Rel'ic, *n.* something that re-

mains, a survival, a surviving trace. **Rel'ict**, *n. leg.* a widow.

Relief', *n.* alleviation, assistance, lessening of pain etc., succour, a sculptured design on flat surface. **Relieve'**, *v.t.* to lighten, take place of, raise siege.

Reli'gion, *n.* belief in a divine power, an organized system of faith and worship. **Reli'gious**, *a.* devout.

Relin'quish, *v.t.* to abandon, give up. **Relin'quishment**, *n.*

Rel'ish, *v.t.* to enjoy greatly. *n.* a taste, sauce.

Reluct'ance, *n.* unwillingness, hesitation. **Reluc'tant**, *a.*

Rely', *v.i.* to depend on, have confidence in. **Reliabil'ity**, *n.* dependability, trustworthiness. **Reli'able**, *a.* **Reli'ance**, *n.* trust, confidence.

Remain', *v.i.* to to stay behind, be left behind, continue in same state. *n. pl.* what is left of a dead person. **Remain'der**, *n.* the part left over, what is still unused.

Remand' (-mahnd), *v.t.* to return to custody pending trial.

Remark', *v.t. & i.* to comment, observe. *n.* **Remark'able**, *a.* worthy of comment, extraordinary.

Rem'edy, *n.* a medicine, anything that cures or helps correct. **Reme'diable**, *a.* capable of being put right or cured. **Reme'dial**, *a.* curative.

Remem'ber, *v.t. & i.* to call to or keep in mind, carry in the memory. **Remem'brance**, *n.* act or power of remembering, memory. **Remem'brancer**, *n.* royal official who collects debts owed to Sovereign.

Remind' (my'nd), *v.t.* to recall to memory. **Remind'er,** *n.* something that does this.

Reminis'cence, *n.* remembering, memories, events recalled or related. **Reminis'cent,** *a.* inducing memories, suggestive of past things.

Remiss', *a.* negligent, careless.

Remit', *v.t. & i.* to forgive, abate, send. **Remis'sion,** *n.* a lessening, a pardon, a remitting. **Remitt'ance,** *n.* the sending of money, the sum involved.

Rem'nant, *n.* remainder, esp. of material.

Remon'strate, *v.i.* to expostulate, protest. **Remon'strance,** *n.*

Remorse', *n.* repentance. **Remorse'less,** *a.* unrepenting, merciless.

Remote', *a.* aloof, far off, isolated.

Remove', *v.t. & i.* to put in another place, take away, move house. **Remov'al,** *n.*

Remunera'tion, *n.* payment, reward. **Remu'nerate,** *v.t.* **Remu'nerative,** *a.* rewarding, profitable.

Renais'sance, *n.* a rebirth, a revival, esp. of the arts during 15th and 16th centuries. **Renas'cence,** *n.* the same, **Rena'scent,** *a.* being reborn, flourishing again.

Rend, *v.t. & i.* to tear.

Ren'der, *v.t.* to give, pay, cause to be, yield, melt down, perform, express. **Render'ing,** *n.* a way of playing or expressing.

Rend'ezvous (-day-voo), *n.* an appointed meeting or meeting-place. *v.t. & i.*

Ren'egade, *n.* traitor, deserter.

Renounce', *v.t. & i.* to disown, give up. **Renuncia'tion,** *n.*

Ren'ovate, *v.t.* to repair, refurbish. **Renova'tion,** *n.*

Renown', *n.* fame, celebrity.

Rent, *n.* periodical payment for use of property. *v.t. & i.* to let out for rent, to occupy as tenant.

Repair', *v.t.* to mend, put in order. *n.* esp. *n. pl.* work done to repair.

Repair', *v.i.* to go.

Repara'tion, *n.* esp. as *n. pl.* compensation for damage done in war.

Repartee', *n.* quick-witted reply.

Repast', *n.* a meal.

Repat'riate, *v.t. & i.* to restore or return to native country. **Repatria'tion,** *n.*

Repeal', *v.t.* to cancel, rescind. *n.*

Repeat', *v.t.* to do or utter again. **Repeti'tion,** *n.* **Repeti'tive,** *a.*

Repel', *v.t.* to check, hold back, reject. **Repell'ent,** *a.* driving back, esp. through disgust.

Repent', *v.t. & i.* to regret wrong action. **Repen'tant,** *a.* **Repent'ance,** *n.*

Repercus'sion, *n.* reverberation, violent reaction.

Rep'ertory, *n.* a collection of songs, plays. **Rep'ertoire** (-twar), *n.*

Repine', *v.t.* to complain, fret.

Replen'ish, *v.t.* to fill again.

Replete', *a.* entirely filled, esp. with food. **Reple'tion,** *n.*

Rep'lica, *n.* duplicate, exact copy.

Reply', *v.t. & i.* to answer. *n.*

Report', *v.t. & i.* to give an account of, to make an official statement, bring back information, inform against. *n.* Report'er, *n.* person who gathers and writes news for newspaper.

Report', *n.* a loud explosive noise.

Repose', *v.t. & i.* to lie, to rest. *n.* rest.

Repose', *v.t.* to put, to lay.

Repos'itory, *n.* a receptacle, a place for safekeeping, a storehouse.

Reprehend', *v.t.* to reprimand, blame. Reprehen'sible, *a.* blameworthy.

Represent', *v.t.* to act for another person, to stand for, portray, describe. Representa'tion, *n.* the act of representing, a portrayal. Represen'tative, *a.* typical. *n.* person who represents.

Repress', *v.t.* to subdue, restrain. Repres'sive, *a.* Repres'sion, *n.*

Reprieve', *v.t.* to let off or free, remit sentence. *n.*

Rep'rimand, *v.t.* to reprehend, rebuke. *n.*

Repri'sal, *n.* retaliation, esp. for damage done by enemy.

Reproach', *v.t.* to rebuke. *n.* Reproach'ful, *a.*

Rep'robate, *n.* dissolute person. *v.t.* to disapprove of greatly. Reproba'tion, *n.*

Reprove', *v.y.* to rebuke, scold, chide. Reproof', *n.*

Rep'tile, *n.* crawling, cold-blooded animal. Reptil'ian, *a.*

Repub'lic, *n.* system of government in which head of state is elected instead of being hereditary as monarch. Repub'lican, *n.* supporter of this as opposed to monarchist. *a.*

Repu'diate, *v.t.* to renounce, disown. Repudia'tion. *n.*

Repug'nance, *n.* extreme disgust. Repug'nant, *a.* offensive.

Repulse', *v.t.* to drive off, rebuff. Repul'sion, *n.* Repul'sive, *a.* loathsome.

Reputa'tion, *n.* esteem, high opinion, standing. Rep'utable, *a.* respectable. Repute', *n.* fame, rumour. Repu'ted, *a.* believed to be.

Request', *v.t.* to ask for earnestly. *n.*

Req'uiem, *n.* solemn rel. service for dead person.

Require', *v.t. & i.* to need, demand, call for. Require'ment, *n.* a need, necessary condition.

Req'uisite (-zit), *n.* an absolute necessity, a requirement. *a.* essential. Requisi'tion, *n.* something needed and taken officially. *v.t.* to demand and seize by authority.

Requite', *v.t.* to repay, esp. e.g. kindness or evil. Requi'tal, *n.*

Re'scind (-sin-), *v.t.* to repeal, cancel.

Res'cue, *v.t.* to save from danger or difficulty. *n.* Res'cuer, *n.*

Research', *n.* expert study to obtain detailed information. *v.i.*

Resem'ble, *v.t.* to be similar to. Resem'blance, *n.* similarity.

Resent', *v.t.* to take umbrage, feel bitterness, be indignant. Resent'ment, *n.* Resent'ful, *a.*

Reserve', *v.t.* to retain for future use, hold over, postpone, retain control of. *n.* qualification, supplementary supply, aloofness, territory devoted to special purpose, substitute. Reserva'tion, *n.* reserving, condition, booking made in advance.

Res'ervoir (-vwar), *n.* a reserve store, large water supply.

Reside', *v.i.* to dwell. Res'idence, *n.* private house. Res'ident, *n* & *a.* person living in a place. Residen'tial, *a.* of district comprised of private houses.

Res'idue, *n.* remainder, balance. Resid'ual, *a.* & *n.* remaining. Resid'uary, *a.*

Resign', *v.t.* & *i.* to give up, retire. Resigna'tion, *n.*

Resil'ient, *a.* elastic, buoyant. Resil'ience, *n.* *fig.* power of recovery.

Res'in, *n.* sticky exudation from trees. Res'inous, *a.*

Resist', *v.t.* & *i.* to repel, oppose. Resis'tance, *n.* act or power of opposing. Resist'ant, *a.*

Res'olute, *a.* steadfast, determined. Resolu'tion, *n.*

Resolve', *v.t.* & *i.* to disintegrate, transform. to determine, decide. Resolu'tion, *n.* a decision confirmed by vote at meeting.

Res'onant, *a.* resounding, echoing. Res'onance, *n.*

Resort', *v.t.* to frequent, turn to esp. for help. *n.* a vacation centre, means, expedient.

Resound', *v.i.* to ring out, sound loudly.

Resource', *n.* ability to deal with difficulty. *n. pl.* reserves, supplementary supply. Resource'ful, *a.* capable.

Respect', *v.t.* to hold in esteem, to head, relate to. *n. pl.* expression of friendship. Respec'table, *a.* presentable, reputable. Respect'ful, *a.* deferential. Respec'ting, *prep.* concerning, in connection with.

Respec'tive, *a.* particular, relating to each of several, individual, comparative.

Respira'tion, *n.* the process of breathing. Respir'atory, *a.* pertaining to this. Respire', *v.t.* & *i.* to breathe.

Res'pite (-pit), *n.* relief, reprieve, breathing-space.

Resplen'dent, *a.* brilliant, magnificent.

Response', *n.* an answer. Respond', *v.i.* Respon'sive, *a.*

Responsibil'ity, *n.* obligation, duty. Respon'sible, *a.* answerable for, reliable.

Rest, *v.i.* to pause from work, to sleep, lie down, lean, be supported, rely, remain. *n.* repose, peace of mind, the remainder, something that supports. Rest'ive, *a.* not resting, fidgety.

Res'taurant, *n.* a public place for eating. Restaurateur', *n.* manager or owner of this.

Restitu'tion, *n.* compensation, return.

Restore', *v.t.* to return, replace, reinstate. Restora'tion, *n.* Restor'ative, *a.* & *n.* means or power of restoring.

Restrain', *v.t.* to hold back, suppress. Restraint', *n.*

Restrict', *v.t.* to confine within bounds. Restric'tion, *n.* Restric'tive, *a.* tending to restrict.

Result', *v.i.* to happen, to arise or follow as consequence. *n.* outcome, effect. Resul'tant, *a.*

Resume', *v.t.* to start again. Resump'tion, *n.*

Resurrect', *v.t.* to bring back from the dead. Resurrec'tion, *n.*

Resus'citate, *v.t.* to revive. Resuscita'tion, *n.*

Retail', *v.t.* & *i.* to sell in small amounts as from ordinary shop, to recount. **Re'tail,** *n.* the sale of goods to ordinary consumers. *a.* **Re'tailer,** *n.* shopkeeper.

Retain', *v.t.* to keep in possession, mind, use, engage services of in advance, esp. barrister. **Retainer,** *n.* fee for latter, servant, esp. in feudal sense.

Retal'iate, *v.t. & i.* to repay for injury by same, to make reprisal. **Retalia'tion,** *n.* **Retalia'tory,** *a.*

Retard', *v.t.* to delay, hinder.

Retch, *v.i.* to vomit or try to.

Reten'tion, *n.* the act of retaining. **Reten'tive,** *a.* possessing power of retaining.

Ret'icence, *n.* verbal restraint or silence. **Ret'icent,** *a.*

Ret'ina, *n.* sensitive membrane at back of eye which receives image.

Ret'inue, *n.* a following of attendants.

Retire', *v.t. & i.* to give up office, withdraw, retreat. **Retire'ment,** *n.* seclusion, state of having given up work. **Retir'ing,** *a.* shy.

Retort', *v.t. & i.* to reply sharply, in kind. *n.* a quick or angry reply.

Retort', *n.* glass vessel used in chem.

Retract', *v.t. & i.* to recant, draw in or back. **Retrac'tion,** *n.*

Retreat', *v.i.* to withdraw, retire. *n.* withdrawal in face of enemy, a solitary place.

Retrench', *v.t. & i.* to decrease, esp. expenses. **Retrench'ment,** *n.*

Retribu'tion, *n.* requital, penalty for sin. **Retrib'utive,** *a.*

Retrieve', *v.t. & i.* to regain possession of, get back, rescue,

recover, fetch. **Retriev'er,** *n.* gun-dog for retrieving.

Ret'rograde, *a.* deteriorating, moving back. **Retrogres'sion,** *n.* **Retrogres'sive,** *a.*

Ret'rospect, *n.* a review of time or events past. **Retrospec'tion,** *n.* a contemplation of these. **Retrospec'tive,** *a.*

Return', *v.t. & i.* to give back, to go back, to answer, to yield, esp. a profit. *n.*

Reveal', *v.t.* to uncover, make known. **Revela'tion,** *n.* a disclosure, a divine communication.

Rev'el, *v.i.* to make merry, enjoy greatly. *n.* festivity. **Rev'-elry,** *n.* merrymaking. **Rev'-eller,** *n.*

Revenge', *n.* retaliation, the inflicting of a counter-injury. *v.t.* to exact satisfaction for wrong done. **Revenge'ful,** *a.*

Rev'enue, *n.* income, esp. government income from taxation.

Rever'berate, *v.t. & i.* to resound, echo. **Reverbera'tion,** *n.*

Revere', *v.t.* to respect greatly, venerate. **Rev'erence,** *n.* respect, honour, sign or gesture of this, clergyman's title. **Rev'-erend,** *a.* worthy of reverence. *n.* also clergyman's title. **Rev'-erent,** *a.* manifesting reverence.

Rev'erie, *n.* deep meditation.

Reverse', *v.t. & i.* to turn or move backwards, go the opposite way. *n.* a defeat, setback. *a.* opposite, backward. **Revers'al,** *n.* **Rever'sible,** *a.*

Revert', *v.i.* to return to subject or condition. **Rever'sion,** *n.* a return.

Review', *v.t. & i.* to revise, re-examine, criticize work of art or lit., to inspect troops. *n.*

Revile', *v.t.* to malign, abuse.

Revise', *v.t.* to correct, alter, reconsider. **Revis'ion**, *n.*

Revive', *v.t.* & *i.* to recover, resuscitate, bring into use again. **Revi'val**, *n.* **Revi'valist**, *n.* person who tries to stimulate interest in rel.

Revoke', *v.t.* & *i.* to cancel, reverse, play card of wrong suit. **Revoca'tion**, *n.*

Revolt', *n.* a rebellion. *v.i.* to rebel.

Revolt', *v.t.* to disgust. **Revol'-ting**, *a.*

Revolu'tion, *n.* violent polit. change, any radical change, the turning of an object round a central point. **Revolu'tionary**, *n.* person who engages in or advocates violent polit. change. *a.* pertaining to sudden change. **Revolu'tionize**, *v.t.* to bring about drastic change.

Revolve', *v.t.* & *i.* to rotate, to turn or cause to turn. **Revol'-ver**, *n.* something that revolves, esp. pistol with revolving cartridge-chamber.

Revue', *n.* theatrical show with mus. and sketches.

Revul'sion, *n.* sudden turning away from, sudden feeling of distaste.

Reward' (Re-), *n.* payment or prize for meritorious conduct, remuneration, payment for information. *v.t.*

Rhet'oric (Ret-), *n.* oratory, showy speech or writing, prop. the art of fine speaking. **Rhetor'ical**, *a.* **Rhetor'ician**, *n.* person skilled in R.

Rheu'matism, *n.* (Room-) painful disease caused by inflammation of joints. **Rheumat'ic**, *a.*

Rhom'bus (Rom-), *n.* diamond-shaped figure. **Rhom'boid**, *n.* & *a.* similar to a rhombus.

Rhyme (Ryme), *n.* identity of sound esp. between ultimate words in lines of poetry. *v.t.* & *i.* to end in corresponding sounds, to cause this. **Rhyme'-ster**, *n.* an inferior poet.

Rhyth'm (Rith'm), *n.* regular and harmonious movement or sound. **Rhyth'mic**, *a.* **Rhyth'-mical**, *a.* marked by regularly repeated movement or stress.

Rib, *n.* one of series of human and animal bones attached to spine and protecting lungs etc., anything resembling a rib. *v.t.* to mark or enclose with ribs.

Rib'ald, *a.* vulgar. **Rib'aldry**, *n.* vulgarity, coarseness.

Rich, *a.* wealthy, fertile, abundant, mellow, very sweet. **Rich'-es**, *n. pl.* great wealth. **Rich'-ness**, *n.*

Rick, *n.* a stack.

Rick, *v.t.* to strain.

Rick'ets, *n.* infantile disease characterized by feeble limbs. **Rick'ety**, *a.* feeble.

Ricochet' (-shay), *v.i.* to glance off without penetrating. *n.*

Rid, *v.t.* to get free of, detach, clear away. **Ridd'ance**, *n.*

Rid'dle, *n.* a puzzle, mystery, conundrum.

Rid'dle, *n.* a sieve. *v.t.* to sift, to pierce with holes as in a riddle.

Ride, *v.t.* & *i.* to travel on horseback or in a vehicle, of ship to lie at anchor, to oppress. *n.* a journey on horseback etc. **Ri'der**, *n.* person who rides a horse.

Ri'der, *n.* qualifying clause.

Ridge, *n.* a long projection, a line of hills, a corrugation. *v.t.*

& i. to mark or become marked with ridges.

Rid'icule, n. derision, mockery. v.t. to make fun of. **Ridic'-ulous,** a. laughable, absurd.

Rife, a. prevalent, widespread.

Riff'-raff, n. rabble, trash.

Ri'fle, n. firearm with long barrel grooved spirally inside.

Ri'fle, v.t. to break open and steal.

Rift, n. a separation, an opening. v.t. to split.

Rig, v.t. to equip ship etc. with necessary sailing items, to erect. n. arrangement of ship's sails etc., style of dress. **Rigg'-ing** n. sailing gear.

Right, a. correct, straight, suitable, honest, right-hand. honourable, just, right-hand side, in polit. conservative, thought. adv. straight, direct. v.t. & i. to correct, put straight, amend. **Rights,** n. entitlement, what is due to one. **Right'ful,** a. fair, proper, have a legal claim.

Right'eous (Ry-chus), a. virtuous, justifiable.

Rig'id (Rij-), a. stiff, harsh. **Rigid'ity,** n.

Rig'marole, n. nonsensical procedure, unnecessary verbiage.

Rig'our, n. severity. **Rig'orous,** a. severe, harsh.

Rile, v.t. to vex, annoy.

Rill, n. a brook.

Rim, n. edge, brim. v.t. to put a brim round.

Rime, n. hoar-frost.

Ri'nd, n. peel, outer skin.

Ring, n. a circular band, metal ornament to go round finger, any circular shape or place, collection of people with common purpose, business cartel. v.t. to encircle, put ring on. **Ring'leader,** n. leader of ring of people, esp. in lawless sense.

Ring, v.t. & i. to to push or work bell to make ringing sound, to telephone, resound, call by bell. n. a sound made by ringing a bell or striking object to make similar sound.

Rink, n. an artificial expanse of ice for skating, etc.

Rinse, v.t. to clean by dipping and squeezing out in water, to wash out with water. n.

Ri'ot, n. disorder, rowdy behaviour. v.i. to start or take part in riot. **Ri'otous,** a.

Rip, v.t. & i. to tear apart, rend. n. a tear.

Rip, n. worthless person, tide-race.

Ripar'ian (-pare-), a. pertaining to a river-bank.

Ripe, a. mature, mellow, fit. **Ri'pen,** v.t. & i. to make or become ripe. **Ripe'ness,** n.

Rip'ple, n. a tiny wave. v.t. & i. to flow gently, form ripples.

Rise, v.i. to go up, get up, ascend, increase, revolt, cope with. **Ri'sing,** n. an elevation, a revolt.

Ris'ible, a. laughable.

Risk, v.t. to hazard, take a chance. n. danger, hazard. **Risk'y,** a.

Rite, n. solemn observance, old-established ceremony. **Rit'ual,** a. pertaining to this. **Rit'ualism,** n. sedulous adherence to rite. **Rit'ualist,** n. **Ritualist'-ic,** a.

Ri'val, n. competitor, opponent. v.t. to compete with, match. a. **Ri'valry,** n. competition.

Riv'er, *n.* large natural flow of water.

Riv'et, *n.* metal bolt for securing metal plates or parts. *v.t.* to secure with rivets, to concentrate (fig.). Riv'eter, *n.* craftsman in riveting.

Riv'ulet, *n.* a rill, small stream.

Road, n. a thoroughfare, a made track for definite use, a way by which something is attained.

Road'stead, *n.* anchorage for ships.

Roam, *v.t. & i.* to wander, ramble.

Roan, *a. & n.* esp. of horse whose dominant colour is interspersed with another, e.g. reddish brown with grey.

Roar, *n.* a deep hoarse cry or sound. *v.t. & i.*

Roast, *v.t. & i.* to bake esp. meat, to cook by heat. *n.* a piece of roasted meat.

Rob, *v.t. & i.* to steal from, thieve. Robb'er, *n.* thief. Robb'ery, *n.*

Robe, *n.* a loose outer garment of formal kind. *v.t. & i.* dress, esp. in robe.

Ro'bot, *n.* machine made to act like human, person who behaves mechanically.

Robust', *a.* vigorous, sturdy.

Rock, *n.* large stone or mass of stone, mineral substance. Rock'ery, *n.* mound of stones interspersed with soil for growing plants whose natural habitat this resembles.

Rock, *v.t. & i.* to move backwards and forwards, to swing, shake violently. Rock'er, *n.* curved contrivance on bottom of chair or cradle to cause rocking movement.

Rock'et, *n.* firework capable of being projected for display, signalling, carrying line etc., *mil.* missile.

Roco'co, *n. & a.* excessively decorated.

Rod, *n.* a long jointed cane or similar contrivance for fishing, a stick for beating, an iron-bar, a measure of length of $5^1/_8$ yds.

Ro'dent, *a.* gnawing. *n.* one of various gnawing animals.

Rode'o (-day-o), *n.* display of cowboy's skill.

Rodomontade', *n.* bragging talk.

Roe, *n.* eggs or spawn of fish.

Roga'tion, *n.* litany preceding Ascension Day.

Rogue, *n.* a scoundrel, savage animal, esp. as applied to elephant. Ro'guery (ger-), *n.* mischievous or dishonest practice.

Ro'guish, *a.* mischievous.

Rois'ter, *v.i.* to swagger, revel noisily. Roist'erer, *n.* Roist'erous, *a.*

Role, *n.* an actor's part, person's function.

Roll, *v.t. & i.* to move or cause to move over and over, to push along on wheels or similar, to wrap oneself up, to utter reverberant sound, undulate, to flatten or smooth by rolling. Roll, *n.* a rolling movement, wrapped up in circular fashion, a reverberating sound, a swelling of the sea, a list of names. Roll call, *n.* a calling out of names from such a list. Roll'er, *n.* a long rolling wave, an instrument for rolling a lawn or pastry. Rolling stock, *n.* movable equipment on railway. Rolling mill, *n.* factory in which iron or steel is made into different forms.

Roll'ick, *v.i.* to frolic. **Roll'-icking**, *a.* gay, merry.

Romance', *n.* orig. a mediaeval story of chivalry and love, now any imaginative, sentimental story, a love encounter. *v.i.* exaggerate fancifully. **Roman'tic**, *a.* idyllic, poetic. **Roman'ticism**, *n.*

Rom'any, *n.* a gypsy, his language.

Romp, *n.* a frolic. *v.i.*

Rond'o, *n.* mus. composition in which main theme is repeated.

Rood, *n.* crucifix.

Rood, *n.* quarter of an acre, any small measure of land.

Room, *n.* division of house, space, chamber. **Room'y**, *a.* with adequate space, spacious.

Roost, *n.* a perch for poultry, a place where birds sleep. *v.i.* **Roost'er**, *n.* cockerel.

Root, *n.* part of plant growing downward into soil and absorbing and processing nourishment from this, a source, a cause, origin. *v.t. & i.* to cause to root, become rooted, to grub about in the soil.

Rope, *n.* thick strong cord. *v.t.* to use rope in various ways. **Ro'py**, *a. sl.* inferior in sense of stringiness.

Ro'sary, *n.* chain of beads used in connection with reciting of prayers.

Rose, *n.* a thorny plant with beautiful and scented flowers, the colour of deep pink. **Ro'seate**, *a.* rose-coloured, flushed. **Rosette'**, *n.* small bunch of ribbon in rose-form. **Ro'sy**, *a.* rose-coloured, hopeful.

Ros'ter, *n.* a schedule of duty.

Ros'trum, *n.* a platform for speaking from.

Rot, *v.t. & i.* to decompose, putrefy. *n.* decay, *sl.* balderdash, *n.*

Ro'ta, *n.* a roster.

Rotate', *v.t. & i.* to revolve, turn or cause to turn in circular fashion. **Rota'tion**, *n.* such a movement. **Ro'tary**, *a.* turning or rotating, pertaining to this.

Rote, *n.* learning by repetition.

Rotund', *a.* corpulent, plump. **Rotund'ity**, *n.* **Rotun'da**, *n.* circular building with domed roof.

Rouge, *n.* red cosmetic for lips and face. *v.t. & i.* to use this.

Rough (Ruf), *a.* harsh, violent, crude, uneven. *v.t.* to make rough, to draw preliminary sketch. *n.* a bully, a sketch, unfinished condition. **Rough'age**, *n.* coarse fodder. **Rough'en**, *v.t.* to make rough or coarse. **Rough-hew'**, *v.t.* to cut or shape with bold strokes. **Rough-rider**, *n.* bareback horse-rider. **Rough-shod**, *a.* esp. as to ride r.-s., to ignore other people's feelings.

Roulette', *n.* gambling game played with revolving wheel and lucky numbers.

Round, *a.* resembling a circle or sphere, full, whole, outspoken, curved, approximate. *adv. & prep.* nearby, in a circular movement, about, on all sides. *n.* a piece of toast, a hand of cards, a volley, a game of golf etc. *v.t.* to travel in a curved direction, to make round or curved, to develop.

Rouse, *v.t. & i.* to stir up, awake from sleep.

Rout, *n.* a defeat, a rabble. *v.t.* to defeat utterly.

Rout, *v.t.* to root out.

Route, *n.* (Root) course of a journey, a way. **Route-march,** *n.* (Rowt) a mil. march or exercise.

Routine' (Rooteen), *n.* customary practice.

Rove, *v.t. & i.* to ramble, wander over.

Ro'ver, *n.* a pirate, esp. as **Sea-rover.**

Row (Ro), *n.* a rank or series of people or objects.

Row (Ro), *v.t. & i.* to propel by means of oars.

Row, *n.* a quarrel, a discordant noise.

Row'dy, *n.* a thug. *a.* noisy and disorderly. **Rowdy'ism,** *n.*

Row'el, *n.* spiked wheel attached to spur.

Row'lock (Rollock), *n.* pegs on gunnel of boat for holding oars and providing leverage.

Roy'al, *a.* pertaining to a monarch or monarchy, magnificent, stately. **Roy'alist,** *n.* supporter of monarchical system. **Roy'alty,** *n.* station or dignity of a monarch, persons belonging to the royal family.

Roy'al, *n.* small sail above topgallant in sailing-ship.

Roy'al, *n.* stag with antlers of twelve or more points.

Roy'alty, *n.* percentage paid to author etc. according to sales.

Rub, *v.t. & i.* to scrape, move one substance against another, to apply friction. *n.* these actions, a hindrance. **Rubb'er,** *n.* an eraser, anything or anyone rubbing, in cards or games a certain number of rounds or contests.

Rubb'ish, *n.* refuse, balderdash.

Rub'ble, *n.* debris from building.

Ru'bicund (Roo-), *a.* red-faced.

Ru'bric (Roo-), *n.* directions in prayer-book, heading of chapter or special wording printed or written in red.

Ru'by, *n.* precious stone of various shades of crimson. *a.* of such a colour.

Ruck, *n.* a confused bunch of people.

Ruck'sack, *n.* haversack for hiker.

Rudd'er, *n.* flat hinged contraption at stern of vessel and connected with steering-wheel.

Rudd'y, *a.* rubicund, flushed.

Rude, *a.* ill-mannered, uncouth, rough.

Ru'diment, *n.* an undeveloped organ. *n. pl.* beginnings, basic principles. **Rudimen'tary,** *a.*

Rue (Roo), *n.* regret, remorse. *v.t. & i.* to regret wickedness or mistake. **Rue'ful,** *a.*

Ruff'ian, *n.* bully, rowdy.

Rug, *n.* small thick carpet or mat, heavy blanket.

Rug'by, *n. esp.* as rugby football, played with oval ball which may be handled as well as kicked. **Rugg'er,** *n.* abbrev.

Rugg'ed, *a.* tough, rough, uneven.

Ru'in, *n.* destruction, downfall. *v.t.* to destroy, cripple financially. **Ruina'tion,** *n.* destruction. **Ru'inous,** *a.* calamitous.

Rule, *v.t. & i.* to govern, decree, influence, direct. *n.* a common usage, a standard of behaviour, a regulation. **Ru'ler,** *n.* person who rules, a strip of wood or metal for measuring or drawing lines. **Ru'ling,** *n.* a decision, a ruled line. *a.* dominant.

Rum, *n.* strong alcohol distilled from sugar-cane.

Rum, *a. sl.* odd.

Rum'ble, *n.* a reverberating noise. *v.i.*

Ru'minate, *v.i.* prop. to chew cud, *coll.* to meditate. **Ru'minant,** *a.* & *n.* cud-chewing animal, e.g. cow. **Rumina'tion,** *n.* **Ru'minative,** *a.*

Rumm'age, *v.t.* & *i.* to search through roughly. *n.* trash.

Ru'mour, *n.* an unverified report. *v.t.* to put this about.

Rump, *n.* the buttocks, hind part of animal.

Rum'ple, *v.t.* to ruffle, crease.

Rum'pus, *n. sl.* trouble, uproar.

Run, *v.t.* & *i.* to move more rapidly than at a walk by putting each foot forward in turn without having both feet on ground at same time, to race, rush, hurry, operate, extend, continue, flow, discharge, be narrated, thrust etc. *n.*

Run'agate, *n.* fugitive, wanderer.

Run'away, *n.* bolting horse, fugitive.

Rune, *n.* (Roon) letter of early Teutonic alphabet, a mysterious primitive verse. **Ru'nic,** *a.* written in or to do with runes.

Rung, *n.* cross-bar in ladder.

Runn'el, *n.* a gutter.

Runn'er, *n.* one who runs or races, a mil. messenger, long narrow keel for facilitating movement of sleigh etc., trailing branch that takes root.

Runt, *n.* smallest pig in a litter.

Rup'ture, *v.t.* & *i.* to burst or break violently. *n.* a breach as of friendship, a hernia.

Ru'ral (Roor-), *a.* pertaining to the countryside or country life.

Ruse, *n.* a trick, a scheme.

Rush, *v.t.* & *i.* to press or drive forward, crowd in disorderly fashion, to capture by surprise. *n.*

Russ'et, *a.* & *n.* reddish-brown colour, kind of apple and cloth.

Rust, *n.* metal oxide formed on iron by exposure to moisture, a plant-fungus causing disease. *v.t.* & *i.* to make or become rusty. **Rust'y,** *a.* affected with rusty, stale, out of practice *coll.*

Rus'tic, *a.* pertaining to the countryside. *n.* a countryman, peasant. **Rust'icate,** *v.t.* to send down from university for misdemeanour, to live a secluded life in country. **Rustica'tion,** *n.*

Rus'tle (Russel), *n.* soft dry furtive movement. *v.i.*

Rus'tle, *v.t.* to steal cattle. **Rus'tler,** *n.* cattle thief.

Rut, *n.* a groove, furrow, *coll.* a dull unchanging existence. *v.t.* to mark with ruts or grooves.

Rut, *n.* periodic sexual activity esp. of deer. *v.i.* to be in sexual heat.

Ruth, *n.* mercy, pity, but us. only as **Ruth'less,** *a.* pitiless.

Rye, *n.* cereal related to wheat and used for bread-flour and basis of some inferior whisky.

S

Sabb'ath, *n.* seventh day of Jewish week observed as day of rest, Christian Sunday. **Sabbat'-ical,** *a.* pertaining to the Sabbath, implying rest from normal work, i.e. a Sabbatical Year allowed for special academic study.

Sa'ble, *n. & a.* black, esp. as heraldic colour, also *poet.*

Sabotage', *n.* deliberate and malicious damage to machinery etc. *v.t.*

Sa'bre (-ber), *n.* heavy curved sword used by cavalry. *v.t.*

Sac, *n.* a baglike organ, a natural pocket.

Sacc'harine (Sak-ar-), *n. & a.* sugar substitute derived from coal-tar.

Sacerdo'tal (Sass-), *a.* to do with priests.

Sachet' (-shay), *n.* small scented bag.

Sack, *n.* a large jute or other fabric bag. *sl. n.* dismissal. *v.t.* to put into sack, *sl.* to discharge. **Sack-cloth,** *n.* fig. mourning-clothes.

Sack, *v.t.* to plunder, destroy, esp. in war. *n.*

Sack, *n.* formerly a Spanish wine resembling sherry.

Sac'rament, *n. rel.* ceremony applied particularly to baptism and Eucharist. **Sacramen'tal,** *a.*

Sa'cred, *a.* consecrated, holy.

Sac'rifice, *n. rel.* offering to God, any act of self-abnegation. *v.t. & i.*

Sacrileg'ious (-lej-), *a.* profane. **Sac'rilege,** *n.* profanity.

Sac'risty, *n.* church vestry.

Sac'rosanct, *a.* most sacred.

Sad, *a.* unhappy through grief, depressed. **Sadd'en,** *v.t. & i.* to make or become unhappy.

Sadd'le, *n.* leather pad or seat for horse-rider, bicyclist etc. *v.t.* to put saddle on in preparation for ride, to burden with something.

Safa'ri (-fahri), *n.* a hunting expedition, esp. in tropical country.

Safe, *a.* secure, not in danger, reliable. *n.* a fire-proof, thief-proof chest for valuables. **Safe-conduct,** *n.* guarantee of safety in enemy territory. **Safe-guard,** *n.* a guarantee or measure of safety. *v.t.* **Safe'ty,** *n.* freedom from harm.

Sag, *v.i.* to droop, flag, become loose.

Sa'ga (sah-gah), *n.* mediaeval Norse legend, heroic story.

Saga'cious, *a.* shrewd. **Sagac'-ity,** *n.* shrewdness.

Sage, *a.* wise. *n.* a wise man.

Sail, *n.* canvas sheeting extended on masts and by rigging to catch wind. *v.i.* to be driven by the wind esp. on water.

Sail'or, *n.* seaman, member of ship's crew.

Saint, *n.* person of extreme virtue, one canonized by church for martyrdom or exemplary life.

Sake, *n.* on behalf, out of consideration for, because of, owing to.

Sala′cious, *a.* lewd.

Sal′ad, *n.* lettuce, dish of uncooked, seasoned vegetables.

Sal′ary, *n.* wages paid by the month.

Sale, *n.* the act of selling, an auction, a reduction of prices.

Sales′man, *n.* itinerant vendor.

Sales′manship, *n.* skill at selling.

Sa′lient, *a.* conspicious, standing out.

Sal′ine, *a.* pertaining to salt.

Sali′va, *n.* spittle, liquid secreted in mouth to help digestion. **Sali′vary,** *a.*

Sall′ow (-o), *a.* sickly yellow, esp. of complexion.

Sall′y, *v.i.* to rush or go forth. *n.* a sudden humorous remark.

Salm′on (Sam-un), *n.* large game fish.

Sal′on, *n.* reception room, art gallery.

Sal′oon, *n.* drinking-bar, large room in liner.

Salt (Solt), *n.* sodium chloride used for cooking and other purposes, a mineral compound, anything imparting flavour or quality, *chem.* crystalline compound resulting from union of acid and base, *coll.* a seaman. *v.t.* to preserve or flavour with salt. **Salt-cellar,** *n.* table container for salt. **Salt-lick,** *n.* place frequented by wild animals for natural surface salt.

Salu′brious, *a.* conducive to health.

Sal′utary, *a.* beneficial.

Salute′, *n.* a gesture of greeting or respect. *v.t. & i.* **Saluta′tion,** *n.* a greeting, courteous words in recognition of another's arrival.

Sal′vage, *v.t.* to rescue property from destruction. *n.* what is rescued thus, payment for this.

Salva′tion, *n.* rescue, being rescued, redemption.

Salve, *n.* a skin ointment, a soothing influence. *v.t.*

Sal′ver, *n.* a small silver tray.

Sal′vo, *n.* simultaneous discharge of artillery or firearms.

Same, *a.* alike, identical, equal. *pron.* **Same′ness,** *n.* similarity.

Sam′ple, (Sahm-), *n.* a pattern, a taste, specimen. *v.t.* to test quality of whole by trying or tasting part.

Sam′pler, *n.* piece of ornamental embroidery as manifestation of skill.

Sanator′ium, *n.* special hospital or health resort. *pl.* -toria.

Sanc′tify, *v.t.* to make holy, devote to sacred purpose. **Sanc′tity,** *n.* sacredness. **Sanctifica′tion,** *n.*

Sanctimo′nious, *a.* ostentatiously pious, hypocritical. **Sanct′imony,** *n.*

Sanc′tuary, *n.* a holy place, a refuge.

Sanc′tum, *n.* us. *iron.* a sacred place, a study.

Sand, *n.* fine powdered rock. *v.t.* to sprinkle with sand.

San′dal, *n.* footwear with open top.

Sand′wich, *n.* meat etc. enclosed between two slices of bread. *v.t.* to make a sandwich, press together as if in s.

Sane, *a.* mentally normal, sensible. **San′ity,** *n.*

San′guinary (-gwin-), *a.* bloody, savage.

San'guine (-gwin), *a.* blood-red, but us. hopeful, confident.

Sanita'tion, *n.* hygiene. San'itary, *a.* hygienic.

Sap, *n.* plant juice.

Sap, *n.* a subterranean gallery esp. under enemy position. *v.t.* to dig this, to undermine.

Sa'pience, *n.* wisdom. Sa'pient, *a.*

Sap'ling, *n.* a young tree, *fig.* a youth.

Sar'casm, *n.* mordant irony. Sarcas'tic, *a.*

Sarcoph'agus, *n.* a stone coffin.

Sardon'ic, *a.* bitterly derisive.

Sartor'ial, *a.* pertaining to tailors and tailoring.

Sash, *n.* an ornamental ribbon.

Sash, *n.* a sliding window-frame.

Satan'ic, *a.* devilish.

Satch'el, *n.* bag with shoulder strap.

Sate, *v.t. arch.* or *iron.* to surfeit, satiate.

Sat'ellite, *n.* planet revolving round larger one, now *fig.* a subservient country.

Sa'tiate, *v.t.* to fill or satisfy to excess, cloy. Sati'ety, *n.* Sa'tiable, *a.*

Sat'in, *n. & a.* fine glossy silk.

Sat'ire (-yre), *n.* mordant irony, facile ridicule. Sat'irist, *n.* satirical person, writer of satire. Sat'irize, *v.t.* to criticize with satire, expose to ridicule. Sat'irical, *a.*

Sat'isfy, *v.t. & i.* to make content, to provide enough, gratify. Satisfac'tion, *n.* fulfilment of needs or desires. Satisfac'tory, *a.* adequate, enough.

Sat'rap, *n.* a petty tyrant, subordinate.

Sat'urate, *v.t.* to soak completely. Satura'tion, *n.* state of not being able to absorb more.

Sat'urnine, *a.* morose.

Sa'tyr (-ter), *n.* myth. forest god.

Sauce (Sawce), *n.* liquid flavouring or relish. *sl.* impertinence. Sau'cy, *a.* impertinent.

Sau'cer, *n.* shallow dish for resting cup, anything resembling a saucer.

Saun'ter, *v.i.* to stroll, walk aimlessly. *n.*

Sau'sage (Sos-ij), *n.* minced meat contained in skin cylinder.

Sav'age, *a.* untamed, brutal, fierce. *n.* a barbarian. Sav'agery (Sav-ij-ri), *n.*

Save, *v.t. & i.* to rescue, preserve, keep, redeem. Sa'ving, *n.* preserving, redeeming. *n.* an economy. *n. pl.* money put by.

Save, *prep.* except.

Sa'viour (Save-yer), *n.* person who rescues or redeems.

Sa'vour, *n.* taste, flavour. *v.t. &* . to taste, have quality of. Sa'voury, *a.* of food having a pleasant smell. *a.* a savoury dish.

Saw, *n.* a toothed cutting tool. *v.t. & i.* to cut with saw, make gesture as if doing this. Sawdust, *n.* wood dust from sawing. Saw'yer, *n.* workman who saws.

Saw, *n.* a proverb.

Sax'ophone, *n. mus.* wind instrument.

Say, *v.t.* to utter verbally. Say'ing, *n.* a remark, quotation.

Scab, *n.* dry protective crust forming over healing wound,

disease of sheep. *sl.* worker who refuses to join strike.

Scabb'ard, *n.* sheath for sword or bayonet.

Scaff'old, *n.* temporary structure to enable building to be repaired or built, raised platform for execution. **Scaff'-olding,** *n.*

Scald (Skawld), *v.t.* to burn with boiling liquid, to steep in hot water, to bring esp. milk almost to boiling-point, *n.* an injury caused by scalding.

Scald, *n.* mediaeval Scandinavian poet.

Scale, *n.* a balance, a standard of measuring, a proportion, in mus. a series of notes. *v.t.* to bring into relation, to represent in scale.

Scale, *v.t.* to climb up.

Scale, *n.* thin flaky plate covering fish or reptile, anything resembling this. *v.t. & i.* to form in scales or peel off in scales.

Scall'op, (Skol-), *n.* bivalve mollusc, shallow pan shaped like shell of this. *v.t.* to incise a border or edge with series of curves.

Scalp, *n.* skin on top of human head. *v.t.* to cut this off.

Scal'pel, *n.* surgeon's knife.

Scamp, *n.* a rogue.

Scamp, *v.t.* to do badly or hurriedly.

Scan, *v.t. & i.* to read over, to have proper metre.

Scan'dal, *n.* a disgrace, spiteful gossip. **Scan'dalous,** *a.* outrageous. **Scan'dalize,** *v.t.* to offend by behaviour. **Scan'dal-monger,** *n.* retailer of gossip.

Scant, *a.* meagre. **Scan'ty,** *a.* sparse.

Scape'-goat, *n.* person who takes the blame for others.

Scape'-grace, *n.* scatterbrained person frequently in trouble.

Scar, *n.* mark left by injury, effect of distress. *v.t. & i.* to mark thus.

Scarce, *a.* not plentiful, insufficient. **Scarce'ly,** *adv.* hardly, barely. **Scar'city** (Scare-), *n.* an insufficiency.

Scare, *v.t.* to frighten. *n.*

Scarf, *n.* wrapping to keep throat warm.

Scar'ify, *v.t.* to lacerate, *fig.* to criticize harshly.

Scar'let, *a. & n.* vivid red colour.

Scath'ing, *a.* blistering, esp. as s. remarks.

Scatt'er, *v.t. & i.* to fling here and there, to separate in various directions. **Scattering,** *n.* a small quantity.

Scav'enge, *v.t. & i.* to feed on carrion, to carry away refuse. **Scav'enger,** *n.*

Scene (Seen), *n.* division of theatrical play, place or setting of incident, an emotional display. **Sce'nery,** *n.* theatrical hangings, landscape. **Scenar'io,** *n.* film-play. **Scen'ic,** *a.* pertaining to scenery.

Scent (sent), *n.* perfume, sense of smell, trail. *v.t.* to catch scent of.

Scep'tic (Skep-), *n.* person habitually inclined to doubt. **Scep'tical,** *a.* **Scep'ticism,** *n.*

Scep'tre (Sep-ter), *n.* emblem of royal power.

Sched'ule (Shed-), *n.* timetable, detailed explanation of arrangements. *v.t.* to plan in relation to time.

Scheme (Skeem), *n.* a plan. *v.t. & i.* to plan, plot. **Sche'ming**, *a.* underhand.

Schism (Siz'm), *n.* a split esp. in a polit. party or church. **Schismat'ic**, *a.* tending to divide or cause division.

Schizophre'nia (Skitz-), *n.* mental disorder characterized by split personality.

School (Skool), *n.* a place for teaching and learning, a body of thought. *v.t.* to instruct, educate. **Schol'ar**, *n.* pupil. learned person, person awarded scholarship. **Schol'arship**, *n.* learning, erudition, award for further education. **Scholast'ic**, *a.* pertaining to education or learning.

School (Skool), *n.* a shoal of fish.

Schoon'er, *n.* (Skoon-) sailing vessel rigged fore-and-aft and having two or more masts.

Sciat'ica, (Sy-), *n.* neuralgia in hip and thigh. **Sciat'ic**, *a.* pertaining to the hip.

Sci'ence (Sy-), *n.* knowledge, esp. systematic and formulated, any organized body of knowledge. **Scientif'ic**, *a.* **Sci'entist**, *n.* person pursuing or practising a science.

Scim'itar (Sim-), *n.* curved oriental sword with double point at end.

Scin'tillate (Sin-), *v.i.* to glint, sparkle. **Scintilla'tion**, *n.* **Scintill'a**, *n.* a spark, but esp. a particle.

Sci'on (Sy-), *n.* a shoot, a descendant.

Sciss'ors (Sizz-), *n. pl.* implement with two attached blades for cutting.

Scoff, *v.t.* to mock.

Scold (Scold), *v.t. & i.* to rebuke, nag. *n.* a nagging woman.

Sconce, *n.* crown of head.

Sconce, *n.* small fort.

Scone (Skon or Skone), *n.* flat round oatmeal cake.

Scoop, *n.* a ladle, shovel, *coll.* a journalistic feat. *v.t.* to ladle or shovel up, to hollow out.

Scope, *n.* outlet, range of activity or talent.

Scorbu'tic, *a.* afflicted with scurvy.

Scorch, *v.t. & i.* to burn lightly, dry up through drought. *n.*

Score, *v.t. & i.* to keep tally in game, to achieve a success, to mark with notches, to strike out. *n.* points scored in game, a mus. composition in detail, a debt, a set of twenty.

Scorn, *n.* disdain, contempt. *v.t.* to deride, despise. **Scorn'ful**, *a.*

Scot, *n. arch.* tax, now us. as **scot-free**, *a.* escaping punishment.

Scotch, *v.t.* to disable, frustrate.

Scoun'drel, *n.* rogue.

Scour (Skowr), *v.t.* to clean thoroughly by rubbing.

Scour, *v.t.* to search thoroughly.

Scourge (Skurj), *n.* a whip for punishment, *fig.* an affliction or punishment. *v.t.* to whip brutally.

Scout (Skowt), *n.* person Sent out to reconnoitre enemy position. *v.t.*

Scout, *v.t.* to reject contemptuously.

Scowl, *n.* an angry or sullen frown. *v.t.*

Scrag, *n.* scrawny meat or person. **Scragg'y**, *a.* thin. *sl.* to seize by neck.

Scram'ble, *v.t.* to clamber with

difficulty, to jostle and push, to mix up.

Scrap, *v.t. & i.* to break up and discard. *n.* a broken piece. **Scrapp'y,** *a.* bitty, uneven.

Scrap, *n. sl.* a fight. *v.i.*

Scrape, *v.t. & i.* to scratch, rub harshly, clean by grating or scratching, to bow clumsily. *n.* an escapade.

Scratch, *v.t. & i.* to injure with claws, to be injured by rough material, to make a grating sound, to cancel. *n.* a mark or sound caused by scratching, starting point in race. *a.* starting from this, not handicapped, improvized.

Scrawl, *v.t. & i.* to write carelessly, scribble. *n.*

Scream, *n.* a shrill cry. *sl.* something laughable. *v.i.*

Scree, *n.* slope covered with loose material.

Screech, *n.* a shrill, harsh cry. *v.i.*

Screed, *n.* tiresome interminable letter or speech.

Screen, *n.* a contrivance for covering or protecting, a sheet for projecting films, a sieve for coal. *v.t.* to protect by a screen. *coll.* to ascertain person's dependability, to sift.

Screw (Skroo) *n.* nail-like piece of metal with spiral groove called thread round lower half for firmer grip in other metal or wood, anything similar to a screw, a twist, a ship's propelling device. *v.t.* to fasten with a screw, make a screw tighter, extort by pressure. **Screw'driver,** *n.* tool for screwing. **Screw'y,** *a. sl.* daft.

Scrib'ble, *v.t. & i.* to scrawl, write hastily or meaninglessly.

n. **Scrib'bler,** *n. iron.* a worthless writer.

Scribe, *n.* a writer, a journalist.

Scrimm'age, *n.* a scrum, a disorderly struggle.

Scrimp, *v.t. & i.* supply inadequately, be mean, esp. as scrimp & scrape.

Scrim'shanker, *n.* shirker.

Scrip, *n.* provisional share & financial certificate or receipt.

Scrip, *n. arch.* a satchel, wallet.

Script, *n.* style of handwriting, finished material for publishing or broadcasting.

Scrip'ture, *n.* holy writings esp. the Bible. **Scrip'tural,** *a.*

Scriv'ener, *n. arch.* a clerk, a scribe.

Scrof'ula, *m.* morbid disease characterized by glandular swellings and tendency to tuberculosis. **Scrof'ulous,** *a.*

Scro'll, *n.* parchment manuscript, ancient document.

Scrounge, *v.t. & i.* to cadge, thieve. **Scroun'ger,** *n.* (-jer).

Scrub, *v.t.* to clean by vigorous rubbing esp. with stiff brush. *n.*

Scrub, *n.* a shrub, stunted tree, land covered with such. **Scrubb'y,** *a.*

Scruff, *n.* back of neck.

Scru'ple, *n. arch.* an apothecary's weight, thus a small amount, a prick of the conscience. *v.i.* to hesitate because of conscience. **Scru'pulous,** *a.* conscientious.

Scru'tinize, *v.t. & i.* to examine carefully. **Scru'tiny,** *n.* a careful inspection or overseeing. **Scrutineer',** *n.*

Scud, *v.i.* to move rapidly and lightly. *n.* wind-blown foam.

Scuf'fle, *n.* a confused brief brawl. *v.i.*

Scull, *n.* light oar. *v.t. & i.*

Scull'ery, *n.* kitchen annexe.

Scull'ion, *n.* formerly a kitchen-servant.

Sculp'ture, *n.* the art of carving figures in stone or wood, an object so produced. *v.t.* **Sculp'-tural,** *a.* **Sculp'tor,** *n.*

Scum, *n.* impure matter rising to surface of liquid as froth, *fig.* anything worthless.

Scupp'er, *n.* hole in ship's bulwark to drain off water. *sl.* *v.t.* to defeat, take aback.

Scurf, *n.* dandruff.

Scurr'ilous, *a.* grossly abusive. **Scurril'ity,** *n.*

Scurr'y, *v.i.* to scamper. *n.*

Scur'vy, *n.* a disease formerly prevalent among sailors & caused by deficiency in diet. *a.* *fig.* contemptible.

Scut'tle, *n.* covered aperture in ship's deck or side. *v.t.* to sink deliberately by opening this.

Scut'tle, *v.i.* to run away hurriedly. *n.*

Scut'tle, *n.* receptacle for coal.

Scythe (Sythe), *n.* hand-tool with long curved blade and handle for cutting grass or corn. *v.t.*

Sea, *n.* the ocean, salt water, movement of the sea. **Sea'-board, Sea'coast,** *n.* land bordering the sea. **Sea'farer,** *n.* sailor, sea-voyager. **Sea'man,** *n.* sailor. **Sea'manship,** *n.* **Sea'-worthy,** *a.* a ship in proper state.

Seal, *n.* amphibious mammal. **Seal'er,** *n.* ship used for hunting seals, member of crew of this.

Seal, *n.* stamp or die with private or official emblem for impressing wax fastening or disk on document. *v.t.* to mark or fix with a seal, to keep secure, to settle, to confirm. **Seal'ing wax,** *n.*

Seam, *n.* a join in cloth or other material, a wrinkle or layer resembling a seam. *v.t. & i.* to join together, to mark in lines. **Seam'y,** *a.* of the underside of things.

Se'ance (Say-), *n.* meeting of organization, but esp. gathering of spiritualists.

Sear, *v.t.* to scorch.

Search (Surch), *v.t. & i.* to seek, examine in order to find. *n.* **Search'ing,** *a.* thorough, keen. **Search'light,** *n.* powerful light capable of turning in any direction.

Seas'on, *n.* one of four main periods of the year with different characteristics, any suitable time, a legal period, a time for particular activity. *v.t. & i.* to bring to the fittest condition. **Seas'onable,** *a.* appropriate to the season. **Seas'-onal,** *a.* pertaining to the seasons.

Seas'on, *v.t.* to flavour. **Seas'-oning,** *n.* flavouring, relish.

Seat, *n.* a structure for sitting on, a way of sitting, part of body on which one sits, part of garment covering this, a base, site, a right to sit in an assembly. *v.t.* to cause to sit, to provide seating accommodation.

Sec'ateurs, *n. pl.* gardener's pruning shears.

Secede' (Sesseed), *v.i.* to withdraw formally. **Seces'sion,** *n.*

Seclude', *v.t.* to withdraw to or place in solitude. **Seclu'sion,** *n.*

Sec'ond, *n.* sixtieth part of minute, a moment, assistant at boxing-match or duel, person coming after the first. *a.* next in order after first. *v.t.* to support. Second', *v.t.* to lend person for temporary duty elsewhere. Sec'onder, *n.* one who supports, esp. a motion at committee meeting. Sec'ondary, *a.* of subordinate or inferior position or quality.

Second-hand, *a.* not new, indirect. Second-sight, *n.* professed power of forecasting events. Second nature, *n.* ingrained habit.

Se'crecy, *n.* concealment, state of being kept secret.

Se'cret, *a.* private, important enough to be hidden, hidden. *n.*

Sec'retary, *n.* person who keeps records, writes letters, etc. for individual or organization. Secretar'ial, *a.* Secretar'iat, *n.* body of secretaries in large organization.

Secrete', *v.t.* to conceal. Secre'tive, *a.* furtive, tending to conceal.

Secrete', *v.t.* to produce by secretion. Secre'tion, *n.* physiological process of producing matter from blood and through certain organs, matter so produced.

Sect, *n.* group of people holding common views, esp. rel. Sectar'ian, *a.* of a sect, narrow, bigoted.

Sec'tion, *n.* a part, a cross-wise exposition, a division of a lit. work. *v.t.* to divide into sections. Sec'tional, *a.* consisting of sections. Sec'tionalism, *n.* narrow self-interest on part of section of community.

Sec'tor, *n. geom.* part of circle between two radii and the appropriate arc, part of mil. or industrial activity.

Sec'ular, *a.* pertaining to temporal things as opposed to rel. Sec'ularize, *v.t.* to make secular, take out of rel. hands. Secular'ism, *n.*

Secure', *a.* safe, free from danger, safely guarded. *v.t.* to make safe, to bind, to obtain, imprison. Secu'rity, *n.* state of being safe or secure, guarantee for loan.

Sedate', *a.* calmly dignified.

Sed'ative, *a. & n.* of, anything having a tranquillizing effect.

Sed'entary, *a.* sitting, characterized by or involving sitting.

Sedge, *n.* marsh plant, tract of land covered by this.

Sed'iment, *n.* dregs, deposit. Sed'imentary, *a.*

Sedit'ion, *n.* polit. agitation, insurrection, incitement to this. Sedit'ious, *a.* pertaining to these.

Seduce', *v.t.* to tempt or lead astray. Seduc'tion, *n.* the act of doing this. Seduc'tive, *a.* tempting, alluring.

Sed'ulous, *a.* ponderously diligent.

See, *v.t. & i.* to perceive optically, to comprehend, experience, visit, reflect. See'ing, *n.* act or power of seeing. *conj.* because of, inasmuch as.

See, *n.* diocese or office of bishop.

Seed, *n.* reproductive fruit of plant, any source or origin that leads to development, offspring. *v.t. & i.* to sow with seed. Seed'ling, *n.* small plant recently emerged from state of being seed.

Seek, *v.t. & i.* to look for, to attempt.

Seem, *v.i.* to appear, look. **Seem'ing,** *a.* apparent.

Seem'ly, *a.* proper, becoming.

Seep, *v.i.* to leak, ooze. **Seep'-age,** *n.*

Seer, *n.* person who sees, a prophet.

Seethe, *v.i.* to boil, *fig.* to be greatly agitated.

Seg'ment, *n.* a section, *geom.* part of circle between an arc and its chord.

Seg'regate, *v.t.* to keep apart, separate from others. **Segrega'-tion,** *n.* **Segrega'tionist,** *n.* esp. person who advocates undemocratic separation of races.

Seine (Sain), *n.* a fishing-net operated in a circle between two points on shore or between boats. *v.i.*

Seis'mic (Size-), *a.* pertaining to an earthquake. **Seis'mograph,** *n.* instrument for recording earthquake. **Seis'mology,** *n.* scientific study of earthquakes.

Seize (Seez), *v.t.* to take hold of violently, grasp, comprehend. **Sei'zure,** *n.* act of doing this, a sudden attack of illness.

Sel'dom, *adv.* not often.

Select', *v.t.* to choose carefully, esp. the best. **Select',** *a.* choice. **Selec'tion,** *n.* a choice, a representative choice. **Selec'-tor,** *n.* one who selects, esp. one appointed to select.

Self, *n.* one's own personality, advantage, interests, individuality. **Self'ish,** *a.* considering only one's own interests. **Self'-less,** *a.* the opposite of this. **Selves,** *n. pl.* of self.

Self- as *pref.* indicating action by oneself or itself, acting concerning oneself or itself, direct or indirect reflexive action, automatic or independent.

Sell, *v.t. & i.* to give in return for money, market, betray. **Sell'er,** *n.* person who sells, thing that sells well.

Sel'vage, Sel'vedge, *n.* stitched, finished edge of material.

Seman'tics, *n. pl.* as *n.* scientific study of evolution of words and language.

Sem'aphore, *n.* a system of and apparatus for signalling by means of flags or mechanical arms. *v.t.*

Sem'blance, *n.* an external appearance, representation.

Semes'ter (Se-mes-), *n.* an academic half year.

Sem'i- *pref.* meaning half.

Sem'inary, *n.* educational institution esp. rel.

Semp'stress (Sem-), *n.* **Seam'-stress,** *n.* needlewoman, garment-maker.

Sen'ate, *n.* part of a legislative body, university council. **Sen'-ator,** *n.* member of these. **Senator'ial,** *a.* pertaining to a senate or senator, dignified.

Send, *v.t. & i.* to despatch, cause to go or be conveyed, cause to come, as send for.

Se'nile, *a.* pertaining to old age. **Senil'ity,** *n.*

Se'nior, *a.* older, higher in rank. *n.* an older person. **Senior'ity,** *n.*

Sense, *n.* feeling, understanding, appreciation, mental or physical faculty. *v.t.* to be aware of, conscious of. **Sense'less,** *a.* useless, stupid, unconscious. **Sensa'tion,** *n.* the act of feeling or using a sense, the reaction to something external, a condition of great and excited interest. **Sensa'tional,** *a.* exciting, remarkable. **Sensation'-alism,** *n.* philos. theory that ideas are produced only by sensation, tendency to exaggerate. **Sensibil'ity,** *n.* capacity to feel. **Sen'sible,** *a.* perceptible by senses, noticeable, conscious, judicious. **Sen'sitive,** *a.* readily perceptive, readily responsive, easily hurt or offended.

Sen'sory, *a.* pertaining to the senses.

Sen'sual, *a.* pertaining to bodily pleasures, carnal. **Sensual'ity,** *n.* indulgence in bodily pleasures.

Sen'suous, *a.* appealing to or acting on the senses.

Sen'tence, *n. gram.* a complete and meaningful set of words, a phrase, a penalty for wrong-doing, a term of imprisonment. *v.t.* to pass sentence on, condemn.

Senten'tious, *a.* pompous *esp.* verbally.

Sen'tient, *a.* capable of feeling.

Sen'timent, *n.* an emotion, feeling, opinion. **Sentimen'tal,** *a.* emotional, mawkish. **Sentimental'ity,** *n.*

Sen'tinel, *n.* a sentry, a guard.

Sen'try, *n.* person esp. soldier entrusted with guarding.

Se'pal, *n. bot.* leaf of calyx in flower.

Sep'arate, *v.t.* to part or divide, to place apart, to go different ways. *a.* divided, together no longer, distinct. **Sep'arable,** *a.* **Separa'tion,** *n.* **Sep'aratism,** *n. esp.* polit. movement advocating unity with another country instead of one actually ruling.

Se'pia, *n. & a.* dark brown colour.

Septem'ber, *n.* ninth month of year.

Septenn'ial, *a. & n.* happening every seven years.

Sep'tic, *a.* infected, *esp.* of blood or wound. **Sep'sis,** *n.* blood poisoning. **Septice'mia,** *n.* the same.

Sep'ulchre (-ker), *n.* a tomb. **Sepul'chral,** *a.* pertaining to a tomb, solemnly gloomy. **Sep'-ulture,** *n.* burial.

Se'quence (-kwence), *n.* the act of following or coming after, a series. **Sequa'cious,** *a.* following, easily led. **Sequac'ity,** *n.* **Se'quel,** *n.* a continuation in chain of events or story.

Sequest'er, *v.t.* to isolate, set apart, confiscate *leg.* **Seques'-trate,** *v.t.* the same. **Sequestra'-tion,** *n.*

Se'quin, *n.* ornamental spangle for dress.

Seragl'io (-ahlio), *n.* a harem.

Ser'aph, *n.* first-class angel. *pl.* **Ser'aphim.** **Seraph'ic,** *a.* angelic.

Sere, *a. poet.* withered, dry.

Serenade', *n.* song played or sung at night by lover beneath sweetheart's window. *v.t.*

Serene', *a.* tranquil. **Seren'ity,** *n.* tranquillity.

Serf, *n.* formerly in mediaeval times or Tsarist Russia, peasant owned by landlord, a slave. **Serf'dom,** *n.*

Serge (Surj), *n.* stout woollen material for suits.

Serg'eant (Sar-jant), *n.* non-commissioned officer in army, police officer above constable.

Serj'eant, *n.* esp. serjeant-at-arms, leg., parliamentary and city official; common serjeant, officer of City of London.

Se′ries, *n.* a sequence of events or parts. Se′rial, *a.* pertaining to a series. *n.* a story in several connected parts.

Se′rious, *a.* grave, earnest.

Ser′mon (Sur-), *n.* a rel. discourse, a moral lecture. Ser′monize, *v.i.* to moralize pompously.

Ser′pent, *n.* a snake, mus. windinstrument. Ser′pentine, *a.* curved like a snake.

Serra′ted, *a.* indented with teeth or notches. Serra′tion, *n.*

Serr′ied (Serrid), *a.* crowded, close.

Se′rum, *n.* lymph, water fluid left after coagulation of blood.

Serve (Surv), *v.t. & i.* to work for, be employed by, be useful, deliver, undergo, to act as serviceman, in tennis to initiate a game or bout, to help at table. Ser′vant, *n.* person employed to serve, a follower. Ser′vice, *n.* condition of serving or being employed, period of mil. employment, rel. ceremony, set of table utensils, act of serving in tennis. *v.t.* to make fit for use.

Ser′viceable (-vis-able), *a.* fit to use, useful.

Serviette′, *n.* mistakenly a tablenapkin, properly a small towel.

Ser′vile (Sur-), *a.* grovelling, like a slave. Servil′ity, *n.*

Ser′vitor, *n. arch.* a servant.

Ser′vitude, *n.* bondage, slavery.

Ses′sion, *n.* official meeting or assembly, sitting of court. Ses′sional, *a.*

Set, *v.t. & i.* to put, pose, erect, prepare, sink, settle, put in place, mend, determine, tend.

a. fixed, settled, mended, regular, etc. *n.* a collection of things, a series, a series of games in tennis, a posture, a clique. Sett′ing, *n.* a background. Set-back, *n. & v.t.* reverse.

Settee′, *n.* a sofa.

Sett′er, *n.* gun-dog.

Set′tle, *v.t. & i.* to decide, to fix or become fixed in position, to calm, to pay a debt, to adjust, agree, to colonize, arrange, bestow. Set′tlement, *n.* the act of settling, a colony. Sett′ler, *n.* a colonist.

Set′tle, *n.* wooden bench with high back and arms.

Sev′er, *v.t. & i.* to cut off, separate. Sev′erance, *n.*

Sev′eral, *a.* separate, distinct, various, some.

Se′vere (-veer), *a.* harsh, exacting, stern, acute. Sever′ity, *n.*

Sew (So), *v.t. & i.* to stitch.

Sew′age, *n.* waste matter, excrement. Sew′er, *n.* drain for removal of this. Sew′erage, *n.* system of drainage.

Sex, *n.* state of being male or female, males or females collectively. Sex′ual, *a.* pertaining to sex or sexes.

Sext′ant, *n.* navigator's instrument for measuring altitudes.

Sextet′, *n. mus.* composition for six instruments, the players of this.

Sex′ton, *n.* church caretaker, gravedigger.

Shabb′y, *a.* threadbare, mean.

Shack, *n.* a hovel, a hut.

Shac′kle, *n.* a fetter, anything that restricts. *v.t.*

Shade, *n.* partial darkness, degree of colour, protection

from heat or light, a device to screen a light, a shadow, a ghost. *v.t.* to screen from heat or light, to intensify degree of colour. **Sha'dy,** *a.* cool and pleasant, *coll.* disreputable.

Shad'ow, *n.* shade caused by interception of light. *v.t.* to cause a shadow, to follow secretly. **Shad'owy,** *a.* like a shadow, insubstantial.

Shaft, *n.* vertical boring in earth, entrance to mine, beam of light, streak of lightning, one of two projecting poles between which horse is harnessed to cart, the stem of an arrow, any long slender straight rod, rod in engine to which rotating parts are connected.

Shagg'y, *a.* hairy, matted.

Shagreen', *n.* shark-skin, untanned leather.

Shah, *n.* Persian king.

Shake, *v.t. & i.* to tremble, vibrate, move rapidly to and fro, to cause to waver. *n.* **Sha'ky,** *a.* weak, tumbledown.

Shak'o, *n. hist.* a kind of mil. hat.

Shale, *n.* kind of clayey rock resembling soft slate.

Shall'op (Shal-), *n.* small light open boat.

Shallot', *n.* kind of onion.

Shall'ow (Shal-o), *a.* not deep, superficial. *n.* **shoal,** shallow water.

Sham, *n. & a.* an imitation, a pretence. *v.t. & i.* to feign.

Sham'ble, *v.i.* to shuffle, walk awkwardly.

Sham'bles, *n. pl.* as *n.* lit. a slaughter-house, *fig.* any place or scene of bloodshed.

Shame, *n.* emotion induced by guilty feeling, disgrace, dis-

honour. *v.t.* to disgrace, cause to feel shame. **Shame'faced,** *a.* embarrassed through guilt. **Shame'ful,** *a.* disgraceful. **Shame'less,** *a.* blatant, unabashed.

Shampoo', *v.t.* to wash head and hair with special lather. *n.* the act of doing this, a special preparation.

Shanghai' (-hy), *v.t.* to kidnap seaman for service in another ship.

Shank, *n.* human lower leg, shinbone. **Shank's pony,** on foot.

Shant'y, *n.* hovel, shack.

Shant'y, *n.* properly Chanty, a sailor's song.

Shape, *n.* form or figure, outline, pattern, object not clearly seen or identified. *v.t.* to form, fashion, give shape to. **Shape'less,** *a.* cumbersome, unformed. **Shape'ly,** *a.* with handsome figure.

Shard, *n.* a fragment of pottery etc.

Share, *n.* a portion, a part, an entitlement to business dividend. *v.t. & i.* to divide in portions, to use or enjoy something with others.

Share, *n.* blade of plough.

Shark, *n.* large carnivorous fish, *coll.* a swindler, rapacious person.

Sharp, *a.* having a good cutting edge, keen, pungent, quick, violent, intense, prompt, *mus.* above true pitch. *n.* in mus. a tone or note above true pitch. **Sharp'en,** *v.t.* to make sharp or sharper, to become brisker. **Sharp'er,** *n.* cheat. **Sharp'shooter,** *n.* first-class rifle-shot. **Sharp'sighted,** *a.*

Shatt'er, *v.t.* to break into fragments, destroy utterly. *coll.* to disturb greatly.

Shave, *v.t. & i.* to remove hair from face with razor, to pare finely, to miss colliding narrowly. *n.* a shaving or being shaved, a narrow escape, esp. as near shave. **Sha'ving,** *n.* thin paring of wood.

Sha'ver, *n. sl.* a small boy.

Shaw, *n.* small wood, thicket.

Shawl, *n.* broad scarf for shoulders and head.

Shawm, *n.* obs. mus. instrument resembling oboe.

She, *pron.* female previously mentioned or implied, *n.* a female.

Sheaf, *n.* a bundle of reaped corn, any bundle of material. *pl.* sheaves.

Shear, *v.t.* to clip, esp. wool from sheep's back, to cut with shears. **Shears,** *n. pl.* cutting implements working on same principle as scissors. **Shear'er,** *n.* farm-hand who shears sheep. **Shear'ling,** *n.* sheep first time shorn.

Sheath, *n.* a scabbard, close-fitting cover. **Sheathe,** *v.t.* to cover with sheath, put sword into scabbard.

Sheave, *n.* pulley wheel.

Shed, *v.t. & i.* to cast off, pour out or off, spill, spread.

Shed, *n.* a hut, small store-building.

Sheen, *n.* lustre, brightness, glossiness.

Sheep, *n.* gregarious woolly ruminant. *pl.* same.

Sheep'ish, *a.* stupidly bashful.

Sheer, *a.* precipitous, straight, utter, complete, absolute, mere, unqualified.

Sheer, *v.i.* to deviate from course, swerve.

Sheer'legs, *n. pl. naut.* hoisting tackle.

Sheet, *n.* part of inner bedclothes, any large flat piece of material, a wide expanse.

Sheet, *n. naut.* rope attached to lower corner of sails. *n. pl.* part of rowing or sailing boat immediately inside bows and stern.

Sheet'anchor, . *n.* emergency anchor, *fig.* dependable person.

Sheikh (Shake), *n.* petty Arab tribal chief.

Shelf, *n.* a ledge for resting things on, anything resembling a shelf.

Shell, *n.* hard or brittle external covering for egg, nut etc, the essential frame of a structure, metal container for explosive. *v.t. & i.* to bombard with shells, to remove covering from egg etc.

Shel'lac, *n.* substance used in making varnish. *v.t.* to treat with or apply shellac.

Shel'ter, *v.t. & i.* to protect or seek protection. *n.* a refuge, anything that affords protection.

Shelve, *v.t.* to put on a shelf, to put off.

Shelve, *v.i.* to slope.

Shep'herd, *n.* guardian of sheep, *fig.* to guide rel. *v.t.* to herd, conduct.

Sher'iff, *n.* head administrative officer in county, in U.S.A. a law-enforcement officer.

Sherr'y, *n.* fortified Spanish wine.

Shibb'oleth, *n.* a slogan or catchword.

Shield, *n.* a large plate or oblong

carried on the arm to parry sword strokes, anything that protects. *v.t.*

Shift, *v.t. & i.* to move, transfer, to get along, improvise. *n.* a change, an expedient, a system of working in relays. **Shift'less,** *a.* improvident. **Shif'ty,** *a.* untrustworthy.

Shift, *n. arch.* a woman's undergarment.

Shill'y shall'y, *v.i.* to vacillate. *n.* feeble indecision.

Shimm'er, *v.i.* to gleam tremulously. *n.* a flickering sheen.

Shin, *n.* front part of lower leg. *v.i. sl.* to climb tree etc.

Shind'y, *n.* commotion, brawl.

Shine, *v.t. & i.* to emit rays of light, to glitter, sparkle, polish, direct beam of light. *n.* a lustre, a brightness.

Shin'gle, *n.* collectively pebbles on beach.

Shin'gle, *n.* wooden roof-tile, style of fem. hairdressing.

Shin'gles, *n. pl.* nervous disease characterized by inflammation of skin.

Ship, *n.* large sea-going vessel of various kinds. *v.t. & i.* to send by ship, load on ship, transport, fit in position, to finish with and put down as ship oars. **Shipmate,** *n.* fellow seaman. **Ship'ment,** *n.* the shipping of cargo, a cargo shipped. **Shipp'ing,** *n.* ships collectively, the business of ships. **Ship'shape,** *a.* in proper condition. **Ship'worm,** *n.* the teredo, a wood-eating mollusc. **Ship'wreck,** *n.* sinking or damaging of a ship at sea. **Ship'yard,** *n.* place where ships are built or repaired.

Shire, *n.* a county, a region.

Shire-horse, *n.* particular breed of strong farm-horse.

Shirk (Shurk), *v.t. & i.* to dodge or evade work or responsibility. **Shir'ker,** *n.* dodger, loafer.

Shirt (Shurt), *n.* man's sleeved undergarment.

Shiv'er, *v.t.* to tremble from cold or fright etc. **Shiv'ery,** *a.*

Shiv'er, *v.t. & i.* to shatter or cause to shatter in fragments.

Shoal (Shole), *n.* large number of fish.

Shoal, *n.* submerged sandbank uncovered at low tide, a shallow place in sea.

Shock, *n.* a violent blow, impact, collision, a sudden emotional upset, physical exhaustion through this, effect on nerves through contact with elec. *v.t.* to horrify, agitate greatly, apply live elec. to. **Shock'ing,** *a.*

Shock, *n.* an untidy mass or lock of hair, a collection of corn sheaves.

Shodd'y, *a.* inferior. *n.* waste woollen material.

Shoe (Shoo), *n.* outer foot-covering not reaching above ankle, metal rim to protect hoof of horse etc., anything serving a similar purpose to a shoe. *v.t.* to provide or protect with shoes. **Shoe'black,** *n.* person who polishes footwear. **Shoe'-horn,** *n.* tongue-like implement for easing on shoe.

Shoo, *v.t. & i.* to drive or scare off mildly. *interj.* a cry.

Shoot, *v.t. & i.* to discharge from gun, fire with bow and arrow, send out missile, hit with missile, let fly, dart out, move quickly, to spurt, to grow rapidly, put forth. *n.* a shooting-party, a young growing branch of a tree or plant.

Shop, *n*. building or room for retail sale, factory building, technical talk. *v.i*. to go out to purchase. **Shopp'ing,** *n*. & *a*. **Shop'keeper,** *n*. retailer. **Shop'-lifter,** *n*. thief who steals shop goods while pretending to be customer. **Shop-soiled,** *a*. damaged or spoilt through being exposed for sale. **Shop-steward,** *n*. factory workman elected as spokesman. **Shop-walker,** *n*. superintendent in large stores.

Shore, *n*. edge of sea or lake or river, beach.

Shore, *n*. baulk of timber as temporary support for beached ship etc. *v.t*.

Short, *a*. brief, deficient, not tall or long, abrupt, crumbling, not prolonged, **Shor'tage,** *n*. a deficiency. **Short circuit,** *n*. fault in elec. **Short'coming,** *n*. a failing. **Shor'ten,** *v.t*. & *i*. to make or become short or shorter in length or time. **Short'hand,** *n*. abbreviated system of writing by means of symbols. **Short'handed,** *a*. without enough crew or workers. **Short'horn,** *n*. breed of cattle.

Shot, *n*. lead pellets as part of missile, the act of shooting, an attempt, a marksman, a drink of spirit, a scene in a film, range of a gun. *a*. variegated in colour.

Shoul'der (Shole-), *n*. part of body to which arm, foreleg or wing is connected, part of garment covering shoulder, anything resembling a shoulder. *v.t. i*. to carry on shoulder, to use shoulder. **Shoulder-blade,**

n. scapula, large flat triangular bone of shoulder.

Shout, *n*. a loud cry. *v.t*. & *i*.

Shove (Shuv), *v.t*. & *i*. to push strongly, jostle. *n*.

Shov'el (Shuv-), *n*. broad bladed tool for scooping up material. *v.t*.

Show (Sho), *v.t*. & *i*. to exhibit, to disclose to the view, to appear, demonstrate, be visible. *n*. an exhibition. **Show'y,** *a*. ostentatious. **Show-off,** *n*. & *v.t*. self-exhibition. **Show up,** *v.t*. to appear, expose. **Show-down,** *n*. a confrontation.

Show'er, *n*. fall of rain, large number, a discharge or scattering. *v.t*. & *i*. to fall in a shower. **Show'ery,** *n*. tending to rain.

Show'ing (Sho-), *n*. a presentation, exhibition.

Shrap'nel, *n*. shell filled with bullets to shower down on target.

Shred, *n*. a strip or scrap. *v.t*. to tear into pieces.

Shrew (Shroo), *n*. insectivorous animal with long snout and nervous disposition, *coll*. a scolding woman. **Shrew'ish,** *a*.

Shrewd, *a*. astute. **Shrewd'ness,** *n*. sagacity.

Shriek, *n*. & *v.t*. & *i*. loud piercing cry.

Shrift, *n*. confession esp. on deathbed, absolution.

Shrill, *a*. high and piercing in tone. *v.t*. & *i*. to utter thus.

Shrimp, *n*. edible shellfish, *coll*. tiny person. *v.i*. to go after shrimps.

Shrine, *n*. a holy place esp. one associated with saint.

Shrink, *v.t*. & *i*. to become smaller, to draw back. **Shrink'-age,** *n*. act or amount of shrinking, tendency to diminish in size or number.

Shrive, *v.t. arch.* to hear confession of and give absolution to. **Shrift,** *n.* above.

Shriv'el, *v.t. & i.* to wither, fade.

Shroud, *n.* covering for a corpse. *v.t.* to hide in a shroud.

Shrouds, *n. pl. naut.* ropes supporting ship's mast.

Shrub, *n.* a bush, small treelike plant. **Shrubb'ery,** *n.* ornamental collection of shrubs.

Shrug, *v.t. & i.* to gesture by hunching shoulders. *n.*

Shudd'er, *v.i.* to tremble violently. *n.*

Shuff'le, *v.t. & i.* to walk carelessly or flatfootedly, to rearrange pack of cards, to move about confusedly. *n.*

Shun, *v.t.* to avoid.

Shunt, *v.t. & i.* to switch from one place or line to another, esp. train. **Shunting-yard,** *n.* part of railway where wagons and carriages are rearranged.

Shut, *v.t. & i.* to close.

Shutt'er, *n.* hinged screen for window, device in camera for controlling light.

Shut'tle, *n.* device in weaving or sewing machine. *v.t. & i.* to move backwards and forwards like a shuttle. **Shuttle-cock,** *n.* cork stuck with feathers and used instead of ball in badminton. **Shuttle-service,** *n.* emergency transport service with train or vehicle journey in opposite directions alternately.

Shy, *a.* retiring, timid, diffident. *v.i.* to start back from nervously.

Shy, *v.t. & i. sl.* to throw. *n.* a throw, thing to be thrown at.

Sib'ilant, *n.* a hissing sound or letter. *a.*

Sib'yl (-il), *n.* woman who prophesies.

Sic, *adv.* so, thus, used esp. to emphasize that questionable word or statement is as printed.

Sick, *a.* unwell, stricken with nausea. **Sick'en,** *v.t. & i.* to become ill, to disgust. **Sick'-ness,** *n.* **Sick-bay,** *n.* ship's hospital, any place for invalids. **Sick-list,** *n.* roll of sick men esp. in services.

Sic'kle, *n.* hand cutting-tool with curved blade.

Side, *n.* outer or inner wall or face, edge, part of surface of a body, direction, a team, a body of opinion, conceit, line of descent through one parent or the other. *v.i.* to join with one as against another opinion. **Side'board,** *n.* piece of dining-room furniture for implements and utensils. **Sidelong,** *a.* sideways. **Side-track,** *v.t.* to evade an issue. **Sideways,** *adv. & a.* towards the side instead of straight. **Si'ding,** *n.* railway track for wagons etc. not in use.

Sider'eal (Sy-deer-e-al), *a.* pertaining to the stars.

Si'dle, *v.i.* to progress sideways.

Siege, *n.* in war the encirclement of a town or fortress by enemy. **Siege-train,** *n.* artillery and other equipment for besieging a place.

Sienn'a, *n.* brownish-yellow or reddish-brown ochrous earth from which pigment is obtained.

Siest'a (See-est-), *n.* afternoon rest.

Sieve (Siv), *n.* utensil with meshed or perforated base for sifting. *v.t.*

Sift, *v.t.* to pass finer material through sieve leaving coarser separate, to go through carefully as with a sieve.

Sigh, *n.* a profound audible breath expressing some emotion. *v.t. & i.*

Sight, *n.* the ability to see, vision, the act of seeing, something remarkable or ludicrous, range of vision, way of regarding, opinion, device on rifle etc. for taking aim. *v.t. & i.* to perceive with the eye, to aim, direct. Sight'less, *a.* blind. Sight'ly, *a.* pleasant to see, handsome. Sight'seeing, *n.* the visiting of objects of interest. Sight'seer, *n.*

Sign, *n.* a symbol, mark, gesture, proof, trade advertisement. *v.t. & i.* to write one's signature, to gesture, show.

Sig'nal, *n.* a formulated sign for conveying intention or message. *v.t. & i.* to convey information or message by signal.

Sig'nalize, *v.t.* to render memorable or remarkable. Sig'nally, *a.* in a remarkable manner.

Sig'nature, *n.* a person's signed name, an autograph. Sig'natory, *n.* person who signs, esp. officially.

Sig'net, *n.* a private seal. Signet-ring, *n.* finger ring with seal.

Signif'icance, *n.* meaning, import. Signif'icant, *a.* meaningful, expressive, noteworthy.

Sig'nify, *v.t. & i.* to make known, to imply, mean. Significa'tion, *n.*

Si'lage, *n.* green cattle fodder processed with molasses for future use.

Si'lence, *n.* absence of noise or any disturbance. *v.t.* to become silent or cause to be. Si'lencer, *n.* device on gun or engine for subduing sound. Si'lent, *a.* quiet, unspoken, not speaking.

Silhouette' (Sil-oo-et), *n.* an outline of a person or object esp. when this shows up darkly, a portrait in profile with subject coloured black. *v.t.* to cause to show up in silhouette.

Sil'ica, *n.* hard mineral occurring in flint and quartz. Sil'icate, *n.* one of various natural salts. Sil'icon, *n.* non-metallic element occurring in rocks and sand. Sil'icosis, *n.* pulmonary disease caused by inhaling quartz dust.

Silk, *n.* fine soft strong thread made from fibres of silkworm's cocoon, fabric made of this. *a.* Silk'en, *a.* made of or like silk. Silk'y, *a.* soft and smooth, *coll.* smoothly plausible.

Sill, *n.* flat structure of wood, tile or stone at foot of window or doorway.

Sill'y, *a.* senseless, absurd.

Si'lo, *n.* pit or tower for storing silage.

Silt, *n.* deposit of fine soil and mud left by river. *v.t. & i.* to block or become blocked with this.

Silu'rian, *a. & n. geol.* division of earth's development during which first air-breathing land animals appeared.

Sil'van, Syl'van, *a.* pertaining to trees and woods.

Sil'ver, *n.* white precious metal, anything made of this. *a.* made of silver and fig. resembling silver, that is pleasant and fine. *v.t. & i.* to coat with silver, to turn silver in colour. **Sil′very,** *a.* smooth, lustrous. **Silversmith,** *n.* craftsman in silver. **Silverware,** *n.* the things he makes.

Sim′ian, *a.* like or relating to an ape. *n.* an ape.

Sim′ilar, *a.* like, resembling, approaching in likeness. **Similar′ity,** *n.*

Sim′ile (Sim-i-lee), *n.* expressive comparative figure of speech.

Simil′itude, *n.* likeness, similarity.

Simm′er, *v.t. & i.* to boil gently and long, *coll.* be on verge of anger or laughter.

Si′mony, *n.* the offence of trafficking in church offices or preferment.

Sim′per, *v.i.* to smirk or grimace in affected fashion.

Sim′ple, *a.* uncomplicated, plain, clear, straightforward, humble. **Sim′pleton,** *n.* mentally defective person. **Simplic′ity,** *n.* condition of being simple or unadorned, humility. **Sim′plify,** *v.t.* to make simple. **Simplifica′tion,** *n.* **Sim′ply,** *adv.* clearly, merely, only.

Sim′ulate, *v.t.* to feign, imitate. **Simula′tion,** *n.*

Simulta′neous, *a.* done or happening at same time.

Sin, *n.* a moral crime. *v.i.*

Since, *adv.* subsequently, from a specific past time to the present, ago. *prep.* from the time of. *conj.* from the time that, because.

Sincere (-seer), *a.* straightforward, candid, honest. **Sincer′ity,** *n.*

Si′necure, *n.* easy job with little or no work.

Sin′ew, *n.* tendon linking muscle and bone, strength, anything that gives power, *esp.* as *n. pl.*

Sing, *v.t. & i.* to utter in mus. voice, to sing a mus. composition for voice, to pipe, to celebrate in poetry.

Singe, *v.t. & i.* to burn surface of lightly, remove or seal hair by this, remove feathers or down. *n.* a scorch, a surface burn.

Sin′gle, *a.* one only, unmarried, performed by one person, for the use of one person, purposeful, sincere. *v.t. & i. esp.* as single out, to select. *n.* a ticket for outward journey only, one run in cricket. **Single file,** people moving in line one after the other. **Single handed,** *a.* performed by oneself. **Single-hearted,** *a.,* **single-minded,** *a.* straightforward, sincere.

Sing′song, *a.* in a monotonous voice. *n.*

Sin′gular, *a. gram.* relating to the singular, one person or thing, remarkable, eccentric. **Singular′ity,** *n.* peculiarity, oddness.

Sin′ister, *a.* foreboding, evil in appearance, threatening, in heraldry on the left.

Sink, *v.t. & i.* to submerge or cause to submerge, to decline, to place under the surface. *n.* a fixed kitchen basin, *fig.* a haunt of iniquity. **Sink′er,** *n.* weight or device for causing object to sink.

Sinn′er, *n.* transgressor.

Sin′uous, *a.* curving, winding. **Sinuos′ity,** *n.*

Si'nus, *n.* pocket in bone or tissue.

Sip, *v.t. & i.* to drink in small mouthfuls. *n.*

Si'phon, *n.* device for drawing off liquids by atmospheric pressure. *v.t.*

Sir, (Sur), *n.* term of respect to man older or in superior position, title of knight or baronet.

Sire, *n. arch.* title of respect when addressing king.

Sire, *n.* father, male ancestor. *v.t.* to beget.

Si'ren, *n.* a sea-nymph, any alluring woman, an instrument for signalling time or warning. *a.* alluring.

Sir'loin, *n.* choice part of loin of beef.

Sis'ter, *n.* female having same parents as another person, a nun, a nurse in responsible position. **Sis'terly,** *a.* helpful in the manner of a sister. **Sis'-terhood,** *n.* the relationship of sisters, a rel. society or community. **Sister-in-law,** *n.* sister of husband or wife.

Sit, *v.t. & i.* to place or rest on a seat or chair, to be in position for riding on horse, to cover eggs for brooding or cause hen to brood these, to be in session, to pose. **Sitt'ing,** *n.* the act of being seated, a session, the period during which one sits.

Site, *n.* place or situation esp. for something to be erected.

Situa'tion, *n.* place or position, employment, predicament. **Sit'uated,** *a.* located, in what circumstances.

Size, *n.* dimensions, largeness, a system of measurement for clothing. *v.t.* to estimate

dimensions etc. **Size'able,** *a.* fairly big.

Size, *n.* glazing substance based on gelatine. *v.t.* to cover or treat with this.

Sizz'le, *v.i.* to make hissing, spluttering sound. *n.*

Skate, *n.* metal attachment for boot to enable one to progress on ice. *v.i.* to move freely on ice. **Roller-skate,** *n.* attachment with small wheels for moving on special surface. **Ska'ter,** *n.* **Ska'ting-rink,** *n.*

Skein (Skane), *n.* coil of wool etc.

Skel'eton, *n.* bone structure of human or animal body, any framework. **Skel'etal,** *a.* pertaining to a skeleton. **Skeleton-key,** *n.* specially designed key to operate number of different locks and used by criminals.

Sketch, *n.* a simple or preliminary drawing, the outline of an idea or project. a light theatrical entertainment. *v.t.* to draw lightly or simply.

Sketch'y, *a.* vague, not properly done.

Skew, *a.* slanting, not straight.

Skew'er, *n.* long metal or wooden pin for holding cooking meat in position. *v.t.* to fasten or pierce with skewer.

Ski (Skee), *n.* long narrow wooden runner with curved fore-end, strapped to each foot to enable easy progress over snow. *v.i.* to move on skis. **Ski'er** (Skee-er), *n.* person who skis.

Skid, *v.i.* to slide sideways while temporarily out of control. *n.* act of skidding, a form of brake, a wooden runner substituted for wheels on aircraft landing on ice.

Skiff, *n.* light rowing-boat.

Skill, *n.* competence, dexterity, applied experience. **Skil'ful,** *a.* adroit. **Skilled,** *a.* trained, expert.

Skill'et, *n.* cooking-pot with handle and sometimes on legs.

Skim, *v.t. & i.* to pass over lightly, to remove surface of liquid, take off the best, to glance through.

Skimp, *v.t. & i.* to scamp, perform perfunctorily, economize. **Skimp'y,** *a.* meagre.

Skin, *n.* outer covering of human body, animal's hide, rind of fruit or vegetable, any protective close-fitting covering. *v.t. & i.* to remove skin from, cover or become covered with skin. **Skin-deep,** *a.* superficial. **Skin-diving,** *n.* underwater diving with face-mask, breathing tube and flippers. **Skin-flint,** *n.* mean person. **Skinn'y,** *a.* scraggy.

Skip, *v.t. & i.* to jump or move in light bounding fashion, to miss out passages in reading. *n.*

Skip, *n.* a bucket or large basket.

Skipp'er, *n.* captain of fishing-boat, *coll.* captain of a team. *v.t.* to captain.

Skir'mish (Skur-), *n.* a confused brief encounter between opposing forces. *v.i.*

Skirt (Skurt), *n.* lower part of woman's dress, a border, outer edge. *v.t.* to border or pass along border.

Skit, *n.* a brief light satire.

Skitt'ish, *a.* flighty, capricious.

Skitt'les, *n.pl.* game in which nine wooden pins have to be knocked down with ball. **Skitt'-le,** *v.t.* to bowl over, defeat.

Skulk, *v.i.* to hang about furtively. **Skulk'er,** *n.* shirker.

Skull, *n.* bony framework of human or animal head.

Skunk, *n.* Amer. mammal able to emit strong offensive smell. *n. sl.* a mean person.

Sky, *n.* the heavens or upper atmosphere, the state of weather as evidenced by clouds. *v.t.* to hit a ball high. **Sky-blue,** *n. & a.* colour of clear sky. **Sky'light,** *n.* window in roof or ceiling. **Sky'line,** *n.* horizon, outline of landscape or buildings against sky. **Sky'scraper,** *n.* very tall building.

Slab, *n.* a thick flat piece of anything.

Slack, *a.* dilatory, sluggish, loose, inactive. *n.* part of rope etc. that is slack, worthless dusty coal. *v.t. & i.* to loosen, work lazily. **Slacks,** *n.pl.* as *n.* informal trousers. **Slack-water,** *n.* turn of tide. **Slack'en,** *v.t. & i.* to loosen, reduce speed. **Slack'er,** *n.* shirker.

Slag, *n.* refuse from mine.

Slake, *v.t. & i.* to satisfy, quench, mix with water esp. e.g. lime.

Slam, *v.t. & i.* to shut violently, put down noisily. *n.*

Slan'der, *v.t.* to defame by false or injurious verbal statements. *n.* **Slan'derous,** *a.*

Slang, *n.* jargon, popular but not standard speech.

Slant, *v.t. & i.* to slope, incline, tilt. *n.* an inclination, an oblique direction or position, *coll.* an attitude.

Slap, *n.* a blow with open hand. *v.t.*

Slap'dash, *a.* careless.

Slash, *v.t. & i.* to slit, cut violently, lash. *n.*

Slat, *n.* a long thin batten.

Slate, *n.* kind of rock readily divisible into thin plates, a shape made of this for covering roof. **Sla'ter,** *n.* craftsman who makes slates.

Slate, *v.t. sl.* to criticize harshly.

Slatt'ern (-turn), *n.* a slut.

Slaugh'ter (Slaw-), *v.t.* to kill violently, butcher, massacre. *n.* a great killing. **Slaugh'terer,** *n.* killer, butcher. **Slaughterhouse,** *n.* abattoir, place for killing meat-animals.

Slave, *n.* person owned by someone else, a drudge, addict of drink or drugs etc. *v.i.* to toil, work like a slave. *a.* pertaining to slaves. **Sla'ver,** *n.* person obtaining and selling slaves, the vessel he ships them in. **Sla'very,** *n.* state of being a slave, bondage. **Sla'vish,** *a.* servile, like a slave.

Slav'er, *v.t. & i.* to dribble.

Slay, *v.i.* to kill. **Slay'er,** *n.*

Slea'zy, *a.* disreputable.

Sled, *n.* a sledge, vehicle with curved bottom-runners for being hauled over snow. **Sledge,** *n. v.t. & i.* to go or transport by sled or sledge.

Sledge, *n.* esp. as sledge-hammer, large heavy hammer.

Sleek, *a.* smooth and glossy, *coll.* plausible.

Sleep, *n.* the condition of not being conscious, not awake. *v.t. & i.* to repose through sleep, to spend time, pass night. **Sleep'-er,** *n.* one who sleeps, compartment on train for sleeping, baulk of timber attached at right angles to railway-line. **Sleep-walking,** *n.* somnambulism, **Sleeping-car,** *n.* railway carriage equipped with beds.

Sleeping-partner, *n.* partner who invests money in project but takes no part in management. **Sleeping-sickness,** *n.* fatal Afric. sickness characterized by somnolence and paralysis of nerves.

Sleet, *n.* mixture of rain and snow. *v.i.* to fall as this.

Sleeve, *n.* part of garment that encloses person's arm, anything resembling this.

Sleigh (Slay), *n.* wheelless vehicle drawn by horses or reindeer for use on snow or ice. *v.i.* to travel by this.

Sleight (Slite), *n.* esp. as s. of hand, deftness, jugglery.

Slen'der, *a.* slim, slight.

Sleuth (Sluth), *n. iron.* a detective.

Slew (Sloo), *v.t. & i.* to turn round sharply.

Slice, *n.* thin flat wide piece. *v.t.* to cut in slices. *n.* an implement for doing this.

Slick, *a.* smart, quick, plausible.

Slide, *v.t. & i.* to glide, pass smoothly over, slip. *n.* a patch of ice or smooth place for sliding.

Slight, *a.* fragile, flimsy, insignificant. *v.t.* to treat as unimportant, to snub. *n.* a snub, insult. **Slight'ly,** *adv.* to an insignificant extent.

Slim, *a.* slender, not enough. *v.i.* to reduce weight by eating less.

Slime, *n.* filth, semi-liquid secretion of snail etc. **Sli'my,** *a. coll.* fawning.

Sling, *n.* a device for hurling missile, a support for injured limb, any support when lifting or carrying. *v.t.* to hurl, swing.

Slink, *v.i.* to skulk, move furtively.

Slip, *v.t. & i.* to make a mistake, to trip, slide, lose foothold, to move unobtrusively into place, put on a garment quickly, unleash dog. *n.* a place for launching ship, an undergarment, sleeveless pullover, fieldsman and position in cricket, a mistake. **Slip-knot,** *n.* a sliding knot. **Slip-stream,** *n.* stream of air driven astern by aircraft propeller. **Slipway,** *n.* launching place for ship. **Slipshod,** *a.* slovenly, down at heel, careless in work.

Slipp'er, *n.* comfortable indoor footwear.

Slipp'ery, *a.* with polished or smooth surface liable to cause one to slip, *coll.* unreliable, evasive.

Slit, *v.t.* to cut lengthwise. *n.*

Slith'er, *v.i.* to slip or slide, esp. out of control.

Sliv'er, *n.* a flake, splinter, small piece.

Slobb'er, *v.t. & i.* to drool, dribble, slaver. *n.*

Sloe, *n.* fruit of blackthorn.

Slog, *v.t. & i.* to work painfully and sedulously, to hit hard. *n.*

Slo'gan, *n.* formerly and properly a war-cry, now a catchword.

Sloop, *n.* one-masted sailing-vessel rigged fore-and-aft.

Slop, *n. esp. n.pl.* liquid refuse, in navy clothing. *v.t. & i.* splash over or spill. **Slopp'y,** *a.* liquid, sentimental, careless.

Slope, *n.* a slanting line or surface, the side of a hill or mountain. *v.t. & i.* to incline, slant.

Slot, *n.* a groove for admission of coins etc.

Slot, *n.* track of deer.

Sloth, *n.* laziness. **Sloth'ful,** *a.* lazy, dilatory.

Slouch, *v.i.* to move awkwardly with rounded shoulders. *n.* a shambling gait, a lazy person. **Slouch hat,** *n.* soft trilby.

Slough (-ow), *n.* a mire.

Slough (Sluff), *v.t. & i.* to shed skin as with snake. *n.* cast off skin.

Slov'en (Sluv-), *n.* a slatternly, unkempt person.

Slow (Slo), *a.* not fast, mentally dull, behind proper time. *v.t. & i.* to slacken speed, hinder.

Slug, *n.* animal resembling snail but without shell.

Slug, *n.* a crude bullet.

Slug, *v.t. coll.* to punch hard. **Slugg'ard,** *n.* lazy person. **Slugg'ish,** *a.* lazy, slow-moving, indolent.

Sluice (Slooce), *n.* artificial channel for water. **Sluice-gate,** *n.* gate for controlling this. **Sluice,** *v.t.* to wash with water.

Slum, *n.* a neglected overcrowded quarter of town. *v.i.* now *iron.* to visit people below one's putative station.

Sium'ber, *v.i.* to sleep. *n.*

Slump, *n.* a collapse of prices or market. *v.i.* to collapse, fall heavily.

Slur, *v.t.* to pronounce indistinctly, pass over hurriedly. *n.* a reproach, in mus. a connecting mark above notes.

Slush, *n.* melting snow, *coll.* sentimental nonsense.

Slut, *n.* slattern, dirty untidy woman. **Slutt'ish,** *a.*

Sly, *a.* furtively cunning, underhand.

Smack, *n.* a fishing-boat.

Smack, *n.* a slap with open hand. *v.t.*

Smack, *v.t. & i.* to taste of, to savour with smacking noise. *n.* a flavour.

Small (Smawl), *a.* not large, little, unimportant, insignificant in quantity or number etc., trivial.

Small-pox, *n.* contagious disease characterized by fever and skin eruptions.

Smart, *a.* well-dressed, lively, clever, fashionable. **Smart'en,** *v.t.* to make smart or tidier in manner or dress.

Smart, *v.i.* to experience stinging or tingling pain, to cause this, to feel offence or distress. *n. & a.*

Smash, *v.t. & i.* to break or shatter into fragments, to destroy. *n.* an accident, breakage.

Smatt'ering, *n.* slight superficial knowledge esp. of language.

Smear, *v.t. & i.* to spread paint or dirty matter, blotch, *coll.* to hint derogatorily. *n.*

Smell, *v.t. & i.* to exercise sense of smell through nose, to have a fragrance or unpleasant odour. *n.* a perfume, odour, olfactory sense. **Smell'y,** *a.* unpleasantly odorous.

Smelt, *v.t.* to melt esp. ore for separation of metal. **Smel'ter,** *n.* craftsman in this.

Smile, *n.* a facial and labial expression of pleasure or amusement, etc. *v.t.*

Smirch (Smurch), *v.t.* to soil, stain. *n.*

Smirk, *n.* an affected conceited smile. *v.i.*

Smite, *v.t.* to strike mightily, to affect.

Smith, *n.* craftsman who works in metal. **Smith'y,** *n.* his workshop. **Black'smith,** *n.*

Smock, *n.* long loose pleated garment once worn by farm-workers, a loose outer working garment. *v.t.* to stitch in pleats.

Smoke, *n.* visible vapour from burning matter. *v.t. & i.* to emit smoke, to preserve by smoke-treatment, to partake of tobacco. **Smo'ker,** *n.* person who indulges in tobacco, railway compartment in which smoking is allowed. **Smoke'-stack,** *n.* factory chimney, steamer's funnel.

Smooth, *a.* of polished or even surface, of uninterrupted action, not rough or harsh, plausible in manner. *v.t.* to make smooth, to soothe.

Smoth'er (Smuth-), *v.t. & i.* to cover up so as to suppress or suffocate, to lack air, feel restrained.

Smoul'der (Smole-), *v.i.* to burn slowly without flame, to feel emotion while suppressing it.

Smudge, *n.* a smear, blotch. *v.t.*

Smug, *a.* self-satisfied.

Smug'gle, *v.t. & i.* to traffic in goods without paying excise duty, to bring or take anything secretly. **Smug'gler,** *n.*

Smut, *n.* small piece of soot or burning material, *coll.* foul jokes or talk. **Smutt'y,** *a.*

Smutch, *v.t.* to sully with soot or smoke. *n.* **a smudge.**

Snack, *n.* a light hurried meal.

Snaf'fle, *n.* horse's jointed bit. *v.t.* to control by means of this.

Snag, *n.* a difficulty, a projection from a broken part.

Snail, *n.* mollusc with spiral shell, dullard, slow-moving person. **Snail's'pace,** *n.* a very slow pace.

Snake, *n.* a serpent, reptile, *coll.*

a mean wretch. *v.t. & i.* to move like a snake, crawl, wind.

Snap, *v.t. & i.* to speak angrily, express anger, to break suddenly, shut sharply, make sharp noise, make as if to bite, to seize, to take photograph. *n.* a spell of weather esp. cold, a photograph, a snapping, *a.* simple card game. *a.* quick, hasty. **Snapp'y**, *a.* brisk, irritable. **Snap'shot**, *n.* informal photograph.

Snare, *n.* a trap in the form of a noose, anything resembling a trap of this kind. *v.t.* to trap, entangle.

Snarl, *v.t. & i.* to utter a savage growling sound, to speak in angry fashion. *n.*

Snarl, *v.t. & i.* to become entangled.

Snatch, *v.t. & i.* to grab at, seize suddenly. *n.* a snatching, fragment of a song.

Sneak, *v.i.* to slink, proceed furtively, to inform against. *n.* an underhand person. **Sneak'-ing**, *a.* cowardly.

Sneer, *v.i.* to express contempt by word or look. *n.*

Sneeze, *v.i.* to expel air from nose explosively through cold or foreign body. *n.*

Sniff, *v.t. & i.* to draw in breath audibly through nose, to smell, to express doubt or contempt. *n.*

Sniff'le, *v.i.* to sniff repeatedly.

Snigg'er, *n.* suppressed derisive laugh. *v.i.*

Snip, *v.t.* to clip, cut lightly with scissors. *n.* a small piece.

Snipe, *n.* gamebird with long straight bill and swift zigzag flight.

Snipe, *v.i.* to shoot at from hid-

den place, esp. mil. **Sni'per**, *n.* hidden marksman.

Sniv'el, *v.i.* to sniffle, to to whimper. **Sniv'eller**, *n.* constantly complaining person.

Snob, *n.* social-climber, person who values wealth more than ability or intellect. **Snobb'ish**, *a.* **Snob'bery**, *n.*

Snook'er, *n.* game played on billiard table.

Snoot'y, *a. sl.* snobbish.

Snooze, *n.* a short sleep, a nap. *v.i.*

Snort, *n.* a noise caused by forcing air suddenly through nose. *v.i.*

Snout, *n.* muzzle of pig or other animal.

Snow, *n.* frozen water vapour falling as flakes or crystals. *v.t. & i.* to fall as snow, pour down as or like snow.

Snub, *v.t.* to rebuff. *n. a.* esp. as snubnose, short and turned up.

Snuff, *v.t.* to extinguish, to smell at.

Snuff, *n.* powdered tobacco for inhaling through nostrils.

Snuf'fle, *n.* a tendency to sniff repeatedly. *v.i.*

Snug, *a.* warm and cosy. **Snug'-gle**, *v.t. & i.* to hold or nestle close for warmth or affection. **Snugg'ery**, *n. coll.* a cosy nook or room.

So, *adv.* in such manner, to such a degree. *conj.* therefore.

Soak, *v.t. & i.* to wet or become thoroughly wet. *n.* a downpour, *coll.* an inveterate drunkard.

Soap, *n.* cleansing substance made of alkali and fat or oils. *v.t.* to use this.

Soar, *v.i.* to fly high.

Sob, *n.* a choking sound as of weeping. *v.i.*

So'ber, *a.* not intoxicated, temperate, level-headed. *v.t. & i.* to make or become sober or serious. **Sobri'ety,** *n.* state of being sober, seriousness.

So'briquet (-kay), *n.* a nickname.

Soci'ety, *n.* people collectively, an organized community, *iron.* the wealthy and notorious, an association. **So'cial,** *a.* pertaining to an organized community or human relationships. **So'-ciable,** *a.* tending to be friendly. **Sociabil'ity,** *n.* **Sociol'ogy,,** *n.* the study of human relationships. **So'cialism,** *n.* the doctrine that the good of the many is more important than that of the individual. **So'cialist,** *n.* person believing in this. **Socialist'ic,** *a.* **So'cialize,** *v.t.* to turn from private to public ownership.

Socc'er, *n.* Association Football in which ball may only be kicked with feet and not handled.

Sock, *n.* a covering for man's or child's foot.

Sock'et, *n.* a device with hole or holes for fitting plug or other object into.

Sod, *n.* turf, a piece of turf.

So'da, *n.* sodium carbonate, sodium bicarbonate etc. **So'da water,** *n.* water charged with carbon dioxide.

Sodd'en, *a.* thoroughly soaked.

Sod'omy, *n.* homosexuality. **Sod'-omite,** *n.*

So'fa, *n.* couch.

Soft, *a.* pliant, smooth, not hard or harsh, kind, mild, weak, out of condition, quiet. **Sof'ten** (Soff'n), *v.t. & i.* to make soft or softer, to reduce force.

Sogg'y, *a.* wet and heavy.

Soil, *n.* fertile earth, the land in general. *v.t. & i.* to make or become dirty.

Sojourn' (-jurn), *n.* a stay. *v.i.* to stay or dwell.

Sol'ace, *v.t.* to console, comfort in distress. *n.*

So'lar, *a.* pertaining to the sun.

Sol'der, *n.* metallic alloy which when melted is used for joining metals. *v.t.*

Sol'dier (Sole-jer), *n.* man serving in army esp. in ranks as opposed to officers. *v.i.* to serve as soldier, to struggle, esp. as soldier on. **Sol'diery,** *n.* troops in general. **Sol'dierly,** *a.* military, upright of carriage.

Sole, *n.* bottom of shoe or foot. *v.t.* to provide with sole.

Sole, *a.* alone, only, single.

Sole, *n.* edible flat-fish.

Sol'ecism, *n.* a verbal blunder, social rudeness.

Sol'emn (-em), *a.* serious, formal, grave. **Solem'nity** (em-ni-), *a.* solemnness, gravity. as *n.pl.* solemn ceremony. **Sol'-emnize,** *v.t.* to observe ceremonially, to make legal.

Solic'it, *v.t.* to ask for persistently, to importune, seek. **Solicita'tion,** *n.*

Solic'itor, *n.* a lawyer.

Solic'itude, *n.* concern, anxiety, for someone else. **Solic'itous,** *a.*

Sol'id, *a.* neither liquid, vapourous or hollow, compact, substantial, unyielding, unbroken. *n.* a solid body, a body of three dimensions *geom.* **Solid'ify,** *v.t. & i.* to make or become solid or rigid. **Solid'ity,** *n.*

Solidar'ity, *n.* an agreement or unity of opinion or effort.

Solil'oquize (-kwyze), *v.i.* to talk to oneself. **Sol'iloquy,** *n.*

Sol'itary, *a.* alone, secluded,

deserted. **Sol'itude,** *n.* the condition of being solitary.

So'lo, *n.* a performance carried out by one person alone. **So'loist,** *n.* particularly in mus. a person performing alone.

Sol'stice (-stiss), *n.* time when sun reaches farthest distance *n.* or *s.* of equator, esp. as summer or winter s.

Sol'uble, *a.* capable of being dissolved in liquid. **Solubil'ity,** *n.* **Solu'tion,** *n.* act of dissolving, liquid with other substance dissolved in it.

Solve, *v.t.* to discover explanation of or answer to problem or mystery. **Solu'tion,** *n.* the answer to a problem, **Sol'vent,** *n.* liquid capable of dissolving other substance. **Sol'vency,** *n.* position of being able to cover all one's debts. **Sol'vent,** *a.*

Som'bre (-ber), *a.* gloomy, dark. **Sombre'ro,** *n.* wide-brimmed. S. Amer. hat. for giving shade.

Some (Sum) *a.* a certain number, particular but unspecified, an indefinite amount. *pron.* particular but unspecified person. *adv.* nearly, about. **Some'body,** *pron.* an unknown or unspecified person. **Some'how,** *adv.* by some means. **Some'one,** *pron.* somebody. **Some'thing,** *pron.* **Some'time,** *adv.* at an unspecified time. **Some'times,** *adv.* occasionally.

Som'ersault (Summer-salt), *v.i.* to turn over rapidly by going head over heels. *n.*

Some'what, *adv.* to an indefinite extent. **Some'where,** *adv.* in an unspecified place.

Somnam'bulism, *n.* sleep-walking. **Somnam'bulist,** *n.*

Som'nolent, *a.* sleepy. **Som'nolence,** *n.*

Son (Sun) *n.* a male child. **Son-in-law,** *n.* husband of a daughter.

Sona'ta (-ahtah), *n.* mus. composition with several movements, esp. for piano.

Song, *n.* words set to mus. **Song'ster,** *n.* *iron.* or of bird, one who sings.

Son'ic, *a.* pertaining to sound.

Sonn'et, *n.* poem of fourteen lines with special rhyme scheme.

Sonor'ous, *a.* resonant. **Sonor'ity,** *n.*

Soon, *adv.* shortly, before long.

Soot, *n.* black powdery deposit caused by burning. **Soot'y,** *a.*

Sooth, *n.* arch. truth. **Sooth'sayer,** *n.* fortuneteller, person claiming power to forecast future.

Soothe, *v.t.* to pacify, calm.

Sop, *n.* any food dipped in liquid, a trivial compensation.

Soph'istry, *n.* facile but fallacious reasoning. **Soph'ism,** *n.* **Soph'ist,** *n.* person whose reasoning is facile but faulty. **Sophist'ical,** *a.* quibbling. **Sophist'icate,** *v.t. & i.* to indulge in sophism, to corrupt, spoil naturalness of. **Sophistica'tion,** *n.* experience of subtle or material ways. **Sophis'ticated,** *a.* contemptuous of innocence, professing great experience.

Soporif'ic, *a. & n.* inducing sleep.

Sopra'no (-prah-), *n.* highest female or boy's voice, mus. for this. *a.*

Sor'cerer, *n.* a magician, wizard. **Sor'cery,** *n.* witchcraft.

Sor'did, *a.* squalid, degraded.

Sore, *a.* painful, *coll.* resentful. *n.* a sore place.

Sore'ly, *adv.* greatly, severely.

Sorr'el, *n.* & *a.* reddish brown colour.

Sorr'ow (-o), *n.* grief, mental distress. *v.i.* to feel sorrow. **Sorr'owful,** *a.*

Sorr'y, *a.* regretful, wretched.

Sort, *n.* a kind or species. *v.t.* to arrange in different sorts.

Sor'tie, *n.* a sudden attack by defenders.

Sot, *n.* a drunkard. **Sott'ish,** *a.*

Sough (Sow), *n.* murmuring sound as of wind. *v.i.*

Soul (Sole), *n.* the essential spirit, the spiritual part of man, personification. **Soul'ful,** *a.* us. *iron.* full of lofty sentiment. **Soul'less,** *a.* ignoble, dull.

Sound (Sownd), *a.* in good condition, unharmed, without fault, thorough. **Sound'ly,** *adv.* thoroughly.

Sound, *n.* what is heard, noise, range of hearing, anything audible. *v.t.* & *i.* to make or cause to make a sound, to seem.

Sound, *v.t.* & *i.* to ascertain depth of water, find out views, to dive deeply esp. of whale. **Soun'ding,** *n.* act of measuring depth of water. *n. pl.* water shallow enough to allow measuring-line and lead to be used.

Soup (Soop), *n.* hot liquid food with vegetables or meat etc.

Sour (Sowr), *a.* acid in taste through fermentation or unripeness or character, disagreeable. *v.t.* & *i.* to turn or cause to turn sour.

Source, *n.* a spring, origin.

Souse (Sows), *v.t.* to drench, pickle. *n.*

South (Sowth), *n.* point opposite to the n., point of compass, region lying to the s. *a.* pertaining to the s. *adv.* to the s. **South'erly,** *a.* (Suth-) & *adv.* pertaining to, toward or coming from the s. **South'ern** (Suth-), *a.* in or of the south. **South'erner** (Suth), *n.* native of the south. **South'ward, south'wards,** *a.* & *adv.* to or towards the s.

Sou'wester (Sow-), *n.* oilskin hat worn by sailors.

Sou'venir (Soo-), *n.* a memento.

Sov'ereign (Sov'rin), *n.* a monarch, a British gold coin equivalent to £1 sterling. *a.* supreme, independent. **Sov'ereignty,** *n.* supreme power or dominion.

So'viet, *n.* a council, orig. revolutionary but becoming basis of Russian government.

Sow, *n.* female pig.

Sow (So), *v.t.* & *i.* to plant seed or scatter for planting. **Sow'er,** *n.* one who sows.

Spa (Spah), *n.* a health resort esp. with med. waters.

Space, *n.* limitless expanse surrounding and containing universe, extent, room, interval between things. *v.t.* to arrange at intervals or with intervals between. **Spa'cious,** *a.* vast, roomy. **Spa'tial,** *a.* pertaining to space.

Spade, *n.* an implement for digging.

Spade, *n.* in cards one of a suit called spades.

Spaghett'i (-getti), *n.* type of thin macaroni.

Span, *n.* the distance between

two connected points, distance between outstretched thumb and little finger, distance covered by bridge etc. *v.t.* to measure, to extend across.

Span'gle, *n.* ornamental metallic disk. *v.i.* to glitter.

Spank, *v.t. & i.* to beat person on posterior esp. with flat hand. *n.* **Spank'ing,** *n.* a beating thus.

Spank'ing, *a.* lively, fine.

Spann'er, *n.* a tool with adjustable head for gripping.

Spar, *n.* a ship's mast or boom.

Spar, *n.* a crystalline mineral.

Spar, *v.i.* to box lightly, argue lightly. **Spar'ring partner,** *n.* person one practises boxing with or habitually argues with.

Spare, *v.t.* to do without, to use economically, save, refrain from, let off. *a.* lean, meagre, in reserve. **Spar'ing,** *a.* frugal.

Spark, *n.* burning particle coming from fire, flash produced in engine or by elec. *v.i.* to give off sparks, as spark off, to start, ignite. **Spark,** *n. coll.* a gay young person resembling a spark. **Spar'kle,** *v.i.* to glitter like sparks.

Sparse, *a.* thinly distributed.

Spar'tan, *a.* tough, unwavering. *n.*

Spasm, *n.* a sudden muscular seizure, sudden onset of emotion. **Spasmod'ic,** *a.* marked by spasms, intermittent. **Spas'tic,** *a. med.* defect accompanied by continued spasm.

Spat, *n.* protective gaiter for ankle and instep.

Spate, *n.* sudden river flood after downpour.

Spatt'er, *v.t.* to splash with liquid. *n.*

Spat'ula, *n. med.* instrument for

pressing down or moving tongue for inspection, similar tool for spreading paint or ointment. **Spat'ulate,** *a.* shaped like a spatula, in long flat blade form.

Spav'in, *n.* disease causing lameness in horses. **Spav'ined,** *a.*

Spawn, *n.* eggs of fish, frogs etc. *v.i.* to produce spawn.

Speak, *v.t. & i.* to express or utter in words, to say, mention, communicate with verbally.

Speak'er, *n.* person who speaks, presiding officer of House of Commons.

Spear, *n.* a weapon with sharp pointed blade attached to long shaft. *v.t.* to pierce with this. **Spear'head,** *n.* the vanguard of a force.

Spec'ial, *a.* particular, unusual, with characteristics out of the ordinary, devoted to or meant for a particular purpose. **Spec'ialist,** *n.* person skilled at and working in one particular subject or branch of this, a specializing med. practitioner. **Spec'ialize,** *v.i.* to work as a specialist. **Special'ity,** *n.* something person is particularly good at, an article specialized in, something distinctive.

Spe'cie (Spe-shi) *n.* gold or silver coin.

Spe'cies, *n.* class of animals or plants with common characteristics. *pl.* same.

Specif'ic, *a.* relating to a definite object, precise, possessing curative quality. *n.* a definite remedy. **Specif'ically,** *adv.* definitely, in particular. **Spec'ify,** *v.t.* to mention or state definitely. **Specifica'tion,** *n.* the act of specifying, detailed description of items needed or work to be done.

Spec'imen, *n.* a representative example.

Spe'cious, *a.* plausible, superficially convincing.

Speck, *n.* a particle.

Spec'kle, *n.* a small mark or blotch. *v.t.* to mark with speckles.

Spec'tacle, *n.* something remarkable to see, a public show. **Spectac'ular,** *a.* exciting or remarkable to see.

Spec'tacles, *n. pl.* framed lenses for correction of vision.

Specta'tor, *n.* an onlooker.

Spec'tre (-ter), *n.* a phantom. **Spec'tral,** *a.*

Spec'trum, *n.* coloured band into which beam of light can be divided by passing through prism etc. **Spec'troscope,** *n.* instrument used for viewing spectrum or spectra (pl.).

Spec'ulate, *v.i.* to guess, theorize, deal in stocks and shares in hope of making profit. **Spec'ulator,** *n.* person who engages in financial dealings. **Spec'ulative,** *a.* pertaining to speculation. **Specula'tion,** *n.* a guess, a conjecture, dealing in stocks and shares.

Speech, *n.* the act or power of speaking, language, a formal address. **Speech'ify,** *v.i. iron.* to talk at length or pompously.

Speed, *n.* swiftness, rate of motion. *v.t. & i.* to move fast, to hasten, bid farewell to, prosper. **Speed'y,** *a.* **Speedom'eter,** *n.* device for calculating speed of vehicle.

Spell, *v.t. & i.* to form words with letters, to put letters of word in proper order, *fig.* to mean.

Spell, *n.* a charm, a magic influence. **Spell'bound,** *a.*

Spell, *n.* a short period, a short period of work.

Spel'ter, *n.* zinc.

Spend, *v.t.* to pay out money, to pass time, use up energy. **Spend'ing,** *n.* the act of spending, money paid out. **Spend'thrift,** *n.* wastrel, extravagant person.

Sperm (Spurm), *n.* male fertilizing fluid.

Sperm, *n.* yellowish oil from head of Sperm whale. **Spermacet'i,** *n.* waxy substance from head of Sperm whale.

Spew, *v.t. & i.* to vomit.

Sphere, *n.* a globe, round solid body, extent of influence or knowledge etc. **Spher'ical,** *a.* round or like a sphere. **Sphe'roid,** *n.* solid body almost but precisely a sphere.

Sphinx, *n.* legendary Greek monster with woman's bust and lion's body who made people answer her riddles on pain of death if they failed, an Egyptian monument, any mysterious or enigmatic person.

Spice, *n.* aromatic powder obtained from certain plants and used for flavouring. *v.t.* to flavour with spices. **Spi'cy,** *a.* well flavoured, racy, slightly daring.

Spick, *a.* us. only as s. and span, smart and neat.

Spi'der, *n.* insectlike, wingless animal with eight legs which us. spins a web as snare for prey. **Spider'y,** *a.* like a spider, scrawling, very thin and delicate.

Spig'ot, *n.* plug for air-hole in barrel or cask.

Spike, *n.* a pointed projection, an ear of corn, cluster of flowers, sharp piece of metal. *v.t.* to pierce or fasten with spike.

Spike'nard, *n. Bib.* fragrant ointment made from plant of same name.

Spile, *n.* a spigot, a foundation pile or stake.

Spill, *v.t. & i.* to flow over or cause to flow over.

Spill, *n.* twisted paper or strip of wood as taper.

Spin, *v.t. & i.* to draw out wool etc. and draw into threads, to revolve or whirl rapidly, to draw out, to make thread, to form web, lengthen. *n.* a trip (coll.). **Spind'le,** *n.* tapering rod for twisting and winding thread, pin or rod on which something revolves. **Spinn'ing-wheel,** *n.* domestic machine for spinning wool etc.

Spin'drift, *n.* foam blown across sea.

Spine, *n.* the backbone, spinal column, a thorn. **Spi'nal,** *a.* to do with the back or spine. **Spinal column,** *n.* the backbone. **Spine'less,** *a.* feeble in character, invertebrate.

Spin'et, *n.* mus. instrument resembling but preceding harpsichord.

Spinn'aker, *n.* large triangular sail used by racing yacht.

Spinn'ey, *n.* a copse, small wood.

Spin'ster, *n.* unmarried woman.

Spi'ral, *a.* coiled like a screw. *n.* a spiral body or shape.

Spire, *n.* pointed part of steeple.

Spir'it, *n.* the soul, essential non-material part, motivating force, a ghost, courage, attitude of mind, alcohol. *v.t.* esp. as spirit away, cause to disappear. **Spir'itless,** *a.* listless, without courage. **Spir'itual,** *a.* pertaining to the spirit, not material, elevated in thought. **Spir'ituality,** *n.* **Spir'itualism,** *n.* belief that souls or spirits of dead persons can communicate with the living through a medium.

Spirt (Spurt), *v.t. & i.* to pour or gush out suddenly. *n.*

Spit, *v.t. & i.* to eject saliva etc. from mouth, to make hostile noise as with cat. **Spit'tle,** *n.* saliva.

Spite, *n.* malice, animosity. **Spite'ful,** *a.*

Splash, *v.t. & i.* to spatter with mud or liquid, to move about noisily in water. *n.*

Splay, *v.t. & i.* to spread out, dislocate, slope. **Splayed,** *a.* spread out. **Splay-footed,** *a.* with feet habitually turned outwards.

Spleen, *n.* organ adjoining stomach which affects blood, *fig.* ill temper.

Splen'did, *a.* fine, magnificent, excellent.

Splen'dour, *n.* brilliance, magnificence, grandeur.

Splenet'ic, *a.* pertaining to the spleen, ill-tempered.

Splice, *v.t.* to join by interweaving strands of rope, to join by overlapping. *n.* a splicing, connecting part of handle and blade in cricket bat.

Splint, *n.* appliance for holding broken bone in place while setting.

Splin'ter, *n.* thin sharp fragment

of wood or metal. *v.t. & i.* to break into splinters.

Split, *v.t. & i.* to chop, divide, break apart, quarrel. *n.* Splitt'ing, *a.*

Splotch, *n.* a blotch, stain. *v.t.*

Splutt'er, *v.t. & i.* to talk incoherently, to make a confused noise of excitement or anger, make a hissing noise. *n.*

Spoil, *v.t. & i.* to damage, harm, decay, plunder, indulge. *n.* or *n. pl.* booty.

Spoke, *n.* one of bars connecting hub with rim of wheel.

Spoke'shave, *n.* carpenter's tool for planing curved surface.

Spokes'man, *n.* person who speaks officially for others.

Spolia'tion, *n.* the act of spoiling, damage, plunder.

Sponge (Spunj), *n.* porous absorbent material obtained from marine animal of this name. *v.t. & i.* to cleanse with a sponge, *coll.* to scrounge. Spon'ger, *n.* human parasite. Spon'gy, *a.* of the texture of a sponge.

Spon'sor, *n.* person who introduces another person or project or is responsible for these. *v.t.*

Sponta'neous, *a.* happening or done without outside influence. Spontane'ity, *n.*

Spook, *n.* a ghost. Spook'y, *a.* with an eerie atmosphere.

Spool, *n.* cylinder for winding film or thread etc.

Spoon, *n.* eating implement with shallow bowl at end of handle. *v.t.* to take up with a spoon.

Spoon'erism, *n.* unintentional transposition of sounds or letters in successive words us. with amusing effect.

Spoor, *n.* track of a wild animal.

Sporad'ic, *a.* intermittent, occasional.

Spore, *n.* small reproductive cell in flowerless plant such as fungus.

Sporr'an, *n.* pouch worn in front of Highlander's kilt.

Sport, *n.* outdoor recreation, organized games or other activities, amusement, *coll.* a person who plays for enjoyment and does not mind losing. *v.t. & i.* to play, *coll.* to show off. Sport'ing, *a.* Sports'man, *n.* person who plays or indulges in sport, fair-minded person. Sports'manship, *n.*

Spot, *n.* a small mark or stain, a place. *v.t. & i.* to mark with a spot or spots, *coll.* to catch sight of. Spot'less, *a.* unblemished. Spot'light, *n.* strong beam of light thrown on particular spot on stage, *fig.* public prominence. Spott'y, *a.* covered in spots or pimples, *coll.* irregular.

Spouse, *n.* husband or wife.

Spout, *v.t. & i.* to jet or gush out, *sl.* to talk verbosely. *n.* projecting device for facilitating pouring, drainpipe.

Sprain, *v.t.* to wrench, twist. *n.* injury to muscles or ligaments through spraining.

Sprawl, *v.t. & i.* to sit, lie or pose in any way in untidy fashion, to cause to do this. *n.* an ungainly position or movement.

Spray, *n.* a small bunch of flowers, a growing branch with flowers.

Spray, *n.* water or other liquid dispersed or flying in small drops, a device for sending out liquid in very fine form. *v.t.*

Spread (Spred), *v.t. & i.* to cover or cause to cover with, to extend, to send out, disperse. *n.* growth, extension, a bed-covering, *sl.* a feast.

Spree, *n.* a pleasure outing or party.

Sprig, *n.* a small plant-shoot, *coll.* a son, youth.

Spright'ly, *a.* lively, spirited.

Spring, *v.t. & i.* to bound, jump, rise up from, come or gush forth, originate from, reveal, develop, strain. *n.* the act of springing, a springing device, a water-source. **Spring'board,** *n.* elevated jumping stand for diving. **Spring tide,** *n.* time when variation between high and low tide is greatest. **Spring'y,** *a.* lissom, elastic.

Spring, *n.* season of year following winter and preceding summer. *a.* **Spring-tide,** *n.* springtime.

Sprin'kle, *v.t. & i.* to water lightly, to pour out particles c.g. of salt, to rain lightly. **Sprin'kling,** *n.* a very small amount.

Sprint, *v.i.* to run very fast for a short distance. *n.* **Sprint'er,** *n.* athlete specializing in short distances.

Sprit, *n.* small spar in sailing-vessel. **Sprit'sail** (-s'l), *n.* fore-and-aft sail extended by sprit.

Sprite, *n.* a goblin.

Sprock'et, *n. esp.* s.-wheel, toothed wheel on bicycle etc. working in conjunction with chain.

Sprout (Sprowt), *v.i.* to start to grow, to put forth. *n.* a new shoot, a kind of green vegetable.

Spruce, *a.* smart and tidy. *v.t. & i.* to tidy oneself, dress smartly.

Spruce, *n.* coniferous tree.

Spry, *a.* alert.

Spud, *n.* gardener's digging-tool.

Spume, *n.* foam.

Spur, *n.* device with small toothed wheel worn by horseman for goading on horse, *fig.* anything that encourages action or effort, fighting-claw on cockerel's leg, a mountain-ridge. *v.t. & i.* to use a spur, urge on, hurry on.

Spu'rious, *a.* bogus, sham.

Spurn, *v.t.* to reject contemptuously.

Spurt, *v.t. & i.* to make a short sudden effort. *n.*

Spu'tum, *n.* saliva.

Spy, *n.* a secret agent who obtains information for another country or works against his own in same way. *v.t. & i.* to act thus, to watch keenly, to catch sight of. **Spy'glass,** *n.* (not us.) telescope.

Squab (Squob), *n.* a young pigeon.

Squab'ble, *n.* an unpleasant quarrel. *v.i.*

Squad (Skwod), *n.* small detachment of soldiers parading or drilling.

Squad'ron, *n.* a formation of cavalry, tanks, aircraft, battleships.

Squal'id, *a.* sordid, wretched. **Squal'or,** *n.*

Squall (Skwawl), *n.* a stormy gust, *sl.* trouble. *v.t. & i.* to make a noise like a squawk, to cry peevishly.

Squan'der (Skwon-), *v.t.* to waste, spend extravagantly.

Square, *n.* rectangular figure with four equal sides, a public place surrounded by buildings, anything resembling a square, *math.* the product of multiplying a number by itself, implement for checking or drawing right-angles. *a.* square in shape, *coll.* honest, above-board, *sl.* liking classical mus. as opposed to more modern effusions. *v.t. & i.* to make square, to settle, arrange. **Square-rigged**, *a.* of sailing ship rigged thus as opposed to fore-and-aft. **Square-dance**, *n.* group dance of gay and complicated character.

Squash, (Skwosh) *v.t. & i.* to crush, mash, crowd together, subdue, rebuff. *n.* anything squashed, crowded conditions.

Squash, *n.* a game played in walled court with racket and hard rubber ball.

Squash, *n.* a kind of gourd, a fruit-drink.

Squat (Skwot), *a.* short and dumpy. *v.i.* to crouch on bent knees and heels touching or near haunches.

Squat, *v.i.* to occupy land or house illegally. **Squat'ter**, *n.*

Squaw, *n.* Amer. Indian woman.

Squawk, *n.* loud harsh cry. *v.i.*

Squeak, *n.* small shrill cry. *v.i.* **Squeak'y**, *a.* thin and high-pitched.

Squeal, *n.* long piercing cry, esp. of pig. *v.i.* to utter this, *sl.* to inform against, betray. **Squeal'er**, *n.*

Squeam'ish, *a.* easily shocked or sickened, excessively scrupulous.

Squeeze, *v.t. & i.* to compress, apply pressure to. *n.*

Squelch, *v.t.* to make splashing sound, walk through mud.

Squib, *n.* a small firework, *coll.* a trivial essay or remark.

Squid, *n.* kind of cuttlefish.

Squint, *n.* a defect of eyesight in which eyes are not properly adjusted, *sl.* a sideways or quick glance. *v.t.* to have a cross-eyed look.

Squire, *n. arch.* a knight's attendant, a country landowner exerting influence over a village. *v.t.* to escort esp. a woman. **Squire-arch'y** (-arki), *n.* country gentry.

Squirm (Skwurm), *v.i.* to wriggle.

Squirr'el, *n.* small arboreal rodent.

Squirt (Skwurt), *v.t. & i.* to force out jet of water etc., to issue forth in jet.

Stab, *v.t. & i.* to wound or pierce with pointed weapon, feel sudden pain. *n.*

Stabil'ity, *n.* condition of being stable, firmness, steadiness. **Sta'bilize**, *v.t.* to make firm or stable. **Sta'ble**, *a.* firm, steady.

Sta'ble, *n.* building for horses, training-establishment for race-horses. *v.t. & i.* to put horse in stable.

Stacca'to (-kah-), *a. mus.* in abrupt style, sharply accented. *adv.*

Stack, *n.* a large pile of hay or timber etc, a chimney structure. *v.t.* to pile up, arrange in stack.

Sta'dium, *n.* sports arena.

Staff, *n.* a long walking-stick, a pole.

Staff, *n.* persons collectively employed in business, educational, or mil. operation, servants. *v.t.* to provide with staff.

Stag, *n.* male deer.

Stage, *n.* the theatre or theatrical profession, a raised platform for performing on, point or period in development, place of any event, part of a journey. *v.t.* to put on a play. **Stage'-coach,** *n.* formerly a regular means of horse-drawn conveyance between regular stages or stops.

Stagg'er, *v.t. & i.* to totter or cause to totter, to make as if to fall, *coll.* to shock, to arrange in shifts.

Stag'nate, *v.i.* to cease to flow, to become spiritless. **Stag'nant,** *a.* sluggish, stale through not moving. **Stagna'tion,** *n.*

Staid, *a.* sedate.

Stain, *v.t. & i.* to blemish, mark with spot, spoil honour or reputation. *n.* **Stain'less,** *a.* unblemished. **Stainless steel,** *n.* untarnishable steel.

Stair, *n.* one of set of steps in stairway. **Stair'case,** *n.* flight of steps inside building. **Stair'way,** *n.*

Stake, *n.* a sharp-ended post, *arch.* death by burning while tied to a stake. *v.t.* to mark out with stakes, to claim by doing this.

Stake, *n.* money put down in betting. *v.t.* to wager.

Stal'actite, *n.* carbonate of lime hanging like icicle from roof of cave.

Stal'agmite, *n.* carbonate of lime dripping from cave of roof and causing inverted icicle-like formation on floor.

Stale, *a.* not fresh, worn out, out of condition. *v.i.* to become stale, of horses to urinate.

Stalk (Stawk), *n.* stem of flower or corn etc.

Stalk, *v.i.* to approach secretly, follow closely. **Stalk'ing,** *n.* the act of doing this. **Deer'-stalking,** *n.*

Stall (Stawl), *n.* front seat in theatre, a church pew or seat in choir, a compartment for cow etc. in byre, an open-air temporary shop in market.

Stall, *v.t. & i.* to stop suddenly and unintentionally, esp. of engine.

Stall'ion (stal-), *n.* uncastrated male horse.

Stal'wart, *a.* sturdy, dependable. *n.* a man of this quality.

Sta'men, *n.* male pollen-bearing flower organ.

Stam'ina, *n.* power of endurance.

Stamm'er, *n.* a defect in speech causing repetition of words or syllables. *v.t. & i.*

Stamp, *n.* a gummed decorated label as token of payment for postage, a die. *v.t. & i.* to affix a stamp to, to mark with a die, to crush, to put down foot violently.

Stam'pede, *n.* a sudden violent panic or scattering esp. of animals or humans. *v.i.* to rush off or scatter in panic.

Stance (stahnce), *n.* a posture, a way of standing.

Stanch'ion, *n.* a supporting post under ceiling or deckhead.

Stand, *v.t. & i.* to be in an erect position, to place upright, to remain firm, to represent. *n.* a resistance, a structure for hanging or placing things on, an outdoor seating arrangement for spectators, an exhibitor's stall at show.

Stand'ard, *n.* a flag, emblem, a reliable or established measure or comparison, a tall upright post or support. **Stan'dardize,** *v.t.* to bring into conformation with a recognized standard. **Stan'ding,** *n.* reputation.

Stand'point, *n.* point of view.

Stan'nary, *n.* tin-mine, tin-mining area.

Stan'-za *n.* group of lines of poetry.

Sta'ple, *n.* important or principal material or commodity, a standard or classification of wool, a place where wool is brought for assessing, a U-shaped double-pointed piece of metal. *a.* regularly used or produced.

Star, *n.* a heavenly body, anything made in the shape of a star, *coll.* a renowned sportsman or actor etc. *v.t.* to mark with stars, to feature prominently.

Star'board, *n.* right-hand side of ship facing bows. *a. v.t.* to turn to starboard.

Starch, *n.* substance occurring in corn, potatoes etc. and necessary in food, preparation made from this and used in stiffening laundry. *v.t.* to apply starch to. **Starch'y,** *a.* containing starch, *coll.* stiff in manner.

Stare, *v.t.* to regard long and fixedly. *n.*

Stark, *a.* utter, rigid.

Start, *v.t. & i.* to begin, set in motion, to make a sudden movement, *n.*

Star'tle, *v.t. & i.* to frighten by sudden action, scare.

Starve, *v.t. & i.* to die or suffer from hunger, to deprive of food. **Starva'tion,** *n.* extreme hunger. **Starve'ling,** *n.* starving person or animal.

State, *n.* condition, civil government, sovereign community or nation, dignity, pomp, rank. **State'ly,** *a.* dignified. **States'-man,** *n.* person engaged in state affairs. **States'manship,** *n.* **State'room,** *n.* large private cabin in liner.

State, *v.t.* to express in words, declare, say emphatically. **State'ment,** *n.* a verbal expression, a formal description or account, a detailed account of items purchased.

Stat'ic, *a.* motionless. *n. pl.* branch of physics concerned with motionless bodies or forces in balance.

Sta'tion, *n.* usual position of person or thing, position in life, regular stopping place on railway, official building of police or fire-fighting force. *v.t.* to put in a definite post or position. **Sta'tionary,** *a.* not moving.

Sta'tionery, *n.* paper and other writing materials. **Sta'tioner,** *n.* person who manufactures or supplies such.

Statist'ics, *n.pl.* numerical data collected, arranged and applied scientifically. **Statisti'cian,** *n.*

Stat'ue, *n.* a decorative or memorial sculpture of a figure or other subject. **Stat'uary,** *n.* collection of statues. **Statuesque',** like a statue, of a formal kind of dignity or beauty.

Stat'ure, *n.* height of a person.

Sta'tus, *n.* position, rank. **Sta'-tus symbol,** *n. iron.* any material possession which is proof one's equality with neighbours.

Stat'ute, *n.* an officially enacted law. **Stat'utory,** *a.* enacted or defined by law.

Staunch (Stawnch) *v.t.* to arrest the flow of, esp. blood.

Staunch, *a.* loyal, dependable.

Stave, *n.* a staff, curved narrow strip of wood for including in side of barrel, a verse of song, in mus. set of five horizontal lines and intervening spaces on which notes are written. *v.t.* to break a hole in or ward off as with a staff.

Stay, *v.t. & i.* to remain, postpone, satisfy, dwell for a short time. *n.* a visit, a postponement.

Stay, *n.* a prop or support, a rope for supporting.

Stays, *n.pl.* corsets.

Stead (Sted), *n.* place, advantage.

Stead′y, *a.* firm, unshakeable, unwavering. **Stead′ily,** *adv.* progressively. **Stead′fast,** *a.* resolute, unflinching. **Stead′y,** *v.t. & i.* to make or become firm or steady.

Steak (Stake), *n.* slice of beef.

Steal, *v.t. & i.* to thieve, move stealthily. **Stealth** (Stelth), *n.* secrecy, underhand behaviour. **Stealth′y** (Stelthy), *a.* furtive.

Steam, *n.* vapour from boiling water. *v.t. & i.* to emit steam or vapour, to boil or treat with steam, to progress by steam power. **Steam′boat, steam′ship,** *nn.* vessels powered by steam engines. **Steam′er,** *n.* steamship. **Steam roller,** *n.* heavy roller powered by steam. **Steam engine,** *n.* railway locomotive. **Steam shovel,** *n.* excavator powered by steam.

Steed, *n.* a riding-horse.

Steel, *n.* alloy of carbon and iron processed to produce hard tough metal, anything made of steel, steel tool for sharpening knives. *a.* made of steel. *v.t.* to treat or make with steel, *fig.* to brace oneself.

Steep, *a.* precipitous, almost vertical. *n.* a steep place. *coll.* excessive.

Steep, *v.t. & i.* to soak or cause to be soaked.

Stee′ple, *n.* church spire or tower with spire. **Steeple-chase,** *n.* cross-country horse-race. **Steeple-jack,** *n.* workman who repairs steeples or high chimneys etc.

Steer, *n.* a castrated bull.

Steer, *v.t. & i.* to control course of vessel or vehicle by means of rudder, tiller, steering-wheel, to guide, be guided. **Steer′age,** *n.* cheapest accomodation in passenger ship. **Steering-wheel,** *n.* wheel for steering vessel or vehicle. **Steers′man,** *n.* sailor who steers.

Stell′ar, *a.* pertaining to the stars.

Stem, *n.* the main stalk of a plant, the shaft of a wine-glass, the main upright in a ship's bows, main part of word.

Stem, *v.t.* to check, stop.

Stench, *n.* a stink, disagreeable odour.

Sten′cil, *n.* hollow outline of letters which can be painted over so that complete letter appears on paper underneath. *v.t.*

Stenog′raphy, *n.* shorthand. **Stenog′rapher,** *n.* person skilled in this.

Stentor′ian, *a.* extremely loud esp. of voice.

Step, *v.t. & i.* to move foot forward or upward, to walk, measure in steps, set up mast. *n.* a small pace, a tread, movement of foot in walking, a short distance, a degree in progress, rank.

Step-, *pref.* indicating a relationship by remarriage, e.g. step-father etc.

Steppe, *n.* Russian prairie.

Ster'eoscope, *n.* optical instrument producing clearly defined single image of two pictures. **Stereoscop'ic,** *a.*

Ster'eotype, *n.* printing plate cast from mould of printing composed in movable type. *a.* printed from this, of anything perfunctory, monotonous.

Ster'ile, *a.* infertile, barren, free from germs. **Steril'ity,** *n.* barrenness. **Ster'ilize,** *v.t.* to make barren, to free from germs. **Steriliza'tion,** *n.*

Ster'ling (Stur-), *a.* of standard weight or quality, pertaining to British currency. *n.* British currency.

Stern (Sturn), *a.* strict, determined.

Stern, *n.* after-part of ship.

Ster'num, *n.* the breast-bone.

Ster'torous, *a.* emitting snore-like sounds, breathing heavily.

Steth'oscope, *n. med.* instrument for examining heart and lungs by aural means.

Ste'vedore, *n.* docker.

Stew, *v.t. & i.* to boil slowly in saucepan. *n.* dish of meat & vegetables so cooked.

Stew'ard, *n.* waiter or attendant on board ship or in club, race-course official.

Stick, *n.* a broken branch, long thin piece of wood, club used in hockey, anything resembling a stick.

Stick, *v.t. & i.* to affix, to paste, fasten, pierce, push, thrust, stay, persevere, protrude. **Stick'y,** *a.* having adhesive quality, *coll.* difficult.

Stick'ler, *n.* esp. as stickler for, person who obstinately insists on things being carried out in detail.

Stiff, *a.* rigid, firm, not working smoothly. **Stiff'en,** *v.t. & i.* to make or become stiff or stiffer. **Stiff'necked,** *a.* stubborn.

Sti'fle, *v.t.* to smother, suppress. **Sti'fling,** *a.* unbearably hot and stuffy.

Stig'ma, *n.* mark of disgrace. **Stig'mata,** *n.pl.* wounds left by crucifixion on the body of Christ. **Stig'matize,** *v.t.* to mark out in disgrace.

Stile, *n.* series of steps or other device for getting through or over bank or hedge.

Stilett'o, *n.* a small slender dagger, a needlework tool.

Still, *n.* apparatus for distilling alcohol.

Still, *adv.* up to present time, continuing, nevertheless, even. *conj.* yet, however.

Still, *a.* peaceful, quiet, motionless. *n.* quiet, silence. *v.t.* to quieten, calm. **Still'born,** *a.* dead at birth. **Still'y,** *a. poet.* silent, tranquil.

Stilt, *n.* one of pair of long poles with elevated foot-rest for trick walking.

Stil'ted, *a.* stiff in manner.

Stim'ulate, *v.t.* to rouse to activity, to incite, to increase activity or response. **Stim'ulant,** *n.* anything that stimulates. **Stimula'tion,** *n.* **Stim'ulus,** *n.* incentive, anything that activates or motivates.

Sting, *n.* sharp defensive or killing organ of various insects or animals. a sharp pain caused by this, any sharp pain mental or physical. *v.t. & i.* to apply sting to, to cause stinging pain, to offend.

Stin'gy (-ji), *a.* mean.

Stink, *n.* a stench, an unpleasant smell. *v.i.* to emit a stench.

Stint, *v.t. & i.* to supply in sparing fashion.

Stint, *n.* an adequate amount of work.

Sti'pend, *n.* salary. **Stipend'iary**, *a.* paid.

Stipp'le, *v.t. & i.* to draw or paint with dots.

Stip'ulate, *v.t.* to specify as a condition, to put forward as terms. **Stipula'tion**, *n.*

Stip'ule, *n.* leaf-like attachment at base of side stem.

Stir, *v.t. & i.* to move, cause or make circular motion, rouse. *n.* excitement. **Stirr'ing**, *a.* exciting, inspiring.

Stirr'up, *n.* horse-rider's foot-rest attached to saddle.

Stitch, *v.t. & i.* to join or mend with needle and thread, to sew. *n.* a loop of thread made by needle, a style of stitching.

Stitch, *n.* sudden sharp pain in side.

Stoat (Stote), *n.* member of weasel family, ermine.

Stock, *n.* goods or material in possession or reserve, cattle, invested money, a post, block, ancestry, meat or vegetable juice as basis for soup, main stem. *v.t.* to lay in supply of. **Stocks**, *n.pl.* wooden cradle for ship under construction, *arch.* a wooden frame with holes for securing ankles of petty criminal who was exposed to public ridicule. **Stock'broker**, *n.* dealer in stock and shares. **Stock'-holder**, *n.* person holding shares in company. **Stock'still**, *a.*

motionless. **Stock'market**, *n.* **Stock'Exchange**, *n.* official place where business is done in stocks and shares.

Stockade', *n.* an enclosure of palings or stakes for defence or keeping cattle.

Stock'ing, *n.* tight fitting enclosure for entire leg.

Stocky', *a.* thickset and strong.

Stod'gy, *a.* heavy and dull.

Sto'ic, *n.* person who suffers without complaining. **Sto'ical**, *a.* toughly enduring. **Sto'icism**, *n.* endurance, self-control under pressure.

Stoke, *v.t. & i.* to supply fire or furnace with fuel. **Sto'ker**, *n.* person in ship or factory who tends furnace.

Stole, *n.* long narrow scarf worn by women and bishops.

Stol'id, *a.* phlegmatic, unemotional. **Stolid'ity**, *n.*

Stom'ach (Stum-ak), *n.* sack comprising main digestive organ, appetite, *fig.* desire, inclination. *v.t.* to tolerate.

Stom'acher (Stum-acher), *n. arch.* part of front of woman's dress.

Stone, *n.* piece of rock, specially cut and shaped piece of this, a pebble, anything resembling a stone, an ailment of the bladder, a measure of weight equalling 14 pounds, the seed of certain fruit. *v.t.* to remove stone from fruit, to pelt with stones. **Stone** as pref. meaning completely, e.g. **stone-blind, deaf** etc. **Stonewalling**, *n.* obstructive tactics.

Stool, *n.* seat with neither back nor sides, sometimes of low form for kneeling or squatting. **Foot'stool**, *n.* stool for resting feet, *coll.* stooge bearing weight of another's responsibility.

Stool pigeon, *n.* decoy.

Stoop, *v.i.* to lower the body from waist, to bear oneself with drooping head and rounded shoulders, to condescend, to surrender. *n.*

Stop, *v.t. & i.* to halt, to hinder, to fill up, desist from. *n.* a stopping, a wedge, in mus. certain organ pipes, means of regulating pitch in instrument, a fullstop in punctuation. **Stop'gap,** *n.* something that fills a gap, an improvisation. **Stopp'age,** *n.* a stopping, a blockage. **Stopp'er,** *n.* a cork or plug. **Stopwatch,** *n.* watch that can be stopped or restarted at will for accurate timing. **Stop'cock,** *n.* a main controlling tap. **Stop'press,** *n.* news coming in after presses have stopped.

Store, *v.t.* to stock up, put away, keep in reserve. *n.* a shop, a reserve of goods, a place for keeping them, a collection of anything. **Stor'age,** *n.* the act of storing, space for storing. **Store cattle,** *n.* cattle kept for fattening. **Store-keeper,** *n.* **Store'house,** **Store'room,** *n.*

Stor'ey (-i), *n.* all the rooms in one horizontal section of a building.

Storm, *n.* tempest, violent weather condition, an angry outburst. *v.t. & i.* to blow furiously, to attack, to rage.

Stor'y, *n.* tale, piece of fiction.

Stoup (Stoop), *n. arch.* a drinking-cup.

Stout (Stowt), *a.* tending to fatness, bulky, resolute, strong, sound, sturdy, well-built. **Stout-hearted,** *a.* resolute.

Stout, *n.* strong kind of porter, dark ale.

Stove, *n.* heating or cooking apparatus.

Stow (Sto), *v.t.* to pack away compactly. **Stow'age,** *n.* things stowed or space for stowing them. **Stow'away,** *n.* person who hides on ship to obtain free passage.

Strad'dle, *v.t. & i.* to sit astride, to stand with legs apart, of warship to fire shells on both sides of target simultaneously so as to adjust range.

Strag'gle, *v.i.* to lag behind, become dispersed, grow weakly.

Straight (Strate), *a.* direct, undeviating, properly placed or arranged, honest, correct, tidy. **Straight'en,** *v.t. & i.* to make or become straight. **Straightforward,** *a.* honest, direct. **Straightaway,** *adv.* at once.

Strain, *n.* race, breed, descent.

Strain, *n.* manner, characteristic.

Strain, *v.t. & i.* to exert, to damage through exertion, to stretch excessively, to filter. *n.* damage through strain, exhaustion. **Strain'er,** *n.* perforated instrument for filtering.

Strait, *n.* a narrow passage of sea. *a.* narrow. **Straits,** *n.pl.* difficult position. **Strait jacket,** *n.* coat-like device for restraining violent lunatics. **Strait'-laced,** *a.* austere, formal in manner.

Strand, *n.* a seashore. *v.t. & i.* to run aground, leave high and dry, *fig.* to leave in difficulty.

Strand, *n.* a thread or fibre.

Strange, *a.* unusual, remarkable. unfamiliar. **Stran'ger** (-jer), *n.* person from a different place, a newcomer, a foreigner.

Stran'gle, *v.t. & i.* to choke, kill

by pressure on windpipe, *coll.* to suppress. **Stran'gler,** *n.* **Strangle-hold,** *n.* unshakable grip. **Strangula'tion,** *n.* act of strangling or being strangled.

Strap, *n.* long narrow piece of leather or other material for fastening. *v.t.* to fasten with a strap.

Strapp'ing, *a.* upstanding, sturdy.

Strat'egy (-ji), *n.* military science, practice of manoeuvring large mil. forces, any similar practice or skill. **Strate'gic,** *a.* pertaining to strategy, advantageous. **Strat'agem** (-jem), *n.* a ruse. a mil. manoeuvre.

Strat'osphere, *n.* upper layer of atmosphere commencing seven miles above earth.

Stra'tum (Strah-), *n.* a layer, esp. geol. *pl.* **Strata. Stra'tify,** *v.t.* to arrange in strata. **Stratifica'tion.**

Straw, *n.* stalks of harvested corn.

Straw'berry, *n.* red juicy ground fruit and plant producing it.

Stray, *v.t. & i.* to deviate from direction, become lost. *a.* intermittent. *n.* a strayed animal.

Streak, *n.* a stripe, a long smear, a characteristic. *v.t.* to mark with streaks. **Streaki'ness,** *n.* unevenness. **Streak'y,** *a.* .

Stream, *n.* flowing water, a small river, anything resembling this. *v.i.* to flow or float smoothly. **Stream'er,** *n.* long narrow pennant or ribbon. **Stream'lined,** *a.* smoothly shaped in flowing manner.

Street, *n.* a road with houses or buildings on either side, a public thoroughfare.

Strength, *n.* power, muscular force. **Strength'en,** *v.t. & i.* to make stronger.

Stren'uous, *a.* energetic, unflagging, arduous.

Stress, *n.* strain, emphasis. pressure. *v.t.* to emphasize, accent, apply stress or pressure.

Stretch, *v.t. & i.* to reach, to pull out, extend. *n.* extent of reaching, an expanse, a period of time. **Stretch'er,** *n.* any device for stretching, a canvas covered frame for conveying sick or injured person, foot-rest in rowing boat.

Strew (Stroo), *v.t.* to scatter.

Strick'en, *a.* struck down, afflicted.

Strict, *n.* stern, precise, rigorous.

Stric'ture, *n.* a constriction, harsh criticism.

Stride, *v.t. & i.* to walk in long paces. *n.* a long pace.

Stri'dent, *a.* loud and harsh.

Stridula'tion, *n.* shrill rasping sound made by grasshoppers etc.

Strife, *n.* conflict.

Strike, *v.t. & i.* to hit, collide be afflicted, to dash, arrange, to ignite, refuse to work, impress, to find. *n.* an organized refusal to work, a discovery of oil etc. **Stri'king,** *a.* remarkable, very noticeable.

String, *n.* cord or thread, wire or gut in certain mus. instruments. *n.pl.* stringed mus. instruments. *v.t. & i.* to tie or furnish with strings, to hang on a string. **String'y,** *a.* long and thin like string. **Strings,** *n.pl. coll.* conditions.

Strin'gent, *a.* strict, rigid. **Strin'gency** (-jen-), *n.*

Strip, *v.t. & i.* to take off covering, tear off, deprive of, undress, take to pieces. *n.* long narrow band or piece.

Stripe, *n.* a narrow band of different material or colour superimposed on main material or background, the mark of a blow, a mark of rank. *v.t.* to mark with stripes.

Strip'ling, *n.* a youth.

Strive, *v.i.* to try earnestly, struggle.

Stroke, *n.* a blow, the act of dealing a blow. a sudden action or idea, a seizure, a mark in writing or painting, a smooth movement, single pulling of oar etc., oarsman nearest stern in racing boat.

Stroke, *v.t.* to pass hand over gently.

Stroll (Strole), *v.i.* to walk idly or slowly. *n.* a walk for pleasure.

Strong, *a.* powerful, physically robust, influential, violent, positive, solid. **Strong'hold,** *n. a.* fortified place. **Strong'room,** *n.* special place for keeping valuables.

Strop, *n.* leather strap for sharpening open razor. *v.t.*

Struc'ture, *n.* anything constructed, a building, bridge etc., the manner in which something is constructed. **Struc'tural,** *a.*

Strug'gle, *v.i.* to strive, fight with, try strenuously. *n.*

Strum, *v.t. & i.* to pluck strings of instrument, to play this in desultory fashion.

Strum'pet, *n.* a blatant woman, a prostitute.

Strut, *v.t.* to walk with conceited step. *n.*

Strut, *n.* a supporting bar or beam.

Strych'nine (Strikneen), *n.* deadly

poison but in minute quantities a stimulant.

Stub, *n.* a stump, a counterfoil. *v.t.* to strike esp. toe against object.

Stub'ble, *n.* short stalks of grain left in ground after harvest, hairs on unshaven face.

Stub'born, *a.* obstinate, refractory. **Stub'bornness,** *n.*

Stucc'o (Stukko), *n.* form of plaster for outside walls.

Stud, *n.* a removable device for fastening shirt sleeves or front, *a.* decorative knob in belt etc., upright strut. *v.t.* to furnish with studs, mark with studs.

Stud, *n.* a collection of pedigree racehorses esp. for breeding.

Stu'dent, *n.* person who studies, university undergraduate.

Stud'y, *n.* the process of gaining knowledge, a particular subject specialized in for this, careful examination or mental effort, a room for studying in. *v.t. & i.* to apply oneself in order to learn, to examine, meditate on.

Stuff, *n.* material, cloth, fabric, what contributes to making something. *v.t.* to fill with stuff, to pack tightly, to eat excessively, to fill skin of dead animal and model to lifelike representation. **Stuff'ing,** *n.* any material for stuffing, a seasoned mixture for stuffing table-poultry.

Stuff'y, *a.* airless, having difficult in breathing. *coll.* dull, pompous.

Stul'tify, *v.t.* to spoil the effect of.

Stum'ble, *v.i.* almost to fall in walking or running, to falter, to find by chance esp. as stumble on. **Stumbling block,** *n.* an obstacle.

Stump, *n.* any part left after main body has been removed, a mutilated limb, the remains of a felled tree, part of wicket in cricket. *v.t.* & *i.* to walk heavily, to dismiss or be dismissed in cricket through having wicket broken when moving beyond crease, to go about making polit. speeches.

Stun, *v.t.* to render senseless or dazed by a blow or news.

Stunt, *v.t.* to impede development or growth.

Stunt, *n.* a spectacular feat, a publicity device.

Stu'pefy, *v.t.* to bemuse, deprive of wits. **Stupefac'tion,** *n.* utter astonishment.

Stupen'dous, *a.* gigantic, amazing.

Stu'pid, *n.* senseless, foolish, **Stupid'ity,** *n.*

Stu'por, *n.* partial unconsciousness.

Stur'dy, *a.* robust, tough, vigorous.

Stur'geon (-jun), *n.* large fish from which caviar is obtained.

Stutt'er, *v.t.* & *i.* to speak defectively. *n.* an impediment in speech.

Sty, *n.* a building for pigs.

Sty, *n.* an inflamed swelling on eyelid.

Style, *n.* manner of acting, behaving, writing, dress etc, mode of address or title, distinctive way of working in art or architecture, an engraving-tool, an arch. writing implement. *v.t.* to fashion, name. **Styl'ish,** *a.* fashionable. **Styl'ist,** *n.* person fastidious in style. **Sty'lus,** *n.* a style, writing-instrument,

Sty'lize, *v.t.* to conform to certain style, paint in conventional way.

Styp'tic, *a.* & *n.* substance used to stop bleeding.

Suave (Swahve), *a.* smooth in manner. **Suav'ity,** *n.*

Sub-, *pref.* meaning under, inferior, lower, nearly, e.g. subconscious, subdivide, subhuman, subnormal etc.

Sub'altern, *a.* of lower rank, but *esp. as n.* junior mil. officer below captain.

Subdue', *n.* to suppress.

Sub'ject, *a.* under control or power of another, liable to. *n.* person under authority or owing allegiance, person or thing under discussion, the conscious self. **Subject',** *v.t.* to make liable to, put under control, cause to be treated or exposed. **Subjec'tion,** *n.* the act of subjecting or being subjected, control. **Subjec'tive,** *a.* **Subjectiv'ity,** *n.* Subject matter, *n.* matter being discussed or described.

Sub'jugate, *v.t.* to subdue. **Sub'juga'tion,** *n.*

Subjunctive, *n.* & *a.* gram. mood of verb expressing possibility or wish.

Sublime', *a.* exalted. **Sub'limate,** *v.t.* to raise to more exalted or higher level. **Sublim'ity,** *n.*

Sub'marine, *a.* underwater, beneath surface of sea. *n.* submersible warship.

Submerge', *v.t.* & *i.* to go or cause to go beneath the surface of water. **Submer'sible,** *a.* **Submer'sion,** *n.*

Submit', *v.t.* & *i.* to yield, put forward, suggest. **Submis'sive,** *a.* yielding. **Submis'sion,** *n.* act of yielding or putting forward, a proposal or suggestion.

Subord'inate, *n. & a.* lower in rank, secondary in importance. *v.t.* **Subordina'tion,** *n.*

Suborn', *v.t.* to induce to commit perjury or other crime.

Subpoen'a (-pena), *n.* a legal order obliging person to attend law-court as witness. *v.t.*

Subscribe', *v.t.* to contribute, sign one's name, assent. **Subscri'ber,** *n.* **Subscrip'tion,** *n.*

Sub'sequent, *a.* later.

Subside', *v.i.* to sink, settle, become quieter. **Sub'sidence,** *n.* a settling down, a fall of earth. **Sub'sidiary,** *a.* supplementary, of secondary importance. **Sub'sidy,** *n.* financial support. **Sub'sidize,** *v.t.*

Subsist', *v.i.* to exist. **Subsist'ence,** *n.*

Sub'stance, *n.* matter, stuff, essential part, property. **Substan'tial,** *a.* of substance, real, considerable.

Substan'tiate, *v.t.* to proove veracity of, make real. **Substantia'tion,** *n.*

Sub'stantive, *a.* substantial. *a. & n.* gram. expressing existence, a noun or compound.

Sub'stitute, *v.t. & i.* to put in place of or take place of something else. *n.* something or someone substituted, a reserve, an artificial thing. **Substitu'tion,** *n.*

Sub'terfuge, *n.* a trick, ruse.

Subterra'nean, *a.* underground.

Sub'tle (Sutt'l), *a.* crafty, evasive, delicate. **Sub'tlety,** *n.*

Subtract', *v.t.* to take away part. *n.* **Subtrac'tion,** *n.*

Sub'urb, *n.* residential quarter near or outside town. **Subur'-** ban, *a.* pertaining to this, dull.

Sub'vention, *n.* a subsidy, a loan or advance.

Subvert' (-vurt), *v.t.* to overthrow polit., corrupt. **Subver'sion,** *n.* the act of overthrowing. **Subver'sive,** *a.* inciting or tending to work against established regime.

Succeed' (Suk-seed), *v.t. & i.* to achieve object, be successful, to follow after, take place of. **Success',** *n.* the achievement of an object, the attainment of esteemed position, riches etc. **Success'ful,** *a.* **Succes'sion,** *n.* a following after, a series or sequence, a line of descent, act or right of succeeding. **Success'ive,** *a.* consecutive. **Success'or,** *n.* person who follows another in rightful order.

Succinct' (Suk-sinkt), *a.* concise.

Suc'cour (Sukk'er), *v.t.* to assist, sustain. *n.*

Suc'culent (Suk-), *a.* juicy. *n.* plant with thick and fleshy stem. **Suc'culence,** *n.*

Succumb' (Suk-kum), *v.i.* to die, yield, give way to.

Such, *a.* of that or like kind. *pron.* a certain person or object.

Suck, *v.t. & i.* to draw in liquid by pursing lips as opposed to drinking or lapping, to consume by constant working of tongue and lips. **Suck'er,** *n.* anything that sucks, an offshoot of plant, an animal organ for gripping. *sl.* a gullible person.

Suc'kle, *v.t. & i.* to give or take milk from breast. **Suck'ling,** *n.* unweaned child or animal.

Suc'tion, *n.* act of sucking, process of drawing liquid by partial vacuum.

Sudd'en, *a.* abrupt, unexpected.

Su'dorific, *a.* promoting sweat. **Sudorif'erous,** *a.*

Suds, *n. pl.* froth of soap and water, esp. as soap-suds.

Sue, *v.t. & i.* to initiate a leg. action, to prosecute, to entreat.

Suede (Swade), *n.* undressed kid-leather. *a.*

Su'et, *n.* hard fat protecting animal kidneys.

Suff'er, *v.t. & i.* to experience or be subjected to pain or distress, to endure, undergo pain etc., to allow. **Suff'erance,** *n.* endurance, power of enduring, permission. **Suff'erer,** *n.*

Suffice', *v.t. & i.* to be enough, satisfy, serve. **Suffi'cient,** *a.* enough. **Suffi'ciency,** *n.* an adequate supply.

Suff'ix, *n.* syllable added to end of word to qualify meaning.

Suff'ocate, *v.t. & i.* to stifle, smother, kill by depriving of air, to feel lack of air or die from this. **Suffoca'tion,** *n.*

Suff'ragan, *n.* esp. as 5. bishop, assistant bishop.

Suff'rage, *n.* the right to vote, the entire voters. **Suffragette',** *n.* woman who agitated for granting of suffrage to women.

Suffuse', *v.t.* to spread over. **Suffu'sion,** *n.*

Su'gar (Shoog'er), *n.* sweet substance obtained mainly from sugar cane or beet. *v.t.* to apply sugar to. **Su'gary,** *a.* very sweet.

Suggest' (Sujjest), *v.t.* to put forward as idea, to bring into mind, propose. **Sugges'tion,** *n.* something proposed or insinuated, idea put forward or brought to mind. **Sugges'tive,** *a.*

Su'icide, *n.* the slaying of oneself, person who kills himself. **Suici'dal,** *a.* pertaining to suicide, so dangerous as to amount to suicide.

Suit (Sute), *n.* a legal process, a courtship, a man's set of outer clothes, one of four sets in pack of cards. **Suit'case,** *n.* travelling-case. **Suit'or,** *n.* one who sues or woos. **Suit,** *v.t.* to fit, meet requirements of, be convenient. **Suit'able,** *a.* appropriate, fitting. **Suitabil'ity,** *n.*

Suite (Sweet), *n.* set of furniture, rooms, a retinue.

Sulk, *v.i.* to be ill-tempered or sullen. **Sul'ky,** *a.* morose, resentful.

Sull'en, *a.* surly, unsociable.

Sull'y, *v.t.* to blemish, stain.

Sul'phur, *n.* yellow non-metallic inflammable element. *a.* of colour of this. **Sul'phurous,** *a.*

Sul'tan, *n.* Moslem ruler. **Sulta'na (-tah-),** *n.* his wife. **Sul'tanate,** *n.* his country or jurisdiction.

Sul'try, *a.* hot and humid.

Sum, *n.* total, amount, math. problem. *v.t.* to add up or as sum up to summarize.

Summ'ary, *n.* a brief account, abridgement. *a.* concise, done or carried out at once. **Summ'arize,** *v.t.* to sum up, give brief account.

Summa'tion, *n.* addition, adding up.

Summ'er, *n.* season of greatest warmth and growth, between spring and autumn. *v.i.* to pass the summer. **Summer'y,** *a.* warm, pleasant.

Summ'it, *n.* a peak, highest point.

Summ'on, *v.t.* to call, to order to appear, send for. **Summ'ons,** *n.*

a call, a court order to appear.

Sump'tuous, a. lavish, costly.

Sun, n. heavenly body round which earth and other planets revolve.

Sund'er, v.t. to break apart, divide, separate.

Sup, v.t. & i. to take supper, to sip a small mouthful.

Su'per, n. additional frame and sections added to beehive.

Su'per- pref. meaning above, over, more than, in excess.

Su'perable, a. able to be overcome.

Superann'uate, v.t. to pension off, retire. Superannua'tion, n.

Superb', a. fine, excellent.

Supercil'ious, a. contemptuously haughty.

Supereroga'tion, n. the performing or paying out of more than duty demands. Supererog'-atory, a.

Superfic'ial, a. pertaining to the surface, shallow, trivial. Superficial'ity, n.

Super'fluous, a. unnecessary. Superflu'ity, n.

Superintendent', v.t. to supervise, direct. Superintend'ent, n. Superintend'ence, n.

Super'ior, a. better in quality, higher in rank. n. Superior'-ity, n.

Super'lative, a. best, highest in degree or quality. n. gram. expressing highest or greatest degree.

Supernat'ural, a. & n. unearthly, beyond what is known or usual in nature.

Supernu'merary, a. extra, esp. beyond necessary number. n.

Supersede', v.t. to take place of.

Supersti'tion, n. belief in imaginary powers or beings. Supersti'tious, a.

Supervene', v.i. to occur unexpectedly, follow immediately after. Superven'tion, n.

Su'pervise, v.t. to watch over, control superintend, oversee. Supervis'ion, n. Supervi'sor, n.

Su'pine, a. reclining, inactive.

Supp'er, n. evening meal.

Supplant', v.t. to take place of, supersede.

Sup'ple, a. lissom, flexible, pliant. Sup'ply (-pli), adv.

Sup'plement, n. something extra, an additional part. Supplement', v.t. to add to, fill out. Supplement'ary, a. additional.

Supp'licate, v.t. & i. to entreat, beg for earnestly. Supplica'tion, n. Supp'licatory, a. Supp'-licant, n. person who entreats.

Supply', v.t. to provide, furnish. n. a providing, required goods.

Support', v.t. to hold up, prop up, encourage. n. something that supports, a prop, assistance. Support'able, a. Support'er, n.

Suppose', v.t. to assume, imagine, take for granted. Supposi'tion, n. an assumption, a theory. Suppositi'tious, a. not genuine.

Suppress', v.t. to crush, subdue, restrain, conceal. Suppres'sion, n. Suppress'or, n.

Supp'urate, v.i. to fester. Suppura'tion, n.

Supreme', a. highest in power, quality, importance etc. Suprem'acy, n. state of being supreme, highest power or authority.

Surcease', v.i. to cease. n. cessation.

Sur'charge, *n.* an extra charge.

Sure (Shoor), *a.* certain, reliable, accurate.

Sure'ty, *n.* guarantee of appearance in court.

Surf, *n.* foam of waves breaking on shore.

Sur'face, *n.* the exterior, the outer side of solid body. *v.t.* to provide with surface, treat surface.

Sur'feit (-fit), *n.* excess, satiety. *v.t. & i.* to indulge to excess.

Surge, *n.* a huge rolling wave or anything similar. *v.i.* to move like this.

Sur'gery, *n.* the skill and practice of med. treatment by operation, a medical practitioner's consulting-room. **Sur'geon** (-jun), *n.* skilled practitioner of surgery. **Sur'gical,** *a.*

Sur'ly, *a.* morose.

Surmise', *v.t. & i.* to guess, conjecture. *n.*

Surmount', *v.t.* to overcome.

Sur'name, *n.* family name.

Surpass', *v.t.* to exceed, excel.

Sur'plice (-plis), *n.* priest's garment.

Sur'plus, *n. & a.* anything over and above what is used or needed.

Surprise', *v.t.* to take unawares, to astonish. *n.*

Surre'alism, *n.* modern movement in art and lit. in which expression of the unconscious takes precedence over skill. **Surreal'ist,** *n.*

Surren'der, *v.t. & i.* to submit, yield. *n.* the act of surrendering.

Surrepti'tious, *a.* clandestine, secret.

Surr'ogate, *n.* a bishop's deputy.

Surround', *v.t.* to encircle completely. **Surround'ings,** *n. pl.* immediate neighbourhood, background.

Surveill'ance (-vay-), *n.* close supervision or observation.

Survey', *v.t.* to regard broadly, look over, to map land. **Survey,** *n.* **Survey'or,** *n.*

Survive', *v.t. & i.* to remain alive, outlive, escape danger. **Survi'val,** *n.* **Survi'vor,** *n.*

Suscep'tible (Suss-), *a.* impressionable. **Susceptibil'ity,** *n.*

Suspect', *v.t.* to doubt, to feel something possible, to question person's innocence etc. *a. & n.* of someone suspected. **Suspi'cion,** *a.* mistrust, impression that something is wrong or that person is guilty.

Suspend', *v.t.* to hang up, defer. **Suspen'der,** *n.* device for holding up. **Suspen'sion,** *n.* the act of hanging or being held up.

Suspense', *n.* undetermined state, anxiety.

Sustain', *v.t.* to support, maintain, suffer, uphold.

Sus'tenance, *n.* food, maintenance, support.

Su'ture, *n.* the stitching up of a wound.

Su'zerain, *n.* a sovereign, a ruler. **Su'zerainty,** *n.*

Swab (Swob), *n.* a mop, a surgical pad. *v.t.* to clean with swab, apply medicine with swab.

Swad'dle (Swod-), *v.t.* to wrap in. **Swad'dling,** *n.* cloth for wrapping baby in.

Swag, *n. sl.* booty.

Swagg'er, *v.i.* to walk in boastful manner. *n.*

Swain, *n. arch.* or *iron.* young lover, country youth.

Swall'ow (-o), *v.t. & i.* to pass or

allow food to pass down throat to stomach, *fig.* to accept with or without difficulty. *n.* the act of swallowing, the amount swallowed.

Swamp (Swomp), *n.* bog, marshy place. *v.t.* to overwhelm, cause to sink.

Swank, *n. coll.* conceit, ostentation. *v.t.* to show off.

Swarm (Sworm), *n.* an organized collection of bees, esp. when leaving hive to start new colony, any great number of things. *v.t. & i.* to crowd together in great numbers.

Swarm, *v.t. & i.* to climb tree etc. by clasping with hands and legs.

Swar'thy (Swor-), *a.* of dark complexion.

Swas'tika, *n.* a cross with broken arms adopted as symbol of Nazis.

Swat (Swot), *v.t.* to strike, hit.

Swath (Swawth), *n.* separate line of grass or grain mown.

Swathe, *v.t.* to bandage, wrap. *n.*

Sway, *v.t. & i.* to move from side to side, to stand unsteadily, to influence, rule. *n.* act of swaying, rule, influence.

Swear (Sware), *v.t. & i.* to declare solemnly on oath, to use foul language.

Sweat (Swet), *n.* perspiration. *v.t. & i.* to exude perspiration, to exploit. **Sweat'er,** *n.* woollen sports jersey. **Sweat'shop,** *n.* formerly factory where workers were employed in very bad conditions and for very small pay.

Sweep, *v.t. & i.* to clean with a broom, brush up with this, make extensive movement, pass rapidly. *n.* a sweeping motion, an operation to cover certain area, a cleaning with a broom, a long oar, person who cleans chimneys, properly chimney-sweep. **Sweep'ing,** *a.* extensive, wide. **Sweep'stake,** *n.* a gamble on horse-race.

Sweet, *a.* tasting like sugar, not sour, pleasant, fragrant, melodious. *n.* a confection. **Sweet'en,** *v.t. & i.* to make or become sweet. **Sweet'bread,** *n.* pancreas of animal as food. **Sweet'heart,** *n.* a lover.

Swell, *v.t. & i.* to increase in volume etc., become bigger or higher, become inflated, grow louder. *n.* the undulation of the sea, *sl.* an overdressed person. **Swell'ing,** *n.* a lump, a tumour.

Swel'ter, *v.i.* to suffer from intense heat.

Swerve (Swurv), *v.t. & i.* to deviate or cause to deviate suddenly in curving manner. *n.*

Swift, *a.* fast, rapid.

Swig, *n. sl.* a drink. *v.t.* to drink eagerly.

Swill, *n.* liquid food for pigs. *v.t. & i.* to eat greedily.

Swim, *v.t. & i.* to progress unaided through water. *n.* a bathe. **Swimm'er,** *n.*

Swim, *v.i.* to feel giddy.

Swin'dle, *v.t. & i.* to cheat esp. for money. *n.* **Swin'dler,** *n.*

Swine, *n.* pigs collectively.

Swing, *v.t. & i.* to move to and fro or cause to do this while suspended, to turn easily, to move as a gate or door. *n.* a suspended seat for swinging on.

Swipe, *v.t. & i.* to strike forcibly. *sl.* to filch.

Swirl (Swurl), *v.t. & i.* to move

round rapidly in air or water, to eddy. *n.*

Swiv'el, *n.* device consisting of two parts one of which can revolve independently. *v.t. & i.* to turn on a swivel.

Swoon, *v.i.* to faint. *n.* a fainting-fit.

Swoop, *v.i.* to descend on suddenly. *n.*

Sword (Sord), *n.* weapon with long pointed blade.

Syb'arite, *n.* (Sib) luxurious and effete person.

Syc'ophant (Sic-), *n.* toady, servile follower, yes-man. **Syc'-ophancy,** *n.*

Syll'able (Sil-), *n.* unit of pronunciation, division of word.

Syll'abus, *n.* programme of study.

Syll'ogism (-jism), *n.* form of argument or reasoning with two intermediary steps leading to a conclusion. **Syllogist'-ic,** *a.*

Sylph (Silph), *n.* ethereal being, *fig.* a beautiful girl.

Syl'van, Sil'van, *a.* pertaining to trees and woods.

Sym'biosis, *n.* union of different organisms for mutual benefit. **Sym'biotic,** *a.*

Sym'bol, *n.* a mark, emblem or thing that represents something else. **Symbol'ic,** *a.* **Sym'bolize,** *v.t.* to represent.

Symm'etry, *n.* exact balance between two halves of same thing. **Symmet'rical,** *a.*

Sym'pathy, *n.* compassion, consideration for another's distress, a sharing of feeling esp. in trouble. **Sympathet'ic,** *a.* **Sym'pathize,** *v.i.* to understand and share someone else's emotions or difficulties.

Sym'phony, *n.* a major mus. composition for full orchestra, an agreeable harmony of sound. **Symphon'ic,** *a.*

Sympo'sium, *n.* a meeting for serious discussion, a collection of essays on same subject by different authors.

Symp'tom, *n.* perceptible change in condition of body manifesting disease, a sign, an indication. **Symptomat'ic,** *a.*

Syn'agogue, *n.* a Jewish rel. building.

Syn'chronize, *v.t. & i.* to coincide, to adjust so as to agree, as of clocks etc. **Synchroniza'-tion,** *n.*

Syn'copate, *v.t. mus.* to change rhythm by commencing on unaccented beat and sustaining into accented beat. **Syncopa'-tion,** *n.*

Syn'cope (-copi), *n. med.* a fainting, loss of consciousness.

Syn'dicate, *n.* a combination of persons for project or enterprise. *v.t.* to form into a syndicate, to sell through this. **Syndica'tion,** *n.*

Syn'od, *n.* church council or court.

Syn'onym (Sin-o-nim), *n.* word having similar meaning to another. **Synon'ymous,** *a.* **Synonym'ity,** *n.*

Synop'sis, *n.* a summary, esp. of story or play.

Syn'tax, *n. gram.* the arrangement of words, the construction of a sentence.

Syn'thesis, *n.* a combination of separate parts or elements. **Synthet'ic,** *a.* artificial.

Syr'inge, *n.* a hand-pump for spraying or applying liquid.

Syr'up, *n*. solution of sugar in water. Syr'upy, *a*. sweet and sticky.

Sys'tem, *n*. an organized way of working or arranging, the working of the human body. Systemat'ic, *a*. organized, regular, methodical. Sys'tematize, *v.t*. to organize or arrange in a system.

T

Tab, *n*. small label, tag, *coll*. as keep tabs on, keep check on.

Tab'ard, *n*. short loose garment worn over armour, short coat worn by herald.

Tabb'y, *n*. & *a*. cat with variegated colouring.

Tab'ernacle, *n*. Jewish place of worship, *rel*. receptable for eucharistic objects, *bib*. a temporary dwelling or tent.

Ta'ble, *n*. piece of household furniture with flat top raised on legs for taking meals etc., *fig*. food or fare in general, systematic arrangement of information or facts. *v.t*. to lay on the table, to put forward.

Tab'leau (-lo), *n*. a representation in dumb-show of an event or an idea.

Tab'let, *n*. small flat piece of material for writing on, a small writing-pad, a wall panel, medicine in concentrated form, piece of soap.

Tab'loid, *n*. a tablet, *coll*. a small highly illustrated newspaper. *a*. summarized.

Taboo', *n*. Tabu', *n*. in primitive rel. the setting apart of people or objects either sacred or accursed. *v.t*. to set apart in this way, to ban. *a*. forbidden, prohibited.

Tab'ular, *a*. arranged systematically in tables or columns. Tab'ulate, *v.t*. to arrange thus. Tabula'tion, *n*.

Tac'it (Tass-it), *a*. implicit, understood without being said.

Tac'iturn (Tass-), *a*. not communicative, using few words. Taciturn'ity, *n*.

Tack, *n*. small nail, temporary stitching, *naut*. rope for securing part of sail, direction or change of direction of sailing vessel according to wind, course of action, *coll*. *naut*. food. *v.t*. to fasten with tacks, to stitch temporarily, to adjust course of vessel.

Tack'le, *n*. (*naut*. Ta'ckle), pulleys and ropes for working sails or as lifting device, equipment in general, in some sports an approach to opponent to rob him of ball. *v.t*. to grapple with, attempt to solve.

Tact, *n*. intuitive knowledge of right behaviour to avoid offence. Tact'ful, *a*. Tact'less, *a*. undiplomatic, socially clumsy.

Tac'tics, *n*. *pl*. as *n*. science of disposing mil. forces in warfare, any similar manoeuvring for advantage. Tac'tical, *a*. Tactic'ian, *n*. person skilled in tactics.

Tac'tile, *a*. pertaining to the sense of touch.

Tad'pole, *n*. larva of frog etc,

between emerging from egg to completed form.

Taff'eta, *n.* glossy silk or linen fabric.

Taff'rail, *n.* guard rail round stern of ship.

Tag, *n.* a small label, metal point at end of shoelace, loop at back of boot for pulling on, any loose end, a children's game. *v.t. & i.* to tie a tag on, to play tag, *coll.* follow persistently.

Tail, *n.* extension of animal's spine, any appendage resembling this, lower part of garment, reverse side of coin. *v.t. & i.* to provide with a tail, remove tail.

Tai'lor, *n.* garment-maker. *v.i.* **tai'loring,** *n.* the trade of making garments, esp. outer ones.

Taint, *n.* a hint or trace of corruption. *v.t. & i.* to spoil or become spoilt, to defile.

Take, *v.t. & i.* to grasp, seize hold of, accept, carry, consume, breathe, perform, do, attract, make, proceed, understand, come upon, succeed. **Ta'king,** *a. coll.* attractive. **Ta'kings,** *n. pl.* receipts. **Take' off,** *n.* a satire, parody, departure of aircraft.

Tale, *n.* a story.

Tal'ent, *n.* ability, skill, *bib.* a coin. **Tal'ented,** *a.* skilled, gifted.

Tal'isman, *n.* a charm.

Talk (Tawk), *v.t. & i.* to speak, discourse, express verbally, discuss. *n.* an address, informal lecture, a discussion, rumour. **Talk'ative,** *a.* voluble.

Tall, *a.* of considerable height. **Tall'boy,** *n.* tall narrow piece

of furniture with drawers and cupboard.

Tall'ow (Tal-o), *n.* melted animal fat for candles etc.

Tall'y, *n.* orig. piece of wood notched to mark items of account and afterwards split in two to provide debtor and creditor with identical record, now an account, score, reckoning. *v.t. & i.* to conform, be exactly equal.

Tal'on, *n.* predatory bird's claw.

Tambourine' (-reen), *n.* small hand drum with movable disks in rim. **Tam'bour,** *n.* bass drum.

Tame, *a.* tractable, not wild, domesticated. *coll.* dull. *v.t. & i.* to subdue, domesticate.

Tamp, *v.t.* to ram down, fill in.

Tam'per, *v.i.* to meddle or interfere with.

Tan, *n.* crushed oak bark as basis of tannic acid, the colour of this or resembling this, sunburn. *v.t. & i.* to treat with tannic acid, become sunburnt. **Tann'er,** *n.* workman in tanning. **Tanner'y,** *n.*

Tan'dem, *a. & adv.* one behind another, arranged thus. *n.* a bicycle with seats for two, pair of carriage horses in tandem.

Tang, *n.* a sharp flavour.

Tan'gent (-jent), *a.* touching but not intersecting. *n.* geom. straight line touching but not penetrating surface. **Tangen'tial,** *a.*

Tan'gible, *a.* capable of being felt, touchable, actual.

Tan'gle, *v.t. & i.* to become interwined, confuse. *n.*

Tank, *n.* a large receptacle for liquid, a water reservoir, an armoured mil. vehicle working on caterpillar tracks.

Tank'ard, *n.* a drinking vessel with handle.

Tank'er, *n.* oil-carrying ship or lorry.

Tann'ic, *a.* esp. t. acid, *n.* strong acid found in tea, oak bark etc. **Tann'in,** *n.* tannic acid.

Tan'talize, *v.t.* to torment by constantly arousing hopes without realizing them.

Tan'tamount, *a.* equivalent.

Tan'trum, *n.* peevish outburst.

Tap, *n.* device for controlling flow of liquid. *v.t.* to broach or pierce, to let out liquid, to open up a source.

Tap, *n.* a light touch. *v.t. & i.*

Tape, *n.* a long narrow band for binding, a streamer of paper for messages, a measuring device, a finishing line in race. *v.t.* to provide with tape, fasten with tape, *coll.* to size someone up.

Ta'per, *n.* long thin candle. *v.t. & i.* to narrow to a point as this, to decrease gradually.

Tap'estry, *n.* ornamental fabric decorated with scenes or figures.

Tap-root, *n.* the main root of a plant.

Tar, *n.* oily black substance obtained from coal, wood etc. and used for preservative or mixing with road materials. *v.t.* to treat with tar.

Tar'dy, *a.* slow, behindhand.

Tare, *n.* allowance made for weight of wrappings, container, packing etc.

Tare, *n. bib.* weeds.

Tar'get, *n.* a mark for shooting at, esp. in series of concentric circles, any mark for shooting or attack, the object of criticism etc., an object aimed at or aspired toward.

Tar'iff, *n.* price list at hotel etc., tax imposed on imported or exported merchandise, detailed list of this.

Tarn, *n.* a small mountain lake.

Tar'nish, *v.t. & i.* to spoil or lose lustre, dull.

Tarpaul'in (paw-), *n.* waterproof covering for boat or ship's hatch etc.

Tar'ry, *v.t.* to linger, delay.

Tar'sus, *n.* ankle, bird's leg between joint and claw. **Tar'sal,** *a.* pertaining to the tarsus.

Tart, *a.* sharp in taste, piquant, biting.

Tart, *n.* small open pie with fruit.

Tar'tan, *n.* woollen fabric marked with colours of Sc. clan. *a.*

Tar'tar, *n.* calcium phosphate deposit on teeth, deposit in wine cask. **Tartar'ic,** *a.*

Tar'tar, *n.* orig. member of marauding nomadic Mongol race, now *fig.* a difficult person.

Task, *n.* (Tahsk) a job, a piece of work, esp. burdensome.

Tass'el, *n.* an ornamental tuft hanging from other object. *v.t. & i.* to form in or decorate with tassels.

Taste, *n.* sense of identifying and appreciating different flavours by means of palate, a sample of food, a flavour, inclination, liking, ability to choose well. *v.t. & i.* to experience or test by taste. **Taste'ful,** *a.* having good taste or discrimination. **Taste'less,** *a.* insipid, unattractive. **Ta'sty,**

a. well flavoured, pleasant to eat.

Tatt'er, *n.* a rag, a torn piece of clothing. *v.t.* to tear.

Tatt'le, *n.* us. as tittle-tattle, *n.* gossip.

Tat'too, *n.* mil. pageant by floodlight, a mil. evening call by drum or bugle, a continuous drum beat or something resembling this.

Tat'too, *n.* sentimental design made on skin by puncturing and applying indelible ink. *v.t.*

Taunt (Tawnt), *v.t.* to deride, mock, jeer. *n.*

Taut (Tawt), *a.* tight, stretched, tense.

Tautol'ogy, *n.* an unnecessary verbal repetition. **Tautolog'ical,** *a.*

Tav'ern, *n. arch.* an inn.

Taw'dry, *a.* flashy and tasteless. *n.* worthless finery.

Taw'ny, *a.* light brownish-yellow.

Tax, *n.* an official charge on income or property. *v.t.* to assess for tax, exact tax, to burden, accuse, strain. **Taxa'tion,** *n.* act of taxing, amount exacted. **Tax'able,** *a.* **Tax'payer,** *n.*

Tax'i, Tax'i-cab, *n.* motor-vehicle for public hire. **Tax'i,** *v.i.* to ride in taxi but esp. of aircraft to move on ground before taking-off or after landing.

Tax'idermy, *n.* skilled practice of mounting dead animals for display. **Tax'idermist,** *n.*

Tea, *n.* a plant of camellia family cultivated for leaves which after treatment are used as beverage, the beverage made from tea, an afternooon meal.

Teach, *v.t. & i.* to instruct, educate, act as teacher. **Teach'er,** *n.* person who works at teaching.

Teak, *n.* tropical tree with very hard heavy wood.

Team, *n.* an organized set of players, a set of draught animals. *v.i.* esp. as t. up, to join forces, work as team.

Tear (Teer), *n.* drop of fluid secreted by eye-gland. **Tear'ful,** *a.* apt to weep, sad.

Tear (Tare), *v.t. & i.* to rend, pull apart, become torn, to rip out, to move or act in excited haste. *n.*

Tease, *v.t.* to comb, separate, to ridicule gently. **Tea'sel,** *n.* plant producing stiff spiny burr which when dried is used for combing.

Teat, *n.* nipple on female breast or udder, anything resembling this.

Technol'ogy (Tek-), *n.* the science, study and application of the mechanical arts. **Tech'nical,** *a.* pertaining to these. **Technical'ity,** *n.* quality characterizing a specific subject or art. **Technique** (Tek-neek), *n.* method of execution in a specific subject or art.

Ted, *v.t.* to turn hay in order to dry. **Tedd'er,** *n.* machine for this.

Te'dious, *a.* boring, wearisome. **Te'dium,** *n.*

Tee, *n.* peg or small pile of sand on which golf ball may be placed for first stroke at commencement of each hole, mark aimed at in various games.

Teem, *v.t. & i.* to be abundant or overflowing, to pour down heavily.

Teens, *n.pl.* years of age marked by numbers ending in teen, i.e. from thirteen to nineteen. **Teen'age, teen'ager,** *n.*

Teethe, *v.t.* to grow teeth.

Teeto'tal, *a.* abstaining from alcohol. **Teeto'taller,** *n.* person who never drinks alcohol.

Teg'ument, *n.* natural covering, skin.

Tel'e- (Tel-i), *pref.* meaning far, at a distance, e.g. **Tel'egraph,** *n.* system of sending and receiving messages at a distance, **Telep'athy,** *n.* the transmission of thought from one person to another, **Tel'ephone,** *n.* apparatus for conversing at a distance, **Tel'escope,** *n.* instrument for viewing at a distance etc.

Tell, *v.t. & i.* to inform, narrate, decide, distinguish, make an impression. **Tell'er,** *n.* person who counts voters in parliament etc. **Tell'ing,** *a.* striking, effective.

Temer'ity, *n.* boldness, rashness. **Temera'rious,** *a.* rash.

Tem'per, *n.* anger, mood, disposition.

Tem'per, *v.t.* to harden by alternately heating and cooling, to modify, moderate.

Tem'perament, *n.* disposition, character. **Temperamen'tal,** *a.* liable to change in mood.

Tem'perance, *n.* abstinence from alcohol, moderation.

Tem'perate, *a.* moderate, not extreme.

Tem'perature, *n.* degree of heat or cold, *med.* degree of heat in human body.

Tem'pest, *n.* a violent storm. **Tempes'tuous,** *a.*

Tem'ple, *n.* a place of worship.

Tem'ple, *n.* side of forehead.

Tem'ple, *n.* device for tautening cloth on loom.

Tem'po, *n.* time or rate in mus.

Temp'oral, *a.* secular, earthly, not spiritual, pertaining to time. **Temporal'ity,** *n.*

Temp'orary, *a.* not permanent, lasting only a certain time.

Tem'porize, *v.i.* to gain time by delay.

Tempt, *v.t.* to try to allure or persuade, esp. for dubious reasons. **Tempt'er,** *n.* one who tempts. **Tempta'tion,** *n.*

Ten'able, *a.* capable of being held or occupied. **Tena'cious,** *a.* dogged in holding on. **Tenac'-ity,** *n.* firmness of grip or purpose.

Ten'ancy, *n.* the occupation for a stipulated rent of somebody else's property. **Ten'ant,** *n.* person who occupies property thus. **Ten'antry,** *n.* tenants collectively esp. on one estate.

Tend, *v.i.* to incline towards, go in certain direction. **Ten'dency,** *n.* a characteristic inclination, direction.

Tend, *v.t.* to watch over. **Ten'der,** *n.* small vessel taking supplies or passengers to liner.

Ten'der, *a.* sensitive, soft, easily damaged. **Tender-hearted,** *a.* kind, sympathetic. **Tender-ness,** *n.*

Ten'der, *v.t.* to offer, propose. *n.* an estimate, an offer.

Ten'don, *n.* sinew connecting bone and muscle.

Ten'dril, *n.* delicate curling plant-organ by means of which plant climbs or gains support.

Ten'ebrous, *a.* gloomy, dark. **Tenebros'ity,** *n.*

Ten'ement, *n.* block of flats or

dwelling-place of inferior kind.

Ten'et, n. a principle, belief.

Tenn'is, n. ball game played with rackets between two or four people.

Ten'on, n. in carpentry a projection for joining with a mortise. v.t. to join thus.

Ten'or, n. mus. highest adult male voice, part for this, general tendency or direction.

Tense, a. taut, manifesting strain, highly strung. Ten'sion, n.

Tense, n. in gram. verb form indicating time of action.

Ten'sile, a. pertaining to tension, capable of being stretched.

Tent, n. portable canvas shelter of varying design.

Ten'tacle, n. long thin flexible appendage in certain animals for grasping or moving.

Ten'tative, a. experimental, provisional, suggestive.

Ten'terhook, n. lit. hook for stretching cloth, us. fig. as on tenterhooks, in state of suspense or anxiety.

Ten'uous, a. slender, fine, fragile.

Ten'ure, n. the right or fact of occupying property or office.

Tep'id, a. slightly warm. Tepid'ity, n.

Term (Turm), n. a mode of expression, a definite period of time, a spell of office, a division of school, university year, period when law courts are sitting, math. part of a ratio. v.t. to name, designate.

Ter'magant (Tur-), n. quarrelsome woman.

Ter'minal, a. pertaining to an end, forming an end, device in elec. circuit. Ter'minus, n. starting or ending point of transport system. Ter'minate, v.t. & i. to end or bring to an end, to conclude. Termina'tion, n.

Terminol'ogy, n. specialized mode of expression.

Ter'mite, n. ant-like insect.

Terr'ace (Terris), n. long platform cut out of sloping side, a row of attached houses. v.t. to form into a terrace.

Terr'a cott'a, n. pottery made of baked clay and left unglazed, the colour resembling this. a. made of terra cotta, reddish-brown in colour.

Ter'rain, n. a specific tract of land as scene of battle or under discussion.

Terres'trial (-tre-al), a. pertaining to the earth or globe.

Ter'rible, a. dreadful, horrible, fearful.

Ter'rier, n. one of various kinds of small dog.

Terrif'ic, a. alarming, terrible. Ter'rify, v.t. to frighten extremely.

Ter'ritory, n. a region, the extent of land owned or governed. Territo'rial, a. pertaining to a specific country. n. abbrev. for T. soldier, n. volunteer part-time soldier.

Ter'ror, n. extreme fear. Ter'rorize, v.t. to fill with extreme fear. Ter'rorism, n. government by fear or the attempt to gain one's polit. aims by fear and violence. Ter'rorist, n. person who believes in this.

Terse (Turse), a. verbally brief.

Ter'tiary, a. third in order of rank or time. n. the third geol. period, a bird's flight feather in third row.

Tess'ellate, v.t. to chequer, pave

with small blocks or shapes.
Tessella'tion, *n.*

Test, *n.* proof, trial, examination. *v.t.* to try out, put to test to find out quality.

Tes'tament, *n.* a will, covenant. **Testamen'tary**, *a.* pertaining to a will, done according to a will. **Testa'tor**, *n.* person who makes will. **Tes'tate**, *a.* leaving a will.

Tes'tify, *v.t. & i.* to declare under oath, bear witness.

Testimo'nial, *n.* a gift on retirement or going to another job, a written summary of person's character by previous employer.

Tes'timony, *n.* evidence.

Tes'ty, *a.* short-tempered, touchy.

Tet'anus, *n.* dangerous disease caused by blood-poisoning.

Teth'er, *n.* a rope for securing an animal. *v.t.*

Tetra-, *pref.* denoting four.

Teu'ton (Tu-), *n.* member of Germanic race. **Teuton'ic**, *a.*

Text, *n.* the actual words of any written or printed matter, a selected passage from the Bible. **Text'book**, *n.* a book for instruction. **Tex'tual**, *a.* pertaining to the text of a book.

Tex'tile, *n. & a.* woven, woven cloth.

Tex'ture, *n.* the structure or arrangement of a fabric.

Than, *conj.* introducing second element in comparison.

Thank, *v.t.* to express gratitude. *n.pl.* expression of this. **Thank'ful**, *a.* grateful. **Thank'less**, *a.* ungrateful, arduous. **Thanks'giving**, *n.* the act esp. rel. of expressing gratitude.

That, *a., conj. & relative pron.*

indicating person or object observed or drawn attention to, introducing subordinate clause, which, who, with a purpose etc.

Thatch, *v.t.* to roof with straw or reeds. *n.*

Thaw, *v.t. & i.* to melt. *n.* a melting, state of weather when thaw sets in.

The'atre, *n.* building where dramatic works are performed, dramatic art collectively, a surgical operating room, a place where important event or action unfolds. **Theat'rical**, *a.* pertaining to the theatre, exaggeratedly dramatic. **Theat'ricals**, *n.pl. iron.* us. for emotional behaviour.

Theft, *n.* the act of stealing.

Theme, *n.* a central connecting subject. **The'matic**, *a.*

Thence, *adv.* from that place or time, from that cause.

Theoc'racy, *n.* government by God, government by the church.

Theod'olite, *n.* surveyor's instrument for calculating angles.

Theol'ogy, *n.* (-ji) the science of religion. **Theolog'ical**, *a.* **Theolo'gian**, *n.* a professor or philosopher of rel. doctrine.

The'orem, *n.* proposition that can be proved by reasoning.

The'ory, *n.* a supposition as explanation for something, a conjecture. **Theoret'ical**, *a.* **The'orize**, *v.i.* to speculate, express or form beliefs meant to explain facts.

Ther'apy, *n. med.* the treatment of disease. **Therapeut'ic** (-pu-), *a.* curative, to do with healing. *n.pl.* therapy.

Ther'mal (Thurm-), *a.* pertaining to heat.

Thermom'eter, *n.* instrument for measuring temperature.

Thermo'stat, *n.* device for controlling heat.

Thermodynam'ics, *n.pl.* as *n.* science treating of relationship between heat and mechanical energy and work.

Thesaur'us, *n.* a lexicon, cyclopedia.

The'sis, *n.* a proposition in argument, an essay summing up research carried out for degree or doctorate. *pl.* **Theses.**

Thes'pian, *a.* pertaining to the theatre or drama.

Thews, *n.pl.* muscles, sinews, strength.

Thick, *a.* of lesser or greater breadth between surfaces, relatively large or small in diameter or cross-section, not thin, dense, compact, abundant, opaque. *coll.* very friendly esp. derogatorily. **Thick'en,** *v.t. & i.* to make or become thick or thicker. **Thick'ness,** *n.* condition of being thick.

Thick'et, *n.* a small compact mass of undergrowth and trees.

Thick'set, *a.* of person broad in comparison with height.

Thief, *n.* person who steals. *pl.* **Thieves. Theft,** *n.* the act of stealing. **Thieve,** *v.t. & i.* to steal. **Thiev'ish,** *a.* sneaking.

Thigh, *n.* part of leg between body and knee.

Thim'ble, *n.* metal protective sheath for tip of finger when sewing. **Thimbleful,** *n.* a very small amount, esp. of liquid.

Thin, *a.* slender, slim, meagre, not thick.

Thing, *n.* an object that can be perceived through the senses, a tangible or material thing.

Think, *v.t. & i.* to use mental power, to imagine, meditate, form or hold an opinion.

Thirst (Thurst), *n.* desire for drink, any great desire. *v.i.* **Thirst'y,** *a.*

Thith'er, *adv.* to that place, in that direction.

Thole, *n.* one of two pins in boat's gunnel for holding oar.

Thong, *n.* thin leather strap.

Thor'ax, *n.* human chest, middle section of insect body.

Thorac'ic (-as-), *a.* pertaining to the chest.

Thorn, *n.* a spiny projection on plant. **Thorn'y,** *a.* prickly, difficult.

Thor'ough (Thur-), *a.* finished, complete, careful. **Thoroughbred,** *a. & n.* of pure breed, esp. of horse. **Thorough-fare,** *n.* a public highway, a street. **Thorough-going,** *a.* uncompromising, utter. **Thorough-paced,** *a.* experienced, practised.

Thorp, thorpe, *n.* village, hamlet, esp. as place name in eastern England.

Those, *pron. pl.* of that.

Though (Tho), *conj. & adv.* even if, notwithstanding the fact that, however.

Thought (Thawt), *n.* mental process or activity, meditation, consideration, deliberation.

Thou'sand, *n. & a.* ten hundreds. a cardinal number.

Thrall, *n.* a serf or bondsman. **Thrall'dom,** *n.* bondage.

Thrash, *v.t. & i.* to beat severely, to thresh grain, to discuss in detail as thrash out a problem, to toss about. **Thrash'ing,** *n.* a flogging.

Thread (Thred), *n.* fine strand or

fibre, a connecting theme, the spiralled ridge of a screw. *v.t.* to put thread through, link with thread, make one's way through. **Thread'bare,** *a.* shabby, worn out.

Threat'en (Thret-), *v.t. & i.* to warn of intention to harm, to intimidate, to portend evil. **Threat,** *n.*

Thresh, *v.t. & i.* to beat out grain, to thrash. **Thresh'ing-machine,** *n. agric.* machine for threshing grain.

Thresh'old, *n.* properly a doorsill, an entrance.

Thrice, *adv.* three times.

Thrift, *n.* frugality, careful economic management. **Thrift'less,** *a.* prodigal. **Thrift'y,** *a.* careful in expenditure.

Thrill, *v.t. & i.* to excite, stir emotionally, vibrate with emotion. *n.*

Thrive, *v.i.* to prosper, succeed, grow.

Throat (Throte), *n.* front part of neck containing gullet etc., any narrow passage resembling a throat. **Throat'y,** *a.* guttural.

Throb, *v.i.* to pulsate, palpitate. *n.*

Throe, *n.* esp. as *pl.* acute agony or distress.

Throne, *n.* ornamental chair for sovereign or eccl. dignitary, sovereign power.

Throng, *n.* a huge crowd, multitude. *v.t. & i.* to gather in vast numbers.

Thros'tle (Thros'l), *n.* the song thrush.

Throt'tle, *v.t.* to choke, strangle. *n.* a device in motor engine for controlling steam or fuel.

Through (Throo), *prep., adv. & a.* passing along the entire inside length or across the breadth, from end to end, by means of, because of, to a finish, from one place to another. **Throughout',** *adv.* everywhere. *prep.* during.

Throw (Thro), *v.t.* to hurl, project, cause to fall, place. *n.*

Thrum, *v.t. & i.* to pluck stringed instrument idly, to tap pointlessly with fingers.

Thrust, *v.t. & i.* to pierce or attempt to pierce, to push violently. *n.*

Thud, *n.* a dull sound of body falling. *v.i.*

Thug, *n.* properly member of Hindu society committing ritual murder, any ruffian or killer.

Thumb (Thum), *n.* thickest, two-jointed finger of hand able to work in opposition to other fingers. *v.t.* to handle or soil with thumb. **Thumb'screw,** *n.* instrument of torture for squeezing thumb.

Thump, *n.* a heavy blow, sound as of this. *v.t. & i.* to strike or fall heavily, make a sound or throb like this.

Thun'der, *n.* loud reverberation accompanying lightning, any loud sound resembling this. *v.i.* to emit thunder or reverberating noise. **Thun'derous,** *a.* **Thun'der-struck,** *a.* startled.

Thus, *adv.* in such a manner, so, therefore.

Thwack, *v.t.* to strike with flat object, beat. *n.*

Thwart (Thwort), *v.t.* to frustrate, outwit.

Thwart, *n.* seat in rowing-boat.

Thy'roid, *n.* as t. cartilage or t. gland in neck.

Tiar'a (Te-ah-), *n.* a woman's jewelled coronet.

Tib'ia, *n.* shin bone.

Tic, *n.* a facial twitching.

Tick, *n.* small regular sound as of clock, a mark for checking. *v.t. & i.* to make a ticking sound, to mark off items with a tick.

Tick, *n.* parasitic blood-sucking insect.

Tick'et, *n.* a voucher for payment entitling one to travel or enter etc.

Tick'ing, *n.* covering for mattress.

Tick'le, *v.t. & i.* to tingle faintly, itch, cause to itch, *coll.* to amuse, please. *n.* **Tick'lish,** *a.* easily tickled, awkward, esp. as ticklish problem.

Tid'bit, *n.* **Tit'bit,** *n.* choice morsel of food.

Tide, *n.* the regular twice-daily rise and fall of sea under influence of moon, anything resembling a tide, a season, time. *v.t. & i.* to drift or be carried with the tide, esp. as to tide over, to cope with temporarily. **Ti'dal,** *a.* pertaining to tides.

Ti'dings, *n.pl.* news.

Ti'dy, *a.* neat, orderly. *coll.* considerable. *v.t. & i.* to make tidy, neat, arrange.

Tie, *v.t. & i.* to fasten in a knot with string, to fasten in a bow, to attach, to limit, equal in score at sport. *n.* a decorative band for wearing round shirt collar, a limit, a restriction, a connection, a contest with joint winners.

Tier (Teer), *n.* one of series of seats or rows in terrace formation.

Tiff, *n.* a slight quarrel.

Ti'ger, *n.* large carnivorous animal of cat family. **Ti'gerish, ti'grish,** *a.* fierce, ruthless.

Tight, *a.* taut, fastened securely, compact, firm, *coll.* mean, drunk. **Tight'en,** *v.t. & i.* to make or become tight or tighter. **Tights,** *n.pl.* dancer's or acrobat's close-fitting outfit. **Tight'rope,** *n.* acrobat's trick of walking across stretched rope above ground.

Tile, *n.* shaped piece of baked clay as part of roofing material. *v.t.* to cover with tiles.

Till, *n.* a cash drawer in shop.

Till, *v.t. & i.* to cultivate, plough. **Till'age,** *n.* cultivation, land cultivated.

Till, *prep & conj.* up to, up to the time when.

Till'er, *n.* a boat's steering device.

Tilt, *v.t. & i.* to lean or cause to lean, incline, orig. to charge on horseback in armed combat, to engage in argument against.

Tilth, *n.* cultivation, land under cultivation.

Tim'ber, *n.* wood cut and processed for use, a large piece of such wood, beam used for ship or building.

Tim'bre (Timber or as Fr.), *n.* in mus. distinctive quality of voice or instrument.

Time, *n.* period, particular moment or hour, passage of life, measure of duration, continued existence, an era, *mus.* rhythm, occasion. *v.t.* to mark time, adjust or regulate time, calculate speed. **Time'ly,** *a.* well timed, suitable. **Time'table,** *n.* schedule of work, details of transport arrangements.

Tim'id, *a.* lacking in boldness, easily frightened. **Timid'ity**, *n.* **Tim'orous**, *a.*

Tin, *n.* white malleable metal used for containers and utensils etc., anything made of this. *a.* **Tin'smith**, *n.* craftsman in tin. **Tin'streamer**, *n. arch.* surface tin-digger. **Tinn'y**, *a.* resembling tin, cracked.

Tinc'ture, *n. med.* solution in alcohol.

Tin'der, *n.* very dry powdery inflammable substance for starting fire by spark from flint. **Tinder'y**, *a.*

Tine, *n.* spike of antler, prong.

Tinge, *v.t.* to stain or flavour slightly. *n.*

Tin'gle, *n.* a slight stinging feeling. *v.i.*

Tin'ker, *n.* itinerant and semi-skilled mender of household utensils. *v.t. & i.* to work at in desultory or unskilled way.

Tink'le, *n.* slight sound as of bell. *v.t. & i.*

Tin'sel, *n.* spurious brilliance, glittering metallic material for decorations. *a.*

Tint, *n.* a faint or delicate colour. *v.t.* to colour slightly.

Tintinnabula'tion, *n.* a tinkling, a sound of bells.

Ti'ny, *a.* very small.

Tip, *v.t. & i.* to overturn, slope, tilt, slant. *n.*

Tip, *n.* a place for dumping rubbish.

Tip, *n.* a pointed end. *v.t.* to provide with pointed end.

Tip, *n.* an additional payment for service, information about racehorse's prospects. *v.t. & i.*

Tip'ple, *v.t. & i.* to drink alcohol habitually or excessively. **Tipp'-ler**, *n.* **Tip'sy**, *a.* slightly intoxicated.

Tip'toe, *v.i.* to walk softly and carefully on toes.

Tip'top, *a.* excellent, fine.

Ti'rade, *n.* censorious violent speech.

Tire, *v.t. & i.* to make or become weary, fatigued. **Tire'less**, *a.* unflagging, indefatigable. **Tire'-some**, *a.* tedious.

Tiss'ue, *n.* thin transparent fabric, substance covering, connecting, forming bodily organs in animals.

Titan'ic, *a.* gigantic.

Tithe, *n. lit.* a tenth part, *agric.* tax payable to church. **Tithe-barn**, *n.* barn where priest or monastery kept produce paid as tax.

Tit'illate, *v.t.* to stimulate sense of pleasure. **Titilla'tion**, *n.*

Tit'ivate, *v.t. & i. coll.* to dress up, tidy oneself.

Ti'tle, *n.* official or usual style of name, indication of ennoblement, name of painting, book, etc. **Ti'tle page**, *n.* page at beginning of book giving details of author etc. **Ti'tled**, *a.* having a title of nobility. **Tit'ular**, *a.* pertaining to a title, nominal.

Titt'er, *v.i.* to laugh in sniggering fashion. *n.*

Titt'le, *n.* very small part or mark.

Titt'le-Tatt'le, *n.* gossip.

Toad, *n.* froglike animal.

Toad'stool, *n.* mushroomlike fungus of various kinds.

Toad'y, *n.* servile person. *v.t. & i.* to curry favour in abject way.

Toast, *v.t.* to heat slightly, esp. bread in front of fire. *n.* slice of bread heated until browned and crisp.

Toast, *n.* a pledge in drink to someone's health or success. *v.t.* to drink such a pledge. **Toast'master,** *n.* master of ceremonies at banquet.

Tobacc'o, *n.* plant from whose dried leaves snuff and smoking-material are made, the substance so obtained.

Tobogg'an, *n.* kind of sled for moving down snow-covered slope. *v.i.*

Toc'sin, *n.* an alarm bell.

Today, *adv.* on the present day, in the present time or period. *n.* the present day.

Todd'le, *v.i.* to walk uncertainly like small child.

Todd'y, *n.* alcoholic drink made from sap of palmtree, whisky and hot water sweetened.

Toe, *n.* digit of foot, front of sock or footwear etc., anything resembling a toe. *v.t.* to touch with the toe.

To'ga, *n. arch.* outer garment worn by ancient Romans.

Togeth'er, *adv.* simultaneously, in company.

Toil, *n.* heavy, arduous labour, a snare, now only in *n.pl. v.i.* **Toil'er,** *n.* a worker. **Toil'some,** *a.* arduous. **Toil'worn,** *a.* worn out by work.

Toil'et, *n.* style of dress, process of dressing.

To'ken, *n.* a symbol, sign, indication.

Tol'erate, *v.t.* to put up with, endure, permit. **Tol'erable,** *a.* endurable, acceptable. **Tolera'tion,** *n.* forbearance. **Tol'erant,** *a.* forbearing. **Tol'erance,** *n.* willingness to allow other people's actions or opinions.

Toll (Tole), *n.* a charge for a particular use or privilege.

Toll, *v.t. & i.* to sound a bell solemnly and slowly.

Tom'ahawk, *n.* N. Amer. Indian hatchet as weapon or tool.

Tomb (Toom), *n.* a grave esp. with ornate structure.

Tome, *n.* us. *iron,* a heavy, serious book.

Tomorrow (-o), *n. & adv.* the day after the present day.

Ton (Tun), *n.* measure of weight, twenty hundredweight. **Tonn'age,** *n.* weight of ship's cargo, carrying capacity of ship, displacement of ship, shipping collectively.

Tone, *n.* sound, mus. sound, quality of sound, modulation of voice, condition of health, quality of colour. *v.t. & i.* to adjust tone, bring into condition. **To'nal,** *a.* pertaining to sound or tone.

Tongs, *n. pl.* pair of hinged metal arms for grasping & lifting small objects.

Tongue (Tung), *n.* muscular organ in mouth used in tasting, eating, speaking, uttering sound etc., anything resembling a tongue in shape, a language.

Ton'ic, *a.* having the effect of strengthening or reviving, pertaining to sound or mus. keynote. *n.* a strengthening medicine, *mus.* keynote.

Tonight, *n.* the present or approaching night. *adv.* on or during this.

Ton'sil, *n.* gland on either side of base of tongue. **Tonsili'tis,** *n.* inflammation of tonsils.

Ton'sure, *n.* ritual shaving of crown of head of monk on taking vows, the bare part of head exposed by this, *fig.* admission into holy orders.

Too, *adv. & a.* as well as, excessively.

Tool, *n.* implement for working with. *v.t.* to use a tool, shape or design with tool.

Tooth, *n.* one of series of bonelike projections set in jaw and used for masticating or attacking, anything resembling a tooth. *pl.* teeth. **Tooth'some,** *a.* tasty.

Top, *n.* the summit, highest part, zenith. *v.t.* to surpass, cut off top, provide with top.

Top, *n.* child's spinning toy used with whip.

To'paz, *n.* precious stone of different hues, esp. yellow.

To'per, *n.* tippler, drunkard.

Topi'ary, *a. & n.* of the skill of shaping shrubs by clipping.

Top'ic, *n.* a subject of discussion or writing. **Top'ical,** *a.* pertaining to a current topic or subject, of immediate interest.

Topog'raphy, *n.* the geographical features of a particular region, the study of these. **Topog'rapher,** *n.* person skilled in this. **Topograph'ical,** *a.*

Top'ple, *v.t.* to fall down lengthways, collapse.

Top'sy-Tur'vy, *a.* in utter confusion, upside down.

Toque (Toke), *n.* woman's close-fitting hat without brim.

Tor, *n.* a rocky hill.

Torch, *n.* a portable light.

Tor'eador (-re-ador), *n.* bullfighter.

Tor'ment, *n.* intense mental or physical suffering. **Torment',** *v.t.* to afflict with this, to annoy greatly. **Tormen'tor,** *n.*

Torna'do, *n.* violent tropical storm.

Torpe'do, *n.* cigar-shaped self-propelling underwater projectile fired by submarine or other warship. *v.t.* to sink by torpedo.

Tor'pid, *a.* sluggish, inactive.

Tor'por, *n.* **Tor'pids,** *n. pl.* inter-college boat races at Oxford University during spring.

Torr'ent, *n.* a violent, turbulent stream, violent downfall of rain. **Torren'tial,** *a.*

Torr'id, *a.* intensely hot, esp. as t. zone, region of the world between the tropics.

Tor'sion, *n.* twisting, state of being twisted in spiral fashion.

Tor'so, *n.* the trunk of human body, trunk of statue without head and limbs.

Tort, *n.* in law, a wrong.

Tor'tile, *a.* twisted, curved.

Tor'tuous, *a.* winding, devious, complicated.

Tor'ture, *v.t.* deliberately to inflict severe pain on. *n.*

Tory, *a. & n.* polit. member or supporter of Tory or Conservative party.

Toss, *v.t. & i.* to throw or be thrown up, jerk, pitch, thrash.

Tot, *n.* small child, small amount of drink. *v.t. & i.* esp. as tot up, to add up.

To'tal, *n.* the entire amount, everything. *a.* entire. *v.t.* to add up, to amount to. **Total'ity,** *n.* **Totalisa'tor** (abbr. tote), *n.* mechanized betting arrangement. **Totalitar'ian,** *a.* of a dictatorial form of government.

To'tem, *n.* sacred tribal emblem.

Tott'er, *v.i.* to stagger, to be in danger of falling.

Touch (Tuch), *n.* sense of feeling, act of contacting physically with hand or part of person. *v.t. & i.* to have physical contact with, to reach, to move emotionally. Touch'ing, *a.* affecting. Touch'wood, *n.* tinder. Touch'y, *a.* easily offended.

Tough (Tuf), *a.* not easily broken. stubborn, rugged, pliable and durable, difficult to eat. *n.* a bully. Tough'en, *v.t. & i.* to make or become tough or tougher.

Toupée (Too-pay), *n.* a small wig, false hair.

Tour (Toor), *n.* an extended journey for pleasure. *v.t. & i.* to travel round or extensively. Tour'ist, *n.*

Tour'nament, *n.* orig. armed combat between mounted knights, now any sporting contest.

Tour'ney (Turn-i), *n.* a tournament. *v.i.* to take part in this.

Tour'niquet (Toornikay), *n.* med. device for stopping serious bleeding by screwing action on bandage.

Tou'sle (Towz'l), *v.t.* to ruffle, rumple.

Tout (Towt), *n.* person who seeks custom, acts as informant for bookmaker. *v.i.*

Tow (Toe), *n.* coarse hemp.

Tow (Toe), *v.t.* to haul or drag at end of rope. *n.* act of dragging thus, rope used for this.

To'wards (Too-), *prep.* in the direction of, as regards. To'-ward (Toe-erd), *a. arch.* promising, going on.

Tow'el, *n.* cloth for drying after bathing or washing. *v.t. & i.* to use a towel, rub oneself down.

Tow'er, *n.* tall square or circular structure rising above but attached to main building or standing on its own, us. part of castle or church. *v.i.* to rise up like a tower, to stand high.

Town, *n.* a large organized community. Town council, *n.* elected body administering town. Town Hall, *n.* building where town affairs are dealt with.

Tox'ic, *a.* of or resulting from poison. Tox'aemia (-e-), *n.* blood poisoning. Toxicol'ogy, *n.* scientific study of poisons.

Toxoph'ilite, *n.* devotee of archery.

Toy, *n.* a child's plaything, anything for pleasure but worthless. *v.i.* to play with something, treat idly.

Trace, *n.* part of harness in horse-drawn vehicle.

Trace, *v.t. & i.* to track, to make a design, to copy, mark out, decorate. *n.* a sign, trail, small quantity. Tra'cery, *n.* delicate interwoven pattern.

Tra'chea (-ke'a), *n.* the windpipe.

Track, *n.* a mark left by someone or something passing, a trail, a path, a race course, place for athletics, railway line. *v.t.* to follow or attempt to follow by means of signs left.

Tract, *n.* a rel. pamphlet.

Tract, *n.* a certain area of land, a system of physical organs.

Trac'table, *a.* easily led, docile. Tractabil'ity, *n.*

Trac'tion, *n.* the act or power of hauling, the force entailed in this. Traction engine, *n.* steam-engine used on roads.

Trac'tor, *n.* powerful open motor-vehicle for hauling.

Trade, *n.* occupation, specific manner of working, commerce, business. *v.t. & i.* to exchange, carry on trade. **Trade-mark,** *n.* brand-mark, distinguishing symbol for brand of goods. Trade name, *n.* distinguishing name for firm or its goods. **Tradesman,** *n.* shopkeeper. **Trade union,** *n.* association of workmen for promotion of their interests. **Trade wind,** *n.* wind blowing continuously towards equator from N.E. or S.E.

Tradit'ion, *n.* custom, belief, etc. passed on to successive generations and continued by them, the act of doing this. **Tradit'ional,** *a.* customary through long practice.

Traduce', *v.t.* to calumniate, slander.

Traff'ic, *n.* trade, passage of people, goods, ships, vehicles. *v.i.* to trade.

Trag'edy (Traj-), *n.* a disastrous or calamitous event, a play ending in misfortune to main characters. **Trag'ic,** *a.* calamitous, pertaining to tragedy. **Trage'dian,** *n.* actor who specializes in tragic parts.

Trail, *n.* a track left by moving object, a train. *v.t. & i.* to hang down, to draw or drag behind, to straggle. **Trail'er,** *n.* an unpowered vehicle drawn behind a motor-vehicle, a trailing plant, sequence of shots from forthcoming film.

Train, *n.* a series of railway carriages and engine, a retinue of servants, long tail of dress, a series as of events, a mil. convoy, long explosive charge. *v.t. & i.* to instruct, educate, make obedient, condition oneself. **Train'ing,** *n.* the act of instructing, conditioning.

Trait (Tray or Trate), *n.* a characteristic.

Trai'tor, *n.* person who betrays his friends, cause, country. **Trai'torous,** *a.*

Trajec'tory, *n.* path followed by projectile.

Tram, *n.* public conveyance running on rails in streets, wagon in coalmine. **Tram'car,** *n.*

Tramm'el, n. kind of fishing-net, shackle. *v.t.* to hamper, impede.

Tramon'tane, *a.* living beyond the mountains, foreign.

Tramp, *v.i.* to walk steadily. *n.* the sound of marching, a vagabond.

Tram'ple, *v.t. & i.* to tread down, crush with feet.

Trance (Trahnce), *n.* deep sleep induced by hypnotism, unnatural condition of insensibility.

Tran'quil, *a.* peaceful, calm. **Tranquill'ity,** *n.* **Tran'quillize,** *v.t.* to soothe, make peaceful.

Trans-, *pref.* meaning across, beyond, through, on or to another side, altogether. Where meanings are clear from reference to main word entries under this heading have been omitted.

Transcend' (-send), *v.t.* to surpass, excel. **Transcen'dent,** *a.* **Transcenden'tal,** *a.* surpassing natural experience or knowledge.

Transcribe', *v.t.* to copy out. **Trans'script,** *n.* a copy of something previously written.

Tran'sept, *n.* transverse part of cruciform church.

Transfer', *v.t.* to convey from one person or place to another,

change over. **Trans'fer,** *n.*
Trans'ferable, *a.* **Trans'ference,**
n. the act of making over,
transferring.

Transfuse', *v.t.* to transfer
liquid. **Transfu'sion,** *n.* esp. as
blood-t., the transfer of blood
from one person to another.

Transgress', *v.t.* to sin. **Trans-
gres'sion,** *n.* **Transgress'or,** *n.*

Tran'sient, *a.* brief, passing.
Tran'sience (-zee-ence), *n.*

Tran'sit, *n.* a passage, conveying.

Transit'ion, *n.* a changing from
one state to another. **Transit'-
ional,** *a.*

Tran'sitive, *a. gram.* of verb
governing a direct object.

Translate', *v.t.* to change from
one language into another, to
elevate a bishop to another
diocese. **Transla'tion,** *n.* **Transla'tor,** *n.* person skilled at
translating languages.

Translit'erate, *v.t.* to represent
in corresponding letters of
another language. **Translitera'-
tion,** *n.*

Transmigra'tion, *n.* the migra-
tion of a soul into a different
body.

Transmit', *v.t.* to send out, pass
on, transfer. **Transmis'sion,** *n.*

Transmute', *v.t.* to change form,
nature, matter. **Transmuta'-
tion,** *n.*

Tran'som, *n.* horizontal bar
across window or top part of
door, window attached to
this.

Transpar'ent, *a.* capable of
being seen through clearly,
clear, open, obvious. **Transpar'-
ency,** *n.* state of being transparent, positive photograph as
lantern slide.

Transpire', *v.t. & i.* to emit,
exhale, come to be known, *coll.*
happen. **Transpira'tion,** *n.*

Transplant', *v.t.* to plant in
another place, to remove
forcibly and cause to settle
elsewhere. **Transplanta'tion,** *n.*

Transport', *v.t.* to convey from
one place to another, stir
emotionally, carry away. *n.* the
means of conveyance, vehicles,
ships, railways etc. in general,
a ship used for transporting
troops or mil. stores, an excess
of emotion. **Transporta'tion,** *n.*
the act of conveying, carrying,
sending away.

Transpose', *v.t.* to alter the
order of. **Transposi'tion,** *n.*

Transubstantia'tion, *n.* conversion or change into a different
substance. **Transubstan'tiate,**
v.t.

Transverse', *a.* situated in cross-
wise position. *n.* object that
lies in crosswise position.

Trap, *n.* a snare, an apparatus
for catching animals, a deceit,
trick. *v.t. & i.* to catch by
means of a trap. **Trapp'er,** *n.*
hunter who catches animals for
their fur.

Trap, *n.* pony-cart.

Trap-door, *n.* door in ceiling or
roof.

Trapeze', *n.* gymnastic apparatus consisting of footbar
suspended by ropes.

Trappings, *n. pl.* ornamental
harness, ceremonial dress.

Trash, *n.* worthless rubbish.

Trau'ma, *n.* shock through
injury. **Traumat'ic,** *a.*

Trav'ail, *n.* esp. agony in childbirth, any great agony. *v.i.*
make laborious effort.

Trav'el, *v.t. & i.* to make a

journey, move across long distances, proceed, voyage. Trav'eller, n.

Trav'erse, v.t. to cross, travel over.

Trav'esty, n. a ridiculous imitation. v.t.

Trawl, n. a large bag-net used in sea-fishing and hauled at stern of trawler. v.t. & i. to fish thus. Trawl'er, n. fishing-boat equipped with trawl. Trawler'man, n.

Tray, n. shallow flat receptacle with or without handle and rim for carrying articles.

Treach'ery (Trech-), n. deeply disloyal behaviour, betrayal of trust, perfidy. Treach'erous, a.

Trea'cle, n. syrup obtained in refining sugar, molasses.

Tread (Tred), v.t. & i. to walk or step, put the foot down, press down with foot. n. a step, a mark of stepping, a manner of walking, top part of a step, patterned surface of tyre. Tread'mill, n. orig. a mill worked by human or animal labour, now any drudgery. Tread'le (Tred'l), n. foot-pedal for turning wheel.

Trea'son (-zn), n. betrayal of one's country, attempt to depose monarch or overthrow government by violent means. Trea'sonable, a.

Treas'ure, n. hoarded or stored wealth or precious objects, anything of great value. v.t. to value greatly, to store up carefully. Treas'urer, n. guardian of treasure, esp. as money. Treas'ury, n. place where wealth is kept, office that administers a country's finances. Treasure trove, n. treasure found in secret hiding-place by other than person who put it there.

Treat, v.t. & i. to behave, act towards, deal with, negotiate, put through special process, entertain without charge. n. a special outing or source of pleasure. Treat'ment, n. method of treating, special med. curative process.

Trea'tise (-iz), n. serious written account of specific subject.

Trea'ty, n. a formal agreement esp. between states.

Treb'le, a. triple, threefold, multiplied by three. n. in mus. highest voice or part. v.t. & i. to multiply by three.

Tree, n. large perennial plant with formation of branches growing from main trunk, fig. a line of descent, esp. as family tree. v.t. to cause to take refuge in tree.

Tre'foil, n. archit. ornament resembling clover-leaf.

Trek, n. a journey across country. v.i.

Trell'is, n. metal or wooden framework for supporting garden plants.

Trem'ble, v.i. to shudder, shiver, shake. n.

Tremen'dous, a. huge and frightening, remarkable.

Trem'olo, n. in mus. a deliberately trembling tone.

Trem'or, n. a trembling or shaking.

Trem'ulous, a. trembling, unsteady.

Trench, n. long narrow deep excavation in earth for defence or laying pipes etc. v.i.

Tren'chant, a. keen, incisive. Trenchan'cy, n.

Tren'cher, *n.* carving board, old fashioned plate.

Trend, *n.* tendency, general direction or inclination. *v.i.* to move in general direction.

Trepan', *n. v.t. surg.* to remove part of bone from skull.

Trepida'tion, *n.* apprehension, alarm.

Tres'pass, *v.i.* to sin, encroach on someone else's property, meddle, intrude, presume. *n.* **Tres'passer**, *n.*

Tress, *n.* a long lock of hair.

Trest'le (Tres'l), *n.* movable framework for supporting flat top.

Tri-, *pref.* meaning three or threefold, e.g. **tri'angle**, *n.* geom. figure with three sides and three angles. **tri'angular**, *a.* **tri'colour**, *a.* having three colours. **trienn'ial**, *a.* lasting or happening every three years etc.

Tri'al, *n.* the process of testing, a legal hearing, a test, anything difficult to endure.

Tribe, *n.* a loosely organized group of primitive people. **Tri'bal**, *a.*

Tribula'tion, *n.* severe hardship or distress.

Tribu'nal, *n.* special legal court, judicial assembly.

Trib'une, *n. arch.* platform for public speaking, in ancient Rome a magistrate.

Trib'ute, *n.* expression of respect or appreciation, payment made to superior power. **Trib'utary**, *a.* having to make such payment, subordinate. *n.* a smaller branch of larger river.

Trice, *n.* a moment, instant.

Trice, *v.t. naut.* to haul up and secure.

Trick, *n.* a dextrous action, clever device, a deceitful act. *v.t.* to deceive, delude, cheat. **Trick'ery**, *n.* cheating. **Trick'y**, *a.* deceitful, difficult.

Trick, *v.t.* to deck out, dress.

Tric'kle, *v.i.* to flow gradually. *n.*

Tri'corn, *a.* three-horned. *n.* three-cornered hat.

Tri'dent, *n.* three-pronged fork esp. as weapon or fishing-implement.

Tri'fle, *n.* something insignificant or trivial, a sweet pudding. *v.t. & i.* to dally, deal with or behave insincerely.

Trigg'er, *n.* device for firing gun.

Trigonom'etry, *n.* branch of math. treating of relations between sides and angles of triangles.

Tril'by, *n.* man's soft hat with brim.

Trill, *n.* a vibrating tone. *v.i.* to sing thus.

Tril'ogy (-ji), *n.* a series of three compositions with connecting theme.

Trim, *a.* neat, tidy. *v.i.* to make tidy, cut lightly in order to tidy, to adjust, to equivocate in order to seize opportunity. **Trimm'er**, *n.* polit. opportunist.

Trin'ity, *n.* a trio, something comprised of three parts, rel. conception of Father, Son & Holy Ghost.

Trink'et, *n.* trifling ornament.

Tri'o (Tre-o), *n.* group or set of three, in mus. composition for three instruments or singers, the players or singers of this.

Trip, *v.t. & i.* to stumble or cause to stumble, to run lightly. *n.* a mistake, a stumble, a short journey.

Tri'partite, *a.* consisting of three parts.

Tripe, *n.* edible part of ox's stomach, *sl.* nonsense.

Trip'le, *a.* threefold, in sets of three, done three times. Trip'let, *n.* one of three children of same birth. Trip'licate, *a.* threefold, done in sets of three or three at a time.

Tri'pod, *n.* three-legged apparatus for supporting other object.

Trite, *a.* stale, commonplace.

Tri'umph, *n.* a great success, a victory, exultation because of this. *v.i.* to exult at success. Trium'phal, *a.* Trium'phant, *a.* victorious.

Trium'virate (Tri-um-), *n.* a trio of persons, esp. in authority.

Triv'et, *n.* three-legged stand for kettle etc.

Triv'ial, *a.* insignificant, paltry. Trivial'ity, *n.*

Tro'chee (-kee), *n.* two-syllabled foot in verse.

Trog'lodyte, *n.* a cave-dweller.

Tro'jan, *n.* tough hardworking person.

Troll (Trole), *n. myth.* mountain-dwarf.

Troll (Trole), *v.t. & i.* to sing lightheartedly or in parts.

Troll (Trole), *v.i.* to fish while being rowed along in boat.

Troll'ey (Trol'i), *n.* powered or unpowered vehicle for transporting things.

Trom'bone, *n.* large wind-instrument.

Troop, *n.* a company of people, a unit of cavalry. *n. pl.* soldiers collectively. *v.i.* to throng in large numbers, to move troops by ship. Troop'er, *n.* a cavalry-man. Troop'ship, *n.* ship for transporting troops.

Trope, *n.* figurative expression.

Tro'phy, *n.* symbol of a victory presented or won.

Trop'ic, *n.* parallel of latitude 23 degrees 27 minutes N. or S. of equator, the region between these latitudes, esp. as Tropics. Trop'ical, *a.* pertaining to the tropics, torrid.

Trot, *v.t. & i.* to proceed at a pace between walking and running. *n.* Trott'er, *n.* horse trained to run with high stepping action.

Troth, *n.* a pledge, trust.

Trou'badour (Troo-ba-door), *n.* mediaeval wandering poet or minstrel.

Troub'le (Trub'l), *n.* worry, distress, inconvenience. *v.t. & i.* to worry, inconvenience, upset, concern. Troub'lesome, *a.* Troub'lous, *a.* calamitous.

Trough (Trof), *n.* long narrow open receptacle for containing animal fodder, anything resembling this, the hollow between waves.

Trounce (Trownce), *v.t.* to beat decisively.

Troupe (Troop), *n.* a troop or company esp. of performers.

Trou'sers (Trowzers), *n. pl.* two-legged outer garment for lower part of body.

Trou'sseau (Troo-so), *n.* bride's outfit.

Trout (Trowt), *n.* freshwater fish.

Trow (Tro or Trow), *v.t. arch.* to believe, think.

Trow'el, *n.* small hand-tool for plastering or gardening.

Troy, *n.* esp. as t. weight, system of weight for precious metals or gems.

Tru'ant, *n.* person who absents himself unlawfully from school or duty. *a.* **Tru'ancy**, *n.*

Truce, *n.* an armistice, a temporary suspension of fighting etc.

Truck, *n.* a wheeled vehicle for transporting.

Truck, *n.* barter, payment in kind instead of money. *v.t. & i.* to deal with, barter.

Truc'kle, *v.i.* to give in ignominiously.

Truc'kle, *n.* esp. as t. bed, a movable bed.

Truc'ulent (Truk-), *a.* excessively aggressive. **Truc'ulence**, *n.*

Trudge (Truj), *v.i.* to walk laboriously, wearily. *n.* a long tiring walk.

True (Troo), *a.* in accordance with the facts, exact, reliable, genuine, accurate. **Tru'ism**, *n.* something obviously true. **Tru'ly**, *adv.*

Truff'le, *n.* edible underground fungus.

Trump, *n.* in certain card games suit designated as temporarily superior to others. *v.i.* to play trump, win with trump.

Trump'ery, *n.* trashy finery. *a.* showy but worthless.

Trum'pet, *n.* wind-instrument regulated by valves. *v.t. & i.* to utter loud noise, to spread abroad.

Trun'cate, *v.t.* to sever top.

Trun'cheon (-shun), *n.* a policeman's baton, a defensive stick

Trun'dle, *v.t. & i.* to roll along, move along slowly on wheels.

Trunk, *n.* a large chest for travelling or storing, the main stem of a tree, main upper part of human body, the proboscis of an elephant. *n. pl.* short trousers. *a.* main, esp. as trunk-road, trunk-call.

Truss, *n.* a supporting bandage or device, a supporting framework. *v.t.* to support with a truss, to tie up or otherwise fasten.

Trust, *n.* confidence, faith, belief in person's reliability, legal administration of property for another's benefit, guardianship, business cartel. *v.t. & i.* to have confidence in, to believe, rely on. **Trus'tee**, *n.* legal administrator of someone else's property. **Trust'ful**, *a.* confiding. **Trus'ting**, *a.* having trust in others. **Trust'worthy**, *a.* worthy of being trusted, dependable. **Trus'ty**, *a.* reliable, faithful.

Truth (Trooth), *n.* veracity, quality of being true, accordance with facts. **Truth'ful**, *a.* true, sincere.

Try, *v.t. & i.* to attempt, make an effort, test, trouble, put on trial, experiment. *n.* an attempt or effort, a score in rugby football. **Try'ing**, *a.* aggravating.

Tryst (Trist), *a. arch.* a rendezvous, a meeting or meeting-place of sweethearts.

Tsar, *n.* title of former ruler of Russia, also Czar. *fem.* **Tsari'na**, *n.*

Tub, *n.* a wooden bath, an open cask.

Tu'ba, *n.* large low-pitched brass wind instrument.

Tube, *n.* a long thin hollow cylinder, a pipe for conveying gas or fluid, underground railway. **Tu'bular**, *a.* shaped like tube.

Tu'ber, (-bur) *n.* lumpish rooting part of certain plants such as potato, dahlia etc, a swelling part. **Tu'berous,** *a.*

Tu'bercle, *n.* diseased lump, natural protruberance.

Tuberculo'sis, *n.* consumption esp. of lungs. **Tuber'cular,** *a.* affected with tuberculosis, having tubercles.

Tuck, *v.t. & i.* to fold or gather in material, fold under, pack away neatly. *n.* a tucking, a fold. *sl.* food.

Tuft, *n.* prominent lock of hair, cluster of grass etc., crest.

Tug, *n.* a small powerful vessel for towing or moving larger ships or hauling barges.

Tug, *v.t. & i.* to pull jerkily, to drag at, haul.

Tuit'ion, *n.* teaching, instruction.

Tum'ble, *v.t. & i.* to fall over suddenly, cause to fall, fall and roll, to somersault. *n.* **Tum'bler,** *n.* an acrobat, a kind of pigeon, a drinking glass without a stem.

Tum'bril, *n.* horse-drawn cart, esp. associated with victims of the Terror in Fr. Revolution being taken to guillotine.

Tu'mid, *a.* swollen. **Tumid'ity,** *n.*

Tu'mour, *n.* morbid swelling.

Tu'mult, *n.* violent uproar. **Tumul'tuous,** *a.* turbulent.

Tun, *n.* a large wine cask.

Tun'dra, *n.* undulating barren marshy land in arctic.

Tune, *n.* a harmonious, melodious arrangement of mus. notes, proper mus. adjustment of instrument etc., harmonious mood. *v.t. & i.* to adjust mus. pitch, to adjust, put right, be in concord.

Tu'nic, *n.* upper garment of a uniform.

Tunn'el, *n.* an underground passage. *v.t. & i.* to make a tunnel, bore.

Tur'ban, *n.* oriental headdress of cloth bound round head in intricate fashion.

Turb'ary, *n.* ancient right of digging turf on common land.

Tur'bid, *a.* muddy, confused.

Tur'bine, *n.* engine powered by steam, water, air, driving against bladed wheel.

Tur'bulent, *a.* riotous, greatly agitated, uncontrollable. **Tur'bulence,** *n.*

Tureen', *n.* large lidded table-dish for soup.

Turf, *n.* grass including the soil it grows in. *pl.* **Turves.** *v.t.* to cover with turf. *Coll.* horse-racing.

Tur'gid (-jid), *a.* morbidly swollen, *fig.* pompous esp. of speech.

Tur'key, *n.* large wild or domestic bird of Amer. origin.

Tur'moil, *n.* commotion, confusion.

Turn, *v.t. & i.* to go round or cause to go round, to revolve, to face about, to go in a different direction, to change, transform, hinge, make, fashion, reel, spoil, upset. *n.* the act of turning or revolving, a performance, a shock, a deed, a change etc.

Turn'coat, *n.* deserter, esp. polit.

Tur'ner, *n.* craftsman who works with lathe.

Turn'key, *n.* arch. janitor, person entrusted with keys of gaol.

Turn'over, *n.* a kind of pie, the total money handled in a business.

Turn'pike, *n. arch.* barrier across a toll-road where payment had to be made.

Turn'stile, *n.* revolving device for controlling and counting people entering an exhibition, sports-ground etc.

Turn'table, *n.* device for changing direction of railway engine in railway yard.

Tur'pentine, *n.* fluid obtained from resin of coniferous trees.

Tur'pitude, *n.* extreme wickedness.

Tur'quoise, *n.* precious stone of azure colour, this colour. *a.*

Tur'ret, *n.* a small tower, an armoured revolving gun-shelter in ship or tank.

Tusk, *n.* long projecting tooth. **Tusk'er**, *n.* animal with long tusks, esp. wild boar or elephant.

Tus'sle, *n.* a scuffle, brief struggle. *v.t.*

Tuss'ock, *n.* tuft of grass.

Tu'telage, *n.* guardianship. **Tu'telary**, *a.* pertaining to tutelage or a guardian.

Tu'tor, *n.* a teacher, esp. in university or privately. **Tutor'ial**, *a.* to do with this. *n.* a special conference or lesson with tutor.

Twad'dle (Twod-), *n.* foolish talk. *v.i.*

Twain, *n. arch.* two, a pair.

Twang, *n.* a metallic, vibrating sound, a nasal way of speaking. *v.t. & i.*

Tweak, *v.t.* to pinch, twist suddenly. *n.*

Tweed, *n.* strong woollen material with hairy surface and us. at least two shades of colour in pattern.

Twee'zers, *n. pl.* small tongs or pincers for handling very small objects.

Twid'dle, *v.t.* to twist rapidly.

Twig, *n.* piece of a branch, a shoot.

Twi'light, *n.* faint light preceding dawn or following sunset.

Twill, *n.* cloth with ribbed texture.

Twin, *n.* one of an identical or almost identical pair, esp. of two children of same birth. *a.*

Twine, *n.* strong thread, tough string. *v.t. & i.* to wind round, twist, entangle.

Twinge (Twinj), *n.* a sudden sharp pain.

Twin'kle, *v.t.* to sparkle, shine flutteringly. *n.*

Twirl (Twurl), *v.t. & i.* to spin round rapidly.

Twist, *v.t. & i.* to contort, bend, distort, wrench, wind. *n.* a twisting, roll of tobacco. **Twist'er**, *n. sl.* a cheat.

Twit, *v.t.* to deride, tease.

Twitch, *v.i.* to pull jerkily, to move jerkily. *n.*

Twitt'er, *n.* a chirping sound, nervous talk. *v.i.* to chirp, talk in nervous way.

Ty'coon, *n.* a business magnate.

Tym'panum (Tim-), *n.* the eardrum, middle ear.

Type, *n.* a particular kind or example, a class, group distinguished by common characteristics. **Typ'ical**, *a.* characteristic of a type or class, representative. **Typ'ify**, *v.t.* to represent, be typical of.

Type, *n.* representation of letter or character cut or cast in wood or metal for printing,

printing-matter. *v.t.* to write on a typewriter. Typesetter, *n.* type compositor. Typescript, *n.* material written on typewriter. Type'writer, *n.* hand operated writing machine. Ty'-pist, *n.* person skilled in using typewriter. Typog'raphy, *n.* the art or style of printing.

Ty'phoid, *n.* infectious water-borne disease.

Ty'phoon, *n.* violent hurricane esp. in China seas.

Ty'phus, *n.* severe feverish disease characterized by eruptions on skin and delirium.

Ty'rant, *n.* a cruel despot, absolute ruler. Tyrann'ical, *a.* like a tyrant, harsh, severe, oppressive. Tyr'annize, *v.i.* to oppress cruelly. Tyr'anny, (Tir-) *n.* oppression, government by a tyrant.

Tyre, tire, *n.* wheel-rim, rubber covering for this.

Ty'ro, *n.* a novice.

U

Ubiq'uitous, *a.* omnipresent, being everywhere at once. Ubiq'uity, *n.* omnipresence.

Udd'er, *n.* mammary gland of cow, goat etc.

Ug'ly, *a.* repulsive, displeasing to the eye, threatening.

Ukase', *n.* an official decree.

Ul'cer (-ser), *n.* open, pus-secreting sore, anything corrupting. Ulcer'ous, *a.* Ulcerate', *v.t. & i.* to make or become ulcerous.

Ull'age, *n.* difference between capacity of cask and contents.

Ul'ster, *n.* long loose belted overcoat.

Ulter'ior (-teer-), *a.* more than is expressed, further than in meaning.

Ul'timate, *a.* final, last.

Ul'timatum, *n.* final demand or condition for making an agreement.

Ul'timo, *adv.* of last month.

Ul'tra, *pref.* meaning extreme, excessive, beyond.

Ulu'late, *v.i.* to howl. Ulula'tion, *n.*

Um'bel, *n.* compact flower-cluster characteristic of certain plants. Umbell'iferous, *a.*

Um'ber, *n.* brown pigment, rich brown colour. *a.*

Umbili'cal, *a.* pertaining to the navel, esp. as u.-cord.

Um'brage, *n.* offence, sense of injury, formerly or *poet.* shade. Umbrage'ous, *a.* shady.

Umbrell'a, *n.* a folding device for protection against rain or heat.

Um'pire, *n.* a referee, person who settles dispute between others. *v.t. & i.*

Un-, *pref.* meaning negative, opposite, reversal of, lack of. The meaning of relevant words will be clear from reference to main word and application of sense of *pref.* explained here.

Unanim'ity (U-na-), *n.* complete agreement, accord. Unan'im-ous, (U-nan-) *a.* completely agreeing, united in opinion.

Uncann'y, *a.* unearthly, ghostly.

Un'cle, *n.* brother of father or mother, husband of aunt.

Uncouth (-kooth), *a.* boorish, clumsy.

Unc'tion, *n.* a ritual anointing, an o ntment for this or a med. ointment, insincere courtesy or fervour. **Unc'tuous** (-tu-us), *a.* oily in manner.

Un'der, *prep.* below, beneath, deficient, less than, subject to, *adv.* in or to a lower position or condition. *a.* lower in position.

Un'der- as *pref.* meaning below, insufficient, subordinate.

Undergrad'uate, *n.* student working for degree.

Un'derground, *a.* beneath the earth, clandestine.

Un'derling, *n.* a lackey, a subordinate.

Understand', *v.t.* to comprehend, perceive mentally. **Understand'ing,** *n.* the act of comprehending, an agreement.

Undertake', *v.t.* to agree to do, accept responsibility. **Underta'king,** *n.* a task undertaken, an enterprise.

Un'dertaker, *n.* person engaging in business of organizing funerals. **Underta'king,** *n.*

Un'derwrite, *v.t. & i.* to support large-scale insurance e.g. in shipping, accept partial liability for loss. **Un'derwriter,** *n.*

Un'dulate, *v.i.* to progress in wavy movement. **Undula'tion,** *n.*

Ungain'ly, *a.* awkward, clumsy.

Un'guent (-gwent), *n.* ointment, greasy substance.

U'nicorn, *n.* fabulous and heraldic beast resembling horse but with long straight horn in forehead.

U'niform, *n.* official dress. *a.* unchanging, unvarying, following a set pattern.

U'nify, *v.t.* to unite, make alike or uniform. **Unifica'tion,** *n.*

Unilat'eral, *a.* one-sided, applying only to one side.

U'nion, *n.* the act or fact of being united, an association of mutual interests, a combination, confederation. **U'nionist,** *n.* advocate of union esp. in polit. sense.

Unique (U-neek), *a.* unequalled, unmatched, utterly remarkable.

U'nison, *n.* concord, agreement, mus. harmony.

U'nit, *n.* single part of a whole, individual person or thing, a quantity representing a standard.

Unitar'ianism, *n. rel.* belief that God is one person instead of Trinity. **Unitar'ian,** *n.*

Unite (U-nite), *v.t. & i.* to join together, make into whole. **U'nity,** *n.*

U'niverse, *n.* all natural matter, the entire creation. the world. **Univer'sal,** *a.* pertaining to the universe, generally applicable. **Universal'ity,** *n.* the condition of being universal.

Univer'sity (U-ni-), *n.* institution for higher education with power of conferring degrees in various subjects.

Unkempt', *a.* uncombed, untidy in appearance.

Unless', *conj.* if not, except.

Unru'ly, *a.* turbulent, ill-behaved.

Until', *prep.* up to that time. *conj.* to the time or place that.

Un'to, *prep.* to.

Un'toward, *a.* inconvenient, awkward.

Up, *adv.* in, to, a higher quality, position, in a standing position, in action. *prep.* toward in a higher way, to or near the top. **Up'ward, Up'wards,** *a. & adv.* moving up, in a higher direction. **Up-** also as *pref.* with similar sense to up.

Upbraid', *v.t.* to reprove harshly.

Uphol'ster (-hole-), *v.t.* to furnish room with curtains and carpets, to cover, stuff or repair furniture. **Uphol'sterer,** *n.* craftsman or merchant in this. **Uphol'stery,** *n.* soft furnishings.

Upon', *prep.* on.

Up'right, *a.* standing up, honest. *n.* a vertical post. **Up'rightness,** *n.* condition of being erect, integrity.

Up'shot, *n.* outcome, result.

Up'start, *n.* person lacking dignity to go with sudden success.

Ura'nium, *n.* radioactive metallic element obtained from pitchblende.

Urano-, *pref.* meaning heaven and chiefly as e.g. **Uranog'raphy,** *n.* descriptive astronomy, **Uran'ology,** *n.* astronomy, etc.

Ur'ban, *a.* pertaining to a town or city.

Urbane', *a.* courteous, polished in manner. **Urban'ity,** *n.*

Urch'in, *n.* mischievous child, ragamuffin.

Urge, *v.t.* to encourage, drive on. try vehemently to persuade. **Ur'gent,** *a.* requiring immediate action, insistent. **Ur'gency,** *n.*

U'rine, *n.* waste fluid from bladder. **U'rinate,** *v.i.* to discharge urine from bladder. **Urina'tion,** *n.*

Urn, *n.* decorative vase, sometimes as container for ashes of dead person, a large vessel for hot beverages.

Use, *v.t. & i.* (Uze) to employ for specific purpose, to avail onself of, to handle as tool or implement, to exploit, exercise, treat, be or make accustomed to. *n.* (Use), the fact of using, custom, employment, application. **U'sable** (Uze-), *a.* **U'sage,** *n.* method of using, practice. **Use'ful,** *a.* **Use'less,** *a.*

Ush'er, *n.* official who directs or escorts to appointed seat or place, doorkeeper, formerly an assistant school-teacher. *v.t.* to escort esp. to seat or place.

U'sual (Uze-), *a.* customary.

Usurp (U-zurp), *v.t.* to take possession of illegally. **Usurp'er,** *n.* **Usurpa'tion,** *n.*

U'sury (Uzury), *n.* money-lending at extortionate rate. **U'surer,** *n.* moneylender. **Usu'rious,** *a.* extortionate.

Uten'sil, *n.* vessel or implement for domestic use.

U'terus, *n.* womb of female mammal.

U'tilize, *v.t.* to make use of. **Util'ity,** *n.* usefulness, useful thing, organization for public service. **Utiliza'tion,** *n.* **Utilitar'ian,** *a.* intended for material use only without aesthetic consideration.

Ut'most, *a.* greatest, most extreme, farthest. **Utt'ermost,** *a.*

Uto'pia, *n.* an imaginary perfect place. **Uto'pian,** *a.* idealistic, *a.*

Utt'er, *v.t.* to speak, pronounce, emit, publish. **Utt'erance,** *n.* act of uttering, a pronouncement.

Utt'er, *a.* absolute, complete.

U'vula, *n.* fleshy projection at back of palate. **U'vular,** *a.*

Uxor'ious, *a.* over-fond of or over-attentive to one's wife.

V

Va'cant, *a.* empty, unoccupied, blank. **Va'cancy.** *n.* emptiness. **Va'cate,** *v.t. & i.* to give up occupation, make empty.

Vaca'tion, *n.* a holiday.

Vac'cinate (Vak-si-), *v.t.* to make immune by inoculation. **Vaccina'tion,** *n.* inoculation. **Vac'cine** (Vak-seen), *n.* substance used for vaccination, esp. virus of cowpox.

Vac'illate (Vass-), *v.i.* to fluctuate, oscillate, hesitate. **Vacilla'tion,** *n.*

Vac'uum (Vak-u-um), *n.* an entirely vacant space esp. when devoid of air. **Vacu'ity,** *n.* an emptiness, an empty space. **Vac'uous** (Vak-), *a.* vacant, expressionless.

Vag'abond, *n.* an idle wanderer.

Vagar'y, *n.* a whim, fancy.

Va'grant, *n.* a vagabond, wandering beggar. *a.* wandering.

Vague, *a.* indefinite, not clear, obscure.

Vain, *a.* useless, unavailing, conceited. **Vain-glorious,** *a.* excessive proud or boastful. **Van'ity,** *n.* conceit, empty pride.

Val'ance, *n.* narrow curtain round bed or across top of window curtains.

Vale, *n.* a valley.

Valedic'tory (Val-e-), *a. & n.* saying farewell, a speech of farewell esp. formal. **Valedic'tion,** *n.*

Val'entine, *n.* amorous greeting sent on St Valentine's Day, 14 February, the object of such a greeeting.

Val'et (-lay), *n.* gentleman's manservant esp. to look after clothes and personal needs. *v.t.* to act as valet.

Valetudinar'ian, *n.* person unduly concerned for his health.

Val'iant, *a.* courageous, heroic.

Val'id, *a.* admissible, legally sound. **Valid'ity,** *n.* **Val'idate,** *v.t.* to make valid.

Valise' (-eez), *n.* hold-all for travelling.

Vall'ey, *n.* a natural trough between ranges of higher ground.

Val'our, *n.* bravery. **Val'orous,** *a.*

Val'ue, *n.* worth, esteem, equivalent worth in money. *v.t.* to regard as precious, to calculate value. **Val'uable,** *a.* costly, precious, of much value. **Valua'tion,** *n.* the act of estimating a value. **Val'uer,** *n.* person practising business of valuation.

Valve, *n.* mechanical or membranous device for opening and shutting pipe, wireless appliance for conversion of waves. **Val'vular,** *a.* of, like or affecting a valve.

Vamp, *v.t.* to repair or adapt with previous material.

Vam'pire, *n.* blood-sucking bat, fictionally a blood-sucking phantom.

Van, *n.* the front or leading part.

Van'guard, *n.* leading part of an army in action.

Van, *n.* covered vehicle for merchandize.

Van'dal, *n.* orig. a marauding Teutonic tribesman, now anyone who deliberately destroys or damages beautiful or valuable things. **Van'dalism,** *n.* wilful destruction of such things.

Vane, *n.* weathercock, blade of propeller.

Vanill'a, *n.* flavouring extract obtained from orchid of this name. *a.*

Van'ish, *v.i.* to disappear.

Van'ity, *n.* empty pride, conceit.

Van'quish, *v.t.* to defeat.

Van'tage (Vahn-), *n.* advantage, esp. as e.g. vantage-point.

Vap'id, *a.* stupid, pointless, insipid. **Vapid'ity,** *n.*

Va'pour (-per), *n.* gaseous form of liquid or solid, mist, steam. **Va'porize,** *v.t. & i.* to turn into vapour. **Va'porous,** *a.* **Va'pouring,** *n.* or esp. *n.pl.* empty talk.

Var'icose, *a.* pertaining to a varix or varices. **Var'ix,** *n. med.* abnormal dilatation esp. of vein.

Var'iegate, *v.t.* to mark with different colours, change appearance by this. **Variega'-tion,** *n.*

Var'nish, *n.* resinous preparation for treating woodwork. *v.t.*

Var'y (Vare-), *v.t. & i.* to change, alter, differ, undergo change. **Var'iable,** *a.* **Variabil'ity,** *n.* **Var'iance,** *n.* state of varying or differing. **Var'iant,** *a. & n.* a differing, differing form. **Varia'-tion,** *n.* a varying, a diversity. **Vari'ety,** *n.* an assortment, a diversity, condition of being different. **Var'ious,** *a.* assorted, different.

Vas'cular (Vask-), *a.* pertaining to or furnished with fluid-carrying vessels esp. in animals or plants.

Vase (Vahz), *n.* an ornamental vessel.

Vass'al, *n.* a serf, feudal tenant. **Vass'alage,** *n.*

Vast (Vahst), *a.* immense.

Vat, *n.* large tank or tub for brewing liquor or making dyes.

Vaude'ville, *n.* variety entertainment.

Vault (Vawlt or Volt), *v.t. & i.* to leap or jump with aid of pole or by using hand or hands for leverage. *n.*

Vault, *n.* an underground tomb, an underground room for tombs, wines or valuables, *archit.* an arched ceiling or roof.

Vaunt (Vawnt), *v.t. & i.* to boast, boast of.

Veal, *n.* meat of ox-calf.

Veer, *v.i.* to change direction, esp. of wind but *fig.* of opinion.

Veg'etable (Vej-), *n.* a plant, plant cultivated for food. *a.* **Vegetar'ian,** *n.* person who never eats meat or fish. **Vegetar'ianism,** *n.* **Vegeta'tion,** *n.* plant life in general.

Veg'etate (Vej-), *v.i.* to grow or live like a plant, us. *fig.* as to lead a dull pointless life.

Ve'hemence (Ve-em-), *n.* vigour, violence in action or speech. **Ve'hement,** *a.*

Ve'hicle (Ve-ik-), *n.* a means of conveyance on land, *fig.* a means of expression. **Vehic'-ular,** *a.*

Veil (Vale), *n.* a covering for the

face, any covering. *v.t.* to cover as with a veil, to obscure.

Vein (Vane), *n.* tubelike vessel for conveying blood or sap, a layer or streak of mineral, a characteristic. *v.t.* to mark with veins or streaks.

Veldt, *n.* S. Afric. prairie.

Vell'um, *n.* calfskin parchment for fine writing.

Veloc'ity (-os-), *n.* speed, rate of motion of projectile, mechanical body.

Vel'our, *n.* plush, velvety material.

Vel'vet, *n.* thickly woven silk material with soft pile. *a.* **Vel'-vety,** *a.* soft of surface. **Velveteen',** *n.* imitation velvet.

Ve'nal, *a.* corrupt, corruptible by bribery. **Venal'ity,** *n.*

Vendett'a, *n.* blood-feud esp. among relations.

Ven'dor, *n.* a seller.

Veneer', *n.* an extra surface of better wood or material to cover inferior material, a superficial gloss. *v.t.* to cover or conceal with veneer.

Ven'erable, *a.* respected because of age, revered. **Ven'erate,** *v.t.* to reverence. **Venera'tion,** *n.*

Vener'eal, *a.* relating to sexual intercourse, affected by this.

Ven'ery, *n. arch.* hunting.

Ven'geance (-jance), *n.* retribution, the exaction of payment or retaliation for a wrong committed. **Venge'ful,** *a.* seeking vengeance.

Ve'nial, *a.* excusable, of sin not grave.

Ven'ison, *n.* meat of deer.

Ven'om, *n.* natural poison, malice. **Ven'omous,** *a.*

Vent, *n.* an outlet, *v.t.* to release, let out.

Ven'tilate, *v.t.* to purify by fresh air, cause fresh air to circulate, to bring subject into open. **Vent'ilator,** *n.* device for ventilating. **Ventila'tion,** *n.*

Ven'tral, *a.* relating to the belly.

Ven'tricle, *n.* a hollow organ, esp. one of chambers of heart.

Ventril'oquism, *n.* power of throwing or directing voice so that it seems to come from another person. **Ventril'oquist,** *n.*

Ven'ture, *n.* a bold or dangerous enterprise. *v.t. & i.* to dare, embark on hazardous enterprise. **Ven'turesome,** *n.* adventurous, bold.

Ven'ue, *n.* meeting-place.

Verac'ity (-as-), *n.* truth, truthfulness. **Verac'ious,** *a.* truthful.

Veran'da, (Veran'dah), *n.* roofed open-fronted gallery along wall of house.

Verb (Vurb), *n. gram.* part of speech expressing action or being.

Verb'al, *a.* pertaining to words. **Verba'tim,** *adv.* literally, word for word. **Ver'biage,** *n.* wordiness. **Verbose',** *a.* using too many words. **Verbos'ity,** *n.* prolixity.

Ver'dant, *a.* fresh, green, profuse in foliage.

Ver'dict (Vur-), a decision after consideration, a legal decision.

Ver'digris, *n.* green rust forming on copper.

Ver'dure, *n.* green foliage, grass.

Verge, *n.* a boundary, edge, margin. *v.i.* to be on the edge of, approach closely.

Ver'ger, *n.* (Vurjer) minor church official, church usher.

Ver'ify, *v.t.* to ascertain or check

truth of. **Ver'ifiable**, *a*. **Ver-ifica'tion**, *n*.

Verisimil'itude, *n*. appearance of actuality or truth.

Ver'itable, *a*. genuine, actual, true. **Ver'ity**, *n*. truth.

Ver'ily, *adv. arch*. or *bib*. truly.

Ver'juice (Vur-), *n*. sour liquor obtained from unripe grapes etc.

Vermicell'i (-sell- or -chell-), *n*. kind of thin macaroni.

Ver'miform, *n*. shaped like a worm. **Verm'icide**, *n*. worm-killer.

Vermil'ion, *n*. & *a*. bright scarlet, the pigment from which this colour is obtained.

Ver'min, *n*. us. as *pl*. (same) anything considered by mankind to be inimical to his interests. **Ver'minous**, *a*.

Vernac'ular, *a*. colloquial. *n*. colloquial language.

Ver'nal, *a*. fresh, springlike, of the spring.

Ver'satile, *a*. capable of performing many things, skilled in a number of subjects. **Versatil'ity**, *n*.

Verse, *n*. poetry, a stanza of poetry. **Ver'sify**, *v.t.* & *i*. us. *iron*. to write verse, turn into verse. **Versifica'tion**, *n*.

Versed, *a*. esp. as versed in, thoroughly acquainted with.

Ver'sion, *n*. an account or description esp. when opposed to another one, a translation.

Ver'sus, *prep*. against.

Ver'tebra, *n*. segment of backbone. *a*. having a backbone.

Ver'tex, *n*. *pl*. vertices, apex, peak.

Ver'tical, *a*. upright. *n*.

Verti'go, *n*. giddiness. **Vertig'-**

inous (-tij-), *a*. giddy or causing giddiness.

Verve (Vurv), *n*. dash, enthusiasm.

Ver'y, *a*. & *adv*. actual, extremely.

Ves'icle, *n*. small blister.

Ves'per, *a. poet*. relating to the evening. a *n.pl*. rel. evening prayers.

Vess'el, *n*. a ship, a receptacle for liquids, a vein, a means of conveying a fluid.

Vest, *n*. an under garment.

Vest, *v.t.* & *i*. to confer upon, furnish, endow, esp. regarding property or office.

Ves'tal, *a*. pure, virgin.

Vest'ibule, *n*. entrance lobby, hallway.

Ves'tige (-tij), *n*. faint trace, sign. **Vestig'ial**, *a*. of biol. part or organ no longer used but still present.

Vest'ment, *n*. a ceremonial robe, esp. as *n.pl*.

Vest'ry, *n*. room attached to church where priest robes himself or church meetings are held.

Ves'ture, *n*. clothing, robes.

Vet'eran, *n*. person with great experience, old serviceman.

Vet'erinary, *a*. pertaining to the study and treatment of animal ailments or injuries. **Vet'erinary surgeon**, *n*. skilled practitioner in treatment of sick animals. **Veterinar'ian**, *n*.

Ve'to, *n*. the power to prohibit or ban. *v.t.* to prohibit by exercising right.

Vex, *v.t.* to irritate, annoy, ruffle. **Vexa'tion**, *n*. **Vexa'tious**, *a*.

Vi'a, *prep*. by way of.

Vi'aduct, *n*. road or rail bridge

esp. when supported by series of arches.

Vi'brant, *a.* vibrating.

Vi'brate, *v.t. & i.* to quiver, oscillate. **Vibra'tion,** *n.* **Vibra'tory,** *a.*

Vic'ar, *n.* a parish priest. **Vic'arage,** *n.* his dwelling.

Vicar'ious, *a.* acting through or for another.

Vice, *n.* evil, wickedness, an evil habit.

Vice, *n.* double-jawed adjustable tool for gripping.

Vice-, *pref.* meaning acting in place of another, e.g. **Viceroy,** *n.* acting for the king, etc.

Vicin'ity (Vis-), *a.* neighbourhood.

Vic'ious (-shus), *a.* malicious, full of vice.

Viciss'itude (-sis-), *n.* change of fortune esp. for the worse.

Vic'tim, *n.* the object of misfortune or attack. **Vic'timize,** *v.t.* to persecute.

Vic'tory, *n.* triumph over an enemy, attainment of a difficult object. **Vic'tor,** *n.* one who gains victory. **Victor'ious,** *a.* triumphant.

Vict'ual (Vitt'l), *v.t.* to supply with food esp. as applied to services. **Victuals,** *n.pl.* foodstuffs. **Vict'ualler,** *n.*

Vie (Vy), *v.i.* to contend with, compete with.

View (Vu), *n.* outlook, prospect, range of vision, landscape, picture, opinion, intention. *v.t.* to look at, survey. **View-point,** *n.* personal attitude.

Vig'il (Vij-), *n.* a staying awake to watch or guard. **Vig'ilance,** *n.* wakefulness, watchfulness. **Vig'ilant,** *a.* alert, keenly observant.

Vig'nette (Vin-yet), *n.* archit. decoration of leaves, informal sketch, decoration round capital letter of manuscript, illustration incorporated in page without definite delimitation.

Vig'our, *n.* energy, strength. **Vig'orous,** *a.*

Vi'king, *n.* Scandinavian pirate during 8th to 10th centuries A.D.

Vile, *a.* ignoble, mean, horrible. **Vile'ness,** *n.* **Vil'ify,** *v.t.* to speak vilely of, defame.

Vill'a, *n.* country house, prop. a Roman farmhouse.

Vill'age, *n.* a small country community and the dwelling-places of it. **Vill'ager,** *n.* inhabitant of a village.

Vill'ain (-en), *n.* a wicked person, character in story or play who contends with hero. **Vill'ainy,** *n.* the committing of evil, wickedness. **Vill'ainous,** *a.* very wicked, heinous.

Vill'ein, *n.* feudal serf.

Vin'dicate, *v.t.* to justify, prove innocent. **Vindica'tion,** *n.*

Vindic'tive, *a.* revengeful, deeply resentful. **Vindic'tiveness,** *n.*

Vine, *n.* grape-bearing climbing plant. **Vine'yard** (Vin-), *n.* farm or garden where grapes are cultivated esp. for wine. **Vi'nous,** *a.* pertaining to wine. **Vin'tage,** *n.* the harvesting of grapes and subsequent making of wine, wine of a certain year. **Vint'ner,** *n.* wine-merchant. **Vin'iculture,** *n.* grape-growing.

Vin'egar, *n.* sour liquid obtained from fermented liquors and used for culinary purposes.

Vi'ol, *n.* mediaeval stringed instrument preceding violin.

Vio′la, *n.* large tenor or alto violin.

Vi′olate, *v.t.* to abuse, trespass, transgress. **Viola′tion**, *n.* **Vi′olator**, *n.*

Vi′olence, *n.* extreme physical force, intensity, vehemence. **Vi′olent**, *a.*

Vi′olet, *a.* & *n.* bluish-purple colour, flower of this colour.

Violin′ (Vy-), *n.* four-stringed instrument played with bow. **Violin′ist**, *n.* performer on this.

Violoncell′o (-chel-), *n.* us. abbrev. to 'cello (chello), large instrument of same class as violin.

Vi′per, *n.* a poisonous snake, an adder. **Vi′perous**, *a.* venomous, malicious.

Vira′go, *n.* termagant, shrewish woman.

Vir′gin, (-jin) *a.* pure, chaste, unused, unspoilt. *n.* a chaste woman. **Vir′ginal**, *a.* pure. **Virgin′ity**, *n.* state of being virgin.

Vir′ginal, *n.* a kind of spinet.

Vir′ile, *a.* robust, masculine. **Viril′ity**, *n.*

Vir′tual (Vur-), *a.* existing in effect if not nominally.

Vir′tue (Vur-), *n.* integrity, moral excellence, high merit. **Vir′tuous**, *a.* morally upright, good.

Virtuos′ity, *n.* special skill or knowledge in art or mus. etc. **Virtuo′so**, *n.* person having this.

Vir′ulence, *n.* poisonous quality, bitter vehemence. **Vir′ulent**, *a.*

Vi′rus, *n.* a venom, a cause of disease.

Vi′sa (Veeza), *n.* endorsement on passport.

Vis′age (Viz-ij), *n.* the face.

Vis′cera (Vis-), *n.pl.* the intestines. **Vis′ceral**, (Vis-) *a.*

Vis′cid, (Vis-) *a.* sticky. **Viscid′ity**, *n.*

Vis′count (Vy-kownt), *n.* title of nobility ranking below earl, an earl's son.

Vis′cous (Vis-kus), *a.* sticky.

Vis′ible, *a.* able to be seen, in sight. **Visibil′ity**, *n.* range of being visible.

Vis′ion (Vizh-), *n.* sense or power of seeing, imagination, a dream, a phantom visitation. **Vis′ionary**, *a.* & *n.* impractical, impractical person.

Vis′it, *v.t.* & *i.* to call on, make a stay with, go or come to see, to send down upon. *n.* **Vis′itor**, *n.* person who visits. **Visita′tion**, *n.* calamity, affliction, visit in official or iron. sense.

Vis′ta, *n.* a confined view.

Vis′ualize, *v.t.* & *i.* to envisage, imagine. **Visualiza′tion**, *n.* **Vis′ual**, *a.* pertaining to sight, visible.

Vital′ity, *n.* life, life-force. **Vi′tal**, *a.* concerned with or affecting life, essential to life. **Vi′talize**, *v.t.* to instil with life or energy.

Vi′tamin, *n.* one of various ingredients of food essential for health or normal growth.

Vi′tiate, *v.t.* to render ineffective. **Vitia′tion**, *n.*

Vit′iculture, *n.* grape-growing.

Vit′reous, *a.* of or like glass. **Vit′rify**, *v.t.* & *i.* to turn into glass or something resembling glass.

Vit′riol, *n.* sulphuric acid, *fig.* bitter sarcasm. **Vitriol′ic**, *a.*

Vitu′perate, *v.t.* to scold abusively. **Vitupera′tion**, *n.* **Vitu′perative**, *a.*

Viva'cious, *a.* spirited, gay, jocose. **Vivac'ity** (-vas-), *n.*

Viv'id, *a.* brilliant, descriptively clear.

Viv'ify, *v.t.* to animate, imbue with life.

Vi'viparous, *a. Zool.* producing young alive as opposed to hatching from egg.

Viv'isection, *n.* the practice of experimenting on live animals for research purposes. **Viv'isect,** *v.t. & i.*

Vix'en, *n.* a female fox.

Vi'zor, vi'sor, Vi'zard, *n.* adjustable part of mediaeval helmet protecting face, now projecting peak of cap or helmet.

Vocab'ulary, *n.* a systematic arrangement of words, range of words habitually used in language or by person or particular group of people.

Vo'cal, *a.* to do with the voice, uttered by the voice, making use of voice. **Vo'calist,** *n.* a singer.

Voca'tion, *n.* calling in life, profession, occupation. **Voca'tional,** *a.*

Voc'ative, *a. & n.* gram. case used in addressing person or thing.

Vocif'erate (Vos-), *v.t. & i.* to utter loudly or emphatically. **Vocifera'tion,** *n.* **Vocif'erous,** *a.*

Vogue, *n.* current fashion.

Voice, *n.* expressive sounds uttered through human or animal mouth, esp. human utterance caused by vibration of vocal cords, the power of speech, an expression of opinion. *v.t.* to express vocally.

Void, *a.* empty, null, vacant. *n.* an empty space. *v.t.* to empty, render useless.

Vol'atile, *a.* evaporating swiftly, *fig.* of person changeable, unpredictable. **Volatil'ity,** *n.*

Volca'no, *n.* opening in earth's crust, us. on mountain, through which subterranean action expels lava etc. **Volcan'ic,** *a.* of, like, caused by volcano, explosive, violent.

Volit'ion, *n.* the exercise of will-power, choice, preference.

Voll'ey, *v.t. & i.* to fire number of weapons simultaneously, return tennis ball to opponent before it bounces, discharge rapid series of remarks. *n.*

Volt, *n.* unit of electromotive force. **Vol'tage,** *n.* electric power measured in volts.

Vol'uble, *a.* talkative, fluent. **Volubil'ity,** *n.*

Vol'ume, *n.* one part of a series of books, a book, certain number of consecutive issues of magazine. **Volu'minous,** *a.* occupying many volumes, bulky in this way.

Vol'ume, *n.* amount of cubic space occupied by a body, any large bulk, roundness of voice.

Vol'untary, *a.* done of one's own volition, intentional.

Volunteer', *v.t.* to serve or offer of one's own will. *n.* serviceman joining through own choice as opposed to being conscripted, anyone similar.

Volup'tuary, *n.* person indulging in sensual pleasures. **Volup'tuous,** *a.* pertaining to sensuous or sensual pleasure.

Volu'tion, *n.* a spiral shape or turn.

Vom'it, *v.t. & i.* to spew, throw up from stomach. *n.* the matter vomited.

Voo'doo, *n. & a.* West Ind. sorcery.

Vorac'ity (-as-), *n.* gluttony, greed in eating. **Vora'cious,** *a.*

Vor'tex, *n.* a whirlpool. *pl.* **Vor'tices** (-ti-seez).

Vo'tary, *n.* devotee, ardent en'husiast.

Vote, *v.t. & i.* to express one's choice by ballot or other means, to approve or elect by expressing one's choice formally. *n.* the act of voting, votes collectively. **Vo'ter,** *n.*

Vo'tive, *a.* dedicated in consecration of a vow.

Vouch (Vowch), *v.t. & i.* to answer for, uphold, bear witness.

Vouch'er, *n.* a receipt or token of payment, free pass.

Vouchsafe', *v.t.* to deign, condescend, to give or grant.

Vow, *n.* a solemn pledge. *v.t. & i.* to promise solemnly.

Vow'el, *n.* open sound uttered in speaking, as opposed to consonant, i.e., a,e, i, o, u.

Voy'age, *n.* a long journey by water. *v.t. & i.* to travel by sea. **Voy'ager,** *n.*

Vul'canize, *v.t.* to harden esp. rubber by treating with sulphur at high temperature. **Vulcaniza'tion,** *n.*

Vul'gar, *a.* coarse, ill-bred, pertaining to the common people. **Vul'garism,** *n.* method of expression in common use but incorrect. **Vul'garity,** *n.* coarseness. **Vul'garize,** *v.t.* to make vulgar, cheapen.

Vul'nerable, *a.* exposed to injury or attack, liable to penalty. **Vulnerabil'ity,** *n.*

Vul'ture, *n.* carrion-eating raptorial bird, *fig.* predatory person.

Vul'va, *n.* an opening, an entrance, esp. the external opening of the female genitals.

Wad (Wod), *n.* small shape of soft material for keeping something in place, shaping other material, stopping a hole, making powder and shot compact in muzzle-loader, any small mass of soft material. *v.t.* to use a wad in various ways. **Wadd'ing,** *n.* soft material used for wads.

Wad'dle (Wod-), *v.t.* to walk in swaying clumsy movement as a duck. *n.*

Wade, *v.t. & i.* to walk through water or anything else entailing

effort, *fig.* to work at something laboriously. **Wa'der,** *n.* various kinds of long-legged waterbird. *pl.* rubber-boots.

Wa'fer, *n.* a very thin us. oblong biscuit, a coloured paper seal.

Waf'fle (wof-), *n.* kind of pancake, *sl.* inane talk. *v.i.*

Waft (Wahft), *v.t. & i.* to pass lightly through air or along surface of water, a tiny gust, scent.

Wag, *n.* an amusing person, a wit. **Wagg'ish,** *a.* droll.

Wag, *v.t. & i.* to move or cause to move from side to side. *n.*

Wage, *v.t.* to carry on, engage in.

Wage, *n.* earning, payment for work or service, esp. as *n. pl.* **Wage-earner,** *n.* paid worker.

Wa'ger (-jer), *v.t. & i.* to bet, gamble. *n.*

Wag'gle, *v.t. & i.* to wag, wriggle.

Wag'on,(Waggon),*n.*unpowered four-wheeled vehicle for conveying goods or articles and drawn by locomotive or draught animals. **Wag'goner,** *n.* driver of animal-drawn wagon.

Waif, *n.* a lost or homeless child.

Wail, *n.* a melancholy cry, a lament. *v.t. & i.*

Wain, *n. arch.* a wagon.

Wain'scot, *n.* skirting-board round bottom of wall, panelling.

Waist, *n.* narrow part of human trunk below ribs and above hips, the corresponding part of a garment, middle part of ship, anything resembling a waist. **Waist'coat,** *n.* man's sleeveless garment worn under coat. **Waist'line,** *n.* cause of concern among women.

Wait, *v.t. & i.* to stay, linger, delay action, serve, attend. *n.* the act of waiting, a delay. **Wai'ter, Wai'tress,** *n.* person who serves at table in restaurant. **Wait'ing,** *n.* act of lingering or remaining, attendance, serving. In waiting, esp. in attendance on a sovereign, e.g. lady in waiting. **Waits,** *n. pl.* carol singers.

Waive, *v.t.* to forgo, give up right etc. **Wai'ver,** *n.* the act of waiving, a clause allowing this.

Wake, *v.t. & i.* to cease to sleep, rouse from sleep, stir up. *n.* an Irish ritual of sitting up with corpse on night immediately after death. **Wake'ful,** *a.* alert. **Wa'ken,** *v.t. & i.*

Wake, *n.* the visible track of a vessel.

Wale, *n.* a weal, mark left by stroke of whip. **Wa'ling,** *n.* a thrashing.

Walk (Wawk), *v.t. & i.* to proceed on foot or cause to go on foot, to ride a horse slowly. *n.* a gait, a distance walked, a promenade, a manner esp. as walk in or of life.

Wall (Wawl), *n.* side of a building, a partition of brick or stone, a barrier, the vertical side of any structure. *v.t.* to build a wall, surround or close up with a wall.

Wall'et (Wol-), *n.* a small canvas or leather bag, folding pocket-case.

Wall'eye, *n.* defect of eye causing excess of white. **Wall-eyed,** *a.*

Wal'lop (Wol-), *n. sl.* a resounding or heavy blow. *v.t.* to beat severely.

Wal'low (Wol-o), *v.i.* to splash and roll about in mud, to enjoy grossly. *n.* a rolling about, a muddy place where deer etc. wallow at certain times.

Wal'nut, *n.* nut-bearing tree, its fruit or timber.

Wal'rus, *n.* large arctic mammal of seal-family bearing ivory tusks.

Waltz (Wolse), **valse,** *n.* graceful gyratory dance for two, the mus. for this. *v.i.* to dance a waltz.

Wan (Won), *a.* pale and sickly.

Wand (Wond), *n.* a slender rod.

Wan'der (Won-), *v.i.* to roam, stray, walk purposelessly, meander, talk deliriously. **Wan'derer,** *n.* roamer. **Wan'derlust,** *n.* yearning to travel.

Wane, *v.i.* to decrease in size, decline. *n.*

Want (Wont), *v.t. & i.* to need, be without, lack, desire. *n.* a need, a deficiency, poverty. **Wan'ting,** *a.* lacking, deficient in.

Wan'ton, *a.* wilful, playful, unrestrained.

War (Wor), *n.* violent conflict between nations, hostilities. *v.i.* to make war against, fight. **War'fare,** *n.* state of war, the waging of war. **War'like,** *a.* threatening war, aggressive. **War'head,** *n.* explosive part of projectile.

War'ble (Wor-), *v.t. & i.* to sing gaily. *n.* **War'bler,** *n.* a singer, one kind of singing bird.

Ward, *v.t.* to protect, avert, esp. as ward off. *n.* the act of protecting, a minor protected by someone other than parents, a division of a town for polit. purposes, a sick-room. **Ward'ship,** *n.* guardianship.

Ward'en, *n.* a guardian, a keeper.

Ward'er, *n.* a keeper, prison-officer.

Ward'robe, *n.* a cupboard for keeping clothes in, a stock of clothes.

Ware, *n.* manufactured articles for sale esp. of specific kind, **e.g.** table-ware, hard ware.

Warehouse, *n.* place for storing goods or merchandize.

Ware, *v.t.* to beware of, avoid. *a.*

Warm (Wor-), *a.* fairly hot, of moderate temperature, emitting moderate heat, affectionate, lively, deep in tone. *v.t. & i.* to imbue with warmth, heat slightly. **Warm-blooded,** *a.* of animals having blood of constant and comparatively high temperature. **Warm-hearted,** *a.* kindly, affectionate. **Warmth,** *n.* state of being moderately hot, emotion.

Warn (Wor-), *v.t.* to alert to danger, to caution. **War'ning,** *n.* a notification of danger or imminent happening.

Warp, *v.t. & i.* to distort or twist out of shape, bend, *naut.* to manoeuvre vessel by means of hawser attached to bollard on quayside. *n.* a hawser, in weaving the lengthwise thread crossed by the woof.

Warr'ant, *n.* an authoritative document empowering action, a voucher, a guarantee, permission. *v.t.* to guarantee, justify. **War'rantable,** *a.* **War'rant officer,** *n.* non-commissioned officer of higher rank.

War'ren, *n.* a colony of rabbits, rough land used for shooting.

War'rior, *n.* a man who takes part in war, a fighting-man.

War'ship, *n.* a man-of-war, a vessel equipped to take part in war.

Wart, *n.* a hard excrescence on the skin. **Wart'y,** *a.* covered with warts.

War'y, (Ware-) *a.* suspicious, vigilant.

Wash (Wosh) *v.t. & i.* to clean or make clean esp. with soap and water, to separate in water, to cover or sweep away with water, to paint with weak colouring. *n.* washing, clothes to be washed, rough water, a liquid for washing or painting. **Wash'ing,** *n.* laundry. **Wash-out,** *n. sl.* a flop.

Wash'er, *n.* metal or leather ring for tightening screw-hold.

Wasp, *n.* winged insect with venomous sting. **Was'pish,** *a.* like a wasp, sharp-tongued.

Was'sail, *n.* Saxon drinking-bout, festive celebration. *v.i.*

Waste, *v.t. & i.* to use extravagantly or purposelessly, to dissipate, squander, wear away, destroy. *n.* act of wasting, waste material, a barren place. *a.* **Waste'ful,** *a.* prodigal. **Wa'-strel,** *n.* loafer, good-for-nothing.

Watch, *v.t. & i.* to regard, observe, perceive with the eyes, guard. *n.* the act of watching, state of guarding or being wakeful, observation, look-out, vigilance, a division of hours esp. for turn of duty, a time-keeping instrument, a watchman. **Watch'dog,** *n.* guard-dog, alert person. **Watch'ful,** *a.* **Watch'maker,** *n.* maker of timepieces. **Watch'-man,** *n.* guard, caretaker. **Watch'tower,** *n.* observation tower. **Watch'word,** *n.* password, countersign.

Wa'ter (Waw-), *n.* natural liquid of which rivers, lakes, rain are formed, compound of oxygen and hydrogen, anything resembling water, the sea. *v.t. & i.* to apply water to, to give water to drink, dilute with water. **Water-colour,** *n.* pig-

ment mixed with water instead of oil. **Water-logged,** *a.* so soaked with water as to be unable to float. **Water-mark,** *n.* indicating mark in paper or banknote proving genuineness or quality etc. **Water-proof,** *a.* resistant against water. **Water-shed,** *n.* mountain ridge on either side of which different rivers have their origins. **Water-tight,** *a.* sealed against water.

Wat'tle (Wot-), *n.* framework of small pliant branches, pendulous red flesh on neck of turkey etc.

Wave, *n.* a curving movement or formation of water, anything resembling this, a sweeping movement or tendency, a gesture of the hand. *v.t. & i.* to gesture with hand in greeting or farewell, to form into waves, to brandish. **Wa'vy,** *a.*

Wa'ver, *v.i.* to hesitate, begin to lose courage, flutter.

Wax, *v.i.* to swell, increase in size or intensity.

Wax, *n.* pale yellow viscous plastic substance manufactured by bees for honeycomb cells, any substance resembling this. *v.t.* to treat with wax. **Wax'en,** *a.* made of wax.

Way, *n.* a direction, a method or manner, a path, habit. **Way-bill,** *n.* list of goods delivered. **Way-farer,** *n.* foot-traveller. **Way-lay,** *v.t.* to lie in wait for with hostile intent. **Wayside,** *n.* at the side of the main path or road. **Wayward,** *a.* wilful, disobedient.

We, *pron.* first person plur.

Weak, *a.* feeble, not strong, flimsy, ineffective, faulty.

Weak'en, *v.t. & i.* to make or become weak or weaker. **Weak'ling,** *n.* puny or feeble person. **Weak'ly,** *a.* feeble, sickly. **Weak'ness,** *n.*

Weal, *n. arch.* prosperity, welfare.

Weal, *n.* same as wale, mark left by blow of whip.

Weald, *n.* district in s.e. England having special geol. characteristics.

Wealth (Welth), *n.* riches, abundance. **Wealth'y,** *a.*

Wean, *v.t.* to accustom child or young animal to eating solid food instead of mother's milk. **Wean'ling,** *n.* child or animal just weaned.

Weap'on (Wep-), *n.* instrument for attack or defence.

Wear (Ware), *v.t. & i.* to use as a garment, to carry on or about the person, to show, fly, spoil by usage, to pass gradually, endure. *n.* act of wearing, things worn, deterioration caused by wearing or using.

Wear (Ware), *v.t. & i. naut.* to bring or put ship about.

Wea'ry, *a.* tired, tedious. *v.t. & i.* to tire, bore, irritate. **Wea'riness,** *n.* **Wea'risome,** *a.* tedious, arduous.

Wea'sel, *n.* small slim carnivorous mammal. **Weasel-faced,** *a.* sharp and lean of feature.

Weath'er (Weth-), *n.* atmospheric conditions. *v.t. & i.* to expose or accustom to the weather, to survive bad weather conditions, *naut.* to get or sail to windward.

Weave, *v.t. & i.* to construct material by intertwining thread, to make material on a loom, to pursue a winding course, to interlace or become so. **Wea'ver,** *n.* craftsman who works at loom.

Web, *n.* a spun or woven fabric, a spider's device for catching flies, an intricate arrangement, membrane between toes or claws of certain creatures. **Web-footed,** *a.* having toes or claws joined by membrane, as in ducks.

Wed, *v.t. & i.* to marry. **Wedd'ed,** *a.* married, joined.

Wedge, *n.* a tapering piece of wood or metal for jamming door, window etc. or splitting object in conjunction with hammer. *v.t.* to fasten with wedge, drive wedge into, drive something into opening tightly.

Wed'lock, *n.* marriage, matrimony.

Wee, *a.* tiny.

Weed, *n.* any plant growing in wrong place, noxious plant, wild plant growing in cultivated soil. *v.t. & i.* to remove such plants, to remove anything inferior, esp. as weed out. **weed'y** *a.* straggly.

Weed, *n.* a garment but us. only as weeds or widow's weeds, mourning clothes.

Week, *n.* a period of seven days. **Week'day,** *n.* any working day, not Sunday. **Week-end,** *n.* Saturday and Sunday as free time. **Week'ly,** *a.* happening every week. *n.* a publication appearing once a week.

Ween, *v.t. & i. arch.* to be of opinion, suppose. **Over-weening,** self-assertive, self-opinionated.

Weep, *v.t.* to shed tears, cry.

Wee'vil, *n.* small beetle sometimes found in flour.

Weft, *n.* the woof in weaving, threads crossing warp.

Weigh (Way), *v.t. & i.* to ascertain the heaviness of, to have as weight, to bear down heavily, to be of importance, to consider carefully. **Weight** (wate), *n.* heaviness, standard of measuring weight, importance, any heavy object. *v.t.* to load down, oppress. **Weight'-less,** *a.* unaffected by gravity. **Weight'y,** *a.* heavy, important, ponderous.

Weir (Wir), *n.* dam in river for controlling water.

Weird (Weerd), *a.* uncanny, unearthly, odd.

Wel'come, *v.t.* to receive gladly or as a guest. *n.* a friendly greeting on arrival. *a.* accorded or received gladly.

Weld, *v.t. & i.* to unite pieces of metal by hammering or pressing after partially melting, to join together. *n.*

Wel'fare, *n.* general well-being, prosperity.

Wel'kin, *n. poet.* the sky.

Well, *n.* a natural exploited source of water, a shaft excavated in earth to tap source of water or oil. *v.i.* to flow as from a well.

Well, *a. & adv.* satisfactory, in good health, rightly, favourably, advisable. interj. of surprise etc. **Well-being,** *n.* welfare. **Well-nigh,** *adv.* almost. **Well-to-do,** *a.* prosperous.

Welsh, Welch, *v.t. & i.* to cheat, esp. of bookmaker who decamps without paying. **Welsh'er,** *n.*

Welt, *v.t.* to beat, thrash. *n.* mark left by this, weal.

Welt, *n.* bordering of leather attaching upper to sole of boot or shoe. *v.t.* to furnish with a welt.

Wel'ter, *v.i.* to wallow, roll clumsily. *n.* a violent confusion.

Wel'ter, *n.* formerly a heavy rider now us. only as welterweight, a category in boxing between lightweight and middle-weight.

Wen, *n.* a harmless tumour, *fig.* a large crowded city.

Wench, *n.* a girl, a maidservant.

Wend, *v.t. & i.* to go one's way.

Were'wolf (Wer-), *n.* legendary person with power of changing into a wolf.

West, *n.* one of four points of compass, opposite east, quarter where sun sets, the Occident, *a. & adv.* coming from or toward the west. **Wes'terly,** *a.* from the west, as of wind. *adv.* in direction of west. **Wes'tern,** *a.* pertaining to the west. **Wes'terner,** *n.* person living in or coming from the west. **West'ward, West'wards,** *adv.* towards the west.

Wet, *a.* consisting of or affected by liquid, moist, damp, not dry, soaked. *v.t.* to affect with moisture. *n.* **Wetness,** water, moisture, liquid.

Weth'er, *n.* castrated ram.

Whack, *v.t.* to slap hard, hit with resounding blow. *n.* such a blow, the sound of this.

Whale, *n.* large sea mammal almost extinct through excessive exploitation for oil etc. **Wha'-ling,** *n.* the practice of hunting whales. **Wha'ler,** *n.* vessel or man engaged in whaling, warship's rowing-boat.

Whale, *v.t.* to beat harshly, flog **Wha'ling,** *n.* a beating.

Wharf (Worf), *n.* quay for loading and unloading cargo ships. **Wharf′age,** *n.* quaside accommodation and facilities, also payment for this. **Wharf′-inger** (-jer), *n.* wharf-owner.

What (Hwot),'*pron.* which thing, that which. *a.* which, how much. **Whatever,** *pron.* all that, anything which, no matter what. **Whatsoever,** *pron.* & *a.* whatever.

Wheat, *n.* cereal plant with highly nutritious seeds used for making flour. **Wheat′en,** *a.*

Whee′dle, *v.t.* to cajole.

Wheel, *n.* circular disk, circular frame with spokes, revolving on axle and used for various mechanical purposes. *v.t.* & *i.* to move on wheels, revolve, turn, change direction. **Wheelbarrow,** *n.* one-wheeled handcart for garden purposes etc. **Wheel′wright,** *n.* craftsman who makes or repairs wheels.

Wheeze, *v.i.* to breathe in gasping manner. *n.* **Wheez′y,** *a.*

Wheeze, *n. sl.* a crazy idea.

Whelk, *n.* edible shellfish.

Whelm, *v.t. poet., arch.* to overwhelm.

Whelp, *n.* young of various animals such as dog, a self-opinionated youth. *v.t.* & *i.* to give birth.

When, *adv.* at what time. *pron.* what time. *conj.* at the time, during. **Whenever,** *adv.* at whatever time, as often as.

Whence, *adv.* from what place, how.

Where, *adv.* in or to what place. *pron.* what place. *conj.* considering that, whereas. **Where′-abouts,** *adv.* in or near what place. *n.* position or questioned position. **Where′as,** *conj.* considering that, while on the contrary. **Where′at,** *adv.* upon which. **Where′by,** *adv.* by which. **Where′fore,** *adv.* why, for what reason. **Where′upon,** *adv.* upon which, after which.

Wherr′y, *n.* sailing-barge, kind of rowing-boat.

Whet, *v.t.* to sharpen. **Whet′-stone,** *n.* stone for sharpening bladed tools.

Wheth′er, *conj.* introducing first of two alternative questions or choices.

Whey (Whay), *n.* watery part of milk after separation from curds. **Whey′faced,** *a.* sickly looking.

Which, *pron.* what one, that, who, the one that. *a.* what one. **Whichever,** *pron.* any one or ones that. *a.* any, no matter which.

Whiff, *n.* faint breath or smell. *v.t.* & *i.* to blow lightly, waft.

Whig, *n.* member of polit. reform party which developed into Liberal Party.

While, *n.* a period of time. *conj.* during the time that. *v.t.* to pass the time, esp. as while away. **Whilst,** *conj.* while.

Whim, *n.* a fad, a caprice. **Whim′sical,** *a.* capricious, fantastic. **Whimsical′ity,** *n.* idiosyncrasy. **Whim′sey,** *n.* whim, fancy.

Whim′per, *n.* a faint doleful cry. *v.i.*

Whine, *n.* a thin complaining cry. *v.i.*

Whinn′y, *n.* sound made by horse, a neigh. *v.i.*

Whip, *n.* a rod or stick with lash or cord attached for flicking horse and making it go faster, an implement for beating, parl. party official, a parl. order to members of party to attend certain sitting. *v.t. & i.* to strike with a whip, move like a whip, beat, act or speak suddenly.

Whip'hand, *n.* domination, advantage.

Whipp'er-in, *n.* assistant huntsman.

Whipp'er-snapper, *n.* impertinent person.

Whipp'et, *n.* coursing dog related to greyhound or result of cross with greyhound.

Whir (Whur), *v.i.* to revolve rapidly while making a humming sound. *n.*

Whirl (Whurl), *v.t. & i.* to spin or cause to spin rapidly. *n.* a movement caused by this.

Whirl'pool, *n.* vortex.

Whirl'wind, *n.* violently circling current of air.

Whisk, *v.t. & i.* to beat lightly into a froth, to dart, cause to disappear suddenly. *n.* a small implement for beating eggs etc.

Whis'ker, *n.* a bristle, a hair, esp. growing on face.

Whisk'y, *n.* strong alcoholic liquor distilled from barley.

Whis'per, *v.t. & i.* to speak extremely quietly or secretly, murmur. *n.*

Whist, *n.* card game, forerunner of bridge.

Whis'tle (Whis'l), *v.t. & i.* to utter a shrill long or continuing sound by forcing air through small opening, e.g. puckered lips or mechanical device. *n.* such a sound or anything similar, a small pipe or mechanical device for making a whistle.

Whit, *n.* a tiny particle, insignificant amount.

White, *a.* colourless, pale, of the colour of newly fallen snow, unblemished. *n.* white colour, albumen of egg, so-called white-skinned person. **Whi'ten,** *v.t. & i.* to make or become white. **White'wash,** *n.* solution of lime for whitening walls, *fig.* a contrived clearing of suspected person.

Whith'er, *adv.* to what place, wherever.

Whit'low (-lo), *n.* inflamed tumour or swelling round fingernail.

Whitt'le, *v.t. & i.* to cut away gradually, shape with knife, *fig.* to reduce gradually esp. as whittle away, whittle down.

Who (Hoo), *pron.* what or which person. **Whoever,** *pron.* whatever person. **Whom** (Hoom), *pron.* objective case of who.

Whole (Hole), *a.* intact, complete. *n.* a complete thing, an entity, total amount. **Wholl'y,** *adv.* entirely. whole-hearted, *a.* sincere. **Whole'meal,** *n.* unadulterated flour. **Whole'sale,** *n.* sale of goods to people in same trade. **Whole'some,** *a.* salubrious.

Whoop (Hoop), *v.t. & i.* to shout or gasp hoarsely, urge on by shouting. *n.* a raucous shout, a gasping cough. **Whoop'er,** *n.* a kind of swan. **Whoop'ing-cough,** *n.* an infectious disease marked by paroxysms of coughing.

Whore (Hor), *n.* a prostitute.

Whorl (Hwurl), *n.* circular arrangement of leaves round a plant stem, spiral turn.

Whose (Hooz), *pron.* possessive

case of who and occasionally of which.

Whosoev'er, *pron.* whoever.

Why (Hwy),*adv.* for what reason, for which.

Wick, *n.* piece of thread or material conducting oil or grease to flame of lamp or candle.

Wick'ed (Wick-ed), *a.* sinful, evil. **Wick'edness,** *n.*

Wick'er, *n.* osier or willow twigs woven into material for baskets etc. **Wicker-work,** *n.* articles made from wicker.

Wick'et, *n.* a small side gate or door, in cricket one of two sets of stumps and bails at either end of pitch, the pitch itself, each batsman's spell at wicket. **Wicket-gate,** *n.* **Wicket-keeper,** *n.* fieldsman in cricket who fields behind stumps where batsman is batting.

Wide, *a.* broad, extensive from side to side, inaccurate. **Wi'-den,** *v.t. & i.* to make or become wide or wider. **Wide'-spread,** *a.* spread out fully, distributed extensively. **Width,** *n.* extent from side to side, breadth.

Wid'ow (-o), *n.* woman whose husband is dead. **Wid'ower** (-o-er), *n.* man whose wife is dead.

Wield (Weeld), *v.t.* to brandish, hold or use in the hands.

Wife, *n.* married woman.

Wig, *n.* artificial head of hair as official headdress, ornament or to conceal baldness.

Wigg'ing, *n.* a rebuke, scolding.

Wild (Wile-), *a.* untamed, uncultivated, living naturally, not domesticated. uncontrollable. **Wild'ness,** *n.* **Wild'fire,** *n.* orig. burning chem. used by ancient

Greeks in naval warfare, now us. as to spread like wildfire, to spread rapidly.

Wil'derness, *n.* a natural region unspoiled by man.

Wile, *n.* a ruse, trick. **Wi'liness,** *n.* **Wi'ly,** *a.* crafty.

Wil'ful, *a.* deliberate, obstinate.

Will, *n.* mental power of decision, choice, intention, wish, resolution, a testament. *v.t. & i.* to intend or wish strongly, determine, bequeath. **Will'ing,** *a.* agreeable, ready.

Will-o'-the-wisp, *n.* marsh gas causing elusive light, *fig.* anything elusive.

Will'ow (-o), *n.* tree growing near water or in damp soil and whose timber is used in making cricket-bats. **Will'owy,** *n.* slender and graceful, like a willow-tree.

Will'y-nill'y, *adv.* without choice, obligatory.

Wilt, *v.t. & i.* to droop, wither, flag.

Wim'ple, *n.* head cloth worn by nuns, mediaeval head covering for women.

Win, *v.t. & i.* to achieve by victory or effort, to prevail, obtain. *n.* a victory or acquisition. **Winn'ing,** *a.* attractive. **Winn'er,** *n.* the person who gains victory.

Wince, *v.i.* to flinch, recoil at pain or threat of. *n.*

Winch, *n.* a windlass, apparatus for lifting.

Wind, *n.* (occasionally in poet. pronounced wynd), air in natural motion, strong breeze, breath, scent, abdominal gas. *v.t.* to have difficulty in breathing, make breathless, to get the scent or news of. **Wind'break,**

n. protection against wind.
Wind'fall, *n.* unexpected legacy or gift.

Wind (Wynd), *v.t.* to make sound by blowing, esp. e.g. a horn.

Wind (Wynd), *v.t. & i.* to pursue a twisting course, to turn a handle or crank, to entwine, wrap, tighten spring in clockwork machine. *n.* a turn, a bend. **Wind up,** *v.t.* to crank up, finish up, settle up.

Wind'jammer, *n.* formerly a large sailing-vessel.

Wind'lass, *n.* a winch.

Wind'mill, *n.* mill powered by action of wind on large sails.

Win'dow (-o), *n.* aperture us. glazed in wall to admit light. **Window-pane,** *n.* sheet of glass for this.

Wind'ward, *n. & a.* side facing wind.

Wine, *n.* fermented juice of grape as liquor.

Wing, *n.* one of flight organs of bird, insect, bat, anything resembling this and used for flight, the flank of an army, an outside position in some sports, a projecting part of a building, a formation in air force. *v.t. & i.* to fly, to bring down by hitting in wing.

Wink, *v.t. & i.* to close and open eyelids rapidly esp. as signal, *fig.* to pretend not to notice, to twinkle, gleam. *n.* the act of winking, a moment, esp. as forty winks, a short nap.

Win'kle, *n.* edible sea-snail. *v.t. sl.* as winkle out, prise out, obtain with difficulty from someone.

Winn'ow (-o), *v.t.* to separate chaff from grain by blast of air from hand machine or by throwing up in air, to separate.

Win'some, *a.* sentimentally charming.

Win'ter, *n.* coldest season of year coming after autumn. *v.t. & i.* to pass the winter, look after during winter. **Win'try,** *a.* cold, bleak.

Wipe, *v.t. & i.* to clean or dry by rubbing on dry material, as. wipe out, to obliterate, destroy. **Wi'per,** *n.* device for wiping.

Wire, *n.* thin metal thread, a cable, *coll.* a telegram. *v.t.* to provide or fasten with wire, to send a telegram. **Wire'less,** *a.* radio. **Wir'y,** *a.* thin and tough like wire.

Wis'dom, *n.* sagacity, great learning or experience, common sense. **Wise,** *n.* possessed of wisdom, sensible. **Wise'acre,** *n.* person possessing less wisdom than he professes.

Wise, *n.* manner, way. Also as suff. denoting manner or direction.

Wish, *v.t. & i.* to desire, want, express an inclination. *n.* **Wish'ful,** *a.* hopeful.

Wish'y-wash'y, *a.* feeble, lacking in strength.

Wisp, *n.* a thin stream of smoke, flimsy bundle of material.

Wist'ful, *a.* yearning, wishful.

Wit, *n.* intelligence, humour, mental power or alertness. **Wit'ticism,** *n.* humorous saying. **Witt'ingly,** *a.* intentionally.

Witch, *n.* female sorcerer. **Witch'craft,** *n.* sorcery, magic. **Witch'ing,** *a.* pertaining to witchcraft.

With, *prep.* by side of, in company with, by means of, as result of, in relation or opposition to. **With'al,** *adv.* moreover.

Withdraw', *v.t. & i.* to take or go back, leave. **Withdraw'al,** *n.*

With'er, *v.t. & i.* to shrivel, or cause to shrivel, dry up, decline.

With'ers, *n.pl.* ridge between horse's shoulder-blades.

Withhold, *v.t.* to keep back, decline to give.

With'in, *adv.* inside, indoors. prep. inside limit of.

Without', *adv.* outside. *prep.* lacking in, beyond, outside of.

Withstand', *v.t.* to resist, oppose.

Wit'ness, *v.t. & i.* to see something happen, to testify, give evidence. *n.* person who gives evidence, testimony.

Wiz'ard, *n.* magician, sorcerer.

Wiz'ened, *a.* dried up, wrinkled.

Woad (Wode), *n.* plant from which blue dye of same name is made.

Wob'ble, *v.t. & i.* to shake, rock, hesitate. **Wobb'ly,** *a.*

Woe, *n.* sorrow, grief. **Woe'begone,** *a.* sorrowful. **Woe'ful,** *a.* calamitous.

Wold (Wole-), *n.* downland, moorland.

Wolf (Woolf), *n.* wild animal of canine order. *v.t.* to eat greedily. *pl.* wolves.

Wom'an (Woom'an), *n.* adult human female. **Woman'hood,** *n.* state of being a woman, women collectively. **Wom'anly,** *a.* proper to a woman.

Womb (Woom), *n.* organ in female mammals in which young are conceived and developed prior to birth.

Won'der (Wun-), *n.* a marvel, source of astonishment or admiration, feeling evoked by this. *v.i.* to feel wonder, to doubt, query. **Won'derful,** *a.*

marvellous. **Won'drous,** *a. poet.* wonderful.

Wo'nt, *n.* habit or custom. **Wo'nted,** *a.* customary, usual.

Woo, *v.t.* to make love to, coax. **Woo'er,** *n.* a suitor.

Wood, *n.* extensive collection of trees, timber. **Wood'en,** *a.* made of wood, stupid. **Wood'land,** *n.* land characterized by many trees.

Woof, *n.* the weft in weaving.

Wool, *n.* soft curly thick hair of sheep and similar animals, material made from this. **Wooll'en,** *a.* made of wool. **Wooll'y,** *a.* like wool, dim-witted. **Wool'gathering,** *n.* formerly practice of gathering wool left on brambles etc., now absent-mindedness.

Word (Wurd), *n.* written or spoken representation of an idea or image or part of these made up of combination of sounds symbolized by letters. *v.t.* to put into words. **Word'y,** *a.* verbose.

Work (Wurk), *v.t. & i.* to make mental or physical effort, persevere, labour, to pursue particular calling. *n.*

World (Wurld), *n.* the earth, organized society, humanity. **World'ly,** *a.* material.

Worm (Wurm), *n.* crawling limbless invertebrate animal working in and feeding on soil, anything resembling such, a rotating screw. *v.t. & i.* to move like a worm.

Worm'wood, *n.* bitter herb used for flavouring absinthe and vermouth, anything extremely bitter.

Worr'y, *n.* anxiety, cause of this. *v.t. & i.* to trouble, disquiet, to pester, shake or pull about while holding in teeth.

Wor'ship (Wur-), *v.t.* to adore, admire, revere. *n.*

Wor'sted (Woos-), *n.* & *a.* woollen yarn.

Worth (Wurth), *n.* merit, value. *a.* **Worth'y,** *a.* respectable, meritorious. **Worth'while,** *a.* worth doing.

Wound (Woond) *v.t.* to injure by weapon or attack, *fig.* to hurt feelings. *n.*

Wrack (Rack), *n.* ruin, wreckage, sea-weed.

Wraith (Raith), *n.* a phantom.

Wran'gle (Ran-), *v.i.* to quarrel, argue noisily. **Wran'gler,** *n.* noisy quarreller.

Wran'gler, *n.* student winning first-class math. honours at Cambridge University.

Wrap (Rap), *v.t.* & *i.* to cover all round, to protect with paper. *n.* a loose garment. **Wrapp'er, Wrapping,** *n.* material for wraping, protective material.

Wrath (Rawth), *n.* great anger. **Wrath'ful,** *a.*

Wreak (Reak), *v.t.* to commit, inflict.

Wreath (Reeth), *n.* a garland of flowers or leaves or anything resembling this. **Wreathe,** *v.t.* to decorate with a wreath, to encircle.

Wreck (Reck), *v.t.* & *i.* to damage severely, destroy, spoil. *n.* a wrecked vessel, a ruin, anything damaged severely. **Wreck'age,** *n.* debris from a wreck. **Wreck'er,** *n.* person who causes wreck deliberately.

Wrench (Rench), *v.t.* to pull or twist violently, strain. *n.* a painful sprain, a parting, a tool for wrenching.

Wrest (Rest), *v.t.* to pull or take away forcibly.

Wres'tle (Res'l), *v.i.* to struggle hard, contend with in sport while using all limbs for gaining hold over opponent. **Wres'tler,** *n.* **Wres'tling-match,** *n.*

Wretch (Retch), *n.* a mean or miserable person. **Wretch'ed,** *a.* mean, poor, despicable.

Wrig'gle (Rig-), *v.t.* & *i.* to squirm. *n.*

Wring (Ring), *v.t.* to squeeze and twist simultaneously, to extort, distress. **Wring'er,** *n.* rolling machine for forcing bulk of water out of wet laundry

Wrin'kle (Rin-), *n.* a crease, pucker, ridge, *coll.* a hint. *v.t.* & *i.* to wrinkle or make wrinkled.

Wrist (Rist), *n.* joint between hand and forearm.

Writ (Rit), *n.* any authoritative writing, legal order.

Write (Rite), *v.t.* & *i.* to express in words on paper by various means, to communicate with by doing this. **Wri'ter,** *n.* person who writes, an author, a clerk in navy.

Writhe (Rithe) to squirm esp. from pain or distress.

Wrong (Rong), *a.* incorrect, mistaken, morally reprehensible, not in proper working order. *n.* moral wickedness, an injury. *v.t.* to do harm or wrong to. **Wrong'ful,** *a.* unjust, harmful.

Wroth (Rawth), *a.* wrathful.

Wry (Ry), *a.* distorted, twisted.

X

X-ray, *n.* electromagnetic ray of very short wavelength capable of penetrating many substances such as human body for photographic examination or treatment, a photograph or examination made by means of this. *v.t.* to apply X-rays to.

Xe'bec (Ze-), *n.* three-masted Mediterranean sailing-vessel.

Xe'nial (Ze-), *a.* pertaining to hospitality or relations between host and guest.

Xeno'gamy (Ze-), *n. bot.* cross-fertilization.

Xenopho'bia (Ze-), *n.* morbid hatred or fear of foreigners. **Xenopho'bic,** *a.*

Xy'lo- (Zy-), *pref.* meaning of or like wood, thus **Xylograph,** *n.* a wood-engraving, **Xy'loid,** *a.* like wood, **Xyloph'agous,** *a.* wood-eating, **Xy'lophone,** *n.* ancient mus. instrument composed of parallel, graduated wooden bars which are struck with small wooden mallets.

Xy'ster (Zy-), *n. surg.* tool for scraping bones.

Xy'stus (Zy-), *n.* roofed gallery used by ancient Greek athletes for indoor exercise.

Y

Yacht (Yot), *n.* sailing-vessel for pleasure. *v.i.* to sail in yacht. **Yachts'man,** *n.*

Yap, *v.i.* to bark shrilly. *n.*

Yard, *n.* an enclosure surrounded by buildings, esp. farm buildings.

Yard, *n.* a unit of linear measure equalling thirty-six inches.

Yard, *n.* a ship's spar for holding sail. **Yard'arm,** *n.* either end of a yard.

Yarn, *n.* spun thread, woollen thread, *coll.* a story. *v.i.* to tell a story.

Yaw, *v.i. naut.* to deviate from or fail to hold course. *n.*

Yawl, *n.* small two-masted fore-and-aft rigged sailing boat, small boat.

Yawn, *v.t. & i.* to open wide, gape, esp. of mouth as expression of fatigue or boredom. *n.*

Ye, *pron. arch.* you.

Yea (Yai), *interj. arch.* yes.

Year, *n.* period of time taken by earth to complete one revolution round sun, human division of time based on this, twelve months. **Year'ly,** *a.* happening once a year.

Year'ling, *n.* animal entered upon its second year.

Yearn (Yurn), *v.t. & i.* to long for greatly, to pity.

Yeast, *n.* substance composed

of fungoid cells which cause fermentation.

Yell, *n.* a shout, a loud cry. *v.i.*

Yell'ow (-o), *a. & n.* colour between orange and green, colour of buttercup, primrose, gold etc., *fig.* cowardly.

Yelp, *n.* a sharp shrill cry of distress, esp. by dog. *v.i.*

Yeo'man (Yo-), *n.* prosperous farmer owning own land, sturdy countryman. *a.* sturdy, reliable. **Yeo'manry,** *n.* yeomen collectively, territorial cavalry.

Yes, *adv.* indicating affirmative. *n.* an affirmative answer. **Yes'-man,** *n.* sycophantic person.

Yes'terday, *n.* the day preceding present day.

Yet, *adv.* still, hitherto, even now. *conj.* nevertheless.

Yield, *v.t. & i.* to submit, give in, produce. *n.* what is produced.

Yo'del, *v.t. & i.* to sing in ululating fashion characteristic of Swiss mountaineers.

Yo'ga, *n.* Hindu metaphysical system entailing conquest of mind over matter. **Yo'gi,** *n.* teacher or devotee of yoga.

Yoke, *n.* a wooden harness to link draught animals side by side, a shaped shoulder-bar to facilitate carrying of full buckets. *v.t.* to furnish with a yoke, join together thus. **Yoke-fellow,** *n.* person or animal other is joined to.

Yo'kel, *n.* a peasant, a country bumpkin.

Yolk (Yoke), *n.* yellow part of egg.

Yon'der, *a. & adv.* over there, farther on, at a distance esp. when in view. **Yon,** *adv. poet.* yonder.

Yore, *n.* the past.

You (U), *pron.* second person *sing.* or *pl.* **Your,** *a.* belonging to you, possessive form of you. **Yours,** *pron. & a.* something belonging to you. **Yourself',** *pron.* reflex. or emphatic form of you. *pl.* **Yourselves.**

Young (Yung), *a.* still growing, not fully developed, not old, in the early part of life. *n.* offspring. **Young'ling,** *n.* young creature. **Young'ster,** *n.* a child, youth. **Youth,** *n.* state of being young esp. after childhood, a lad, young man. **Youth'ful,** *a.* being young, vigorous.

Yule'tide, *n.* old Norse festival which has developed into Christian celebration of birth of Christ, Christmas.

Z

Za'ny, *n.* a fool, buffoon.

Zeal, *n.* ardour, enthusiasm. **Zeal'ous** (Zel-), *a.* eager, enthusiastic. **Zeal'ot** (Zel-), *n.* fanatical partisan.

Zen'ith, *n.* the greatest height, highest point, point of sky immediately overhead.

Zeph'yr (Zeffer), *n.* a faint breeze, properly the west wind.

Zepp'elin, *n.* an airship, esp. of German design.

Ze'ro, *n.* nothing, nought, point from which reckoning of temperature or time begins. **Zero hour,** *n.* us. of time of commencement of mil. attack.

Zest, *n.* lively enjoyment, relish. Zest'ful, *a.*

Zig'zag, *n.* formation or direction comprising series of short angled turns. *a. v.t. & i.* to form in zigzag or move in zigzag fashion as of convoy avoiding submarines.

Zinc, *n.* bluish-white metal unaffected by exposure. *a.*

Zi'onism, *n.* a movement for the establishment of a modern Jewish nation in Palestine now realized as the state of Israel. Zi'onist, *n.*

Zip, *n.* a sharp thin sound as of flying object, a sliding fastener, esp. as Zip-fastener.

Zo'diac, *n.* ancient conception of the heavens embracing all the heavenly bodies which were divided into twelve regions each named after the predominant constellation.

Zone, *n.* a circular region or belt, geographical division. Zo'nal, *a.* pertaining to a zone.

Zool'ogy (Zo-ol-), *n.* natural history of animal, scientific study of this. **Zoolog'ical** (-loj-), *a.* Zool'ogist, *n.* scientic worker in zoology. **Zoolog'ical garden,** *n.* us. abbrev. to zoo, garden where animals are displayed.

Zoom, *v.i.* of aircraft to climb sharply and abruptly. *n.* a long booming noise as of this.

Zo'ophysics, *n.* scientific study of structure of animals.

Zo'ophyte, *n.* kind of plant-like animal such as jelly-fish.

Zo'otheism, *n.* deification or worship of animals.

Zymo'sis, *n.* fermentation.

WEIGHTS AND MEASURES

AVOIRDUPOIS

7000 grains . . . . 1 pound
16 drams . . . 1 ounce (oz.)
16 ounces . . . 1 pound (lb.)
14 pounds . . . 1 stone (st.)
28 pounds . . 1 quarter (qr.)
4 quarters . . . 1 hundredweight (cwt.)
20 hundredweights . 1 ton (tn.)

BRITISH LINEAR MEASURE

12 inches (in.) . . 1 foot (ft.)
3 feet . . . . . 1 yard (yd.)
2 yards . . . . 1 fathom (f.)
5$^1/_2$ yards . . 1 pole (rod or
perch)
4 poles . . . . . . 1 chain
10 chains. . . 1 furlong (fur.)
8 furlongs . . . . 1 mile (m.)
1 mile . . . . . . 1,760 yds.

SQUARE MEASURE

144 square inches . . 1 square
foot
9 square feet. . . 1 square yard
30$^1/_4$ sq. yards . . 1 square pole
40 sq. poles . . . . . 1 rood
4 roods . . . . . . 1 acre
640 acres . . . 1 square mile

IMPERIAL DRY MEASURE

2 pints . . . . 1 quart
4 quarts . . . . . 1 gallon

2 gallons . . . . . . 1 peck
4 pecks . . . . . 1 bushel
8 bushels . . . . 1 quarter

METRIC MEASURE

1 kilometre . . . 1,000 metres
1 decimetre 1/10th
of a metre
1 centimetre 1/100th
of a metre
1 millimetre 1/1000th
of a metre

METRIC WEIGHT

1 kilogram . . . 1,000 grams
1 decigram . . 1/10th of a gram
1 centigram 1/100th
of a gram
1 milligram . . . 1/1000th
of a gram

TROY WEIGHT

24 grains . . . 1 pennyweight
(dwt.)
20 pennyweights . . . 1 ounce
12 ounces . . . . . 1 pound

APOTHECARIES WEIGHT

20 grains . . . 1 scruple (scr.)
3 scruples . . . . 1 dram (dr.)
8 drams . . . . . 1 ounce (oz.)
12 ounces . . . . 1 pound (lb.)

COMMON ABBREVIATIONS

A

A.A., Automobile Assoc.
A.A.A., Amateur Athletic Assoc.
A.B., able-bodied seaman.
A.D., anno Domini (in the year of our Lord).
ad lib. (itum) (= to the extent desired).
A.F.A., Amateur Football Assoc.
a.m., ante meridiem (= before noon).
anon., anonymous.
A.R.A., Associate of the Royal Academy.
A.R.C.M., Associate of the Royal College of Music.
A.R.I.B.A., Associate of the Royal Institute of British Architects.

B

b., born.
B.A., Bachelor of Arts.
Bart., baronet.
B.B.C., British Broadcasting Corporation.
B.B.B.C., British Boxing Board of Control.
B.C., before Christ.
B.C.L., Bachelor of Civil Law.
b.h.p., brake horse-power.
B.P., British Pharmacopoeia.
B.P.C., British Pharmacopoeia Codex.
B.Sc., Bachelor of Science.
Bt., baronet.
B.Th.U., British Thermal Unit.

C

C., centigrade.
c., cent; chapter; circa (about)

C.B., Companion of the Bath.
C.B.E., Commander of the British Empire.
c.c., cubic centimetre(s).
Cent., centigrade.
cf., confer (Lat.=compare).
Co., company; county.
c/o, care of.
C.O.D., cash on delivery.
Col., colonel.
c.p., candle-power.
cwt., hundredweight.

D

d., daughter; denarius (=penny); departs &c.; died.
D.C., District of Columbia.
deg., degree.
D.F.C., Distinguished Flying Cross.
D. Lit., Doctor of Literature.
D. Litt., Doctor of Letters.
do., ditto.
dol., dollar(s).
D.Sc., Doctor of Science.

E

E., East.
Ed., editor &c.
e.g., exempli gratia (=for instance).
Esq., esquire.
etc., etcetera (=and the rest).
E. & O.E., errors & omissions excepted.

F

F., Fahrenheit; Fellow (of learned society).
f., feet; feminine; foot; franc(s).
F.A., Football Assoc.

Fahr., Fahrenheit.
F.C., football club.
fig., figure; figuratively.
F.O., Foreign Office.
Fr., French.
F.R.I.B.A., Fellow of the Royal Institute of British Architects.
F.Z.S., Fellow of the Zoological Soc.

G

G.C.B., Grand Cross of the Bath.
Gib., Gibraltar.
Gk., Greek.
G.P., general practitioner.
G.P.O., General Post Office.

H

h., hour(s).
H.C.F., highest common factor.
H.E., his Excellency; high explosive.
H.H., His (or Her) Highness.
H.M., His (or Her) Majesty.
H.O., Home Office.
Hon. Sec., Honorary Secretary.
h.p., horse-power.
H.Q., head-quarters.
H.R.H., His (or Her) Royal, Highness.
hr(s)., hour(s).

I

ib., ibid., ibidem (=in the same place).
i.e., id est (that is).
ILO., International Labour Organisation.
inst., instant (= in present month).
Ir., Irish.
It., Italian.

J

J.P., Justice of Peace.
Jr., jun., junr., junior.

K

K.B.E., Knight Commander of the British Empire.
K.C.B., Knight Commandor of the Bath.
K.C.M.G., Knight Commander of the Order of St. Michael & St. George.
K.C.V.O., Knight Commander of the Victorian Order.
K.G., Knight of the Garter.
K.P., Knight of St. Patrick.
K.T., Knight of the Thistle.
Kt., Knight.

L

l., left; libra(e) (=pound(s); lira; lire; litre(s).
lat., latitude.
lb., libra(e) (=pound(s) weight).
l.c., lower case.
L.C.M., lowest common multiple.
loc. cit., loco citato (=in the place quoted).
long., longitude.
Ltd., Limited.

M

M., Monsieur.
m., mark(s) (coin); masculine; metre(s); mile(s); minute(s).
M.A., Master of Arts.
M.B., medicinae baccalaureus (=Bachelor of Medicine).
M.B.E., Member of the Order of the British Empire.
M.C., Master of Ceremonies; Member of Congress; Military Cross.

M.C.C., Marylebone Cricket Club.
M.D., medicinae doctor (=doctor of Medicine).
M.F.H., Master of Fox-Hounds.
Mlle., Mademoiselle.
Mme., Madame.
M.O., Medical Officer.
mod., modern.
M.O.H., Medical Officer of Health.
M.P., Member of Parliament.
m.p.h., miles per hour.
M.R.C.V.S., Member of the Royal College of Veterinary Surgeons.
MS manuscript.
Mt., mount.
M.V.O., Member of the Victorian Order.

N

N., North.
N.B., nota bene (note well).
n.p., new paragraph.
N.S.P.C.C., National Soc. for the Prevention of Cruelty to Children.
N.Y., New York.
N.Z., New Zealand.

O

ob., obiit (=died).
O.B.E., Officer of the British Empire.
O.H.M.S., on H.M.'s service.
O.M., Order of Merit.
op. cit., opus citatum (=the work cited).
O.S., ordinary seaman; outsize.
oz., ounce(s).

P

p., page.
p.a., per annum.
P.C., post-card; police constable; Privy Council(lor).

p.c., per cent.
P.E.P., Political & Economic Planning.
per pro., per procurationem (by proxy).
Ph.D., philosophiae doctor (=Doctor of Philosophy).
P.L.A., Port of London Authority.
P.M., Prime Minister; Police Magistrate; Provost Marshall.
p.m., post meridiem (=after noon); post mortem (=after death).
P.M.G., Post Master General.
pp., pa s.
P.P.S., post-postscriptum (further P.S.).
P.R., Proportional Representation; Public Relations.
Prof., Professor.
prox., proximo (=in the next month).
P.S., post script.
P.T.O., Please Turn Over.

Q

Q.C., Queen's Counsel.
Q.E.D., quod erat demonstrandum (=which was to be proved).
q.s., quantum sufficit (= as much as suffices).
q.v., quod vide (=which see).

R

r., right.
R.A., Royal Academy.
R.A.F., Royal Air Force.
R.A.C., Royal Automobile Club.
R.A.M., Royal Academy of Music.
R.C.P., R.C.S., Royal College of Physicians, Surgeons.
R.D., refer to drawer.

R.D.C., Rural District Council.
recd., received.
ref., reference.
Revd., Reverend.
R.S.P.C.A., Royal Soc. for the Prevention of Cruelty to Animals.
R.S.V.P., repondez s'il vous plait (=please answer).
Rt. Hon., Right Honourable.
Rt. Rev., Right Reverend.
R.U., Rugby Union.
R.W.S., Royal Soc. of Painters in Water-colours.

S

S., Saint; South; soprano.
s., shilling; son.
Salop., Shropshire.
Sec., secretary.
sec., second.
sect., section.
sen., senr., senior.
Soc., society.
S.P.C.K., Soc. for Promoting Christian Knowledge.
S.P.G., Soc. for Propagation of the Gospel.
sq., square.
Sr., Senior.
S.S., steamship.
SS., Saints.
St., Saint.
st., street.

T

T.B., tuberculosis.
temp., tempore (=in the period of).
T.N.T., trinitrotoluol.

U

u.c., upper case.

U.D.C., Urban District Council.
U.K., United Kingdom.
ult., ultimo (=in last month).
UNESCO, United Nations Educational Scientific & Cultura Organisation.
UNICEF, United Nations Children's Fund.
UNO, United Nations Organisation.
U.S.A., United States of America.
U.S.S.R., Union of Soviet Socialist Republics.

V

v., versus (=against); vide (=see).
V.C., Vice Chancellor; Victoria Cross.
Ven., Venerable.
viz.. videlicet (=namely).
vol., volume.
vv., verses.

W

W., West.
w., wide; with.
w.c., water closet.
WHO, World Health Organisation.
wt., weight.

X

Xmas, Christmas.

Y

yd., yard.
Y.M.C.A., Young Men's Christian Assoc.
Y.W.C.A., Young Women's Christian Assoc.